THE ECLIPSE OF THE
BIG GUN

The Eclipse of the BIG GUN

The Warship 1906-45

Editor: Robert Gardiner
Consultant Editor: David K Brown, RCNC

CONWAY

© Conway Maritime Press, 1992

This paperback edition first published in 2004 by Conway Maritime Press
The Chrysalis Building
Bramley Road
London W10 6SP
www.conwaymaritime.com

An imprint of **Chrysalis** Books Group

A CIP catalogue record of this book is available from the British Library

ISBN 0 85177 953 0

Distributed in North America by:
Casemate Publishing, 2114 Darby Road,
Havertown, PA 19083, USA

Series Consultant: Dr Basil Greenhill CB, CMG, FSA, FRHistS
Series Editor: Robert Gardiner

Printed and bound by JCG, Spain

Leading maritime historians and specialists from around the world have been brought together to ensure that the book is informative, authoritative and fully international in outlook.

Consultant Editor
David K Brown is now retired after an eminent career as a warship designer with the Royal Corps of Naval Constructors. He has published widely on historical as well as professional topics. His books range from *Before the Ironclad*, a major study of technical change in the 1815–60 period, to *The Future British Surface Fleet*, which analyses future technical and strategic developments.

Ian Buxton is a naval architect and Reader in Marine Transport at the University of Newcastle upon Tyne; he is also a leading member of the British Shipbuilding History Project.

N J M Campbell is an authority on naval weaponry, and the author of the standard work of reference, *Naval Weapons of World War Two*.

John English specialises in the study of smaller warship; he has produced a book on 'Hunt' class destroyers and has written extensively for naval journals.

Norman Friedman is probably America's leading naval analyst and the author of over a dozen highly regarded warship studies.

Brian Friend has made a particular study of the history of amphibious craft.

David Lyon, of the National Maritime Museum at Greenwich, is an authority on the development of torpedo warfare.

Keith McBride is a frequent contributor to naval journals, who specialises in unusual and neglected topics.

Al Ross is a ship draughtsman and historian, with a particular interest in coastal forces. He is co-author of the definitive work, *Allied Coastal Forces*.

Robert F Sumrall, curator of the US Naval Academy Museum, is a much-published authority on modern warships, such as *Iowa Class Battleships*.

David Williams is author of *Liners in Battledress*.

Michael Wilson, a submariner by profession, joined the Naval Historical Branch after his sea service and has written two books on underwater operations and numerous articles.

Contents

Preface

THIS volume launches *Conway's History of the Ship*, an ambitious programme of twelve volumes intended to provide the first detailed and comprehensive account of a technology that has shaped human history. It has been conceived as a basic reference work, the essential first stop for anyone seeking information on any aspect of the subject, so it is more concerned to be complete than to be original. However, the series takes full account of all the latest research and in certain areas will be publishing entirely new material. In the matter of interpretation care has been taken to avoid the old myths and to present only the most widely accepted modern viewpoints.

To tell a coherent story, in a more readable form than is usual with encyclopaedias, each volume takes the form of independent chapters, all by recognised authorities in the field. Most chapters are devoted to a ship type, but some broader topics are necessary to give added depth to the reader's understanding of developments. Some degree of generalisation is inevitable when tackling a subject of this breadth, but wherever possible the specific details of ships and their characteristics have been included (a table of typical ships for each relevant chapter includes a convenient summary of data from which the reader can chart the evolution of the ship type concerned). Except for the earliest craft, the series is confined to seagoing vessels; to have included boats would have expanded an already massive task.

The history of the ship is not a romanticised story of epic battles and heroic voyages but equally it is not simply a matter of technological advances. Ships were built to carry out particular tasks and their design was as much influenced by the experience of that employment – the lessons or war, or the conditions of trade, for example – as purely technical innovation. Throughout this series an attempt has been made to keep this clearly in view, to describe the *what* and *when* of developments without losing sight of the *why*.

The series is aimed at those with some knowledge of, and interest in, ships and the sea.

It would have been impossible to make a contribution of any value to the subject if it had been pitched at the level of the complete novice, so while there is an extensive glossary, for example, it assumes an understanding of the most basic nautical terms. Similarly, the bibliography avoids very general works and concentrates on those which will broaden or deepen the reader's understanding beyond the level of *Conway's History of the Ship*. The intention is not to inform genuine experts in their particular area of expertise, but to provide them with the best available single-volume summaries of less familiar fields.

Each volume is chronological in approach, with the periods covered becoming shorter as the march of technology quickens, but organised around a dominant theme – represented by the title – that sums up the period in question. In this way each book is fully self-sufficient, although when completed the twelve titles will link up to form a coherent history, chronicling the progress of ship design from its earliest recorded forms to the present day.

This first title, *The Eclipse of the Big Gun*, describes the evolution of the warship from the launch of the *Dreadnought* in 1906 to the end of the Second World War. Its central theme is the growing challenge to the primacy of the big gun surface ship, the traditional arbiter of naval power since the sixteenth century. The challenge was already well mounted by 1906 in the form of underwater weapons – the mine and torpedo – whose technology was established and effective. However, mines were regarded as a primarily defensive weapon, so of less importance to 'blue water' sea powers whose strategy was based on a battlefleet; the threat of the torpedo, and its principal launch platform, the torpedo boat, was considered to have been diminished, if not neutralised, by the British invention of the torpedo boat destroyer (or destroyer for short). Nevertheless, whereas previous battlefleets had required small craft only for reconnaissance and support duties, henceforward they were increasingly needed for the actual protection of the expensive capital ships.

The threat increased significantly with the first practical submarines – effectively submersible torpedo boats – which preceded the *Dreadnought* by a few years. However, in the long term, the greatest threat was to be posed by the aircraft; barely capable of carrying a man aloft when *Dreadnought* was launched, during the active lifetime of this vessel it became a potent ship-killer, capable of deploying torpedoes, mines and aerial bombs.

The new weapons demanded novel countermeasures and so the First World War saw a growth of specialist craft, like minesweepers and anti-submarine vessels, to deal with them. Total war meant the mobilisation of whole national economies, inspiring on the one hand the pursuit of commerce warfare with unprecedented savagery (torpedoing merchantmen without warning, for example), and on the other, huge programmes of cheap, expendable escorts. By contrast, major warships became larger, more technologically complex, and hence more costly, in response to the more complicated conditions of modern sea warfare.

In straightened postwar circumstances the Great Powers made a concerted, and relatively successful, attempt to control the naval arms race with treaties, and this introduced a new element of constraint into warship design, naval architects being forced to work to strict tonnage limitations. With battleship construction all but prohibited for fifteen years, some navies turned their attention to naval aviation, and this was to be proved far-sighted by the events of the Second World War. Big guns did see action against one another, but usually where air power could not do the job – at night or beyond its range – and from Pearl Harbor to Leyte Gulf, large surface ships fell easy victim to aircraft. By 1945 battleships had been largely reduced to the subsidiary roles of escorting aircraft carriers and shore bombardment in support of amphibious assaults.

Robert Gardiner
Series Editor

Introduction

THE following chapters will show that all classes of warship improved in capability with more and bigger weapons, higher speed and greater endurance during this period. Much of this improved capability was made possible by developments in the hull and machinery, unseen and little recognised. Stronger and better shaped hulls were developed while machinery became more powerful and much lighter as well. Reliability and economy were also much improved. To a considerable extent, the machinery improvements depended on apparently trivial changes to detail components or material.

Protection against enemy weapons was strengthened by improved quality and disposition of armour and, later, by effective measures against underwater attack.

Only a few improvements were made to habitability and the sailor of 1906 would have found the living quarters of 1945 all too familiar, though more crowded.

There was not much difference in the pace of development between the Great Powers though there is an indication that technical progress is most likely in the wealthier powers. It would be a wise man who could prove which was cause and which effect. Most hull and machinery developments before 1918 were initiated in the Royal Navy while in the later period, the US Navy had an even clearer lead.

The technical changes and the limits of the Washington Treaty make a natural break and hence this section is in two parts, 1906–1919 and 1919–45.

Technical developments: 1906–19

Machinery development – turbines

The steam turbine first went to sea in *Turbinia* in 1897 but, by 1906, there were few such installations and these had a number of problems. The fundamental cause of these problems was that turbines were most efficient at very high rotational speed (rpm), such as *Turbinia*'s 2000rpm, while propellers work best at low rpm. In the first turbine destroyers speed was reduced to 1200rpm and soon 900rpm became common practice for fast ships. Even this was too high for the propeller and too low for the turbine and many early destroyers failed to make their design speed on trial while most suffered from rapid erosion of the propeller.

In these circumstances, it was a very brave decision to commit *Dreadnought* to turbine machinery and the engineers involved, Durston, Watts and Froude, deserve great credit. However, the turbine machinery saved some 300 tons directly with about another 700 tons consequential saving in the hull. The other great advantage of the turbine was its reliability, particularly at sustained high power. Reciprocating machinery run hard would overheat due to lubrication problems while the vibration would even shake rivets out of the hull.

One problem associated with turbine plants which was not apparent until the war brought frequent use of high speed was 'condenseritis': failure of the brass sea water pipes in the condenser, letting salt into the feed water. This type of failure, known as impingement attack, is dependent on the speed of the water in the pipes, higher in turbine plant, and increasing with ship speed. It was a problem which affected all navies until about 1930 when it was much alleviated by the addition of one per cent aluminium to the brass.

From 1906, turbine machinery was virtually universal in the Royal Navy with other navies following suit. The US Navy briefly reverted to triple-expansion after problems, including poor fuel consumption, with early units. Early British turbines were of the Parsons reaction type while the US Navy used the Curtis impulse design. Up to the war, first one then the other showed an advantage but eventually both designers adopted a mixed blading combining the advantages.

Gearing

The next step forward was to reconcile the rotational speed requirements of turbine and propeller. In 1909, Parsons bought the cargo ship *Vespasian*, removed her machinery and fitted her with a geared turbine plant. The gearing reduced the turbine speed of 1700rpm to 74rpm at the propeller. This greatly improved fuel consumption and increased propeller life.

However, gear-cutting machinery was not common in the sizes required and could not be made quickly, while the standard of accuracy was not sufficient in some cases. For these reasons, the introduction of geared turbines was necessarily slow, starting with two British destroyers in 1912. By 1915 it was decided that all new warships ordered for the Royal Navy should have geared turbines. The later US 'flush deckers' had geared turbines as did a few German ships but the Royal Navy was the only navy to operate geared turbine ships in numbers during the war.

The effect on fuel consumption and hence on endurance due to increased efficiency of both turbine and propeller was dramatic. The 'R' class destroyer with geared drive needed 28 per cent less fuel at 25kts and 12 per cent at 18 compared with the similar but ungeared 'M' class. The first cruiser with gearing, *Calliope*, burnt 420 tons per day compared with 530 for her direct-drive sisters. In geared drive the thrust had to be taken outside the gearbox, made possible by the Michell thrust bearing or the similar Kingsbury (US) design.

The only significant alternative to gearing was electric drive in which turbines drove generators which, in turn, drove motors, turning the propeller shaft at lower speed. The US Navy used this system in some battleships and aircraft carriers but it was heavy, demanding in space and less efficient than geared drive. Electric drive did permit very close subdivision of the machinery spaces with boilers, turbines and motors in separate rooms which could be cross-connected in the event of damage. In the US ships, this advantage was nullified since there was only a single switchboard, badly protected, whose loss would immobilise the ship.

Boilers

During the 1890s the Royal Navy had been very dissatisfied with the reliability of early watertube boilers and following bitter arguments – known as the 'Battle of the Boilers' – settled on the Babcock large tube boiler, also used by the US Navy, for capital ships and the Yarrow small tube for smaller ships. Neither was entirely satisfactory; the Babcock was big and heavy though very reliable while the Yarrow was less reliable. The German Schultz-Thornycroft was smaller and reliable as well.

There was a general move to higher steam temperatures and pressures, superheaters being tried from about 1910, with further gains in economy.

Oil fuel

Trials with oil fuel began in the UK about 1898 but there were many problems to be overcome before the benefits could be realised. Oil gives out about 30 per cent more heat per pound than coal but only when it is fully burnt. Early spray nozzles were unable to achieve complete combustion and in the first trials thick black smoke was seen as a disadvantage of oil compared with coal.

These problems had largely been overcome by 1909 when the Royal Navy decided that all future destroyers should burn oil exclusively. A comparison was drawn up between the latest coal-burning *Beagle* and the oil-fired *Defender*.

	Beagle	Defender
Boiler heating surface, 1000sq ft	26	19
Boiler room weights, tons	187	142
Boiler room length, ft	92	61
Fuel required for same endurance, tons	225	175
Engine room complement	58	24
Cost of complete ship, £000s	106	86

In Britain, various objections were raised to the use of oil: it came from abroad, its source was insecure and fuelling stations were infrequent. Oil was seen as a fire risk and did not

provide the protection against shell fire given by a coal bunker. However, the advantages were overwhelming; other than those shown above, refuelling became quick and easy. Soon all British ships were to be oil-fired, culminating in the first battleships to be oil-fired exclusively, the *Queen Elizabeth*s of 1912. US developments were very similar and the oil-fired *Nevada* was also started in 1912.

Weight saving in machinery could be put to good use elsewhere and by 1914 such savings were very considerable as shown below. Note that these figures relate to ungeared installations. Comparison with other navies is not possible because of different definitions of machinery weight.

Date Ship	Dispt (tons)	Power (shp)	Speed (knots)	Machinery weight (lbs) shp
Capital ships				
1905 Dread-nought	17,900	23,000	21.3	184
1909 *Lion*	26,350	70,000	25.8	154
1912 *Malaya*	27,500	75,000	24	108
1914 *Repulse*	26,500	112,000	31.0	113
Destroyers				
1907 'Tribal'	850	14,500	33	64
1908 *Beagle*	900	12,000	27	64.5
1909 *Acorn*	760	13,500	27	51.5
1910 'M' class	1100	25,000	34	33.6

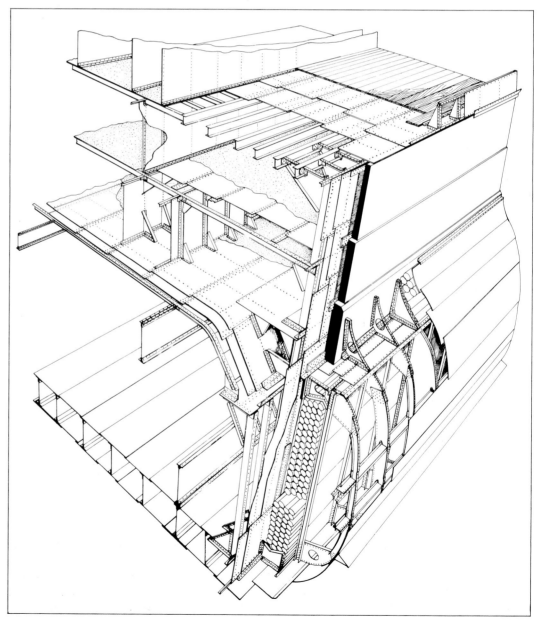

The hull of a capital ship was a complex structure: this cutaway shows the British battlecruiser Hood *of 1918. Note the combination of three thicknesses of belt armour above the anti-torpedo bulge, itself fitted with tubes designed to absorb the shock of torpedo detonation.* (John Roberts)

It should be re-emphasised that much of the success achieved in machinery design depended on quite detailed improvements such as the profile of a gear tooth, a thrust block, the quality of bricks in the boiler, the purity of feed water, etc.

Hull development

Since William Froude opened the first model test tank at Torquay in 1872, the hull form of British ships was developed by the use of model tests and by 1906 most navies had access to such tanks. The UK still had an advantage in that Edmund Froude took over on the death of his father in 1879 and remained in charge until 1919, giving him unique experience in the shaping of ships. The increase in speed of battleships from 18 to 21kts with the introduction of *Dreadnought* led to a marked change in shape as the speed/length ratio entered a region where resistance was more associated with wave making than friction.

Edmund Froude's work on propellers had made their design straightforward except for destroyers working at high rpm. Though Parsons correctly identified the problem – cavitation – he and Froude, who collaborated closely, were unable to find a solution until gearing brought lower rpm. Manoeuvring tests had begun, including those for submarines in the vertical plane, and the behaviour of models in head seas was studied.

Armour

In the years up to 1906, there had been enormous developments in the composition and manufacture of armour leading to the almost universal use of Krupp cemented plate for thick belts. Such armour was equivalent to iron two and a half times the thickness. Most major navies carried out full scale trials of armour protection using old ships, much modified, to represent modern practice. One such trial was that against HMS *Belleisle* in 1900 which demonstrated the dramatic effect of large (12in) high explosive (HE) shells against unarmoured structure. For this reason, the Royal Navy believed a thin, upper belt to keep out HE shells to be essential. A later trial against *Edinburgh* in 1909–10 showed that British AP shells were seriously defective. This trial also showed that protective decks, intended to prevent splinters from shells bursting above from entering lower spaces – magazines, machinery – were less effective than had been assumed.

In 1906, battle practice was at 6000yds and 'long' range seen as 10,000yds at which shells

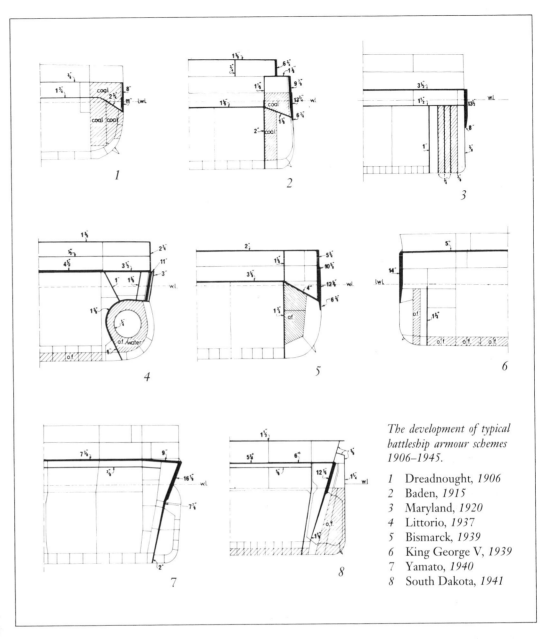

The development of typical battleship armour schemes 1906–1945.

1 Dreadnought, *1906*
2 Baden, *1915*
3 Maryland, *1920*
4 Littorio, *1937*
5 Bismarck, *1939*
6 King George V, *1939*
7 Yamato, *1940*
8 South Dakota, *1941*

would impact at about 5 degrees to the horizontal (up to 20 degrees allowing for roll). It was never expected that intact shells would reach the protective deck – a not unreasonable assumption as only in 1913 was firing tried at 16,000yds when the angle of descent was 17 degrees, plus roll.

In consequence, battleships of almost all navies had a thick (c13in) main belt at the waterline over vital spaces with a thinner, (6–9in) upper belt which would defeat big HE shells. The uppermost (forecastle) deck was about 1in thick for structural reasons which was enough to initiate the fuse of shells falling at steeper angles. The thick deck was never more than 2in thick and more often 1in. Though this was barely adequate as splinter protection, only one splinter was found below such decks in British ships after Jutland.

The US Navy introduced an entirely different system – the so-called 'all-or-nothing' scheme – of armouring in the *Nevada*, with a thick main belt and a thicker than usual (3in) deck. There was no armour at all above this citadel or at the ends. For such a protective system to work, it would have been essential that no important systems were exposed in the unprotected areas.

Earlier light cruisers relied entirely on a protective deck at the level of the waterline but when this was shown to be of limited value, later ships were given a side belt. Even this thin belt (2–3in) proved most effective in war, keeping out all HE and most SAP shells from enemy cruisers.

Structural strength had been put on a sound basis by the British naval constructor Sir Edward Reed and his assistants in 1870 but the loss of *Cobra* in 1901 showed that there were gaps in the knowledge of dynamic loading in waves and in design to resist such loading as well as some deficiencies in building practice. The Torpedo Boat Destroyer Committee which studied the lessons of this tragedy made a number of important recommendations, most of which were published, which prevented serious failures even in the light and heavily loaded structure of destroyers.

In 1912 the destroyer *Ardent* was built with longitudinal framing but the shipbuilders complained that this much stronger style of structure was too difficult to build and its use was abandoned for some twenty years in destroyers. Larger ships had longitudinal framing with intercostal transverse frames.

Subdivision and torpedo protection

The sinking in collision of HMS *Victoria* in 1893 showed the danger of flood water spreading through doors, hatches and ventilation trunking, particularly when structure was distorted by damage. By the time of *Dreadnought* unpierced bulkheads were the rule in the Royal Navy though the lesson was not fully implemented in detail, as the loss of *Audacious* was due to flooding through sanitary piping and ventilators.

German ships had closer subdivision with a very elaborate pumping and drainage system which proved more of a liability as, after damage, broken pipes and valves allowed the spread of flood water. It is not unfair to say that all navies appreciated the need for close subdivision but there was an equally general failure to get the vital details right. The point is further emphasised by the remarkable ability of British and German light cruisers to withstand damage. Because they had very few services, bulkheads were kept intact and ships remained afloat after severe damage.

The Royal Navy carried out a number of trials before the war to guide in the development of protection against torpedoes and a few trials were held by other navies. Again, the principle was clear: the torpedo had to be detonated a considerable distance from an inner longitudinal bulkhead which would remain tight after the hit. The space between would be arranged to absorb the high pressure gas from the explosion and to prevent splinters from puncturing the inner bulkhead.

The 'bulge', designed by Tennyson d'Eyncourt, was capable of giving almost complete protection against torpedoes of the day at the cost of about 1–2kts speed in a battleship. The conventional side torpedo protection was too often interrupted by wing turrets or submerged torpedo flats and often weakened by poor details.

Lessons and developments of the war

The loss of several ships from magazine explosions (some accidental) focused attention on the need to prevent flash from entering magazines and on the need for much improved deck protection. These changes, though valuable, distracted attention from the need to produce a more stable propellant, which was only partially achieved by the Royal Navy in the 1930s. The need for better torpedo protection was also clear.

These new requirements implied much bigger ships. A one-inch steel plate weighs 40 pounds per square foot and decks as thick as 8in over very many square feet were envisaged. Torpedo protection systems needed to be about 20ft deep each side. Whilst it still seemed possible to design capital ships which could resist all forms of attack available in 1919, such ships would be very big – over 50,000 tons – and very expensive.

Both the British and Americans introduced the unit system of machinery in cruisers in which engine and boiler rooms alternated so that a single hit by bomb or torpedo would usually leave at least one of each and, provided that they could be connected, the ship could still move.

Apart from 'condenseritis', machinery had proved reliable. It was realised that fuel consumption could be reduced by universal adoption of geared drive and by using superheated steam at higher pressures. Wetness was a problem, particularly in cruisers, and the need for increased freeboard was seen, together with flare. There were no serious structural problems though strained rivets led to many minor leaks, serious if in feed water tanks, deemed acceptable in mess decks.

By the end of the war the Royal Navy had the first true aircraft carrier, *Argus*, with the first effective torpedo bomber squadron embarked, a considerable number of seaplane carriers and with about 100 aircraft carried in ships of the Grand Fleet. Postwar ships would clearly have to carry aircraft.

Other developments were forgotten after the war or died of financial stringency. Mines had not been a serious threat to warships in the later years of the war, once effective sweeping gear was developed, but the number of sweepers needed was forgotten. The successful use of magnetic mines by the Royal Navy in 1918 was known to few and the prototype acoustic mine to even fewer so effective countermeasures were not put in hand.

The hydrophone – passive sonar – was the only method used in the war to locate a submerged submarine and considerable progress had been made in 'silent propulsion' so that the noise of the hunter would not drown that of the prey. With the development of ASDIC – active sonar – it was understandably but mistakenly assumed that silent propulsion was no longer required.

One lesson which was accepted by all navies was the value of the giant submarine. Most navies built such craft derived from the German U-cruisers and all were expensive failures.

Technical developments: 1920–1945

The Washington Treaty

The need for deck armour, torpedo protection and aircraft arrangements led to the design of enormous capital ships, many of which were even ordered. The crippled economies of the major powers could not afford such mastodons and the US proposal for a naval arms limitation treaty was welcomed by Treasuries everywhere.

The simple concept of limitation by displacement and gun calibre was only possible because ship types were clearly defined – everyone knew what was meant by a battleship, cruiser or destroyer – and because the gun was seen as the dominant weapon. Technically the Washington Treaty led to an emphasis on weight saving and many ingenious ideas were adopted to make the most of treaty limits or to disguise the breaking of them.

Legal measures included the extensive use of aluminium in minor structure, welding, the novel use of an exceptionally deep hull in the British *Kent* class to reduce stresses and hence save structural weight and, in the same class, an attempt to increase the effective armament by giving the 8in guns a very high rate of fire. The simpler approach of making false declarations on displacement was much more widely adopted and it is a reflection on the lack of technical expertise in intelligence departments that these lies were not recognised much earlier. An extra 15 per cent on displacement does wonders for speed or armament.

Arc welding

A limited amount of electric arc welding was carried out during the First World War. There was intense enthusiasm in the design departments of the UK and the USA and following the latter's entry into the war, there was a very active exchange of information and ideas. It was expected that all-welded warships would be introduced very soon. In fact, the first all-welded ship was the small merchant ship *Fullagar*, built by Cammell Laird in 1920.

Problems, real and imaginary, soon appeared. Shipbuilders were very reluctant to adopt new procedures, particularly those interfering with traditional trade demarcations, an attitude which lasted in some British yards until 1945. It was gradually realised that many steels, particularly high strength alloys, were unsuitable for welding and the supporting industries needed for electrodes, transformers, etc were almost non-existent. It is interesting that the first all-welded British warship, *Seagull*, was built in Devonport Dockyard as no commercial yard was willing to weld to this extent. *Seagull* was a success, needing far fewer man-hours to build than her riveted sister.

The more adventurous navies suffered for their rashness. The German 'pocket battleships' used welding extensively and suffered from frequent cracking. The Japanese *Mogami* class cracked so badly that the welded shell had to be removed and replaced with a much heavier riveted skin. The more cautious British approach had fewer problems, though it was not until the end of the Second World War that there were steels with enough ductility after welding to resist explosive loading.

Protection

Most navies used ships due for disposal under the Treaty for trials on the effect of bombs and torpedoes. A major problem of these tests was the inability of aircraft to hit a stationary and unprotected battleship from realistic heights (Mitchell's attack on *Ostfriesland* was *not* realistic). The Royal Navy solved this problem by firing bombs from howitzers at targets on land to measure penetration and then placing and detonating bombs on board the trial ship at key points. As a result of such trials in the 1920s, navies believed that battleships could be protected against most bombs and wartime experience largely confirmed this view. Modernisation of older battleships was limited by treaty to a weight growth of 3000 tons for battleships and even more severely by financial shortage. The danger of bombs to smaller ships was not recognised as it was assumed that bombing was too inaccurate to hit them.

Elaborate torpedo protection systems were designed which, in full-scale trials, gave complete security against all current torpedoes. Most of these tests were made against targets in the form of large rectangular pontoons which failed to reveal the problems of real ships. It becomes increasingly difficult to incorporate deep torpedo protection as the ship narrows towards the ends and it is further weakened at the stern where the shafts pass through it. The US Navy used forms with a long parallel section which reduced these problems at the cost of some loss of hydrodynamic performance. Finally, these simple trials did not reproduce all the pipes etc in a real ship which could act as struts and carry the force of an explosion direct from the shell to the inner bulkhead.

Both the success and failure of these systems are shown by the *Prince of Wales*. The only torpedo which hit her protection system caused little damage but she was sunk by damage from torpedoes hitting the exposed shafts aft.

If a torpedo or mine explodes underneath the bottom, the ship will flex violently – whipping – and the shock will break cast iron fittings such as machinery feet, hull valves, etc and may shake turrets and directors off their rollers; the ship may even break her back in severe cases. The crew will suffer from broken legs and fractured skulls if they are thrown against the deckhead.

Under-bottom explosions will usually rupture both inner and outer bottoms. British trials showed that triple bottoms were of little value though the US Navy reached different conclusions and fitted triple bottoms in some classes. If the double bottom space is half filled with liquid, it gives some protection. Very hard cemented armour will fracture under the shock of a very large charge such as a torpedo warhead throwing fragments into the ship, as torpedo protection needs tough, ductile steel.

Surprising improvements were made in cemented armour about 1930 in the UK and Germany though not in the USA. The depth of the cemented face was increased while at the same time the carbon content was reduced to increase toughness. As a result the new armour could resist penetration as well as older style plate 30 per cent thicker. Tough, non-cemented armour was developed for decks and turret roofs.

Since there were very few hits on armour during the war, it is hard to comment on its value in action. *Bismarck* was the only modern capital ship to be hit by a large number of shells and her thickest armour was penetrated by many shells, though at close range. She had been disabled much earlier by the destruction of her gunnery control system which had too many unprotected components. This action also confirmed that gunfire is not a very effective way of sinking a ship.

A major advantage of US ships in the Second World War was the particular efficiency of their high pressure steam machinery, giving a greater power to weight ratio and better fuel economy, manifested in greater range. The 600psi, 850-degree boiler conditions were introduced with the Somers *class of 1937 – Jouett is shown here – which became standard for wartime units. (USN)*

Machinery

Since the Washington Treaty made weight saving essential, small tube boilers and geared drive were universal. The next step was to raise the temperature and pressure of the steam. At the end of the Great War, modern British ships used saturated steam at 235psi and other navies were fairly similar. Early postwar destroyers worked at 300psi and 625 degrees F with a fuel consumption of 0.81lbs/shp/hr. In 1930 an experimental plant was fitted in *Acheron* with 500psi, 700 degrees, which gave 0.61lbs/shp/hr. There were teething problems with the high pressure turbine and the Royal Navy settled for 400psi and 700 degrees F.

Even these quite moderate steam conditions gave big savings over earlier plants: when the *Queen Elizabeth* was modernised in the late 1930s the original twenty-four boilers and the turbines were replaced with eight boilers giving a 50 per cent reduction in weight, 33 per cent in floor area while the endurance at 10kts was trebled.

The US Navy's early postwar plants worked at similar conditions to the Royal Navy's but rapid developments were made after 1930. Early teething troubles were overcome and American wartime machinery was very reliable.

Class	Pressure (psi)	Temperature (degrees F)
Porter	426	648
Mahan	400	700
Somers	600	850

The *Somers* conditions became standard in the US Navy driving through double reduction gearing. Such machinery was light in weight; cruisers were about 60shp/ton compared with 50shp/ton for British ships and was economical and reliable. Major problems were rare in Royal Navy ships but steam leaks were commonplace, boiler cleaning and brick maintenance needed far more frequently than in the US Navy (Home Fleet routine was 10 days steaming, 3 days maintenance) and they were kept running by dedicated staff.

The British marine engineering industry was badly hit by the inter-war slump and was unable to manufacture enough turbines and gearing sets for the Second World War fleet of escort vessels and minesweepers, most of which had to make do with reciprocating engines. It is a widely held fallacy that such 'simple' machinery is reliable and needs less maintenance than

the more advanced designs. In fact, the turbo-electric 'Captain' class, built in the USA, with Royal Navy crews, needed much less maintenance than UK-built primitives.

It is always possible to go too far, too fast. The German Navy went to very advanced designs, up to 1100psi, 930 degrees F in the 'Narvik' type destroyers but their numerous problems were not overcome. The machinery was so tightly packed that repairs and maintenance was very difficult.

The US Navy gained a further bonus on fuel consumption when, at the outbreak of war, they introduced a hot plastic antifouling paint which almost halved the rate at which resistance increased with time out of dock due to fouling.

The British were interested in diesel engines for cruisers in the 1920s but the diesel-electric cruising plant for *Adventure* was the only outcome and was not successful. The German Navy, backed by an excellent diesel industry, adopted an all-diesel plant for the 'pocket battleships' and as cruising engines in light cruisers. Even the best diesels of the day were big and heavy, offsetting their much lower fuel consumption and in the battleships the vibration which they caused interfered with gunnery control.

Electrical equipment

The requirement for electrical power did not grow rapidly between the wars. Bigger Royal Navy cruisers were close to 1.2kW/ton displacement throughout the period with small cruisers a little higher but the wartime additions, such as radar, brought an explosive increase in electrical demand.

Weight of Electrical Plant	
	Tons
Fiji, as designed	219
Fiji, as completed	305
Tiger, design	450

American industry gave their ships a most important bonus in lightweight electrical equipment. *Worcester*'s electrics, with 6000kW steam generated and 1000kW diesel, weighed 400 tons while the plant for the contemporary and similar British *Minotaur* was estimated at 650 tons. The US made further savings in more extensive welding, more austere equipment etc so that *Worcester*'s hull and equipment weighed 500 tons less than the British design, equivalent to the weight of an extra twin turret.

Auxiliary equipment

Aircraft carriers needed a wide range of flight deck machinery to operate effectively – lifts, accelerators, arresting gear and crash barriers. Though most of these were pioneered by the the British at or soon after the First World War, their real value was perceived only by the US Navy as they operated much larger numbers of aircraft in single strikes. Catapults for battleships and cruisers also needed considerable development between the wars.

It was realised soon after the First World War that rolling would seriously degrade the accuracy of anti-aircraft fire, particularly from smaller ships. The first attempts at roll reduction in several navies used a very large gyroscope: the results were not very good and there were fears that, if the rotor were damaged in action, it might shatter causing very severe damage. Various tank systems, derived from the work of Watts or Frahm were also tried without great success. In the mid-1930s, Denny Brown designed an active fin stabiliser which was fitted to the sloop HMS *Bittern*. Results of her trials were sufficiently encouraging for fin stabilisers to be fitted to many British sloops and 'Hunt' class destroyers though, due to lack of a good control theory, results were not as good as had been hoped.

Habitability

The Royal Navy, operating from the Arctic to the tropics, found that wartime conditions exposed a number of serious problems; indeed, one submarine reporting temperature and humidity was told that the figures given would not support human life. Peacetime cruising, in

The relatively spartan living conditions of British ships is apparent in this drawing of a typical mess in an inter-war capital ship. The crew still slept in hammocks (stowed to the left of the kit lockers) and the table and benches were folded away when not in use. There was little or no privacy. (John Roberts)

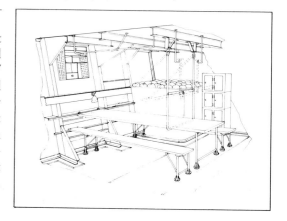

temperate waters, with scuttles open and awnings spread, did not expose the environmental problems of wartime operation with openings welded shut, overcrowded mess decks and the heat generated by all the additional electrical equipment.

Ship side lagging was applied – unhappily, with sprayed asbestos whose effects are today still killing those who applied it – heating was added for the Arctic and a very limited amount of air conditioning installed for the tropics. In most ships, fresh water distillers were inadequate for hot climates.

Other aspects of living quarters were greatly inferior to those of the US Navy, vividly illustrated by a comparison of the Royal Navy 'River' class with the US built version, the 'Colonies'. Though UK resources were scarce, the improvement in crew efficiency would surely have justified better habitability.

There was continuing debate on the value and arrangement of open bridges. The British were sure that an open bridge was essential as it was possible to see a bomb released from an enemy aircraft in time to dodge it. There was also a view that fresh air would keep lookouts and other bridge personnel awake – it is now realised that this is quite the reverse of the truth and cold air leads to rapid exhaustion.

Some wartime problems

Increased topweight in the form of extra anti-aircraft weapons and their splinter protection and of radar, with the heavier masts it needed, led to stability problems. Smaller ships had to be ballasted or restrictions imposed on the use of fuel and the main armament of many classes was reduced (partly to provide the space for close range weapons). The only major warships which capsized were four US destroyers during 1944 but many other ships of all navies had stability no better or worse than the unfortunate US ships. In addition, a small French destroyer, *Branlebas*, broke in half in a gale in the English Channel in 1940.

Production

The use of welding increased rapidly in all countries and was almost universal in the USA. There were still problems, particularly with steel ductility in low temperatures, and cracks were liable to form and spread at alarming speed. With some justice, the Royal Navy preferred riveted ships for Arctic service as though cracks would still start, they would usually stop at a seam.

It soon became clear that welded construction was most economical and speedy if prefabricated units were built under cover and finally assembled on the slip. This technique was first used extensively in the USA and largely accounted for the extraordinary speed with which they built warships. Good planning and sufficient people with the right skills for fitting out were also necessary. German and British yards were badly affected by blackout, air raids and by severe labour shortages but even making every allowance, their productivity does not compare well with US yards.

British yards introduced prefabrication with the 'Loch' class and it was found that, though building time was reduced, the man-hours needed, increased. The German Type XXI U-boats were prefabricated but had a very considerable number of problems, mainly in the hydraulic system, which prevented any of them playing a part in the war. Rivalry between Vickers and Chatham Dockyard led to two different schemes for prefabrication for the Royal Navy's 'A' class submarines, both rapid and relatively problem free.

Submarines

There has been little mention of submarine technology in either part since in these vessels technology is so closely linked with other aspects of submarines that most developments are covered in a later chapter. However, one or two specific points need mention.

In the First World War German submarine designs had the great advantage of diesels which could give 300hp per cylinder; the best British engines could only manage 100hp/cylinder. It was the inability to obtain powerful diesels which led to steam propulsion in the 'K' class, with all the problems which that involved.

The fast 'R' class, with a submerged speed of about 15kts, had a safe diving depth little greater than their length and with hydroplanes operated by rod and cable must have been frightening to control, perhaps a contributory cause of their early disposal, which mainly seems to have been due to the mistaken belief that ASDICs had made submarines ineffective and specialist anti-submarine submarines were no longer needed.

In the 1930s the US Navy joined with the railway industry to develop powerful and reliable high speed diesels. Once sorted out, these were very successful and enabled a 3kt increase in surface speed. Since the components of these high speed units were small and standardised, repair and maintenance was easy. Considerable attention was paid to habitability, so

The fast Type XXI U-boats were designed for modular prefabricated construction. Here the stern section and a No 3 section can be seen prior to assembly. (CMP)

important for long patrols in the Pacific. US submarines were air conditioned and were not short of fresh water.

Second World War U-boats were able to achieve considerably greater diving depths than submarines of other nations – though not so much as is sometimes claimed. In part, this was due to earlier adoption of welded pressure hulls, to lightweight (short life) batteries and to highly loaded engines. To a greater extent, their diving depth was due to a theoretical breakthrough by von Mises in the design of cylinders exposed to external pressure. For the first time, the strength of frames and plating could be considered together, showing that older designs had devoted far too much weight to frames. The new designs which resulted made much more effective use of their structural weight and so could dive deeper.

Conclusion

The battleship of 1906 was the most complicated artifact of its day and ships were to increase greatly in complexity by 1945. It became increasingly clear that a powerful navy could only be built by a country with an industry which was advanced and efficient in many different areas of technology. A simple count of guns and comparison of displacements was little guide to the capability of the later ships in battle.

David K Brown, RCNC

1

The Battleship and Battlecruiser

WITH the evolution of the modern warship, the battleship was considered the primary combatant, or capital ship, in all navies. It carried the heaviest of guns and was the best protected of all of the ships in the fleet. The battleship was viewed as symbolic of a nation's industrial capability and scientific achievement. It was, truly, a projection of national power – vital to the large colonial powers in order to maintain their empires, necessary to the smaller states for the preservation of their sovereignty.

Genesis of the *Dreadnought*

Just after the turn of the century, a typical battleship carried a mixed battery of heavy guns and an assortment of lighter weapons. For example, the British battleships of the *King Edward VII* class laid down between 1902 and 1904, displaced 16,350 tons, carried four 12in, four 9.2in and ten 6in guns, fourteen 12pdrs, fourteen 3pdrs and two Maxim machine-guns. They were capable of 19kts speed. All of these guns were intended to be used against other battleships. The lighter calibres were also meant to defend against attacking torpedo boats.

In the early 1900s, the efficiency and accuracy of the 12in guns limited the effective fighting range of battleships to about 6000yds. Because the slow-firing, heavy 12in guns had limited accuracy but considerable penetrating power, they were aimed to make destructive hits on the main battery or armour belt of an adversary. Fire from the medium calibre weapons was directed at the more lightly armoured areas which they could penetrate and where their higher rate of fire could be expected to score a greater number of hits. Finally, at the prevailing battle ranges, the light weapons with their high rate of fire were used to rake the decks and superstructure of the opposing ship.

The sides and turrets of battleships were protected with heavy belt armour thick enough to defeat the largest shells which were expected to be used against them. The smaller calibre guns in the superstructure were enclosed with lighter armour under the same theory. Because trajectories were nearly flat at the effective battle ranges, the decks were protected with thinner armour so that a shell would glance off rather than punch through, and would protect the vitals from splinters caused by bursts over the deck.

While numerous classes of multi-battery battleships continued to be built by all major naval powers, vast improvements in naval gunnery were taking place. Acutely aware of the need for greater accuracy, Captain Percy Scott, RN, began the revolution in naval gunnery when, in 1898, he invented the technique of continuous aiming and introduced salvo firing and spotting with optical rangefinding equipment. His innovations more than doubled the accuracy of large calibre guns. Within the next few years, they enabled battle ranges to be extended as far as 8000yds. Across the Atlantic, Scott's counterpart in the US Navy, Captain William Sims, was working along much the same lines to reform US naval gunnery. And thus, steadily, the science of fire control for naval gunnery began to evolve.

Another important factor that gave impetus to gunnery improvements was the torpedo. In 1903, the maximum effective range of torpedoes was 3000yds. Newer models, however, were expected to be capable of 4000yds or more. Since battleships also carried torpedoes, there was considerable advantage in extending the battle range for gunnery beyond torpedo range. That would obviate the use of torpedoes except in a closing action.

It soon became apparent that when all of a battleship's batteries were firing, it was impossible to accurately distinguish 12in shell splashes from those of 9.2in, 8in, 7in or even 6in shells. A solution was to use salvoes from the 12in shells to establish range and deflection from which were devised elaborate methods of correction for the other calibres. The secondary calibres, however, were becoming less effective in armour penetration as battle ranges were extended. From a technical standpoint, it was far better to have a ship with a uniform battery of the same calibre – the savings in weight and space by eliminating the secondary calibres allowed the doubling of the number of

Dreadnought at a pre-1914 fleet review, heading a line of typical pre-dreadnoughts. The magnitude of the step forward represented by this ship is apparent in her greater size and the asymmetrical layout necessary to accommodate the all-big-gun armament. (CMP)

The Invincible *class (this is* Indomitable *about 1910) introduced the all-big-gun concept to the armoured cruiser. Originally called 'dreadnought cruisers' or 'battleship-cruisers', eventually the term 'battlecruisers' evolved.* (CMP)

heaviest guns. The genesis of the all-big-gun ship was at hand.

The concept of a single calibre, all-big-gun ship took shape almost simultaneously with a number of designers world-wide. In 1900 Admiral Sir John Fisher spent considerable time in the Royal Dockyard at Malta discussing his ideas with Chief Constructor W H Gard. At about the same time, Italian Naval Constructor Vittorio Cuniberti, designer of the *Regina Elena* class light battleships of 1901, submitted a paper on 'An Ideal Battleship for the British Grand Fleet' which was published in the 1903 edition of *Jane's Fighting Ships*. In the United States in 1901, Commander H C Poundstone, USN, attracted the attention of President Roosevelt with a paper on the merits of an all-big-gun ship. The matter was also discussed in the US Naval Institute *Proceedings* by Professor P R Alger, the US Navy's gunnery expert, and Naval Constructor David W Taylor.

Having determined the role of future battleships to be the destruction of other battleships and repulsing torpedo attacks, the US Navy's General Board initiated design studies for an all-big-gun battleship in the autumn of 1903. On 3 March 1905, the Congress authorised the construction of two such vessels that became the *South Carolina* and *Michigan*. Both ships were completed early in 1910, and mounted eight 12in guns in twin turrets for the main battery and twenty-two 3in guns in their torpedo defence battery; their speed was 18.5kts. The main battery was arranged with two turrets forward and aft all on the centreline, turrets No 2 and 3 firing over No 1 and 4 which provided an eight-gun broadside.

In 1902, Admiral Sir John Fisher became the Second Sea Lord, and in 1903, was appointed the Commander-in-Chief, Portsmouth. While at Portsmouth, he was able to pursue his interest in an all-big-gun super-ship. Aware of similar American efforts, Fisher had W H Gard, now the Manager of the Constructive Department at Portsmouth, prepare a number of schemes for his super-ship, nicknamed HMS *Untakable*.

Admiral Fisher became the First Sea Lord in October 1904 and transferred W H Gard to Whitehall as Assistant Director of Naval Construction where he was to complete the super-ship design studies. In December, Fisher appointed a Committee on Designs and became

its Chairman. The Committee first convened on 3 January 1905 to consider a number of designs and gun arrangements. The action the previous August off Port Arthur during the Russo-Japanese War was fresh in their minds. During that engagement, 12in salvoes were exchanged at the extreme range of an estimated 14,000yds (although 10,000yds seems more likely). Two 12in shells struck the Russian flagship *Czarevitch* killing the admiral and all personnel controlling the ship. The Russian fleet, following the erratic movements of its flagship, was led into confusion. Two 12in shells, fired at 14,000 yards, were thought to have decided the battle.

The Committee decided upon a design which became *Dreadnought*, displacing 17,900 tons, with ten 12in guns mounted in twin turrets for her main battery, twenty-seven 12pdr (3in) for the torpedo defence battery and a speed of 21kts, produced by the revolutionary new turbine machinery. Her main battery was arranged with one centreline turret forward, two wing turrets between the funnels and two turrets on the centreline aft, allowing an eight-gun broadside.

As a result of the Committee's decisions, the *Dreadnought* was to be laid down as soon as possible and completed within a year. Trials were to be conducted without delay to gain experience for further ships, and no new battleships were to be ordered until these trials were completed and analysed. Construction of the *Dreadnought* was assigned to HM Dockyard, Portsmouth. Her keel was laid on 2 October 1905, less than nine months after her design was fixed, and she was launched just over four months later on 10 February 1906 by King Edward VII. The *Dreadnought* was pronounced completed and ready for trials on 3 October

1906, just a year and a day after her keel was laid. This feat was an impressive demonstration of Britain's industrial capabilities.

So it was that *Dreadnought* became the first of a new type of capital ship after which all future battleships and battlecruisers would be patterned. The genius of the *Dreadnought* design would make all existing battleships obsolete. Nearly a century later, the *Iowa*s, last of the world's battleships in service, are still often referred to as dreadnoughts.

Genesis of the battlecruiser

Traditionally, cruisers have been used for independent operation or employed with a main battle force performing valuable scouting and dispatch services. Operating independently, they maintained a naval presence in peacetime and were effective in showing the flag. During hostilities, their primary role was the protection of friendly shipping and the interdiction and destruction of an enemy's commerce. Cruisers eventually developed along three lines of specialisation: light unarmoured units for dispatch service and picket duty with a battle force; protected types for battlefleet scouting and support of independent operations; and the armoured cruiser to reinforce the battle line and to serve as a powerful leader for independent operations.

The armoured cruisers of the early 1900s were armed with medium calibre guns, similar in size and number to a battleship's secondary batteries, and were protected against these

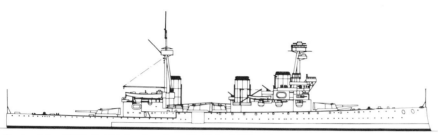

Dreadnought, *1906, British battleship, 21,850t, 527ft*

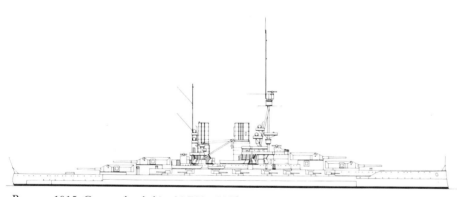

Invincible, *1907, British battlecruiser, 20,100t, 567ft*

Bayern, *1915, German battleship, 31,700t, 590ft*

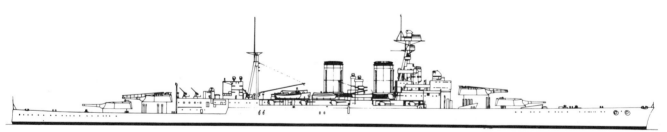

Hood, *1918, British battlecruiser, 45,200t, 860ft*

CAPITAL SHIP GROWTH 1906–1945

Date is of launch; tonnage is full load; length is overall; scale is 1/1500.

weapons with both belt and deck armour. Fast and powerful, armoured cruisers were, in effect, an auxiliary capital ship. For example, the American armoured cruisers of the *Tennessee* class, laid down between 1903 and 1905, displaced 14,500 tons, carried four 10in, sixteen 6in and twenty-two 3in guns and could make nearly 23kts.

When Fisher's Committee on Designs met in December 1904, the matter of a new armoured cruiser design was also on the agenda.

It was taken up in January 1905, at the same time the *Dreadnought* issue was being settled. Just before the Committee convened, it learned that the Japanese would soon begin the construction of two *Tsukuba* class cruisers of 13,750 tons, mounting four 12in guns, twelve 4.7in and two 14pdrs, with a rated speed of 22kts. They appeared to be patterned after the Royal Navy's *Duncan* class battleships but with a lighter armour scheme and 3kts more speed. The Committee began its considerations with

the knowledge that the new ships should be armed with 12in guns and they would need a speed advantage of at least three knots. In March 1905, they selected a design which became *Invincible*, which displaced 17,250 tons, had eight 12in guns mounted in twin turrets for her main battery, sixteen 4in guns for her torpedo defence battery and a speed of 25kts (all exceeded 26kts on trials). The arrangement of the main battery featured one turret forward on the centreline, two turrets amidships offset

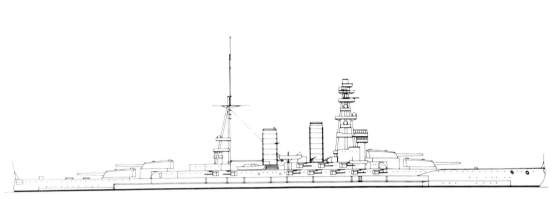

Nagato, *1920, Japanese battleship, 38,500t, 700ft*

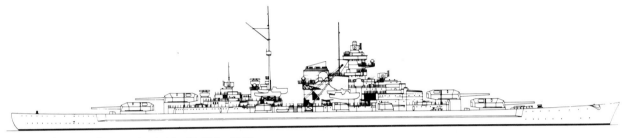

Bismarck, *1939, German battleship, 50,900t, 814ft*

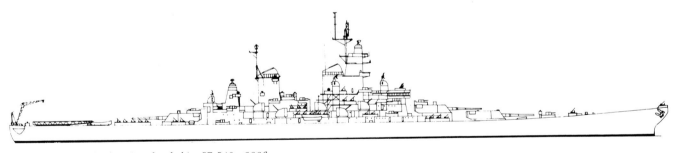

Yamato, *1940, Japanese battleship, 69,990t, 840ft*

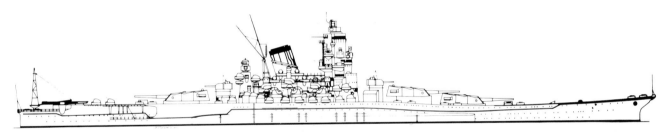

New Jersey, *1942, American battleship, 57,540t, 888ft*

en echelon and one turret aft on the centreline offering a broadside of eight guns. The importance of greater speed for the new cruisers was proved at the Battle of Tsushima during the Russo-Japanese War. A six-knot speed advantage gave the Japanese a choice of tactical positions and enabled them to maintain a minimum rate of change in target range.

Unlike the fanfare of publicity surrounding the *Dreadnought*, details of the new cruisers were kept secret. The three *Invincible*s were completed by mid-1908. After their entry into service, when their details and armament became known, the new ships were called battleship-cruisers and finally, more simply, battlecruisers. The battlecruiser was clearly designed to fight against armoured cruisers with an inferior battery, either when scouting against them in a fleet action or when hunting them down on the trade routes. During the First World War they performed exceptionally well in the latter role when the *Invincible* and *Inflexible* easily overpowered the German armoured cruisers *Scharnhorst* and *Gneisenau* at the Battle of the Falklands on 8 December 1914. The basic premise of their existence was to engage inferior units with their superior firepower and, with their superior speed, to avoid action with ships of equal or greater firepower. That premise was later upset at the battle of Dogger Bank on 24 January 1915 when the German Navy appeared with their own battlecruisers.

The pre-1914 naval arms race

The construction of the *Dreadnought* and *Invincible* incited a naval arms race between Great Britain and Germany which only ended with the First World War. Other nations also built dreadnoughts, and some of their designs and concepts had a profound and lasting effect on all future dreadnought-type ships. A brief summation of each country's building programme follows.

Germany

The *Dreadnought* and *Invincible* took the world's navies, and particularly the German navy, by surprise. It made all existing battleships obsolete and provided the German navy with the opportunity and incentive to attempt to achieve parity with the Royal Navy. Until the late 1890s, the German navy was primarily a coastal defence force, but with the accession of Kaiser Wilhelm II in 1888, naval policy gradually changed to include operations on the high seas for the protection of German overseas trade and colonial commitments. In 1897, Wilhelm II appointed Admiral Alfred von Tirpitz to the post of Secretary of State for Naval Affairs and in 1898 he convinced the German Reichstag to pass the First Navy Law authorising a fleet of nineteen battleships and eight coastal defence ships and mandated their replacement within twenty-five years. The Second Navy Law was passed in 1900, increasing the number of capital ships to thirty-eight battleships and eight large cruisers, its passage facilitated by Royal Navy seizures of German ships during the Boer War.

In response to the German building programme, Great Britain formed alliances with Japan, Russia and France. This realignment of

world powers was viewed as an attempt to contain the German Empire, and the Reichstag amended the Navy Law in 1908, reducing the replacement time of capital ships from twenty-five to twenty years and directing the eight large cruisers of the 1900 law to be battlecruisers. The German navy never attained numerical superiority or even parity, but in only twenty years, it went from a coastal defence force to the second largest and most powerful navy in the world.

The four *Nassau* class battleships, the first authorised under the Navy Law of 1900, were not laid down until mid-1907. They were Germany's first dreadnoughts and all were completed by 1910. Although outgunned by *Dreadnought* herself, they featured a greater distribution of armour but the tight subdivision of the hull was compromised by an overly elaborate pumping and flooding system which was itself vulnerable to underwater damage. These features became characteristic of all German capital ships. As completed, the *Nassau* class displaced 18,900 tons, had twelve 11in guns mounted in twin turrets for their main battery. For torpedo defence, their battery included a number of 5.9in (15cm) and 3.4in (8.8cm) guns which became the standard secondary calibres in German capital ships throughout the Great War. Their main battery was arranged with one centreline turret forward, two wing turrets on each side amidships and one turret aft on the centreline for an eight-gun broadside. They retained reciprocating machinery and their speed was over 19kts.

Germany's first battlecruiser, the *Von der Tann*, was not laid down until March 1908. Her main battery consisted of eight 11in guns, in an arrangement similar to that in the *Invincible*. She had a design speed of nearly 25kts, but exceeded 27kts on trial. As in the *Nassau* class battleships, the *Von der Tann* was outgunned by her British counterparts, but enjoyed generally

superior protection. She was completed in 1910.

The first German ships built under the amended Naval Law of 1908 were the four ships of the *Helgoland* class. The gun calibre of the main battery was increased to 12in to match the British shell size and weight of broadside but the battery was still arranged as in the *Nassau* class. The last of the class was completed in 1912. They displaced 22,800 tons and had a speed of 20kts.

The two *Moltke* class battlecruisers were also part of the 1908 programme. Essentially enlarged versions of the *Von der Tann* displacing 22,600 tons, they were the first European capital ships to use superfiring turrets as in the American *South Carolina* class. They carried ten 11in guns in twin turrets; one turret was mounted forward, two were *en echelon* amidships and two were aft with Turret No 4 firing over No 5. A ten-gun broadside was possible with this arrangement. Their armour was heavier than in the *Von der Tann* and they were designed to do 25.5kts, although both reached 28kts on trials. An improved unit with greater horsepower, the *Seydlitz*, was slightly larger, displacing 24,610 tons and achieving 28kts on trials. The *Moltkes* were completed in 1912 and the *Seydlitz* in 1913.

In 1910, five 24,380-ton *Kaiser* class battleships were laid down. Their main battery of ten 12in guns was arranged as in the *Moltke* class to fire a ten-gun broadside. Introducing turbines to German battleships, they could achieve 21kts. The last ship of the class was completed in 1913.

Work on the four *König* class battleships ran almost concurrently with the *Kaiser* class. They were slightly larger and improved versions of the *Kaiser*s with all of the main battery on the centreline. The ten 12in guns were mounted in twin turrets with two forward and two aft in a superfiring arrangement and one amidships between the funnels. They displaced 25,390 tons and could make 21kts. All were completed in 1914.

The construction of the three large battlecruisers of the *Derfflinger* class began in January 1912. They carried the same 12in gun as in the *König* class battleships, but with eight guns in twin turrets, two forward and two aft in a balanced, superfiring arrangement. Their speed was around 27kts. The last of these 26,180-ton ships was not completed until 1917.

The first German dreadnoughts were the Nassau *class, which adopted a symmetrical, if inefficient, layout of main armament with two twin turrets on each broadside.* Westfalen *is pictured here in July 1910. (CMP)*

German battlecruisers, like the Moltke *seen here, were generally less heavily armed than their British opponents, with less emphasis on speed, but a greater proportion of displacement devoted to protection. The anti-torpedo net defences carried by all German capital ships before the war can be seen stowed along the armour belt. (CMP)*

The Germans did not match the Royal Navy's 13.5in gun but when the British developed a 15in gun for the *Queen Elizabeth* class battleships, the Germans designed a comparable 15in gun for the four 28,000-ton *Bayern* class battleships. The first two were completed in 1916 but the exigencies of war prevented the finishing of the last two. Eight 15in guns were mounted in twin turrets, two forward and two aft as in the *Königs*. Their speed was a little over 21kts.

The last German capital ships of the First World War were the four *Mackensen* class battlecruisers. They were armed with a new 13.8in (35cm) gun designed belatedly to match the British 13.5in and American and Japanese 14in guns. These large 31,510-ton ships were essentially an enlargement of the *Derfflinger* class with their eight main armament guns mounted in the same battery arrangement. They were designed for 28kts, but none was completed. Work on three improved *Mackensens*, the *Ersatz Yorck* class, began in 1916. They were to be 33,000 tons and mount eight 15in guns; none was ever launched.

Great Britain

The design of British capital ships was characterised by progressive improvements over the previous class. Both size and armament gradually increased in order to accommodate new technical developments in gunnery, protection and machinery. While drawings for the *Dreadnought* were being finalised, a design for the next generation, the *Bellerophon* class, proceeded. The *Bellerophon* class was an 18,800-ton version of the *Dreadnought* design, with increased underwater protection and a rearranged topside. All four ships were completed in early 1909. Overlapping the design and construction of the three *Bellerophons* were three 19,560-ton ships of the *St Vincent* class. Nine feet longer but otherwise similar, they introduced a more powerful 12in gun. The last unit was completed in 1910. Both classes were designed to make 21kts.

The *Neptune* and her two half-sisters completed in 1911 featured a new main battery arrangement for the ten 12in guns. There was one turret forward, two amidships *en echelon* as in the *Invincible* class battlecruisers, and two aft with turret No 4 firing over No 5. This was the first superfiring arrangement to be used in the Royal Navy. The *Neptune*s displaced 19,680 tons and had a speed of 21kts.

The three 18,500-ton battlecruisers of the *Indefatigable* class were almost a duplication of the *Invincible*s, being only slightly longer to give the centre turrets better arcs of fire. Although they had the new 12in gun, their protection was inferior to the German *Von der Tann* and *Moltke*s. Their 25kt design speed matched the *Tann*'s but in practical terms they were a knot or so slower than the *Moltke*s. The last ship was completed in mid-1913.

The four 22,200-ton battleships of the *Orion* class introduced the 13.5in gun in a new main battery arrangement, and were quickly dubbed super-dreadnoughts. Ten 13.5in guns were mounted in twin turrets all on the centreline. Two superfiring turrets were located forward and aft with a single turret placed amidships. The new gun gave them a much heavier weight of broadside than their German contemporaries. They had heavier armour and could make 21kts. All were completed by mid-1912.

Two *Lion* class battlecruisers and an improved near-sister, the *Queen Mary*, were

The Grand Fleet at Scapa Flow in 1917, displaying the main lines of British battleship development: in the foreground is the Neptune *with another early 12in dreadnought astern; beyond them is a line of three* Orion *class ships (the first 13.5in-armed battleships); further off to the right can be seen the requisitioned* Erin *(ex-Turkish* Reshadieh) *with funnels close together, and* Canada *(ex-Chilean* Almirante Latorre), *with two single-funnelled* Revenge *class 15in dreadnoughts; in the centre distance are two* Iron Dukes *and a 'light battlecruiser' of the* Courageous *class, and in the left distance the battlecruisers* Australia *and* New Zealand. *The main absentees are the majority of the battlecruisers and the* Queen Elizabeth*s. (CMP)*

armed with eight of the new 13.5in guns in twin turrets all on the centreline. Two turrets were forward as in the *Orion*s but the third turret was amidships between the funnels; the fourth turret was aft. The *Lion*s displaced 26,270 tons and had a speed of 27kts. The *Queen Mary* was 26,770 tons and half a knot faster. The last ship was completed in 1913.

The next eight battleships were improved editions of the *Orion*s with the same main battery. Four ships of the 23,000-ton *King George V* class were followed by four 25,820-ton units of the *Iron Duke* class. Both classes were capable of 21kts. The main difference between them was an increase in the secondary armament to 6in in the *Iron Duke*s. All were completed by 1914.

In 1911, three battleships had been laid down in British yards to the order of foreign governments: the 22,780-ton *Reshadieh* for Turkey; the 28,600-ton *Almirante Latorre* for Chile; and the 27,500-ton *Rio de Janeiro* for Brazil. All were 21-knot ships. They were completed in 1914 and 1915, after the start of the First World War, and as a result all were taken over by the Royal Navy as the *Erin*, *Canada* and *Agincourt* respectively.

The 28,430-ton battlecruiser *Tiger* was an improved *Queen Mary* influenced by the battlecruiser *Kongo* being built for Japan. Her armament was the same as in the *Queen Mary* except that the amidships turret was placed aft of the funnels for an unobstructed arc of fire. The secondary battery was increased to 6in. Her speed was 28kts and she was completed in late 1914.

The first all-big-gun ships to be designed were actually the American South Carolina *class, but* Dreadnought *was the first to be completed. However, the US ships had the advantage of superfiring turrets fore and aft which with two guns less than* Dreadnought *permitted the same eight-gun broadside. This is* USS Michigan *as completed.* (USN)

Between 1915 and 1917, ten battleships mounting the new 15in gun were completed. Five were of the 27,500-ton *Queen Elizabeth* class; five comprised the 28,000-ton *Revenge* class. They had a balanced main battery of two twin turrets forward and aft, and fired a heavier broadside, even with two less guns, than the *Iron Duke*s. The *Queens* had a speed of 24kts and the *Revenges* could make better than 21kts. The ten ships were the last British battleships built during the First World War, while a further unit of each class was cancelled in August 1914, and two *Revenges* reordered as battlecruisers.

These two ships of the *Renown* class were very fast, lightly armoured, shallow draft vessels displacing 27,947 tons. They were both completed by September 1916, and mounted six 15in guns. Two turrets were located forward and one aft and their secondary armament was a reversion to the 4in gun. They had a speed of over 30kts.

Another pair of even more lightly armoured 'battlecruisers' – officially 'large light cruisers' – was completed in 1917. The 18,600-ton *Courageous* class had only four 15in guns in one turret forward and one aft. Their speed was 31kts. A modified near-sister was completed in July 1917 as the 19,500-ton *Furious*; she was to have mounted two single 18in guns, but an aircraft hangar and flying platform was fitted in place of the after gun.

The last British capital ship to be built during the First World War was the 36,300-ton battlecruiser *Hood*, but she was not completed until 1920. Eight 15in guns were mounted in a balanced battery as in the *Queen Elizabeth* class, and the *Hood* was capable of 32kts.

United States

The naval building programme in the United States progressed at a slower pace, and had the Americans felt compelled to match Great Britain and Germany, the *South Carolina*s might well have been the first all-big-gun ships. A significant contribution to battleship design was the superfiring main battery guns all arranged on the centreline which was eventually adopted by all navies. This was made possible by moving the vulnerable sighting hoods from the top to the sides of turrets.

Freed from a 16,000-ton Congressional Limit, the two 20,500-ton *Delaware* class battleships were 25 per cent larger than the *South Carolina*s and carried ten 12in guns in five turrets on the centreline with two superfiring forward and three aft. Turret No 3 fired over Nos 4 and 5 which were back to back. The

The last pre-treaty US capital ships were the four Colorados *(one not completed) which were similar in appearance to the preceding* Tennessee *class, but introduced the twin 16in gun in place of the triple 14in. They were not heavily modified between the wars, and apart from the catapults and aircraft,* Maryland *seen here in the 1930s was substantially as completed. (USN)*

secondary battery was increased to 5in which became the standard for American battleships. Their speed was 21kts and they were completed in 1910. Two improved *Delaware*s, of the 21,825-ton *Florida* class were completed in 1911. The main battery duplicated that in the *Delaware*s as did the 21kt speed.

The two 26,000-ton *Wyoming* class battleships introduced a new, more powerful 12in gun. Essentially enlarged *Florida*s, the main battery had twelve 12in guns in three pairs of turrets, one pair forward and two pairs aft. The speed was over 20kts. Both ships were completed in 1912.

A new 14in gun was introduced in the two *New York* class battleships completed in 1914. The guns, developed to match those in the Japanese *Kongo*s, were mounted in five twin turrets and in an arrangement similar to the *Wyoming* class except one turret replaced the centre pair. They displaced 27,000 tons and had a speed of 21kts.

The two *Nevada* class battleships which followed introduced the revolutionary all-or-nothing concept of protection where only the vital parts of the ship were covered with heavy armour. In theory, the armour provided immunity against specific weapons between certain ranges. This created an immune zone which was an expression of expected battle ranges. The inner edge was the shortest range at which the side belt could not be penetrated and the outer edge the shortest range at which plung-

ing fire would penetrate the deck armour. Eventually, this theory was accepted universally. The 27,500-ton *Nevada*s carried ten 14in guns in two twin and two triple turrets, with two of each mounted forward and aft, with the twins firing over the triples. This was the first triple gun mounting in the US Navy. They had a speed of over 20kts. Both ships were completed in May 1916.

Enlarged versions of the *Nevada*s, the *Pennsylvania* class displaced 31,400 tons and carried twelve 14in guns in a fore and aft, balanced, triple-turret arrangement. Their standard speed was 21kts and they were completed in 1916. The three 32,000-ton *New Mexico* class battleships continued to develop the basic design concepts of the *Nevada*. The gun calibre and turret layout were the same as in the *Pennsylvania*, but the twelve 14in guns were a new and more powerful model. A new type of turbo-electric machinery produced the standard 21kts. The last unit was completed in 1918.

In October 1916, the two 32,300-ton *Tennessee* class battleships were begun. The main battery of twelve 14in guns was arranged the same as in the *New Mexico*, and turbo-electric machinery also produced the 21kt speed but their underwater protection was greatly improved. The last ship was not completed until October 1921.

The four ships of the *Colorado* class were identical to the *Tennessee*s except for their main battery of eight 16in guns in twin turrets and a modest increase in displacement to 32,600 tons. The gun calibre was increased to match the 16in model used in the Japanese *Nagato*s. The last ship was completed in 1923.

Six large 43,200-ton *South Dakota* class battleships were authorised in 1917 and laid down in 1920. All were cancelled under the Washington Treaty and broken up on the shipways. They were to have been enlarged *Colorado*s with twelve improved 16in guns in four triple turrets and capable of making 23kts.

The first and only American battlecruisers were the six 43,500-ton *Lexington*s begun in 1920. All fell victim to the Washington Treaty of 1922 but two were allowed to be completed as aircraft carriers. They would have been 33kt versions of the *Colorado*s using the same main battery layout but with an improved 16in gun.

Later American ships mounted more guns but sided turrets as popular in European navies were never adopted, all guns in US capital ships being in centreline mountings. After Dreadnought *arguably the next major step forward was the 'all-or-nothing' concept of armouring introduced with the* Nevada *class of 1916. The 5in secondary armament was mounted on the main deck, the casemates being sealable with the prominent weather flaps seen amidships in this view of* Nevada *in 1918. (USN)*

16in guns and the same high speed. The main battery layout was as in the American *New York* class.

The last Japanese capital ships to be started before the Washington Treaty were the four 40,000-ton *Amagi* class battlecruisers. They were to have been 30kt enlargements of the *Tosa* design with the same main battery.

Italy

Italy entered the twentieth century as a technically competent industrial country with considerable shipbuilding experience. She was concerned about the dreadnought race to the extent that it affected her position in the Mediterranean. There was concern about the Austro-Hungarian Empire in the Adriatic and French expansion in North Africa when the first dreadnought-type battleship, the *Dante Alighieri*, was laid down in June 1909. It was the first battleship to use triple turrets in its main battery with twelve 12in guns arranged in four centreline turrets; one forward, two amidships between the funnels and one aft, providing a twelve-gun broadside. The secondary battery was a mix of 4.7in and 3in guns which was also carried in the next class. The *Dante Alighieri* displaced 19,552 tons and made nearly 23kts on trials. She was completed in 1913.

The three *Conte di Cavour* class ships which followed carried thirteen 12in guns in three triple and two twin turrets. Both forward and aft twin turrets fired over triple turrets and one triple turret was mounted amidships between the funnels. The three ships were completed

Japan

After soundly defeating the Russian Navy in 1905, Japan did not feel compelled to enter the capital ship race. The war had strained Japan's economy and it was not until 1909 that the first all-big-gun ships of the *Settsu* class were laid down (even these had main armament guns of two different lengths so were not true dreadnoughts). The two ships displaced 21,420 tons and carried twelve 12in guns in an arrangement similar to Germany's *Westfalen* and *Helgoland* classes. The secondary battery was a mix of 6in and 4.7in guns. Their speed was 21kts.

To benefit from British experience, the battlecruiser *Kongo* was ordered from the firm of Vickers in 1910. Three additional ships of the class were later ordered from Japanese yards. They were fast, powerful ships with a high standard of protection. Displacing 26,320 tons, they could make 27.5kts. They were armed with eight 14in guns in twin turrets, all on the centreline, with turret No 2 firing over No 1 forward and Nos 3 and 4 widely separated aft. The last unit was completed in 1915.

In 1912, the first of four battleships was begun in response to the American *New York* class. The first two ships became the 29,326-

ton *Fuso* class with twelve 14in guns in six twin turrets. A centreline arrangement was now standard in the Japanese Navy, and there were superfiring turrets forward and aft with the turrets amidships separated by the second funnel. The second pair of ships was the 29,980-ton *Ise* class with the same main battery but arranged in three pairs of superfiring turrets as in the American *Arkansas* class. The last of the four was completed in 1917. All were capable of 23kts.

Two 32,720-ton *Nagato* class battleships were begun in 1917 to counter the American *Colorado* and British *Queen Elizabeth* classes. Their main battery of eight 16in guns had the same arrangement as in their foreign contemporaries. They had a speed of nearly 27kts. The last ship was completed in 1921.

Two large 38,500-ton battleships of the *Tosa* class, begun in 1920, were cancelled in 1922 under the Washington Treaty. They were to have been enlarged *Nagato*s with ten improved

The Nagato *class, the first entirely Japanese designed capital ships, were the largest battleships in the world when completed (although the battlecruiser* Hood *was larger). They were also the fastest, the Japanese concealing their true speed of over 26kts for most of the inter-war period. The ships were completed with straight funnels but exhaust gases affected the bridge platforms and after trying a funnel cap in 1921, the fore funnel was angled aft in 1924 as seen here on* Nagato. *Both ships were heavily rebuilt in the mid-1930s. (CMP)*

France was late to enter the dreadnought race (with the four Courbet *class ships laid down in 1910) and progress was virtually stopped by the overriding needs of the land war in Flanders. The* Courbet *class, of which this is the name-ship, were able to adopt superfiring turrets but still carried two on the broadside. The succeeding* Bretagnes *were similar but replaced the twelve 12in guns with ten 13.4in, all in centreline turrets. (CMP)*

by 1915. Their displacement was 22,800 tons and their best trials speed was 22.2kts.

Two improved dreadnoughts of the *Andrea Doria* class had the same dimensions as the *Cavour*s and the same gun calibre and arrangement but their displacement was 22,956 tons. Part of the weight increase was due to the replacement of the 4.7in guns in the secondary battery with sixteen 6in guns. They were commissioned by 1916, and were the last Italian battleships to be completed before the naval arms race of the 1930s.

In 1914, four 34,000-ton *Caracciolo* class battleships were begun. They were to have been 28kt ships armed with eight 15in guns in a balanced four-turret layout but none was completed.

France

By 1900, the primary concern of the French navy was maintaining communications with her colonies in North Africa and protecting her flanks from the Italians. For several years, the navy had been in a state of decline as a result of an incoherent naval policy, political patronage and general mismanagement. France and Great Britain had been rivals for centuries, which had sustained France's naval programmes in the past, and the 1904 entente between them only further eroded the position of the French navy. It was not until 1909, after the Anglo-German naval rivalry was well under way, that the rebuilding of the French navy began.

France's first dreadnoughts were the four ships of the 23,100-ton *Courbet* class laid down in 1910. They carried twelve 12in guns mounted in twin turrets, and a standard secondary battery of 5.5in guns. The main battery was arranged with two superfiring turrets forward and aft and two wing turrets amidships giving a ten-gun broadside. Their speed was 20kts. The last units were completed in 1914.

The *Courbet* class hull design was repeated on the three ships of the *Bretagne* class which were fitted with a new 34cm (13.4in) gun. There were five twin, centreline turrets; two were in superfiring positions forward and aft and one was amidships between the funnels. The 20kt *Bretagne*s displaced 23,230 tons. The last ship,

completed in 1916, was the last French battleship completed before the Washington Treaty.

Five 25,230-ton ships of the *Normandie* class were begun in 1913 to a radical new design featuring three 13.4in quadruple turrets. One turret was located forward, one amidships and one aft. Their speed was to be 21kts. None was completed but one survived to be converted into an aircraft carrier after the Washington Treaty. Five *Lyon* class ships, a 27,500-ton enlargement of the *Normandie*, were planned with a fourth quadruple turret superfiring aft. The project was cancelled after the First World War started.

Russia

After a staggering defeat by the Japanese in 1905, the Russians began to rebuild a fleet worthy of a world naval power. With a vast coastline to protect, their naval resources were geographically organised into Baltic, Black Sea, White Sea and the Pacific fleets. Vessels were constructed and supported in each of these areas because of the difficulty in transferring forces between operational areas. Although Russia had great technical and industrial potential, her backward political system continually inhibited progress and growth.

The first Russian dreadnoughts were the four 23,360-ton ships of the *Gangut* class laid down in Baltic yards during 1909. In many ways they represented Russia's reading of the lessons of the Japanese War, being heavily armed but protected by lighter if more extensive armour. They generally resembled the Italian *Dante Alighieri* class with four triple 12in turrets in a similar arrangement, and a

speed of 23kts. The last unit was completed in 1915. In 1911, three *Imperatritsa Mariya* class battleships were laid down in Black Sea yards in response to two dreadnoughts ordered by the Turks from British firms. These 22,600-ton ships were slightly smaller, 21kt versions of the *Gangut*s. These seven ships were the only Russian dreadnoughts ever to be completed.

Four large 32,500-ton *Borodino* class battlecruisers were begun in 1913. They were enlarged *Gangut*s with twelve 14in guns mounted in triple turrets with the same arrangement. Their speed was to have been 26.5kts. None was completed. Finally, the 27,300-ton *Imperator Nikolai I*, an improved *Imperatritsa Mariya*, was begun in 1915 but she too was never completed.

Austria–Hungary

The Austro-Hungarian navy was a small but effective Adriatic force which had proved adequate in the defence of its coastline against the Italians. Tensions in the Adriatic increased sharply when Italy laid down the *Dante Alighieri* in 1909 followed by the three *Cavour*s in 1910. Finally, in 1911, the Austro-Hungarian state ordered their first dreadnought-type battleships.

The four 20,000-ton ships of the *Tegetthoff* class carried twelve 12in guns in triple turrets mounted in superfiring positions forward and aft. The triple turrets were a product of the Skoda Works and were very advanced for their time. The ships' speed was 20.5kts and they were completed between 1912 and 1915.

Four 24,500-ton improved versions of the *Unitus* class were planned but never built. They were designed to carry ten 14.8in guns in two triple and two twin turrets arranged as in the American *Nevada* class. Their speed was to have been 21kts.

Other countries

Although ten other countries attempted to build or acquire dreadnoughts, only Argentina, Brazil, Chile, Spain and Turkey were successful in their efforts.

In 1907, Brazil ordered two 19,280-ton *Minas Geraes* class dreadnoughts from British shipyards. Armed with twelve 12in guns, when delivered in 1910 they were the most powerful battleships in the world. In reply, Argentina purchased two 27,940-ton battleships armed with twelve 12in guns from yards in the United States which were delivered in 1914 and 1915. To keep pace with her neighbours, Chile ordered two 28,600-ton ships from British yards in 1910. They were to mount ten 14in guns and were clearly the most powerful of the South American dreadnoughts. The lead ship, *Almirante Latorre*, was taken into service in the Royal Navy in 1915 as the *Canada* and was finally delivered to Chile in 1920. The second ship was later completed as the Royal Navy aircraft carrier *Eagle*.

Three small dreadnoughts, more properly classified as armoured ships, were built in Spain between 1910 and 1921. Although they mounted eight 12in guns, with their light armour and 19kt speed, they were inferior to any other ship with the same calibre guns.

In 1911, two 22,780-ton ships of the *Reshadieh* class were ordered from British shipyards by the Imperial Ottoman Navy. After the 1912–1913 Balkan war and the demise of the Ottoman Empire, one ship was cancelled. The lead ship, instead of being delivered to Turkey, was taken over by the Royal Navy to serve as the *Erin*. Turkey also purchased the 27,500-ton *Rio de Janeiro* building in Britain for Brazil, as the *Sultan Osman I*, but she too was commandeered by the Royal Navy on the outbreak of war and commissioned as

HMS *Agincourt*. The only dreadnought-type ship to serve in the Turkish navy was the *Yavuz Sultan Selim*, the former German battlecruiser *Goeben*, transferred in 1914.

The First World War

War is the ultimate test of any weapon, strategy and order of battle, and so it was for the dreadnoughts and battlecruisers of the First World War. Extensive naval campaigns were carried out in the Mediterranean, North Sea and Baltic involving many pre-dreadnought battleships and some dreadnought types. There were only a few actions, however, in which the dreadnoughts and battlecruisers faced their own kind to fight in the manner for which they were intended, to decide the control of the seas. Those actions are outlined here in order to point out some of the more important lessons learned as a result of combat. It is also important to mention that the tactical doctrine which dominated operations on both sides was one of extreme caution – the fear of the disaster of defeat outweighed the prize of victory. This policy was further promoted by the new silent weapons, the torpedo and the mine.

Battlecruisers were the first capital ships to see action when the Royal Navy dispatched *Invincible* and *Inflexible* to the South Atlantic to destroy a raiding force of German armoured cruisers. This was the type of action for which the battlecruiser was designed, and in December 1914 at the Battle of the Falkland Islands they ran down and sank the more lightly armed German *Scharnhorst* and *Gneisenau*, although it took a vast expenditure of ammunition to do so.

At the Battle of the Dogger Bank in January 1915 a superior force of five British battlecruisers intercepted three German battlecruisers and one armoured cruiser. The action was significant in that it was fought at ranges of

over 15,000yds. It was a tactical victory for the British: the armoured cruiser *Blücher* was lost but the *Seydlitz* and *Derfflinger* received only three hits each, to sixteen hits scored on the *Lion* and six on the *Tiger*.

The only time whole battlefleets of capital ships ever clashed was at the Battle of Jutland in the North Sea in May 1916. In numbers of capital ships, the British committed twenty-eight dreadnoughts to Germany's sixteen and nine battlecruisers to their five.

The battlecruisers exchanged the first heavy fire and the British *Indefatigable* and *Queen Mary* blew up and sank, followed by the *Invincible* after the main fleets had engaged. The German fleet broke off the action and headed south, with the British declining pursuit for fear of being led into waiting U-Boats or minefields. Many ships on both sides were badly damaged. The German battlecruiser *Lützow* was damaged so severely that she had to be sunk the next day.

The battle was a tactical victory for the Germans in terms of losses and they escaped a numerically superior British force. However, they had not seriously hurt the British fleet and the strategic situation remained unchanged for the duration of the war.

The lessons of the First World War

Combat operations provided a number of lessons in design and tactics. For instance, battleships were best employed in formations and fleets where full advantage could be gained from their concentration of firepower. Battle ranges were established at which their guns were the most efficient and their armour was the most effective. New fire control techniques had extended battle ranges to well over 15,000yds. At the greater battle ranges, shells came in at steeper angles and deck armour was easier to penetrate.

The *Seydlitz* was nearly lost during the Dogger Bank battle due to the instability of cordite propellant charges and their tendency to flash, but the Germans had elaborate precautions to prevent explosions or fires in turrets from flashing into the magazines below via the barbettes. The British measures were less than thorough and the loss of three battlecruisers at

At Jutland in 1916 many German ships survived considerable punishment. One that did not was the battlecruiser Lützow – *seen here during her short active career of three months – although she was hit by at least two dozen heavy shells before the decision was made to abandon her. She was dispatched by a German destroyer torpedo, and sank in two minutes. (CMP)*

Jutland could well have been due more to cordite handling procedures and the lack of flash protection than inadequate armouring.

In addition to inhibiting tactical operations, torpedoes and mines had a considerable effect on later warship construction. To counteract the threat of underwater explosions, new designs featured expanded side protection systems and external bulges were fitted to existing ships. Secondary batteries were reworked to provide more power and efficiency against attacking destroyers, while new guns with a high angle capability were introduced for protection against aircraft.

After Jutland, there were dreadnought sorties by both fleets, but the giants never met again. Construction slackened and when the war ended in November 1918 the German fleet was surrendered at Scapa Flow and scuttled there the following June. Although greatly slowed, dreadnought construction continued in the United States, Japan, France, Italy, Russia and Great Britain.

The Treaty Era

The Washington Treaty

By 1921, participants in the Great War were facing a postwar recession with some on the brink of financial disaster. Massive naval building programmes could not be continued and the practical solution was negotiation, the outcome of which was the Washington Treaty signed by Great Britain, the United States, Japan, France and Italy on 6 February 1922. The Treaty created a 'building holiday' for ten years and restricted the total tonnage for each country. It also established a maximum displacement of 35,000 tons and a gun calibre of 16in for capital ships.

The total tonnage limitations imposed were:

Great Britain – 580,450
United States – 500,320
Japan – 301,320
France – 221,170
Italy – 182,000

This allocation was referred to as the '5-5-3' ratio. Capital ship age was set at twenty years and replacements could not be built before this age was reached. Reconstruction was limited to improvements against aerial and underwater attack, but with a displacement increase of 3000 tons. A 'standard displacement' was established and defined as the weight of the vessel complete, fully manned and ready for sea. It included ammunition, provisions, potable water and all other items carried in war but excluded fuel and reserve feed water. Displacement weight was defined as 2240 pounds or 1016.05 kilogrammes per ton.

Some vessels under construction were allowed to be completed if they met all of the Treaty restrictions. Most new construction, however, had to be scrapped in order to comply. It was also necessary to dispose of many older vessels in order to reach the tonnage allotments. As a measure of economy, each country was allowed to convert two capital ships into aircraft carriers not to exceed 33,000 tons each.

The negotiations produced a great deal of dissension. There was bitter disagreement over the question of displacement and type allocation. Japan was never satisfied with the '5-5-3' ratio established for the top three powers. She felt forced into a position of inferiority and by 1936, had withdrawn from treaty participation.

In signing the Washington Treaty, Japan agreed to dispose of the two *Tosa* class battleships and the four *Amagi* class battlecruisers under construction. The battlecruisers *Amagi* and *Akagi* were to be completed as aircraft carriers but when the hull of the *Amagi* was badly damaged in an earthquake in 1923, it was replaced by the battleship *Kaga*, a sister of the *Tosa* which had been expended as a target. Japan was also permitted to retain the *Nagato* and *Mutsu*, both of which were completed just before the Treaty was signed.

In the United States, the battleship and battlecruiser programmes were cancelled. The hulls were broken up on the ways except for the battlecruisers *Lexington* and *Saratoga*, which were completed as aircraft carriers. The US Navy was allowed to retain the *Maryland*, completed just before the Treaty went into effect, and complete her two sisters, the *Colorado* and *West Virginia*. A fourth ship, the *Washington* was sunk as a target.

There was no new capital ship construction in Great Britain after 1917, due mainly to the diminishing threat from the German navy, but the Treaty forced the cancellation of four 48,000-ton 'G3' type battlecruisers which had just been ordered. Because of severe financial conditions, both France and Italy had abandoned the completion of their wartime construction. Only the French *Béarn* survived to be completed as an aircraft carrier. To compensate for this, special clauses in the Treaty permitted Britain, France and Italy to design and construct two battleships each in accordance with the new regulations.

The London Treaties

The Washington Treaty had provided for a conference to be held at London in 1930, a year before the expiration of the capital ship 'building holiday'. By the late 1920s, the postwar recession had worsened and the financial atmosphere was hardly conducive to the beginning of another naval arms race. Yet those countries not at par with Great Britain and the United States wanted equity, even if they could not afford it. The prestigeous floating fortresses were viewed as symbolic of a nation's industrial capability and scientific achievement. Furthermore, most of the Treaty signatories possessed overseas colonies so control of the sea lanes became even more important in the projection and maintenance of national power.

When the second naval arms limitation conference was convened at London in 1930, the same grievances foreshadowed the proceedings. Undoubtedly, Great Britain and the United States hoped to continue their naval superiority. Conditions were in their favour, for by 1930, the recession had become a depression and most nations were not in a position to fund capital ship construction. The world economy was the most compelling factor in bringing about a limited agreement to extend the 'building holiday' for another five years.

In 1929, Germany laid down the *Deutschland*, her first major warship since the Great War. German naval construction was regulated by the Treaty of Versailles, which formally ended the First World War, but was not bound by any other agreement. The limits imposed were 10,000 tons per vessel and a maximum 11in gun calibre. France refused to ratify the new agreement because of the *Deutschland* and intelligence that indicated at least two more German ships, possibly even larger in size, were about to be laid down. France's vital link to North Africa had to be maintained. New, unrestricted ships were necessary as a countermeasure. As expected, Italy refused to support the Treaty; if France built new capital ships, then Italy's position in the Mediterranean would be threatened. Japan agreed to the five-year extension but later gave notice that she did not intend to renew the Treaty when it expired.

Because the *Deutschland* disrupted the calculated capital ship strength of the Treaties, it had a significant political impact on the world's naval powers. It also touched off a second arms race, which was well under way when the next naval arms limitation conference met at London in 1936. The remaining Treaty particip-

The first – and for many years the only – post-Washington capital ships were the British Rodney *and* Nelson. *Emphasising firepower and magazine protection over speed, they had a radical layout with all the turrets forward, and benefited from much of the design work done on the abortive 1921 capital ships.* (CMP)

ants agreed to an 'escalator clause' allowing an increase in tonnage and gun calibre to match any increases by non-participants. While it did not match the original hopes at Washington in 1922, the Treaty did work for ten years.

Treaty construction

The first new construction was undertaken by the Royal Navy, which on the cancellation of the 'G3' type battlecruisers was badly outclassed by the 16in gun building programmes in the United States and Japan. The new battleships *Nelson* and *Rodney* carried nine 16in

guns in triple turrets mounted forward, displaced 33,950 tons and made 23kts. Completed in 1927, they were the only British ships to mount 16in guns.

The German design selected in 1927, which resulted in the *Deutschland* (later renamed *Lützow*), produced a ship that displaced 11,700

tons, mounted six 11in guns and was capable of over 26kts. Officially referred to as a *panzerschiffe* (armoured ship), the *Deutschland* soon became known as a 'pocket battleship'. She was intended to operate as a commerce raider and not as a battleship or battlecruiser in a battle line. The 'pocket battleship' had deficiencies

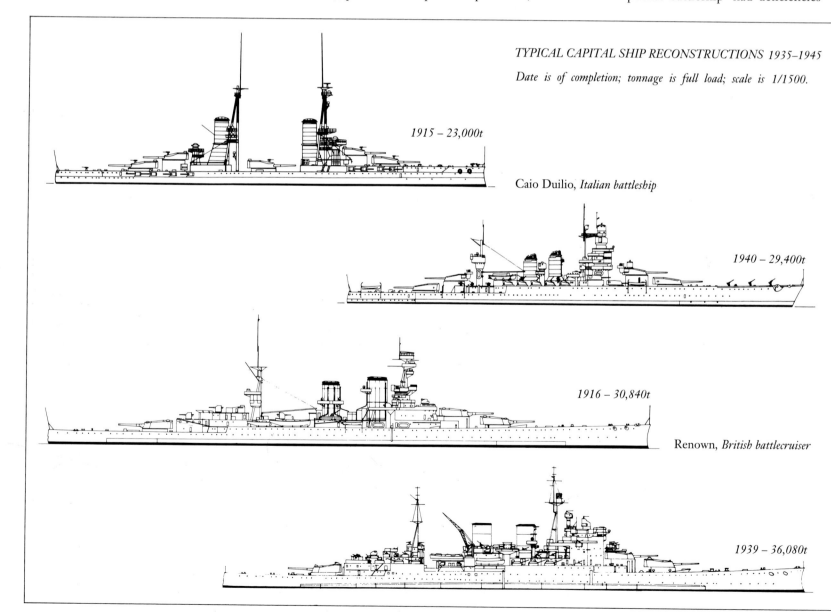

TYPICAL CAPITAL SHIP RECONSTRUCTIONS 1935–1945

Date is of completion; tonnage is full load; scale is 1/1500.

1915 – 23,000t

Caio Duilio, *Italian battleship*

1940 – 29,400t

1916 – 30,840t

Renown, *British battlecruiser*

1939 – 36,080t

With the rearmament of Germany, France began to consider the emergence of a new naval threat, building the two Dunkerque *class battlecruisers to counter the* panzerschiffe *of the* Deutschland *type. Germany then responded with* Scharnhorst *(seen here during the war) and* Gneisenau *– grossly under-declared at 26,000 tons, when they actually displaced nearly 35,000. (CMP)*

but its greatest impact was the psychological effect it had on naval strategy and tactics.

The French responded to the *Deutschland* threat with the battlecruiser *Dunkerque* in 1932 and the *Strasbourg* in 1934. They were handsome vessels of 26,500 tons, with eight 13in guns in two quadruple turrets mounted forward. Completed in 1937 and 1938, they made over 30kts on trials.

Impressed with the French *Dunkerque*s, the Italians built two Treaty battleships, the *Littorio* and *Vittorio Veneto*. Officially described as 35,000-tonners, they were actually over 40,000 tons, carried nine 15in guns in triple turrets and were capable of 30kts. A third ship, the *Roma*, had improvements which pushed her tonnage to 41,000 tons. It was completed in 1942. A fourth unit, the *Impero*, was never finished.

In 1935, two nominally 35,000-ton *Richelieu* class battleships were ordered by the French navy as a direct response to Italy's *Littorio*s. The *Richelieu* was completed in July 1940 at a designed standard displacement of nearly 38,000 tons. The *Jean Bart* was laid down in January 1939 but was not completed until ten

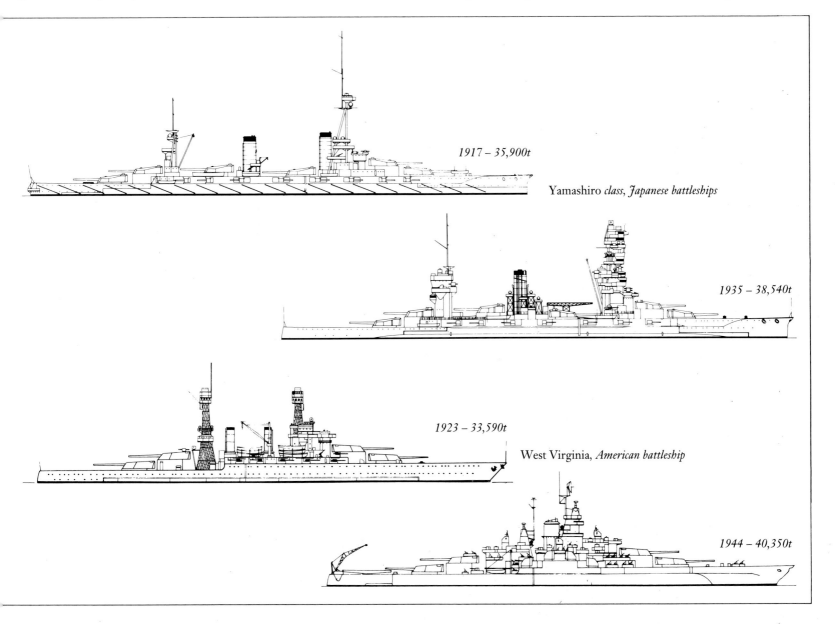

1917 – 35,900t

Yamashiro *class, Japanese battleships*

1935 – 38,540t

1923 – 33,590t

West Virginia, *American battleship*

1944 – 40,350t

years later. They were designed along the lines of the *Dunkerque*, carrying eight 15in guns in two quadruple turrets mounted forward. Their designed speed was 30kts. Two additional units, the *Clemenceau* and *Gascogne*, were ordered, but they were not completed.

Germany laid down two additional 'pocket battleships', the *Admiral Scheer* in 1931 and the *Admiral Graf Spee* in 1932. A total of six *panzerschiffe* was planned and ordnance and material for the next three were ordered. With the appearance of the *Dunkerque* class, the last three ships were re-ordered as two enlarged units to accommodate a third 11in turret. The need for additional speed and protection made the idea impractical and a new battlecruiser design emerged.

The battlecruisers *Scharnhorst* and *Gneisenau* were laid down in 1935. The displacement was stated to be 26,000 tons, but they were actually 34,800 tons when completed and could do over 31kts. The six 11in turrets planned for the cancelled *panzerschiffe* were used to arm each new battlecruiser with nine 11in guns. The last ship was completed in January 1939. The design allowed for replacement of the triple 11in turrets with twin 15in turrets.

In the United States, the building holiday effectively froze all capital ship design. The US Navy was awaiting the appearance of the Royal Navy's *Nelson* and *Rodney* to set the standard for future capital ship design and replacement under the Treaties. Serious design work on battleships did not resume until spring 1935 with the first replacements allowed under the Treaties.

Treaty modernisations

Many ships retained under the Treaties were modernised in the 1920s and 1930s. Improvements up to 3000 tons per vessel were allowable under the Washington Treaty to offset the effects of aerial bombing and underwater explosions. Many ships were modernised in the 1920s and again during the 1930s.

General modernisation features included the addition of bulges, or blisters, to increase the depth of torpedo protection and the stability; upgrading the side and deck armour; refurbishing or replacing boilers and machinery to increase efficiency; and upgrading the fire control equipment and secondary batteries.

Experiments conducted on target ships, such as the *Tosa* in Japan and the *Washington* in the United States, greatly affected the modernisation programmes and the design of new Treaty replacement ships.

The Royal Navy blistered the *Queen Elizabeth*, *Revenge* and *Renown* classes in the 1920s and some of each class had extensive topside renovations in the 1930s. The US Navy also blistered most of its older ships with only *West Virginia*, *Tennessee* and *California* left untouched when the Second World War began.

The reconstructions undertaken by the Japanese were extensive and paid little heed to treaty restrictions. In addition to blistering, they were fitted with new boilers and turbines allowing smaller subdivision of the machinery spaces. Finally, they were lengthened to reduce hull resistance. With the new machinery and streamlined hull, they were able to retain or increase their speed on a much greater displacement. For example, after their second modernisation, the *Kongo*s were rerated as battleships and were known to have made over 30kts.

However, the Italian reconstructions of the *Conte di Cavour* and *Andrea Doria* classes were the most extensive, in effect, making them new battleships. Their hulls were completely gutted, the centre turret was removed and modern machinery was installed. New bows were fitted, increasing their length, and the side protection system was reconstructed without blistering. The efficiency attained with the new hull shape and machinery increased their speed to 27kts. Their guns were relined to 12.6in calibre and mounted in reconstructed turrets.

The first US treaty battleships were the two North Carolina *class. They were powerfully armed with nine 16in guns, but because treaty restrictions were taken seriously they could not be armoured against 16in shellfire (they were actually designed under a treaty limiting main armament to 14in guns).* USS Washington *was the victor in a gun duel with the 14in-armed* Kirishima *off Guadalcanal in 1942. (USN)*

Yamato, one of the two largest battleships ever built, fitting out at Kure in 1941. Sheer size reduces the compromises forced on a battleship designer, but in naval warfare individual quality has never been an answer to superior numbers; both were sunk at sea by overwhelming US carrier air power, marking the final transfer of sea power from the big gun to the naval aircraft. (CMP)

The last dreadnoughts

The naval arms limitation treaties of Washington and London all but collapsed after the 1936 negotiations in London. The final generation of dreadnoughts was in the minds of their designers, if not already on the drawing boards, when the delegates returned home from the conference. Here follows a brief summation of each country's building programme up to the present date. The table at the end of the section lists the basic specifications of capital ship classes built or reconstructed after 1922.

United States

The first Treaty ships were the *North Carolina* class completed in 1941. Treaty limitations of 35,000 tons were taken seriously, although the final standard displacement was 37,500 tons. The main restrictions were met, but armour protection was marginal. They carried nine 16in guns in triple turrets with two mounted forward and one aft. Their secondary armament was twenty 5in dual purpose guns in twin mountings. Their speed was 27.6kts.

It was felt that the *North Carolina*s represented the limit of what could be attained on a nominal 35,000 tons. However, the next generation of battleships, the *South Dakota* class, had the same main and secondary armament, the same 27kt speed, was afforded adequate armour protection and did not exceed the *North Carolina*s' displacement. This was achieved with more efficient machinery in a unique arrangement requiring a shorter protected length. It allowed an increased weight of armour per foot on the same tonnage. All four *South Dakota*s were commissioned in 1942.

To match the speed of foreign contemporaries, a high speed 33kt version of the *South Dakota* class was developed. They carried the same armament but the 16in guns were of a new and more powerful type. Six 45,000-ton *Iowa* class battleships were ordered but only four were completed. They were the last battleships to be built by the US Navy and saw action in the Second World War and the Korean War. The *New Jersey* fought in Vietnam and all four were on active service in 1990.

The *Missouri* and *Wisconsin* were deployed in 1990 and 1991 in support of Coalition forces during the conflict with Iraq.

The last capital ships ordered by the US Navy were the six 27,000-ton *Alaska* class large cruisers. They carried nine 12in guns in triple turrets, two forward and one aft and a secondary battery of twin 5in guns. The 33kt *Alaska*s were lightly armoured and protected and were designed for screening, raiding and counter-raiding operations. Two of the class were completed in 1944. A third ship was never completed and the last three were cancelled.

The culmination of American battleship design was the 60,500-ton *Montana* class. They were enlarged, but slower versions of the *Iowa*s, with twelve 16in guns mounted in a four-turret balanced battery. The twin 5in secondary battery guns were of an improved model. The *Montana*s' designed speed was 28kts. Five ships were authorised in 1940 but construction was cancelled in 1943.

Japan

Design work for the largest battleships ever built, the 64,000-ton *Yamato* class, was begun in 1934 when Japan announced her intent to abrogate the London Treaty. The Japanese knew they could not match the numerical superiority of the US Navy and hoped to offset this difference with individually superior ships. Two ships were completed by 1942. The third unit was converted to an aircraft carrier and the last was cancelled. They carried nine 18.1in guns mounted in triple turrets, two forward and one aft. This was the heaviest gun armament ever carried by a warship. They carried 6in guns for protection against light surface units and 5in anti-aircraft guns. Their speed was 27kts.

Great Britain

The five ships of the *King George V* class were the first Treaty replacements. Displacing 36,727 tons and armed with ten 14in guns, they were all completed between 1940 and 1942. The main battery was arranged in one twin and two quadruple turrets. The quadruples were mounted forward and aft, the twin superfiring forward. Their secondary armament was sixteen 5.25in dual purpose guns in twin mountings. Their speed was 28kts.

Four 40,550-ton *Lion* class battleships were ordered in 1938 and two units were laid down in 1939. They were enlargements of the *King George V* class with nine 16in guns in triple turrets. Their speed was to be 30kts. They were cancelled because of wartime labour and material shortages and the long lead time required to design and build the new 16in mountings.

In 1939, a new design was developed to use the twin 15in turrets from the First World War battlecruisers *Courageous* and *Glorious* which were converted to aircraft carriers. They were reliable weapons which could be satisfactorily remounted to modern standards. A single ship, the *Vanguard*, was completed in

Like the USA, Britain also took treaty limitations seriously, but the King George V *class preferred protection to firepower. It was originally hoped to fit twelve 14in guns, but when weight proved critical two guns were given up to preserve the requisite level of armouring. Like all genuine treaty battleships, wartime conditions showed them to be very cramped.* HMS Duke of York, *seen here in 1948, carries many of the additional sensors and anti-aircraft guns required by war service.* (CMP)

1946. Her design was along the lines of the *King George V* and *Lion* classes on a 44,500-ton displacement with a speed of 30kts.

Germany

Although not a party to the 1930 London Treaty, an Anglo-German Naval Agreement was reached in 1935 which, in effect, nullified the Treaty of Versailles. It allowed Germany to build up to 35 per cent of the Royal Navy strength if she would honour any future world naval agreements. After the 1936 London Agreement, it was apparent from the 'Escalator Clause' that the Treaty would soon be useless. With this interpretation, Germany began an unrestricted rebuilding of her navy and in 1939 renounced the Anglo-German Agreement.

In 1936, two ships were laid down, the 41,700-ton *Bismarck* and the slightly modified 42,900-ton *Tirpitz*. In many respects they were similar to the *Bayern* class battleships of the First World War, using the latest technology and modern equipment. They were armed with eight 15in guns in a twin turret balanced arrangement. Their secondary armament consisted of 5.9in guns for close-in surface defence and 4.1in anti-aircraft guns. Their speed was 29kts. The *Bismarck* was completed in August 1940 and the *Tirpitz* six months later.

Six 55,453-ton 'H' class battleships were planned and two were actually laid down. Essentially enlargements of the *Bismarck* design mounting eight 16in guns in twin turrets, they were to be diesel powered with a speed of

30kts. They were cancelled shortly after the war began.

The last German capital ships designed were the 'O' class battlecruisers. Three units were ordered in 1939 but cancelled after the outbreak of war. They were to be a 30,500-ton improved *Scharnhorst* with six 15in guns in twin turrets. Designed for 33kts, a combination of steam turbines and diesel engines was planned.

Soviet Union

In 1938, the Soviet Union began a massive naval reconstruction programme which included four 59,150-ton battleships of the *Sovyetski Soyuz* class and two 35,240-ton *Kronshtadt* class battlecruisers. The *Sovyetski Soyuz* class would have carried nine 16in guns and had a speed of 28kts. The *Kronshtadt*s would have been armed with nine 12in guns with a speed of 33kts.

This was an ambitious undertaking after a costly civil war had decimated technical skills and greatly reduced industrial capacity. Considerable foreign technical assistance was received from Italy, the United States and even Germany before its invasion of Russia in 1940. In view of these major difficulties confronting their building programme, it is remarkable how much actual construction progress was made on these vessels. Two of the *Sovyetski Soyuz* class were about 75 per cent complete and two *Kronshdadt*s may have been as much as 50 per cent complete when abandoned in 1940.

The Second World War

When the Second World War broke out in September 1939, the world's battlefleets were considerably smaller than in the Great War because of the Washington and London Naval Treaties. Again, caution dominated tactical operations: with fewer ships, capital ship losses were even less acceptable. The objective, the control of the seas, had not changed but the means of exercising such control had. The new dimension was aircraft. They could deliver torpedoes, aerial bombs and even plant mines, all of which were as lethal as gunfire from another capital ship. Control of the air tended to be an equaliser for a numerically inferior surface fleet.

Battleships in action

Capital ships played an important part in naval operations but they were not always employed in the role for which they were designed. Battleships and battlecruisers became multipurpose, indispensable vessels, protecting convoys, providing shore bombardment and screening aircraft carriers, as well as fighting their own kind. The actions most remembered, such as between the *Bismarck* and *Hood*, were few compared to the overall scope of the naval war.

The first capital ship action of the war was between the *Admiral Graf Spee* and three British cruisers. After a three month commerce raiding cruise, the *Spee* was intercepted off the South American coast on 13 December 1939. After a fierce battle, the *Spee* entered Montevideo harbour for emergency repairs. A large British force was dispatched to the area and the *Spee*, low on ammunition and fuel, was scuttled outside the harbour to prevent a disastrous battle and possible capture.

After successful raiding sorties in the Atlantic by the *Gneisenau* and *Scharnhorst*, the newly completed *Bismarck* and the cruiser *Prinz Eugen* left the Baltic for Atlantic operations in

1941. They were spotted in the North Sea and pursued by three British forces totalling seven battleships, two aircraft carriers and twelve cruisers. In the first contact, the *Hood* was hit several times and blew up and the *Prince of Wales* was damaged, but not before she landed an important hit on one of *Bismarck*'s fuel tanks. Forced to make for Brest, she was attacked and her rudder disabled by torpedo bombers, allowing the *King George V* and *Rodney* to intercept the ship. They reduced the *Bismarck* to a wreck in about 45 minutes, although she remained afloat for over an hour longer.

When Italy entered the war in June 1940, the Royal Navy's very existence in the Medi-

A contrast in the final generation of dreadnoughts: USS New Jersey *in New York harbour in September 1943 with the French* Richelieu *beyond. The latter carried all her 15in main armament in two quadruple turrets forward in an attempt to reduce the proportion of hull requiring heavy armour; the more conventional layout of the US ship with two triple turrets forward and one aft, had the advantage of minimising the risk of a single hit knocking out much of her firepower.* (USN)

terranean was threatened. There were many clashes between British and Italian battleships protecting their respective convoys and although these actions were hard fought, there was no decisive engagement. When not escorting convoys, the British battleships bombarded numerous shore targets on both the European and African coasts. Perhaps the most significant battle in the Mediterranean was fought when a British force, centred on the carrier *Illustrious*, attacked the Italian fleet in the harbour at Taranto in November 1940 using twenty-one Swordfish aircraft carrying torpedoes. Three Italian battleships were sunk, and although they were later raised and two were returned to service, this was the first time a battlefleet was crippled without gunfire from the opposing naval surface force. The Japanese paid particular attention to this action in planning the Pearl Harbor attack.

By late 1941, the situation in the Pacific was serious due to the continued Japanese expansion. As a deterrent, the Royal Navy dispatched the battleship *Prince of Wales* and battlecruiser *Repulse* to Singapore.

On the morning of 7 December 1941, the Japanese dealt the US Navy's Battle Force a crippling blow at Pearl Harbor. The battleship *Arizona* exploded after a bomb hit; the *Oklahoma* capsized and the *West Virginia*, *Nevada* and *California* sank in shallow water from multiple torpedo hits. The *Maryland*, *Tennessee* and *Pennsylvania* escaped serious damage but were blocked in the harbour by sunken ships.

With reports that a Japanese invasion force was landing troops in northern Malaya and Siam, the *Prince of Wales* and *Repulse* left Singapore on 8 December to intercept them. They were sighted early on the morning of the 10th and the Japanese attacked with bombers and fighters. Without air cover, both British ships were lost from multiple bomb and torpedo hits.

The Japanese advanced steadily toward Australia but in early May 1942 were turned back at the Battle of the Coral Sea. The battle was fought entirely by carrier aircraft at long range. There were no capital ships in either fleet and the surface units never sighted each other. A

month later, in an attempt to take Midway Island, the Japanese were again turned away in a similar action at the Battle of Midway.

After the action at Midway, there were strong feelings in Britain, the United States and Japan that the aircraft carrier had become the primary capital ship. The British continued work on their lone *Vanguard*, while the Japanese converted the incomplete *Shinano* to an aircraft carrier. The US Navy cancelled the *Montana* class and concentrated on carrier construction. From this point on, the battleship was gradually subordinated to the carrier.

There were, however, several more engagements between battleships. On the night of 14–15 November 1942 off Guadalcanal, the Japanese battleship *Kirishima*, with four cruisers and nine destroyers, was engaged by the American battleships *South Dakota* and *Washington* and four destroyers. The *South Dakota* suffered considerable topside damage from a number of 14in and 8in shells, but her armour was not penetrated. The *Kirishima* was reduced to a wreck by 16in and 5in fire and, in a hopeless condition, she was scuttled.

While trying to break up an Allied convoy *en route* to Russia off North Cape on 26 December 1943, the *Scharnhorst*, with four de-

The most constrained of US treaty battleships was the South Dakota *class, which attempted to provide protection from 16in shellfire on the same displacement as the preceding* North Carolinas. *The armour belt had to be inclined steeply for maximum effect which meant positioning it inside the wing tanks (visible in this photo of* South Dakota *herself by virtue of the deep recess in the hull amidships which provided a catwalk to fill the tanks). In the November 1942 battle with* Kirishima, South Dakota *was hit by both 14in and 8in shells but the belt was not penetrated. (USN)*

stroyers, was engaged by the *Duke of York*, four cruisers and four destroyers. The *Duke of York* scored several 14in hits and the *Scharnhorst* was also hit by several torpedoes. Dead in the water, the *Scharnhorst* was battered by the British ships until she capsized and sank.

The last engagement between battleships was fought during the night of 24–25 October 1944 in the Surigao Straits in the Philippines. An American force of six battleships, nine cruisers and thirty destroyers effected the classic manoeuvre of crossing the 'T' on a Japanese force of two battleships, four cruisers and eleven destroyers. Attacking destroyers sank the *Fuso* with torpedoes. The entire American battle line then concentrated its fire on the *Yamashiro* and sunk her. The American battleships were all of First World War vintage; five of them were at Pearl Harbor, the *California* and *West Virginia* having been raised from the bottom and rebuilt.

Second World War reconstructions

A number of battleships underwent major reconstruction during the war. It was usually as a result of being severely damaged, since otherwise they could not have been spared from service.

The American battleships damaged at Pearl Harbor received the most extensive refits. The *West Virginia*, *Tennessee* and *California* were blistered and completely rebuilt from the weather decks up, with their superstructure resembling that of the *South Dakota* class. The *Nevada* and *Pennsylvania* had their topsides rebuilt and, with the remaining older battleships, had their anti-aircraft batteries and fire control systems modernised.

To compensate in part for their heavy carrier losses at Midway, the Japanese converted the battleships *Ise* and *Hyuga* into hybrid battleship-carriers which could carry twenty-two aircraft. The aftermost 14in turrets were removed and replaced with a hangar two decks high supporting a flight deck serviced by a lift from the hangars. Catapults were fitted on either side amidships and outboard of the two centre 14in turrets. Aircraft were never operated, however, due to the shortage of planes and pilots.

The lessons of the Second World War

Combat experience from the Second World War provided many tactical and material lessons. There would be no future generations of battleships to benefit from this knowledge, but the underwater protection systems of large carriers built after 1945 were enhanced by the knowledge of underwater explosions gained in the war.

Unlike shell fire, which normally required a lucky magazine hit to be lethal, a torpedo could very easily sink a large warship. This was demonstrated by the losses of the British *Barham*, *Repulse* and *Prince of Wales*; the Japanese *Fuso*, *Kongo*, *Yamato* and *Musashi*; the American battleships at Pearl Harbor and Italian battleships at Taranto, all of which suffered from extensive flooding. The flash a torpedo generates can also penetrate deep into a ship. This phenomenon may have touched off the magazine explosion in the *Barham*. This flash effect was also noticed when the *North Carolina* was torpedoed in September 1942. Magazines in the area were immediately flooded.

Aerial bombing caused considerable topside damage and near misses, resulting in underwater explosions, caused serious flooding in many ships. This damage usually required periods of repair, but aerial bombing did not become a serious threat to capital ships until aircraft became large enough to carry very heavy bombs that could penetrate deck armour from high altitudes. For example, hits from several 5.5-ton bombs caused the *Tirpitz* to capsize on 12 November 1944. They were dropped from a height of between 12,500 and 16,000ft by British Lancaster bombers specially equipped to carry one bomb each.

After the events at Taranto, Pearl Harbor and Malaya, it was obvious that battleships should not be sent into combat without adequate air cover. Had a reasonable air defence been mustered in any of these actions, like the combat air patrol for subsequent carrier operations, battleships certainly would not have fared worse than the more vulnerable carriers.

Battleships were especially effective for shore bombardment; their accuracy of fire could not be matched by aircraft. The penetration of their shells was several times that of even the heaviest of bombs, and a battleship could deliver the same weight of ordnance over twice as fast as a carrier. All four of the *Iowa*s provided regular naval gunfire support during the Korean War. For example, they prevented the Chinese from overrunning United Nations forces during the evacuation of Hungnam in December 1950. During her brief deployment to Vietnam in 1968–1969, the *New Jersey* fired over 3000 rounds from her 16in guns, destroying hundreds of targets ashore which were only marginally damaged by aircraft.

The new battleships also proved their worth in screening the fast carriers. Their modern anti-aircraft batteries and fire control equipment performed exceptionally well. For example, while escorting the *Enterprise*, the *South Dakota* claimed twenty-six planes shot down on 26 October 1942 in the Battle of Santa Cruz.

Capital ship design

Warship design is a compromise between armament, armour, displacement, dimensions, speed and power. A balance of these features is necessary if the battleship or battlecruiser is to achieve its intended purpose.

The construction time for a capital ship was effectively set by the time required to design and build the main battery guns and turrets. Since capital ships were normally protected against a comparable adversary, the calibre of the main battery determined the thickness of the armour. The amount of speed required affected the size, or length of the machinery plant. The vitals – main battery, magazines and machinery – all had to be protected with armour and supported by scantlings heavy enough to retain the strength of the hull girder. Therefore, weight was a balance between guns, armour and machinery. It was also proportional to total cost and nations could only build what they could afford.

Armament

Capital ships existed as platforms to carry their heavy guns into combat. Improvements in the operation and handling of heavy calibre guns increased their rate of fire from one round every four or five minutes to two rounds per minute. This made the concept of the all-big-gun ship practical. Gun calibres ranged from 12in in the early dreadnoughts to 18in in the *Yamato* class. The *Dreadnought* carried ten 12in guns on 17,000 tons, while the *Yamato* required 64,000 tons to mount nine 18.1in guns.

The desire to improve armour penetration drove the designers to produce more efficient guns. In an approximate penetration formula, the calibre (diameter) of the armour-piercing shell was roughly equal to the thickness of armour it would penetrate at a given velocity and distance. Since penetration depended on the striking velocity of the shell, a more efficient, hence more powerful gun could be made by lengthening the barrel. This increased the shell's velocity.

Increasing gun calibre also increased the penetration. The weight of the shell increased by the square of its diameter and the increased weight gave the shell greater striking power. The heavier shell could carry a heavier explosive charge, was more stable in flight, retained its velocity longer and was more accurate.

During the 1930s, considerable efforts were made by the major naval powers to improve their capital ships' abilities to cope with attacking destroyers and aircraft. Some powers, including Germany, France and Italy developed two separate types of secondary batteries, a gun for surface use against destroyers and a lighter, high-angle gun for aircraft. In some respects, this was a reversion to the pre-dreadnought era. The United States, Britain and Japan opted for a single calibre secondary battery with a high-angle capability which would be effective against aircraft and destroyers.

Fire control

The finest of naval artillery was of little value if it was not accurate and capable of hitting its target quickly and consistently. Accuracy depended on ranging and spotting. Ranging is the process of determining the distance and bearing to the target and spotting is the assessment of where the shells fall relative to the target. Before radar, high grade optical instruments, rangefinders and telescopes, were used and good visibility was essential. They furnished the target's position to a plotting table where tracks of the target and one's own ship were made. The target position was continuously predicted from these tracks and aiming was then mechanically calculated from the predictions. After firing a salvo, the position of the shell splashes in relation to the target was measured. Aiming was then recalculated for the next salvo. Radar, made it possible to make the same calculation in poor visibility and at night.

As battle ranges approached 20,000yds, it was necessary to locate the ranging and spotting equipment high enough aloft to begin tracking the target well in advance of opening fire. A position 90ft above the water could range to over 25,000yds. In modern battleships, designed after the First World War, the equipment was usually mounted atop a tower in the superstructure. In the *Iowa* class, the forward rangefinder was 116ft above the water.

Protection

One of the most important aspects of battleship design and construction was the ship's ability to survive an attack by the weapons that were expected to be used against it. Protection against gunfire was provided by heavy armour. Protection against the effects of underwater explosions was provided by multi-layered sides and bottoms.

The arrangement of armour can be visualised as a box, or citadel, into which all of the vital equipment, such as magazines, plotting rooms, machinery and so on necessary for survival, was fitted. The sides of the box were a heavy armour belt which was covered over by lighter layers of deck armour and closed forward and aft by armoured bulkheads. Normally, the bottom of the box was not ballistically protected. Items outside the box requiring protection, such as turrets, barbettes, conning tower, directors and steering gear, formed armoured appendages.

Armour was intended to defeat projectiles by reducing their velocity in a very short space. In general, armour was either face-hardened or

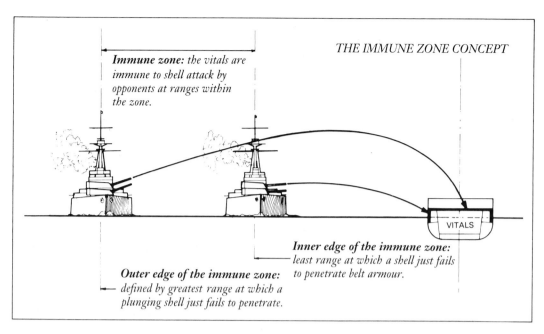

THE IMMUNE ZONE CONCEPT

Immune zone: the vitals are immune to shell attack by opponents at ranges within the zone.

Inner edge of the immune zone: least range at which a shell just fails to penetrate belt armour.

Outer edge of the immune zone: defined by greatest range at which a plunging shell just fails to penetrate.

VITALS

layout of these areas affected the armoured length and thus the final displacement, so designers always strived to produce more efficient, compact and lighter weight machinery.

Steam was the primary source of power for all capital ships from the *Dreadnought* to the *Vanguard*. It was generated in boilers and piped to the engines where it was converted into rotating energy and transmitted to the propeller shafts. Although diesel and combined diesel-steam plants were proposed and designed, none was ever built. Only the German 'pocket battleships' used diesels for propulsion and they were not truly capital ships.

At the beginning of the dreadnought period in 1905, coal-fired, large tube boilers were in common use but small tube boilers were preferred by some navies. Mixed coal-and-oil firing was tried but by the outbreak of the Great War, the advantages of burning only oil were clear. The science of steam engineering advanced very rapidly as demands for speed and horsepower increased. In 1910, Normand introduced a superheater, in which efficiency was increased by raising the steam temperature and pressure which required less fuel for weight of steam produced. The dry, superheated steam

homogeneous. Face-hardened, or cemented, armour had a hard face and a ductile back. The hard face was intended to break up the shell, while the soft and tougher back prevented the plate from shattering. Homogeneous armour was uniform in composition and physical properties. Its strength was in ductility and the ability to spread the impact of a shell over a wider area. Main belts, turret faces, barbettes and conning towers were usually face-hardened, while auxiliary belts and decks were of homogeneous armour. Auxiliary belts were a lighter, downward extension of the main belt to defeat a projectile which fell short but continued its trajectory underwater.

Protection against the effects of torpedoes, mines and near-miss bombing consisted of layers of vertical compartments along the sides of the ship with more than one bottom sandwiched between them. These compartments were intended to absorb the energy from the shock wave produced by an underwater explosion and limit the amount of flooding. The more elastic the system, the better its resistance to leakage. Heavy, face-hardened armour was not elastic, therefore it was not worked into the structure of the compartments. Light homogeneous armour was often used to contain the shower of fragments generated by an explosion.

Machinery

About one-third of a battleship's internal volume was devoted to the machinery spaces which contained the boilers, main engines and auxiliary equipment. The shape and location of these spaces often determined the arrangement of the main armament, magazines, and the volume available for torpedo protection. The

The battleship's curtain call? The four remaining battleships of the US Iowa *class have been employed since 1945 in Korea, Vietnam and most recently in the 1991 Gulf conflict in between long periods of reserve. Huge sums were spent on them in the 1980s to modernise them for surface action and shore bombardment, for which roles Tomahawk and Harpoon cruise missiles considerably increased their striking range, but in the post 'Cold War' era, their future once again seems in doubt. The most visible features of the refitted ships – the box launchers for the missiles, and the white domed Close In Weapon System (CIWS) gatling guns in the bridge wings and before the after funnel – can be seen in this November 1986 view of* USS Missouri. *(USN)*

was also less corrosive to the boilers and engines. The steam operating conditions in the *Iowa* class of 1940 were 850 degrees F at 565psi.

The *Dreadnought*, fitted with Parsons machinery, was the first large warship to have steam turbines as the main propulsion engines and much of her success can be attributed to this feature. In both Germany and the US, machinery manufacturers were producing stationary steam turbine-driven electrical power generating plants but were slow to adapt them to the requirements of naval service. As a result, a number of early dreadnoughts were fitted with triple-expansion steam engines but they were large, heavy, and unreliable. The more efficient, less mechanically complex steam turbine soon became the standard engine for all capital ships.

Modern steam turbines operate at high rotational speeds but propellers are efficient at far lower rpm, so it became necessary, therefore, to provide reduction gearing at the turbine output to furnish an optimum speed for the propeller design.

With the rapid development of electrical equipment after 1890, propulsion by electrical drive became practical. Designed after stationary steam turbine power plants, a turbo-generator produced power for an electrical drive motor with output speeds in the range of propeller efficiencies. Turbo-electric propulsion eliminated the need for reduction gearing (gear-cutting of sufficient quality was a problem in the US at the time), and the propulsion motors were located well aft requiring shorter propeller shafts. The smaller individual units allowed greater subdivision within the hull to control flooding but the cable runs between compartments were vulnerable and the system was considerably heavier than a geared turbine drive.

This system became popular in the US Navy after the successful installation in the collier *Jupiter* in 1913. Beginning with the battleship *New Mexico* in 1915, all subsequent American capital ships built before the Washington Treaty of 1922 used turbo-electric drive. Because of tonnage restrictions imposed by the Treaty and great technical advances in boilers and turbines, the *North Carolina* class of 1937 adopted geared turbine drive.

The battleship today

The US Navy's four *Iowa* class ships are the only surviving battleships in active naval service today. Except for four preserved as memorials in the United States, they are the sole survivors of the great fleet of battleships that began with *Dreadnought* in 1905.

The *Iowa*s were completely modernised during the mid-1980s to mount the latest weapons, radar and electronics. They still mount their original nine 16in, plus twelve 5in guns, but their surface warfare capabilities now include thirty-two long range Tomahawk cruise missiles in armoured box launchers and sixteen medium-range Harpoon cruise missiles in armoured canister launchers. Their air defence has been upgraded with four CIWS gatling guns.

Robert F Sumrall

Capital Ships: Typical Vessels 1906–1945

Ship or Class	Nationality	Dispt (tons) Normal/Std Full load	Dimensions (loa × breadth × deep draught) Feet–Inches Metres	Armament Main Secondary	Armour Belt/Turrets/ Deck (max ins)	Speed (max design kts)	Launch dates	Numbers built
DREADNOUGHT	British	18,110 21,845	527–0 × 82–0 × 31–0 160.6 × 25.0 × 9.4	10–12in 27–12pdr	11/11/3	21	1906	1
SOUTH CAROLINA	American	16,000 17,617	452–9 × 80–5 × 24–7 138.0 × 24.5 × 7.5	8–12in 22–3in	12/12/2.5	18.5	1906–08	2
INVINCIBLE	British	17,373 20,078	567–0 × 78–6 × 26-2 172.8 × 22.1 × 8.0	8–12in 16–4in	6/7/2.5	25.5	1907	3
NASSAU	German	18,570 21,000	479–4 × 88–5 × 29–3 146.1 × 26.9 × 8.9	12–11.1in 12–5.9in	12/11/3	19.5	1908	4
LION	British	26,270 29,680	700–0 × 88–6 × 27–8 213.4 × 27.0 × 8.4	8–13.5in 16–4in	9/9/2.5	27	1910–11	2
CONTI DI CAVOUR	Italian	22,992 24,250	557–5 × 91–10 × 30–6 176.0 × 28.0 × 9.3	13–12in 18–4.7in	10/10/4.5	22	1911	3
COURBET	French	22,189 25,000	551–2 × 91–6 × 29–6 168.0 × 27.9 × 9.0	12–12in 22–5.4in	10.6/12.6/2.75	20	1911–12	4
GANGUT	Russian	23,360 25,850	549–6 × 87–3 × 30–2 181.2 × 26.6 × 9.2	12–12in 16–4.7in	9/8/3	23	1911	4
TEGETTHOFF	Austro-Hungarian	20,014 21,595	499–3 × 89–8 × 29–0 152.2 × 27.3 × 8.9	12–12in 12–5.9in	11/11/1.75	20.3	1911–14	4
KONGO	Japanese	27,500 32,000	704–0 × 92–0 × 27–7 211.0 × 28.0 × 8.4	8–14in 16–6in	8/10/2.25	27.5	1912–13	4

Ship or Class	Nationality	Dispt (tons) Normal/Std Full load	Dimensions (loa × breadth × deep draught) Feet–Inches Metres	Armament Main Secondary	Armour Belt/Turrets/ Deck (max ins)	Speed (max design kts)	Launch dates	Numbers built
IRON DUKE	British	25,000 29,560	622–9 × 90–0 × 29–6 189.8 × 27.4 × 9.0	10–13.5in 12–6in	12/11/2.5	21.25	1912–13	4
KÖNIG	German	25,390 29,200	575–6 × 96–9 × 30–6 175.4 × 29.5 × 9.3	10–12in 14–5.9in	14/12/4.7	21	1913–14	4
DERFFLINGER	German	26,180 30,700	690–3 × 95–2 × 31–0 210.4 × 29.0 × 9.5	8–12in 12–5.9in	12/10.7/3.2	26.5	1913	2
QUEEN ELIZABETH	British	27,500 31,500	645–6 × 90–6 × 28–9 196.8 × 27.6 × 8.8	8–15in 14–6in	13/13/13	23	1913–15	5
FUSO	Japanese	30,600 35,900	665–0 × 94–0 × 28–6 202.7 × 28.7 × 8.7	12–14in 16–6in	12/12/3	22.5	1914–15	2
NEVADA	American	27,500 28,400	583–0 × 95–6 × 28–6 177.7 × 29.1 × 8.7	10–14in 21–5in	13.5/18/3	20.5	1914	2
BAYERN	German	28,074 31,690	589–10 × 98–5 × 30–9 179.8 × 30.0 × 9.4	8–15in 16–5.9in	14/14/4.7	21	1915	2
HOOD	British	42,670 45,200	860–0 × 104–0 × 28–6–0 262.1 × 31.7 × 8.7	8–15in 12–5.5in	12/15/3	31	1918	1
TENNESSEE	American	32,300 33,190	624–0 × 97–5 × 30–2 190.2 × 29.7 × 9.2	12–14in 14–5in	13.5/18/3.5	21	1919	2
NAGATO	Japanese	33,800 38,500	700–0 × 95–0 × 30–0 213.4 × 29.0 × 9.1	8–16in 20–5.5in	12/12/3	26.5	1919–20	2
NELSON	British	33,313 41,250	710–0 × 106–0 × 33–6 216.4 × 32.3 × 10.2	9–16in 12–6in	14/16/6.25	23	1925	2
DUNKERQUE	French	26,500 35,500	703–9 × 102–0 × 28–6 214.5 × 31.1 × 8.7	8–13in 16–5.1in	9.75/13.25/5	29.5	1935–36	2
LITTORIO	Italian	40,724 45,236	780–0 × 107–5 × 31–5 237.8 × 32.8 × 9.6	9–15in 12–6in	11/13.7/6.4	30	1937–40	3
BISMARCK	German	41,700 50,900	813–8 × 118–1 × 34–9 248.0 × 36.0 × 10.6	8–15in 12–5.9in	12.25/14.25/4.75	29	1939	2
KING GEORGE V	British	36,727 42,076	745–0 × 103–0 × 32–7 227.1 × 31.4 × 9.9	10–14in 16–5.25in	15/13/6	28	1939–40	5
NORTH CAROLINA	American	37,484 44,377	728–9 × 108–4 × 32–11.5 222.1 × 33.0 × 10.0	9–16in 20–5in	12/16/5.5	28	1940	2
YAMATO	Japanese	62,316 69,990	862–9 × 121–1 × 34–1 263.0 × 36.9 × 10.4	9–18.1in 12–6.1in	16.1/25.6/9.1	27	1940	2
IOWA	American	48,110 57,540	887–3 × 108–2 × 36–2 270.4 × 33.0 × 11.0	9–16in 20–5in	12/19.7/6	32.5	1942–44	4
VANGUARD	British	44,500 51,420	814–4 × 108 × 34–10 248.2 × 32.9 × 10.6	8–15in 16–5.25in	14/13/6	30	1944	1

Notes:

The data apply to ships as originally built.

Displacement is given in Imperial tons of 2240 pounds. The upper figure is 'Normal' (approximately one-third fuel) for pre-Washington Treaty ships and 'Standard' (without fluids) for later.

Draught is maximum at deep load wherever possible.

Armament includes only main and secondary calibres.

Armour thicknesses are maximum values, which would be very restricted in area. The detailed layout of an armour scheme is usually more important than crude measures of thickness so these figures are at best only a rough comparison.

Speed is the design maximum.

Numbers are those completed as capital ships.

2

The Aircraft Carrier

VICE-ADMIRAL Sir Arthur Hezlet RN once remarked that the three greatest influences on modern naval warfare have been the aeroplane, the submarine, and electronics. Aircraft extended the area over which naval war could be fought; they allowed navies to attack land forces and land targets directly. Submarines introduced a new and invisible element into naval warfare, among other things upsetting the previous concept of the capital ship. Electronics made it possible to exploit the capabilities of the airplane and, to some extent, to control the submarine. In some ways naval aircraft equipped with (and supported by) the appropriate electronics have been the most effective counter to submarines, at least in the period since 1945.

The genesis of the aircraft carrier

The point of a carrier (*ie* of aircraft operating with the fleet) was that the carrier's aircraft could go far beyond the reach of those based ashore. At the very least, the carrier could launch tactical aircraft, such as fighters, which might be able to compete with comparable shore-based types, whereas any shore-based aeroplane flying great distances (to support a fleet near a hostile shore, for example) could not possibly do so. Moreover, a carrier with a fleet could provide aircraft instantly, whereas

The aircraft of the First World War needed very little space in which to take off, so fighters were often carried on board capital ships and flown off platforms built over their turrets. This was actually an intermediate step; initially aircraft were merely carried on board ship and then hoisted into the water for take off. The final step was to provide for the aeroplanes to return to their carriers. This Sopwith Camel is shown on board the US battleship Texas, *about 1919. The markings on the turret are deflection scales, indicating angle of train to other ships in her group. (USN)*

co-ordination with distantly based units was (and, for that matter, remains) difficult. Conversely, carrier tactics were always shaped by the limitations inherent in any self-contained seagoing unit: the limited number of aircraft (not to mention pilots) available, and also by the limits (on total aircraft operating hours) set by the amount of aircraft fuel carried on board.

The essential features of a carrier

Between 1914 and 1945 the sea-based aircraft evolved from a useful fleet auxiliary to a dominant factor in naval warfare. That was partly because aeroplanes themselves became vastly more powerful, but it was also because navies solved three fundamental problems to produce viable aircraft carriers:

(i) making it possible for aircraft to take off in a seaway;
(ii) making it possible for aircraft to be recovered in a seaway;
(iii) making sustained or repeated air operations possible at sea.

Problem (i) was approached first. An aircraft first flew from a deck rigged on board a warship as early as 1910, but as of 1914 this had not been repeated on a regular basis, and not in the open sea. Through much of the First World War seaplanes (actually floatplanes) seemed preferable to wheeled aircraft, because they could take off from the sea itself, and re-

turn to land on it, without any need to solve (ii), the really difficult problem. The earliest carrier air raid, on Cuxhaven, was mounted by such floatplanes in December 1914. However, the floats which made such operation possible also drastically limited performance, motivating the Royal Navy to concentrate on wheeled airplanes, *ie* on solving problem (ii) as well as (i).

Problem (ii) mattered because almost by definition a viable carrier would have to launch her aircraft beyond range of land. Unless they could be recovered in a seaway, then, any airplanes carried to sea would have to be expended once they were used. That was marginally acceptable during the First World War, when aircraft were quite cheap. It became almost entirely unacceptable afterwards, as improving aircraft performance cost increasing aircraft unit price, not to mention much more pilot training (expending an airplane too often meant losing the pilot). In any case, sustained operations required recovery, since no carrier could be expected to accommodate an infinite number of aeroplanes.

Problem (iii) includes the issue of how many aircraft a ship of a given size can support. That is not merely how many she can accommodate. Aeroplanes have finite endurance. Generally a carrier of 1914–45 configuration could launch only one at a time. Her effective capacity, then, was set by a comparison between launch/recovery interval and aircraft endurance. For example, a very small fighter might be able to remain aloft for only two hours. If it took five minutes between launchings, and five minutes between recoveries, then the carrier could launch only twenty-four fighters before the first one had to be recovered. Conversely, anything which greatly speeded up the carrier operating cycle would also greatly increase her capacity. This lesson was only slowly absorbed between wars.

By 1918, the Royal Navy had largely solved problems (i) and (ii). Wheeled aircraft could take off under their own power after rolling down a sufficiently long flat deck. Aircraft had

The earliest seaplane carriers were mercantile conversions, the British favouring the relatively fast short sea passenger ferry. The initial modifications were minimal (essentially canvas shelters fore and aft) but a permanent hangar was added aft from 1915. This is Engadine, *with the later modifications; she took part in the Cuxhaven raid in 1914 and scouted for the British fleet at Jutland. (CMP)*

to warm-up their engines on deck. Carriers generally warmed up their aircraft *en masse* on the after part of the flight deck; its area was one measure of how many could be launched together. The farthest forward airplane had to have enough deck to run down for take-off. Thus one measure of carrier operating capacity (not approached in many cases until the Second World War) was the capacity of the deck area aft of the beginning of the take-off run of the first airplane, which by 1940 might be 300ft or 400ft from the bow.

During the Second World War, as aircraft take-off weight increased, they needed longer and longer take-off runs. As the beginning of the rolling run crept aft, it ate into the carrier's capacity to launch a single intense strike. That was unacceptable; indeed, there was intense pressure to increase the number of aircraft any given carrier could operate. The US solution was to launch the first few aeroplanes by hydraulic catapult set into the flight deck (British carriers introduced catapults for other reasons). This was not the short cruiser or battleship catapult which limited British aircraft designs (see below); it was much longer and thus could develop a much higher end speed. Catapult shots took longer than rolling

take-offs, so in wartime they were often limited to the first few aircraft on deck (once they were off, the rest had sufficient space for rolling take-offs). Postwar, catapulting was essential for jets, which did not develop sufficient thrust for short take-offs. That is generally the case now, although newer aircraft may actually be capable of rolling take-offs, particularly if (as in the new Soviet carrier) the deck is angled up in a ski-jump. In that case the issue is, as in 1944, to what extent the rolling take-off reduces the size of the possible deck park and thus of the operable carrier air group.

The earliest projects for full aircraft carriers (by the Royal Navy, 1917[7]) showed separate decks aft for landing-on and forward for taking off, but experiments aboard *Furious* showed clearly that existing aircraft could not deal with the air currents generated by a ship's superstructure. The solution was a single continuous flat deck, introduced in 1918 in *Argus*, a converted liner. The single long deck had the ad-

ditional advantage that heavier aircraft could make a longer take-off run, and thus that torpedo bombers could finally be launched in any weather. Thus by late 1918 it seemed that the expectations of 1914 could finally be met. *Argus* was, in effect, the prototype of all modern carriers. Although she looked quite modern, she did not represent a really efficient solution to the third problem. It took most of the interwar period for the major carrier navies, the Royal Navy, the Imperial Japanese Navy, and the US Navy, to solve the third problem. The result was not too different from that we see today, half a century later.

Argus could not launch in very bad weather, but compared to her predecessors she was an all-weather carrier. Aircraft landed on the same deck, caught by arresting wires. They were needed to keep the very light airplanes of the time from being knocked over the side by gusts of wind. As aircraft became heavier, this was no longer necessary, and the Royal Navy abandoned arrester gear about 1926, reviving it only in the late 1930s. It was characteristic of British practice that each aircraft was struck below, into the hangar, before the next was allowed to land. Overall, British practice made for a slow operating tempo and that in itself limited carrier capacity. Limited carrier capacity meant a small Fleet Air Arm, which could not order aircraft in sufficient quantities to gain much industrial attention. Nor could it employ very many pilots. Heavy losses early in the Second World War virtually wiped out the prewar cadre of carefully-trained pilots and other aircrew. A British official historian sug-

HMS Argus, *a converted liner building in Britain on the outbreak of war in 1914, was completed as the first fully flush-decked carrier. Note the effects of no superstructure: a small retractable charthouse forward, and the absence of funnel uptakes, smoke being vented aft, a solution also adopted by Japanese carriers with no substantial islands. (CMP)*

gested postwar that the reason for relatively poor performance in 1941 (*eg* the near-fatal attack on the cruiser *Sheffield* during the *Bismarck* chase) was that the prewar men had gone. The question of preserving a cadre for future expansion versus making early attacks was to become important postwar, when the Royal Navy again operated a very small Fleet Air Arm.

Britain was not alone in developing aircraft-carrying ships during the First World War, but she was by far the most advanced in that direction. In 1918, in addition to *Argus*, she had two more full-deck carriers under construction (*Eagle*, a converted battleship, and *Hermes*). *Furious*, a large cruiser, had been decked over fore and aft, but retained enough of a conventional superstructure amidships to ruin her aerodynamics. Similarly, the cruiser *Vindictive* had been only incompletely converted. There were also several wartime seaplane carriers.

Britain's wartime allies, particularly Japan and the United States, were well aware of British development, and began their own carrier programmes before the end of the war. At least in the US case, the close relationship lasted through to about 1920, and surviving archival papers suggest that British ideas heavily influenced the US constructors who developed the first true US carriers, the two *Lexington*s. A British naval air mission visited Japan in 1921. Although the Japanese were already building their prototype carrier, *Hosho*, the mission undoubtedly proved quite influential. Finally, considerable design data was provided to the French navy about 1924, to support the con-

struction of the prototype French carrier, *Béarn*. Thus the British First World War experience led directly to the formation of the major naval air arms which would fight the Second.

Aircraft operating procedures

However, the other navies developed their own operating techniques, some of which drastically changed the potential represented by any particular ship. By the early 1920s, the US Navy was trying out carrier tactics on the gaming floor at the Naval War College at Newport. The main conclusion was that it was essential to maximise the number of aircraft operated by the fleet. When Captain Joseph Reeves went from Newport to command the prototype carrier, the converted collier *Langley*, he rejected the existing operating technique. Instead, the ship was fitted with arresting gear and a crash barrier. Upon landing, an aeroplane was pushed forward beyond the barrier rather than being struck below. In theory, the arresting gear would catch a landing airplane before it hit the barrier, but in any case the barrier would protect the parked aircraft forward. This practice made for a much faster operating cycle, and for a much larger carrier air group, since carrier operating capacity was now proportional to flight deck area. Aircraft which did not fit in the hangar were parked permanently on deck; the hangar was often more a repair than a storage area. The US philosophy supported mass air strikes, since aircraft would normally be lined up on

the flight deck and their engines started *en masse*.

US landing practice was much more dangerous than British, since airplanes often missed the arresting wires and hit the barrier. Reeves was able to insist on the new practice, however. To make US practice workable at all, pilots had to submit to rigid discipline as they landed, enforced by the landing signal officers (LSOs) who corrected their glide paths and told them when to cut their engines. In turn, such rigid operating practice made for very quick landings and a fast operating cycle. The combination of arresting gear and LSOs made for very abrupt and relatively fast landings (US landings are sometimes called 'controlled crashes' and US aircraft had to be relatively robust). Aircraft were little affected by the details of airflow around the carrier island and deck. One consequence was that US carrier designers paid little attention to issues of airflow, in decided contrast to their British counterparts.

By way of contrast, the Royal Navy could not apply pressure for larger carrier air groups or for faster or more efficient deck cycles, probably largely because it did not control the aircraft its ships carried. That power had been handed over to the new Royal Air Force in 1918. Indeed, at the crucial time of carrier innovation after the First World War, the land-orientated RAF seems not even to have been aware that something better was possible. By the time the Royal Navy awoke to the need for larger air groups in 1931, the RAF refused to allow for them for fear that larger naval aircraft purchases would eat into its appropriations, and that enlargement of the Fleet Air Arm would reduce its own size (in view of treaty negotiations, ultimately abortive, then underway). As for the operating cycle and the LSO, as late as the late 1930s US observers (at least in the Far East) found British practice both slow and remarkably sloppy.

British operating procedures had profound implications for ship and aircraft design. A pilot landing as he would ashore was much affected by airflow, and to smooth it British carriers were provided with carefully streamlined islands (particularly funnels) and rounded-off flight decks. Unlike the US Navy, the Royal Navy could not mount medium calibre guns on deck, because of the consequent disruption of airflow. The prewar standards for aircraft operation made relatively delicate aircraft acceptable to the Royal Navy. It is also possible that prewar operating practices made relatively short flight decks acceptable to the Royal Navy. When existing carriers were operated in US style, they proved quite dangerous. For example, during the Okinawa campaign in 1945, British carrier squadrons tended to lose far more pilots to operational accidents than to enemy fire.

Aircraft capacity and hangar design

The Royal Navy was always well aware that the fleet needed large numbers of aircraft; indeed, its staff made more of an attempt to estimate the total number needed than did its counterpart in Washington. The difference was the squeeze in capacity due to the Washington Treaty (see below), and also due to the overhang of early carriers designed during the First World War, with very small hangars (these ships were satisfactory enough that reconstruction did not seem essential, and in any case there was never enough money to rebuild them for greater efficiency).

In an attempt to increase fleet capacity, the British converted three ships (*Furious*, *Courageous*, and *Glorious*) with double-deck hangars, a feature which made them much more complex. That helped, but even a double-hangar ship did not have the capacity which the US Navy associated with her flight deck size. Moreover, nothing in the double-hangar design really improved operating tempo. The ships initially could launch fighters from their hangar decks (so that in theory launch rate could double, larger aircraft flying from the full flight deck), but that capability soon had to be abandoned.

The double hangar had another implication. Although it was built out above the original hull, it was a continuation of the solid hull structure, and each hangar was enclosed. British practice was to fuel airplanes below decks,

and hangars were operated under magazine conditions. There was really no other way to build a structure as tall as a double hangar, so the first really modern British carrier built as such from the keel up, *Ark Royal*, also had her hangars integral with her hull. British constructors followed a similar practice in later single-hangar ships. One consequence was that British hangars were very tight. Even slight increases in aircraft dimensions could drastically reduce the numbers accommodated. Unfortunately for the Royal Navy, aircraft developed particularly rapidly just as the new carriers were being built, *ie* just at the time that they could not be stretched in any way – hence the desperate need to provide deck parking once war experience had shown that existing air groups just were not large enough.

The Imperial Japanese Navy also adopted integral hangars. The US Navy did not; after the *Lexington*s, and until the postwar *Forrestal* class, its flight decks were light superstructures built atop the hull. The space between flight and hangar decks was enclosed by light rolling shutters. Because the hangar deck was open, aircraft could run up their engines on it, and engines could be tested there. In theory, then, a US open-hangar carrier could launch a deck load of aircraft while running up more airplanes on the hangar deck before lifting them up to the flight deck for take-off. The Second World War Royal Navy was sufficiently impressed with this capability that its last wartime carrier design, prepared in 1944–45 for the abortive *Malta*, had a US-style open hangar deck.

Prewar, the Admiralty Staff sought other so-

lutions to the numbers problems. One was to insist that as many aircraft as possible be capable of several different roles; that in turn limited their performance. Another was to use the catapults of surface ships as a way of augmenting fleet air power. Aeroplanes like the Swordfish were designed so that they could be catapulted *fully armed*. That again limited their performance, since they had to be able to lift torpedoes at the limited end speed available from the catapults. Since the British did not use a deck park, they had little interest in arresting gear. Aircraft landed and came to a rolling stop before being struck below. Such a practice limited allowable landing speed. The combination of limited take-off speed (due to the planned, though not practised, use of cruiser and battleship catapults) and the limit on landing speed made for large wings and low performance, even in fighters. It was often suggested before the war that fighter performance was further compromised by the demand for a second seat, for a navigator, but even a single-seat fighter (the Blackburn Firebrand) designed to British requirements for landing and take-off and for endurance proved quite sluggish compared to contemporary land aircraft.

Japanese operating practice seems to have been closer to that of the Royal Navy than to the US Navy, although the Japanese did adopt arresting gear quite early. Aircraft were serviced and armed in the double closed hangars, and there is no evidence of crash barriers or deck parks in surviving documents or photographs. The result was probably a relatively slow deck cycle, and certainly limited capacity per ship (typically about sixty-three compared

HMS Courageous, *a converted light battlecruiser, shows clearly where the old hull deckline has the new double, enclosed hangar added. Although the front of the upper hangar is closed, the downward sloping flying-off deck is apparent.* (CMP)

One of the two Japanese capital ships allowed to be converted under the Washington Treaty, Kaga (seen here about 1928) has many of the features of the first generation of British carriers – separate flying-off deck forward, minimal island superstructure and funnels trunked aft. (CMP)

to a nominal capacity of about eighty for contemporary US ships, and one hundred by the end of the war). In at least one case, that of the carrier *Taiho*, the closed hangar (lightly armoured in this case) had disastrous consequences. Gasoline fumes trapped in it exploded and destroyed the ship, after fuel mains had been broken by a submarine torpedo hit. A similar explosion in an open-hangar carrier would have blown the roller curtains out, but would not have blown in the hangar deck (the flight deck would not have contained the pressure).

Unlike Britain, after 1918 Japan did not suffer from an overhang of existing obsolescent carriers. Although the overall size of her carrier force was limited by treaty (nominally to 60 per cent of the tonnage of the US and British forces; in fact she evaded this restriction), she never seems to have considered the British approach of using catapults for combatant aircraft. Thus her aircraft did not suffer from the attendant performance limits. Japan did differ from the United States in depending mainly on cruiser floatplanes for reconnaissance (although torpedo bombers were also adapted for this role). During the Second World War, however, the Japanese navy lost some of its largest carriers at Midway; and lacked the industrial base to replace them. One expedient was to fit two old battleships with powerful catapults, by means of which they could have launched combat aircraft (flat decks built abaft the catapults replaced some of their main battery; they were intended for aircraft to warm up before take-off and there was no landing-on capability).

For both the United States and Japan, the Washington Treaty was an important factor in carrier development, since it encouraged the conversion of very large capital ship hulls. USS Saratoga is shown, heavily modernised, about 1944. She was the last US carrier before the 1950s to have a hangar integral with her hull. As a consequence, it was relatively small and limited her operations. (USN)

Land-based naval aircraft

Before the war, Japan had adopted another solution to the inadequacy of her treaty-limited carrier force. By about 1935 it appeared that what seemed extraordinary speed and range could be achieved by a twin-engine land-based scout bomber. It could be based in the Japanese-controlled island chains of the Central Pacific, through which the US fleet was expected to pass en route to a decisive battle in the western Pacific. These aircraft (G3M 'Nells') sank *Prince of Wales* and *Repulse* in 1941.

The US Navy also wanted long-range reconnaissance and bombing aircraft to supplement those aboard its carriers, but it lacked any network of island bases. Its solution was to build special seaplane tenders, each of which would support thirty-six patrol bombers operating from an isolated atoll. The tenders were much slower than contemporary US carriers, but they were armoured and they had command and control facilities almost on the same scale as carriers. Unfortunately, even though the seaplane which inspired this concept, the famous Catalina (PBY) had sterling performance, it could not match landplanes. It never really justified the bomber part of its designation. Once the navy actually began seizing island bases, moreover, it turned out that airfields were not too difficult to build. The US Navy therefore acquired a land-based long range air arm equivalent to what the Japanese

had developed. The P-3 Orion is the modern heir to this force.

In neither case did the long-range bombers supplant smaller carrier-based tactical aircraft. The Royal Navy's situation was rather different. The Royal Air Force, its competitor for funds, controlled seaplanes and long range land-based aircraft. Between the wars they were often touted as cheaper alternatives to sea-based aircraft (as well as to conventional naval forces). Perhaps the most notorious example is the small obsolete torpedo bomber unit at Singapore, which the RAF maintained removed the necessity for coast defence artillery (similarly, the RAF claimed that it could deal with any Japanese advance down the Malay Peninsula). Postwar, land-based maritime patrol aircraft were advanced as an alternative to British anti-submarine carriers.

The roles of naval air power

Virtually from their beginning, sea-based aircraft have had three roles: strike, reconnaissance/observation, and air defence. Each places quite different demands on a seagoing aircraft platform.

Anti-ship strike

The first carriers, three converted British cross-channel steamers of 1914, were intended to support a torpedo bomber attack on the German fleet in harbour. The German fleet was clearly inferior to the British Grand Fleet,

and the Admiralty's central strategic fear was that it would remain in harbour, as a 'fleet in being', tying down the British fleet. That is actually what happened. Once the Allied and German armies were locked into the trenches of France and Flanders, only the mobility associated with naval forces could have broken that horribly expensive stalemate. The British actually contemplated several amphibious operations (one of which was in fact executed, at Gallipoli). A more direct attack was planned to turn the flank of the German army in Flanders. It had to be abandoned because the British could not risk the expected losses of capital ships, which would have reduced the vital margin of superiority enjoyed by the Grand Fleet. Thus, from August 1914 on, the Admiralty concentrated its attention on destroying the German High Seas Fleet, either in harbour or by bringing it to battle in the open sea.

The Royal Navy had already abandoned the possibility of a seaborne assault on German harbours, because mines and torpedoes made it too likely that any close approach would fail. Indeed, in 1908 the Royal Navy abandoned its traditional policy of close blockade for just this reason.

Through the First World War, air strikes seemed to offer a way out of the problem. By 1913 the Admiralty was intensely interested in airplanes powerful enough to lift a torpedo. As soon as war broke out, Captain Murray Sueter, RN, secured permission to convert three fast steamers to convey aeroplanes into position to attack. They only had to fly off once. Recovery was desirable, but not essential. Existing airplanes could barely lift even lightweight torpedoes, and to do that they needed long take-off runs. The obvious solution at the time was to use floatplanes, which could take as long as they liked as long as the water was calm. Using floatplanes also greatly simplified the ship design problem: all that was required was reasonably dry stowage on deck and a crane heavy enough to hoist the airplanes into the water.

The technology of 1914 was not up to expectations. The North Sea was so rough that the heavily-loaded and badly underpowered

floatplanes often could not even take off. Even aboard ship, they absorbed so much moisture that their performance suffered noticeably. Moreover, a hard-pressed British merchant fleet could not supply enough hulls for conversion to attack carriers. Even when sea-based aircraft could operate, they could not lift heavy torpedoes from the North Sea. However, they still offered a valuable potential. From late 1914 to the spring of 1916 the British carriers attacked vital inland German targets (such as a radio station and a Zeppelin base) in hopes that the German fleet would have to come out to deal with the carriers. It would then encounter the British battlefleet. The Germans never took this bait, presumably because the attacks could not be severe enough (aircraft still had insufficient performance) to make them risk their fleet.

Even so, the lesson the British drew was that the single greatest strategic problem of future war might well be to deal with an inferior 'fleet in being' in a protected harbour. A Harbour Attack Committee met through much of the inter-war period; among its products was an unsuccessful remote-controlled semi-submersible torpedo (controlled by a torpedo bomber, but carrying far more explosive than an aerial torpedo). Through the second half of the 1930s, for example, the Mediterranean Fleet developed plans to destroy its likely enemy, the Italian fleet, in harbour at Taranto. This work culminated in the torpedo bomber strike on Taranto in November 1940, which did indeed solve the problem of the Italian battlefleet for some months.

The Battle of Jutland demonstrated the other side of this coin: if an inferior fleet was tempted to sea, it might still avoid destruction if it could flee quickly enough. Even though

they might be unable to sink enemy capital ships (see below), aircraft at sea could slow an enemy fleet sufficiently to allow the British fleet to catch up and win with conventional gunfire and shipboard torpedoes. Only they would have the reach to do so. The motto of the Fleet Air Arm is 'find, fix, and strike'; this is the 'fix' element. That was certainly the case with the *Bismarck* in 1941.

In the context of problem (iii), the single mass strike on a fleet required only that a large number of aircraft be launchd together, not that they be recoverable nor that the carrier be able to attack again in a short time. Moreover, at least during the First World War, it could be assumed that the strike could wait for sufficiently good weather. After 1918 strikes against land targets became increasingly attractive, at least to the Japanese and US navies, and such tactics often required multiple attacks. Ironically, this situation reversed in the main scenario studied by the US Navy in the 1950s and early 1960s, the carrier-based nuclear strike. In that case it was assumed that the carrier would operate on a hit-and-run basis, launching only one strike at one set of targets. If her aircraft could be recovered, they would not be launched again until she had run quite some distance towards another set of targets.

Reconnaissance, spotting and patrol

The second great aircraft role at sea was reconnaissance. The single determining issue in naval tactics has always been to find a few enemy ships in a vast sea space. Even fleets are difficult to find in the open sea. Before the advent of aircraft, the only means of achieving contact was to stretch a line of scouts (frigates and then cruisers) across the line along which a

HMS Hermes was the first carrier in the world to be designed and built as such. For many years she was an essential element of British naval power in the Far East, the sole carrier of the China Fleet (she is shown at Chefoo, in 1931). As in other British carriers, her aircraft-carrying capacity was determined by the size of her hangar, which was much smaller than might have been achieved on her displacement. By the Second World War she was considered quite obsolescent, but no more powerful ship could be spared for her station. (USN)

Although most carrier development was confined to the three largest navies, the other maritime powers, France, Italy and Germany, attempted to provide at least one ship – Italy by converting a liner to become the Aquila, *Germany by designing the* Graf Zeppelin *from scratch, and France by completing a suspended battleship, the* Béarn *seen here in 1932. Only the French ship entered service, the other two being incomplete on the outbreak of war.* (CMP)

fleet would go. To avoid missing any enemy passing through it, the scouting line had to be quite dense: adjacent ships had to be almost within visual touch, probably not more than a few miles apart. As a consequence, even the most numerous fleet could only sweep a very limited width. It could come into contact with another fleet in the open sea, but only if the two were fairly close together in the first place. That is why, historically, fleets generally came into contact almost within sight of land: it was quite unlikely that they would collide in the open ocean.

Appearing almost simultaneously, aircraft and radio promised to solve this problem.

If an enemy used his own radio, he could be tracked by shore (and later shipboard) direction finders. During the First World War, radio direction finding promised that a fleet in the open ocean could be tracked for the first time, even if only approximately. Even without direction finding, code-breaking (signals intelligence) was often sufficient to indicate the details of enemy operations, and thus the likely track of the enemy fleet. The Royal Navy made particularly good use of such data during the Great War. Given such tracking, a fleet commander could try to search the area defined by radio intelligence. Aircraft greatly increased the area which could be searched, since they could cover a far larger area than could a conventional scouting line. Moreover, they could radio back their sighting reports. They could provide a fleet commander with a near-instantaneous picture of the area hundreds of miles beyond it. Given such information, the fleet commander could accept or refuse action, and he could ambush an enemy not supplied with similar intelligence.

As it happened, the British were quite successful in gathering and using signals intelligence during the First World War; the Germans were not. The British therefore had relatively little interest in what might now be called strategic scouting. For them, scouts promised more a useful tactical picture of a developing battle. Thus it is often suggested that the British failed to win a decisive victory at Jutland because of a failure of the British

scout aircraft. The surface scouts (the cruisers and battlecruisers) could not see enough of the very large battle area to provide Admiral Jellicoe with the information he needed, although his intuitive grasp of the battle did help. Jellicoe did have a carrier-based scout with him, but technical failures drastically limited its value.

Strategic scouting was much more important to the inferior German High Seas Fleet, forced (largely by internal political pressures) to eschew the role of 'fleet in being' but vulnerable to destruction if it encountered the whole of the British fleet. The Germans developed a force of land-based rigid airships (Zeppelins) to maintain watch over the North Sea. For example, the German High Seas Fleet managed to avoid a potentially decisive defeat in August 1916 because Zeppelins attached to it detected the British Grand Fleet waiting for it.

The British were well aware of the role of the Zeppelin, and from 1914 onwards saw ship-based aircraft as the best counter. From about 1915 on, that meant fighters. In contrast to strike aircraft, fighters would have to be launchable in almost any weather. Moreover, a fleet at sea would have to be able to fly its fighters several times during a sortie. That made it important to be able to recover aircraft at sea. Similar considerations applied to tactical scouts, except that the British could hope that radio intelligence would tell them when they were approaching an enemy fleet, and they could also expect that a battle would not last longer than the endurance of a few scout aircraft.

Spotting was a related role. The accuracy of battleship fire depended on seeing the fall of shot, and by the First World War guns could fire beyond the visual horizon. The obvious solution was airborne observation, either from a captive balloon or from an aeroplane. Both were tried, and by the end of the war the Grand Fleet used airplanes with trained observers and special radios. After 1918, a major naval air mission was to protect friendly spotters while eliminating those of the enemy. This

was a smaller-scale equivalent of the scouting/anti-scouting role.

One other role related to scouting and spotting deserves mention here: anti-submarine patrol. Until well into the Second World War, no submarine was particularly mobile except on the surface. Any measure which forced submarines to dive greatly limited their mobility, considerably reducing their ability to do damage. That was true whatever the ability to follow-on with an actual attack. A submarine commander, moreover, could never know whether the aircraft he spotted could or would attack him. He had to dive to be safe. By 1917, then, the Allies were mounting large-scale air patrols in waters known to be infested with German U-boats. Few or no U-boats were sunk by aircraft (which included non-rigid airships, or 'blimps'), but it is clear that the air patrols had some effect. They included air patrols around and over convoys. The great value of such patrols was that they prevented submarines from moving at speed beyond the convoy's horizon.

The aircraft had little prospect of finding a submerged U-boat, although a few flying boats were fitted with hydrophones (passive sonar) for use after they had landed on the sea. They could be guided to U-boat operating areas on the basis of signals intelligence, but they could only patrol those areas in hope of a visual sighting. Even so, they were clearly useful.

Similar operations were mounted during the Second World War.

Air defence

All of these air roles explain the importance of ship-based air defence. Shipboard guns and shipboard aircraft were always complementary. The guns could not reach very far, but they could help discourage aircraft coming close to ships either for observation or for attack. Generally fighters were needed to drive enemy aircraft off, or to destroy them. The perceived value of the fighters depended very much on how much warning the carrier could receive.

The most important prewar US carriers were the three Yorktowns; Hornet *is shown. Note the aircraft on deck, ready to fly off. A sister ship is in the background of this 1942 photograph. This design led directly to the wartime* Essex *class. (USN)*

The tactics of carrier employment

Anti-ship strike warfare, and direct defence against strike aircraft, came to dominate carrier roles after 1918. There was little expectation at this time that carriers could immediately replace gun-armed capital ships, simply because existing carrier aircraft could not hope to sink large armoured ships. The only credible means of attack was the torpedo, and hits against fast ships were difficult at best. The torpedo itself was not very much faster than its target, and it had to be released very near the target to prevent successful evasion. Moreover, because aircraft could not easily lift very heavy loads, carrier-based torpedo bombers did not carry weapons powerful enough to sink large warships. It is well to keep in mind that the first two capital ships sunk at sea by aircraft, *Repulse* and *Prince of Wales*, were sunk by *land-based* naval bombers quite large enough to lift substantial torpedoes. The ships at Pearl Harbor could reasonably be written off as obsolete, with limited torpedo protection, and in some cases with key elements of their protective systems left open. Similar things might be said of the Italian ships sunk at Taranto. Carriers did not actually sink modern battleships at sea until 1944–45 (in the cases of the huge *Yamato* and *Musashi*), and then it took several carriers per battleship.

Dive bombing

A new attack technique, dive bombing, was developed between wars, initially by the US Navy. A dive bomber pointed its nose directly at the target, and the bomb built up its speed while carried by the diving bomber (which could change the point of aim to match the target's manoeuvres). The bomb was released at its 'terminal' (maximum) velocity, the bomber pulling up. The need to pull up limited that velocity to penetrate thick armoured decks. However, its accuracy did mean that even fast, manoeuvrable ships could be hit from the air. Moreover, dive bombers were much more difficult to counter than torpedo or level bombers, whose motions were relatively predictable (and for which, therefore, anti-aircraft shell fuses could effectively be set). A dive bomber

flew anything but a steady, level, predictable course: it suddenly fell from perhaps 10,000ft to 2000ft. The counter was to abandon conventional gunnery in favour of rapid-firing automatic weapons, whose smaller shells could fill the tube down which the bomber dived. Even so, it was generally admitted in the late 1930s that carriers could be sunk relatively easily by carrier-based aircraft.

The US Navy

Air defence, either of a fleet or of a carrier herself, was not a simple issue. On land, defended areas were quite large, and standing fighter patrols could be mounted on their periphery. A fleet at sea was at once a more concentrated target and one possessing many fewer fighters. Standing patrols were possible, but not in great numbers. The US Navy was typical. About 1930, its doctrine was to spread out a screen of destroyers. Observers on board the destroyers could hope to see approaching enemy aircraft in time for the carrier fighters to scramble to intercept them, particularly in the relatively cloudless Pacific. Destroyer pickets as much as 50nm from a carrier could provide 30 minutes warning of 100kt attackers. However, as aircraft speeds improved towards and beyond 200kts, and as aircraft flew higher (*eg* above clouds), the screening concept became less and less viable.

The US conclusion was that only a successful first strike could ensure the survival of the carriers. Thus, by the late 1930s, US fleet exercises generally began with a phase in which two carrier fleets sought each other out and then struck. The carriers had to stay relatively far from the battleships, because the battlefleet was far easier to recognise from a distance from the air, and also because it was relatively slow. Answering a battleship commander who complained that he was fighting a private war and not supplying essential air services, Admiral E J King, then commander of the fleet air compo-

nent, replied that until he had won that war he could not ensure the survival of the aircraft, and if the carriers were sunk the battleships would be entirely without air support. By 1939 this view seems to have been well understood within the US fleet.

Such tactics were viable only because of the large capacity of the US carriers. Normally they supported four squadrons: one of fighters (primarily to escort strikes), one of heavy bombers (level and torpedo attack), one of dive bombers, and one of specialised scouts, a total of seventy-two aircraft (plus auxiliaries).

The Royal Navy

The British response was different. Carrier capacity was inherently limited; the first new British carrier built in the 1930s, *Ark Royal*, was designed to support a maximum of seventy-two aircraft (normally about sixty) in her double-decker hangar. Moreover, the crisis with Italy in 1935 demonstrated that carriers might have to fight within range of land air bases. No matter how good the reconnaissance, they could not hope to destroy the enemy air arm on the ground. In 1935–36, therefore, the British designed a new generation of armoured carriers (the *Illustrious* class), their hangars protected sufficiently well that they could ride out enemy air attacks. The cost, given limited overall displacement (the British Government hoped to reduce the carrier limit to 23,000 tons at the 1936 naval arms limitation conference), was half the aircraft capacity (*ie* one hangar rather than two). Even so, to provide 3½in of armour so high in these ships was a considerable technical achievement. The choice of armour over aeroplanes per ship was acceptable partly because the limit on total carrier numbers lapsed in 1936; in effect the Royal Navy doubled the number of carriers it wanted, to achieve the same total naval air force in a more robust way.

The US Navy did not consider flight deck armour an option, because it was unwilling to

THE EVOLUTION OF THE AIRCRAFT CARRIER 1914–1930

Date is completion; scale is 1/1500.

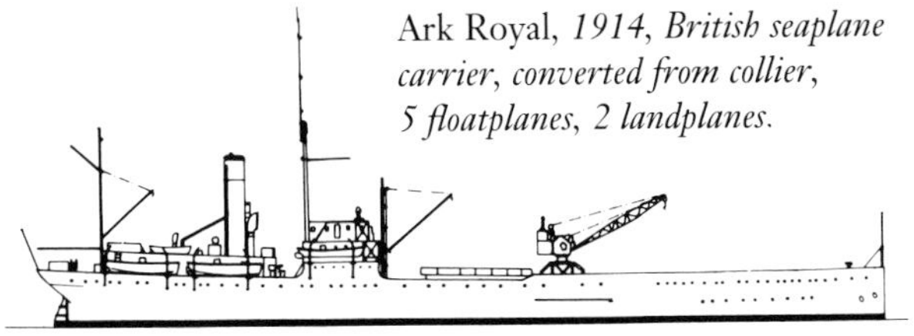

Ark Royal, *1914, British seaplane
carrier, converted from collier,
5 floatplanes, 2 landplanes.*

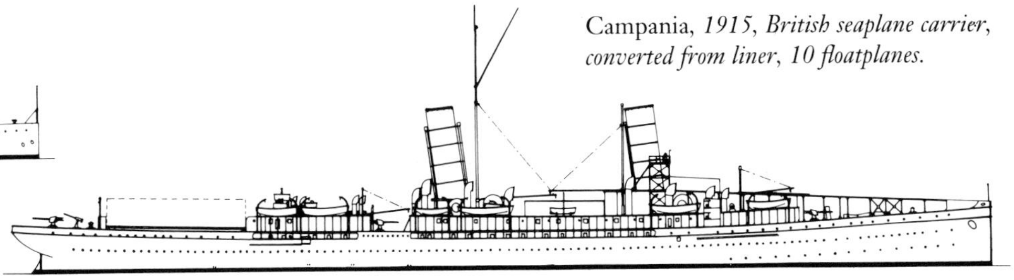

Campania, *1915, British seaplane carrier,
converted from liner, 10 floatplanes.*

Furious, *1917, British aircraft carrier,
converted from light battlecruiser, 8 aircraft.*

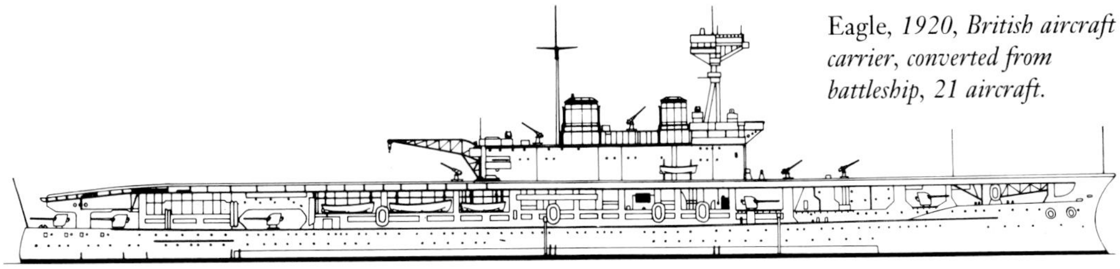

Eagle, *1920, British aircraft
carrier, converted from
battleship, 21 aircraft.*

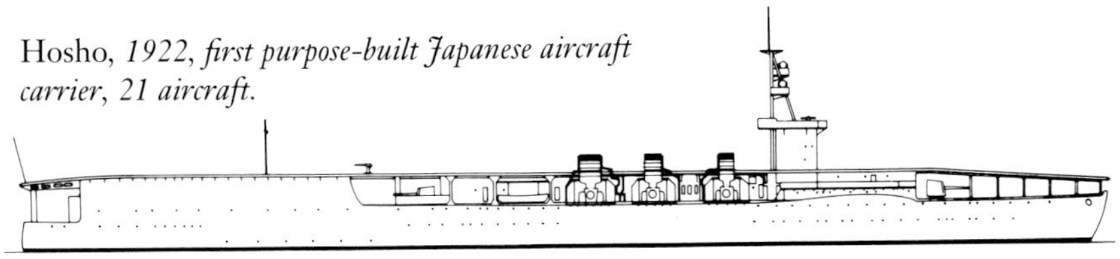

Hosho, *1922, first purpose-built Japanese aircraft
carrier, 21 aircraft.*

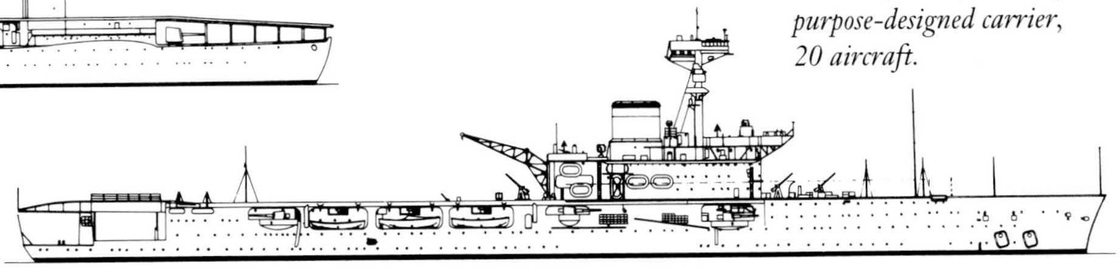

Hermes, *1924, world's first
purpose-designed carrier,
20 aircraft.*

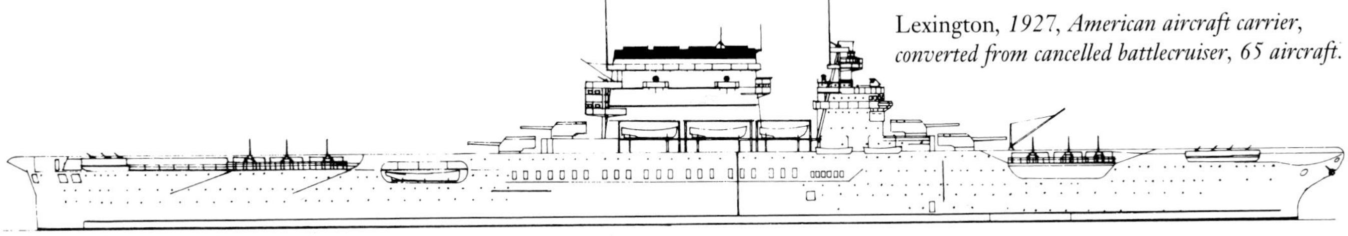

Lexington, *1927, American aircraft carrier,
converted from cancelled battlecruiser, 65 aircraft.*

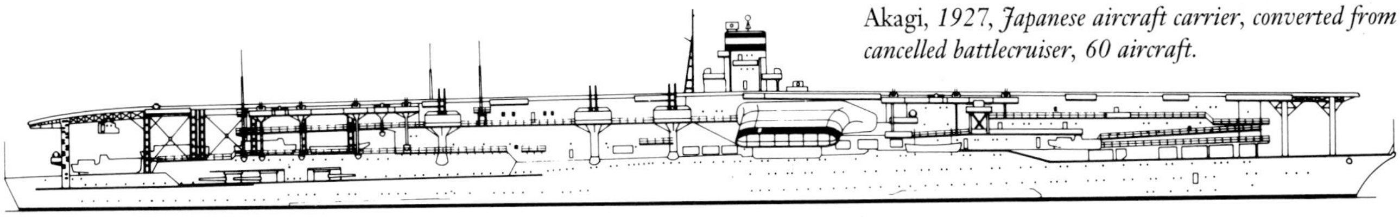

Akagi, *1927, Japanese aircraft carrier, converted from
cancelled battlecruiser, 60 aircraft.*

surrender numbers of aircraft within ships of limited total displacement. Instead, it built its flight decks of wood, on the theory that damage from bombs tearing up those decks could be relatively easily repaired. Substantial deck armour lower in US ships was intended to preserve them from any more serious effects of such attack. Ironically, as each navy became more aware of the other's designs (from 1940 on), each tended to see the other's approach as better. In the US case, very favourable impressions formed of *Illustrious* while she was under repair at Norfolk in 1941 contributed materially to the decision to armour the flight deck of what became the *Midway* class. That in turn was possible mainly because by that time the treaty limits had been abandoned altogether.

The Imperial Japanese Navy

The Japanese approach was different again. During the 1930s, the Japanese carriers were used both to attack targets ashore and to provide fighter escorts to land-based bombers attacking China. Carrier air groups were roughly evenly divided between fighters and bombers. By the mid-1930s, however, like the US Navy, the Japanese navy carried far more attack aircraft than fighters. For example, the large carrier *Kaga* carried twenty-four dive bombers, thirty-six torpedo bombers, and twelve fighters. Similarly, the new *Shokaku* was designed to operate twenty-seven dive bombers, twenty-seven torpedo bombers, and eighteen fighters. As the Pacific War approached, the problem

Most modern of the Japanese carriers at the outbreak of war, Shokaku (seen here) and Zuikaku fought in most of the early carrier battles, the former surviving serious damage on a number of occasions. Both were sunk in 1944. (CMP)

was how to provide worthwhile defences for carriers without compromising the weight of the attack. Until 1941, Japanese carriers tended to operate independently, like those of the US or British navies. Without radar, they probably would have found self-defence very difficult.

The solution was suggested by a newsreel of US carriers operating, uncharacteristically, in close proximity. In 1941 then, the Japanese formed a six-carrier task force. They were able to concentrate useful numbers of defensive fighters to form patrols over the carrier group. Even so, these patrols could not be fully effective, however, because the Japanese lacked any means of sufficiently early warning (the Japanese apparently achieved limited early warning by means such as acoustics – aircraft flying over the sea produce considerable noise in the sea).

In each case, the conclusion was that the enemy air force had to be destroyed at source, because there was no hope of intercepting it in flight. That made sense in a carrier-versus-carrier engagement, but not in a battle against shore-based aircraft.

The advent of radar

This logic was overthrown by the advent of radar in the late 1930s, both in Britain and in the United States. It could indeed provide just the sort of warning which was needed. About 1939 US doctrine changed to provide a fifth

The prewar Royal Navy doubted that ship-based fighters could reliably intercept enemy bombers, so it designed carriers which traded aircraft capacity for hangar protection. Ironically, they entered service just as radar made exactly such interception possible. This is Victorious *in November 1942, with Fulmar fighters and Albacore torpedo biplanes emphasising the relatively small deck area. (MoD)*

squadron of defensive fighters (at first they were to have been cued by airborne pickets launched by escorting cruisers, but it seems likely that references to the pickets were only a cover for the expectation that radar would soon appear). It was possible to provide the extra fighters only because US carrier aircraft capacity was relatively unconstrained.

Having accepted a virtually fighter-less carrier fleet in the form of the armoured carrier, the Royal Navy soon (1940) suffered the irony of discovering that even a very few radar-directed fighters could indeed break up bomber raids. It became vitally interested in a class of fighters, high-performance interceptors, which had previously been irrelevant, and it soon had to accept deck parking merely to accommodate these aeroplanes (some of which had no folding wings and therefore could not be struck below in any case). Even then aircraft capacity proved very limited.

Even with radar, fighter protection could never be perfect. The armoured hangar could limit the damage bombers could do, as several British carriers demonstrated in the face of kamikazes in 1945 (when US carriers, with much larger numbers of aircraft aboard, were put out of action by flight-deck hits). On the other hand, by that time the Royal Navy itself was not entirely happy with limited air groups. The carrier it designed in 1944–45, planned as *Malta*, was a US-style hull with an open hangar and only a lightly armoured flight deck, optimised to launch the largest possible air strikes. At the same time the US Navy, deeply impressed with the protection the Royal Navy had achieved, was commissioning three *Midway* class carriers with flight deck armour similar to that of the British ships, but with US-style open hangars.

For the Royal Navy, the advent of radar had another important implication. Carriers were now valued not only for their offensive capability but also for their ability to defend a fleet from air attack, by breaking up incoming formations. The losses of *Prince of Wales* and *Repulse*, to Japanese land-based naval aircraft (which could indeed carry battleship-killing torpedoes) made a particularly strong impression; now the Royal Navy needed carriers to accommodate sufficient high-performance fighters specifically to protect capital ships.

The Essex *class was the culmination of US prewar carrier design, at last freed of treaty limitations.* USS Lexington *is shown (she recalled the name of the earlier carrier sunk at the Coral Sea). She was the last surviving operational ship of this type, serving (in much-modified form) as training carrier at Pensacola as late as 1991.* (USN)

The prewar programme of large general-purpose carriers no longer seemed particularly adequate, and a new emergency ship (which became the light fleet carriers of the *Colossus* and *Majestic* classes) was designed in 1942.

For the US Navy, the Pacific War demonstrated just how important such radar control could be. At the Coral Sea and at Midway in 1942, carrier fleets fought at long range in much the way envisaged prewar. At Midway, for example, the two fleets virtually annihilated each other. The US force did enjoy the advantage of radar, but the radar could not be used efficiently enough to arrange interceptions far enough from the fleet to preclude serious damage. For their part, the Japanese, lacking radar entirely, could not detect the US attackers long enough in advance to perceive their attack plan. Their fighters, orbiting right over their ships, could indeed break up the initial torpedo attack, but none was held back to deal with the dive bombers which followed, and which sank four carriers.

For the next two years, the US Navy learned to collate the information obtained by its increasingly sophisticated radars in combat information centres (CICs) which could direct defending fighters. At the Philippine Sea, in 1944, the Japanese did indeed detect the US fleet first. However, the CICs and the fighters they controlled were able to break up the attacks far short of their targets, and thus to destroy much of the Japanese fleet air arm. The

Japanese concluded that conventional air attacks were no longer viable.

Each carrier CIC could handle only a few raids at a time, but as long as they were making conventional attacks, the Japanese had to bunch their aircraft into only a few large raids, since it took many aircraft to penetrate dense anti-aircraft fire to make useful hits. Kamikaze tactics were very different. A kamikaze pilot tended to steer into intense fire, so that in theory it took many fewer aeroplanes to make a useful hit. In any case, many kamikaze pilots were too inexperienced to fly in dense formations. As a result, the CICs were faced with many more separate raids, more than they could track. The carrier-controlled fighter organisation broke down. The solution, adopted in 1945, was twofold. First, fighter control was decentralised so that other ships, such as converted destroyers, were assigned fighter (combat air patrol) sections. Second, much greater efforts were made to destroy kamikazes on the ground. Both solutions demanded more carrier fighters, and the carrier air groups were reorganised to provide them at the cost of conventional attack bombers. Again, larger aircraft capacity made for tactical flexibility.

Trade protection

Quite aside from their role in fleet operations, carriers proved extremely important in the Second World War in protecting trade against

As the war progressed carrier efficiency was increasingly dependent on the electronic gathering and marshalling of information. Even carriers with big islands, like the US Essex class, found it difficult to make room for new radar and electronics. Yorktown (CV 10) shown here in September 1944 has a large air search radar (SK) sponsored out from the funnel on the port side, with a secondary set (SC-2) on the opposite side; the tripod carries a fighter control radar (SP) on the platform with a surface search (SG) set on the topmast and a YE aircraft beacon above it. Because of crowding some radars did not have all-round coverage, so back-ups were required (note the second SG at the rear of the funnel). (USN)

THE EVOLUTION OF THE ESCORT CARRIER 1941–1945

Date is completion or conversion; scale is 1/1500.

Audacity, *1941, British conversion of captured German merchantman, 6 aircraft.*

Avenger, *1942, American converted merchantman for British, 15 aircraft.*

Chuyo, *1942, Japanese converted merchantman, 27 aircraft.*

Casablanca, *1943, American purpose-built escort carrier, 27 aircraft.*

Commencement Bay, *1944, American purpose-built escort carrier, 33 aircraft.*

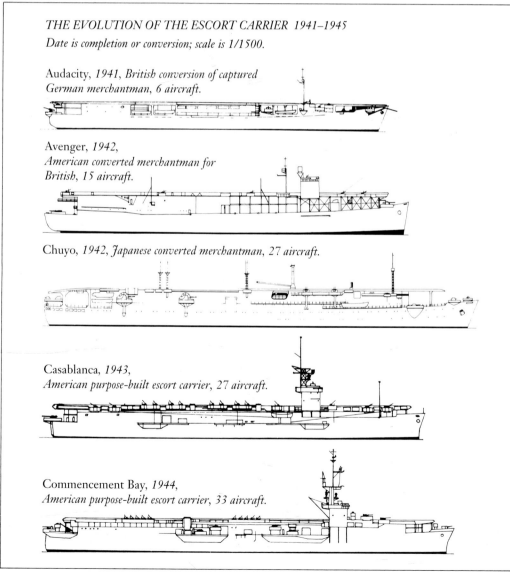

submarines. Here one great virtue of the carrier was that her aircraft could cover a substantial radius. That was important in two ways.

First, a carrier in a convoy could attack submarines trying to approach the convoy. Most Second World War submarines could not sustain speed underwater. They approached a convoy on the surface, submerging only when they crossed the horizon of the escorts (and thus had to become effectively invisible). Air patrols extended that horizon so far that approach became virtually impossible, since the submarine could not travel very far underwater, at least at a speed sufficient to deal with the convoy. This tactic, of holding down submarines, was used during the First World War, but it became particularly effective during the Second, with the advent of more reliable aircraft and carriers.

Second, aircraft could attack submarines at a considerable distance. During the Second World War, many German submarines were detected, not by sonar but rather by interception of the radio signals they had to send to the central submarine command. Such a submarine might be quite far from any naval force at the time it transmitted, but carrier-based aircraft could make up for much of that distance.

Fortunately, carrier anti-submarine aircraft made relatively few demands on the ships carrying them, so that inexpensive trade-protection carriers could be built in large numbers, mainly in the United States. They were called escort carriers, and many were converted merchant ships. Others were specially built, but on hulls originally designed for merchant service. The Royal Navy also added flight decks to some tankers and grain carriers, without eliminating their cargo-carrying role. These ships were called Merchant Aircraft Carriers (MAC ships).

Trade protection carriers also had another role. In some areas, such as the convoy run from Britain to Murmansk, the main threat to

In the Pacific escort carriers were employed in support of amphibious operations. Five US Casablanca class escort carriers, their decks crammed with aircraft, lie at anchor at Ulithi in February 1945. (USN)

merchant shipping was enemy shore-based aircraft. Escort carriers could support existing fighters, and the Royal Navy in particular operated some of its ships as fighter carriers.

Both the Royal Navy and the US Navy used carriers intended for trade protection to provide fighter and attack aircraft in support of amphibious operations, covering the landing areas until sufficient air forces had been assembled ashore. The US Navy also used its escort carriers as aircraft transports. One variation on this theme was to carry land-based fighters to an amphibious assault, and then fly them off to land ashore for immediate use.

Many of the wartime trade protection aircraft imposed very limited requirements on the ships operating them, because very limited performance was quite tolerable. However, as in the case of the postwar convoy escorts, postwar anti-submarine aircraft imposed much more severe requirements, partly because they had to carry heavier sensors and weapons. They in turn could not operate from surviving wartime trade protection carriers, and had to be placed aboard surviving wartime fleet carriers, modified for this new role. This problem was solved only with the advent of viable helicopters, which could operate not only from small carriers, but also from surface ships such as large frigates.

Land attack

During the Second World War, carriers were important, too, because they added a new dimension to naval warfare: deep strikes against land targets. As early as 1929, the US Navy practised just such attacks, with its new large carriers, against the Canal Zone, and in the inter-war period exercises regularly included strikes on Los Angeles and Pearl Harbor. However, just as the Royal Navy of the mid-1930s feared the land-based air arm it would face in the Mediterranean, the US Navy of the same period felt that long-range land-based reconnaissance aircraft, such as its own new PBY, would make possible pre-emptive

The treaties determined each navy's total carrier tonnage; US legislation was based on these figures even after the limit lapsed in 1936. USS Wasp, shown here, was a victim; she was about a quarter smaller than the similar-looking Yorktowns. She was famous for carrying Spitfires to Malta in 1942. (USN)

strikes by overwhelmingly powerful land-based air forces. The Japanese naval air arm actually executed attacks against land targets in China from 1937 on. For its part, the prewar Royal Navy was prohibited from considering strikes on land targets because that was reserved to the land-based bombers of the Royal Air Force. This distinction was, however, abandoned after 1939.

Wartime strikes ranged from supporting amphibious operations to attacks against strategic targets such as Tokyo itself, in 1945, in effect in competition with land-based heavy bombers. The same radar and CIC and fighter organisation which triumphed at the Philippine Sea also restored the viability of land strikes, even in the presence of very powerful enemy air forces. For the US Navy, the strategic attacks of 1944–45 were the basis of postwar planning, for war against a new enemy which lacked a fleet of its own, the Soviet Union.

The impact of treaties

Carrier development was also deeply influenced by the inter-war treaty system. Indeed, the rapid rise of the carrier might be considered almost a consequence of the structure of the Washington Naval Arms Limitation Treaty of 1922 and of its 1930 and 1936 successors (the two London treaties). The Washington Treaty was probably responsible for the form the first really useful carriers took in the US and Japanese navies, and it made carriers

more important earlier than they might otherwise have been. Treaty limitations also dominated the designs of the carriers which fought the Second World War, even in cases in which ships were designed and built after they had lapsed.

The principal goal of the treaties was to limit the cost of naval competition by limiting both the total size (global tonnage) of important warship categories and also by limiting the size (and therefore the cost) of individual warships (qualitative limitations). The treaties were also designed to reduce the incentives for new capital ship construction by freezing what seemed to be the most important offensive naval weapon, the heavy gun. For example, modifications to existing gun mountings, which would have been needed to extend range, were prohibited. Existing battleships could be rebuilt to improve their deck and anti-torpedo protection, partly to make reconstruction an adequate alternative to new construction.

Carrier size

No such freeze could be applied to carriers and their offensive weapons, aircraft, simply because the same ship could and did carry several successive generations of aeroplanes of increasing capability. The only real limit on increased carrier air capability was carrier size, and that was just the limit the Washington Treaty did not really apply. Because carriers were so embryonic in 1922, it was clearly inappropriate to limit their size unduly. The effect of setting the upper tonnage limit so high (27,000 tons in most cases, 33,000 for two ships per major sig-

natory converted from existing capital ships) was to encourage the construction of carriers much larger than contemporary aircraft technology might have justified, hence capable of operations beyond what was envisaged in 1922. In particular, new capital ships converted to carriers in Japan and in the United States had to be very large because the hulls on which they were based were so large. Had there been no treaty in 1922, carriers would surely have been built, but they would probably have been relatively small (about the size of large cruisers), with limited inherent capacity.

By 1930, the British Government in particular saw further treaty limitations as a way of cutting defence costs without sacrificing security. The British carrier designs of the 1930s were limited to match the new limits the government sought, 22,000 tons (after 1936, 23,000 tons was accepted in the last of the inter-war treaties). It is possible that the British preferred smaller tonnages because their own converted ships (based on First World War 'large light cruisers') displaced less than 20,000 tons, compared to the 33,000 tons of the US *Lexingtons* and the 36,000 of the Japanese ships (actually the US ships also displaced about 36,000 tons, the extra 3000 tons being covered, according to US interpretation, by a Treaty clause allowing that much for modernisation to protect a capital ship against bomb and torpedo damage).

The British were more limited because they had suspended capital ship construction in 1917 and therefore had no big partly-complete new ships to convert (unlike Japan and the United States, the British merely cancelled newly-ordered ships in 1922). Instead, the British converted two ships generally considered useless in their existing form, *Courageous* and *Glorious*. Worse, because she had invested so heavily in naval aviation during the First World War, Britain still had carriers of that design vintage: *Argus*, *Eagle*, and *Hermes*. There was no hope of scrapping them postwar to free up allowable tonnage for more modern ships, even though their very small hangars made them virtually obsolete (particularly considering British operating practice). They were just satisfactory enough to preclude any demand for complete reconstruction. A fourth wartime ship, *Furious*, was completely rebuilt postwar.

By treaty, no carrier could mount guns over 8in calibre, to preclude the construction of illegal gun-armed capital ships under the guise of carriers, a practice which could have been attractive given the large allowable carrier unit tonnage. The first US and Japanese carriers did

mount 8in guns, partly to fend off most of the warships fast enough to bother them, cruisers and destroyers. For a time there was considerable debate as to whether such guns were worthwhile, or whether they merely posed a threat to aircraft aboard the ship (due to their blast). By the Second World War, carrier guns were intended for anti-aircraft protection, and the important question was how much they should be allowed to impinge on flight deck shape and area. Only postwar did carriers suffer a progressive loss of anti-aircraft guns in favour of better aircraft-handling facilities.

Carrier numbers

The vital question for the three main carrier navies was how to divide the remaining total allowable carrier tonnage most efficiently. Carrier capacity was clearly related directly to flight or hangar deck area; consequently the smallest practical carrier, built in the largest allowable numbers, would (in theory) provide the largest overall force (deck area rises more slowly than displacement as a carrier becomes larger). The US Navy tried just this route with the 14,500-ton carrier *Ranger*, designed while the two big ex-battlecruisers were still being converted. However, once they became operational, the much larger ships showed that this logic was flawed; larger hulls bought higher sustained speed, better seakeeping, better internal arrangements, better survivability and, incidentally, greater flexibility to take new aircraft. Instead of repeating the *Ranger*, as had been planned, the United States built a class of three much larger carriers, the 20,000-ton *Yorktowns* (there was not enough tonnage for three ships of the maximum allowable size). Japan learned a similar lesson once her big ex-capital ships entered service.

Both the US and the Japanese navies soon realised that large-scale Pacific operations would require more carriers than the treaty permitted. Both therefore developed mobilisation concepts for auxiliary carriers. The Japanese navy built three fast auxiliaries (seaplane and submarine tenders) specifically designed for wartime conversion into full carriers. It also subsidised liners which were designed for ultimate conversion. The US Navy also studied liner conversions, but the weak US merchant fleet did not provide many candidates. By the late 1930s, moreover, projections of the time such a conversion would take seemed so long as to be pointless. Even so, the new Maritime Commission, which was formed in 1936 to rejuvenate the US merchant fleet (and, incidentally, to provide sufficient auxiliaries in

wartime) developed a liner (P-4P) specifically for conversion, with its funnels and uptakes to one side of the hull to clear a future flight deck. This ship, announced in 1940, was overtaken by war. In the event, much simpler merchant conversions were built much more quickly than prewar estimates suggested.

The 1930 treaty, which limited cruiser numbers as well as capital ships, had another effect on British carrier doctrine. To the Royal Navy, numerous cruisers were an essential protection for world trade routes. In 1930 the British Government agreed to go below the previously accepted minimum figure, seventy, in order to secure an agreement with the United States (particularly to eliminate large expensive cruisers). By about 1935, the Royal Navy was pressing for trade protection carriers, whose aircraft could cover large areas and thus replace the cruisers. These ships were not built; instead the Royal Navy bought its six armoured fleet carriers. However, it was the need for carriers to replace cruisers which opened up the question of more carriers for the Royal Navy.

Had there been no treaty, the steeply rising unit cost of gun-armed capital ships (which were becoming much faster and therefore much larger) would probably have crowded out very much carrier construction. It was not so much that naval officers were hidebound, as that carriers were perceived as very useful but not essential in large numbers. However, the effect of the treaty was to end battleship construction essentially until the late 1930s. The treaty did permit cruiser construction, and indeed a cruiser-building race ensued, but that was a very different proposition.

Limits on total carrier tonnage were abandoned in 1936, but that did not lead immediately to large carrier-building programmes, partly because replacement battleship construction was first permitted at the same time (and thus sopped up available funds and industrial potential). The Royal Navy, which had the keenest perception of how far it was from the carrier capacity it needed, did press for a large programme; indeed, at the outbreak of war in 1939 it had the largest carrier programme of all, six fleet carriers. Once war had begun, British building capacity was shifted to the most urgent requirements: a few cruisers, but mainly destroyers, submarines, and escorts. No new carriers could be ordered until 1942, and given the lack of capacity no fleet carriers ordered after the outbreak of war could be completed in wartime.

The US situation was very different. From 1936 to 1939, the US Navy concentrated on battleships, which had the longest lead times

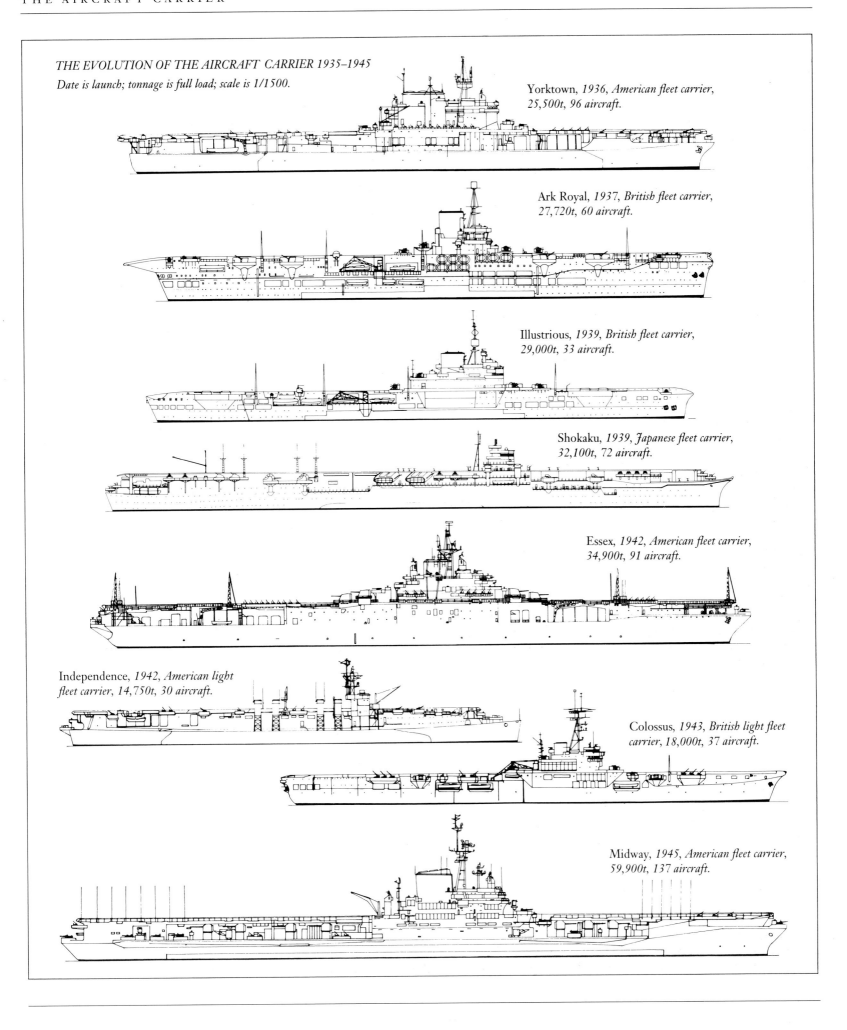

THE EVOLUTION OF THE AIRCRAFT CARRIER 1935–1945
Date is launch; tonnage is full load; scale is 1/1500.

Yorktown, *1936, American fleet carrier,*
25,500t, 96 aircraft.

Ark Royal, *1937, British fleet carrier,*
27,720t, 60 aircraft.

Illustrious, *1939, British fleet carrier,*
29,000t, 33 aircraft.

Shokaku, *1939, Japanese fleet carrier,*
32,100t, 72 aircraft.

Essex, *1942, American fleet carrier,*
34,900t, 91 aircraft.

Independence, *1942, American light*
fleet carrier, 14,750t, 30 aircraft.

Colossus, *1943, British light fleet*
carrier, 18,000t, 37 aircraft.

Midway, *1945, American fleet carrier,*
59,900t, 137 aircraft.

(for their guns and their heavy armour). President Franklin D Roosevelt, who had a keen sense of the potential of air power, pressed for a much more aggressive carrier programme, and in 1940 the United States ordered eleven large fleet carriers (the first series of the *Essex* class). Roosevelt also sought ways of enlarging the carrier fleet more quickly, and urged the conversion of some of the light cruisers then under construction. That was not done, however, until after the outbreak of war.

The Second World War

The effects of the treaties outlasted them. Unit tonnage restrictions lapsed in 1939 with the outbreak of war. However, it takes time to design new ships. Thus the main wartime US carrier, the *Essex* class, which was designed in 1940, inevitably incorporated experience with the earlier *Yorktown* class, which had been limited by treaty (it displaced about 20,000 tons), although it was enlarged to 27,500 tons. The first newly-designed fleet carriers, the *Midways*, were not ordered until 1943 and did not appear until the very end of the war. Britain was even less lucky. She had laid down six carriers, all treaty-limited to 23,000 tons, prewar. Once the war began, industrial capacity was shifted to smaller ships desperately needed in wartime. No new fleet carriers could be ordered until 1942, and they were too late for the war. However, both Britain and the United States converted merchant ships to carriers in time to see action, as noted above. They were not nearly as efficient as specially-designed carriers of similar tonnage, but they often operated in circumstances in which even a very few aircraft could make an enormous difference. The escort carriers and merchant aircraft carriers did not long survive the end of the war, because of the severe limits they imposed on their aircraft.

The United States also converted nine *Cleveland* class light cruisers into the *Independence* class fleet carriers. Apart from their high speed, they were not too different from the escort carriers; as a consequence, they could be completed very quickly, in time to enter com-

bat in 1943. Japan tried a similar conversion of a heavy cruiser hull, but it was not ready in time for action.

Japan was even more tightly limited by her industrial base. She managed to lay down several ships in wartime, but she had lost most of her experienced pilots by the time they were ready in 1944–45, and they had little impact on the war.

Carriers were much less expensive than battleships partly because they were much less heavily armoured. Pre-1939 battleship proponents tended to emphasise their vulnerability, and they turned out to be correct. The United States began the war with seven, but by the end of 1942 four had been sunk. Fortunately, by that time the big programme of *Essex* class construction was well advanced, and the first of the new ships were in combat by mid-1943.

Britain was not so lucky. She lost her only really modern prewar carrier, *Ark Royal*, in 1941, and by the end of 1942 a total of five prewar ships had been sunk, leaving only two. Four new carriers, the result of the prewar programme, were in service. Most major naval construction was suspended during the desperate years of 1940–41. When a major new construction programme was framed in 1942–43, it included numerous carriers, which were to fill the gaps left by the prewar programme. However, Britain's shipbuilders were badly strained, and they could not hope to build fleet carriers like the *Essex*es at anything like American speed. The British therefore designed a second-line fleet carrier, which they called a light fleet carrier, for relatively quick construction. Such ships proved limited in their capacity to accept major modification postwar. Of the larger carriers planned in wartime, only six (two large and four smaller ones) could be completed postwar, the last as late as 1959 (to a radically altered design).

Aircraft and carrier design

As for aircraft, although they evolved enormously between 1914 and 1945, one important consideration did not change. The combination of unit weight and engine power was always such that, given a reasonable wind over the deck generated by a ship, an aircraft could generally take off in less than about 400ft. Thus, as late as 1945, virtually any substantial ship with a flat deck on top could function as a carrier. Ship size was not unimportant, but it did not preclude air operation. It determined how many planes a ship could operate, and how often (given fuel capacity and maintenance space), and also how much ordnance could be delivered by those airplanes. Thus a navy intent merely on having some sort of carrier could get by with something quite small and inexpensive, but substantial operational capability demanded much more. The situation changed with the introduction of jets, which could not take off without catapults. It has changed back with the current generation of vertical take-off fighters, such as the Harrier. Once more, even the smallest ship can operate as a carrier of sorts (say, with one Harrier); but one aircraft provides very little operational power, and a ship supporting fifty or ninety Harriers must be quite large.

It may seem odd to leave the aircraft themselves for last as a major influence on carrier design. However, examination of carriers built during the prewar period will show that the same ship, essentially unmodified, quite successfully operated several different generations of naval aircraft. Moreover, most of those aircraft were quite the equal of contemporaries ashore. Carrier design acted more as a constraint on aircraft designers than the other way

The loss of two capital ships in the Far East to Japanese land-based torpedo bombers convinced the Royal Navy that special fighter carriers, fast enough to accompany battleships, were essential. This concept evolved into the light fleet carrier shown here. Though much less capacious than a fleet carrier, these ships could operate postwar aircraft. They introduced carrier operations to the Argentine, Brazilian, Dutch and Indian navies. This is Theseus *in 1950. (CMP)*

During the Second World War the US Navy decided to build British-style armoured carriers (the Royal Navy ultimately decided it liked the US open-hangar unarmoured type better). However, it rejected the British closed hangar design, and was unwilling to cut the air group or the sheer size of the flight deck. What began as an armoured version of the 27,500-ton (standard) Essex ended up as the 45,000-ton Midway, shown here in 1947. Although the hangar sides were open, it was argued that the row of gunhouses along them would keep out kamikazes. The original battery of eighteen 5in/54 guns was gradually reduced as the ships were modernised. (USN)

around. Postwar, new heavy jets required much more in the way of carrier characteristics.

For the period of interest, the most important impacts of aircraft on carriers were in factors such as the clear height in their hangars. The US Navy required 17ft 6in; the Royal Navy, with its double hangars, could not generally afford as much. After 1942, however, the Royal Navy depended heavily on Lend-Lease aircraft, and its wartime designs (the light fleet carriers and the later *Ark Royal, Malta,* and *Hermes* classes) all incorporated the US hangar deck requirement. Other major features are aircraft fuel and ammunition stowage. To at least some extent both are proportional to the overall size and characteristics of the carrier air group. Aviation gasoline (avgas) presented the designer with particular problems, because it could easily form an explosive vapour (the Japanese *Taiho* was torn apart by the explosion of just such a vapour, comparable to that of a modern fuel-air bomb). Avgas thus must be stowed underwater, competing for scarce hull volume with machinery, magazines, and underwater protection.

Typically a carrier was designed for a nominal air group with some expected hourly consumption of avgas. Avgas capacity therefore corresponded to several days of operation, and that sort of operation had some tactical logic. Unfortunately, aircraft changed very rapidly in the late 1930s and early 1940s. Their increased performance was bought at the price of much increased fuel consumption. It was difficult for navies to project ahead the sort of growth involved. Yet it was also very difficult to provide much more internal volume in a hull already tightly designed (carriers were the first real examples of volume-constrained, rather than weight-constrained, hull design). This problem became much worse as jets appeared postwar, and it was solved only when jets adopted fuels sufficiently benign that they could be stowed like ship fuel oil.

Finally there is aircraft weight. A flight deck is designed to take a particular maximum landing load; arrester gear can absorb only so much energy; elevators can lift only so much weight. The standard for individual aircraft weight roughly doubled (in some cases, more than doubled) during the Second World War. Ships had to be strengthened to match. Much the same might be said of weapons elevators.

The significance of carrier limits on aircraft design changed radically between the world wars due very largely to changes in aero-engine performance and, to a lesser extent, to the development of sufficiently strong lightweight structures. In 1914 the highest performance single-seat aircraft used engines of about 100hp, whereas in 1918 similar aircraft had 200 or 300hp engines. By about 1930, 700hp was practical in a single-seater, and by 1939, about 1000hp (as in the case of the Merlin). The very high performance naval aircraft of the Second World War relied on engines in the 2000hp class, like the US R-2800. In each case a much more powerful single engine was available, but it was too heavy for a high-performance aircraft. Greater power (and greater specific power, *ie* power per unit engine weight) translated not only into higher speed, but also into greater range with a larger payload. Thus in 1914 it took a very large, clumsy, airplane to lift a small torpedo. In 1944 US single-seat fighters, such as Hellcats, could carry torpedoes, although they did not typically do so in combat.

Norman Friedman

Aircraft Carriers: Typical Vessels 1906–1945

Ship or Class	Nationality	Dispt (tons) Normal/ Std Full load	Dimensions (loa × breadth × deep draught) Feet Metres	Armament Guns Aircraft	Armour Belt/Decks (max ins)	Speed (max design kts)	Launch dates	Numbers built
ARGUS	British	14,550 15,775	566 × 68 × 21 173 × 21 × 6	6 – 4in 20	–/–	20	1917	1
HERMES	British	10,850 13,000	598 × 70 × 19 182 × 21 × 6	10 – 5.5in 20	3/1	25	1919	1
COURAGEOUS	British	22,500 27,560	783 × 91 × 28 240 × 28 × 9	16 – 4.7in 48	3/–	30	1916	2

Ship or Class	Nationality	Dispt (tons) Normal/ Std Full load	Dimensions (loa × breadth × deep draught) Feet Metres	Armament Guns Aircraft	Armour Belt/Decks (max ins)	Speed (max design kts)	Launch dates	Numbers built
LEXINGTON	American	37,600 43,055	888 × 105 × 33 271 × 32 × 10	8 – 8in, 12 – 5in 63	7/1.25	33.25	1925	2
AKAGI	Japanese	36,500 42,750	855 × 95 × 27 261 × 29 × 8	10 – 8in, 12 – 4.7 60	10/?	31	1925	1
BEARN	French	22,146 28,400	599 × 89 × 31 182 × 27 ×9	8 – 6in, 6 – 3in 40	3/1/1	21.5	1920	1
HIRYU	Japanese	17,300 21,900	746 × 73 × 26 227 × 22 × 8	12 – 5in 64	3.5/1	34.3	1937	1
RANGER	American	14,575 17,577	769 × 80 × 22 234 × 24 × 7	8 – 5in 76	2/1	29.25	1933	1
ARK ROYAL	British	22,000 27,720	800 × 95 × 28 244 × 29 × 8	16 – 4.5in 60	4/3	31	1937	1
SHOKAKU	Japanese	25,675 32,105	845 × 85 × 29 256 × 26 × 9	16 – 5in 72	1.8/3.9	34.2	1939	2
YORKTOWN	American	19,875 25,484	825 × 83 × 26 251 × 25 × 8	8 – 5in 96	4/1.5	32.5	1936–40	3
ILLUSTRIOUS	British	23,000 29,110	753 × 96 × 29 230 × 29 × 9	16 – 4.5in 33	4.5/3/3	30.5	1939	3
ESSEX	American	27,208 34,881	872 × 93 × 28 266 × 28 × 8	12 – 5in 91	4/2.5	32.7	1942–45	24
INDEPENDENCE (CVL)	American	10,662 14,751	622 × 72 × 24 190 × 22 × 7	Light AA only 36	5/2	31.6	1942–43	9
IMPLACABLE	British	23,450 32,110	766 × 96 × 29 234 × 29 × 9	16 – 4.5in 60	4.5/3/3	32	1942	2
CASABLANCA (CVE)	American	8,188 10,902	512 × 65 × 21 156 × 20 × 6	1 – 5in 27	–/–	19	1943–44	50
COMMENCEMENT BAY (CVE)	American	18,908 21,397	557 × 75 × 28 170 × 23 ×9	1 – 5in 33	–/–	19	1944–46	19
TAIHO	Japanese	29,300 37,720	855 × 91 × 32 260 × 28 × 10	12 – 3.9in 53	2.2/3.1/4.9	33.3	1943	1
SHINANO	Japanese	62,000 71,890	873 × 119 × 34 266 × 36 × 10	16 – 5in 47	8.1/3.1/7.5	27	1944	1
UNRYU	Japanese	17,150 22,400	746 × 72 × 26 227 × 22 × 8	12 – 5in 65	1.8/1	34	1943–44	6
COLOSSUS (CVL)	British	13,190 18,040	695 × 80 × 23 212 × 24 × 7	Light AA only 37	–/–	25	1943–44	8
MIDWAY	American	47,387 59,901	968 × 113 × 35 295 × 34 × 11	18 – 5in 137	7.6/3.5/2	33	1945–46	3

Notes:

Length is overall; often flight decks were much longer than the hulls supporting them.

Beam is on waterline; flight decks often overhung by a considerable margin, which could vary as ships were modified in wartime.

Armament includes only guns of calibre greater than 3in; note that some ships were armed only with lighter weapons. Number of aircraft is the operational maximum, not the somewhat larger number carried (which would include spares to make up battle damage).

Armour When two deck thicknesses are given, the first number is flight deck armour. Deck and side are generally armour over machinery (armour over magazines was often thicker).

3

The Cruiser

BY the end of the nineteenth century, the diverse duties expected from cruisers had led to several different types. The perceived roles included:

1. Scouting for, and shadowing, the enemy battlefleet
2. Trade war, raiding and defence
3. Colonial police work
4. Destroyer leader

In addition, there was a role for the cruiser acting as a capital ship in areas remote from the battlefleet.

Scouting presented the greatest problems, though the development of wireless (radio) eased these considerably. There were two schools of thought, one advocating large, powerful ships which could fight off the enemy cruiser screen to contact the enemy battle fleet, the other believing that small, high-speed ships could achieve their objective by evasion.

Before the treaties

Most British cruiser designs sprang from four pairs of scouts completed in 1905. They were fast – 25kts – which could be sustained at sea but had a very weak armament of ten 12pdrs. Two pairs had a thin belt over their machinery whilst the others relied on a protective deck. These ships could have formed the starting point for a steady development but Admiral Fisher disrupted the cruiser programme by maintaining that there was no need for ships between the battlecruiser and the big destroyer.

The lessons of the Battle of Tsushima (1905) could be read in more than one way. Since the Japanese operating base was close to Port

Arthur, and the water was shallow, most of their scouting was carried out by destroyers. The postwar Japanese admiralty seems to have taken the same line as Fisher, building the pre-dreadnought 'battlecruisers' of the *Tsukuba* and *Ibuki* classes and only the three impressive light cruisers of the *Chikuma* class in the 1907 programme.

The very large first class protected cruisers had died out as a result of high cost and vulnerability while the very small, third class cruiser also disappeared as the role of colonial policing became less military and could be carried out by sloops. Britain and Germany were the only countries which built cruisers in substantial numbers up to 1918 and this section will concentrate on these navies.

German developments

German development was steady and continuous from the small protected cruisers of the *Gazelle* class of ten ships, launched from 1898 to 1902. They carried ten 105mm (4.1in) guns and had a speed of 21kts. The armament was the same in subsequent classes until the *Wiesbaden*, launched 1915, introduced the 150mm (5.9in). There was a steady increase in speed, bringing with it a considerable growth in displacement from the 2900 tons of *Gazelle* to the 6350 tons of *Graudenz* with the same armament but a speed of 28kts.

Technical development was quite rapid;

Lübeck, launched 1904, introduced the turbine with four propellers on each of her two shafts. Following classes usually had one ship with turbines until the *Kolberg* class of 1908, all four of which had turbines. *Karlsruhe* was the only ship to complete with fully geared turbines.

The *Magdeburg* class of the 1908–9 programme marked a considerable step forward in design introducing a thin, 60mm, waterline belt extending over some 80 per cent of the length, worked into the ship as part of the structure. *Magdeburg* was the first German ship to carry oil as well as coal. A raked stem replaced the traditional ram shape and the lines were improved. The poop disappeared to make way for a mining deck capable of carrying 120 mines.

British developments

The scout *Attentive* was the starting point for British cruisers after 1906. Turbines replaced triple expansion machinery in all classes and all earlier ships carried both coal and oil fuel. Armament increased from six 4in in *Boadicea* to ten in *Blonde* and later. The five ships of the *Bristol* class were given a 6in at each end as well as ten 4in, sided. These grew rapidly into the *Weymouth*s with eight 6in and the *Chatham*s also with eight 6in but with a 2in nickel steel belt over 1in structural plating. Further development led to the *Birmingham* with nine 6in. This design was then adapted by Cammell

The Magdeburg *class introduced a new look to the German cruiser and, with it, a thin armour belt and some capability to burn oil. This is* Strassburg *as completed.* (CMP)

Laird for two cruisers with ten 5.5in guns, ordered by Greece but taken over by the Royal Navy in 1915.

Three more 25kt scouts were launched in 1911 but by this time destroyer speeds were approaching 30kts, even in moderate seas and a faster cruiser was needed as a leader. Fisher wanted an improved *Swift* with speed increased to 37kts whilst there was also pressure to stay with the well-liked *Chatham*s. These latter were expensive at £350,000 and the majority view, including Churchill as First Lord, recommended an improved scout.

These ships, the *Arethusa*s, were to have destroyer-type machinery which it was hoped would give 30kts though the design team knew that such a speed was not possible. There was considerable debate over the merits of an all-6in or all-4in armament and what seemed a sensible compromise of two 6in and six 4in was agreed. They were given a 3in belt, worked structurally. Though they did not quite make 30kts, they were regarded as very successful ships and formed the basis for most British cruisers of the First World War.

The first of the 'C' classes had a novel arrangement of guns with two superfiring 6in aft and eight 4in sided and forward arguing that she would run away from cruisers, engaging with the 6in, and chase destroyers using the 4in with its higher rate of fire. Two similar ships introduced geared turbines, discussed in the Introduction, and all later classes had gearing. From the *Centaur*s, launched 1916, a 6in armament, with all guns on the centreline was adopted. The *Arethusa*s and early 'C's were

very wet and the last five were given a 'trawler bow', increasing freeboard forward.

The 'D' class were stretched 'C's with a sixth 6in and other minor improvements including lower rpm machinery which, with increased length, enabled them to make the same speed as the 'C's on the same power even though displacement had gone up from 5000 to 5780 tons. The 'E' class, completed after the war, were very much bigger ships with twice the power giving an increase in speed to 33kts. They mounted seven 6in and, after modification, sixteen 21in torpedo tubes. Their machinery was divided into units so that they would retain mobility after any likely damage.

Technical developments in cruisers 1906–1918

Arrangement of guns. Initially, it was seen as essential that the guns should be widely separated, partly to ensure that no one hit would put more than one gun out of action and partly to protect the crews of these open mountings from the severe blast from their neighbours. This led to a disposition with one or two guns at each end and the rest spaced down either side, limiting the number which could fire on either broadside to about half the total. Since it was expected that these ships would fight destroyers at close range, it was even seen as an advantage that there were guns on both sides to engage multiple targets – a fallacy which persisted as late as the American *Minneapolis* of 1917.

As effective range increased, particularly

under director control, the advantage of mounting all guns on the centreline, where they could fire on both sides, became apparent. It was some time before *ad hoc* tests showed that blast screens would permit superfiring guns, even in open shields. The German navy never did move to guns all on the centreline nor did they adopt director firing though they did use superfiring guns aft in several classes.

Size of gun. Before the war, the Royal Navy debated for each class the merits of all-4in, all-6in or a mix. The 4in, firing a 31lb shell, was quite big enough for use against destroyers. During trials in 1909–10, 4in Lyddite shell blew holes 29ft × 20ft in the side of the old destroyer *Ferret* while powder filled common shell made a hole 8ft × 5ft. The light weight of the shell permitted a high rate of fire whilst the gun was light enough for rapid changes in training and elevation; the combined effect being to give a much greater chance of lethal hits on a destroyer than from a 6in.

On the other hand, the effective range of the 4in was less than that of the 6in and it was unlikely to penetrate the thin belt fitted to later cruisers or even to inflict serious damage on their unprotected areas. The choice was made more difficult by the effect of the motions of the ship in even moderate seas. A 100lb shell is not easy to handle even on a stationary platform and it is almost impossible when the ship is rolling. Training and elevating a heavy gun by hand against the motions of a ship is also very difficult and for this reason the early 6in, 50-calibre, Mk XI was replaced by the 45-calibre, Mk XII, which was 2 tons lighter in the *Chatham* and later classes. The lighter gun had the same maximum range of 14,000yds, though during the war, fire was normally opened at about 12,000yds and 9000 was seen as the effective range. The best choice for a hand operated mounting was probably the 5.5in with an 82lb projectile but it only became available after the outbreak of war.

The German 4.1in was a good gun, slightly superior in range to the British 4in, but unable to penetrate the 2–3in belt of most British ships. Both navies were to adopt all 6in/5.9in armaments during the war as cruiser duels became more frequent.

Seakeeping. These ships, with few exceptions, were quite small, much the size of today's frig-

Phaeton, *an Arethusa class ship which formed the basis for most British cruiser designs in the First World War. Note the big Blue Ensign worn in addition to the White since the latter had been confused with the German ensign.* (CMP)

ates. There were a number of seakeeping problems but, with little theory and only limited model tests, designers were unable to find a full solution. They were fairly deep draught ships so slamming was not a problem. On the other hand, freeboard was deliberately kept low to reduce silhouette and topweight and to limit the extent of unarmoured structure. Even before the war, the forecastle was extended aft and waist guns moved up but these steps were insufficient as later classes were still wet.

Gradually, empirical solutions were found. Flare and freeboard were both increased. The ram bow was replaced, first by a 'plough' and later by a straight raked stem. The 'trawler bow', added to the later 'C' and 'D' classes, increased freeboard but, since it was an addition, there was a knuckle in the section which helped to throw the spray aside. Rolling was the biggest problem for men moving heavy weights, as when loading and training guns. By the end of the nineteenth century it was well understood that rolling could be much reduced by bilge keels which, in British light cruisers, were about 2ft deep, considerably less than a modern designer would select.

Based on trial data from modern ships, a 450ft ship should be able to steam at 20kts in sea state 6, though these cruisers would probably have been slowed more due to their low freeboard.

Armour. The earlier ships of all navies relied on a protective deck, sloped down at the sides, to protect magazines and machinery; coal bunkers were arranged to give additional protection. The deck, 2in thick at most, would not resist the direct impact of a shell but such hits were unlikely. Normally, the fuse would be actuated as the shell hit the ship's side and it would burst above the protective deck which was thought

to be strong enough to keep out blast and splinters. Full scale trials, particularly those against *Edinburgh* in 1910, showed that these decks were much less effective than had been believed.

Until the development of nickel steel armour, it was not possible, within the weight limits of a fast cruiser, to fit a belt which would resist the impact of shells of any size. Effective belts appeared in the Royal Navy in the *Chatham* and in the German Navy in *Magdeburg*, both launched in 1911. The British ship had 2in protection over 1in shell plating which would resist any 4in shell at fighting ranges and probably keep out 6in HE. *Southampton* was hit at Jutland by a nose-fused 5.9in HE shell which burst on impact and though the belt was punctured, there was little damage behind. *Arethusa*'s 3in plates easily resisted 4.1in shells at Heligoland.

These ships were well subdivided transversely, without longitudinal subdivision, making them hard to sink by torpedo. *Falmouth* was hit by four torpedoes, *Nottingham* by three, both remaining afloat for many hours. Several hit by a single torpedo survived. Pride of place must go to *Wiesbaden*, hit by fifteen heavy shells (mostly 12in), six 9.2in or 7.5in and many 6in as well as a torpedo; however, she was immobilised by the very first hit which put both engine rooms out of action. As in their bigger ships, the German cruisers had a very elaborate pumping system which was seen by British designers as a hazard because of the number of bulkhead penetrations.

Radio. The scouting task was greatly eased by the introduction of radio, as was that of tracking down enemy raiders. In particular, the scout could radio a sighting report immediately instead of having to find its own fleet or rely on

a line of repeating ships. The Tsushima campaign showed the value of radio and by 1905 the Royal Navy was fitting wireless in all ships bigger than destroyers. Most ships were re-equipped about 1907 with improved sets when 'Instructions for the conduct of WT signalling' were issued.

At the outbreak of war, the distant German cable and wireless installations were captured or destroyed depriving their raiders of intelligence. Conversely, the British stations helped considerably in the hunt for enemy ships such as *Emden*.

It should not be forgotten that radio was in its infancy in the First World War and, even by the time of Jutland, it took 10–20 minutes to get a message from bridge to bridge. Failures to get through were not uncommon.

Machinery. All the British cruisers of this era were driven by steam turbines, the Germans following a little later in the *Kolberg* class. The development of machinery is discussed in the Introduction and will not be repeated here. The turbine was far superior to the reciprocating engines for sustained speed but suffered a little in consumption until gearing was introduced just before the war in British ships.

Boilers were 'small tube' type in all classes of both navies, the *Arethusa*s adopting destroyer practice. British boilers were taller than those in German ships making it impossible to run a continuous main deck through the boiler rooms, contributing to the high stresses in the *Arethusa*s. The upper deck amidships was about 1in thick for structural reasons and provided some protection against splinters.

British cruisers prior to the *Arethusa*s could burn either coal or oil and carried both, but later ships burnt oil only. Boilers burning only oil were more efficient and oil-burning ships were about 1½–2kts faster. *Magdeburg* (1909 programme) was the first German to introduce mixed firing and none were all oil-burning. Oil-fired boilers did not choke with clinker and ash and were far superior in sustaining high speed.

Wartime changes and alterations

The earlier British light cruisers from *Arethusa* onwards were given extra 6in in place of some or all of their 4in guns. Some German cruisers also had 4.1in replaced by 5.9in guns. The value of the bigger gun was greatly enhanced on British ships by the introduction of director firing during 1917–18, a change made visible by the fitting of tripod masts. Anti-aircraft guns were added, the number of torpedo tubes was increased and searchlights increased in size and number. The heavy conning tower, little used in action, was removed from most ships as weight compensation.

The most dramatic change was the addition of aircraft and launching platforms. By the end of the war twenty Grand Fleet cruisers carried aircraft in addition to full armament, often in a hangar and seven others could tow a kite balloon. The aircraft were usually fighters to attack German airships. No German cruiser carried aircraft except the *Stuttgart* in her late-war seaplane carrier conversion.

There were many other detail changes contributing to fighting efficiency, such as pneumatic message transmission from the signal office to bridge. Ammunition, both propellant and shells, was improved in effectiveness and made safer to stow.

Bigger cruisers

The British light cruisers were small and fairly short endurance ships, intended mainly for North Sea operations. A bigger ship was needed to protect distant sea lanes with longer endurance and, it was thought, a more powerful gun. The outcome was the *Hawkins* class, designed in 1915 as a development of the *Birmingham*, which they resembled in gun disposition. Because of the lack of oil fuel depots in the more distant areas they were designed to burn both oil and coal. All but the first two were converted to oil-only before completion, with power increased by 10,000shp, and the others were changed later. After some debate, the armament became seven 7.5in guns which were given electric elevation and training. The 200lb shells were hand loaded, an almost impossible task except in a dead calm.

Minneapolis class

The US Navy began to think of 'Scouts' in 1915 and by 1917 these had developed into the *Minneapolis* class of ten ships. With four thin funnels and a mainly sided armament they looked, and to a considerable extent were, archaic. There were twelve 6in carried in a twin turret fore and aft with the remainder

Hawkins: this class was more highly esteemed abroad than at home. They can be seen as the direct ancestor of the world's Washington Treaty cruisers.

sided. The turret guns were very close together leading to slow firing and the lower guns on the side were washed out in a seaway.

They had very powerful machinery giving trial speeds close to 35kts. The machinery was well subdivided and, with widely separated engine rooms, they were well able to retain mobility after damage. The space needed for these powerful engines left the rest of the ship very cramped and wild heat made them unbearably hot in the tropics. Their length, 555ft, led to considerable structural problems, only partially solved.

From 1918 onwards, Japan launched twelve fine light cruisers of the *Tenryu*, *Kuma* and *Nagara* classes, generally similar to the British 'C' and 'D' classes but with 5.5in guns.

Between the Wars

The Washington Treaty

US Navy studies showed that they needed big ships with high speed and 8in guns for scouting in the Pacific while the British were keen to retain the *Hawkins* class of 9750 tons, with 7.5in guns. Hence it was easy to agree a limit on individual ships, accepted by other countries, of 10,000 tons and 8in guns.

No agreement was reached on numbers: the Royal Navy had accepted a report from Admiral Jellicoe which said that the requirement was 70 cruisers, a target for which the Navy was to press up to the outbreak of war. The US Navy was unwilling either to accept British superiority in numbers or to build their fleet up to 70, while Japan was also not prepared to accept an inferior position.

The Washington Treaty is often claimed to

have caused an escalation in the size of cruisers but this seems unlikely since 10,000 tons had often been equalled or exceeded at the beginning of the century. Another fallacy is that the Washington Treaty emasculated the Royal Navy. In fact, during the depression it enabled the Admiralty to argue with Ministers that they were contracted to build up to the Treaty limits and these limitations probably left the navy stronger than it would otherwise have been.

This section covers a period of nearly twenty years during which there were steady, if undramatic, developments in engineering. Machinery and equipments tended to reduce in weight and further weight savings came from the increasing use of welding, making more weight available for military capability. A ship of the late 1930s cannot be compared with one built in the early 1920s, except as a measure of this progress. Comparison is also made more difficult by the way in which several countries ignored the agreed limits on displacement: a naval architect can do a lot for fighting capability with an extra 1000 tons and some of the later ships were as much as 6000 tons over the limit.

Early 8in gun ships

The British designs for the *Kent* class introduced a number of novel features, not always obvious. They were long ships and, to meet Treaty limits, the hull had to be light. Stresses are reduced in a ship which is deep from deck to keel permitting a lighter structure whilst the resulting high freeboard made them good seaboats and provided airy mess decks. The armament was even more novel; the twin 8in turrets were designed for 70 degrees elevation to act as AA guns, though the rates of training and elevation were inadequate for such a role, and they were intended to fire five rounds per

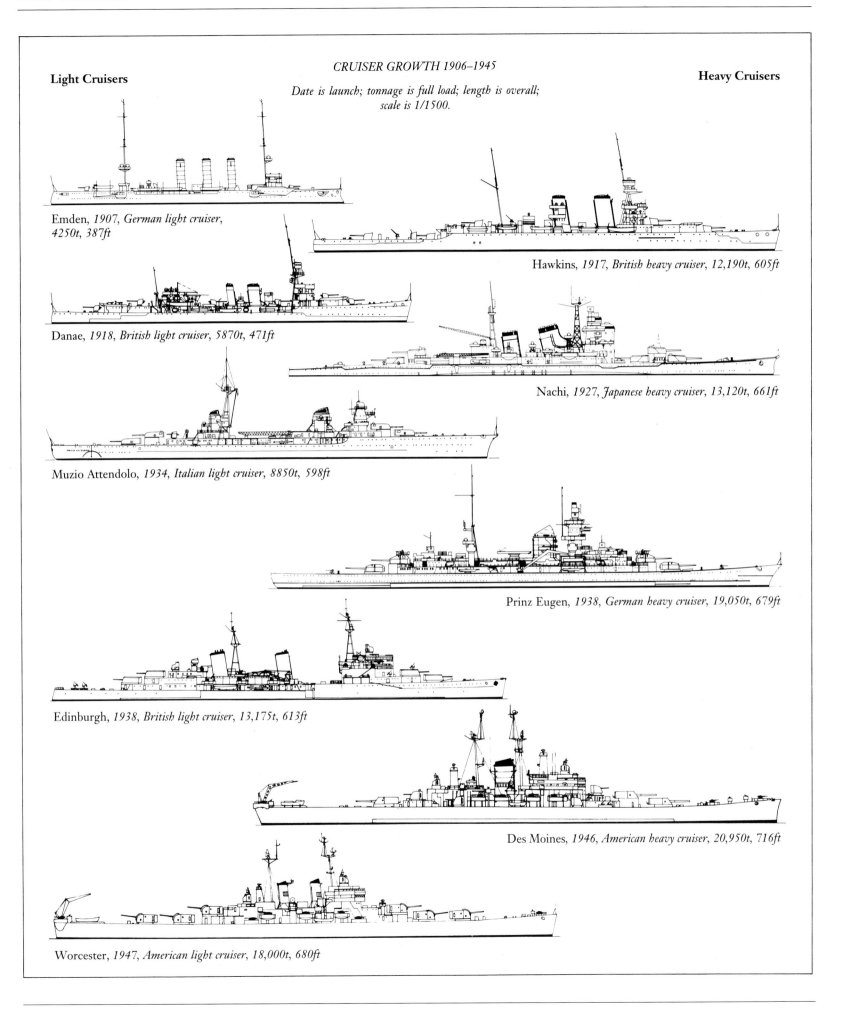

Light Cruisers

Heavy Cruisers

CRUISER GROWTH 1906–1945

*Date is launch; tonnage is full load; length is overall;
scale is 1/1500.*

Emden, *1907, German light cruiser,
4250t, 387ft*

Hawkins, *1917, British heavy cruiser, 12,190t, 605ft*

Danae, *1918, British light cruiser, 5870t, 471ft*

Nachi, *1927, Japanese heavy cruiser, 13,120t, 661ft*

Muzio Attendolo, *1934, Italian light cruiser, 8850t, 598ft*

Prinz Eugen, *1938, German heavy cruiser, 19,050t, 679ft*

Edinburgh, *1938, British light cruiser, 13,175t, 613ft*

Des Moines, *1946, American heavy cruiser, 20,950t, 716ft*

Worcester, *1947, American light cruiser, 18,000t, 680ft*

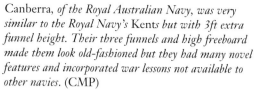

Canberra, of the Royal Australian Navy, was very similar to the Royal Navy's Kents but with 3ft extra funnel height. Their three funnels and high freeboard made them look old-fashioned but they had many novel features and incorporated war lessons not available to other navies. (CMP)

minute, a figure occasionally achieved in service though not very reliably. They also carried four 4in AA guns and were intended for two 8-barrel 2pdr pom-poms, an exceptional AA armament for the time.

Staff debate centred on protection; it was clear that there was no weight to spare for protection against 8in shells and that, unless speed was drastically reduced, most of the ship would be vulnerable even to 6in fire. It was decided to confine effective protection to the magazines whilst shell rooms and machinery only had splinter protection. They were given small bulges, of little value against contemporary torpedoes and though the machinery was well subdivided it lacked the benefits of the alternating unit system introduced in the 'E' class. The *Kent*s were probably the most technically advanced of the first wave of 'Treaty' cruisers but the three tall funnels and high freeboard gave them an old-fashioned look.

Great attention was paid to weight saving during the detailed design and construction and they completed much lighter than the design figure (*eg Berwick* 9750 tons). A catapult and seaplane were added soon after completion using some of the spare weight. It is perhaps worth noting that aircraft of the 1920s were too flimsy to land on the sea except in a dead calm and too expensive to be expendable as in

the war. As soon as suitable aircraft became available, most navies began to use them.

The first two US Navy ships of the *Pensacola* class carried ten 8in but the cramped mountings, combined with heavy rolling, limited the rate of fire to two rounds per minute at best. They were designed without a director though this was added during building and only then did the US Navy appreciate the possibility of hitting at long range, even up to 30,000yds, and hence the desirability of protecting against such hits. These two ships completed some 900 tons below the limit.

The Japanese, under the 1921 programme, built a very small, experimental cruiser, the *Yubari*. On a design displacement of 2890 tons she was to carry six 5.5in guns, achieve 35.5kts and have a thin belt. The armour was worked structurally to save weight but, even so, she came out very heavy at 3387 tons, a 17 per cent error. Her style – including bad weight estimating – was adopted in following classes.

The first two 8in ships of the *Furutaka* class, with six 8in in open mounts, can be seen as a direct response to *Hawkins*. The next two, the *Aoba*s, were generally similar but carried their guns in three twin turrets; the earlier pair were altered to this configuration in 1936–39. All four were well over their declared weight but within Treaty limits.

These ships introduced the 'wavy' deckline characteristic of Japanese cruisers, with high freeboard at the bow to keep the ship dry and also amidships for a good range of stability, dropping in the way of the turrets and aft to give a low centre of gravity. They had a centreline bulkhead in the engine and most boiler rooms intended to prevent minor damage from flooding a major part of the machinery but it also ensured that major damage would lead to rapid capsize (eight out of twelve Japanese cruisers hit in this region capsized). Originally, they were very fast ships with a speed of about 34.5kts, reduced to 33kts when bulges were fitted to improve their inadequate stability.

Postwar French cruiser building began with two *Duguay Trouin* class mounting eight 6in in twin turrets, very little protection and a speed of 33kts. These were followed by two *Duquesne* class with eight 8in, a speed of 33.75kts and a total of 430 tons of protection, none more than 1in thick. French practice was to run a short trial at 10 per cent overload power and frequently only the speed on the fastest run, with wind and tide, was published, much exaggerating their capability at sea. Weight saving in the hull was carried to excess and their overstressed hull suffered from leaky seams.

The two Italian ships of the *Trento* class also put a premium on speed, the Ministry paying one million lire for each knot over the design speed on trial. By over-forcing the machinery, they approached 36kts on trial and could probably make 34kts at sea in fair weather. They had a 70mm belt and a light deck, and were over the limit by 300 tons.

Second wave

The pace of building was so rapid that the second class followed so close to the first that few, if any lessons could be incorporated. The Royal Navy was well satisfied with the seven *Kent*s and followed with four *London*s and two *Norfolk*s which were generally similar. The shallow bulges were omitted and the lines improved giving an extra ¾kt in speed. The Mk II turret was introduced in the *Norfolk* class limit-

Pensacola, the first US Navy design, after the Washington Treaty. Her turrets were very cramped and the ship completed 900 tons under the treaty limit. (CMP)

Duquesne, *an early French 8in cruiser with light protection and high speed.* (CMP)

ing elevation to 50 degrees. The mechanism was simplified to improve reliability and it was also hoped that the Mk II would be lighter than the earlier mount, which was 50 tons over weight; however, the Mark II was a further 15 tons heavier.

In 1928, Spain ordered two modified *Kent*s of the *Canarias* class. They had a little more power and a striking new profile. Their 'modern' bridge and massive single funnel made them much more highly esteemed than the *Kent*s from which they differed little in capability.

The British could not afford sufficient numbers of big cruisers and sought an effective design of smaller ship. *York* with six 8in was followed by *Exeter*, technically similar, but with vertical funnels to make it difficult to estimate her bearing and range and, with a lower bridge, she looked the more modern ship. Some of the weight saved by omitting a turret and reducing freeboard aft of amidships went into a 3in belt over the machinery. These were the last British 8in cruisers to be built; the *Surrey*s planned for 1929 would have had the much lower speed of 30kts and a 5¾in belt with a 2–3in deck, but were cancelled as an economy measure in the Depression.

The US Navy speedily realised that the *Pensacola*s were going to be unsatisfactory, cramped, wet and yet well under the weight limit. The six ships of the *Northampton* class and the two slightly modified *Portland*s attempted to rectify these defects. They all carried three triple 8in turrets, saving space and

The New Orleans *class were much more heavily armoured than earlier cruisers of any navy. In particular, the gun turrets carried armour as opposed to splinter protection. This is* Minneapolis *photographed in September 1941.* (USN)

weight, and the earlier ships had a slight increase in protection, considerably enhanced in the last two which were a little over weight.

The *New Orleans* class carried the same armament and were not dissimilar in appearance but were much more advanced ships. Weight was saved by squeezing the machinery which was closely subdivided into four boiler and two engine rooms but these were not in true units so reducing their resistance to torpedoes and bombs. More weight was saved by the considerable use of welding which enabled them to carry a 5in belt and a 2½in deck. Perhaps more valuable than these, the guns were protected for the first time with 6in turret faces and a 2½

roof instead of the 1in or so on most ships of other countries.

The next Japanese ships were the four *Myoko*s with five twin turrets, a speed of 35½kts and a 3.9in belt, but a standard displacement 1000 tons over the treaty limit. This excess weight caused both strength and stability problems and as a result they were reconstructed in 1940–41 when bulges were fitted raising their displacement to 13,000 tons, a reasonable figure for their capability but a gross breach of the treaty under which they had been designed.

The following *Takao* class were generally similar with a standard displacement of 11,350 tons as completed, 13,400 as rebuilt. The torpedo armament of both classes was very heavy with twelve 24in tubes and up to thirty-six torpedoes. Their designer recognised the danger of so much high explosive (and compressed oxygen) on the upper deck and the tubes were sponsored out from the hull to reduce the effect of an explosion and the spare warheads were protected. Even so, several ships were lost in the war following detonation of their own torpedoes.

Both France and Italy fitted more protection in their second group of ships. The four *Suffren*s sacrificed 2kts for a 2–2¼in belt and remained under 10,000 tons. The Italian navy asked for a 4–6in belt as well as eight 8in and

Takao. *One of two classes of Japanese cruisers heavily armed with ten 8in guns and very fast but grossly over treaty weight limits. Stability, strength and damage resistance were all poor.* (CMP)

were not repeated when greater freedom of design was permitted. Instead, Germany built conventional heavy cruisers with eight 8in, a long 3¼in belt and a speed of 32½kts. The first two were 14,000 tons and *Prinz Eugen*, the only one to complete of the second group scaled nearly 17,000 tons. Endurance was poor at 6800 miles and their high pressure, high temperature machinery was unreliable. They seem to have been structurally weak and, as with other German cruisers of the Second World War, their subdivision leaked seriously after damage.

Small cruisers

Many countries found that they could only afford ships in the numbers needed by building much smaller cruisers. The Royal Navy designed the *Leander* in 1929 with four twin 6in turrets. She had a speed of 32½kts and a 3in belt (over 1in shell). The increasing use of welding, particularly in follow-on ships, saved weight in the hull. The armament was seen as the minimum to deal with armed merchant raiders when used in the trade protection role. However, at a cost of £1.6 million compared with £2 million for the 'Counties', they were not cheap.

The five *Leander*s were followed by three very similar *Amphion*s, later sold to Australia. They introduced alternating engine/boiler room machinery units intended to reduce the chance of losing all power from a single hit and this feature was incorporated in all later British cruisers. This admirable feature was spoilt in detail as the wing compartment arranged alongside the after boiler room led to asymmetrical flooding and capsize of several ships which were hit in that area. The four *Arethusa*s

32kts in the *Zara* and even with lightweight machinery the *design* displacement was still 1500 tons above that of the treaty which Italy had signed. In *Bolzano*, policy changed again with a speed of 36kts and only a 70mm belt but with displacement still well over the limit.

Pocket battleships etc

The Treaty of Versailles allowed Germany to build warships not exceeding 10,000 tons with a maximum gun calibre of 11in. It was envisaged that this would lead to coastal defence ships for the Baltic similar to Swedish vessels. In the late 1920s, work began on a technical *tour de force* using welding extensively to save weight and with diesel engines for very long endurance. The declared aim was to provide a vessel which would be more powerfully armed than any vessel fast enough to catch her and faster, at 28kts, than any more powerful ship. They were to have an endurance of 12,000 miles making them potent, if very expensive,

commerce raiders. It is not clear whether they were originally intended to break the Treaty limit but they completed at 11,700 tons; a useful 17 per cent bonus for military equipment.

However, their belt was only 3in thick and could be penetrated by 8in APC. This meant that they had to be sure of destroying such an opponent before it could reach effective range, about 18,000 yards. With only six guns there was not much chance of many hits outside this range, a chance reduced still further by the effect of vibration from the diesels on the director.

They were a great propaganda success and grossly overrated by other navies but the German opinion was shown by the fact that they

The panzerschiff *(armoured ship) Admiral Graf Spee. Though welding was used extensively to save weight, she was still far heavier than permitted by the Versailles Treaty. Her diesel engines gave her a long range as a commerce raider but at the expense of heavy vibration which affected gunnery control.* (CMP)

HMS Achilles. *The* Leander *class reintroduced the moderate size, 6in cruiser to the Royal Navy and also introduced a considerable extent of welded structure. They were seen as very successful ships but, at £1.6 million, they were not cheap.* (CMP)

looked like cut down *Amphion*s with one less turret but arose from a different requirement, to act as destroyer leaders.

France built a number of similar ships with nine 6in guns in triple turrets with high speed, at least on trials. The six *La Galissonnières* had a speed of 31kts on normal power but made about 35kts on trials on overload. Aircraft arrangements were on the quarterdeck with a very broad transom on which a Hein Mat was stowed to aid recovery of seaplanes.

Italy, too, built ten moderate-sized 6in cruisers in five pairs, collectively referred to as the 'Condottieri' type. There was a steady growth in size from 5110 tons to 9440 with a reduction in speed from a nominal 36.5kts to 34kts. Protection increased very considerably from virtually nothing (25mm side plating) to spaced armour with a 30mm de-capping plate separated from a 100mm main belt. Most carried eight 6in, the last two, ten.

Germany built the 6in training cruiser *Emden*, in 1921, which was followed between 1926 and 1934 by five ships, all of about 6500 tons mounting nine 6in. All had three shafts with steam turbines on the wings and diesels on the centre for long endurance. In the first three ships of the 'K' class the machinery could only be operated as steam *or* diesel, the two later vessels could use all shafts together, a controllable pitch propeller on the centre taking account of the different loading conditions.

Hybrids

The Swedish cruiser *Gotland*, launched in 1933 was a most interesting variant on the conventional light cruiser. On a displacement of 4700 tons she carried six 6in guns, splinter protec-

tion and could steam at 28kts. The whole after end was devoted to aircraft with a catapult, ranging deck and a hangar. Her nominal aircraft complement was eleven but she never seems to have carried more than six Ospreys. A Hein Mat was fitted to ease landing in a rough sea. By 1943 there were no aircraft suitable for such a small ship and she was converted to an AA cruiser. There were many other designs for hybrid cruiser-carriers in both Britain and the USA during the 1930s and 1940s but none were built. The Japanese *Tone*s, and *Mogami* after her 1943 rebuild, were true hybrids with six aircraft embarked.

Luigi Cadorna, one of a group of light, fast Italian cruisers known as the 'Condottieri' type. (CMP)

The London Treaty 1931

This agreement divided cruisers into two categories:

(a) Guns between 6.1in and 8in.
(b) Guns between 5.1in and 6.1in.

The total permitted tonnage for each category was laid down for the three main naval powers as follows:

	USA	British Empire	Japan
Category (a)	180,000	146,800	108,400
Category (b)	143,000	192,200	105,500

It will be noted that this treaty meant that the Royal Navy could build no more 8in ships but gained in total tonnage as well as in category (b). In practice, resources were insufficient

Admiral Hipper, a conventional heavy cruiser which the German navy preferred to the pocket battleship. She was also much over the new weight limits of the Anglo-German treaty. (CMP)

The Japanese Mogami *on trials, when she is said to have reached 36kts at 12,400 tons. She was weak and lacking in stability, which required extensive modifications, further increasing the weight by which she exceeded treaty limits.* (CMP)

to build up to these figures by 1939, gun and armour manufacturing capacity being more limiting than money.

Big 6in gunned ships

In 1931, Japan declared to the other Treaty powers that she was to build the *Mogami* class mounting fifteen 6in guns, with a 3.9in belt and a speed of 37kts, all on a displacement of 8500 tons, a claim which should have been recognised as incredible. The design displacement was actually 9500 tons, already 1000 tons above that declared under the Treaty and provision was made to replace the 6in with ten 8in when the Treaty expired. The first real sign of trouble came in 1934 when the torpedo boat *Tomozuru* capsized in a storm. The overall review of stability standards which followed led to a considerable redesign and *Mogami* completed with a displacement of 11,200 tons and on trials attained an impressive 36kts.

In a storm in September 1935, *Mogami*, *Mikuma* and other ships sustained structural damage. Remedial action brought the displacement to 12,400 tons. In 1937, Japan denounced the treaties and the 8in guns were fitted with

yet another increase in displacement. They were fast, well armed ships but in no way exceptional for their true size. It seems unlikely that the well-trained Japanese naval architects simply made a mistake in every class of cruiser. It is more likely that they were unable to resist naval staff pressure to carry an impossible load.

Eight or six inch?

In several navies the limits placed on the strength of the 8in fleet under the London Treaty led to a re-examination of the relative capability of 8in and 6in ships. The 8in gun had a longer range and considerably better armour penetration and the heavier bursting charge would cause a little more damage. On the other hand, for a given size of ship, more 6in guns could be carried (15:9, for example) and these could fire at 8–10 rounds per minute compared with about 2 for most 8in guns.

The critical issue was whether the 8in guns could destroy a 6in ship in the zone between the maximum ranges of their guns; about 28,000yds for 8in, 20,000yds for a 6in. In peacetime firings the 8in could hit a target at long range but wartime experience showed that

hits on a fast, rapidly manoeuvring ship were almost unknown over 20,000yds. For example, the British cruisers at Matapan were under 'accurate' Italian 8in fire at about 26,000yds for some time without being hit. In the Battle of the Komandorskis, the *Salt Lake City* had some 200 8in shells fall close to her at 16–24,000yds with only one hit.

It was also argued that the 'vitals' of a ship could be protected against 6in shells at fighting ranges but not against 8in. However, the increasing complexity of cruisers, particularly of their gunnery communications, meant that damage to the unarmoured areas could seriously reduce their ability to fight. This argument was further complicated by the US Navy's introduction of much heavier shells with greater penetration. The 8in AP shell went up from 260lbs to 335lbs while the 6in increased from 105lbs to 130lbs. The US Navy also gave up the practice of mounting all three guns in a single cradle which limited rate of fire and caused scatter of the salvo. Mere counting of barrels ceased to be an accurate guide to capability.

Brooklyn class

The *Brooklyn* class introduced a number of novel features of which the most visible was an aircraft hangar under the quarterdeck, permitted by the transom stern. They extended the use of welding and introduced longitudinal framing to save hull weight and further savings probably came from their greater depth. They are among the classic warship designs of all time and almost all later cruisers of the US Navy have a clear line of descent from the *Brooklyn*.

On 9700 tons, they mounted fifteen 6in guns, a 5in belt (over 0.625in shell), a 2in deck, heavily protected turrets and had a speed of 32½ kts. It was intended that they should be immune to 6in fire between 8000 and 23,000yds. The first seven ships had eight single 5in/25-calibre AA guns but the last two had the much superior 5in/38 in twin mounts. These two, *St Louis* and *Helena*, were virtually a

Nashville, *a* Brooklyn *class cruiser from which most wartime US Navy ships were derived. Well protected and heavily armed, they show the clear superiority of US marine industries by the late 1930s.* (CMP)

The British 'Colony' class was a successful attempt to carry a heavy armament on a relatively small hull. Inevitably they were cramped and most (like Kenya shown here in 1949) had 'X' turret removed to compensate for wartime additions. (CMP)

new class, re-introducing alternating machinery units so much improving their resistance to underwater attack.

The might of American industry was beginning to show; their machinery was light in weight and reliable and other equipment, particularly the electrical system, was lighter than those of other countries making more weight available for military features.

Towns and Colonies

The Royal Navy was well satisfied with the *Leander/Amphion* classes but news of *Mogami* and *Brooklyn* forced a change to more powerful ships. To obtain as many ships as possible within the overall Treaty tonnage, size was kept as small as possible and *Southampton* displaced 9100 tons, with twelve 6in, a 4½in belt and a speed of 32kts. In most aspects they were stretched *Amphion*s but they reverted to raking funnels and they were given a fixed athwartships catapult between the funnels with large hangars in the forward superstructure. In action, they were only a little inferior to the *Brooklyn*s as the latter's third turret had limited firing arcs.

The first five had only the usual splinter protection to the turrets but the last three had 4in faces and 2in roofs; they also had a second director aft. They were followed by two *Belfast*s, originally intended to have four quadruple 6in turrets but, due to delays, were built with triples. These were of a new design giving a slightly higher rate of fire whilst needing a smaller crew. The AA armament was increased to twelve 4in and two 8-barrel pom-poms, though with a poor ammunition supply route.

Britain hoped that, as a result of the London Treaty of 1936, future cruisers would be limited to 8000 tons and the *Fiji* class was designed to that displacement with twelve 6in, a 3½in belt and a speed of 31.5kts. Inevitably, they were cramped, with little scope for additions, but were well liked for their heavy armament on a small, economical ship. Several variants

HMS Sirius seen in 1947 has changed little. A few early radars and some light AA are the only visible additions and unlike most of her sisters, she retains ten 5.25in guns. Her AA capability was much less than appears as the guns were slow to load, train and elevate and the control system inadequate. (CMP)

were built during the war, sacrificing a triple turret for increased AA armament.

Smaller cruisers

Several navies perceived a need for smaller cruisers either to stay within overall treaty tonnage or for reasons of economy. The rationale behind such designs differed considerably.

The Italian 'Capitani Romani' class were small cruisers designed to counter the large French *contre-torpilleurs* and were designed for 40kts, maintaining 36 at sea with wartime load. They carried eight 135mm guns with a range of 21,400yds and a rather slow rate of fire of six rounds per minute. Of twelve ships laid down, only three completed during the war and one more later.

The US Navy carried out a variety of studies for 8000-ton, 'London 1936' ships and eventually settled on a uniform armament of twin 5in/38-calibre guns. They were to work with destroyers and to screen the battle line against air attack. The first four *Atlanta*s mounted sixteen 5in with a substantial 3.75in belt and a moderate 32.5kt speed. The four repeats sacrificed the two wing turrets for enhanced light AA etc, whilst the last three had turrets and superstructure lowered to improve stability, a problem with the earlier groups as a result of wartime additions. Their hull form was derived from the *Brooklyn*s as were other lightweight features such as the boilers.

During the mid-1930s the Royal Navy looked at a range of studies for small cruisers to replace the ageing 'C' and 'D' classes which were based on *Arethusa* but with an armament of 5.25in dual purpose guns. The initial requirements for the 5.25s were over-ambitious and the best that could be achieved was eight rounds per minute and 70 degrees elevation. The complete twin mount weighed up to 96

tons and training and elevating at 10 degrees per second was too slow for AA work.

The eleven ships of the *Dido* class were intended to carry five twin mounts, a 3in belt and steam at 32¼kts. Because of production delays, three ships completed with one turret missing and two others were given a main armament of eight 4.5in guns, possibly a more effective AA fit. Most survivors had a turret removed during the war in order to increase light AA armament. The five *Black Prince*s built during the war were basically similar but with only four turrets which permitted a lower bridge and this, combined with vertical funnels, changed their appearance considerably.

Particularly at the time of the Italian attack on Abyssinia, the Admiralty became aware of the weakness of the fleet's AA protection and several of the old 'C' class cruisers were converted to AA ships. The first two conversions carried ten 4in singles (later reduced to eight) and later ones had four twin mounts. Like almost all Royal Navy ships, they suffered from an inadequate AA control system, almost the only mistake in prewar planning. One of the exceptions was the *Delhi*, re-armed in the USA with five single 5in/38 and a Mk 37 director making her a much more effective ship than the 'C's.

Prewar modifications

As war approached, the major powers attempted to improve their ships. The AA armament of British ships was increased from four to eight 4in and multiple pom-poms and four-barrelled 0.5in machine-guns were fitted as they became available. The *Kent*s, well under weight limits, were given a 4½in belt over the machinery and transmitting station together with an athwartships catapult and hangar with three aircraft in most ships. *London* was given a much more elaborate modernisation with a profile resembling a large *Fiji*. She received a 3½in belt and a heavier AA armament. Treaty limits had lapsed and she completed at about 11,000 tons and, as a result, her hull was much over stressed and she suffered badly from leaking seams in both deck and bottom. The bigger cruisers operated the Walrus amphibian for search, spotting and ASW work. This aircraft was rugged and reliable and well suited to its task in the early years of the war.

Prewar modernisation in the US Navy was less extensive but most ships had additional 5in/25s fitted together with the ineffective quadruple 1.1in. After British experience in the early war years, open bridges were fitted to many ships, the better to evade or counter air attacks, and masts were reduced in size. Torpedo tubes were removed from the 8in ships.

Following the capsize of *Tomozuru* and structural damage to other ships, the Japanese reduced topweight and in many cases fitted bulges. Their most interesting conversions were the two torpedo cruisers, *Kitakami* and *Oi*, whose seven 5.5in were reduced to four to make it possible to fit no less than forty 24in torpedo tubes in quadruple mounts. They were intended to play a part in a war of attrition against the US fleet as it moved east across the Pacific.

The War Years

Wichita

She was the only 8in gun variant of the *Brooklyn* class and had a new turret with guns spaced more widely in separate cradles, reducing the spread of salvoes; the rate of fire was also slightly increased. Her belt was 6in over the shell and, with a 2¼in deck, she was immune to 8in AP from 10–22,000yds. She carried six single 5in/38-calibre, later increased to eight when ballast was added to improve stability, which meant that she completed nearly 600 tons heavy.

Cleveland class

The outbreak of war in Europe greatly affected US building plans which were also constrained by production capacity, great as that was. The two cruisers of the 1939 programme were originally to have been of 8000 tons, with ten of the new 6in/47 DP guns but problems with this gun led to a hurried re-design.

The resulting *Cleveland*s were seen as an interim design, a modified *Helena*, with one triple 6in omitted to make way for two more twin 5in. Additional bulkheads were fitted dividing both forward and aft boiler rooms which added

USS Dayton *(in November 1948), one of the* Cleveland*s, the largest cruiser class ever built. Although they suffered topweight problems even before completion, they were adopted as the standard light cruiser because they were the latest completed design when America went to war.* (USN)

USS Helena, *one of the nineteen very successful* Baltimore*s, well armed and well liked.* (L & L van Ginderen*)*

16ft to the length (increased subdivision is valuable but it is not cheap).

These ships had a 5in belt and a design speed of 32½kts. Like the *Brooklyn*s, they had a hangar under the quarterdeck for four aircraft with two catapults above. The inevitable additions seen to be needed as a result of British wartime experience and restrictions on the use of aluminium led to serious weight growth high up; they completed at 11,744 tons and had continuing stability problems.

A limited re-design was undertaken in mid-1942, before any of the class had completed. The 6in turrets were lowered about a foot by minor changes in sheer and the wing 5in were lowered to the upper deck, the handling rooms also moving down. The number of 40mm AA mounts was reduced as was the size of the superstructure. The boiler uptakes were trunked into a single funnel. These long trunks were very vulnerable to bomb damage and a single hit could have severely restricted mobility. Less obvious, transverse bulkheads were unpierced for doors below the second deck as doors can distort and leak after damage. The hangar was halved in size to make more room for accommodation. Only two ships were completed to this *Fargo* design.

Altogether, fifty-two *Cleveland*s were ordered though only twenty-nine completed as cruisers, the largest class ever built anywhere. Though not without fault, they were a valuable group of ships.

Baltimore class

These ships bore the same relationship to *Cleveland* as did *Wichita* to *Brooklyn*. Their design followed that of *Cleveland* and was not so rushed, a further 4ft on the beam taking care of stability and 64ft on the length made them less cramped. They had a 6in belt and a 2½in deck which gave an immunity zone against a 260lb shell of 15,700–24,000yds, reduced to 19,600–21,000yds against the 335lb projectile. The turrets had an 8in face and a 3in roof. They carried nine 8in and twelve 5in/38-calibre in twin mounts, displacing 14,500 tons as completed.

A similar re-design to the *Cleveland*s led to a single funnel variant in the three *Oregon City*s. Since stability was not a serious problem, the 5in were not lowered but the superstructure was simplified and the directors were lowered. Eighteen of these excellent ships were com-

pleted from spring of 1943, including four postwar, and many were active in the post-1945 fleet.

Other navies

As already discussed Royal Navy wartime building was limited to variants on *Fiji* and *Dido*. There were many sketch designs for big 6in, 8in and even 9.2in gun ships but none was developed, due to lack of resources and the probable time scale.

Japan built four *Agano*s of 7590 tons (trial) completing with six 6in and eight 24in torpedo tubes. They had a speed of 35kts to act as destroyer leaders. The *Oyodo* of the 1939 programme was intended to scout for long range submarines and was designed with a 45m catapult and a hangar for six big seaplanes but completed with an 18m catapult and only two smaller planes. She had two triple 6in and a speed of 35kts. Other countries struggled, unsuccessfully, to complete their prewar programmes.

Post-treaty designs

The US *Worcester* design was conceived in early 1941 using the new, dual purpose 6in/47 and was intended to provide long range defence against high level bombers. Well before they completed, this particular requirement had lapsed but it was argued that long range gunfire was needed against the aircraft which controlled guided bombs.

The final design carried six twin mounts with each gun able to fire some 12 rounds a minute, about 50 per cent better than the older mounts. The original requirements for speed and armour were excessive: 33kts and a 5in belt

were accepted with a displacement of 14,700 tons. On completion, *Worcester* had catapults as did *Des Moines*, described below, but these were soon removed.

The light anti-aircraft armament consisted of twenty-four 3in/50 though a dozen 20mm were fitted as well at first. In the postwar fleet, cruiser guns were mainly needed for shore bombardment for which the 8in was superior and the two *Worcester*s had a short active life, paying off in 1958. The Royal Navy was greatly attracted by the concept and developed the *Minotaur* design using the British twin 6in dual purpose gun. US machinery, turrets and particularly the electrical systems were all lighter so that, on about the same displacement, the *Minotaur*s could only carry five turrets. The British turret, however, could fire at 20 rounds per minute, at least for a short time.

The US Navy developed an 8in gun, in triple mounts, based on the 6in/47 which was fitted in the three *Des Moines*. This gun could fire ten 335lb shells per minute and was seen as the answer to the old problem that the 8in fired too slowly and the 6in could not inflict lethal damage in a brief encounter. On a displacement of 17,255 tons they carried three of the new triple turrets, twenty-four 3in/50s with a 6in belt and a speed of 33kts. They were formidable ships and well liked, remaining in service for many years.

In 1940–41, the US Navy saw the logic of the heavy cruiser as leading to battlecruisers of the *Alaska* class with nine 12in and a 9in belt, steaming at 33kts. To the US Navy, they were big cruisers, not small capital ships. To some extent, they were conceived as counters to predicted Japanese battlecruisers which did not then exist, though the Japanese did later design battlecruisers to counter the *Alaska*s.

Glasgow *in 1947, showing wartime alterations. She has lost 'X' turret to provide space and topweight compensation for a much increased light AA armament and she carries many radar and electronic warfare aerials. She retains much of the beauty of the original design.* (CMP)

Wartime lessons and alterations

Most of the lessons were learnt in the first two years of war, before the entry of the USA and Japan. The Battle of the River Plate showed, among other things, the need for splinter protection to exposed personnel and to internal wiring, lessons reinforced by early air attacks. The mining of *Belfast* showed that prewar shock trials, on short sections of a ship did not show the full extent of damage due to whipping; cast iron items had to be replaced and machinery re-designed.

Watertight integrity needed considerable improvement and lower deck scuttles were blanked, coamings fitted to hatches and doors etc. On the other hand, the tragedy of the French *contre-torpilleur Maillé Brézé* destroyed by accidental explosion showed the need for escape scuttles in the side. Damage control procedures had to be improved and more pumps and emergency generators fitted.

It was found that high level bombing was much less of a threat than expected as the bomb could be seen and evaded from an open bridge. The sinking of *Königsberg* by Fleet Air Arm Skuas, the first major success for dive bombers, showed the danger from this form of attack. The multiple pom-pom was too slow in training and had an inadequate muzzle velocity but in the early years there was nothing else. Oerlikon 20mm and Bofors 40mm were fitted as they became available, mainly from 1942 onwards, though there were not many Bofors in the Royal Navy until army guns became available in 1945.

All navies found the need to increase close range AA; the US quadruple 1.1in was ineffective and replaced with Bofors in large numbers,

though Oerlikons were also used. Japan had an effective triple 25mm of which large numbers were fitted. The larger weapons were given radar directors in later years.

Arcs of fire of directors and guns were improved by fitting tripod instead of pole masts with stays and by pruning bridge wings. Radar aerials were not heavy in the early days and could be fitted on existing tripods with a little bracing to reduce vibration. Air warning sets were introduced from 1939 onwards with surface search and gunnery radars from about 1941–2. In the German navy gunnery radar appeared first; *Graf Spee*'s radar was an object of careful study by the British. Various direction finders and radar jammers as well as many communication aerials added to the clutter on the mast and also required more power. The information from the new sensors needed processing and presenting on plotting tables in an operations room ('CIC' or Combat Information Center in US terminology).

Prewar generators were quite inadequate for all the new electronics and gun machinery. Where possible, bigger sets replaced the originals and diesel generators were added where space could be found. All these new equipments encroached on mess decks while at the same time more men were needed to man the extra equipment, making ships very cramped. In many cases ventilation was inadequate, particularly for tropical service. It was also realised that accommodation for officers and senior rates should be divided, fore and aft so that one hit could not kill a large proportion of key personnel, as had occurred when *Southampton* was lost.

Much of the extra equipment had to be fitted high in the ship reducing stability, many Brit-

ish ships and some Japanese sacrificing turrets in compensation. It was fortunate that from 1942 onwards it was possible to remove aircraft arrangements saving a little weight and providing more space.

Protection

In all countries the first post-Washington cruisers sacrificed protection to maintain gunpower and speed under Treaty limits. It is worth noting that British designers, the only ones with direct wartime experience, built the *Kent*s with virtually no armour other than over the magazines. During the next two decades, navies everywhere increased armour as weight was saved elsewhere and even sacrificed speed for protection against shells.

British cruisers were in the thick of the fighting for nearly 6 years:

Damage to British Cruisers

	1939– 40	'40– 41	'41– 42	'42– 43	'43– 44	'44– 45
Number in commission	44	46	42	35	36	29
Number damaged	20	53	45	14	22	9

The type of weapon and its effect can be read from the table below.

Weapon Effects

	Shell	Bomb	Mine	Torpedo	Total
Sunk	3	10	1	13	27
Severely damaged	9	42	8	24	83
Slightly damaged	22	45	2	–	69
TOTAL	34	97	11	37	179

Torpedoes and bombs caused far more losses and serious damage than did shells, a lesson later learnt by the US Navy, particularly faced with the Japanese 24in weapon. British losses to torpedo are inflated by six ships lost due to wing compartments abreast the boiler room and Japanese losses from capsize show the peril of a centreline bulkhead.

US cruisers with their tradition of well subdivided machinery, usually on the unit system, and of good damage control survived well.

US cruisers torpedoed	31
of which, sunk	7
Hit in the machinery space	11
of which, immobilised	2

None was lost to a single torpedo.

Bombs frequently caused fires, sometimes leading to the loss of the ship. Great attention was paid to reducing flammable material in later years, particularly by the US Navy, training in firefighting was improved and more hoses provided. The Royal Navy removed aircraft and their dangerous petrol. Hits in magazines, such as that by a guided bomb on USS *Savannah*, did not cause the magazine to detonate as feared. In part, the fire was extinguished by sea water flooding in but US propellants seem to have been very stable.

With hindsight, it may be suggested that good protection to the magazines and splinter protection elsewhere was sufficient. Good subdivision, with unpierced bulkheads and unit machinery combined with fire precautions and a well-trained crew would make even a small cruiser hard to disable or sink.

Technical developments

Increased fighting capability without great increase in size came from improved technology. There were no spectacular changes but a steady reduction in the weight of hull and machinery.

Whilst a good big ship will always beat a good little one, it would seem that numbers counted more than armament, protection or speed. In European waters, the British *Leander*s did well and, given a better gun, the *Dido*s could have been ideal. They could disable a destroyer or merchant ship quickly and were tough enough to accept a lot of damage. The Pacific is a big ocean, needing big ships and the *Baltimore*s were outstanding. Cramped designs, unable to accept additions, were always unsatisfactory such as most Japanese ships, the British *Fiji*s and American *Cleveland*s.

David K Brown, RCNC

Cruisers: Typical Ships 1906–1945

Ship or Class	Nationality	Dispt Normal/Std Full load (tons)	Dimensions (loa × breadth × draught) Feet–Inches Metres	Armament	Armour Belt/Deck (max ins)	Speed (kts)	Launch dates	Numbers built
BOADICEA	British	3300 3800	405–0 × 41–0 × 14–0 123.4 × 12.5 × 4.3	6–4in 2–21in TT	–/1	25	1908–09	2
MAGDEBURG	German	4570 5587	455–0 × 43–11 × 16–10 139 × 13.5 × 5.1	12–4.1in 2–19.7in TT	2½/2½	27	1911	4
BIRMINGHAM	British	5440 6040	457–0 × 50–0 × 16–0 139.3 × 15.2 × 4.9	9–6in 2–21in TT	2/1½	25.5	1913–22	4
ARETHUSA	British	3585 4400	436–0 × 39–0 × 14.1–0 139.3 × 11.9 × 4.3	2–6in 6–4in 4–21in TT	2/1	28.5	1913–14	8
WIESBADEN	German	5180 6600	476–9 × 45–7 × 19–0 145.3 × 13.5 × 5.8	8–5.9in 2–3.5in 4–19.7in TT	2½/2½	27.5	1915	2
CERES	British	4190 4400	450–0 × 43–5 × 14–8 137.2 × 13.3 × 4.5	5–6in 2–3in 8–21in TT	3/1	29	1917	10
KUMA	Japan	5500 5832	532–0 × 46–6 × 15–9 162.1 × 14.2 × 4.8	7–5.5in 2–3.1in 8–21in TT	2½/1¼	36	1920–21	5
KENT	British	9750 13,500	630–0 × 68–4 × 16–3 192 × 20.8 × 5	8–8in 4–4in 8–21in TT	Box	32	1926–27	7
ZARA	Italian	11,680 14,300	557–2 × 62–10 × 19–5 182.8 × 20.6 × 6.0	8–8in 16–3.9in	6/2	32	1930–31	4
MYOKO	Japanese	10,980 13,800	661–1 × 60–8 × 20–2 200.6 × 18.0 × 6.2	10–8in 6–4.7in 2–24in TT	3.9/2.5	36	1935–37	4
DEUTSCHLAND	German	10,600 16,020	610–3 × 67–9 × 19–0 186.0 × 20.7 × 5.8	6–11in 8–5.9in, 6–4.1in 2–21in TT	3/1.5	28	1931–34	3

Ship or Class	Nationality	Dispt Normal/Std Full load (tons)	Dimensions (loa × breadth × draught) Feet–Inches Metres	Armament	Armour Belt/Deck (max ins)	Speed (kts)	Launch dates	Numbers built
AJAX	British	7030 9400	554–6 × 55–8 × 15–6 161.0 × 17.0 × 4.7	8–6in 4–4in 8–21in TT	3/1.25	32.5	1932–34	5
NEW ORLEANS	American	10,136 12,436	588–0 × 61–9 × (21–9) 179.2 × 18.8 × (6.6)	9–8in 8–5in	5/2.25	32.7	1933–36	7
DUCA D'AOSTA	Italian	8317 10,374	613–2 × 57–5 × 16–4 186.9 × 17.5 × 5	10–6in 6–3.9in 6–21in TT	3/0.75	36.5	1934–35	2
LA GALISSONIÈRE	French	7600 9100	538–11 × 57–4 × 17–7 179.5 × 17.5 × 5.4	9–6in 8–3.5in 4–21.7in TT	4/1.5	31	1935–37	6
MOGAMI	Japanese	11,200 13,800	661–1 × 60–8 × 20–2 200.6 × 18 × 6.2	15–6in 8–5in 12–24in TT	3.9/2.5	36	1935–37	4
PRINZ EUGEN	German	14,680 18,750	680–0 × 71–0 × 19–4 207.7 × 21.7 × 5.9	8–8in 12–4.1in 12–21in TT	3.25/1.25	32	1937–39	5
BROOKLYN	American	9767 12,207	608–4 × 61–9 × 21–9 185.4 × 18.8 × 6.6	15–6in 8–5in	5/2	32.5	1936–38	9
FIJI	British	8350 10,700	555–6 × 62 × 16–6 169.3 × 18.9 × 5.0	12–6in 8–4in 6–21in TT	3/2	32.5	1939–42	11
DIDO	British	5600 6850	512–0 × 50–6 × 14–0 156.1 × 15.4 × 4.3	10–5.25in 6–21in TT	3/2	32.25	1939–41	11
'CAPITANI ROMANI'	Italian	3745 5420	468–10 × 47–3 × 13–3 142.2 × 14.4 × 4.1	8–5.3in 8–21in TT	–/–	41	1940–41	3
CLEVELAND	American	11,744 14,131	610–1 × 66–4 × (24–6) 186.0 × 20.2 × (7.5)	12–6in 12–5in	5/2	32.5	1941–46	29
BALTIMORE	American	14,472 17,031	673–5 × 70–10 × (24) 205.3 × 23.0 × (7.3)	9–8in 12–5in	6/2.5	32	1942–45	18
DES MOINES	American	17,255 20,934	716–6 × 75–4 × (26) 218.4 × 23.0 × (7.9)	9–8in 12–5in 24–3in	6/3.5	33	1946–47	3

Notes:

The predominance of British classes in this table reflects the fact that the Royal Navy built more *classes* over a longer period than any other navy. The vast US Navy building programme of the Second World War was concentrated into a few classes, most of which are listed.

Displacement is given in Imperial tons of 2240 pounds. The upper figure is 'Normal' (approximately one-third fuel) up to *Kuma* and is 'Washington Standard' (no fluids) for later ships. The lower figure is full load displacement. Note also that displacement can vary quite considerably within a class; *Ajax* is listed rather than *Leander* as the latter ship was much heavier than the other ships and hence not typical as a result of increased

welding in the later vessels. *Deutschland* was much lighter than her two sisters though even she was well over the Treaty limit.

Draught corresponds to the Normal/Washington displacement wherever possible. Figures in brackets correspond to full load.

Speed is given at Normal/Washington displacement. Since Washington excluded fuel, such figures are somewhat unrealistic. Full load speed would be 1–2kts less and fouling would take off at least another 1–2kts within one year out of dock.

Consistency. Standard references are not consistent in quoting draught and speed at the displacement given. As a result of much cross checking (see

Bibliography) it is hoped that this table is better, though absolute accuracy cannot be guaranteed and, indeed, is meaningless. It must be doubted of draught can be measured to better than a ½in, displacement to within 100 tons and speed on trial to better than ¼kt.

Armament. Guns smaller than 3in (75mm) are omitted. Data refer to the ship as built; reference to major changes may be found in the text.

Armour. The thickness given is the maximum value which may only extend over a small part of the ship. Shell plating would usually add ¾–1in more to the steel thickness.

Numbers are those completed as cruisers.

4

Coast Offence and Defence Vessels

SHIPS for the line of battle were not the only vessels that mounted big guns. Heavy ordnance was also deployed on coast defence ships – essentially mobile coast artillery – and on coast offence ships – essentially for bombardment of enemy positions ashore. The coast defence vessels were largely the preserve of second line navies, such as the Scandinavian countries, which did not need and could not afford battleships. Coast offence vessels could be considered as 'hostilities only' craft built rapidly during wartime to harrass enemy coastlines. In the nineteenth century, the Crimean gunboats were a good example, but during the First World War, one major power, Britain, built a fleet of thirty-five such specialist vessels, called monitors.

Coast offence vessels

The first British monitors

The outbreak of war in August 1914 opened up opportunities for Allied coast offence ships, since the land based Central Powers (Germany, Austria-Hungary and later Turkey and Bulgaria) were vulnerable to attack by sea on their flanks. The success of a makeshift fleet of bombardment vessels off the Belgian coast in October 1914 as the Germans struck southwest to the Channel coast had shown that heavily armed well-protected shallow draft vessels were of potential value, either where front lines extended to the sea or in support of amphibious operations. Winston Churchill as First Lord of the Admiralty and Admiral Sir John Fisher, First Sea Lord from 30 October 1914, considered that such vessels could be used in support of possible landings off the German North Sea coast, or even on their Baltic coast to strike close to Berlin. It would be

possible to deploy on ships heavy calibre guns with ranges of 10 nautical miles or more, but it would take more than a year to manufacture such ordnance. Early in November 1914, Charles Schwab of the American Bethlehem Steel Company visited Britain and offered the four twin 14in turrets destined for the Greek battlecruiser *Salamis* then building in Germany, which could not be delivered owing to the British blockade. Churchill and Fisher eagerly seized on the offer, and immediately ordered the Director of Naval Construction, Eustace Tennyson d'Eyncourt, and his staff to design a fleet of four vessels each mounting one such turret. Draft was not to exceed 10ft, with designed speed 10kts.

The essential requirements of coast offence vessels were that they should carry the heaviest guns available on the smallest hulls, and to be 'riskable' in a way that a battleship could not be for secondary purposes. Shallow draft was desirable, not only to get close inshore to increase effective range inland but to lessen the hazards of offshore navigation. Mobility was necessary, but high speed and long endurance were not; seagoing capability needed only to be sufficient to reach theatres of operation. Deployed in vulnerable positions close to enemy forces, good protection was required, against mine, torpedo and artillery. Speed of construction

was essential, which required not only simple hulls and machinery, but also the ready availability of suitable armament. Such craft could offer mobility in comparison with shore based artillery and, in comparison with aircraft once they became a potent bombing weapon, accuracy and sustained fire.

The design was entrusted to a young constructor, Charles Lillicrap, who was later to become a DNC himself. Within a fortnight, he had produced a design of a 6000-ton vessel to carry one twin 14in turret, whose revolving weight was 620 tons, which with barbette armour and ammunition represented a concentrated weight of 970 tons or 16 per cent of the full load displacement. The American gun used nitro-cellulose propellant, unlike the British who used cordite, which although expensive gave a long barrel life. It fired a 1400lb projectile to a range of 19,900yds at its maximum elevation of 15 degrees. The turret was sited just forward of midships, almost underneath a tripod mast supporting the gun director and spotting top. Twin-screw steam reciprocating machinery, coal bunkers, crew accommodation and stores took up most of the main hull, which was 335ft long overall and 60ft broad. Outside the main hull, 15ft wide bulges were added below the water each side, partly watertight, partly open to the sea, to give protection

HMS Abercrombie *in April 1919, showing the extended funnel and 6in gun added aft in 1917.* (CMP)

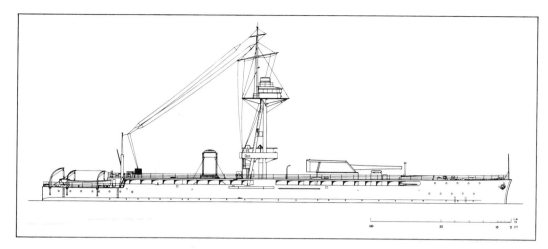

HMS Roberts *as completed. The simplicity of the early monitors is clear from this external elevation.* (Ian Buxton)

against mine or torpedo, by detonating such weapons outside the 1.5in-thick side protective bulkhead on the main hull – a principle used also in capital ships. A 4in sloped armour belt gave protection to magazines and machinery against enemy guns of field artillery type, while the upper deck was mostly of 2in high-tensile steel, giving some protection against primitive aircraft weapons. The turret retained the designed battlecruiser protection: 10in front, 7in sides and rear, 4in roof, 8in barbette. Provision was even made for carrying two small seaplanes abaft the single funnel, recognising that aerial spotting would be the key to effective bombardment. The term 'monitor' was applied to these vessels, although the original American concept of a low freeboard vessel was not adopted.

The monitors had to be constructed quickly, but a massive naval building programme consisting largely of destroyers and submarines was also being put in hand. Builders not normally used by the Admiralty were therefore called upon, notably Harland & Wolff, who had spare shipbuilding capacity with the postponement of passenger liner orders. They received contracts to build three of the monitors in November 1914, two for their Belfast yard, one for their Glasgow, with the fourth going to Swan Hunter & Wigham Richardson on the Tyne. Originally to have been named after American military leaders like *General Grant*, after launch they were renamed after British leaders like (General) *Abercrombie* and (Lord) *Roberts*.

A month later, eight further heavy turrets were obtained by removing the two twin 12in mountings from four of the *Majestic* class pre-dreadnoughts designed in 1893, which were

now of limited military value. Eight more monitors were then ordered, each mounting one such turret, but converted from 13.5- to 30-degree elevation to increase range from 13,700 to 21,300yds. They were also named after British military leaders, including *General Wolfe* and *Lord Clive*.

No sooner had these vessels been ordered (five from Harland & Wolff), than two more turrets became available. When the 1914 programme battleships *Renown* and *Repulse*, mounting 15in guns ranging to 23,400yds, were altered to 32kt battlecruisers in December 1914, they had to reduce from eight to six guns. Hence two twin turrets could be allocated from the production programme to arm two more monitors, the necessary installation to be carried out by Armstrong's Elswick Ordnance Company. Churchill was an advocate of diesel engines, so arranged that these two vessels, to be named after the French military leaders *Marshal Ney* and *Marshal Soult*, would

be engined with twin diesels taken from oilers then building, sufficient for a speed of 6kts. All the other monitors got steam reciprocating machinery of about 2000ihp, although model testing at the Admiralty Experiment Works soon showed that this would be insufficient to achieve 10kts with the proposed hull form. Owing to the urgency of construction, it was too late to make changes, so when the first monitors went on trial in May 1915, they could only make about 6kts – a serious operational handicap for the rest of their lives.

With the Dardanelles campaign opening in February 1915 to attack Turkey, bombardment vessels were required which had a greater 'riskability' than the new 15in gun battleship *Queen Elizabeth*. In May Churchill ordered that the first nine monitors should all go to the Dardanelles, now that Allied forces had been landed on the Gallipoli peninsula in April. Both Fisher and Churchill resigned a few weeks later, but the new Admiralty Board confirmed the decision to send the monitors, but only the four 14in (*Abercrombie*, *Havelock*, *Raglan* and *Roberts*) and two of the 12in (*Earl of Peterborough* and *Sir Thomas Picton*), plus fifteen of the smaller monitors mounting 9.2in and 6in guns. These latter had been ordered in February and March 1915 to make use of surplus guns: ten single 9.2in Mk VI (16,300yds range) removed from elderly *Edgar* class cruisers, and four modern 9.2in Mk X (25,000yds), spares no longer needed for the

A cross section of the 12in monitor Sir John Moore *(portside looking aft), shows the main structural features, particularly the sloping armour and extreme form of the underwater bulge.* (Ian Buxton)

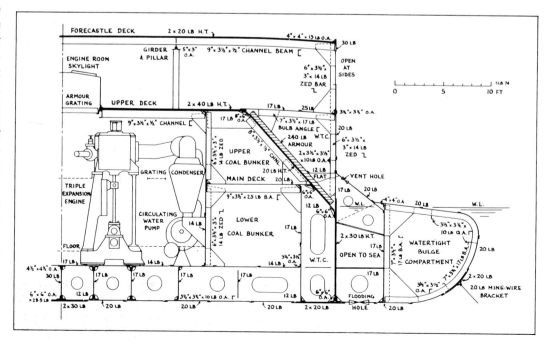

reduced number of *Cressy* and *Drake* class armoured cruisers following war losses. These 600-ton 12kt vessels were 'named' *M19* to *M28* and *M15* to *M18* respectively. Five more vessels (*M29* to *M33*) each mounted two single 6in Mk XII (14,700yds), which could not be used in the five *Queen Elizabeths*' secondary armament owing to their being sited too close to the waterline.

The first monitors arrived off the Dardanelles in July 1915, manned by largely reservist crews of 200 men (large ships) and 70 (small). They were able to give much needed fire support to the Allied troops at Cape Helles and Anzac, and soon afterwards at Suvla. There was a shortage of heavy artillery ashore and the troops were pinned down by strong Turkish defences. With shallow draft and bulges, the large monitors were relatively immune to torpedo attack from U-boats, which had already been responsible for the loss of three British pre-dreadnoughts in May alone.

The monitor fleet also included the ex-river gunboat *Humber*, originally ordered with two sisters by Brazil, but bought by Britain on the outbreak of war. Armed initially with a twin 6in turret, these 1260-ton shallow draft vessels named *Severn*, *Mersey* and *Humber* had played a useful role off the Belgian coast a year earlier. The two former vessels had been sent to East Africa to eliminate the German cruiser *Königsberg* which had taken refuge in the Rufiji river, which was carried out in July 1915.

After the Allied decision to evacuate the Gallipoli peninsula was taken, the monitors covered that operation, which was successfully completed in January 1916. Thereafter two large monitors were retained on patrol in the

Aegean in case the German battlecruiser *Goeben* and the cruiser *Breslau*, which had arrived in Turkey in August 1914, should make a sortie. *Havelock* and *Roberts* were sent back to Britain to coast defence duties following German raids on east coast towns, while the other two large monitors supported the Salonika front, which had been opened by the Allies against Bulgaria to assist Serbia. The small monitors were redeployed either on this front or on local patrols in the Aegean and East Mediterranean, bombarding enemy forces where they were in reach of the coast.

Meantime, the other six 12in monitors (*Lord Clive*, *Prince Rupert*, *Sir John Moore*, *General Craufurd*, *Prince Eugene* and *General Wolfe*), the two 15in monitors and four small monitors (*M24* to *M27*) had been engaged in operations off the Belgian coast. The front line was virtually static just west of Ostend, with the Germans strongly fortifying the coastal strip with heavy artillery to discourage an Allied landing behind their lines. They also used Zeebrugge and other ports as U-boat and torpedo boat bases. Vice-Admiral Reginald Bacon, based at Dover, was determined to use this new bom-

bardment fleet to harry the Germans from August 1915. Targets such as the Zeebrugge lock gates were selected, but it proved very difficult to hit such small targets from nine miles out to sea. There were few aiming marks to assist fire control, gun ballistics at high elevation had not been fully established, and aircraft with wireless spotting were not yet fully effective. The German coast defences were able to range accurately out to 30,000yds, notably the 'Tirpitz' battery with four 280mm (11in) guns just south-west of Ostend.

However in the summer of 1915, new monitors had been designed, which were to mount a modern 15in turret, with elevation increased from 20 to 30 degrees, to give 29,000yds range, and carrying 100 rounds per gun in the magazine. One of these turrets was to be removed from *Marshal Ney*, whose MAN diesel engines had proved unreliable, although performance of her sister's Vickers engines was reasonably satisfactory. The other turret was one of the two spares ordered for the battlecruiser *Furious* should her planned two single 18in turrets prove unsatisfactory. Construction of two new 8000-ton vessels started in October 1915, so that they were able to take advantage of the model test results by having a hull form and machinery which would enable 12kts to be obtained. *Erebus* and *Terror* were completed by Harland & Wolff in late summer 1916 at a cost each of about £390,000 for hull, armour and machinery, plus a further £150,000 for armament – figures which can be multiplied by about forty to get a present day value.

The Monitors 1916–18

From the end of 1916, bombardments off the Belgian coast were normally carried out by the three 15in monitors. The outranged 12in vessels and the small monitors were relegated

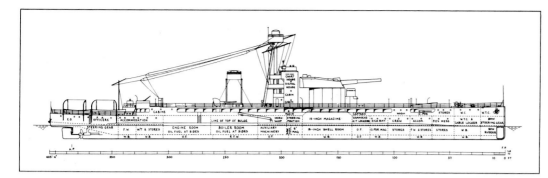

Erebus *as completed; with her sister* Terror, *they were the first to benefit from service experience and their 12kt speed and 15in main armament elevating to 30 degrees made them the most effective of First World War monitors.* (Ian Buxton)

largely to patrol work and subsidiary duties, while *Marshal Ney* was rearmed with six 6in and stationed off Ramsgate as a guardship. Bombardments in 1917 required careful planning to hit specific targets in the face of strengthened German coast defence artillery. Typically about a hundred rounds would be fired during each operation at ports such as Ostend, which forced the abandonment of the latter as a regular naval base. The 12in monitors were prepared for the 'Great Landing', an amphibious operation planned to land one division behind the German lines west of Ostend, using special shallow draft pontoons. In the event, lack of progress in the Allied offensive ashore forced cancellation in September 1917.

During 1917, plans were made to arm three of the 12in monitors with a single 18in gun. *Furious* had been partially converted to an aircraft carrier, so no longer needed her two 150-ton 18in guns and one spare. *General Wolfe*, *Lord Clive* and *Prince Eugene* were therefore converted to carry a single 18in on an athwartship mounting aft of the funnel. Although only limited training was possible, elevation was increased from 30 to 45 degrees, so increasing maximum range from 28,900 to 33,100yds. This could be increased to 40,500yds (20 nautical miles or 37km) by using long pointed projectiles weighing 3320lb with 690lb supercharges. Guns were installed only in the first two by the autumn of 1918, which were used to fire a total of 85 rounds at ranges up to 36,000yds at German positions inland during

the September offensive which led up to the Armistice.

The long range monitors were joined by two ex-Norwegian coast defence ships, renamed *Gorgon* and *Glatton*. Norway had ordered two ships as *Nidaros* and *Björgvin* from Armstrong-Whitworth early in 1913. They were essentially updates of the 1900 *Norge* but more heavily armed with two single 240mm (9.4in) and four 150mm (5.9in). Displacing 4800 tons, the 15kt ships were of the classic coast defence type, with a short hull only 310ft long, but quite well protected with 7in belt and 2in deck slopes. With construction suspended after launching in the summer of 1914, Britain bought the two hulls. Various monitor conversion plans were put forward, the final one in 1917 involving adding bulges, increasing full load displacement to 5700 tons and converting the main guns to long range 9.2in. With elevation increased to 40 degrees and special ammunition, they could range to 39,000yds. *Gorgon* joined *Wolfe* on her autumn 1918 bombardments. *Glatton* however did not get the opportunity, being lost from fire resulting from an overheated magazine in Dover harbour on 16 September 1918; she had to be torpedoed by *Cossack* and *Myngs* to prevent an explosion.

Meantime in the Mediterranean, the two 12in monitors had been transferred to the northern Adriatic to assist Italian operations against the front with Austria-Hungary from early 1917. Possibly inspired by the British monitor concept, the Italians had started to build up a fleet of bombardment craft, more

accurately described as self-propelled floating batteries. With construction of the *Caracciolo* class battleships suspended, a number of 15in guns became available. A twin mounting with limited training was installed on the 1400-ton converted crane barge *Alfredo Cappellini* completed in April 1916. A purpose-built vessel *Faa' di Bruno* also mounting a twin 15in was not completed until July 1917. Of 2800 tons and rectangular hull form, not surprisingly speed was low at 3kts, with manoeuvrability even worse than the British monitors. Six other makeshift craft of around 500 tons were converted from barges, carrying either a single 12in or 15in. Some fifty further floating batteries, mostly non-propelled, were also put into service during 1917–18, mounting a variety of guns from 4in to 8in. All of these craft were intended to support the Italian army, where following the defeat at Caporetto in October 1917 it became possible for such craft to get close to the front using rivers and lagoons. The two bigger monitors were quite unseaworthy and were driven ashore in bad weather in the autumn of 1917, although *Faa' di Bruno* was later salved. She was used as the floating battery *GM194* for the defence of Genoa in the Second World War; all the others were discarded soon after 1918.

The two British 14in and the smaller monitors patrolled off the enemy coastlines of Turkey, Bulgaria and Palestine, but there were few worthwhile targets. In early 1918, *Goeben* and *Breslau* made their long awaited sortie to attack British ships in the Aegean, but the British were caught unawares. The two monitors *Raglan* and *M28* guarding the Dardanelles entrance were at anchor off Imbros on 20 January and quickly sunk by gunfire. The German vessels were not damaged by the few shells aimed at them, but were caught in a British minefield, *Breslau* being sunk and *Goeben* damaged.

After the First World War

Postwar, there was little need in the Royal Navy for coast offence vessels. Most of the monitors returned to home ports and paid off

Lord Clive (foreground) and General Wolff *at Dover in October 1918. The 18in gun aft is clearly visible in the former.* (IWM)

The Norwegian coast defence ship Björgvin *building on the Tyne was taken over as the* Glatton *during the First World War. The modifications for her new role as monitor included the heavy tripod mast and spotting top.* (IWM)

during 1919. Twelve of the small monitors did see action however in support of the White Russians against the Bolsheviks. *M17*, *M18*, *M22* and *M29* were engaged off the Crimea in 1919, while *M24*, *M26*, *M23*, *M25*, *M27*, *M31*, *M33* and *Humber* were in North Russia, now armed with 4in, 6in or 7.5in guns. The latter six were deployed up the Dvina river to allow Allied troops to withdraw to Archangel in the summer of 1919. *Erebus*, *M24*, *M26* and later *M23* were in the White Sea, with the former being transferred to the Baltic for operations in support of the Baltic states in October 1919.

The three 15in monitors were used for training duties such as turret drill ships at the main naval bases. *Erebus* and *Terror* carried out firing trials against surrendered German warships from 1919 to 1921. *Lord Clive* was temporarily fitted in 1921 with three 15in aft in place of her 18in for trials purposes. All the 12in and 14in monitors were sold for scrap from 1921 onwards, as well as *Gorgon*, *Mersey* and *Severn*. *Humber* was sold for conversion into a crane barge, while eight small monitors were sold to Shell for conversion into coastal tankers. Four other small monitors (*M22*, *M29*, *M31* and *M33*) were converted into coastal minelayers between 1920 and 1925, with *M23* becoming a drill ship for the reserves. *Marshal Ney* survived to 1957 as a stoker training hulk at Devonport. Other war losses were *M30* (1916), *M15* (1917), *M21* (1918)

plus *M25* and *M27* abandoned in North Russia in 1919. *M33* renamed *Minerva* as a minelayer, was later used as a floating workshop at Portsmouth until 1984. Sold by the Ministry of Defence, plans were in hand in 1990 for her preservation and possible restoration at Portsmouth.

The Second World War

Terror had been sent out to Singapore in 1933 to act as guardship while the fixed defences of the new base were being built, including the mounting of five single 15in guns. *Erebus* had been a training ship from 1926 but in 1939 was allocated to the defence of Cape Town; however, war broke out before she could sail. By the end of 1939, it had been decided to refit

both monitors including fitting of stronger anti-aircraft armament and thicker deck protection. *Marshal Soult* was found not to be worth refitting, so it was decided to transfer her 15in turret to a new monitor.

Of a similar size to *Erebus* and *Terror*, the new vessel was ordered from John Brown's Clydebank yard in March 1940. The design requirements remained in principle as before: one twin turret just forward of midships, director and spotting facilities on a tripod mast, bulges, moderate speed of 12kts, endurance of about 2500 miles and relatively shallow draft of 13ft. Machinery was twin-screw steam turbines of 4800shp, which permitted a short machinery space and a reduced length of 373ft. The major changes were associated with the stronger threat of air attack off enemy-held coastlines. Deck protection was increased to 3in over machinery (proof against 500lb bombs) with 4in over magazines. Anti-aircraft armament was of cruiser standard: four twin 4in, sixteen 2pdr pom-poms in multiple mountings and eight of the new 20mm Oerlikons, supported by new air warning radar and high angle radar fire control equipment. These and all the modifications from the preceding quarter of a century brought full load displacement up to 9150 tons, and doubled crew number to 442 when the new *Roberts* completed in October 1941.

Meantime *Terror* had been transferred to the Mediterranean where she supplemented Malta's meagre gun defences from June 1940 when Italy entered the war. She then sup-

Marshal Ney at Dover after the removal of her 15in guns. The great breadth of the bulges is apparent. (IWM)

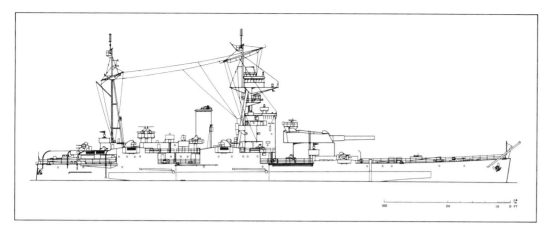

The final monitor design, the Second World War Abercrombie *retained the essential layout of earlier classes but relatively strong anti-aircraft armament reflected the new realities of naval warfare.* (Ian Buxton)

ported the North African campaign, bombarding Italian positions as the British Eighth Army pressed westward into Libya from Egypt in December 1940. Six weeks of intensive firing wore out her 15in guns, each having fired well over 300 equivalent full charges. Air attacks were frequent, so her newly fitted six 4in high angle were equally heavily used. Leaving Benghazi on 22 February 1941, she was caught the following evening by eight German aircraft, bombed and sunk.

It had been hoped that *Erebus* could emulate her Great War Belgian Coast role off the German-held continental shores. Fitted with new anti-aircraft weapons, including rocket launchers, she was deployed in September 1940 to bombard the coast defences being erected by the Germans around Calais. But her general condition and performance had deteriorated and enemy attacks from aircraft and S-boats were strong. In order to replace *Terror* off North Africa, both *Erebus* and *Roberts* sailed for the eastern Mediterranean via the Cape in December 1941. Following Japan's entry into the war, *Erebus* was diverted to the Indian Ocean but saw no action throughout 1942. *Roberts* became anti-aircraft guardship at Suez as Rommel pushed the Eighth Army back into Egypt. She was allocated to support the Allied landings in North Africa in November 1942 (Operation Torch). She did not need to use her heavy guns off Algiers, but was subjected to heavy German air attack. Two bomb hits amidships caused serious damage and fires, but she was able to return to the UK for full repairs.

Meantime a sister ship *Abercrombie* had been ordered on the Tyne as a replacement for *Terror*. She was basically a repeat of *Roberts* but had more up-to-date equipment and anti-aircraft defences. Both vessels were allocated to support the Allied landings in Sicily (Operation 'Husky'), so sailed with the assault convoys in June 1943. *Erebus* joined from the east, so all were in action from 10 July. Over the next six

weeks, the three monitors fired over 600 rounds of 15in at targets such as airfields, batteries, troop concentrations, roads and railways. *Erebus* was sent home to refit and change guns, but *Roberts* and *Abercrombie* supported the Salerno landings in September. The latter was damaged by a mine on 9 September which put her out of action for nearly a year, with repairs being carried out at Taranto dockyard once it was in Allied hands. *Roberts* withdrew to Port Said to refit and change guns before returning home to prepare for Operation 'Neptune', the amphibious phase of the D-Day landings.

No British small monitors were used or built during the Second World War. However the potential value of small inshore fire support vessels carrying medium calibre guns to accompany amphibious operations was recognised. It proved possible to modify tank landing craft to carry two ex-destroyer 4.7in guns. About thirty Mk 3 and Mk 4 LCTs were taken over after launching in 1942–43 and so converted to landing craft, gun (LCG). With a displacement of about 500 tons, speed of about 10kts and shallow draft, they could be considered as the modern counterparts of the First World War small monitors, although they were intended to be used in a beached mode. They were used both in Mediterranean and in northern European landings, some being operated by the US Navy. In 1944, nearly a hundred more British purpose-designed LCGs were ordered carrying either two 25pdr or two 17pdr Army guns, although only a few were completed by the end of the war. A rather similar concept was the LCT(R) or landing craft, rocket, fitted with some 500 fixed 5in rocket launchers to saturate enemy positions ashore. The Americans combined a 5in gun with rocket launchers in the LSM(R) or landing ship, medium, rocket, which were vessels of about 1000 tons and 12kts. Sixty were ordered; some vessels saw service in the Pacific before the end of the war. Postwar, they were reclassified as inshore fire support ships.

Erebus and *Roberts* worked up in the Clyde in the spring of 1944, as part of the heavy Normandy bombarding force comprising the British battleships *Warspite*, *Nelson*, *Rodney* and *Ramillies* and the American battleships *Nevada*, *Texas* and *Arkansas*. *Roberts* opened fire off the easternmost British beach 'Sword' at 0520 on 6 June from 20,000yds at German 155mm (6.1in) batteries. *Erebus* had opened fire off the western American 'Utah' beach at 170mm (6.7in) batteries on the Cherbourg peninsula. Both monitors suffered damage to one of their 15in guns on D-Day, due to shells bursting prematurely while being fired. The extensive damage to *Erebus'* turret required six weeks under repair at Devonport, but *Roberts'* gun was quickly replaced at Portsmouth. Battleships, cruisers, destroyers and LCGs all contributed to gunfire support off the beaches.

For the next three months, one or other of the monitors was on call off the Normandy coastline to fire on targets as much as 15 miles inland. Forward observation officers and Spitfire spotting aircraft proved effective in controlling the 3371 rounds fired by the six British big-gun ships, of which the monitors contributed about one thousand. *Erebus'* last shoot off Normandy was on German heavy batteries defending Le Havre in September. The last European operation by *Roberts* and *Erebus* was in support of the Walcheren landings in November 1944 when, together with *Warspite*, 636 rounds were fired at batteries and strongpoints to assist opening up the river Scheldt and access to the port of Antwerp. LCGs were in close support, and suffered badly.

With victory in Europe near, both *Roberts* and *Abercrombie* were prepared for service in the Indian Ocean, as planned amphibious landings in Malaya would require heavy gun support. *Abercrombie*, further damaged by a mine off Malta in August 1944, was finally out of dockyard hands by July 1945. Both vessels had passed Suez by the time of the formal Japanese surrender, but there was little need for their services now, so they were sent home, arriving in November 1945.

After the Second World War

As in 1919, there was little need for the monitors' services postwar. *Marshal Soult* had been a base ship at Portsmouth throughout the war and was scrapped in 1946. *Erebus* went in 1947.

The Niels Juel, *the last Danish coast defence ship, suffered a long drawn out completion owing to the embargo on her intended armament of German 12in guns. She is seen here in 1937 with the revised armament of 5.9in guns.* (NMM)

Abercrombie and *Roberts* were used in subsidiary roles such as turret drill ships or in reserve, the latter surviving until 1965, the last ship in the Royal Navy still mounting 15in guns. One of her former guns is one of the pair on display outside the Imperial War Museum, London.

In an era of ever more powerful aircraft and precision guided weapons, the potential for both coast offence and coast defence gun-armed vessels was small. However, in the mid-1960s, the US Navy did convert some sixty 80-ton mechanised landing craft to carry one 105mm howitzer for riverine fire support in Vietnam, while other countries with large rivers retained a few gunboats. The battleship *New Jersey* with her 16in guns was reactivated during 1968–69 for fire support off Vietnam, but there were few worthwhile targets. She and her three sisters were again reactivated in the 1980s, and modified to carry thirty-two Tomahawk cruise missiles and sixteen Harpoon anti-ship missiles in addition to their nine 16in guns. They thus formed heavily protected mobile offshore launching platforms, and could be regarded as a form of coast offence vessel. In this role *Missouri* and *Wisconsin* launched their highly accurate Tomahawks at Iraqi targets in the 1991 Gulf conflict as well as using their 16in guns against defences around Kuwait.

Coast defence vessels

Heavily armed coast defence ships were regarded as powerful deterrents by smaller countries which had no designs on others, but which were vulnerable to blockade or attack from the sea. By deploying relatively strong vessels, it was hoped that neutrality could be maintained. While major harbours could be defended by coast artillery, an extended coastline could best be protected from the sea by vessels mounting heavy guns capable of driving off cruisers and other marauding ships, or of drawing such attackers within range of submarines or torpedo boats. Without overseas possessions, such countries did not need to de-

ploy fleets capable of cruising in distant waters. Nor could they afford a fleet able to attack hostile vessels in the latter's home waters. Since an open ocean capability was not needed, comparatively small vessels of short length, low freeboard, shallow draft and moderate speed could be designed to mount guns of up to 12in calibre.

The Scandinavian navies

Classically this was the role of the Scandinavian navies, which had begun building monitor type vessels from the 1860s. By 1906, Sweden, Denmark and Norway had constructed over thirty such vessels of gradually increasing size, most still in service. Denmark completed *Peder Skram* in 1909, the third vessel of her class, mounting two single 240mm (9.4in) guns on a displacement of 3500 tons. A much more powerful vessel, the 4000-ton *Niels Juel* was commenced in 1914 to reinforce Danish neutrality. She was designed to carry two single 305mm (12in) guns, but delivery of these

Krupp guns and their armour was deferred owing to the war. She was not launched from the Royal Dockyard at Copenhagen until 1918. After the Armistice, the Allies forbade the Germans to complete the contract, so a revised armament was planned – ten single 149mm (5.9in) guns ordered from the Swedish Bofors company. The 16kt armoured ship was finally completed in 1923, neither cruiser nor mini-battleship. She was given a stronger anti-aircraft armament in the 1930s, and spent most of her time in harbour. After the Germans overran Denmark in April 1940, she like other Danish warships remained nominally under Danish control. When the Germans moved to disarm all Danish forces on 29 August 1943, *Peder Skram* was scuttled at Copenhagen, while *Niels Juel* attempted to make for neutral Sweden. She was caught by German aircraft and ran aground that same day. Both vessels were salved by the Germans and put into service as the AA ship *Adler* and the training ship *Nordland* respectively. Both were bombed by Allied aircraft near Kiel in the spring of 1945.

The Swedish Gustav V *in 1934. She was modernised during a major refit 1927–30 with her two funnels trunked into one and was to be reconstructed again at the end of the 1930s.* (NMM)

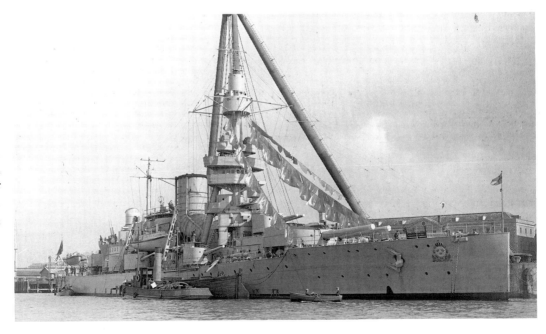

The Väinämöinen, *one of a pair of coast defence ships built in Finland in 1930–33.* (NMM)

Sweden had completed the coast defence ship *Oscar II* in 1907, giving her a fleet of twelve such ships in the 3000-ton bracket, each armed with two 254mm (10in) guns. In 1912 public subscription raised the money to build a much more powerful coast defence ship. The 7000-ton *Sverige* mounted four 283mm (11.1in) guns in twin turrets forward and aft, plus eight 152mm (6in), two torpedo tubes and smaller guns. Steam turbine machinery of 20,000shp gave her the respectable speed of 22.5kts. She was completed by Gotaverken in 1917, and followed by two near-sisters *Drottning Victoria* and *Gustav V* in 1921 and 1922 respectively. Protected by armour up to 200mm (8in), they were intended to form in effect long range offshore artillery, the fixed coast artillery also being a naval responsibility. Various modernisations were carried out between the wars including strengthened AA armament and new boilers. With Sweden's neutrality threatened as the Second World War loomed, two new coast defence ships were proposed, but in the event destroyers and submarines were built. The three 'armoured ships' formed the backbone of Sweden's navy but were not called upon to defend her neutrality in action during the war. They remained in service after the war in training roles, *Gustav V* surviving until 1970 before being broken up.

Norway had become fully independent of Sweden in 1905, then possessing four coast defence ships in the fleet. Two further vessels were ordered in 1913, but were taken over by Britain as described previously. The only two coast defence ships operational at the outbreak of the Second World War (*Norge* and *Eidsvold*) were sunk by German destroyer torpedoes at Narvik on 9 April 1940.

Finland gained its independence from Russia in 1917. Its small navy was considerably strengthened when two coast defence ships were ordered in 1929. They mounted four Bofors 254mm (10in) guns in twin turrets forward and aft. These businesslike 3900-ton ships were designed by IvS in Holland and completed by Crichton-Vulcan at Turku in 1932 (*Väinämöinen*) and 1933 (*Ilmarinen*). Diesel-electric machinery gave them a modest 15kt speed. During the winter war of 1939–40, they defended Turku against Russian air attack. In mid-1941 they protected the strategically important Åland Islands from assault by the Soviets. Both vessels were deployed in the northern Baltic while the Germans launched an attack on the Estonian islands. On 13 Sep-

tember 1941 *Ilmarinen*'s paravanes encountered mines, probably Soviet, which exploded under the ship, capsizing and sinking her in a few minutes. *Väinämöinen* supported light craft operations off the Finnish coast throughout the rest of the war. After the war she was sold to the Soviet Union to help pay off reparations. She was converted into a training ship and renamed *Vyborg* in 1947, surviving until at least 1960.

The Netherlands navy

The only other European navy to build coast defence ships in the twentieth century was the Dutch. The 6500-ton *De Zeven Provincien* was completed in 1910, mounting two single 11in guns to provide heavy artillery to defend the Dutch East Indies. Four 7000-ton vessels with four 11in apiece were planned in 1912, but were not built, nor were projected battleships. *De Zeven Provincien* was relegated to training duties in the East Indies from the mid-1920s. She was converted into a training ship in 1937, being renamed *Soerabaia* and reclassified as a gunboat. She was at her name port when attacked and sunk by Japanese aircraft on 18 February 1942. She was later raised by the Japanese and used as a blockship.

The Thai (Siamese) navy

The last navy to commission coast defence ships was that of Siam in 1938. A coast defence ship had been ordered from Armstrong, Whitworth in 1914. At 1070 tons with two single 6in guns, *Ratanakosindra* would be little more than a river gunboat, but construction was suspended on the outbreak of war. The order was reinstated with her Tyneside hull and machinery builders in 1924, with *Ratanakosindra* being delivered to Bangkok in January 1926. Three

years later, a sister ship was ordered from the Barrow yard of the now merged Vickers-Armstrong. *Sukothai*'s normal displacement was 1030 tons; she made 12.9kts on trial. Two single 6in, one forward, one aft and four single 3in AA guns constituted her armament. She was protected by a 2.5in armour belt and 1.5in high-tensile steel deck.

During the later 1930s, the Siamese navy was strengthened by a number of new ships, including a pair of more powerful coast defence ships delivered in 1938. The name Thailand was adopted in 1939 and thereafter the Siamese navy became the Thai navy. The compact Japanese-built 2265-ton vessels mounted two twin 8in turrets. Twin MAN diesels gave *Sri Ayuthia* and *Dhonburi* a speed of 16kts. In December 1940 Thailand attempted to annex parts of British Malaya and French Indo-China. The French despatched their Indo-China naval squadron to destroy the Thai naval forces. The 6in cruiser *Lamotte-Picquet* and sloops found the Thai ships off Ko Chang on 17 January 1941. In the ensuing action, *Sri Ayuthia* was damaged and beached, while *Dhonburi* was also hit and abandoned in shallow water. Both vessels were salvaged, but *Dhonburi* was thereafter fit only for static use as a headquarters ship.

Sri Ayuthia was involved in a coup when she was bombed and sunk by Thai air force aircraft in the Chao Phya river at Bangkok on 30 June 1951. The other three coast defence ships remained in training roles at Thai naval bases until the late 1960s. *Sukothai* was not deleted until 1971 and was probably broken up locally, the last of the twentieth century coast defence ships afloat. From the 1960s, aircraft and missile-armed fast attack craft (and sometimes submarines) became the coast defence weapons of such navies against seaborne attack.

Ian Buxton

Coast Offence and Defence Ships: Typical Vessels 1906–1945

Ship or Class	Nationality	Dispt (tons) Normal/Std Full load (fl)	Dimensions (loa × breadth × deep draught) Feet–Inches Metres	Armament	Armour Belt/Turrets/ Deck (max ins)	Speed (service (s) design (d) kts)	Launch dates	Numbers built
DE ZEVEN PROVINCIEN	Dutch	6530	339–6 × 56–0 × 20–3 103.5 × 17.1 × 6.2	2–11in 4–5.9in 10–75mm	5.9/9.8/2	16 d	1909	1
HUMBER	British ex-Brazilian	1260 1520	266–9 × 49–0 × 5–7 81.3 × 14.9 × 1.7	2–6in 2–4.7in 4–3pdr	3/4/2	9.5 s	1913	3
GORGON	British ex-Norwegian	5705 fl	310–0 × 73–7 × 16–4 94.5 × 22.4 × 5.0	2–9.2in 4–6in 2–3in 4–2pdr	7/8/2	12 s	1914	2
ABERCROMBIE	British	6150 fl	334–6 × 90–2 × 10–0 102.0 ×27.4 × 3.1	2–14in 2–12pdr 1–3pdr 1–2pdr	4/10/2	6.5 s	1915	4
GENERAL WOLFE (as in 1918)	British	6850 fl†	335–6 × 87–2 × 11–0 102.3 × 26.6 × 3.3	1–18in* 2–12in 2–6in 2–3in 2–2pdr	6/10.5/2	7 s	1915	8*
M15	British	540 650	177–3 × 31–0 × 7–0 54.0 × 9.4 × 2.1	1–9.2in 1–12pdr 1–6pdr	Nil	11 s	1915	14
SVERIGE	Swedish	6852 std 7516	393–8 × 61–0 × 21–4 120.0 × 18.6 × 6.5	4–11.1in 8–6in 6–75mm 2–450mm TT	7.9/7.9/1.6	22.5 d	1915–18	3
EREBUS	British	8000 8450	405–0 × 88–2 × 11–8 123.4 × 26.9 × 3.6	2–15in 2–6in 1–3in 2–12pdr	4/13/2	12 s	1916	2
FAA' DI BRUNO	Italian	2854	182–1 × 88–7 × 7–3 55.5 × 27.0 × 2.2	2–15in 4–3in 2–40mm	9.5ft concrete bulge/2.8/1.6	3 s	1916	1
NIELS JUEL	Danish	3800 4100	295–3 × 53–6 × 16–6 90.0 × 16.3 × 5.0	10–149mm 4–57mm 2–450mm TT	7.7/1.8/2.2	16 d	1918	1
VÄINÄMÖINEN	Finnish	3900 std	305–1 × 55–5 × 14–9 93.0 × 16.9 × 4.5	4–10in 8–105mm 4–40mm	2.2/3.9/0.8	15 s	1930–31	2
SRI AYUTHIA	Thai	2265 std	252–8 × 47–4 × 13–8 77.0 × 14.4 × 4.2	4–8in 4–3in 4–20mm	2.5/4/1.5	16 d	1937–38	2
ABERCROMBIE	British	8536 std 9717	373–4 × 89–9 × 14–5 113.8 × 27.4 × 4.4	2–15in 8–4in 16–2pdr 20–20mm	5/13/4	12 s	1941–42	2

Notes:
The data criteria are generally as outlined for earlier tables.

* Only two were fitted with the 18in gun.
† Displacement as built 5900 tons at 9–7ft (2.9m) draft.

5

The Destroyer and Torpedo Boat

BY the first decade of the twentieth century the torpedo was coming of age as a weapon. The installation of 'air heaters' (using the burning of fuel greatly to increase the effect of the compressed air carried, or – to put it another way – using that air to provide the oxygen for an internal combustion engine) produced much greater range. The use of gyroscopic control permitted the greater accuracy needed to exploit that range. Simultaneously new types of platform were becoming available to launch this form of underwater attack. The submarine was already established as a practical instrument of war, whilst the first aircraft had flown. By the end of the First World War submarines, aircraft and small fast motor boats had all demonstrated their ability to sink ships with torpedoes. Our concern here, however, is with the type of steam-powered ship intended for torpedo attack, but which was to become increasingly the chief surface escort against such attack, whether from on, above or below the surface: in other words we are dealing with the destroyer in all its forms.

Trends in destroyer development

In the forty years between the appearance of the *Dreadnought* and the end of the Second World War there are three main threads which can be picked out in destroyer development. All three can be seen in the Royal Navy at the start of our period. Britain was building the

large destroyers of the 'Tribal' type, the small 'Coastal Destroyers' soon to be re-classified as 'Torpedo Boats' and was putting into service the 'River' type – the first true destroyers.[1] This threefold division between 'superdestroyer', 'torpedo boat' and 'destroyer' continues throughout our period. General trends are a steady increase in size, power and performance of all types. Increasingly obvious towards the end of the period is a change of purpose away from the defence against (and provision of) surface torpedo attack and towards meeting the new submarine and air threats – a development which, in the years after 1945, would result in the disappearance of the 'true' destroyer. The name 'destroyer' would continue to be used – and many of the old destroyer hulls would be altered – but the result was not the same kind of ship. Our period was, indeed, the heyday of the destroyer – if by that is understood a warship which gave approximately equal prominence to guns and to torpedoes, which was of comparatively high speed and was also the largest flotilla vessel – the biggest vessel, that is, which was cheap enough to build in substantial numbers, and which was intended to operate in groups and not singly.

The designing and building of strong, light, fast craft was a specialised business. The torpedo boat market had been dominated by four great firms – Thornycroft and Yarrow in Britain, Le Normand in France and Schichau in Germany with a few other specialist firms (Herreshoff in the United States and J S White in Britain for example) playing a lesser but still important part. These firms (except Herreshoff) were still of significance in the development of the destroyer, but by this time technology in this area was not being pushed quite as much to its limits as was the case in the early days of the torpedo boat and it was therefore possible for many more shipbuilders to be involved. However, the number of countries capable of designing as well as building destroyers was comparatively small, though there was a slow spread of the relevant technology and skills. Initially the only countries capable of the full process of designing and building destroyers were Britain, Germany and the United States; France, for mainly political reasons, was somewhat left behind until the 1920s. Italy did not break completely loose from direct British influence on the designs she built until the 1920s.[2] Much the same story holds

The German torpedo boat S 143 of 1907, seen here prewar, was mined and sunk in 1914 but later raised and put back into service. The well before the bridge and the small size of the guns were both typical of German practice at the time. (BfZ)

1. The Royal Navy was also building a real 'super-destroyer' in the form of the huge *Swift*, a very clear, and not very successful, example of the pursuit of speed and size for their own sake.

2. There is clear indication from Thornycroft's records (now held at the National Maritime Museum) that this firm continued to provide design back-up to Italy until just after 1920 – and it rather looks as if Yarrow was doing the same.

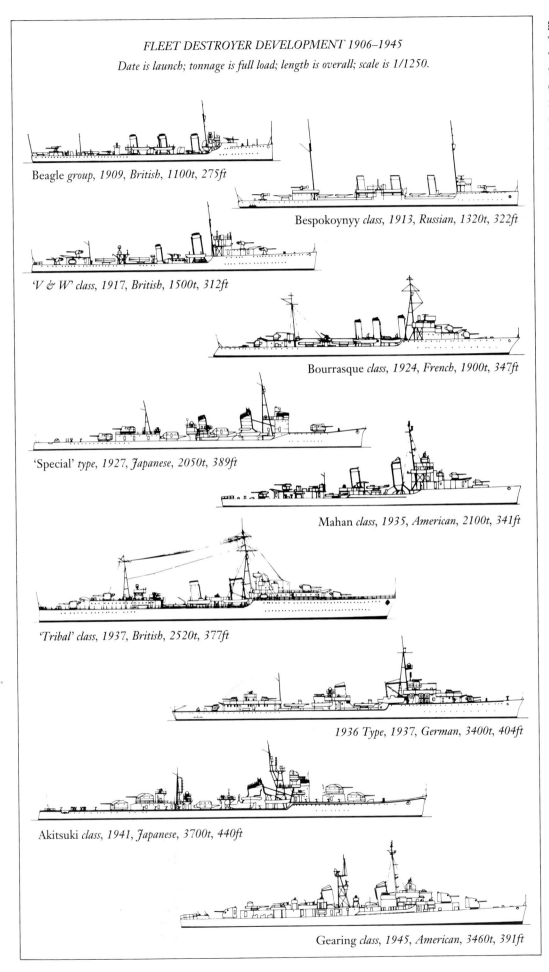

FLEET DESTROYER DEVELOPMENT 1906–1945

Date is launch; tonnage is full load; length is overall; scale is 1/1250.

Beagle *group, 1909, British, 1100t, 275ft*

Bespokoynyy *class, 1913, Russian, 1320t, 322ft*

'V & W' *class, 1917, British, 1500t, 312ft*

Bourrasque *class, 1924, French, 1900t, 347ft*

'Special' *type, 1927, Japanese, 2050t, 389ft*

Mahan *class, 1935, American, 2100t, 341ft*

'Tribal' *class, 1937, British, 2520t, 377ft*

1936 Type, 1937, German, 3400t, 404ft

Akitsuki *class, 1941, Japanese, 3700t, 440ft*

Gearing *class, 1945, American, 3460t, 391ft*

good for Japan. Tsarist Russia, as we shall see, went her own way as far as design requirements were concerned, but had to rely on foreign technical aid in design and construction (mostly from British and German firms). Stalinist Russia had fallen so much behind when expanding its navy in the 1930s that it had to buy in foreign (mostly Italian) design expertise, with an end result that was neither particularly impressive nor of much use to the country concerned once war came. Portugal and Spain relied on British (and, in the latter case, later French) designs built in their own yards. During the Second World War Brazil built her own destroyers – to both British and American designs. Even the Dutch and Scandinavian home-built vessels had a substantial foreign design input, whether from Britain, Germany or Italy. Everyone else merely bought ships from the main destroyer-building nations: sometimes buying what were virtually 'off the peg' copies of designs building for the producer's own navy, at other times getting the builders to produce new designs. The large destroyers ordered by Argentina from Germany, France and Britain in 1910, the small Chilean *Serrano*s built by Thornycroft in the late 1920s and the impressive *Blyskawica* and *Grom* ordered by Poland in 1935 from J S White are all examples of the latter process. In effect this means that the story of destroyer development can be told by considering the shipyards of only six nations: America, Britain, France, Germany, Italy and Japan, though the intentions ('staff requirements') of a few other countries are of relevance.

The torpedo boat destroyer

A decade before our period begins the British had built the first 'torpedo boat destroyers' – basically larger, more powerful and faster torpedo boats which in reality were no more than the continuation of an existing trend towards bigger and more capable torpedo boats, though primarily intended to defend the battlefleet against torpedo boat attack.[3] In the next few years most navies followed the British example and built 'TBDs' in numbers, though all continued to build smaller 'TBs' as well. The emphasis was above all on high speed – trial speed

3. In this way they, with the earlier Torpedo Gunboats (TGBs), can be considered as the first purpose-designed escorts of the steam era.

The British 'Tribal' group destroyer Nubian *running trials in 1909 – a photograph taken by her builders, John I Thornycroft and Sons. The long row of funnels give some indication of how much of the length of the hull was devoted to propulsion.* (CMP)

in smooth water – which was a snare and delusion with the inherent difficulties in running and maintaining high speed reciprocating engines on steam provided from coal-fired boilers. The result was flotillas of fair-weather vessels – too fragile and unreliable to be considered truly seagoing – which never made their design speed except in the unrealistic circumstance of their acceptance trials and whose endurance was strictly limited. The overall appearance and design of these vessels had in general followed the British prototypes: long, narrow craft with 'turtleback' bows, a low silhouette and a mixed armament of 12pdr and 6pdr guns with a couple of 18in torpedo tubes. The main national variants were that Germany concentrated on the torpedo attack function and continued to designate her, somewhat smaller, vessels 'torpedo boats', whilst France built enlarged versions of her own torpedo boat designs rather than direct copies of the British types.

Seaworthiness versus speed

The British 'River' group[4] of destroyers, however, marked a change of direction from the pursuit of speed. The prototype destroyers (Thornycroft's *Daring* and *Decoy*, Yarrow's

4. As there were considerable differences between the designs by different builders for both 'River's and 'TB's it seems more sensible to call these vessels by some other name than 'class', which can then be reserved for a grouping of vessels built to a common design; this is what has been done here, though the looser use of the word 'class' for both 'River's and 'TB's is historically quite valid.

Havock and *Hornet*) were intended for 26kts, while the initial group of destroyers built in quantity for the Royal Navy were significantly called '27-knotters' and their successors '30-knotters'. There were also three 'specials' intended (not very successfully) for 33kts. By the beginning of the new century there was growing pressure from the users for somewhat larger and more substantial vessels of greater seaworthiness and endurance. The speed requirement for the 'Rivers' was a sustainable sea speed of 26kts rather than the higher trial speeds (never approached in service) of the earlier classes. This victory of practicality over publicity was assisted by the replacement of the turtleback bow by a raised forecastle. This made it possible to maintain speed in worse conditions whilst keeping the vessels drier. In some ways the development of the torpedo boat into something larger, sturdier and more seaworthy had produced a vessel with considerable resemblances to the 'torpedo gunboats' of the previous decade – an earlier attempt to produce a seagoing torpedo vessel capable of use as an anti-torpedo boat escort which had foundered on engineering problems.

Simultaneously, the introduction of the steam turbine was making the achieving and, even more importantly, the maintaining, of high speed very much easier. High speed reciprocating engines with their high stresses, liability to vibration and mechanical unreliability disappeared from destroyer design almost at a stroke. The change from coal to oil fuel which was also in train at the same time (the 'coastal destroyers' were the Royal Navy's first oil-fuelled vessels, nicknamed the 'oily wads' in service) was another step in the direction of operational simplicity and reliability, not to mention a life of considerably less hardship for engine room personnel.

Increased armament

With increases in size and seaworthiness came developments in armament. As torpedo vessels became sturdier, bigger guns with heavier shells were needed to sink them. The first generation of destroyers had a typical gun armament of a single 12pdr (3in or 75mm) backed up by a number of smaller 6pdr quick-firing guns. The 'Rivers' introduced a uniform 12pdr armament, but the later ships of the larger 'Tribal' group brought the 4in (102mm) gun to destroyers. Its slower rate of fire would be compensated for by a more destructive projectile. Given the limitations on fire control and accuracy of gunfire from destroyers (limitations which would remain until nearly the end of our period) it is far from certain that this was a real improvement. Gunnery from a small fast vessel was unlikely to be accurate and using a light weapon with a high rate of fire at least increased the possibility of achieving hits, some hits with a light shell being better than none at all with a heavier one. Another step was taken at the end of the first decade of the twentieth century when the 21in (533mm) diameter torpedo was introduced to replace the 18in. This step first occurred in the Royal Navy with the *Beagle* 'class' of 1908–9 programme, a group otherwise notable for being the last coal-fired destroyers (a temporary backsliding) in that navy, and also the last occasion for Britain when the old torpedo boat method of ordering was adopted, with each builder producing their own design to fit general Admiralty requirements. From then on the basic design of each class would be provided by the Admiralty, though the specialist builders, Thornycroft and Yarrow, would still be allowed to build 'specials' to their own designs from time to time. This permitted a degree of experimentation and comparison within an ordering structure

The Sheldrake *of 1911, shown here during the First World War, was one of the* Acorn *class with which the Royal Navy returned to oil fuel. Long hulls were important for high speed in smooth water conditions, but less satisfactory in a seaway as can be seen here.* (CMP)

which emphasised the cheapness and interoperability of individual units (a need which the spectrum of types amongst the earlier TBDs had emphasised) and seems to have been a workable compromise between the requirements for ease of operation and technical development.

The destroyer in other navies

During the first decade of the century the destroyers of most other nations reflected the British pattern, even when they were not actually built in British yards. However, German designers followed their own path: the German navy was particularly devoted to the torpedo boat idea (Tirpitz was a torpedo officer) and their vessels tended to emphasise the torpedo rather than the gun, to be slightly smaller and have a lower silhouette, whilst having their own hallmark of a very short raised forecastle which finished far short of the bridge in a 'well deck' to distinguish them from foreign contemporaries. The Italians, while building destroyers to British designs, also pursued their own course with 'esploratori' (scouts) – small fast torpedo cruisers suited to employment in the Mediterranean – which, with the *Poerio* class (laid down in 1913), entered the super-destroyer category. They also continued to build torpedo boats, both larger ones of 200 tons or so and smaller coastal vessels (the earlier 'PN' series) of just over 100 tons. Italy is a country with a long exposed coastline and large numbers of very small torpedo craft were one way of obtaining a reasonably mobile and flexible coastal defence.[5] The Russian navy, when it finally resumed building destroyers after the disasters of the war with Japan, decided to adopt very large, heavily armed and fast destroyers. The prototype of these was the *Novik* ordered in 1909. Before completion in 1912 her armament was augmented to four 4in guns and eight 18in torpedo tubes. With a design top speed of 36kts (nearly achieved on first trials, exceeded by more than a knot after modifications), she was the most powerful destroyer of her day and set a standard to which other

5. It is not surprising that Italy took a leading part in the development of motor torpedo boats (her MAS boats) in the war that followed.

navies would aspire before long. However it should be added that this very ambitious design could not have been achieved without foreign help: the machinery was sub-contracted to the Vulcan yard in Germany, while the *Bespokoynyy* and *Leitenant Ilin* classes which followed to the same general concept were designed and produced with German and British help.

The American approach

The country that took an entirely separate course was the United States. Despite the official intention that destroyers should have the primary purpose of defending the battle line from torpedo attack, US destroyers had a very powerful torpedo armament compared to their foreign contemporaries (six 18in in the '700-tonners' of 1908–10, eight 18in – then 21in –

in the '1000-tonners' which succeeded them, and finally twelve 21in in the designs that led to the mass-produced flush-decked 'four stackers' of 1917–19. These latter had their tubes in a 'sided' arrangement which meant that in effect the ship had two separate salvoes of six torpedoes each. This showed some realisation that the increased range of both battleship secondary armament and of the torpedoes themselves would have the logical consequence that most attacks would have to be launched at long range. In these circumstances the torpedoes would have to be thought of more as a weapon fired in numbers as a 'shotgun spread' to ensure at least one hit rather than the preci-

Like the British 'M's the American 'four stackers' or 'flush deckers' of the Wickes *(DD 75 – DD 185) and* Clemson *classes were built in vast numbers, as can be seen in this group laid up at San Diego between the wars. Of those visible at least one served in each of the British, Canadian and Norwegian navies in the Second World War, and others as destroyer minelayers, minesweepers, fast amphibious transports and auxiliaries.* (CMP)

sion sniper's instrument that previous practice and the (for the time) high cost of the individual torpedoes seemed to indicate.

Wartime experience

By the time the 'four stackers' appeared, however, they looked somewhat old-fashioned when compared to the similarly armed but considerably more logically laid-out 'V & W's of the Royal Navy. These were the result of wartime experience combined with what had been a steady development of destroyer design. The coal-fired *Beagle*s (1908–9 programme) were enlarged and more powerful 'Rivers' with a single 4in gun forward, three 12pdrs and two torpedo tubes; this was the class where the 21in torpedo replaced the 18in. The 1909–10 programme *Acorn*s marked the definitive return to oil fuel, and had two 4in and two 12pdr guns. The next years' programme *Acheron*s were similar, apart from Yarrow, Thornycroft and the turbine-building firm of Parsons being given orders for 'specials' (the Parsons pair marking the first use of gears in conjunction with turbines) in a successful attempt to improve performance. The 1911–12 programme *Acasta*s had a uniform gun armament of three

4in, the 12pdr being abandoned, whilst the machinery installation was two-shaft rather than the three shafts of earlier turbine-powered destroyers. The 'L' or *Laforey* class of 1912–13, the class which was completing on the outbreak of war in 1914, doubled the torpedo armament by fitting twin tubes. Whereas this and earlier classes had been designed for 29kts, the 1913–14 'M's were given 6kts more speed partly because German destroyers built for Argentina had been considerably faster than British ones and this had upset the new First Lord, Winston Churchill.[6] Fortunately by this time improvements in machinery made this a perfectly possible move which did not seriously affect other aspects of performance or reliability.[7] The 'M' design was built in considerable numbers as the standard 'war emergency' destroyer design, slightly modified into the 'R' design, and finally modified further in the 'S' class building as smaller destroyers for North Sea use at the end of the First World War.

The actual experience of that War proved that destroyers (even old and small ones) made good anti-submarine escorts.[8] They also made excellent fast minelayers – and both British and Germans made much use of them in this role – which, since mines in that war proved to be the most effective anti-submarine weapon, was itself a useful move against the U-boats. However the experience of war also forced an increase in size and armament in destroyer design.

The Thornycroft-built Shakespeare *class (this is* HMS *Spenser) and the similar Admiralty-designed* Scott*s introduced the 4.7in gun and were an immensely influential design. Notice the fifth 4.7in gun positioned between the funnels. (CMP)*

Flotilla leaders

Even before the commencement of hostilities the need for somewhat bigger and more powerful vessels to lead groups of destroyers – the so-called 'flotilla leaders' – resulted in an order for an enlarged destroyer with four instead of three 4in guns to be placed in early 1914 (the *Lightfoot* class). Large destroyers building for foreign navies were impressed into the navies of Britain, France and Germany when war broke out later the same year.[9] The next stage with the British flotilla leader was to move the bridge further back and place a second gun, in a superfiring position, in front of it (*Parker* class), followed by relocating the third gun from amidships to a superfiring position aft. The result was the 'V' class flotilla leader, which, however, almost immediately became the prototype of the next group of destroyers (also given 'V' names). The reason for this was that there were rumours that the Germans were fitting 5in guns to destroyers and new designs for even bigger flotilla leaders to be armed with 4.7in guns were rushed out by both Thornycroft and the Admiralty. These, respectively the *Shakespeare*s and the *Scott*s, had the same basic gun and tube layout as the 'V's but with an extra gun amidships to give a broadside of five in all, and two triple torpedo tube mountings. This took deep load tonnage up to above 2000 (the *Lightfoot*s were 1700, the 'V's only 1400, whilst the standard wartime 'M' class destroyers were about 1250 tons). The big newcomers took over the flotilla leader role, but meanwhile the demands of war had, in any case, indicated a need for a larger destroyer, which led to the 'V leader' design being copied in quantity as the 'V' class destroyer. It was

6. Argentina had ordered large destroyers from British, German and French yards with an ambitious specification which included a top speed of 35kts. The German boats passed their speed trials and were delivered. The British boats were ordered from Cammell Laird (not, it will be noted, one of the true specialist yards, though one with considerable experience of destroyer building) and on trial just failed to meet their contract speed. The problem of what to do with them was solved by their being sold to the Greeks who were in conflict with the Turks at the time – to whom these sturdy if undistinguished vessels gave good service for many years, being completely rebuilt in the 1920s by J S White. As for the French vessels, these languished incomplete and undelivered until they were taken over by the French navy on the outbreak of war in 1914. The German navy made a similar requisition of the replacement orders for British and French destroyers which Argentina placed with German yards.

7. Geared turbines had been introduced with considerable success, and a diesel auxiliary engine for cruising tried with much less success – despite the fact that the Germans were building a diesel powered class of destroyers in 1945, the diesel, which performs best at a steady power output, was not the ideal power plant for destroyers.

8. There was the classic case in 1918 of the old British '30-knotter' *Fairy* which sank after ramming and sinking the German *UC 75*, which was of greater tonnage than herself – not a bad exchange.

9. The *Botha*s (building for Chile) in Britain, destroyers building for Argentina in both France and Germany and ones building for Romania in Italy as well. For both France and Germany the impressed vessels (and, in Germany, the destroyers built to make use of sets of machinery building for Russia) were much bigger than any other of their destroyers, proved very useful and had a considerable influence on future designs as a result.

FLOTILLA LEADERS AND SUPER-DESTROYERS 1906–1945
Date is launch; tonnage is full load; length is overall; scale is 1/1250.

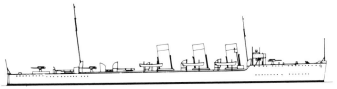

Swift, *1907, British, 2390t, 345ft*

Aventurier, *1911, French (ex-Argentine), 1250t, 290ft*

Faulknor, *1914, British (ex-Chilean), 2000t, 331ft*

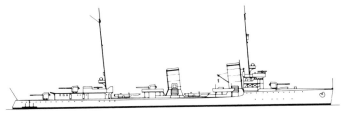

S 113, *1918, German, 2415t, 348ft*

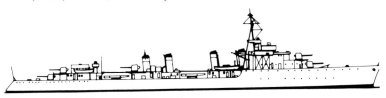

Guepard, *1928, French, 3200t, 427ft*

Grom, *1936, Polish (British-built), 3380t, 374ft*

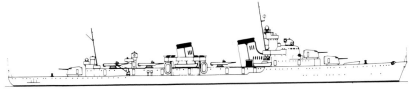

Tashkent, *1937, Russian (Italian-built), 3200t, 459ft*

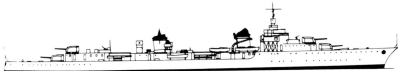

Mogador, *1937, French, 4020t, 450ft*

then decided to upgun the design with 4.7in (120mm) weapons instead of 4in and to give the two torpedo mountings triple instead of twin tubes, producing another large class, the 'W's. The 'V & W' group with the contemporary British flotilla leaders set the fashion for destroyer-building world-wide for the next decade or more.

Meanwhile the Germans were, indeed, building very large destroyers armed with heavy guns – four 5.9in (150mm), plus also four 23.6in (600mm) torpedo tubes – in an over-reaction to their dissatisfaction with their previous pattern of design. The large and seaworthy *B 97* class, built round turbines originally ordered for Russian destroyers and the first German vessels to be classed as 'destroyers' and not 'torpedo boats', had proved a great success. Because the smaller and less powerful (88mm armed) German destroyers were failing to break through screens of British ships armed with 4in (102mm), the more modern classes of the former were rearmed with 105mm guns themselves. This was only partially satisfactory and so the Germans tried to steal a march by going for significantly larger vessels (2400 tons deep load) and guns than the British. This however ignored the fact that the 5.9in was really too heavy a gun to load and operate on the heaving deck of a destroyer, however large; furthermore, the new vessels (the *S 113* and *V 116* classes) proved to be lacking in seaworthiness.

However the French, who with the Italians took the only complete pair of vessels of this type over as reparations after the war, were impressed with the design. It is perhaps significant that they had, for over a decade, been building destroyers which were small and old-fashioned by comparison with their contemporaries. During the inter-war years, when their chief naval rivals were the Italians (which therefore placed an emphasis on high performance in the comparatively restricted arena of the Mediterranean), they proceeded to build a series of super-destroyer classes armed first with five 5in guns (*Chacal* class), then 5.5in guns (*Guépard* class and successors). Besides a powerful armament these ships also possessed high speed, culminating in the extraordinary and extravagant *Fantasque*s of the late 1930s which were capable of steaming in company at speeds in excess of 40kts. One of the class, *Le Terrible*, set a record, which still stands for a ship of any size, of over 45kts. Their even larger successors, the *Mogador*s had four less reliable twin instead of five single mounts for 5.5in guns. One can only wonder whether these large and striking vessels were not a spec-

tacular extravagance, and whether the French would not have done better to concentrate on the classes of more conventional standard-sized destroyers they were also building; an alternative would have been to follow the Italian example in building classes of fast light cruisers, instead of ships too light to be effective as cruisers, but needlessly large and expensive for destroyers. The French were, however, influential in producing a type of curved ('clipper') bow which was eventually copied by all the other major navies.

The Italians, after continuing their line of larger destroyer designs with the 'Navigatori's of the end of the 1920s reverted to the parallel line of development of rather smaller destroyers culminating in the 'Soldati' class of a decade later. From the *Sauro* class of the

mid-1920s the Italians had gone for their own armament pattern, with twin-mounted 4.7in guns disposed forward, amidships and aft, and from the beginning of the 1930s single funnels became characteristic of this nation's destroyers.

Inter-war developments

The British, meanwhile, continued to refine the basic design layout of the 'V & W's in a series of destroyer classes which ran the alphabetical gamut from 'A' to 'I' from the

The French Le Triomphante *of the* Fantasque *class photographed in 1940. A superb looking ship with an incredible performance, but of uncertain role. Too big and expensive for a destroyer, but lacking the size, strength, endurance and gunnery performance to match a cruiser, it rather looks as if the technical possibilities had rather run away with her designers.* (CMP)

mid-1920s to the mid-1930s. The prototypes, built by Thornycroft and Yarrow to their own designs as *Amazon* and *Ambuscade*, repeated the armament and layout of the 'W' class. Their successors, the 'A' class, introduced quadruple instead of triple torpedo tubes, thus giving a full torpedo armament of eight 21in, but were otherwise similar. The flotilla leader (*Codrington*) was built slightly longer, with increased accommodation and an extra 4.7in gun mounted between the funnels on the pattern set by the *Shakespeare* and *Scott* classes. *Acheron* of the 'A' class experimented with the use of high pressure steam, but was not given the special treatment that such an experiment deserved and was accounted a failure. This resulted in the British not moving over to high

This photograph of the French 'super-destroyer' Leopard *of the* Chacal *(or* Jaguar) *class was taken in 1936, twelve years after her launch in 1924. Like all French inter-war destroyers her hull was very highly stressed and her stability low by the standards of British design of the time. Serving under British control during the war she had the fore funnel and two boilers removed – probably as much to give her extra stability as to increase her very poor endurance.* (L & L van Ginderen)

The Italian 'Navigatori' class of large destroyers (this photo is of the Antonio Pigafetta *of 1929) were intended to counter the French super-destroyers like the* Leopard. *Note the typical Italian layout of twin 4.7in guns forward, amidships and on a deckhouse aft.* (Marius Bar)

pressure steam installations until the very end of the Second World War (in the *Daring* class, designed in 1944 but not completed until over a decade later), by which time the Americans had thoroughly proved their benefits in increased range. It is worth noting, however, that the Germans had, like the Americans, adopted high pressure steam before the War, but unlike them had failed to prove the concept by thorough trials, the result being constant mechanical unreliability and a very poor serviceability record in the German flotillas. A similar mistake on the British side could have had catastrophic consequences given Britain's reliance on sea communications and naval protection. Though the British destroyer force suffered under the disadvantage of being comparatively 'short-legged', its machinery was also extremely easily maintained.

Anti-aircraft defence

Another unfortunate failure was the trial installation in the *Bulldog* of the next ('B') class of a comparatively high angle main armament gun, one of the 4.7in being given 60 degrees maximum elevation. As the Second World War was to prove, anti-aircraft armament was a vital necessity for any warship: early in the war one of the two sets of torpedo tubes in most classes of British destroyers would be sacrificed for a high angle gun – virtually *any* high angle gun, and normally an ancient 3in or 4in

weapon. An even greater necessity were heavy automatic guns for close range defence, particularly against that great menace of the early war years, the dive bomber. These, it would prove, would have to be provided in numbers, both to cover all angles of attack and to provide some chance of hitting a small, fast approaching target. It was not that the danger was totally ignored, more that a combination of budgetary restraints and a poor choice of actual weapons meant that British destroyers were particularly badly defended against dive bomber attack. The single 2pdr pom-poms in the 'A' class were probably slightly better than the awkward and inadequate quadruple 0.5in machine-gun which would replace them in the 'D' class (the 'C's had a single 3in gun instead). The quadruple 2pdr gun which was used in the 'Tribal's and in other destroyers completed in the early war years was nearer the size of weapon required to give the range and punch which experience would show to be necessary, but was rendered much less effective than it could have been because of the lack of power of the

already existing round adopted for reasons of economy. The Americans had much the same problems with the 1.1in gun they decided to adopt in the late 1930s. Fortunately before they entered the war they took note of British experience and followed the Royal Navy in adopting the excellent 20mm Oerlikon and 40mm Bofors guns, respectively Swiss and Swedish but coming from designs of German origin. The navy that was in the lead in light AA at the outbreak of the war was the Dutch, whose combination of 40mm Bofors guns with the triaxial Hazemeyer mounting was not the least important feature of the interesting and excellent *Tjerk Hiddes* class which was building as war broke out.[10]

The Japanese 'Special type'

The mid-1920s was the time in which the Japanese very conspicuously went their own way in warship design. This was especially so with destroyers. Japan had already moved away from slavishly copying British designs with a number of classes with short forecastles ending well short of the bridge after the German style. The last of these, the *Mutsuki* class, introduced the 24in (609mm) torpedo, a heavy, long range weapon which was to become characteristic of subsequent Japanese ships and whose development would culminate in the magnificent

HMS Amazon *on trials in 1927 – the 'V & W' class formula only slightly modified and updated.* (CMP)

10. Earlier Dutch destroyers had been barely modified versions of standard Yarrow designs – with the interesting variation, since they were intended to operate in Indonesian waters, that they could carry a seaplane. This class, though Yarrow still had an input in the design, were quite different from any of their contemporaries. Incomplete when the Germans invaded, one (*Isaac Sweers*) was towed to Britain and equipped with British armament, another was completed by the Germans as *ZH 1*.

oxygen-driven weapon known as 'Long Lance'. This devastating weapon gave Japanese destroyers a range and striking power in torpedo attack far greater than any of their Second World War contemporaries. This effect was even greater because the later classes of destroyer built between the wars were built with a torpedo reloading system fitted into deckhouses. This meant that they could fire a torpedo salvo, briefly retreat to reload and then return to the attack. Not only was this facility unparalleled by any other navy, but it and the sheer range,[11] speed and striking power of the 'Long Lance' was unsuspected by the American opponents of the Japanese until after the end of the war. This enhancement of the power of their torpedo armament was complemented by the adoption of a heavy dual purpose gun armament in the 'Special type' destroyers of the *Fubuki* class, the first of which completed in 1928. The early members of this class had three twin 5in gun mounts capable of elevating to 40 degrees for a limited amount of anti-aircraft fire. Later ships had mountings capable of elevating to 75 degrees which made the mounting truly dual purpose. These features made the 'Special type' ships the most advanced destroyers of their time. Subsequent classes refined the basic design but did not alter its essentials, except to improve stability after the 1934 capsizing of the torpedo boat *Tomozuru* in a typhoon showed up the prob-

lems of attempting heavy armament on light displacements. The *Kagero* and *Yugumo* classes, the culmination of this development, were excellent all-round destroyers apart from a weakness in light AA guns shared by all Japanese ships, the 25mm based on a French Hotchkiss design being barely adequate.

Larger British destroyers

A somewhat belated attempt to reply to the heavy gun armament of the *Fubuki*s was produced by the British in the form of the 'Tribal' class of large destroyers. Like so many designs produced as a reaction to foreign designs instead of as a result of clear analysis of needs, these were not a particularly successful concept. To obtain twice the number of 4.7in guns carried in previous classes, the 'Tribals' replaced single mountings by twins. Despite an increase in size this entailed a reduction in torpedo armament to a single quadruple set of tubes. Destroyers at this period did not have

the necessary fire control, nor were they steady enough gun platforms, to take advantage of an increased number of guns. That the advantages given by the increased number of guns were more apparent than real is shown by the fact that, despite prolonged discussion at the design stage as to whether such theoretically powerful ships should be called 'destroyers' any longer, they were consistently used as just another class of destroyers. The half-hearted nature of the 40-degree maximum elevation of the main armament was shown up by the replacement of one of the twin 4.7in mounts by the truly dual purpose capacity of a twin 4in just as soon as early war experience showed the real deadliness of the threat from the air. An even more striking demonstration of this was in the 'L' class where delays in the production of the large and over-complicated mounting for the new and more powerful Mk XI 4.7in gun resulted in four of the class going into service with four twin 4in instead of three twin 4.7in mountings. These improvised anti-aircraft de-

---

11. The range was 22,000yds at 49kts – or up to 40,000yds at slower speeds – greater by a factor of three than was possible for the torpedoes of other nations. The greater size of the torpedo also produced a warhead which was 50 per cent larger than foreign ones. This splendid weapon made the Japanese the greatest and most successful proponents of surface torpedo attack.

The Karl Galster *(or Z 20) was one of the 1936 Type destroyers; the next group of German destroyers and their successors would not have names, bearing only 'Z' (Zerstörer = Destroyer) numbers. A big and handsome ship but crippled like all German destroyers of this generation by unreliable machinery and inadequate seaworthiness. (CMP)*

stroyers proved more useful than their properly-armed sisters.

The 'L' and 'M' classes were an attempt to make full use of a new 4.7in gun firing a heavier shell, and using a heavier gun mounting than their immediate predecessors of the 'J' and 'K' classes. These latter were much better balanced ships than the 'Tribal's with only one less twin 4.7in mounting but two sets of torpedo tubes. They also re-introduced the weight-saving and strength-giving features of longitudinal construction to British destroyer design[12] and were one-funnelled. After war broke out the 'War Emergency' programme required a standard destroyer design to build in quantity, and this design was modified for the purpose. The main change was to go back to the simplicity of four single gun mounts[13], but the hull design was also modified to make the ships slightly smaller – and then the next groups had to be slightly enlarged – so some of the advantages of standardisation were thrown away. The last classes ('Z's and the various groups of the 'C's) of this sequence of destroyers adopted a new 4.5in (114mm) gun which fired a heavier shell than its 4.7in calibre predecessor.

America and Germany: renewed construction

Both the Americans and Germans did not build new destroyers until comparatively late in the inter-war period, the latter because of their position as the defeated power, and the former because of the vast numbers of war emergency programme 'four stackers' to hand. Both navies adopted a similar layout of five single 5in guns. The Americans with the 5in 38-calibre dual purpose gun made an excellent choice of weapon, which with their judicious adoption of high pressure steam after adequate development trials helps to explain the excellence of their eventual 'war standard' design, the *Fletcher* class that was produced in such huge numbers. This design had evolved via a series of very different classes during the mid- to late-1930s. First the *Farragut*s introduced the 5in gun; then the *Porter*s went for gunpower (like the British 'Tribal's, they had four twin mountings and like the British ships this increase in gunpower was more impressive on paper than in practice). These 'super-destroyers' were also intended to some extent to fill the gap left by the lack of light cruisers in the US Navy. The *Mahan*s introduced high-pressure steam, and they had twelve torpedo tubes, while the following *Gridley*, *Bagley* and *Benham* classes mounted as many as sixteen. The final prewar class, the *Benson*s, had eight tubes and were similar in basic layout to the *Fletcher*s, but the latter had 400 tons more displacement (and therefore could absorb the great increases in light AA guns that war experience showed to be necessary) and had a flush deck instead of a raised forecastle. They were eventually succeeded on the stocks by a new class which carried three twin 5in mountings instead of the five singles, which gave less crowding along the centreline of the ship, but had the disadvantage of putting a concentration of weight forward where two of the three main mountings were positioned. This meant that the *Sumner* class were less satisfactory sea-boats than their predecessors, and the same disadvantage applied to the slightly longer *Gearing*s which were the last class of destroyers to be built for the USN before the end of the war.

After her defeat in 1918 Germany was restricted to a small navy for coastal defence only and reverted in the 1920s to her old policy of building small destroyers (later re-classed as torpedo boats) with three 4.1in (105mm) guns and six torpedo tubes. These proved extremely useful ships in the English Channel when war came – excellent escorts capable of inflicting fatal damage on larger adversaries. The tor-

The Americans introduced high pressure steam machinery exemplified here by the Mahan *class destroyer* Drayton *on trials in July 1936. (USN)*

---

12. One destroyer, *Ardent*, had been built longitudinally before the First World War. It was a sign of the times that this ship was built at the suggestion of her builders (Denny of Dumbarton) but that two decades later the Admiralty had to pressure reluctant shipbuilders to adopt this 'new' method of construction with the 'J's.

13. Partly because of supply difficulties with 4.7in mountings, partly to give an enhanced high angle capacity, the majority of the first two 'War Emergency' classes – the 'O's and the 'P's – had old 4in guns instead, and proved very useful ships, once again showing how the theoretically weaker armament was, if anything, *more* useful than the intended one.

pedo role was further emphasised in the 1930s by the building of two groups (1935 and 1937 Types) which had only one 4.1in gun (mounted aft) though with a good light anti-aircraft armament; they were considered undergunned and were less actively employed. The final group of such ships (1939 Type) were enlarged versions with four 4.1in guns and were as successful as the original vessels of the type. The German navy would have done well to build more of these excellent vessels rather than the larger destroyers on which it concentrated from 1934. These resembled American and French contemporaries in having five single 5in (127mm) mountings, but they suffered badly from operating defects. Their problems with high pressure steam machinery, which gave them a very poor record of availability, have already been noted. When they did get to sea their ability to fight their guns in a seaway was noticeably worse than their smaller British equivalents. This was compounded in later classes (the later versions of the 1936 type) by the replacement of the 5in by 5.9in (150mm) weapons – really too large for such comparatively small vessels. The situation was made even worse by the use of a large and complex twin mounting forward, which weighed 97 tons and made the vessels even less suitable for fighting at sea. The classic illustration of the futility of mounting such heavy weapons was seen in an engagement in the Bay of Biscay in 1943 when two British cruisers (*Glasgow* and *Enterprise*) took on and defeated a large German destroyer and torpedo boat force which had more heavy guns of approximately the same calibre – a clear demonstration of the importance of having a good gun platform and the superior gunnery control possible in a larger ship. The failures of machinery and armament were reflected in the reversion to 5in guns and the adoption of diesel engines in the late war designs.

Torpedo boats and escort destroyers

During the inter-war years the Italians, French and Japanese all built somewhat similar torpedo boats – in essence smaller destroyers – whilst the destroyers built by the Scandinavian navies were nearly all of this type.[14] These were useful vessels in the context of fighting in more confined waters like the Mediterranean, the Baltic, or the seas around Britain. Neither the British nor Americans, however, built vessels of this type at that time. The former instead built escort sloops, which were in effect slower, sturdier destroyers without a torpedo armament at all (vessels which were to prove invaluable when war came). However there was still a requirement for a smaller destroyer for escort work in confined waters, and this was the origin of the 'Hunt' class, designed just before the war. As the result of a most uncharacteristic error in design calculations made by both the Admiralty designers and by the lead yard, these were made just too small and proved too unstable to take the original design armament of three twin 4in anti-aircraft guns and one set of triple tubes. A hasty re-design left them with only two 4in mountings and no torpedo tubes at all – in effect a sloop armament on a somewhat faster hull. With a broader hull the second group of these ships

carried the intended original gun armament, whilst the third group reverted to two gun mountings so they could incorporate a triple torpedo tube mounting.

Only the fourth group – the *Brecon* and *Brissenden* built by Thornycroft to their own design – carried the full armament as originally conceived. This pair were very interesting ships, with the forecastle deck extended nearly the whole length of the vessel and other hull form innovations that prefigured later frigate developments. They were, however, considerably more expensive than their Admiralty-designed sisters. The 'Hunts' did indeed prove useful escorts and particularly anti-aircraft vessels in the Mediterranean, North Sea and English Channel but as they were very 'tight' designs with hardly any capacity for accommodating necessary growth and alterations, it is scarcely surprising that they went out of service very rapidly after the end of the War. Larger destroyers had greater flexibility for modification to suit changed circumstances, as would be shown both by the conversion of old 'V & W's to first anti-aircraft 'Wairs' and then long range anti-submarine escorts in the late 1930s and early '40s[15] and by the alteration to the

A wartime photograph of the torpedo-armed Type III 'Hunt' class escort destroyer HMS *Talybont. This group was distinguishable from the Types I and II by an upright funnel with a sloping top, visibly thinner than the slightly raked funnels of the other groups.* (CMP)

14. Though in the 1940s, following Italian models, the Swedes began to build larger destroyers.

15. The 'Wairs' were given a 'Hunt' type anti-aircraft armament of two twin 4in mounts plus lighter weapons. The torpedo tubes were removed. The long range escort conversion (done during rather than before the war) was less elaborate, involving the removal of the fore boiler-room to make way for extra oil bunkerage, plus a couple of the guns and the addition of a large depth charge armament. Speed was reduced to 25kts which was still quite adequate for the convoy escort task.

American destroyer escorts (DEs) were built in vast numbers not only for the US Navy itself but for the navies of allies as well – this is DE 109 which was completed in 1943 for the French navy as Marocain. *After the war many more of these American ships found new homes in other navies (as did quite a few British destroyers and escort destroyers). The last of the war-surplus DDs and DEs have only recently been leaving the service of a range of smaller navies.* Marocain *herself was returned to the USA in 1964. (CMP)*

large number of 'war emergency' destroyers available in the early 1950s to stop-gap anti-submarine frigates.

The Americans also had a large stock of old destroyers in the form of the 'four stackers', of which many went to Britain in the 'destroyers for bases' Lend-Lease deal of 1940. A more crowded design than their British contemporaries, they were less suited for radical conversion; but converted they were, both the British and Americans producing long range anti-submarine versions and the latter also producing destroyer-minesweeper, seaplane tender and amphibious transport versions. Other nations also used old destroyers for escort functions, but their conversions tended to be less radical and elaborate.

The Americans followed up the example set by the 'Hunt' class by producing their own design for a small destroyer. However it seemed that a full size destroyer could be produced for not much more and the design was about to be abandoned as a poorer use of resources when the British, desperate for destroyer hulls of any kind to be provided in the minimum time, placed an order. The Americans then built what became known as 'Destroyer Escorts' (DEs) in huge numbers for themselves as well as the British. The armament of three 3in guns was principally intended for anti-aircraft work and was supplemented by one twin or triple torpedo tube mounting in some of the versions. As the British had also found, the manufacture of both turbine blades[16] and gears were bottlenecks which held back mass-production of the hulls, so various groups of these smaller and slower destroyers were built, some with geared diesels, some with diesel-electric and some with turbo-electric machinery.

16. Steam turbines, during this period, were the obvious machinery for destroyers, giving both speed and flexibility in producing power. They replaced reciprocating steam machinery (never very reliable or satisfactory at the higher speeds) almost as soon as they appeared. Diesels never appeared to be a viable competitor – the German attempts to build diesel-powered destroyers were aborted by the end of the war in 1945, at which time gas turbine technology had not yet reached the stage at which it was a possible alternative.

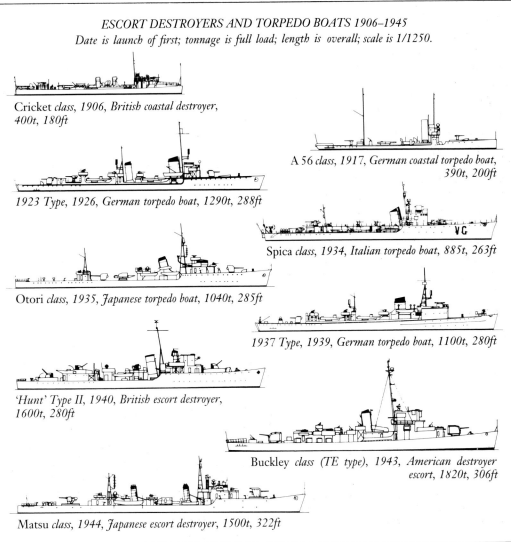

ESCORT DESTROYERS AND TORPEDO BOATS 1906–1945
Date is launch of first; tonnage is full load; length is overall; scale is 1/1250.

Cricket *class, 1906, British coastal destroyer, 400t, 180ft*

A 56 *class, 1917, German coastal torpedo boat, 390t, 200ft*

1923 Type, 1926, German torpedo boat, 1290t, 288ft

Spica *class, 1934, Italian torpedo boat, 885t, 263ft*

Otori *class, 1935, Japanese torpedo boat, 1040t, 285ft*

1937 Type, 1939, German torpedo boat, 1100t, 280ft

'Hunt' Type II, 1940, British escort destroyer, 1600t, 280ft

Buckley *class (TE type), 1943, American destroyer escort, 1820t, 306ft*

Matsu *class, 1944, Japanese escort destroyer, 1500t, 322ft*

The Italian destroyer Carabiniere *of the 'Soldati' class, seen here postwar, was completed at the end of 1938. She shows the standard Italian layout of twin gun mountings fore and aft, and single funnel. She also had a fifth standard 4.7in gun mounted on the deckhouse between the two sets of torpedo tubes unlike the rest of her classmates which had a short gun for firing starshell in this position. (CMP)*

New roles for the destroyer

From the start the experience of the Second World War emphasised the anti-aircraft and anti-submarine side of destroyer design at the expense of, though not to the exclusion of, surface gun and torpedo attack. No nation had provided adequately for close-in defence against aircraft so Oerlikons, Bofors and similar weapons were added wherever space could be found on destroyers' already crowded superstructures. Nor had any nation realised the extent of the need for heavy anti-submarine armament,[17] so depth charges proliferated on sterns and later new ahead-throwing weapons ('Hedgehog' and 'Squid') were introduced. New sensors were developed – by 1939 other navies were following the Royal Navy's example in fitting their destroyers and other escorts with some form of sonar whilst soon afterwards radar reached a sufficient stage of development to become available for use at sea. As soon as production permitted (and, usually,

rather before reliability was adequate), radar sets for both detection and fire control purposes were rushed into service aboard destroyers. By the end of the War the concept of using such ships for fighter and coastal craft control and as radar pickets for the defence of the fleet were well advanced. Corresponding improvements were made in radio communications, and the use of 'Huff Duff'[18] and countermeasures to glider-bomb attacks on escorts marked the origins of electronic warfare at sea. All these new devices required manning and the accommodation of them and their crews on board added to the never ceasing demand for increases in size and tonnage as well as indicating new directions for warship design. By the middle of the Second World War these trends meant that the torpedo boat destroyer was becoming something entirely different.

In 1939 the Japanese produced a design for a fast anti-aircraft escort for carriers based around four twin 3.9in (100mm) dual purpose fully enclosed gun mountings. The design was modified by adding a single quadruple torpedo tube mounting to make these large (3700-ton full load) ships capable of destroyer duties as well. These very successful *Akitsuki* class ships were designed to fill a purpose for which the British and Americans built anti-aircraft cruisers.

In the end the Americans reached very much the same goal by a different route in the

Sumner and *Gearing* classes. A similar process of development of the destroyer into a fleet escort with a primary anti-aircraft role can be seen in the Royal Navy. Again, as with the American twin 5in mounting, a weapon first designed as secondary anti-aircraft armament for a larger vessel – the twin 4.5in 'between decks' mounting – was adopted for destroyer use. This appeared in the 1942 'Battle' class design, where both gun mountings carried were mounted forward. A formidable armament of Bofors guns guarded against close attack from astern. The modified design of the second group showed the influence of conservative criticism from senior naval officers in the unnecessary addition of two extra torpedoes and a single extra 4.5in gun. However a step forward was the equipping of these ships before completion with a 'Squid' ahead-throwing anti-submarine weapon.

The destroyer was being modified to be a ship whose primary weapons were beginning to be anti-aircraft or anti-submarine rather than anti-surface ship. After the war, torpedoes (except anti-submarine ones) would begin to be neglected in favour of guns and missiles in one line of development, and anti-submarine devices in another. Already destroyers were becoming too large to be flotilla vessels – so big that they were beginning to resemble the light cruisers of an earlier era. To an extent the role

A June 1942 photograph of the new Japanese anti-aircraft destroyer Akitsuki. *The big twin turrets for 3.9in guns are clearly her main armament – the single quadruple torpedo tube mounting was literally an afterthought. The destroyer's postwar fate as an AA escort is foreshadowed in this impressive ship. (CMP)*

17. Britain, with the greatest need – because her trade was the most vulnerable to submarine attack – had partially noted the lessons of the First World War and had produced suitable designs for escorts (sloops and destroyer conversions) before the war began. However unrealistically high hopes for the performance of 'Asdic' (sonar) and the unexpected and unpredictable fall of the entire Atlantic coast of North West Europe to the Axis in 1940 combined to falsify expectations. Those who like to use hindsight to condemn the unprepared have better targets in the US Navy's wilful rejection of convoy in 1941 and even more so in the failure of the Japanese to begin to consider trade defence before they found the US submarine campaign in the Pacific destroying their capacity to wage war.

18. High frequency direction finding (HF/DF or 'Huff Duff') – perhaps even more important than radar or code-breaking in achieving the defeat of the U-boat. The Germans could not believe that an adequate direction finder could be fitted aboard an escort and continued to use their radios (which were, indeed, essential to the form of centralised control of wolf-pack attacks practised by U-boat command) and therefore advertised their location.

A postwar photograph of the Gearing class destroyer USS Turner of 1945 is a clear illustration of the disadvantages of having the weight of two gun mountings, concentrated forward. (CMP)

of surface torpedo attack (in any case diminishing in importance) would revert to a smaller type of fast torpedo boat – MTBs and FPBs – themselves involved in a seemingly inevitable rise in size and power. Destroyer speed would increasingly be vital for escorts intended to counter new fast submarine designs, but absolute high speed became increasingly less relevant in an era where the margin of speed of aircraft over ship literally rocketed to enormous levels.

Even towards the end of the Second World War in bad weather or at night – or just in cases of dire necessity – traditional destroyer tactics using torpedo attack (and the threat of torpedo attack) against larger ships continued to be used. The skilful and gallant defence of an Arctic convoy by Sherbrooke and his flotilla against *Admiral Hipper* and *Admiral Scheer* can be matched by American destroyer and DE at-

Right: No big guns facing aft at all: merely massed batteries of 40mm Bofors guns – it is no wonder that the more hidebound senior officers were dismayed by the 'Battle' class. The first British fleet destroyers to be designed from the start for AA work, their two twin 4.5in mountings were both forward. This picture shows Corunna *and* Barrosa *in 1952. (CMP)*

Below: One of the largest class of destroyers ever built, USS Kidd (DD 661) photographed just after completion in 1943 was some two-thirds through the sequence from the name-ship Fletcher *of 1942 to* Rooks *of 1944. A good balanced design well suited to the needs of Pacific warfare, the Fletchers were armed with perhaps the best destroyer gun of the time, the 5in/38-calibre dual purpose weapon in a single mount.*

tacks against *Yamato* and her companions off Cape Engano in defence of the escort carrier force. The successful use of PT-boats and destroyers (which included one Australian) by the Americans against the Japanese fleet advancing to its doom in Surigao Strait compares to an even more textbook attack by a British flotilla which sank the Japanese cruiser *Haguro*. However by 1945 the day of the traditional destroyer was almost over: the fate of remaining British and American war construction destroyers would symbolise this as they became improvised anti-submarine frigates or fleet escorts with guided anti-aircraft missiles. In many ways the new frigates would be destroyers with a primary anti-submarine function whilst those ships which would be called 'destroyers' were more accurately the successors of the anti-aircraft cruisers of an earlier generation.

David Lyon

Destroyers: Typical Vessels 1906–1945

Ship or Class	Nationality	Dispt (tons) Normal Full load	Dimensions Feet – Inches Metres	Armament Main guns Torpedoes	Speed (max design kts)	Launch Year	Numbers built
Coastal Destroyer TB group	British	225* c400	175–0 × 17–6 × 6–0 53.3 × 5.3 × 1.8	2–12pdr 3–18in	26	1906	36
G 132 class	German	414 544	215–6 × 22–11 × 8–6 65.7 × 7.0 × 2.6	4–52mm 3–45cm	28	1906	5
TARTAR ('Tribal' group)	British	850 1200?	207–0 × 26–0 × 10–0 82.3 × 7.9 × 3.0	3–12pdr 2–18in	33	1907	12
SWIFT	British	2170* 2390	353–9 × 34–2 × 10–6 107.8 × 10.4 × 3.2	4–4in 2–18in	35	1907	1
SMITH class	American	700 900	293–8 × 26–0 × 8–0 89.6 × 7.9 × 2.4	5–3in 3–18in	28	1908	5
BEAGLE group	British	945* 1100	275–0 × 28–1 × 8–6 83.8 × 8.6 × 2.6	1–4in 3–12pdr 2–21in	27	1909	16
NOVIK	Russian	1280* 1590	336–3 × 31–3 × 9–10 102.5 × 9.5 × 3.0	4–4in 8–18in	36	1911	1
V 25 class	German	812 975	257–7 × 27–3 × 10–1 78.5 × 8.3 × 3.3	3–88mm 6–50cm	33.5	1914	30
Admiralty 'M' class	British	900 1100	273–4 × 26–8 × 8–6 83.3 × 8.1 × 2.6	3–4in 4–21in	34	1914	6 + 73
POERIO class leaders	Italian	1028* 1216	278–10 × 26–3 × 10–2 85.0 × 8.0 × 3.1	6–4in 4–45cm	31.5	1914	3
WICKES class	American	1090* 1247	314–4 × 30–10 × 9–2 95.8 × 9.4 × 2.8	4–4in 12–21in	35	1917	111
'V' leaders	British	1188 1400	312–0 × 29–6 × 10–6 95.1 × 9.0 × 3.2	4–4in 4–21in	34	1917	5 + 23
SHAKESPEARE	British	1554 2009	329–0 × 31–6 × 12–6 100.3 × 9.6 × 3.8	5–4.7in 6–21in	36	1917	5 + [2]
S 113 class	German	2060 2415	347–9 × 33–6 × 11–1 106.0 × 10.2 × 3.4	4–150mm 4–60cm	36	1918	1 + [2]
CHACAL class	French	2126 3000	415–11 × 37–2 × 13–5 126.8 × 11.4 × 4.1	5–130mm 6–550mm	35	1923	6
1923 Type TBs	German	924 1290	287–9 × 27–8 × 9–2 87.7 × 8.4 × 2.8	3–105mm 6–500mm	33.6	1926	6
FUBUKI class	Japanese	1750 2090	388–6 × 34–0 × 10–6 118.4 × 10.4 × 3.2	6–5in 9–24in	38	1927	20

Ship or Class	Nationality	Dispt (tons) Normal Full load	Dimensions Feet – Inches Metres	Armament Main guns Torpedoes	Speed (max design kts)	Launch Year	Numbers built
'NAVIGATORI' class	Italian	1900 2850	352–0 × 33–5 × 11–2 107.3 × 10.2 × 3.4	6–120mm 6–533mm	38	1928	20
'A' class	British	1337 1747	323–0 × 32–3 × 12–3 98.5 × 9.8 × 3.7	4–4.7in 8–21in	35.25	1929	8
LE FANTASQUE class	French	2569 3300	434–4 × 40–6 × 16–5 132.4 × 12.4 × 5	5–138mm 9–550mm	37	1933	6
FARRAGUT class	American	1358 2064	341–3 × 34–3 × 11–7 104.0 × 10.4 × 3.5	5–5in 8–21in	36.5	1934	8
BAGLEY class	American	1646 2245	341–4 × 35–6 × 12–10 104.0 × 10.8 × 3.9	4–5in 12–21in	38.5	1936	8
PEGASO class TBs	Italian	840 1575	293–0 × 31–9 × 12–3 89.3 × 9.7 × 3.7	2–100mm 6–450mm	28	1936	4
GROM class	Polish [British-built]	2011 3383	374–0 × 36–1 × 10–10 114.0 × 11.0 × 3.3	7–120mm 6–550mm	39	1936	2
'TRIBAL' class	British	1959 2519	377–0 × 36–6 × 13–0 114.9 × 11.1 × 4.0	8–4.7in 4–21in	36.25	1937	16 + 11
SOMERS class	American	2047 2767	381–0 × 36–11 × 12–5 116.1 × 11.3 × 3.8	8–5in 12–21in	37	1937	5
'SOLDATI' class	Italian	1690 2250	350–0 × 33–7 × 11–6 106.7 × 10.2 × 3.5	4/5–120mm 6–533mm	38	1937	12 + 7
KAGERO class	Japan	2033 2490	388–9 × 35–5 × 12–4 118.5 × 10.8 × 3.8	6–5in 8–24in	35	1938	18
'J' class	British	1760 2330	356–6 × 35–8 × 13–8 108.7 × 10.9 × 4.2	6–4.7in 10–21in	36	1938	8 + 16
LE HARDI class	French	1772 2417	348–6 × 36–5 × 13–9 117.2 × 11.1 × 4.2	6–130mm 7–550mm	37	1938	8 + [4]
'HUNT' class, Type III	British	1050 1545	280–0 × 31–6 × 12–3 85.3 × 9.6 × 3.7	4–4in 2–21in	27	1941	28
Z 31–Z 39 class (1936A [Mob] Type)	German	2603 3597	416–8 × 39–4 × 13–1 127.0 × 12.0 × 4.0	5–150mm 8–533mm	38.5	1941	7
AKITSUKI class	Japanese	2701 3700	440–3 × 38–1 × 13–7 134.2 × 11.6 × 4.2	8–3.9in 4–24in	33	1941	13 + [3]
FLETCHER class	American	2325 2924	376–5 × 39–7 × 13–9 114.7 × 12.1 × 4.2	5–5in 10–21in	38	1942	181
BATTLE class, 1st Group	British	2315 3290	379–0 × 40–3 × 15–2 115.5 × 12.3 × 4.6	4–4.5in 8–21in	35.75	1943	16 + 8
SUMNER class	American	2610 3218	376–6 × 40–10 × 14–2 114.8 × 12.5 × 4.3	6–5in 10–21in	36.5	1943	58
BUCKLEY class Destroyer escorts	American	1432 1823	306–0 × 37–0 × 11–3 93.3 × 11.3 × 3.4	3–3in 3–21in	23.7	1943	102

Notes:

Tonnage. First given is 'normal' [marked *] or legend.

Dimensions are length overall × breadth × draught at full load. Names designated 'Groups' had variable dimensions and tonnage.

Launch year is that of the first of class.

Numbers quote original class + similar vessels built later or [never completed].

6

The Submarine

BY 1906 most of the major navies of the world, with the notable exception of Germany, were equipped with submarines. They were primitive in design, limited in their operational capability and were essentially for harbour or coastal defence. In the years leading to the outbreak of the Great War in August 1914 Germany too became a submarine power while development consisted mainly of improvements in existing design. It was left largely to the enthusiasm of the submarine officers themselves to try to point the way in the tactical use of their boats against the die-hard opposition of senior officers who regarded both the boats and their crews with distaste.

Pre-1914 developments

In Britain 1906 saw the completion of the 'B' class and the start of construction of the larger 'C' class. Both these classes were single-hulled vessels of spindle form, that is all transverse sections were circular in form with their centres in a straight line, both had a single propeller powered by a petrol engine for surface running and an electric motor when dived, while both classes relied on an armament of two bow 18in torpedo tubes. Main ballast was carried in tanks internal to the pressure hull, a system both wasteful in space and having the weakness of exposing other adjacent compartments and internal tanks to full external diving pressure. The main difference between the two classes was one of size; the 'C' class at just over 142ft overall and a displacement of 287 tons (surface)/316 tons (dived) was half as big again as the earlier boats.

D1, completed in 1909, was a major advance in submarine design. Compared to the 'C' class, the submerged displacement was nearly doubled, but the main change was the introduction of the saddle tank construction and the change to a diesel engine propulsion system on twin shafts. Like most British, and many foreign, submarines up to the advent of nuclear propulsion, *D1* had the diesel engines for surface propulsion and the electric motors for use when dived in tandem. An engine clutch between the two units allowed for the diesels to be disengaged when dived or manoeuvring. A second clutch aft of the motor, the tail clutch, allowed the propellers to be disconnected from the propulsion systems and for the motors to be used as generators to recharge the batteries.

The saddle tanks were designed to carry most of the water required for main ballast, though some was still carried in internal tanks with all the inherent disadvantages, nevertheless there was a greater longitudinal stability, increased safety from the larger size and greater reserve of buoyancy over earlier designs, while the change to diesel engines eliminated the risk of explosion from petrol fumes and at the same time gave an increase in performance. The armament was increased by the introduction of a stern torpedo tube, while the two tubes at the bow were placed one above the other thus giving finer lines than in the 'C' class where they had been positioned side by side. With the introduction of this class the submarine changed from being a coastal craft to 'overseas', for the first time being capable of operating offensively off an enemy's coast.

The initial contract awarded to Vickers in 1901 for the construction of submarines gave that company a virtual monopoly which would require two years to break, providing development was kept to the basic original Holland design. With other shipyards lacking in experience in building submarines there would be inadequate facilities for rapid expansion in the event of war so that it was fortunate that in August 1911 there was an opportunity for British officers to visit the Fiat San Giorgio Company at La Spezia to inspect submarines building for the Italian navy to a Laurenti design. As a result an order was given to Messrs Scotts at Greenock to build a similar vessel, *S1*,

The British B 2 *underway with periscope raised. Note that the forward casing stops well short of the bows. On 4 October 1912 the* B 2 *was struck while on the surface in the Strait of Dover by the Hamburg-America Company's liner* Amerika. *The submarine was cut almost in two and sank immediately with the loss of all the crew but two. Another submarine of this class, the* B 10, *became the first submarine to be sunk as the result of air attack, sinking after a near miss from a bomb while alongside the depot ship in Venice on 9 August 1916.* (CMP)

The first of the 'E' class was ordered from Chatham Dockyard in February 1911. The class became the mainstay of the British submarine service during the war, fifty-five being completed. The picture shows E 7 alongside the seaplane carrier Ben-my-Chree at Mudros in September 1915 with one of the carrier's Sopwith Schneider seaplanes resting on the fore casing. Other experiments with aircraft at this time included the carriage of a Friedrichshafen FF 29 seaplane on the casing of the German U 12 from Zeebrugge and HMS E 22 which carried two Sopwith seaplanes in the North Sea to give them greater range when intercepting Zeppelins on their way to bomb England. (Michael Wilson)

under licence so that its performance could be compared with similar British designed boats, though before this could be done two more were also ordered. Similarly a British team visited the shipyard at Toulon where submarines of the Laubeuf design were building for the French navy. Although it was thought that they would not be suitable for the Royal Navy two boats of this design, the *W1* and *W2*, were ordered from Armstrong Whitworth & Co, with a further two the following year. In the event none of these foreign designed boats performed well in the inhospitable waters of the North Sea and all were eventually sold to Italy during the war.

As a result of the inspections of the Italian and French designs the Admiralty commissioned a panel of submarine officers to recommend requirements for future designs. A number of criteria were specified for an 'overseas' type, including a surface displacement of 1000 tons able to keep at sea for extended operations in all weather conditions. The first result of these recommendations was the acceptance of a new design by Vickers for a submarine to be named *Nautilus*, laid down in 1913, some 258ft overall and a displacement of 1441/2026 tons, an enormous increase in size compared to the boats already being built: too big perhaps since the boat never achieved its design potential and because of the outbreak of war was late in delivery. As the design could not achieve the specified 20kts expected by the Submarine Committee, the Italian designer Laurenti was asked to produce a design that would meet this requirement. Unwilling to use diesel engines to achieve this speed he produced a steam driven design which Scotts developed and laid down as the *Swordfish*. Like the *Nautilus* it too was unsatisfactory and was eventually converted to a surface patrol craft.

Meanwhile, the 'E' class which followed the conventional development pattern were similar to the earlier 'D' class, but again larger with a displacement of 667/796 tons. Armament was again increased with the introduction of two beam tubes in addition to one in the bow and another aft. Originally it had been planned to omit the bow tube as it was considered that the increased size of the submarine at just over 178ft overall length would not make them sufficiently manoeuvrable to avoid damage after firing a bow torpedo at the close range necessary to ensure a hit. In the event commonsense prevailed and one was fitted, subsequently increased to two, in the light of experience in the *E 9* and later boats. The class was destined to become the backbone of the Royal Navy's submarine effort during the war which broke out in 1914.

It must be mentioned that the French designer Laubeuf favoured the double-hull principle, similar to the British saddle tanks, where the ballast for diving and fuel tanks were retained between the main pressure hull and a lighter outer hull. The Italian Laurenti used a modified double hull principle for his designs. There were several advantages to such a system, not the least being the increased space available inside the main pressure hull while the shape of the outer hull could be adapted to that of the normal surface ship giving better seakeeping qualities and speed. The design also gave greater stability and seaworthiness. The main disadvantage was the increased diving time.

At a time when diesel engines were still in their infancy for surface propulsion the French favoured the steam engine rather than risk the dangers of petrol, though such a design was not without its disadvantages too. There were two major drawbacks; large openings in the hull were needed which had to be shut before diving; while the steam plant took time to close down for diving, or to start up on surfacing, even then there were high residual temperatures inside the boiler which spread throughout the submarine while dived. Diving time in such circumstances was reported to be between 15 and 20 minutes, hardly a desirable trait in war time when the submarine is being hunted.

Germany was the last of the major naval powers to acquire a submarine fleet. *Unterseeboot 1 (U1)* was built at Kiel in 1906 to a French design modified from that of three submarines built by the same yard for the Russian navy. For many years Admiral von Tirpitz had vetoed any proposals for the construction of submarines for the Imperial Navy, stating that he considered them to be of little value. He was eventually persuaded to change his views in 1904 when he authorised the construction of the *U1*. Because of the dangers inherent in the use of petrol engines for surface running, and because of the then unreliability of the recently developed diesel engine, the first German submarines were fitted with Korting paraffin engines. There was a penalty to pay, especially in wartime, in that these engines tended to leave a distinctive exhaust trail which could be seen for miles by day, as could the sparks from the exhaust by night.

Such a late start in submarine construction was in fact to be of minimal handicap since the

The French Ventose, *one of a class of eighteen steam driven submarines completed between 1908 and 1911. Despite their slow diving time many were employed on active operations in the Adriatic during the war. Only one bow torpedo tube was fitted in this class and then subsequently removed from all but five of the class, being retained in* Ventose *where it can be seen in the picture. Also visible are the empty cradles for torpedoes along the saddle tanks, a method of stowage which made the weapons prone to damage in rough weather and meant they could not be fired when on the surface.* (IWM)

Germans were able to take advantage of the improvements already made by other nations, leaving them on the outbreak of war with a more modern fleet with fewer obsolete vessels.

The Royal Navy had had its first submarines built under licence to the American 'Holland' design and the US Navy's first submarines had been similarly constructed at the same time. Subsequent US Navy development followed in succession as improvements to the original rather in the same way that development had taken place in the Royal Navy. By 1914 the American submarine had progressed from being a port defence vessel, to offshore defence and to sea going; the 'K' class first launched in 1913 had a length of 153ft and displaced 392/521 tons, with four torpedo tubes and a surface range of 4500nm (nautical miles) at 10kts.

When war came in 1914, the Royal Navy had some seventy-seven submarines in service with another twenty-five building or ordered compared to the German figures of twenty-nine and nineteen. The French had by 1914

The stern section of the German UB 7 *being lifted off the railway truck prior to being positioned in dock for reassembly at the Austrian naval base of Pola on the Adriatic.* (By courtesy of Michael Wilson)

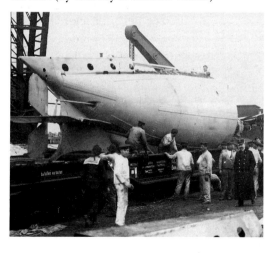

built eighty-nine submarines of which seventy-five were still listed though only about half were in active commission. However, the apparent British predominance at this time was one of numbers only, since only the eight boats of the 'D' class and another eight of the 'E' class then commissioned could be considered suitable for a war. The French, who had started the century as the main submarine power, had lost their initial enthusiasm and impetus and by 1912 had been overtaken by the Royal Navy in both quantity and the quality of new construction. It was the Germans, late starters in the submarine race and who were to make such devastating use of submarines in the war, who were in reality on the outbreak of war, the strongest submarine service.

The Great War

The submarine war of 1914–18 was primarily one for the German and British navies, though French and Italian and Austrian submarines were active in the Adriatic and the French also saw service at the Dardanelles. But the hard service and experiences of war are what stimulate development and it was in the British and German submarine fleets that the greatest development took place.

At the outbreak of war, as has been seen, the Royal Navy had a large number of submarines but comparatively few of them were fit for operational service other than round the coasts of Britain. Prior to 1914 only Admiral Fisher, then in retirement, had pressed for a larger submarine building programme, indeed as recently as May of that year he had written to the Prime Minister, Mr Asquith, saying: 'Myself, I should drop a *Dreadnought* secretly [this from Fisher !] and go in for twenty submarines instead.' There was then a need to expand rapidly

the building programme. One way was to buy from abroad, and this led to an order for twenty submarines from the Electric Boat Company in America. In the event ten were built to this design in Canada to avoid American neutrality laws while the remaining ten American-built were embargoed until after the American entry into the war in 1917. The boats themselves were smaller than the current British 'E' class, being only half the displacement and some 30ft shorter. Nevertheless they were the first submarines in the Royal Navy to have a full bow salvo of four 18in torpedoes. Like most submarines of their time they were built without a gun, but the dictates of war soon altered that and most became fitted at one time or another with a variety of elderly 6pdr guns. Although three 'C' class submarines had reached Hong Kong before the war, these small submarines were the first to cross the Atlantic, albeit with the help of a tow from time to time from the escorting ship. The class became known in the Royal Navy as the 'H' class, where they were unique in that they were the only submarines to be built in a foreign yard. It was also a designation which was later also used by the American, Italian and Russian navies where other units found their place in the order of battle, while six of the batch built for Britain in America were transferred to Chile. Some units of a later, and improved version, built in Britain towards the end of the war remained in service until 1944.

Rumours reached the British Admiralty late in 1914 that the Germans had developed a submarine with a surface speed of 22kts, compared to the 15kts of the British 'E' class. This fitted neatly with the ideas of many Admirals that a submarine should be rather in the nature of a submersible destroyer and thus capable of working with the fleet. Such a concept illustrates the lack of understanding by the Admiralty of the way a submarine operates. At that stage of its development it was not considered as a possible anti-submarine vessel and even in the event of such an action the size and strength of the enemy is immaterial to the out-

The British 'K' class, the largest submarines of their time, were designed as 'submersible destroyers' with a high surface speed so that they could keep up with the battlefleet. Their high speed of 24kts was achieved not by diesel engines but by oil fired steam engines. This photograph of K 12 *shows the large bulbous bow which was fitted to improve seakeeping qualities in bad weather. At the same time the 4in gun, shown here on a platform just forward of the conning tower, was moved from its position on the fore casing where it was too wet for the gun's crew. (CMP)*

come of the action, unlike the meeting of two similar surface ships. Consequently, there should have been no requirement for the Admiralty to order a fleet submarine purely on the basis that the Germans had developed one, which in fact they had not! Nor, as events were to prove, should submarines operate in flotillas as part of the fleet.

Since the two experimental boats, *Nautilus* and *Swordfish*, were not yet complete and in any case would not be fast enough, it was decided to build a new type, the 'J' class. Steam as a means of achieving the high surface speed required was not considered practical, despite the fact that this was used extensively by the French and was incorporated in the *Swordfish*. To avoid designing a new engine the well tried 8-cylinder diesel engine already in service for the 'E' class was adopted, three sets being included in the design. Even so a figure of 20kts for the top speed was never expected, the target being gradually reduced to 19½kts and then 'in excess of 19kts', and so even before the design got passed the drawing board stage it was a failure in that the boats were unable to achieve their aim of working with the fleet. Nevertheless, seven submarines of this class were built. The machinery spaces occupied about 36 per cent of the overall length of 275½ft and they were the first, and only, three-shaft submarines in the Royal Navy.

One of the 'J' class also achieved the distinction of being the only British submarine to be fitted with an internal depth charge 'dispenser'. Two were fitted aft by the main motors and, like small vertical torpedo tubes, were fitted with an inner and outer cap. The idea was not a success since the submarine, even at full speed, took too long to reach the supposed diving position of its target and then was severely shaken by the explosion of the charges. There is one recorded attack on an actual target; in the Strait of Gibraltar within days of the end of the War.

The situation regarding efforts to obtain a fleet submarine by the spring of 1915 was that the *Nautilus* and *Swordfish* were building, albeit slowly, while the 'J' class had been ordered. Yet the speed likely to be achieved by this miscellany was only 17kts, 18kts and 19+kts respectively, while in a renewed demand for submarines to accompany the fleet, made by the Grand Fleet rather than submariners, the speed required had been increased to 24kts. To obtain such a speed, a large submarine would be required and there was the alternative of the use of diesel engines, of which eight of the 12-cylinder engines which were to go into the 'J' class would be required for each submarine, or steam for which two boilers would be fitted. The Admiralty took the steam option, despite the poor showing of the *Swordfish* and the inherent disadvantages of such a power unit which had been well demonstrated by the French.

The 'K' class which evolved were 339ft overall, had a displacement of 1980/2566 tons and as designed were to be fitted with ten 18in torpedo tubes. Two of these tubes were in the upper deck mounting for use on the surface at night, but this had to be removed after trials with the first boats as part of a package to improve seaworthiness. Air to the boiler rooms was through four openings each 3ft in diameter, and the covers of which were telemotor-operated while the funnels folded back when dived. The accident to the *K13* was caused by these air intakes being left opened when the submarine dived, although word had been passed that they were shut. It was one of a number of accidents and disasters that occurred to the boats of this class which led to them being regarded as unlucky, although they did achieve the aim, though faulty in concept, of working with the fleet.

The Germans too made rapid changes to the design of their submarines in the light of experience and the needs of war. On the outbreak of war of the forty-five U-boats either completed or under construction only twenty were available for operations, with the first four boats completed by then only suitable for training duties. Of these the *U5–18* were not suitable for extended patrols and only the six diesel-engined boats, *U19–24*, were fully operational. Immediately orders were placed for a further seventeen boats to be built with a completion date of eighteen months. Also under construction in German yards were five submarines for the Austro-Hungarian navy and with their agreement they were taken over by the Germans in November since it was considered impractical for them to make the passage to an Austro-Hungarian port in the Adriatic under wartime conditions. It was a false premise since in April 1915 the smaller *U21* successfully sailed to Cattaro to begin the German presence in the Mediterranean.

With the capture of most of the Belgian coast the Germans began to consider the building of small submarines to be based at Bruges for operations in the English Channel. Several designs were put forward before an order was placed on 15 October 1914 for seventeen of a new type UB submarine. They were to be of only 127/142 tons displacement and be armed with two 45cm (17.7in) torpedo tubes; no reload torpedoes could be carried. Originally it had been thought that for speed of construction and their small size it would be necessary to complete them with all-electric propulsion with all the inherent limitations that went with such construction. However, the naval view carried the day and a 60hp diesel engine was eventually fitted giving a maximum surface speed of 6½kts, while a range of 1650 miles could be obtained at 5kts. The single

A German Type UC II submarine surrendering at Harwich in November 1918. These UC II boats were considerably bigger than the earlier UC boats which were built and transported in sections and while they still carried external mines they were also armed with torpedo tubes. (IWM)

electric motor gave a dived top speed of 5kts while an endurance of 45 miles at 4kts is quoted. An additional feature was that the submarines could be broken down into three sections for transport by rail. In this way they eventually reached their Belgian base and also Pola, the naval base at the top of the Adriatic, where some units were transferred to Austria-Hungary while others made ready for operations in the Mediterranean and then on to Turkey from where they operated either in the Aegean or the Black Sea. The contract specified a building time of four months, but the first boat was completed in only 75 days, and the last by May 1915.

The design of a similar submarine for minelaying was also considered, and on 23 November 1914 the contract was awarded for the building of fifteen of a new type UC. They were similar to the UB type with a displacement only slightly larger at 168/183 tons, a single diesel engine and again could be broken down into sections for transport by rail. They were unusual in that no torpedo tubes were fitted; instead the bow section contained six mine chutes to carry twelve mines, the chutes being built in at a slight angle aft from the vertical to allow minelaying to be undertaken under way. The first boat was ready in a short space of time and left the yard at the end of April 1915, the whole class going either to Bruges or Pola.

The British also used a similar system of chutes for mining operations from submarines. In October 1915 the Admiralty ordered two of the 'E' class then building, the *E24* and *E41*, to be converted to minelayers, a decision possibly

influenced by the German design, for the *UC2* had been sunk off Great Yarmouth in July 1915 and subsequently investigated by divers who discovered her secrets. In the British case the chutes for twenty mines were placed in the saddle tanks amidships, allowing the bow tubes to be retained but with the loss of the two beam tubes. Six submarines of this class were converted together with six of the subsequent 'L' class, though none of the latter was completed in time to become operational during the war.

Laid down in 1908 the Russian minelaying submarine *Krab* could have been expected to be in service before the German UC type, but Russian shipbuilding delays combined with design faults meant she was not ready for operations until 1915. She was of 512/752 tons displacement but could carry and lay sixty mines at a time, in addition to having two torpedoes in drop collars and a 75mm (3in) gun – in theory a better proposition than the unarmed German boats with their small number of mines. The mines were carried in two horizontal tubes inside the submarine's casing and were laid over the stern by means of a chain conveyor belt. Although she did carry out several operations, *Krab* was not a success and was mechanically unsound.

The small UC boats had their limitations both as a submarine and operationally, with restricted range and speed, the inability to defend themselves and, not least, the fact that the settings on the mines could not be changed

once they had been loaded into the chutes. (This last limitation was also a factor for the British minelayers.) As the war progressed the Germans improved on this basic minelayer introducing first the UC Type II of 417/493 tons displacement, a higher surface speed of 11.6kts from two engines, able to carry eighteen mines and with an armament of two bow and one stern torpedo tubes and a 88mm (3.5in) gun; then the UC Type III of 474/560 tons and improved endurance and performance. Additionally another type of U-boat, designated the Type UE but known as *U71–80*, was developed and built with internal mine storage. Planned as being of 600–700 tons they were of 755/832 tons when completed and in consequence were under-powered and could only attain 10.6kts on the surface. They were fitted with single 50cm (19.7in) torpedo tubes forward and aft and carried thirty-four mines. The mines were laid over the stern by a cog drive through two tubes each 100cm (39in) in diameter and able to carry three mines at a time. A later variant carried even more mines and had the range to enable them to operate in American waters.

France built only four submarine minelayers, and the Italians put three into service including the salvaged *UC12* which sank off Taranto after striking one of her own mines.

From the beginning of the war the British blockade of the German coast played an increasingly important part in the strategic direction of operations and it was in consequence of this blockade that the Germans developed an unarmed submarine uniquely designated and manned as a merchant ship. Completed in March 1916, only 5 months after the contract for her construction was signed, the *Deutschland* was 213ft in length and displaced 1440/1820 tons. On 23 June she sailed from

The German merchant U-boat Deutschland *was taken into naval service as the* U 155 *following America's entry into the war which made her redundant while her sisters were similarly armed and became* U 151–U 154. *Here* U 151 *clearly shows the two large 15cm (5.9in) guns with which she was armed. (CMP)*

The British 'R' class were designed and built as anti-submarine submarines with a high submerged speed to enable them to approach within firing range of their target undetected. The first boat to be completed was R 7, at Vickers shipyard in Barrow, in June 1918 within nine months of the order being placed. The clean lines of the hull are clearly shown in this view of R 7 which was taken in Barrow before completion. (IWM)

Kiel to the then neutral United States carrying some 700 tons of cargo. For the return trip from Baltimore on 2 August she carried vital rubber, nickel, tin, copper and silver, in all some 900 tons, and again successfully evaded the hastily assembled British patrols that were ill-equipped to even seek a submerged submarine let alone attack one. The *Deutschland*, made two round trips to America, though the second boat, the *Bremen* was lost in mid-Atlantic on her first voyage. A third boat, the *Oldenburg*, was not completed in time before America's entry into the war made them unnecessary. The *Oldenburg* and her later sisters were then converted into cruiser submarines with two bow torpedo tubes and two 15cm (5.9in) guns, as was the *Deutschland* herself.

In general submarines were limited to the number of ships that could be sunk in any patrol by the relatively small number of torpedoes that could be carried, but the *Deutschland*, or *U 155* as she was later known, and her sisters introduced the large calibre gun into submarine operations, giving the submarine the potential to sink numbers of ships by gunfire in areas where patrols were infrequent. The British built the 'M' class, coincidentally known also as 'Monitor Submarines' because of their original intended role, or 'mutton boats' from their shape, though the class letter merely happened to be the next in the series. Armed with a single 12in gun it was thought that they would be able to operate with impunity off the Belgian coast to bombard the German defences; indeed there was no need for them to fully surface before firing as long as the muzzle was clear of the water. Building of the four boats was delayed after they had been laid down as it was thought that once their

presence was known the Germans would also build similar boats, and in the event only the *M 1* was commissioned before the end of the war and of the others only two were completed. More practically it was thought that the 12in gun would be more accurate with its flat trajectory than a torpedo at the short ranges used in attacking ships, while the shell would be as damaging as the torpedo warhead. Forty shells could be carried but only eight torpedoes.

Perhaps the most imaginative design of the war was the British 'R' class, built as anti-submarine submarines. With the virtual disappearance of the German merchant fleet from the high seas and the German fleet making only infrequent sorties the main target for British submarines became the U-boat. Yet British boats were unable to convert the many sightings of surfaced U-boats into successful attacks for want of a high submerged speed to be able to reach an attacking position and also a powerful torpedo salvo to ensure at least one hit. The single-hull design was refined to reduce drag as much as possible with superstructure reduced to a minimum to allow for the high underwater speed of 15kts (sustainable for one hour), while six 18in torpedo tubes were fitted forward. An additional feature was the mounting of five sensitive hydrophones forward to aid the detection of approaching targets. The penalties in this design were a low surface speed, only 9½kts, and poor seakeeping

qualities. With the elimination of the U-boat after the Armistice there was no perceived use for this successful class of submarine, of which ten were completed, and they were soon removed from the postwar Navy List.

The inter-war years

With the war over and a reduction in military forces required by the constraints of peacetime finance and the need to demobilise thousands of conscripted personnel, the naval powers took immediate steps to reduce their submarine strength by scrapping the many obsolete boats still in service. There were additional problems for the submariners as political debate arose as to the future of this weapon of war. Britain, for example, as its chief wartime victim wanted the submarine outlawed with all construction prohibited. Such a total ban did not achieve a consensus at the several conferences convened in the inter-war years to control naval armaments, and the best that could be done was to limit their size and numbers. The Washington

During the war the British ordered four big-gun submarines of the 'M' class armed with a single 12in gun and four 18in (21in in the last two) bow torpedo tubes. These giants displaced 1594/1946 tons and were nearly 300ft overall. Only M 1 was completed before the end of the war, and the last was scrapped while incomplete. Although often described as being built for bombardment this would hardly have been practicable since although the gun could be fired with the submarine partially dived reloading had to be done on the surface. More realistic would have been the use of the gun at short range when the flat trajectory would have made the chance of hitting much higher than with a torpedo and the explosion of the shell more effective than that of a torpedo warhead. M 1 is shown here at Barrow with the gun at maximum elevation of 20 degrees; also visible is the 3in HA gun on the after casing. (CMP)

Laid down in 1927 the French Surcouf *took seven years to complete. She displaced 3250/4304 tons and was 361 feet overall. Making this submarine unusual was the small seaplane carried in a hangar aft of the conning tower and a twin 204mm (8in) gun turret forward of the tower, the largest guns permitted in a submarine by the naval treaties in force at that time.* (NMM)

Naval Treaty of 1922 dealt only with capital ships, though it was then known that a second conference was due to be called in 1930 which would place limitations on smaller vessels. The London Naval Treaty of 1930 did affect both the size and numbers of submarines. Firstly, with minor exceptions, no submarine could be built with a standard displacement (a measurement lighter than surface displacement) greater than 2000 tons or a gun armament of greater calibre than 5.1in, though it is strange that a submarine's offensive power should have been measured solely by the calibre of her guns rather than the size and number of her torpedo tubes. Secondly, each contracting nation was given a maximum overall tonnage for the numbers of submarines, and it was agreed that submarines were to be thirteen years old before they could be replaced with newer vessels. In fact this Treaty was never ratified by the French or Italian parliaments while the Japanese paid only lip service to its observance.

Such was the doubt as to the future of the submarine that no new boats were ordered by the British until the end of 1921. The *X1* which was then laid down was a large cruiser-type submarine of 363½ft overall length and displaced 2780/3600 tons with six 21in torpedo tubes and four 5.2in guns in two twin mountings. When completed she was the largest submarine in the world. Although a good sea-boat she had many failings, not the least being the unreliability of her main diesel engines. The future of the three large gun submarines of the 'M' class (the fourth had never been completed with the end of the war) also came under consideration; the *M1* was lost in an accident while the *M2* was converted in 1925–27 with the removal of the gun and gunhouse and the fitting of a small seaplane and its hangar. At sea the aircraft could be launched from a catapult along the forward casing for scouting duties. The returning aircraft had to land on the sea and be hoisted inboard by means of a crane. The *M2* was lost in an accident in 1932 and the project was then abandoned.

The French combined both these ideas in one large submarine, the *Surcouf*, which was

laid down in 1927 but took seven years to complete. She was 361ft long and displaced 3250/4304 tons. Her armament consisted of two 204mm (8in) guns in a twin watertight turret, with two triple external torpedo mountings each of one 55cm (21.7in) and two 40cm (15.7in) tubes and an internal bow salvo of four 55cm tubes. In addition a small seaplane was carried in a hangar abaft the conning tower, though unlike the British *M2* the plane could not be launched by catapult but had to be assembled and then lowered into the water by crane, a task that took up to 30 minutes. Not commissioned until August 1935 her role as an overseas commerce raider was by then hard to defend as the possible enemy was again Germany, but in a controversial career surrounded by myth she had already become a legend before she was accidentally sunk in collision in early 1942.

In July 1920 the Admiralty began an exhaustive investigation into the staff requirements for submarine minelayers. Several designs were considered but the main point in question was whether the mines should be stowed internally, as in the German UE type during the War, or externally in chutes, as was the case in the existing 'L' class conversions. In 1927 the third of the 'M' class was converted to carry 100 standard contact mines with mining rails fitted to the top of the pressure hull along two-thirds of the submarine's length, allowing the mines to be laid over the stern with the submarine either dived or surfaced. The mining arrangements were completely satisfactory and led to the subsequent construction of the *Porpoise* class, though as a submarine the *M3* took an inordinate time to dive – up to 13 minutes in rough weather – due to the slow flooding of the casing which held 600 gallons of water when full. The submarine was scrapped after the completion of the trials.

The United States also built a large minelaying submarine, the *Argonaut*, which was launched in 1927 and which at 381ft overall was the longest American submarine to be built until the *Triton* with her twin nuclear reactors was laid down in 1956. Unlike the British, the

Americans went for internal stowage for the sixty moored mines carried and which were launched through two 40in tubes at the stern of the submarine. This was the only dedicated minelaying submarine built by the Americans. It must be added that the French retained the proven wartime system of having the mines in external chutes and the six boats of the *Saphir* class completed between 1930 and 1937 were all of this design. Each submarine carried thirty-two mines in sixteen chutes located in the side tanks amidships. One submarine of this class, the *Rubis*, laid 683 mines in a record 28 patrols between 1940 and 1944.

At the end of the war, and in the immediate postwar years Japanese submarine design was based on the British 'L' class, French Schneider-Laubeuf or Italian Fiat-Laurenti designs. The Washington Naval Treaty in 1922 and the later London Treaty limited the Japanese navy to a battleship tonnage considerably less than her expectations, especially in relation to that allocated to the United States. Consequently the Japanese navy reconsidered its strategy, which in turn led to the construction of large oceangoing submarines with a high surface speed and long range, capable of operating far out in the Pacific in an attacking role against the American battlefleet. A large number of such boats were built in the period to 1941, with a surface displacement of up to 2919 tons, a surface speed in excess of 20kts and a powerful gun armament to back up the torpedoes. As they might have to operate in flotillas subordinate to the fleet commander some of these boats were built to accommodate a senior officer and staff, and others were designed to carry a small floatplane. Indeed while a number of other navies experimented with the use of a seaplane flown from a submarine only the Japanese persevered with the concept. Here, in the *Samurai* tradition, the Japanese considered its submarines as essentially part of the surface fleet for attacking the enemy's fleet and did not at that time consider at all their use against trade.

For the Royal Navy the biggest postwar change in submarine requirements concerned their role in any future war, since the possible enemy and area of operation changed from Germany and the North Sea with its relatively short passage distances from their bases to Japan and the Pacific where the enemy coast was 1500 miles from the nearest British base at Hong Kong. New 'overseas' types when they made their appearance from 1924 onwards had to reflect this requirement for increased range, and in consequence showed an increase in size; the *Oberon* was of 1480 tons surface displacement compared to the 890 tons of the 'L' class. The subsequent 'P' and 'R' classes were merely improvements on this design for Far East operations.

Once again in 1928 the question of a fast fleet-type submarine arose, with the necessity of a surface speed of 23kts or 24kts, though it was accepted that this could not be achieved and that 18kts or 19kts would be the best that could be hoped for. The result was the *Thames* class with a length of 345ft and a displacement of 2165/2680 tons. They were double-hull boats except near the keel where, in order to reduce weight, the outer hull met the main pressure hull, giving a keyhole effect. Also to reduce weight the diving depth was reduced to 300ft – against the 500ft of the earlier *Oberons* – with an operating depth of 200ft. Diesel engines were fitted and in fact gave a speed of 21.75kts on trials, while the endurance is quoted as 16,000 miles at economical speed. Six 21in torpedo tubes were fitted in the bow only.

Also in 1928 the need for a new class of coastal submarines became apparent, resulting in the similar *Swordfish* and *Shark* classes of about 200ft length, displacing just over 700 tons on the surface and with a bow torpedo armament of six 21in tubes. In all twelve boats of these two classes were built and were commissioned before the outbreak of war, at which time it had been intended that no more of this type would be built, but experience early in the war showed that they were an excellent design and in 1940 this was reviewed and many more boats were then built. A larger class was first ordered in 1935, as the 'T' class. This class were interesting in that as originally designed and built they were fitted with the very heavy bow armament of six internal and four external 21in torpedo tubes (it was thought too dangerous to expose a periscope, and since an Asdic attack was less accurate a shotgun salvo was needed); later two of the externals were

changed so as to fire astern and a stern tube was also fitted.

Another small coastal type made its appearance at this time, the 'U' class. Originally for training purposes the design was for an unarmed submarine under 200ft in length, but this was modified to include four internal bow torpedo tubes. Four of the early construction also had two external bow tubes in a large fore deck bulge but this was not pursued as the bulge caused a noticeable bow wave when running at periscope depth and also made the boat difficult to trim with the shallow periscope depth of these boats. They were of single-hulled construction, and unusually for the Royal Navy, they had diesel-electric drive. Nevertheless, these boats were easy and quick to construct and gave valuable service during the war, particularly in the Mediterranean.

Under the Treaty of Versailles in 1919 Germany was forbidden to build or possess any submarines, but on 16 March 1935 Hitler repudiated the treaty and with it the embargo on submarine construction. In June Germany signed an agreement with Britain which allowed her to build a surface fleet of displacement not greater than 35 per cent of the British, while submarine tonnage was established at 45 per cent of the British – with parity under certain conditions.

In the years after the 1918 Armistice German interest and experience in submarine construction had been kept alive by the design and building of several submarines in shipyards outside Germany for other nations. Thus, two oceangoing boats of 505/620 tons had been built in Holland for Turkey in 1927, five boats of various displacements in Finland between 1930 and 1933 and one in Spain, the *Gur*, of 750/960 tons for Turkey.

This experience undoubtedly allowed the

German shipbuilding industry to begin construction of a new U-boat fleet with little delay and few problems. Indeed, following the signing of the Anglo-German Agreement the first of a new generation of U-boats came into service only a mere four months later, due to this hidden foreign building programme and judicious prefabrication and stockpiling of parts. The first twenty-four boats ordered were based on one of the designs produced for Finland – 250-ton coastal submarines of single-hull construction with three bow torpedo tubes and known as Type II, followed by just two of the unsatisfactory, but larger, Type I.

The first of the Type VII boats, which in various forms became the backbone of the German submarine fleet during the war, followed as the *U27*, launched in June 1936. The original Type VII U-boats were 212ft in length and 626/745 tons displacement, of single-hulled construction fitted with five 53cm (21in) torpedo tubes, four forward and one aft. Diesel engines gave a surface speed of 17kts and a range of 6200 miles at 10kts, while a dived speed of 8kts submerged was possible. Many variants followed as the war progressed, the last being the Type VIIF of 1084/1181 tons and a range of 14,700 miles at 10kts while the maximum surface speed had actually increased by ½kt despite the massive increase in displacement.

The Germans also developed a third type before the outbreak of war, the Type IX. These were double-hulled oceangoing submarines with good seakeeping qualities. During the war a further six variants of the design were produced but the initial boats of this type displaced 1032/1153 tons, were fitted with six 53cm torpedo tubes and had a range of 10,500 miles at 10kts, a figure which had increased to 31,500 miles by the end of the war.

The launch of the Type VIIB submarine U 99. *The Type VII in its various modifications was the mainstay of the German U-boat fleet during the Second World War, over 700 being completed.* U 99 *became famous under the command of Germany's foremost 'Ace' Otto Kretschmer until sunk on 15 March 1941.* (BfZ)

Mention has already been made of the submarine cruiser *Surcouf* built for the French navy in the inter-war years and of the French minelaying submarines of the *Saphir* class. In addition in these years the French also built a number of 600–800 tons submarines suitable for operations in the North Sea or Mediterranean with a number of larger 1500-ton boats with a speed of 17kts for overseas operations around the French Empire. The Italians too built up a considerable submarine fleet between the wars including boats capable of operating outside the Mediterranean.

During these inter-war years in Italy the construction of submarines was given considerable priority and when that country entered the war in June 1940 she had 115 boats in service, one of the largest submarine fleets in the world. They were in the main of two types: medium range types of 600–700 tons surface displacement, and oceangoing classes of about 1000 tons with others exceeding 1500 tons. One of their most remarkable designs of this period was the four-boat *Ammiraglio Cagni* class laid down in 1939. Designed specifically for attacks on merchant ships they had only 457mm (18in) torpedo tubes but their smaller size allowed fourteen to be fitted – eight forward and six aft – while a total of thirty-six torpedoes could be carried. The Italian submariners also had an advantage in that they had

recent operational experience, albeit largely unsuccessful, during the Spanish Civil War.

The Soviet navy did not really start construction of submarines until the early 1930s, until then relying on a number of obsolete Tsarist submarines of various designs, many of them salvaged from where they had been scuttled or sunk. The first design was the 'D' class, with many faults and not very successful. This was followed in turn by the 'L' class – based on the design of the British *L 55* which had been sunk in the Gulf of Leningrad in 1919 and subsequently salved by the Soviets – the Soviet designed 'P' class which was not a success and the numerically large 'Shch' coastal type. Two classes, the 'S' and 'K', were built from 1935 onwards for ocean operations, the former with

German help under the guise of a Dutch company, while in 1939 construction began of the small 'M' class, of only 161/202 tons.

Apart from the one-off minelaying submarine and several cruiser types American development between the wars was dedicated to a possible war in the Pacific where any submarine deployments would be required to travel long distances merely to reach their patrol areas; long endurance and high surface speed were therefore two critical requirements in any design. Completed in the mid-1930s the *Pike* and *Perch* classes had a displacement of 1320/1990 tons, were 300ft in length with a 25ft beam, capable of 20kts on the surface and 8¾kts dived, while their range was 10,000 miles at an economical speed of 10kts. The class also introduced the diesel-electric system of propulsion, a system in which the diesel engines were used solely to provide electric

power as generators and the electric motors were the propulsive force.

Subsequent classes were improvements on this design leading to the appearance in 1941 of the *Gato* class, which were later mass-produced and played such an important role in the Pacific War. Displacing 1525 tons on the surface they could exceed 20kts, had a range of 11,000 miles at 10kts and could operate a 75-day patrol.

The underwater war 1939–1945

The outbreak of war in Europe in September 1939 saw an immediate increase in the submarine building programmes of the nations involved, using the existing peacetime-developed designs. As the war progressed so designs were amended and improved as dictated by the harsh lessons that were learned.

The Germans initially continued to build the three main types developed prewar, though after 1941 production of the Type II ceased. Improvements were constantly sought with more reliable torpedoes, greater speed and range, better manoeuvrability and, after increasing success by Allied escorts and aircraft, greater diving depth. With the use of the French Biscay ports and later with the entry of America into the war at the end of 1941 the Germans introduced the Type XIV, an oceangoing supply submarine known as the '*Milchkuh*', developed from the Type VII and capable of carrying about 600 tons of diesel fuel and a limited number of torpedoes and other stores. It was the introduction of these boats that enabled the Type VIIs to operate in the Caribbean and for the Type IXs to roam at will in the South Atlantic. There was however a factor which contributed largely to their total loss: a rendezvous with supply boats had to be arranged by the use of radio, and for many months the Allies were able to read the German codes so that these meetings were compromised and the boats could be attacked while in company. It is of interest that the Germans were able to carry out trials of refuelling with both submarines submerged, although this was never tested operationally.

Domination of the air by Allied aircraft eventually forced the U-boats to spend more and more time submerged with the loss of freedom to seek out their targets. Efforts to counter the aircraft included the fitting of '*Metox*',

which would detect the radar transmissions of the aircraft, but which in turn was countered by the change of the wavelength of the radar, and by fitting a heavy anti-aircraft gun armament. This too was largely unsuccessful. Another device was the '*schnorkel*' (or 'snort mast' as it is now more usually known), which was an induction mast which allowed the submarine to take in air for the diesel engines while dived. Strangely this had been developed by the Dutch before the war and came to the attention of the Germans when they captured the Dutch dockyards in 1940, though was not then considered worthy of much attention. The British too did not think this device warranted the additional equipment required and it was in fact removed from the Dutch submarines that were fitted with it when they arrived in Britain after the fall of the Netherlands.

A totally new approach was sought to the problems of attack and subsequent rapid disengagement, with a new propulsion system enabling the submarine to proceed submerged at high speeds for long periods. Since 1939 Doctor Walter, a distinguished scientist and engineer, had been testing a closed-cycle engine which, in simple terms, used the oxygen from the breakdown of hydrogen peroxide to burn a fuel which in turn drove a turbine giving a high underwater speed. A special small trials submarine, the *V80* (V for '*Versuchsboote*' or research boat), was tested in 1940 with encouraging results. This was followed by a larger but non-operational boat, the *V300* of 300 tons displacement. Although the boat did not reach the speed requirements promised by Walter it was followed by four U-boats of the *U792* series to continue the trials. During one trial in March 1944 with five Admirals embarked, including Dönitz himself, the *U794* attained a speed of 22kts submerged. However, the transformation to a fully operational submarine was beyond the capabilities of German industry in the closing months of the war, even though several new types of submarine were planned using the HTP (High Test Peroxide) engines of Doctor Walter. By May 1945 only three boats of the Type XVIIB had been completed, though none was operational and they had only one of the Walter turbines giving a submerged speed of 21½kts. Of these boats the *U1407* was taken to Britain after the war for further trials and became HMS *Meteorite* while a second was shipped to the USA, also for trials.

Much more promising were the two designs using conventional propulsion methods of normal diesels and electric motors. They were known as the Types XXI and XXIII, and like the British 'R' class of the previous conflict

German periscopic 'Schnorkel' induction mast for providing air to the diesel engines while at periscope depth (known as Snort in British parlance). The ball float safety valve can be clearly seen. Any rising water level lifts the float and cuts off the supply of air and stops water from entering the submarine. (CMP)

they were perhaps the most radical improvement in submarine design of the whole war. The former was an oceangoing boat with a high submerged speed, while the latter was a small coastal version. The high submerged speed was achieved by radical streamlining of the external hull and fittings and by use of a large high-performance battery.

The Type XXIII consisted of two superimposed pressure hulls, the upper larger in diameter than the lower. The crew's quarters, engines and torpedo tubes were within this upper hull while the lower contained all the battery sections and some of the fuel and diving tanks. There was a large single propeller, a small and streamlined conning tower and no casing. The displacement was only 232/258 tons, the armament was just two 53cm bow torpedo tubes; no reload torpedoes were carried because there was no space available for them. A maximum submerged speed of 12½kts could be maintained for over an hour while an economical speed of 4kts was possible for over 40 hours.

Because of their small size it had been hoped that some could be constructed at yards outside Germany leaving the main submarine building slips free for the larger boats. In this way sections were sent for six boats to be built at Toulon for operations in the Mediterranean with others in Italy and Russia or Romania. Yet the loss of these sites as the German army pulled back prevented any completion of these

Small German Type XXIIIs in a building dock. These boats were built in large numbers to give a small submarine with fast underwater speed, but the war was over before they could become fully effective. Undoubtedly they, and their larger Type XXI equivalents, would have caused considerable problems for Allied escort forces if they had been ready earlier. (CMP)

boats, and all the Type XXIIIs completed were from German shipyards.

The first of these boats, the U2321, was launched on 17 April 1944 and was ready for service in mid-June; in all eighty-three were begun and sixty-two had entered service when the war ended. However, such were the problems of trials and providing training for the crews that only ten operational patrols were carried out between March and May 1945 during which six merchant ships were sunk. Two of the last sinkings of the war are credited to one of these boats, the U2336, off Scotland on 7 May.

The Type XXI was a more sophisticated boat with a length of over 250ft, a displacement of 1621/1819 tons and fitted with six 53cm bow torpedo tubes, twenty-three torpedoes being carried. Like the smaller Type XXIII a double superimposed hull was used, while to aid prefabrication the frames were fitted outside the hull. Heavy plating gave a theoretical crush depth of over 1000ft and an operational diving depth of 650ft. For the first time since the British 'R' class the maximum submerged speed of 17½kts exceeded the 15½kts surface speed, while the power available to the electric motors was greater than that of the diesels. Although built rapidly and in large numbers it is perhaps fortunate for the Allies that only one boat commenced an operational patrol before the war's end, long training periods having slowed the entry into service of the completed boats. Typically, the Germans had already considered

variants of this design even before the first boat was operational. One such design provided for six more torpedo tubes to be fitted, three each side in the bow but firing astern at an angle of 10 degrees outward from the centreline of the boat. Nevertheless, it must be conceded that this design was the most important development in submarine construction of the whole war period and formed the basis of all postwar conventional submarine design.

Japanese submarines, both the large fleet boats and midgets, were involved in the attack on Pearl Harbor in December 1941 but neither in this action or in the months following were they able to make a significant contribution to the attack on Allied warships or trade. They suffered severe losses in the process. During the war production continued with the various cruiser and fleet submarines some of which were still fitted with small scouting aircraft, the Japanese being the only nation to use such aircraft operationally. Medium and short range conventional submarines were also constructed.

Like their German allies the Japanese also began construction of submarines with a high underwater speed. As with the German Type XXI the I201 class had a very streamlined hull cleared of unnecessary projections, large electric motors and a high capacity battery. On trials the first of these boats achieved a submerged speed of 19kts for almost an hour followed by 3kts for 12 hours. Whilst other navies had generally changed to all-welded con-

struction by the closing stages of the War, the Japanese retained riveted hulls for all their large oceangoing boats with the exception of this I201 class, though welding was also used for some of the smaller classes and midgets.

A small submarine with a high underwater speed was also developed, the Ha201 class with some 80 units planned of which only 10 were completed before the end of the war and none was ever operational. Of only 320/429 tons displacement they were armed with just two torpedo tubes but had an underwater speed of almost 14kts.

The Japanese also developed a number of specialised submarine types. Of these the largest was the I400 class, of which three were completed. They were designed to carry three aircraft, with a fourth in a broken down state to replace any loss. With a large range (34,000 miles) and a 120 days endurance it was hoped that they would be able to carry out attacks against American shipping and bases on the west coast of mainland USA and Panama. Submarines of the I351 class were for carrying petrol, bombs and other essential supplies necessary for becoming a floating base for seaplanes. The petrol (365 tons) was carried in tanks outside the pressure hull, but as with so many other Japanese submarines these soon became relegated to the task of supplying outlying garrisons that had been cut off by the American advances across the Pacific. The I361 class was specially designed for just this purpose and could carry 120 armed men or a large quantity of provisions. Later boats of this class were unarmed in that their torpedo tubes were removed to increase stowage of petrol and other fuels. However, in order to build submarines more quickly the class was discontinued in 1944 and small transport submarines of the Ha101 class were substituted.

The Royal Navy at the outbreak of war had a number of submarines still available for service that dated from the 1918 era as well as a number of boats of the 'River', 'O', 'P' and 'R' classes, but more importantly the newer boats of the 'U', 'S' and 'T' classes. It was on these three types that construction was concentrated after the outbreak of war. Development was confined to improving their capability.

As has been mentioned previously the early

The two large submarines I 400 *and* I 401 *capable of carrying three aircraft and a fourth in knock-down condition, together with the smaller* I 14 *which carried only two aircraft. Here seen after the Japanese surrender these monsters were not completed in time for them to carry out any operations, though they had been intended to attack American shipping and installations as distant as the Panama Canal. Note the large waterproof hangar doors and aircraft catapults along the fore casing. (IWM)*

classes, from 300ft to 350ft. With the acceptance of welding techniques following the availability of a suitable steel and the requirement for submarines to travel long distances in the prosecution of the war in the Far East it was possible to convert one pair of ballast tanks to carry emergency oil fuel. In the case of the 'T' class this increased the amount of fuel that could be carried from 132 to 230 tons and a consequent increase of range from 8000 to 11,000 miles at an economical speed of 10kts.

The only new design for the Royal Navy during the war was the 'A' class, which arose from the need for a larger and faster boat for operations in the Pacific theatre. They were 280ft long and had a displacement of 1385/1620 tons with six torpedo tubes forward (two external) and four aft (two external). Their speed was 18½/8½kts. With their welded hulls the safe diving depth was increased to 500ft. Air conditioning was fitted as part of the design in view of their anticipated role in the Far East, but in the event only two were completed before the war was over and neither was to carry out operational patrols.

The Americans started the war with an existing large building programme for the ocean-going submarines of the *Gato* class, which after 73 units had been completed were followed by the largely similar *Balao* class, of which 132 units were planned. Several design changes were made but mainly of a sort that allowed

boats of the 'U' class had two external tubes within a bulge in the bow casing, these two tubes being omitted from later units. Similarly, the 'T' class had their two midships tubes, initially arranged for firing forward, turned so that they constituted a stern salvo with the newly added single external stern tube. Thought was given to converting some of this class to specialised minelayers, as had been done with the 'E' and 'L' classes. Three of the class were planned to be so fitted with four mine chutes on each side within the saddle tanks, and the first, *Tetrarch*, carried out trials in 1940. They were not a success, if only for the fact that there was a unacceptable reduction in surface speed of 1½kts, and the tubes

were removed from the submarine together with those from the incomplete *Torbay* and *Talisman*. This left only the six specialist minelayers of the *Porpoise* class until the development of the tube-launched submarine mine.

All classes of submarine were gradually fitted with both surface and air search radars as the equipment became more readily available and could be made sufficiently compact to be fitted into a submarine. Aerials were fitted on extra periscopic masts.

During the war a transformation from riveted hulls to welded ones took place, speeding up construction and giving an increase in safe diving depth, in the case of the 'S' and 'T'

Arguably the finest looking British submarines ever built, the 'T' class spanned over four decades from when first authorised to when the last was finally removed from the lists of the world's navies, fifty-three being built. Originally fitted with eight bow torpedo tubes and two further tubes amidships by the conning tower aimed also to fire forward, this armament was later altered for the midships tubes to fire astern and with a further stern tube also fitted. The photograph shows HMS Truculent, *one of the later boats of the class built towards the end of the war. Here fitted with both 'Airguard' and 'Seaguard' radar, the aerials being visible aft and forward of the two periscope standards, while at the after end of the conning tower a 'bandstand' platform contains the 20mm Oerlikon gun. The pyramid shape on the after casing is the HF/DF aerial. (CMP)*

A new class of British submarine was introduced towards the end of the war intended for the war in the Pacific against the Japanese where the long transit distances to and from patrol areas demanded a higher surface speed than was available to the older 'S' and 'T' classes. With the end of the war only seventeen of this class were completed though a further twenty-eight were either not finished or cancelled. The photograph shows HMS Auriga, the high bow concealing a bow buoyancy tank which had to be fitted to give greater surface stability. (CMP)

more rapid construction and greater pre-fabrication, while strength was increased to give a greater diving depth. Later, a third class, the *Tench*, was initiated; again basically the same as the earlier boats but with improved internal layout and improved hull strength. Capable of long patrols over the great distances of the Pacific these submarines possessed a degree of habitability that were unsurpassed in submarines of other nations. Compared with

European submarines the larger conning tower gave longer diving times than would have been acceptable in the Atlantic or Mediterranean, but this proved of little importance in the sort of war fought by the US submarines in the Pacific where poor Japanese anti-submarine measures and the American use of radar gave them an advantage.

Through two World Wars the submarine had proved its value as a weapon of war. Dur-

ing the four decades under review it had changed from a rather primitive vessel of only limited coast defence value to a highly sophisticated weapon carrier capable of carrying the war to the enemy over long distances and which had played a substantial part in winning the war at sea in the Pacific in 1945 and which earlier had come near to winning a similar war in the Atlantic. The next few years were to see the continuation of the development of a submarine with a higher underwater speed following the example of the German Type XXI, flirting with further trials of the Walter turbine propulsion system with its HTP fuel until the arrival of the nuclear-powered boats added a new dimension to the underwater war.

Michael Wilson

Submarines: Typical Vessels 1906–1945

Boat or Class	Nationality	Launch dates	Dimensions (loa × breadth) Feet–Inches Metres	Disp (tons) Surface/Dived	Torpedo Tubes	Armament	Speed Surface/ Dived (kts)	Surface endurance (nm @ kts)	Dived endurance (nm @ kts)	Numbers built
SAPHIR	French	1906–08	147–4 × 12–10 44.9 × 3.9	392/425	6–45cm	Nil	11½/9	2000/7½	100/5	6
D 1	British	1908–11	163–0 × 20–6 49.7 × 6.2	483/595	3–18in	Nil[1]	14/9	1750/11	65/5	8
U 9	German	1910	188–4 × 19–8 57.4 × 6.0	493/611	4–45cm	Nil	14/8	1800/13	80/5	4
FARADAY	French	1911–13	170–11 × 17–9 52.1 × 5.2	397/551	1–45cm plus 6 torpedoes externally	Nil	13/8¾	1700/10	84/5	16
U 21	German	1912–13	210–8 × 20–0 64.2 × 6.1	650/837	4–50cm	1–8.8cm	15½/9½	7600/8	80/5	4
E 9	British	1912–16	181–0 × 15–1 55.2 × 4.6	667/807	5–18in	Nil[2]	14/9½	3000/10	99/3	56
L 1	American	1915	167–4 × 17–5 51.0 × 5.3	450/548	4–18in	1–3in	14/10	3300/11	150/5	11
U 71	German	1915–16	186–4 × 19–4 56.8 × 5.9	755/832	2–50cm 2–100cm mining	1–8.8cm	10½/7½	5800/7	83/4	10

Boat or Class	Nationality	Launch dates	Dimensions (loa × breadth) Feet–Inches Metres	Disp (tons) Surface/Dived	Torpedo Tubes	Armament	Speed Surface/ Dived (kts)	Surface endurance (nm @ kts)	Dived endurance (nm @ kts)	Numbers built
U151	German	1916–17	213–3 × 29–2 65.0 × 8.9	1512/1875	2–50cm	1–15cm	12½/5¼	25,000/5½	65/3	6
K1	British	1916–17	330 × 26–7 100.6 × 8.1	1980/2566	8–18in	1–4in 1–3in	24/8	12,500/10	30/4	18
UB48 [UB III Type]	German	1917–18	181–5 × 19 55.3 × 5.8	516/651	5–50cm	1–8.8cm	13½/7½	9000/6	55/4	c90
L1	British	1917–19	231–1 × 23–5 70.4 × 17.2	891/1074	6–18in[3]	1–4in	17/10½	3600/11	65/5	31
R1	British	1918	163–9 × 15–3 49.9 × 4.6	410/503	6–18in	Nil	9½/15	2000/9	150/1½	10
SAPHIR	French	1928–35	216–2 × 23–7 65.9 × 7.2	761/925	3–53cm 2–40[4]	1–75mm	12/8	7000/7½	80/4	6
CASABIANCA	French	1928–37	302–10 × 26–11 92.3 × 8.2	1570/2084	9–53cm 2–40cm	1–100mm	17/9	10,000/10	100/5	31
U1 [Type IIA]	German	1935	134–2 × 13–5 40.1 × 4.1	254/303	3–53cm	Nil	13/6¾	1600/8	35/4	6
U27 [Type VIIA]	German	1936–37	211–7 × 19 64.5 × 5.8	626/745	5–53cm	1–8.8cm	17/8	6200/10	94/4	10[5]
UPHOLDER	British	1937	191 × 16–1 58.2 × 4.9	630/730	4–21in[6]	1–3in	11½/9	4000/2	120/2	49
TRITON	British	1937–44	275 × 26–7 83.8 × 8.1	1330/1585	10–21in	1–4in	15/9	8000/10	130/2½	53
BRIN	Italian	1938	237–8 × 21–11 72.5 × 6.7	1016/1266	8–53cm	1–120mm	17/8	9000/8	90/4	5
I16	Japanese	1938–39	356–7 × 30–6 108.7 × 9.3	2554/3561	8–21in	1–5.5in	23½/8	14,000/16	60/3	5
GATO	American	1941–46	311–9 × 27–3 95.0 × 8.3	1825/2410	10–21in	1–3/4/5in	20¼/8½	11,800/10	95/5	195
I400	Japanese	1944	400–3 × 39–4 122.0 × 12.0	3530/5223	8–21in	1–5.5in 3 floatplanes	18¾/6½	37,500/14	60/3	3
U2501 [Type XXI]	German	1944–45	251–8 × 21–8 76.7 × 6.6	1621/1819	6–53cm	2–20mm	15½/17¼	11,150/12	285/6	119
U2321 [Type XXIII]	German	1944–45	113–10 × 9–10 34.7 × 3.0	234/258	2–53cm	Nil	9½/12½	2600/8	175/4	62
I201	Japanese	1944–45	259–2 × 19–0 79.0 × 5.8	1070/1291	4–21in	2–25mm	15½/19	8000/11	135/3	3
TENCH	American	1944–46	311–8 × 27–3 95.0 × 8.3	1570/1980	10–21in	1/2–5in	20¼/8¾	11,000/10	96/2	31
AMPHION	British	1944–47	279–3 × 22–3 85.1 × 6.8	1385/1620	10–21in	1–4in	18½/8	10,500/11	90/3	16

Notes:

1. The *D4* became the first British submarine to be fitted with a gun, a 12pdr.
2. The 'E' class as built were not fitted with a gun, but various calibres were fitted later.
3. 4–21in plus 2–18inch in *L9* and later.
4. *Saphir* class also fitted with 16 mine chutes amidships, eight each side, for 32 mines.
5. 705 Type VII boats of all variants entered service.
6. Four boats of the class were fitted with 6–21in TT.

7

Mine Warfare and Escort Vessels

THE sea mine and the torpedo, which originally shared the same name, appeared in the nineteenth century; both posed new threats and brought new types of ship into existence to deliver and to counter them. The mine offered the possibility of making a stretch of sea unusable until something was done about it, while the mobile member of the family could destroy the mightiest ship afloat if some intrepid soul could get it into the right place.

Pre-1914 thinking

Mine warfare

For many years it was thought that mines would only be laid in a belligerent's territorial waters, as provided by international law, and, for much longer, that the torpedo would only be used against warships. Hence not much was done about providing either minesweepers, minelayers or escorts.

Virtually all the early mines were moored, and it was soon realised that cutting the mooring wire caused them to float to the surface, where they could be sunk by small arms fire or exploded if a lucky or skilful marksman was available. The obvious craft to do the cutting were fishing vessels or tugs, both of which had the necessary equipment and crews experienced in handling ropes and wires and would be available in great numbers. In Britain, a 'Trawler Reserve' was set up in 1907 and tests carried out to determine the best type of minesweep. Actual fishing gear proved ineffective, but a 'pair sweep' kept at the right depth by 'Kites' based on fishing practice, proved satisfactory and was adopted. It required accurate station-keeping, since a mine would slide irresistibly along the wire to strike whichever ship of a pair fell astern. Theoretically, it left the bows of the sweepers vulnerable or protected only by not very effective 'bow protection gear'

PURPOSE-BUILT MINESWEEPERS 1906–1945
Date is launch of first; tonnage is normal to 1922 and standard thereafter; scale is 1/1250.

Fugas *class, 1910, Russian, 150t*

Acacia *class, 1915, British 'fleet sweeping sloop', 1200t*

M 1 *class, 1915, German, 425t*

'Hunt' *class, 1916, British, 750t*

'Bird' *class, 1918, American, 950t*

W 1 *class, 1923, Japanese, 615t*

1935 Type, *1937, German, 680t*

Vladimir Polukin *class, 1940, Russian, 700t*

Bathurst *class, 1940, Australian version of the British* Bangor, *750t*

W 19 *class, 1941, Japanese, 650t*

– in practice, hits right forward were rare; the mine was usually pushed aside by the bow wave and sucked in again abreast the bridge and machinery spaces, which in a sweeper would be protected by the sweep.

During the years prior to 1914, several designs for minesweepers were produced and proposals made for construction, but, when it came to the point, other calls on available funds always had higher priority. The Fleet Sweeping role was assigned to some of the old torpedo gunboats, which were fairly fast and

had been superseded by destroyers in their original role.

Admiralty studies suggested that a minesweeper would have to be small and simple (to permit large numbers), seaworthy, capable of towing sweeps, ships or other objects, and fairly fast; 600 tons was regarded as the minimum to guarantee seaworthiness, and it was suggested that large seagoing tugs might be suitable. It seemed inevitable that many sweepers would fall victim to mines, which argued for the smallest possible size and crew and

One of the first purpose-built escort vessel designs was the British 'Flower' class of 'fleet sweeping sloops' (this is HMS Celandine, *one of the improved* Arabis class, *in 1917). Originally conceived as minesweepers, they were built to simple mercantile standards for mass-production, and after the introduction of convoys, proved capable anti-submarine vessels.* (IWM)

would rule out carrying any armament. The Director of Naval Construction, Sir Philip Watts, opposed this on grounds of morale and the need to fire at floating objects 'to determine their character'.

Since much work would have to be done at low speed, reciprocating engines and coal-firing were both adequate and advantageous – turbines need a lot of skilled manufacture and maintenance. However, although sketches had been produced, no ships had been put in hand at the outbreak of war.

The submarine threat

In the years before the War, the submarine had matured, and posed a great though ill-understood threat. It obviously had the power to sink large warships if it got within range, and all navies had exercised in the use of destroyers to screen fleets. As yet, all they could do was to charge at a periscope in the hope of ramming or at least spoiling the submarine's shot, and this proved moderately effective. One or two thinkers had raised the possibility of submarines attacking merchant ships, but this would obviously mean killing many of the crews and passengers, and no government seriously contemplated this. Nevertheless, one German officer was sufficiently impressed by English 'future war' speculation to work out the number of submarines needed for a war on commerce; it came out at 222. In a way, this was a resurrection of a French proposal of the 1890s to use torpedo boats – then being touted as the answer to every problem – to stalk merchant ships, closing in at night to torpedo them; this idea was greeted with horror, not least in France, and was dropped.

The Great War

Soon after war started, German U-boats indeed began to attack merchant ships, at first in a casual, sporadic way, but clearly with the potential to do much more. From this was born the escort vessel, in her many forms. The term was not at first appropriate, since she did not

escort. It was obviously impossible to escort every merchant ship, and equally impossible to put ships in convoy, which had been abandoned with the age of sail. It was argued that the owners would not allow it, the captains would not sail in accordance with naval orders, and that even if they did there would be innumerable collisions; furthermore a submarine or warship could easily find a convoy and massacre it. All these things were firmly believed by those who had studied the subject, and all were wrong.

The ideal anti-submarine vessel was the destroyer, which was fast, heavily armed and manoeuvrable, but she was urgently needed for fleet work. Specialist vessels fell into several main groups:

a) The submarine chaser, a fast low-freeboard vessel, somewhere between a very small destroyer and a very large motor launch, operating fairly near shore, usually in a group, and relying on speed to close with any submarine sighted.

b) A larger vessel, often doubling up as a fast minesweeper, more seaworthy and possibly slower than the chaser.

c) The Q-ship or submarine trap: a vessel either converted or specially built, disguised as a merchantman and carrying a concealed armament. Her *modus operandi* was to act innocently and helplessly in the hope of luring a surfaced submarine within close gun range. A lot of effort was put into this type, especially by the British, and some success was obtained, though hardly enough to justify it (see Chapter 14). However, it did bring some early successes when nothing else seemed to work. The reverse of the coin was that U-boats either had to give up commerce raiding or resort to attack without warning. In a war that soon became total, they not unnaturally chose the latter course.

d) The minelayer. There was no need for specialist anti-submarine minelayers, though specialist anti-submarine mines were soon de-

veloped and laid and were rightly much feared.

e) The submarine – least probable of all, but a deadly enemy of her own kind. No submarine could survive a torpedo explosion, and submarines learnt to lie in wait in operating areas and on passage routes. British submarines accounted for about 10 per cent of U-boat losses, plus those caused by submarine-laid mines. In the last two years of the war, much British submarine effort was devoted to anti-U-boat patrols. Attacks on another submarine were normally from periscope depth and were rendered somewhat fraught by the target usually being sighted at something like 2½ miles and by the risk that she would dive into safety before the attack was completed. The British constructed a specialist 'cannibal' submarine, the 'R' class, with a maximum submerged speed of 15kts (see Chapter 6).

Early anti-submarine weapons

For surface ships, the provision of effective anti-submarine weapons proved difficult. Guns were effective against surfaced opponents, but the 3in/12pdr/75mm was about the smallest to be really effective. Bombs of many types – even hand-thrown Lance Bombs – were tried and made a few kills. A 'modified sweep' fitted with several small charges, supported by floats and electrified, had been developed. It could only be towed at slow speed and in good weather – its nickname of 'The Boatswain's Nightmare' tells the story. If it did foul something, a needle flicked over in the towing ship, a switch was thrown, the charges went off and down – occasionally – went the submarine.

Ramming was nearly 100 per cent effective after small craft had been fitted with an anti-submarine spike, but the enemy had to be located and forced either to the surface or to periscope depth. Other devices such as howitzers, stick bombs loaded into gun muzzles in the manner of rifle grenades and depth mines were also tried.

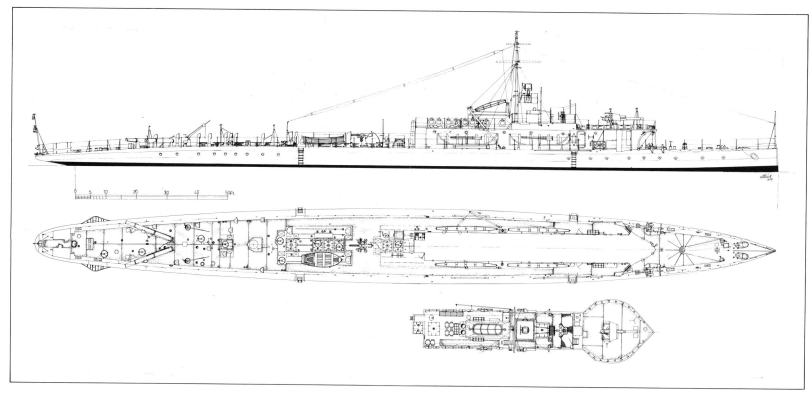

The British 'P-boat', a form of utility destroyer, was designed to resemble a submarine to give them an opportunity to close with unsuspecting U-boats. (Drawing by John Roberts)

The idea of escorting merchant ships, except for a very few troopships or other very important ships, took a long time to be accepted. The first thought was to maintain patrols in focal areas where shipping routes converged, the most important being the western approaches to the British Isles. These were the areas where submarines would find most prey and the patrollers would find most submarines and be at hand to rush to the help of any ship attacked. The fact that the attack, successful or not, would usually be over by the time the patroller arrived, took a long time to register.

British escorts

The 'Flower' class sloops were the first British reaction to the two underwater weapons; they derived from prewar minesweeper studies, with the addition of two 3in guns to engage submarines and – it was optimistically hoped – destroyers, and two pom-poms to drive off the flying machines which sometimes chugged overhead. Great stress was laid on good sea-keeping and the ability to withstand punishment; this was obtained by stout construction, good compartmentation and careful disposition of the bunkers. A single screw was used to reduce the risk of entanglement with sweeps or mine moorings, the magazine was placed aft

and armoured, and great care taken with the arrangement of all hoisting and hauling gear. Minesweepers had more need of old-fashioned 'pulley-hauly' seamanship than almost any other type; their sweeps were in effect their main armament. Their sustained speed of 16kts was intended to enable them to sweep ahead of a fleet.

The general design owed a lot to the old torpedo gunboats, but was drastically modified at the instance of Admiral Oliver, the Chief of Staff, to permit construction in large numbers by merchant shipbuilding firms and operation by ex merchant service personnel. Cylindrical boilers, simple triple-expansion machinery and merchant ship type construction were used, and an improvised but very successful construction programme set up. Guns were mostly old 4.7in – 3in and 12pdrs had insufficient range – fittings were mostly 'off the peg' and Lloyd's did the inspection. There were many rough edges, but the first ship was completed in 17 weeks and was followed by over a hundred others.

In service, they met almost all expectations, proving seaworthy, tough and reliable. The distinctive two-funnelled appearance of the original version and the big turning circle hampered them against submarines, but they sank some, scared off many more and swept many mines.

The next British escort type was utterly different. One of the unexpected lessons of the first winter of the War was that large 'overseas'

submarines could keep moving on the surface in weather which forced 'surface' ships to heave-to. Surfaced submarines were also very hard to see. This suggested the building of escorts like non-diving submarines, which appeared in the form of the P-boat. The first were ordered in May 1915 and construction continued up to 1918. They were of 613 tons, structurally like destroyers but built of mild steel and sufficiently submarine-like to attract a lot of fire from their friends. Their basic armament was a 4in gun, a pom-pom, a ram and, when these arrived, depth charges.

They were good sea-boats, though very lively, and their speed of 20kts was ample for anti-submarine work. Their main field of operations was the English Channel and the Strait of Dover, where they escorted the 'Leave Boat' among many others. The sloping stern was useful for dropping depth charges. At Dover, they might have met enemy destroyers, but apparently never did. In such an event, P-boat men felt that the only chance was to go in and ram, but the designers thoughtfully provided a pair of old 14in torpedo tubes firing over the quarters to give a sailor's farewell to any destroyers encountered. They were considered for the fast minesweeping role, but apparently not so used, although the shallow draught made them fairly safe from mines and torpedoes.

They only scored one confirmed U-boat kill, despite much diligent escort work, but their cousins the PQ, later PC-boats, scored four.

The success of the decoy principle led the British to develop a new class of sloops to follow the 'Flowers' in which the silhouette was virtually identical fore and aft; the mast was placed before the funnel in some and abaft it in others, and to add to the confusion they were dazzle camouflaged, all of which made their course virtually impossible to determine by stalking U-boats. Called the '24' class, the one shown here is HMS Silvio. *(CMP)*

The early success of the Q-ships with their disguised crews and concealed armament, led to the building of many of the later 'Flower' class with a mercantile silhouette, and the same was done with some P-boats, converted on the stocks or built from the keel up. The change from a very low hull to a high one with additional guns made wooden girdling necessary in some cases. In both types, the slim warship hull was a 'give-away' except from the beam, and the coat-trailing role involved casualties, but the PC-boats sank four U-boats and the mercantile 'convoy sloops' a few more.

One other type was based on civilian practice; it proved a disappointment at the time but led to great things in the future. The civilian whalecatcher was designed to pursue large and agile underwater prey, and a militarised version seemed useful as an anti-submarine craft. The 'Z' type were based on a design produced by Smith's Dock for the Russian Government; the Admiralty produced the designs and Smith's Dock built the ships. Emphasis was placed on manoeuvrability rather than speed, and some effort was put into giving a civilian appearance. A dummy harpoon gun was fitted, which seemed like gilding the lily, and the real 12pdr or 3in was stowed athwartships and concealed, while the bridge was disguised to resemble the normal wheelhouse. The stem was strengthened for ramming, and shallow draught, good compartmentation and the best speed attainable on the displacement of 336/346 tons was sought. Coal-fired triple-expansion engines of 1200ihp gave a speed of 13kts. The idea seemed excellent, but the craft turned out very bad sea-boats and construction was stopped after twelve units.

German small craft

With a merchant fleet blockaded in port, the Germans had little need for escort vessels in the First World War, but their minesweepers were sturdy, seaworthy ships with coal-fired reciprocating engines – parallel evolution to their opponents. They also used many 'fish cutters' as 'Vorpostenboote' and 'Minensuchboote', performing similar arduous, monotonous duties to the British. France had to devote

most of her men and industry to the terrible land campaign; she had to obtain destroyers from Japan and 'Flowers' from Britain. For her own small craft she had to cannibalise old torpedo boats for their engines. She built diesel-engined minesweepers and ships analogous to the British convoy sloops. (One of these, the *Ailette*, hit a U-boat from 6000yds, which must be a record.)

The US programme

When the United States came into the war, an immense programme of anti-submarine craft was put in hand; destroyers of the famous

'flush-decker' type were the most powerful, but few were completed before the Armistice. Small submarine chasers were built in great numbers and saw a good deal of action. They were inspired by the 80ft 19kt motor launches built for Britain before America's entry, but were bigger and sturdier.

Their designer, Loring Swasey, planned two 300hp petrol engines, but had to accept three 220hp heavy duty ones 'off the peg' – a typical wartime improvisation. They came out at 110ft long, with a speed of 18kts, a crew of 27 and a

FM 29, *a German shallow draught minesweeper launched at the end of the First World War. Poor seakeeping restricted them to coastal waters. (BfZ)*

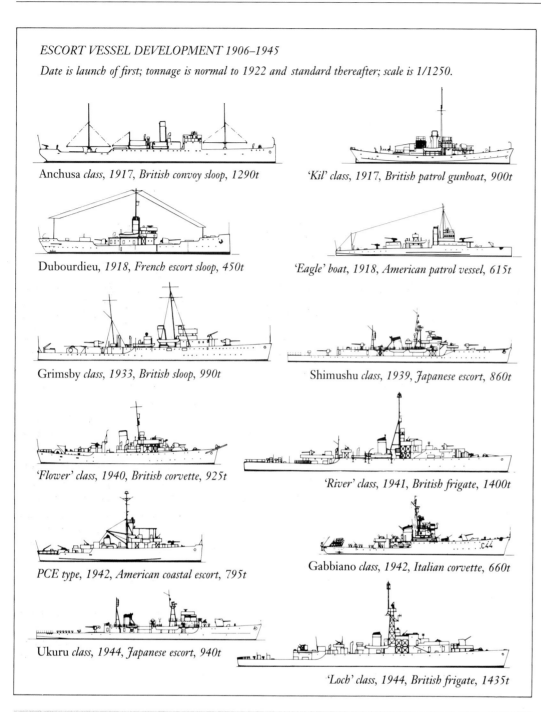

ESCORT VESSEL DEVELOPMENT 1906–1945

Date is launch of first; tonnage is normal to 1922 and standard thereafter; scale is 1/1250.

Anchusa *class, 1917, British convoy sloop, 1290t*

'Kil' *class, 1917, British patrol gunboat, 900t*

Dubourdieu, *1918, French escort sloop, 450t*

'Eagle' *boat, 1918, American patrol vessel, 615t*

Grimsby *class, 1933, British sloop, 990t*

Shimushu *class, 1939, Japanese escort, 860t*

'Flower' *class, 1940, British corvette, 925t*

'River' *class, 1941, British frigate, 1400t*

PCE *type, 1942, American coastal escort, 795t*

Gabbiano *class, 1942, Italian corvette, 660t*

Ukuru *class, 1944, Japanese escort, 940t*

'Loch' *class, 1944, British frigate, 1435t*

radius of 1000nm at 12kts. Armament comprised one short-barrelled 3in as a submarine-killer, two machine guns and a 'Y-gun' for hurling pairs of depth charges.

A useful refinement was the provision of voice radio with a range of 5 miles. By this stage of the war considerable progress had been made with the development of hydrophones, and the SCs were equipped with hull-mounted SC & MB 'tubes' of 3-mile range and towed 'K' fish hydrophones, claimed to have a 30-mile detection range. It seems most unlikely that any such ranges were achieved against U-boats in service, but the sub-chasers proved a considerable nuisance to U-boats in coastal waters, and were the inspiration for the wooden SCs and steel PCs of the Second World War.

A larger type, the PE or 'Eagle Boat' was developed for mass production by Ford. Its general inspiration was the P-boat, whose plans had been taken to the US by Stanley Goodall RCNC. To simplify construction, the straightest lines possible and a single screw were adopted. The PE was of 615 tons full load, 200ft long and carried the remarkably heavy armament of two 4in, one 3in AA, a Y-gun, a machine gun, and depth charge rails. Maximum speed was the same as for the SCs but radius was 3500nm at 10kts, which would probably have enabled them to escort convoys for two or three days out and back, with a margin for eventualities. Despite tremendous efforts, only one of a planned sixty had been completed by 11 November 1918.

Wartime developments

While detection of submerged submarines was still very difficult, the other link in the chain – an effective weapon against them – had appeared in 1915 and became widespread in the following year. This was of course the depth charge. It differed from all previous efforts in relying not on direct hits but on water-borne concussion and in being exploded not by contact or time-fuse but by hydrostatic pressure. It turned the submarine's watery armour against it and provided an instant minefield for setting off wherever a submarine's presence was suspected. German depth charges, on the other hand, were not taken too seriously by British submariners, whose main enemy was the mine.

'Bird' class minesweeper Grebe, *the standard US Navy design of the First World War. They were developed as dual purpose minesweepers/fleet tugs and they could lay mines as well as clear them.* (L & L van Ginderen)

The wartime disruption of French industry restricted all naval shipbuilding, but a limited number of sloops was completed. This is Oise *of the six-ship* Marne *class.* (CMP)

Allied depth charges were mostly of 350lbs weight, containing 290lbs of TNT or Amatol, and originally had two depth settings, 40ft and 140ft. They were credited with a long lethal range, whereas in fact, they could only pierce a pressure hull if exploding within 14ft; out to 28ft they could spring seams or rivets, and out to 60ft they could shake up the target considerably, possibly damaging equipment. Despite these limitations, the depth charge could sink a submarine, and both sides knew it.

At first, supplies were very limited – only four to a destroyer – but by the Armistice, destroyers were carrying 30 to 40 and 2000 were being expended a month. Initially, they were dropped or rolled from racks at the stern, but then the 'Y-gun', a mortar which hurled pairs of charges to either side of the ship, was introduced, permitting the dropping of patterns. About forty-four U-boats were sunk by depth charge in the First World War out of some two hundred losses.

Work on the passive hydrophone was being pushed energetically and it was by now in widespread use, but something better was needed, and the brilliant French scientist Pierre Langevin – also an expert code-breaker – hit on the idea of using underwater sound echoes to locate submarines, icebergs and other menaces. Trials of his device – to be called Asdic in Britain – were just beginning to show promise as the War ended.

About the same time in the mine warfare field, several new ideas for mines and countermeasures were appearing on both sides. The 'Oropesa' sweep, first tested in the armed merchant cruiser of that name, enabled a single sweeper to work effectively, while the paravane permitted each ship to become, within limits, her own sweeper. The 'Flowers' were succeeded by the faster twin-screw 'Hunt' class and the increasing number of bulged ships, almost immune to ordinary torpedoes and mines, led the Germans to try magnetic torpedo pistols and the British, magnetic mines. The latter were made of concrete and lay on the bottom in fairly shallow water. Both types proved temperamental in the early stages, and examples of the British magnetic mine laid in the Dvina river during the anti-Bolshevik 'Intervention' were recovered by the Russians, who passed on the information to the Germans during the 1920s.

Another development which unfortunately led nowhere was the antenna mine. This was intended to sink submarines while leaving the surface unobstructed; it worked on the principle of a 'sea cell' and was developed from an ordinary mine, moored at considerable depth, with a wire rising to a float on the surface. It was used in the vast Northern Barrage, intended to seal off the North Sea, but proved terribly liable to prematures. It may have sunk some U-boats, it certainly sank HMS *Gaillardia*, and unfortunately the idea was repeated in the Second World War, with equal lack of success. As another harbinger of future technology, the British had a prototype acoustic mine tested by 1918.

The inter-war years

Minesweeping

Between the wars, little effort was put into minesweepers; there were plenty in hand, which remained serviceable for many years, and attention tended to drift back to the big ships, as in prewar days. Research and development went on; in Britain large numbers of ships were fitted with Asdic and its use was carefully taught. Unfortunately, its existence tended to convince people that 'the submarine menace' had been mastered. Many lessons, such as the danger of night surface attack, the uses of aircraft and the need for these to operate by night, were forgotten.

Towards the end of the 1920s, new minesweeping sloops were built in small numbers; unfortunately, these were not suited to mass construction. As the 'Flowers' and the 'Hunts' wore out, work began on replacements, but only in small numbers. Aircraft were developing rapidly, especially after 1930, requiring escorts to carry anti-aircraft guns or preferably dual purpose weapons. The Royal Navy had to make do with 0.5in machine guns aimed by eye, but planned a 1.1in replacement, which was a failure. For the inter-war years the problem was usually lack of resources rather than lack of forethought.

As the international scene darkened in the

A successful war emergency minesweeper design was the British 'Hunt' class (this is Leamington *of the later 'Hunt', or* Aberdare, *class); the first group were named after fox hunts, but the later ships adopted small inland towns for a naming scheme.* (CMP)

The First World War 'Flowers' were succeeded in the Second by a smaller and less capable – but more rapidly built – escort, which Winston Churchill dubbed the 'corvette'. Intended for coastal duties, they were pressed into service for ocean convoys and were subject to a huge range of modifications. Alisma, *shown here in April 1942, still has the original short forecastle that was extended aft in later ships.* (IWM)

late 1930s, it was realised that the 'Flowers' were now too old and that new seagoing anti-submarine escorts were needed quickly, and in great numbers. The minimum needed was a ship with an anti-submarine gun, an Asdic, depth charges, a speed comparable with a surfaced submarine and good seakeeping qualities. She was needed to escort convoys through the areas up to two or three days out, where U-boats were expected. Fortunately, Smith's Dock had their latest whalecatcher design available, and this formed the basis for the first fifty-six of the new class ordered shortly before war broke out. At first, they were described as 'whalers', but Winston Churchill found this inappropriate, since they were not meant to hunt whales. He chose a historic if inappropriate name, to which they gave a new significance: that of corvette.

Minelaying

In its purpose-built form, the minelayer was rather a rare bird, but the minelaying task fell into two distinct parts, requiring different types and tactics. Defensive or barrier minelaying was almost a routine job and could be performed by almost any type of ship big enough to carry mines. Merchant ships, old cruisers or battleships could do it. The Royal Navy converted seven old *Apollo* class cruisers before 1914, leaving them with only a token 6pdr armament. Normally an escort was provided and the main problem was navigation; accuracy was vital in both laying and sweeping.

The other, offensive or 'trap' minelaying, was more demanding, requiring entry into enemy waters protected by speed or stealth. As early as 1905, the Japanese had used destroyers for the job, and in some navies virtually all warships were equipped to lay mines. In 1905–7 the Germans built the *Nautilus* and *Pelikan*,

like small cruisers but too slow and small for the job. A 30kt minelayer was designed by Italy in 1902.

The Russians, being a nation of chess-players, subject to seaborne attack over the centuries by the Swedes, British, French, Japanese and other predators, were pioneers in mining, and scored the first success of a contact mine as early as 1855 (off Kronstadt, HMS *Meteor* being the victim). Russia hit on the idea of a submarine minelayer as early as 1908, the potential advantage being invisibility, even though their *Krab* could only lay mines on the surface. However, the country was industrially backward and was not able to complete the *Krab* by 1914, so the Germans appear to have been the first to actually lay mines from underwater. Russian mines were also excellent; Britain had to obtain some to supplement her useless 'British Elias' while the Russian M08 was still catching out the unwary in the Persian Gulf until the late 1980s.

The danger of the minelaying submarine became clear when mines were found off the British coast in areas no surface minelayer could possibly have reached, and much of the vast Allied sweeping effort was devoted to countering their work.

Once they had been supplied with effective Russian-designed mines, the British laid extensive fields, partly to catch submarines and, especially in the latter years, to mine in the High Seas Fleet. The fields further from German bases were laid by converted cross-channel steamers, old cruisers and other large vessels, those close in by submarines and temporarily converted destroyers. A special destroyer flotilla, the 20th, was formed for the job. The ships were a mixture of the 'Leader' *Abdiel*, and 'V', 'I' 'L' and 'R' class. The conversion took the form of removing the aftermost gun and set of tubes, mine rails being

substituted. The job could be done in five or six hours and the mines loaded in an hour. Destroyer minelaying was regarded as very secret, and painted canvas screens showing the normal destroyer fittings were placed along the sides – some humorist even added seagulls and men on deck.

The secrecy earned dividends: the enemy suffered heavy losses from large fields laid secretly in his home waters. Over one hundred German small craft were claimed sunk in the first half of 1918. In an example written up after the War by 'Taffrail', his *Telemachus*, one of the 20th Flotilla, carried out thirty-six 40-mine lays between 19 February and 31 August 1918. The Flotilla often sighted German ships, but were only once sighted themselves – by a Zeppelin which did not realise their significance. Their only setback came from German mines on 2 August, when the *Ariel* and *Vehement* were lost.

The German fast minelayers did not achieve much with their mines late in the war, though the very fast cruiser types *Bremse* and *Brummer* used their speed and guns to destroy a convoy. In the Baltic, Russian mines made things very difficult for the Germans in the Gulf of Riga.

It may be remarked that radio played a vital part in the mine war; radio gave warning of mines located, channels closed, channels cleared, drifting mines sighted and suspicious vessels seen. On the other side, intercepts and direction finding gave clues as to where to lay mines, what success had been gained and where the enemy thought the channels were safe. They might locate a minelayer, though these transmitted as little as possible (Russian minelayers on offensive missions maintained absolute radio silence), and they might permit a warning to be given of enemy forces near the layer's route. Without radio, the menace of minefields would have lasted until survivors from one or more victims had reached the shore, and it would have been difficult to divert approaching ships, or to advise that a channel was now safe again.

After the War, the task of clearance took years and a number of lives, but otherwise the weapon and all to do with it sank back into obscurity; it lacked the glamour of the U-boat

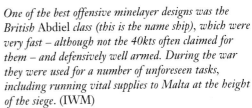

or the surface raider. Skills were kept up, and designers went on designing as far as limited resources allowed.

In the climate of financial stringency, it is very odd that the Admiralty were able to authorise *Adventure* in 1921, and a tragedy that she was such a flop. She was very large (6740 tons), conspicuous, weakly armed (four 4.7in AA) and not very fast (27.7kts). She could carry 340 mines, but otherwise seems a poor bargain. Furthermore, two promising innovations in her, a transom stern and auxiliary diesel engines, got a bad name and were out of favour for years (the transom created a patch of dead water which tended to suck mines back against the stern and break off their horns). The French navy's *Pluton*, of slightly later date, was smaller, better-armed, faster and carried 290 mines.

With regard to armament, a minelayer needed some, though it was obviously desirable to avoid a fight until the mines had been laid and preferable to avoid detection at all. For offensive minelaying, the choice lay between a specialist vessel with such armament as could be fitted, and a cruiser or destroyer with minelaying facilities.

A few British 'E' class destroyers were fitted for quick conversion to minelaying, a few small minelayers were built, and, in the late 1930s, four ultra-fast specialist minelayers, the *Abdiels*,

were authorised. These were of 2650 tons, with six 4in guns, a large mine-load, and a designed speed of 36kts (early hopes and later propaganda made this 40kts). During the war they did well in their designed role and proved invaluable as fast blockade-runners to Malta and elsewhere, but it seems doubtful whether their existence could be justified prewar.

Anti-submarine vessels

In the escort field, as the 1930s went on, the Japanese built a few submarine chasers, the small *Chidori* escorts and sundry small and not very fast minelayers; the primary threat was America and the distances seemed far too great for offensive minelaying or, apparently, for American submarines to be a threat. Although they had participated in the anti-submarine war in the Mediterranean, they seem to have concentrated mainly on the 'big ship' lessons of 1914–18, an attitude not unknown elsewhere.

France built a number of interesting and useful escort types, ranging from the big *Bougainville* class sloops – the true descendants of the sailing corvette – through the *Elan/Chamois* minesweeper/escorts, to steel submarine chasers that succeeded the wooden American-built ones, which were worn out. In 1938–39 the French navy partly adopted the British idea of rugged, primitive ships in which

there was nothing complicated to go wrong, ordering some of the new Smith's Dock corvettes. The big French 'Contre-Torpilleurs' and 'Torpilleurs' (destroyers) were not suited to escort work; the small *Branlebas* class of 'Torpilleurs Legers' made good escorts in summer weather, but their stability was poor and the name ship broke in half in a gale in 1940, indicating structural weakness.

Appearances to the contrary, this was not true of other French types. The *Elan/Chamois* class *looked* fragile but were not; during the brief Franco–Italian combat of June 1940, the 630-ton *La Curieuse* rammed and sank the 1260-ton Italian submarine *Provana* without ill effect. The *Elans* were flush-decked, whereas the *Chamois* type had a forecastle, and all had rounded gunwales; the two 3.9in guns were in a pair aft, which left a blind spot ahead, but otherwise gave a good arc of fire and no doubt improved seakeeping. Their two-shaft diesels gave 20kts and a very wide radius of action. However, it is unlikely that they could have been built rapidly in great numbers.

Across the Atlantic there were many 'flush-decker' destroyers in reserve, and plans to build submarine chasers and patrol craft in quantity. The 'Bird' class tug/minesweepers existed, but attention was concentrated on the Pacific, where a 'big ship' war against Japan seemed the most likely contingency. When war did come, no medium-sized escort was in hand, though there had been plans for small destroyers. Admiral Ernie J King, who was to command the USN during the Second World War, suggested adopting the US Coast Guard's 'Treasury' class cutter design, which was comparable with the *Bougainvilles*, being of 2750 tons, with good gun armament, very good seakeeping and radius, anti-submarine equipment and 20kts speed.

However, it was felt that they were too big and had insufficient compartmentation. Possibly it was also felt that two 5in and four 3in were too weak for such big ships. The decision was to produce something smaller, the de-

A small number of sloops were built in Britain between the wars initially with minesweeping in mind, but by the time the Lowestoft, *shown here, was designed there was a renewed emphasis on convoy escort.* (CMP)

stroyer escort or DE. These were originally designed to meet a British requirement, but the US Navy adopted the type and so it was built in vast numbers, although none was ready before late 1943.

The Second World War

When war finally broke out in 1939, the submarine threat was contained fairly well until the fall of France; the many Asdic-equipped destroyers took a fairly heavy toll of U-boats, which as yet operated as expected, attacking singly from periscope depth by day; their successes were not enough to cause concern. The rapid overrunning of France took the efficient French ships out of the struggle and gave the Germans Atlantic bases which greatly increased the effective size of their force and gave them some air support, while many British escorts had been lost or damaged in the many evacuations.

The Battle of the Atlantic

To the Admiralty's great surprise, U-boats began working in groups, attacking on the surface at night and delivering attack after attack, often spread over several days. The unexpected continuous attacks reminded observers of the party game of deciding who should be thrown to the wolves from the fleeing sledge, and the term 'Wolf Pack' for what the Germans called the 'Rake Tactic' (*Rudeltaktik*), was eagerly seized on by German propaganda.

The newly completed corvette had to be thrown into the breach. However, it was found that without radar, escorts could hardly ever see a surfaced U-boat first, Asdic was equally ineffective against surface targets, hitting by gunfire was difficult, and 16kts – usually 14kts in practice – was not enough to overtake a shadowing U-boat seen on the horizon, while a corvette captain had to think very carefully how long he could search or pursue before beginning the long slow job of catching up with the convoy before it was attacked again.

Having been designed for coastal work, corvettes presented problems when sent into the Atlantic. They were magnificent sea-boats, but so lively that it was said, derisively, that they would roll on wet grass. However, the corvettes were most of the escort force available, and their seasick crews, many just from civilian life learnt to make the best of them.

The German '*Rudeltaktik*' required a lot of radio transmissions and could be very risky with aircraft about, so that the U-boats were steadily driven further and further offshore, while many convoys were successfully diverted thanks to shore-based direction finding and later code-breaking. This thinned their pickings but meant that escorts, too, had to go further and further afield. By mid-1941, convoys were being escorted right across the Atlantic. Refuelling at sea, rather neglected by the Royal Navy, had to be practised in foul conditions. Almost anything that floated could be and was used; the fifty American 'flush-deckers' obtained in the 'Destroyers-for-Bases' deal were invaluable, despite the poor condition of some. Construction of corvettes was pressed on vigorously in Britain and – as is often forgotten – in Canada.

Improved depth charge and Asdic drill, and better teamwork by permanently formed escort groups, successes by code-breakers and the efforts of the RAF and RCAF all helped to turn the tide against the U-boat. Something better than the corvette was needed, but for the time being corvettes and a sprinkling of sloops and old destroyers had to prevent immediate defeat, while plans were made to make use of the time they won. The gradual fitting of radar and other equipment made the escorts more effective but also very crowded. The 'Flower' class corvettes were designed for a crew of thirty-four and by the end of the war were carrying nearly four times that number. That, plus their liveliness, the much longer time spent at sea, and the almost continual danger of attack, put a great strain on their crews.

The 'Hunt' class escort destroyers, after initial stability troubles, proved very useful in the English Channel, Mediterranean and on the Gibraltar run, but they lacked the endurance for the Atlantic. It was worthwhile to convert old 'V & W' class destroyers into slower long range escorts, since their old but sturdy hulls were no longer suitable for high speed steaming. Trawlers were also used in the Atlantic and had great endurance, but were too slow to be optimum U-boat hunters and their crews had the hardest time of all.

The English Channel and North Sea

All this time, several different wars were in progress; in the English Channel and North Sea the enemies were mines, aircraft and S-boats (*Schnellboote*) – fast and skilfully operated German MTBs, using the torpedo and the mine and for some reason called 'E-boats' in Admiralty communiqués. The minesweepers fought against their old horned opponent of the Great War, plus the new magnetic and acoustic ground mines, each of which required special techniques and sweeps. In these areas, sweepers were exposed to air, S-boat and even shore battery attack; around Dover, sweeping had to be done at night, putting an even greater premium on accurate navigation and pilotage.

Prewar, the sloop-like *Halcyon* class had been built; they were good sweepers but tended to be pressed into escort work. Trawlers and drifters kept up their eternal channel clearance work, usually under attack or the threat of it. Easier-built fleet sweepers – the smaller

Large numbers of most war-standard British escort designs were built in Canada, some in Australia and a few in India. HMCS Kenora *was a Canadian-built unit of the* Bangor *class of small seagoing minesweepers.* (RCN)

1940 type were of 543/775 tons and entered service from 1941 onward. Later in the war, the forward 4.1in gun was removed to permit the fitting of many 20mm – up to eight plus a 37mm – to guard against air attack.

These types, plus the many converted fishing and other '*Minensuchboote*' and '*Vorpostenboote*' were usually described as 'flak ships' by the crews of the RAF's Strike Wings. They were built or converted by the hundreds; mine warfare demands numbers and even a small patch of sea needs a lot of sweeping and escort coverage.

The Mediterranean

In the Mediterranean, things were different; mines were less important though not to be despised, air attack could be expected anywhere, and convoys travelled fast under heavy escort. Italy's main problem was to protect her supply line to North Africa, Britain's to keep Malta supplied as a base for harrying the Italian traffic.

At first, normal Italian destroyers were effective against British submarines, though they had only hydrophones. Small destroyers or torpedo boats were equally useful and were supported by many small craft. However, the small British 'U' class submarines were much more elusive and effective. From October 1941, countermeasures were intensified. Active sonar and training were obtained from Germany and first used in February 1942. A specialist escort type was clearly needed, and a programme of

The Bangors *proved too cramped to cope with all the new mine countermeasures gear that became necessary as the war progressed so they were gradually replaced by the larger* Algerine *class, of which* HMS Rattlesnake *was a member.* (CMP)

*Bangor*s and the large *Algerine*s – succeeded the *Halcyon*s and great use was made of smaller craft. These included specialist motor minesweepers and the ubiquitous Fairmile 'B' motor launches (see Chapter 8).

On the other side, German sweepers were coping with the efforts of British layers, and they also had to protect extensive shipping routes along the coasts of occupied Europe from attack by aircraft of many different types and surface ships from cruisers to kayaks. The equivalent of the British ML was the *Räumboot*, (sweeping boat) or R-boat. The fleet sweepers comprised some of the old 1914–18 ships, plus the new 1935 'M' class. These ships were of 717/874 tons, oiled-fired with advanced Wagner or Lamont boilers driving twin-shaft triple expansion engines to give a speed of 18¼kts, with the excellent radius of 5000nm at

The German 1935 Type minesweeper proved to be versatile craft, quite capable of general escort duties as well as laying mines. (CMP)

10kts; armament was two 4.1in dual purpose guns, two 37mm and eight 20mm, which made them a force to be reckoned with in coastal warfare. Draft was 7/8½ft, which often caused torpedoes to run underneath them.

The oil-firing led to difficulty in Hitler's beseiged fortress, and the 1940 type reverted to coal-firing and less advanced machinery. Armament was similar, except in a few boats fitted with torpedo tubes for training purposes. The

The standard American large fleet sweeper was the Raven/Auk *group, similar in size to the British* Algerine*s. This is* Sheldrake *serving postwar as a survey vessel.* (L & L van Ginderen)

sixty, plus sixty submarine chasers, was put in hand. The latter were too small to be effective, but the former were much more useful. One of several designs prepared by Italy's veteran Chief Constructor, Gen da Fea, was used and designated a corvette.

The name ship was *Gabbiano* and the ships were of 670/743 tons, similar to the *Elan/ Chamois* types. They likewise used diesel engines. The real surprise came in the provision of storage batteries and electric 'creep motors', permitting several hours silent search by sonar; diesels, despite their many virtues, make too much noise and vibration for optimum sonar operation. A half-length forecastle ensured good seakeeping and the armament was effective against air, surface and submarine attack.

The main gun was a new dual-purpose 3.9in, backed up by seven 20mm. Early ships (like the old British P-boats) carried two 17.7in (nominally 18in) tubes as a threat to surface attackers, but the main armament comprised two types of sonar, listening gear, eight depth charge throwers and two racks, with a total of eighty-four charges, most kept down below and brought up by a hoist. Above all, the corvettes were given proper training against 'tame submarines', some of them ex-British 'H' boats. The first corvettes were commissioned in 1942, which was most creditable in view of Italy's weak industrial base, and 28 of the 60 were in service by September 1943. Though little time was left to the Italian navy, they made themselves felt. Their tactics were to stalk the target on electric motors until location, course and depth had been established, then make a run. At the last moment, the diesels were started, speed increased and a massed

salvo of twenty to thirty-six charges dropped. This was very like Cdr Walker's 'Creeping Attack' in the Atlantic, and between March and August 1943 it sank HMS/MS *Thunderbolt*, *Sahib* and *Saracen*, all successful submarines with first class captains. The remaining *Gabbiano*s continued in service for many years afterwards.

The Pacific War

Far to the eastward, the Japanese were at first little worried by the American submarine threat; numbers were few and the opposition were hampered by unreliable torpedoes, and, it appears, by a number of unaggressive captains. Nevertheless, Japan's shipping defence authorities were sufficiently worried to request 300 escorts; they were allowed 60. As time went on, the potential threat became actual and more and more escorts were built. Their title was *Kaibokan*, literally 'coast defence vessel', although the Americans called them frigates.

They had the characteristic undulating deck line, twin-screw diesels at first, and two or three old 4.7in guns taken from destroyers, backed up by numerous 25mm. Their anti-submarine armament comprised several depth charge throwers and racks, with a huge outfit of up to 300 charges. Sonar and listening gear were good, but radar, when fitted, was always less advanced than American equivalents. Unlike the Italians, they did not receive intensive training or back-up, and their performance was erratic; sometimes deadly, sometimes feeble. The high speed, good radar, deep diving and high surface speed of American submarines gave the latter the edge, so that unlike its Atlantic parallel the 'Battle of the Pacific' went against the escorts. The American habit of firing 'down the throat' at escorts must have been discouraging, too.

Once its economy was properly geared for war, the United States was able to build minesweepers and escort vessels in great numbers to a limited number of standard designs. Apart from old First World War 'Birds' and commandeered vessels, there were three main minesweeper types: the big *Raven/Auk*s – two-funnelled diesel vessels of 810 to 890 tons, with a speed of 18kts, one or two 3in and close range weapons; the 650-ton *Admirable*s also diesel

The Japanese were slow to mass-manufacture a utility escort, but as the American submarine war against their commerce gained momentum, they designed ever more austere vessels, culminating in the Type D Kaibokan escort, laid down from October 1943. No 8, seen here in February 1944, demonstrates the straight lines and simple fittings that reduced building time to 4–9 months. (CMP)

The US Admirable *class minesweeper was a smaller and cheaper alternative to the* Raven/Auk *class, but in the event coastal escorts were a greater priority and many were completed as PCEs, their poor speed (14kts sustained) being offset by good seakeeping. Many were transferred after the war, including the South Korean* Hansan *(ex-PCE 873) seen here in 1953. (L & L van Ginderen)*

engined, with 15kts speed and one 3in, again plus close range weapons; and the small YMS 'yard minesweepers' of 215 tons and 12kts.

In the escort/anti-submarine role, there were frigates, an inferior equivalent of the DE, built on a mercantile hull, the steel 173ft PC, the wooden 110ft SC, descended from the 1917–18 ones, and two interesting hybrid types, the PCE and PCS, built on *Admirable* and YMS hulls respectively. As it happened, the PCEs proved better escorts than the purpose-built PCs, being better sea-boats though nominally slower, and few if any of

these types encountered submarines or mines. They tended to be used for such tasks as shepherding landing craft, bombardment, attacking enemy small craft traffic in support of PT-boats, and other miscellaneous tasks, which they did very well.

The Pacific theatre was too vast and deep for mines to be a major threat – just a serious nuisance. Nor did the Japanese wage a 'Battle of the Pacific' of their own against the ever-lengthening American supply lines. They might well have done so, in which case the PCs, SCs and others would have been in the

front line. Similarly, if the US Navy had had a hundred of these little ships, with trained crews, on hand in January 1942, the U-boats' 'happy time' off the Atlantic coast would have been shorter and much less happy. Despite her vast industrial resources, the US had some difficulty in providing enough diesel engines of the right kind at the right time, hence the appearance of the hybrid PCE and other improvisations.

US minesweepers were heavily involved in the Normandy landings and the run-up to them, and in clearing the way for amphibious landings. Offensive minelaying by old US destroyer minelayers gained one major success in the Solomons, and the Japanese minelayers, whose mines could be laid in very deep water, snared several US submarines, but in general, the Pacific was not a mine war.

Winning the anti-submarine war

In the Atlantic, 1942 saw the appearance of the frigate, the faster, better-armed successor to the corvette, plus a small number of new sloops on prewar lines. Corvette construction shifted over to the 'Castle' class, which was a cut-down frigate, suited to construction in small, cramped shipyards. Across the Atlantic, great numbers of destroyer escorts appeared from 1943 onwards. Their general conception was inspired by the British 'Hunt's, though they came out very different. They were armed with either three 3in or two 5in guns, many 40mm and 20mm, and in most, one tube mount, plus many throwers and racks for depth charges. All had the ahead-throwing 'Hedgehog' added; it proved particularly effective in the Pacific. Propulsion was by geared diesel, diesel-electric, geared turbine or turbo-electric according to what was available; about half had to be content with 6000hp instead of 12,000, which cut their speed to 21kts from 24kts.

They were lively, especially those with 3in guns, but topweight could be reduced by the

The 173ft PC, or coastal patrol craft, was a purpose-built submarine chaser. Those that continued to serve postwar, like Tooele *(PC 572) were given names. (L & L van Ginderen)*

omission of torpedo tubes (none of the British ships carried them, for example); they were very weatherly and of good endurance. They took a heavy toll of U-boats, but by the time they appeared, the Atlantic tide had been turned, largely by earlier types, aircraft and code-breakers. Some were converted to other duties, used as coastal forces control ships, amphibious landing headquarter ships, and fighter direction ships. Many served in the Pacific, where they stood up well to air attack, typhoons and even battleships. Their appearance permitted the retirement of the many surviving 'flush-deckers', which, like many other veterans, were showing signs of their long, hard service.

The escorts and the minesweepers were fully engaged in the Second World War from the first to the very last (a minesweeper was lost on the final night of the U-boat war). Casualties in both were very heavy, especially after the introduction of the acoustic homing torpedo, which was particularly effective against escorts, and of the many ingenious new types of mine, whose threat lasted long after the war. Few escorts or minesweepers could survive a torpedo or mine hit without heavy casualties, and the normal risks of the trade – men overboard, arms and legs lost in a sweep, legs or skulls broken from a mine hit – were very many. They were also easy targets for air or surface attack; the toll was a long one, and the job attracted little glamour or publicity. The six-year Battle of the Atlantic ended as it began, 'A struggle of groping and drowning, of science and seamanship'; and the struggle of the minesweepers, which required 'the mind of an intelligent ploughman', was equally hard, equally demanding, and equally vital.

K D McBride

Mine Warfare and Escort Vessels: Typical Ships 1906–1945

Ship or Class [Type]	Nationality	Dispt (tons) Normal/Std Full load	Dimensions (loa × breadth × deep draught) Feet–Inches Metres	Armament	Other weapons	Speed (max design kts)	Launch dates	Numbers built
NAUTILUS [Minelayer]	German	1975 2345	331–0 × 36–9 × 14–5 100.9 × 11.2 × 4.4	2–8.8cm	200 mines	20	1906–07	2
FUGAS [Minesweeper]	Russian	150	148–0 × 20–0 × 6–3 45.1 × 6.1 × 1.9	1–63mm	50 mines M/S gear	11.5	1910	5
NATSUSHIMA [Minelayer]	Japanese	420	149–11 × 24–11 × 7–7 45.7 × 7.6 × 2.3	2–76mm 2 MGs	45 mines	12.8	1911–18	13
'FLOWER' class [Minesweeping sloop]	British	1210	268 × 33–6 × 11 81.7 × 10.2 × 3.4	2–12pdr/4in/ 4.7in, 2–3pdr	DCs M/S gear	16	1915–16	72
P-BOAT [Patrol craft]	British	613	244–6 × 23–9 × 8 74.5 × 7.2 × 2.4	1–4in 1–2pdr	2–14in TT DCs	20	1915–18	43
'HUNT' class [Minesweeper]	British	750	231–0 × 28–0 × 7–0 70.4 × 8.5 × 2.1	2–12pdr 2–6pdr	M/S gear	16	1916–17	20
M57 class [Minesweeper]	German	500 539	193–7 × 24–3 × 7–1 59.3 × 7.4 × 2.2	2–10.5cm	30 mines	16	1917–19	52
RD31 class [Minesweeper]	Italian	207	119–9 × 19–0 × 7–3 36.5 × 5.8 × 2.2	1–3in 2 MGs	M/S gear	14	1917–19	7

Ship or Class [Type]	Nationality	Dispt (tons) Normal/Std Full load	Dimensions (loa × breadth × deep draught) Feet–Inches Metres	Armament	Other weapons	Speed (max design kts)	Launch dates	Numbers built
'EAGLE' Boat [Partol craft]	American	500 615	200–10 × 33–2 × 8–6 61.2 × 10.1 × 2.6	2–4in 1–3in	1 Y-gun	18	1918–19	60
BOUGAINVILLE [Colonial sloop]	French	2156 2600	340–3 × 41–8 × 14–9 103.7 × 12.7 × 4.5	3–5.5in 4–37mm 6 MGs	50 mines 1 aircraft	15.5	1931–39	8
BITTERN [Sloop]	British	1190 1790	282–0 × 37–0 × 11–5 86.0 × 11.3 × 3.5	6–4in 2–3pdr	DCs	18	1934–37	3
F 1 [Fast escort]	German	712 1028	249–4 × 28–10 × 10–7 76.0 × 8.8 × 3.2	2–10.5cm 4–37mm 4–20mm		28	1935	10
TRAL class [Minesweeper]	Russian	434 490	203–5 × 25–0 × 7–9 62.0 × 7.6 × 2.4	1–100mm 1–45mm	30 mines	18	1935–40	44
M 35 class [Minesweeper]	German	682 784	224–5 × 27–10 × 8–8 68.4 × 8.5 × 2.7	2–10.5cm 2–37mm 2–20mm	DCs as escort	18	1937–41	69
ELAN class [Minesweeping sloop]	French	750 895	256–11 × 28–6 × 10–9 78.3 × 8.7 × 3.3	2–100m 8–13.2mm	2 DCTs 1 DC rack	20	1938–40	13
'FLOWER' class [Corvette]	British	925	205–0 × 33–2 × 13–7 62.5 × 10.1 × 4.1	1–4in 1–2pdr	40 DCs	16.5	1940–42	137 RN 79 RCN
BANGOR class [Minesweeper]	British	605 780	174–0 × 28.6 × 9–8 53.0 × 6.7 × 3.0	1–3in	40 DCs as escorts	16.5	1940–42	26*
ABDIEL class [Minelayer]	British	2650 4000	418–0 × 40–0 × 13–9 127.4 × 12.2 × 4.5	6–4in 4–2pdr	100–156 mines	37	1940–43	6
PC1084 [173ft sub-chaser]	American	414 463	173–8 × 23–2 × 7–9 52.9 × 7.1 × 2.4	1–3in 1–20mm	2 Mousetrap 2 DCTs 2 DC racks	19	1940–44	328
AUK class [AM, fleet 'sweeper]	American	890 1250	221–2 × 32–2 × 10–9 67.4 × 9.8 × 3.3	2–3in 4–20mm	1 Hedgehog 4 DCTs 2 DC racks	18	1940–45	95
'RIVER' class [Frigate]	British	1320 1920	301–4 × 36–8 × 11–10 91.9 × 11.2 × 3.6	2–4in 4/6–20mm	Hedgehog 126/150 DCs	20	1941–44	57 RN 70 RCN
ALGERINE class [Fleet 'sweeper]	British	950 1265	225–0 × 35–6 × 10–9 68.6 × 10.8 × 3.3	1–4in 4–40mm	92 DCs as escort	16.5	1941–45	48 RN 49 RCN
PCE type [Coastal escort]	American	850 903	184–6 × 33–1 × 9–0 56.2 × 10.1 × 2.7	1–3in 6–40mm 4–20mm	1 Hedgehog 4 DCTs 2 DC racks	15	1942–44	35 USN 15 RN
GABBIANO class [Corvette]	Italian	660 728	211–0 × 28–7 × 8–4 64.4 × 8.7 × 2.5	1–100mm 7–20mm	2–17.7in TT 10 DCTs	18	1942–44	46
YMS type [Motor minesweeper]	American	215	136–0 × 24–6 × 7–9 41.5 × 7.5 × 2.4	1–3in 2–20mm		14	1942–45	c475

Notes:

The data criteria are generally as outlined for earlier tables, but armament (which often varied considerably) can only be regarded as representative. Many of the war-emergency designs could be fitted for more than one role, so numbers completed are often a matter of definition; for British Commonwealth programmes, figures are divided between those built in the mother country (RN) and those built in Canada (RCN) irrespective of the navy in which they served.

* Turbine engined type; there were also 14 diesel and 69 reciprocating steam powered vessels of similar design.

8

Coastal Forces

A BEWILDERING array of small combatants falls within the category of Coastal Forces, particularly with respect to the 1939–45 period. The term 'coastal forces' as used in this chapter refers to small combatants which fall into two relatively distinct functional categories:

1. slow to medium speed craft whose primary role is defensive and which are normally assigned to patrol, escort, anti-submarine, and minesweeping duties; and,
2. high speed craft whose primary role is offensive.

Each category will be discussed separately but, due to space limitations, only the most representative types can be addressed.

Defensive craft

Prior to the First World War few patrol craft of any significance existed; there was neither sufficient need nor technology to justify their existence. Reliable petrol engines of sufficient horsepower were only just becoming available in adequate numbers and the submarine forces of the world were still in their infancy. Established firms such as Thornycroft, Yarrow, Fiat-Muggiano, and Nixon experimented with petrol-powered, torpedo-armed boats as early as 1906, but they were built only in small quantities. A number were exported to Russia, where they were designated SK (submarine chasers) but saw little other service. With the advent of the Great War and the emergence of the submarine as a significant threat, however,

the need for such small craft became readily apparent. Large numbers of privately-owned yachts and workboats were pressed into service, but few were suitable for the tasks required of them. Purpose-built patrol craft were needed in large numbers and design work proceeded apace.

Among the more significant patrol craft to evolve during the 1906–1918 period were the Electric Launch Company's (ELCO) 80ft motor launch, the US Navy-designed 110ft submarine chaser (SC), and the *MAS 115–139* series, developed by the Italian SVAN organisation.

80ft ELCO launches

The ELCO design came about as a result of a Royal Navy requirement for coastal convoy escorts and anti-submarine patrol craft. In the spring of 1915, the Admiralty approached the

Electric Launch Company (ELCO) of Bayonne, New Jersey, to build a series of fifty 75ft motor launches. After delivery of the prototype, a further 500 boats were ordered, albeit to a slightly modified design and lengthened to 80ft. Using mass-production techniques, ELCO was able to build all 550 boats in 488 days. By 1918, a further 30 boats were built for the Royal Navy. In addition, the French navy operated 52 of the ELCOs as *vedettes à moteur*, while 110 more served with the Italian navy as motor anti-submarine (MAS) boats. Between 1918 and 1921, a further 65 boats (*MAS 296, 303–317, 327–376*) were built to a modified design by a number of Italian firms.

The 80ft ELCOs were similar in design to contemporary pleasure craft, being of round-bilge form with an extended raised forecastle. Built of wood and powered by two 220hp Standard Motor Company petrol engines, they were capable of about 19kts and were generally

British 80ft ELCO motor launches patrolling the Otranto anti-submarine barrage in the Adriatic during the First World War. As this suggests, they were relatively seaworthy and could be employed in open coastal waters. The colour scheme is less a form of camouflage than a distinctive pattern of identity markings designed to prevent being mistaken for the enemy. (IWM)

fitted with a 3pdr, although in French service many were fitted with a modified 75mm (3in) gun. Italian boats normally carried a 76mm cannon and small machine-gun. In the original design, anti-submarine weapons were limited to small, hand-thrown charges and towed explosive paravanes; depth charges had not yet been developed. By the end of the war, however, most of the British ELCOs carried up to ten depth charges, while their Italian counterparts carried twice that number.

110ft SC submarine chasers

The other American craft to see wide service during the First World War was the 110ft SC (submarine chaser). Realising that American involvement in the European war was imminent, the US Navy concluded that a large number of coastal patrol and anti-submarine craft would be required. To achieve the numbers needed, and to minimise the need to use strategic materials (namely steel) and skilled labour, these craft would have to be of wooden construction and capable of being built by small commercial boatyards.

Initially, the navy considered buying a number of 80ft ELCO motor launches to meet its needs. Designed for anti-submarine warfare, the 80ft ELCOs were generally well-liked by the Royal Navy, but they were too small and too primitively armed to be truly effective against contemporary submarines. Consequently, the Bureau of Construction and Repair Preliminary Design division began a series of studies that would eventually result in the first 110ft SC design.

The original design had a slender, flush-decked wooden hull powered by three 220hp Standard Motor Company petrol engines and was capable of about 19kts. Trunk cabins were built above the main deck to provide sufficient headroom in the shallow hull. A small, simple wheelhouse with wing extensions was mounted atop the forward trunk cabin. Armament varied somewhat: generally, either a 6pdr or 3in/23 was mounted forward, two .30-calibre machine-guns amidships, and a single Y-gun aft, along with two depth charge tracks.

These first SCs were designed to be built by a number of private and government yards, unlike the ELCOs which were built only by the parent yard. Designed for mass-production, SC construction proceeded rapidly. On 19 August 1917, the US Navy commissioned *SC 6*, the first of its 110ft boats; two years later, on 26 August 1919, it commissioned *SC 444*, the last of 440 SCs eventually built for the USN and France. During their fifteen months of combat service, the SCs conducted patrol and anti-submarine operations along the Atlantic seaboard of the US and in European waters. However, like most war-expedient designs, they had short lives. By 1921, most of those in US Navy service had been decommissioned and sold. Of the survivors, only two, *SC 412* and *437*, were still in commission at the end of the Second World War.

MAS boats

In February, 1917, the SVAN organisation was given a contract for a series of wooden anti-submarine launches (MAS). The resulting craft

(*MAS 115–139*) were superficially similar in appearance to the ELCOs, although they were shorter (59ft compared to 80ft), lighter (19 tons to 42 tons), faster (22kts to 19kts) and far more heavily-armed than their British counterparts, mounting a 76mm (3in) gun and 20 depth charges. A follow-on group (*MAS 233–252*) was built by the Ducroit organisation of Palermo between April 1918 and September 1919. Both groups operated in the Strait of Messina and the Tyrrhenian Sea as convoy escorts and ASW craft. A large number of these craft survived until the end of 1929.

Following the war, patrol craft development languished until the 1930s, when interest in these types was renewed by increasing world tensions. 1931 saw the development of the first of an eventual 325 *Räumboote* (motor minesweepers) for the German navy; in 1937, the US Navy sought a replacement for its ageing SCs, resulting in the *SC 497* class; and, in 1938, the Fairmile organisation proposed the development of a large, mass-produced, multipurpose motor launch, the 'A' type. As the Second World War erupted into an international conflict, the 'A' type ML was superseded by the far more effective 'B' type ML, the Admiralty developed the 72ft Harbour Defence Motor Launch (HDML), and the Italian navy began to acquire a series of large *Vedette Antisommergibili* (VAS) for anti-submarine work.

Räumboote

The *Räumboote* was the result of a joint venture among three firms (Abeking & Rasmussen, Schlichting and Lürssen) and the *K-amt* (the German counterpart of the US Navy's Bureau of Construction and Repair), to develop a small minesweeper. As with most German designs, the various series of *Räumboote* were of composite construction and diesel-powered. The design evolved rapidly from the relatively small (24m or 79ft, 42-ton), lightly-armed minesweeper of 1931 (*R 1*) to the large (39m or 128ft, 150-ton), heavily-armed convoy escort of 1945 (*R 300*).

The first sixteen boats (*R 1–16*), built between 1931 and 1934, were completed with a raised forecastle and relatively long superstructure. An interim series (*R 17–20*), built in 1935, retained the long superstructure but incorporated a flush-deck hull design. Subsequent

The successful inter-war German Räumboot *(or R-boat) could serve in a number of roles. This is a later flush-decked boat operating as a minelayer.* (CMP)

Räumboote were also flush-decked and were fitted with a compact superstructure, leaving more deck area for the constant increases in armament caused by operational demands. To illustrate the latter, in 1933 *R3* mounted a single 20mm aft; by 1944, *R401* mounted a single 37mm and three twin 20mm, along with 12 mines.

110ft SC submarine chasers

Like their Great War counterparts, the *SC497* class sub-chasers were developed in response to the impending US involvement in another war. The design considerations were remarkably similar to those for the earlier craft: large numbers were required quickly, strategic materials and skilled labour were to be conserved, and contracts were to be let to many small boatyards.

In 1938, a patrol craft design competition was held. From the proposals received, two SC designs were selected and, in 1940, two prototypes (initially designated *PC449* and *PC450*) were built. *PC449* was designed by ELCO, but built by Luders Marine Construction Company, while *PC450* was a modernised First World War design built by the American Car and Foundry. Outwardly, both designs differed little in appearance, dimensions, armament, and performance from their

Great War counterparts. Both mounted a 3in/23 forward and *PC450* was fitted with two depth charge tracks at the stern. Interestingly, neither mounted a Y-gun. Each, however, was diesel-powered and twin-screwed, which was a major departure from the earlier gasoline-powered, triple-screw design.

Neither design proved successful, as performance and firepower were well below that needed to deal with modern submarines. On the verge of being cancelled, the SC programme was saved primarily by the introduction of the so-called 'pancake' diesel developed by General Motors, and a revised hull design. Developing twice the horsepower of the original GM 8–268A diesels (2400 *vs* 1200hp), the new engines raised top speed from 17kts to about 22kts, although the range remained the same (about 1500 miles at 12kts).

The new design commenced with *SC497*, built by the Westergard Boat Works. Of all-wood construction, the SC's flush-decked hull incorporated longitudinal yellow pine or Douglas fir planking over 109 frames, sheathed with ¾in white oak. An external keel with extended skeg aft protected the lower part of the hull.

Two trunk cabins about a foot high were incorporated to provide additional headroom in the relatively shallow hull. The aft trunk cabin was very small, extending only over part

of the galley and the after crew's head. On early SCs mounting only two 20mm, a companionway, vegetable locker, several vents, and a wherry were mounted on the roof; later boats had a 'bandstand' built over the after trunk for a third 20mm.

As designed, the *SC497* class boats mounted a 3in/23.5 Mk 14 forward and two single .50-calibre Mk 3 machine-guns on a platform aft of the pilothouse. When the 3in/23 proved unsatisfactory, it was replaced by a 3in/50 Mk 22. Similarly, the .50s gave way to two 20mm Mk 4, which, in turn, were replaced by three of the lighter 20mm Mk 10 mounts, two on the midships platform and a third on a raised platform over the galley.

Owing to a shortage of 3in/50s and a lack of satisfaction with its installation, the navy decided to fit a 40mm Mk 3 to *SC508* in October 1942. Due to its light weight, tracer capability, and higher rate of fire, the 40mm became the standard main armament of the SC soon after.

As first designed, none of the SCs carried radar. In 1942, a number of SCs (including *SC712* and *SC738*) were experimentally fitted with the Canadian SW–1C radar. As it became available in sufficient numbers, the standard SG surface search radar was mounted atop the mast.

Eight SCs (*644, 757, 1035, 1053, 1056, 1071, 1072,* and *1366*) were converted to motor gunboats (*PGM 1–8*) in November 1943. This conversion involved major alterations, including the removal of the pilothouse and all ASW gear. A simple open bridge replaced the original enclosed wheelhouse. Single 40mm Mk 3 mounts were fitted fore and aft within semi-circular splinter shields. Two pairs of Mk 17 twin .50-calibre turrets were installed on either side amidships. SG radar was mounted atop a PT-style bipod radar mast aft of the open bridge.

The PGMs were originally intended to accompany PT-boats on 'barge busting' operations, but proved too slow to keep up with their speedy companions. As a result, the PGMs reverted to convoy escort.

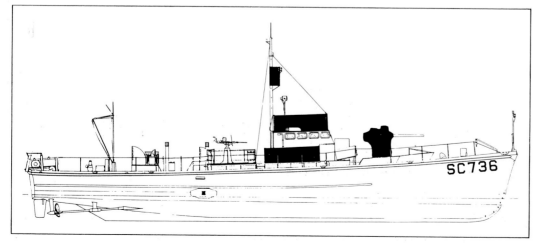

The US Navy developed a new 110ft wooden-hulled sub-chaser at the beginning of the European war. This drawing represents the early configuration with a 3in gun, which was replaced by a 40mm Bofors in most later boats. A motor gunboat (PGM) version was also built. (Al Ross)

One of the most flexible of all Second Wold War small craft designs, the Fairmile 'B' could be converted into a wide variety of roles from inshore patrol to long range rescue. ML 145, seen here in January 1942 carries a 3pdr forward, a 20mm Oerlikon aft and four depth charges. Abaft the funnel there is also a Holman projector, a stopgap weapon of dubious effectiveness that used compressed air (or steam) to fire a Mills bomb (fused grenade) into the path of low flying aircraft. (IWM)

Between 1943 and 1945, 78 SCs were transferred to the Soviet navy, with which they served in the Arctic, Pacific, and Black Sea fleets. *SC1477, 1485, 1507,* and *685* appear to have been lost in action, the remainder being returned to the US Navy, scrapped, or scuttled by 1956.

Fairmile motor launches

The 'A' type ML (motor launch) was the first of a very successful building concept devised by the Fairmile company which culminated in the powerful 'D' class MGB/MTBs, discussed later in this chapter. Fairmile proposed that these motor launches be prefabricated by a large number of subcontractors, then shipped in kit form to the assembling yards. While the 'A' type ML proved the concept effective, the company-designed boat itself was not a success. Due to its hard-chine hull form, the boat pounded heavily in a seaway; there were also problems with its internal arrangement. Only twelve were built and they were soon converted to minelayers. However, they were followed by the Admiralty-designed and highly successful 'B' type ML, a somewhat larger, round-bilge hull with an amazing capacity for conversion. Powered by two 600hp Hall-Scott petrol engines, the 'B' could make about 20kts on a clean bottom.

A wooden 'kit' boat like its predecessor, the 'B' type ML's capacity for conversion came from a series of steel strips built into the deck. These strips were drilled and tapped in patterns corresponding to the base mounts of a broad range of weapons (torpedo tubes, depth

charge tracks, Oerlikons, etc), thus making armament changes a simple process of unbolting the existing mounts and bolting on others. Given this versatility, it is not surprising that the Fairmile 'B' MLs operated as minesweepers, ambulance boats, landing craft control boats, convoy escorts, long range rescue craft, and, at one point, as MTBs.

Originally armed with a single 3pdr, two .303in Lewis machine-guns and twelve depth charges, the Fairmile 'B' went through the normal upgrades dictated by operational requirements throughout the war. By 1945, a typical Burma-based 'B' mounted one 6pdr, one 2pdr, one 20mm, and four .303in machine-guns.

More than 560 Fairmile 'B' MLs were built by over 70 yards between 1940 and 1945. Most operated with the various Commonwealth navies, a large number serving in Asian waters with the 13th, 14th, and 56th ML Flotillas. Fairmile 'B's serving in tropical waters had their bottoms coppered to inhibit marine growth. Eight 'B's built in Canada were transferred to the US Navy in 1942 as *SC1466–1473*.

HDMLs

The Harbour Defence Motor Launch (HDML) was designed by the Admiralty to meet a requirement for a small anti-submarine vessel intended to protect harbour and capable of being transported to its destination aboard ship. Unlike the Fairmiles, the HDMLs were built in a conventional manner, and incorporated double diagonal mahogany planking over transverse frames and longitudinal stringers. Built all over the globe by fifty-seven different yards, the HDMLs were powered by two diesels of varying makes and horsepower (130–160hp), giving them a speed of about 11kts. Armament varied as well, although a typical fitting included one 3pdr forward, two twin .303in Vickers machine-guns in the bridge wings, a single 20mm Oerlikon on a bandstand amidships, and eight depth charges.

Like the Fairmile 'B's, Burma-based HDMLs tended to carry heavier weapons to deal with Japanese barge traffic. *HDML 1385*, for instance, carried a 40mm forward.

VAS boats

In September 1941, the Italian navy contracted with the Baglietto, Picchiotti, Navalmeccanica, Soriente, and Celli yards to produce a series of *vedette antisommergibili* (VAS 201–230). The

The 72ft harbour defence motor launch (HDML) was built in huge numbers for the Royal and Commonwealth navies. Armament and details varied considerably but this sheer elevation of ML 1285 is typical. (John Lambert)

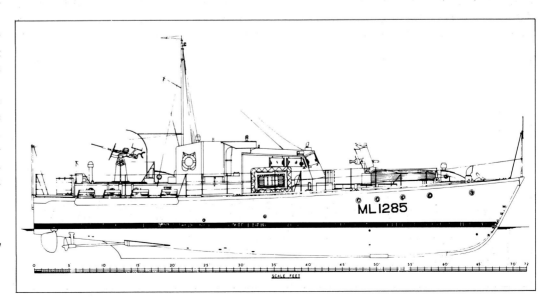

An Italian anti-submarine boat of the second series, VAS 237 is seen here in the Venice lagoon in 1947. Although not visible on this boat, several carried 18in torpedoes which gave them a more offensive capability than their equivalents in other navies. (Aldo Fraccaroli)

first fourteen of these 28m (92ft) boats were of all-wood construction, while the remainder were of composite construction. A second group (*VAS 231–248*) was ordered in January 1942.

The machinery arrangement of the VAS was quite unlike that of its Allied contemporaries. The first series was powered by two 750hp Fiat A25 and one 300hp Carraro petrol engines, while the second series was powered by one 1100hp Isotta-Fraschini ASM 183 and two 300hp Carraros. Despite the disparity in horsepower, the difference in speed between the two types was only half a knot.

Armament generally consisted of two 20mm Bredas and two 18in torpedoes in side launching gear, along with a complement of depth charges. Although originally intended to engage submarines, the inclusion of torpedoes provided the VAS with an effective anti-surface ship weapon. Several boats of the second series were converted to minesweepers in 1943.

Offensive craft

Prior to the First World War, small offensive craft were generally limited to steam pinnaces fitted with a single torpedo tube and one or two small rapid-fire weapons. Advances in torpedoes and internal combustion engines early in the twentieth century, however, provided the impetus for further development of the type. In 1906, Fiat-Muggiano experimented

The first very fast small craft designed for offensive use was the coastal motor boat (CMB), a hydroplane developed by the British firm of Thornycroft's. Initially 40ft long, the hull was soon lengthened to 55ft (CMB 65A is seen here), and eventually to 70ft. The torpedo was dropped stern-first from a trough aft, but as in this example, the boats could also carry depth charges or mines. (IWM)

with a small steel motorboat armed with two 35.6cm (14in) torpedo tubes and a 47mm gun. Thornycroft and Yarrow developed similar types, although they mounted larger (45cm, 17.7in) torpedoes and were about 10kts faster than their Italian counterpart.

It was not until 1915, however, that operational motor torpedo boats of any consequence were developed. These included the 40ft Coastal Motor Boat (CMB) designed by Thornycroft, a broad range of motor anti-submarine boats (MAS) developed for the Italian navy, primarily by SVAN, Orlando, and Baglietto, and a small number of aircraft-engined motor torpedo boats (LM) built by the Lürssen, Naglo, and Oertz yards for the German navy.

CMBs

The CMB was based on the hull of *Miranda IV*, a single-step hydroplane designed by John Thornycroft in 1910. Of all-wood construction, the CMB was 40ft long and carried a single 18in torpedo in a trough on the centre-line aft. The torpedo was launched tail-first, the CMB veering after launching to avoid being struck. Powered by a single 275hp

Thornycroft petrol engine, the CMB was capable of 33kts. In 1917, the 55ft CMB entered service. Almost identical in appearance to the 40ft CMB, the larger boat carried two 21in torpedos in troughs astern and was powered by two 375hp petrol engines. The larger boats served as both motor torpedo boats and motor anti-submarine boats. By the end of the war, the design had been enlarged further to 70ft (designed to lay 'M-Sinker' magnetic mines), although only five were built up to 1922.

MAS boats

While the Royal Navy concentrated on hydroplane hull types, the Italian navy retained the flat-bottomed design of most racing boats of the period and developed a large number of fast, motor anti-submarine motor boats (MAS). Most MAS designs of the period were hard-chined, usually with a very shallow vee bottom. Despite this commonality, the boats varied widely in general arrangement. *MAS 115–139*, for instance, were superficially similar in appearance to the US-built 80ft ELCO launches, while *MAS 23–62* sported a turtle-decked forecastle reminiscent of the larger nineteenth century torpedo boats. Despite their anti-submarine designation, these boats were completed as either motor torpedo boats (*Siluranti*) or motor gunboats (*Cannonieri*). As *Siluranti*, these craft normally carried two 45cm (17.7in) torpedoes and one or two small machine-guns, while the *Cannonieri* generally carried a 47mm or 76mm cannon in lieu of torpedoes. A unique feature of the torpedo craft was their side

capable of 29–30kts. Thirty-three LM boats
were built between 1917 and 1919, some of the
later boats surviving into the 1930s and 1940s
as anti-submarine craft (UZ – *Uboot-Zerstörer*).

Versuchsgleitboot

Although not an operational design, one further craft deserves mention – the Austro-
Hungarian *Versuchsgleitboot*, a torpedo-armed
hovercraft. Designed in 1915 by Lt-Cdr
Dagobert Muller von Thomamuehl and built
to a modified MTK design in 1916, this 13m
boat looked like a section from a large,
constant-chord aircraft wing with an open
cockpit amidships. Two 35cm (13.7in) torpedoes were carried in troughs fitted to either
side of the cockpit, facing aft. Unlike most
stern-launched torpedoes, however, they were
launched warhead first as the hovercraft
headed away from its target. Lift was provided
by a single 65hp engine, while propulsion was
provided by two tandem pairs of 120hp
Austrodaimler engines.

Inter-war development

For more than a decade following 1918, development of small offensive craft waned. Beginning in 1930, however, interest in the type
was renewed. By 1945, the major navies had in

launching gear for the torpedoes, which dis-
pensed with the heavy tubes of their counterparts. Not surprisingly, this lightweight
arrangement was a design feature of MAS
boats to the end of the Second World War.
The only other navies to successfully develop
side launching gear of any significance were
the US and Soviet navies, and this would not
be until the beginning of the Second World
War.

with a single 45cm torpedo tube built into the
bow. A 20mm or 37mm cannon could be fitted
in lieu of the torpedo tube. The first thirteen
boats appear to have been hydroplanes, but the
remainder (*LM 14–33*) reverted to a round-
bilge form more suitable for the English Channel and North Sea. Powered by three 240hp
Maybach petrol engines, the LM boats were

LM types

In contrast to its efforts in the later world conflict, the German navy developed only a token
motor torpedo boat force during the Great
War. Due to a lack of suitable marine engines,
the LM (*Luftschiffmotorboote*) boats were designed from the outset to use airship engines,
as these were the only suitable powerplants
available. As a result, the LM boats were relatively small (15m–16m, 49ft–52ft) craft fitted

*German motor torpedo boats were inspired by the need to
attack the anti-submarine net barrages of the North Sea
coast and their defending destroyers. The boats initially
had a planing hull, but the LM 14 and LM 17 classes
shown here had a more seaworthy round bilge hull.
(BfZ)*

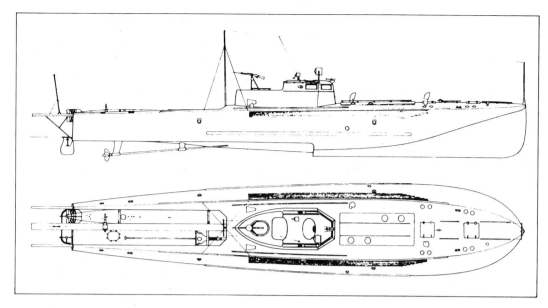

The Soviet G 5 type hydroplane was based on the British 55ft CMB (one of which was captured during the anti-Bolshevik 'intervention' of 1919). The design was developed through the 1930s and many boats saw action right down to the end of the Second World War. (P Budzbon)

their inventories large numbers of highly specialised motor torpedo boats (MTBs) and motor gunboats (MGBs). While most navies standardised on two or three designs, others – most notably the Royal Navy – operated a wide range of types.

The most prevalent designs of the 1930–1945 period fall into five general categories. These categories, and typical examples of each, include:

1. petrol-powered, single-step hydroplanes – Soviet *G 5* MTB;
2. petrol-powered multi-step wooden hydroplanes – Italian *MAS 500* series;
3. diesel- or petrol-powered, round-bilge hulls of composite (wooden planking over metal frames) construction – German S-boats and Italian MS types;
4. petrol-powered, hard-chine, vee-bottom, wooden hulls – ELCO, Higgins, British Power Boat, Vosper, Soviet *D 3*, Japanese *T 14*, and J S White types; and,
5. steam-driven, round-bilge, steel hulls – the seven steam gunboats (SGB)

G 5 MTBs

One of the first designs to emerge during this period was also one of the more unusual – the Soviet navy's *G 5* type MTB. The *G 5* was the successor to the similar *Shya 4* series, which was developed in 1928 and based on the 55ft Thornycroft CMB. Unlike their predecessor, both Soviet types had hulls constructed of duralumin. Built from 1933 to 1940, the *G 5* retained the turtle-back deck and aft launching torpedoes of its predecessor but had a larger enclosed cockpit. Armament varied with the series (7, 8, 9, 10, and 11), but typically consisted of two 21in torpedoes and one or two

12.7mm or 7.62mm machine-guns on ring mounts.

Powered by two indigenously-designed GAM 34 engines, the *G 5* is reported to have been capable of between 49kts and 62kts in light condition, depending on the series of engine fitted. Initially, the GAM 34 engine developed 675hp; by 1940, it was rated at 1250hp.

Approximately 295 of these 62.5ft craft were built and served with the Baltic, Pacific, Northern, and Black Sea fleets. Unfortunately, their usefulness was severely limited by the susceptibility to corrosion of their duralumin hulls. Nevertheless, the *G 5* type saw action until the end of the Second World War.

MAS 500 series

The Royal and Soviet navies were not alone in the successful employment of the hydroplane. In 1932, the Baglietto yard built the experimental *MAS 431*, a single-stepped hydroplane carrying two torpedoes, five depth charges, and two 6.5mm machine-guns. Powered by two 900hp Isotta-Fraschini petrol engines, *MAS 431* could reach 41kts. Further experiments lead to the 1935 development of *MAS 424*, a larger, multi-stepped hydroplane powered by three 500hp Isotta-Fraschini Asso petrol engines, which served as the prototype for the *MAS 500* series.

The *MAS 500* series comprised four distinct groups (*MAS 501–525, 424; 526–550; 451–452; 550–564*) built by a variety of yards, including Baglietto, CRDA, CNA, Celli, and Picchiotti. With the exception of the steel *MAS 525*, all of these boats were of wooden construction. Very similar in appearance, the various groups ranged in length from 17m (56ft) to 18.7m (61ft). Armament varied, but generally included two 45cm (17.7in) torpedoes in side launching gear, a 13.2mm Breda machine-gun, and several depth charges. The machine-gun was replaced by a 20mm/65 Breda cannon in the *MAS 551* group. In 1945, *MAS 540* and *545* were converted to gunboats,

Italian expertise with fast motor boats was kept up between the wars with a series of relatively small torpedo armed craft. Foremost among the builders was Baglietto at Varazze; MAS 451, shown here, was one of their boats, launched in 1940. (Italian Navy)

their torpedoes being replaced by two 20mm/65 mounts.

Two 1000hp Isotta-Fraschini Asso petrol engines provided main propulsion, while two 80hp or 100hp Carraro engines, used for cruising and silent approach, were coupled to the shafts ahead of the main engines.

Schnellboote

Hampered by the Treaty of Versailles, motor torpedo boat development in the German navy was stifled until the end of the 1920s. Then, in 1930, the Lürssen yard produced the prototype of what was to prove to be an extremely successful design, the *S1*. Built under the guise of a dispatch boat, the *S1* was a large (26.85m, 88ft) purpose-built torpedo boat of composite construction. She retained the round bilge of her Great War predecessors and was powered by three 800hp Daimler-Benz petrol engines.

Following the *S1*'s successful trials, four slightly larger production boats (*S2* to *S5*) were ordered. All five boats were eventually fitted with two 21in torpedo tubes and one or two machine-guns. The hulls were scalloped near the bow to provide torpedo clearance. These boats served until 1936, at which time they were paid off, due primarily to the *Kriegsmarine*'s dislike for petrol engines. Subsequent *Schnellboote* were powered by MAN or Daimler-Benz diesels.

Schnellboote up to *S25* retained the exposed tubes of the original design. Beginning with *S26*, the forecastle was raised to improve seakeeping and the tubes were enclosed within. The aft gun mount was supplemented by a second weapon in a well in the raised forecastle. On later boats, the machine-guns were replaced by 20mm cannon; by 1944, a combination of one 37mm and three 20mm was not uncommon.

In 1941, *S67* was fitted with an experimental perspex bridge intended to lower the overall silhouette of the boat; this was not overly practical and subsequent *S-boote* had a light alloy bridge shaped like a skull cap.

As the size, displacement, and armament of the *Schnellboote* increased, so too did the output of the exceptional Daimler-Benz diesels. The *S1* of 1930 had been powered by three 900hp engines; by 1944, *S218* was running on three 2500hp supercharged MB511 diesels.

Another factor contributing to the design's success was the so-called 'Lürssen Effect' rudder arrangement. Basically, two small rudders were fitted aft of the wing propellers and could be rotated outboard 30 degrees without altering the position of the main centreline rudder. This action altered the flow of water aft and resulted in increased acceleration and propeller efficiency, the gain at top end being about 2kts.

MS boats

In April, 1941, the Italians captured six Yugoslavian *S2* type motor torpedo boats that had been built by Lürssen in the late 1930s. Five were sent to Taranto for overhaul and one was handed over to the CRDA organisation for study. Based on this boat, CRDA developed a modified version, and, between April and August, delivered eighteen (*MS 11–16, 21–26, 31–36*) to the Italian navy. Outwardly similar to the original Lürssen design, the MS boats differed from the German design primarily in armament and powerplants. The two exposed 21in torpedo tubes and 'Lürssen Effect' rudders were retained, but single 20mm Bredas were fitted forward and amidships. Lacking suitable diesel powerplants, the boats were powered by three 1150hp Isotta-Fraschini ASM 183 petrol engines. Eighteen more boats built to a modified design were ordered in 1942. The major alterations to this group were the addition of bulwarks forward and the fitting of two 18in torpedoes in side launching gear aft.

British Power Boat Company designs

Following the end of the First World War, Royal Navy Coastal Forces were rapidly run down; by 1930, the only operational types were two of the 70ft CMBs. Increasing world tensions in the early 1930s renewed interest in motor torpedo boats and, in 1935, the British Power Boat Company (BPB) developed from its 64ft air/sea rescue launch a 60ft MTB for use in the Mediterranean. Utilising the increasingly popular hard-chine hull form, the 60ft MTB retained the stern-launched torpedoes of the older CMB, although with a twist. Rather than carry its two 18in torpedoes in open troughs, the BPB design carried them on overhead rails in the engine room. A pair of rail extensions were fitted on the main deck aft. In action, these extensions were pivoted over the transom, the torpedo locks were released, and the boat accelerated rapidly, launching the torpedoes tail-first through ports in the transom. Gun armament consisted of two sets of quadruple .303in Lewis machine-guns on scarf rings fitted on forward and aft centreline hatches. Later, these guns were moved to tubs on either side of the cockpit. Power was provided by three 500hp Napier Lion petrol engines. Eighteen boats (*MTB 1–12, 14–19*) were built, serving in both the Mediterranean and at Hong Kong.

In 1938, British Power Boat took another bold step and, again at its own expense, developed a 70ft MTB quite unlike anything in service. Designated *PV70* (for 'private venture, 70ft'), the new boat was structurally similar to other boats of her type. The hard-chine, stepless hull consisted of two layers of mahogany planks laid diagonally to each other, between which was sandwiched a layer of marine glue-impregnated aircraft fabric. In form, however, she was very different from her contemporaries. In profile, *PV70* displayed a graceful reverse sheer and an S-shaped stem. A long, low streamlined trunk cabin, running perhaps half the length of the boat, was surmounted by two domed, power-operated machine-gun turrets. Completing *PV 70*'s departure from other English designs were her trainable 18in torpedo tubes. Powered by three 1000hp Rolls

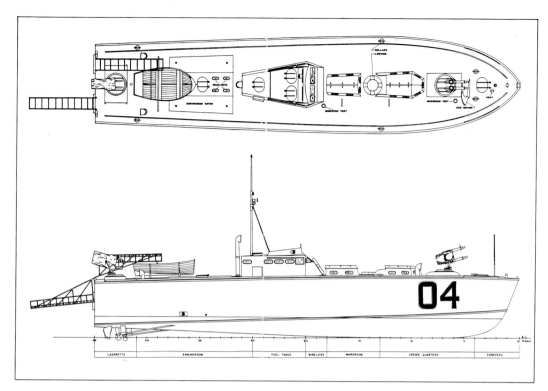

The British Power Boat 60ft motor torpedo boat (MTB) of 1937 revived the Royal Navy's interest in coastal forces. Torpedoes were still launched over the stern as in the earlier CMB, but the hull form is now that of a hard-chine planing boat. (Al Ross)

their poor performance as gun platforms resulted in a new design, the 71ft 6in MGB, the first of which came off the line in February 1942. Designed by George Selman, the new MGBs (*MGB 74–81, 107–138*) were built to Admiralty structural standards and bore little resemblance to the earlier types, other than the retention of the standard double diagonal planking and characteristic BPB bow curve. Powered by three 1200hp Packard 4M2500 petrol engines, the new boats were heavily armed with a single 2pdr and twin 20mm, both in power-operated mounts. MGBs in the second group replaced the power-operated 20mm mount with a lighter manually-operated unit.

As the war progressed, the need for torpedo armament became apparent and, in mid-1943, *MGB 123* was taken in hand to serve as the prototype for a new MTB. The new design retained the MGB hull, but replaced the humped coachroof with an MTB-style cockpit. The forward 2pdr was replaced with a power-operated 6pdr, a twin manually-operated 20mm was placed in a bandstand aft, and two 18in torpedo tubes were fitted abreast the cockpit. Later, the remaining MGBs were re-classified and renumbered as MTBs, although few appear to have actually been fitted with torpedo tubes.

Vosper MTB designs

At the same time that British Power Boat was developing its 60ft MTB, Vosper entered the arena with its 68ft *MTB 102*. Launched in 1937, she was a more robust boat than the BPB types and incorporated some novel, though ultimately unsuccessful, features. The torpedo-firing arrangement was probably the most unusual feature, consisting of both a stern trough like the First World War CMBs and an internal, bow mounted tube similar to German designs of the same era. By June 1938, these were removed and replaced by a pair of 21in tubes abeam the cockpit. Because no suitable English engines were available, she was powered by three 1100hp Isotta-Fraschini petrol engines.

Royce Merlin petrol engines, *PV 70* was capable of 44kts.

Initially designed to compete for a contract from the Royal Navy, this design was regarded as structurally weak and lost out to a Vosper design (*MTB 102*) and was subsequently offered to other navies, nobably those of Canada and the US, which each bought an example. The Canadian boat was taken over by the Royal Canadian Navy as *MTB 1* in 1940. At the same time, the Canadian Power Boat Company, an offshoot of the parent British Power Boat Company, was established in Montreal and began building a series of MTBs based on *PV 70* for both the Canadian and the Dutch navies. Four of this group served in the US Navy as *PT 368–371*. Somewhat later, the design was modified to serve as a rescue launch for the Royal Canadian Air Force. The second example was purchased by the Electric Boat

Company (ELCO) of Bayonne, New Jersey, and served as the prototype for that company's 70ft and 77ft PT boats, described later in this chapter.

PV 70's basic design was carried over to a large number of 63ft and 70ft motor anti-submarine boats (MASB), high speed rescue launches (HSL), and motor gunboats (MGB) built between 1939 and 1941. Most of the MASBs were reclassified as either MGBs or HSLs by early 1941. Engine arrangements and armament varied considerably. Power was generally either two or three 800hp Napier Lions or 1000hp Rolls Royce Merlins. Typical MGB armament consisted of two twin .5in Vickers machine-guns and either a single 20mm or 2pdr, plus two depth charges.

Clashes with *Schnellboote* in the English Channel demonstrated the inherent structural weaknesses of the 63ft and 70ft MGBs, and

The British 6th MGB (motor gunboat) Flotilla in 1942, comprising British Power Boat 70ft MGBs. Originally classed as motor anti-submarine boats (MASBs), they were reclassified in 1941; in this view they are being led by a 'Hunt' class escort destroyer operating as a control ship for the flotilla. (IWM)

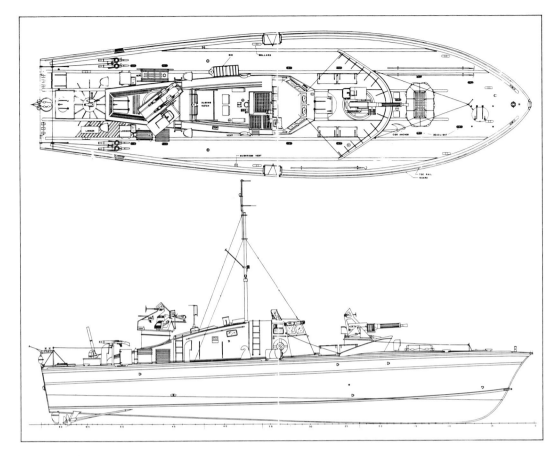

The more robust and better armed MGBs of the 71ft 6in BPB type were later equipped with torpedoes and became MTBs. This is a general arrangement of one of the first, MGB 75, as completed. (Al Ross)

and four 18in torpedo tubes; the second group carried a power-operated 6pdr forward, twin 20mm amidships, and two 18in torpedo tubes aft.

Fairmile 'C' and 'D' types

The Fairmile 'C' and 'D' types shared nearly parallel histories with their 'A' and 'B' type ML sisters. Both were 'kit boats' and were assembled by a number of yards. The Fairmile 'C' was essentially an improved 'A' type fitted with more powerful engines and armament. Designated as an MGB, 24 'C' types were built (*MGB 312–335*) between June and August of 1941. Armed with two 2pdrs, two twin .5in Vickers, and several .303in machine-guns, they saw heavy service in the English Channel and North Sea.

The 'D' type was designed from the outset as a convertible MTB/MGB and was very successful. Designed by William Holt, the 'D' had a unique hull form, often described as a destroyer bow fitted to a fast motor boat stern (basically a round bilge hull form with a knuckle). Only 5ft longer than the 'C' type MGB, the 115ft 'D' displaced an additional 30 tons and was powered by four 1350hp Packards.

More than 200 'D' boats were built, the first (*MGB 601*) completing in February 1942. *MGB 601–632* were completed as motor gunboats, without the deck edge scallops for torpedo clearance, although a number of this group actually carried torpedo tubes. Subsequent boats (*633–800, 5001–5029*, less the cancelled *5027*) had the scallops.

As might be expected, armament varied widely. As completed, *MGB 601* mounted a single 2pdr forward, two twin .5in Vickers on either side of the bridge, and a twin power-operated 20mm mount aft. Various combinations of single and twin 20mm, 2pdr, 6pdr, and 18in and 21in torpedo tubes proliferated throughout the war.

Fairmile 'D' boats served with the British Canadian and Norwegian navies in the North Sea, English Channel, and Mediterranean. Nineteen were completed as long range rescue

As a follow-on to *MTB 102*, Vosper built several 60ft and 70ft MTBs of similar form and power in 1939–40. In 1940, the Royal Navy standardised on the 70ft boat (actually 72ft 6in), albeit to a modified design with a raised forecastle (*MTB 31*). The supply of Isotta engines dried up with the opening of hostilities, so these boats were powered by three 900hp Hall-Scott engines, with a corresponding loss in performance. Fortunately, the Packard 4M2500 became available in quantity in 1941 and became the standard fit commencing with

MTB 73. The type was also built under licence in the US. Armament generally included two 21in torpedo tubes abeam the cockpit and a twin .5in Vickers mount on the centreline amidships.

In 1944, Vosper produced a totally new design, the 73ft MTB. Built to a flush-decked design, the new boats (*MTB 379–385; 523–530, 523–533*) retained the concave/convex underbody of the 72ft 6in MTB, but carried far heavier armament. The first group was fitted with a twin manually-operated 20mm forward

Besides BPB, the other main British designer of fast attack craft was Vosper. The nominal 70ft design, to which MTB 378 belongs, was built in large numbers in the middle years of the war. (IWM)

The Fairmile 'D' type MTB/MGB was the nearest Allied equivalent to a German S-boat. Large, seaworthy and heavily armed, they were not quite as fast as German craft, but were more flexible in their range of employment. Lacking the high speed diesels of the German boats, most Allied coastal forces had to make do with petrol engines, that made them more vulnerable to fire and explosion than diesels. These 'D's are seen entering Algiers in 1944. (IWM)

craft for the RAF, an additional 21 being transferred for the same purpose in 1944.

70ft ELCO PT

The design for the American 70ft ELCO can be traced directly to the British Power Boat Company's 70ft private venture (*PV 70*) MTB. In the summer of 1939, Henry Sutphen and Irwin Chase of the Electric Boat Company purchased an example and the associated manufacturing rights. Arriving in the US in September, the boat received some minor modifications and was demonstrated for a navy trials board in November. Based on these trials, the navy authorised the construction of twenty-two 70ft boats (ten PTs and twelve PTCs) of similar design. *PV 70* was to be placed in service as *PT 9*, while the new construction were to be numbered *PT 10–19* and *PTC 1–12*. Prior to construction, however, the ELCO yard discovered that the plans they had

purchased were not complete. Consequently, to save time and expense, ELCO used *PV 70* as a pattern to develop their own plans.

The boats which resulted from this process were not, however, exact copies of *PV 70*. The hull remained essentially unchanged; the major deviations occurred at deck level and above. The streamlined trunk cabin remained, but the cockpit section was enlarged and raised. The .30 calibre machine-gun turrets were replaced with a similar but larger unit mounting twin .50 calibre weapons.

The primary difference between the PT and the PTC versions was the main armament. While the PTs mounted four 18in torpedo tubes primarily for surface attack, the PTCs carried depth charges for anti-submarine warfare. The depth charges were carried on either side on long rails which led aft to two Y-guns, aft of which were two four-charge racks for dropping charges over the stern.

Upon delivery, the ten PTs, along with *PT 9*,

were formed into PT Squadron Two under the command of Lt Earl Caldwell. During the winter of 1940–41, the boats engaged in rough-water trials off Miami. In March, the squadron was ordered back to New York where the boats were to be transferred to the Royal Navy. Prior to being transferred, however, the ten PTs were modified to British requirements. Essentially, these modifications included the replacement of the four 18in tubes with two 21in fixed Royal Navy pattern tubes, removal of the domes covering the turrets, and installation of a 20mm on the stern. Renumbered *MTB 259–268*, the boats comprised the 10th MTB flotilla and were assigned to the Mediterranean, where they saw constant action.

Only four of the PTCs saw service with the US Navy. In January 1941, *PTC 1–4* headed for Key West to run trials with their experimental sound units, each boat being fitted with a different design. It was soon apparent that the boats did not provide a suitable platform for sonar and they returned to New York. Like their PT sisters, all twelve of the PTCs were modified and transferred to the Royal Navy, this time as MGBs. Reconfiguration for the MGB role included the removal of all anti-submarine warfare equipment and the fitting of a 20mm on the stern. Unlike the PTs, the PTCs retained their perspex turret domes; later, the turrets were removed and replaced by Vickers Mk V turrets on either side of the cockpit. In this latter configuration, they closely resembled the 70ft British Power Boat Company *MGB 50–67*. Assigned to the 5th and 7th MGB Flotillas, the boats operated out of Lowestoft.

77ft ELCO PT

The 77ft ELCO PTs were the direct descendants of the earlier experimental 70ft types. During trials in the Caribbean, deficiencies in the 70-footers became apparent and steps were taken to improve the design. The most obvious change was in length, the new boats being

PT 17, one of the first 70ft ELCO patrol torpedo (PT) boats for the US Navy. (Al Ross)

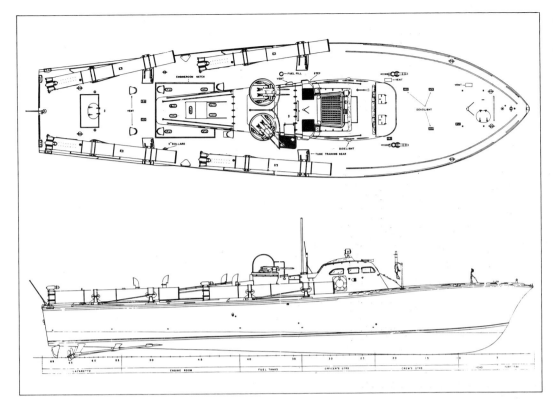

A general arrangement of PT 34, *one of the first series of* ELCO *77-footers. The aircraft-type plexiglass turret domes were removed shortly after the outbreak of war.* (Al Ross)

of their torpedo tubes and fitted with a single 40mm Bofors fore and aft, as well as additional shielded .50 calibre machine-guns along the deck.

The ten boats in British service, *MTB 307–316* (ex-*PT 49–58*), differed from their US Navy counterparts primarily in armament and minor fittings. In place of the four torpedo tubes and twin turrets, the Royal Navy MTBs mounted only two 21in torpedo tubes at a fixed angle and a single Mk V Vickers turret on the centreline of the coachroof; the 20mm aft was retained. A single depth charge on a roll-off rack was fitted on either side of the deck edge, aft of the Oerlikon mount.

The ten British ELCOs were assigned to the 15th MTB Flotilla in the Mediterranean and saw extensive combat. Six were eventually lost in action, including one (*MTB 314*) captured by the Italians during a raid on Tobruk. Following repairs, ex-*MTB 314* operated as the German navy patrol boat *RA 10*, eventually being sunk by the RAF!

80ft ELCO PT

By 1941, the US Navy was able to define more clearly what characteristics were needed for an effective PT. Up to this point, the only PTs operational in any numbers were the 77ft ELCOs. The 'Plywood Derby' had shown inherent weaknesses in the structure of the boats, as well as their comparative strengths. Based on the results, the navy indicated that a heavier, more powerful boat was required. The new specifications required a boat between 75ft and 82ft in length, powered by three muffled Packard engines, and capable of at least 40kts. In the fall of 1941, the ELCO, Higgins, and Huckins companies were invited by the navy to submit designs meeting the new specifications. This invitation resulted in major contracts being awarded to Higgins and ELCO, with Huckins receiving only a minor contract for six boats (eventually, eighteen Huckins PTs were built, but none saw combat).

Only 3ft longer than her predecessor, the 80ft boat was an entirely different design and actually a much larger boat. The hard-chine hull, constructed of two layers of mahogany set diagonally to each other, was sleek, graceful, and deadly in appearance. The superstructure consisted of an angular charthouse and day cabin, on each of which was mounted a Mk 17

lengthened to accommodate four of the standard 21in Mk VIII torpedoes. Other, more subtle changes included a modified cockpit, strengthened frames, and revised domes for the Dewandre turrets.

There were two series of 77ft boats. The first series comprised *PT 20* to *PT 44* and was built to the original design. Combat experience led to the second series, *PT 45* to *PT 68*, which differed from the first series primarily in the shape of the cockpit, armament configuration, and hull stiffness. Ten boats of this second series (*PT 49–58*) were Lend/Leased to the Royal Navy with suitable modifications.

Like their 70ft sisters, the 77ft ELCOs were powered by three 4M2500 Packard petrol engines driving three-bladed screws through vee-drives. Rated at 1200hp (later 1350hp), the Packards gave the ELCOs a top speed of about 41kts with a clean bottom. After a few months in action, top speed dropped radically due to fouling, added weight from soakage and equipment, and general wear and tear on the engines. During the opening months of the Pacific War, the boats of RON 3 in the Philippines had to contend with fuel sabotaged with dissolved wax, requiring it to be filtered through chamois during refuelling.

The early boats were built with the hydraulically-powered, plexiglass-domed Dewandre turrets, but combat experience demonstrated that the domes fogged up when the guns were fired; additionally, the hydraulic training and elevating mechanisms of the Dew-

andre mounts were found to be too slow to track modern aircraft and prone to damage. Consequently, the domes were removed and the hydraulics bypassed on the first series, while the second series were built with the standard Mk 17 manually-operated .50 calibre mounts. A 20mm Oerlikon Mk 4 was also fitted aft on the second series boats.

Both series of 77ft PTs could carry either four 21in torpedoes in tubes, or two tubes and eight Mk 6 depth charges. The tubes were trainable and were normally trained in line with the keel. When going into action, the tubes were trained outboard (aft tubes 12 degrees, forward tubes 8.5 degrees) by hand-operated cranks. The torpedoes were fired either electrically from the cockpit, or by percussion at the tube should the electrical firing circuit fail. Late in the war, the tubes of some surviving boats were replaced with the Mk 1 roll-off racks for the Mk 13 torpedoes normally fitted to the 80ft ELCO and 78ft Higgins PTs.

One of the more interesting modifications applied to the 77ft boats was the conversion of *PT 59, 60,* and *61* to MGBs during the summer of 1943. Torpedo targets in the Pacific theatre were becoming scarce, and the PTs were being diverted to interdict the large numbers of Japanese barges used to supply their beleaguered garrisons in the islands. As these barges were generally armoured against the .50 calibre machine-guns carried by the PTs, heavier firepower was required to sink them. Consequently, the three old 77-footers were stripped

PT 117, one of the 80ft ELCO boats, on completion. These craft were radically different from their predecessors and as the war progressed were steadily modified, including replacing the tubes with lighter release gear and much augmenting the gun armament. (Al Ross)

ELCO also developed the Thunderbolt, a powered mount containing four 20mm guns that was mounted on the stern of several boats in the Pacific and Mediterranean. Although capable of delivering a withering volume of fire, it lacked the punch needed to deal with heavily armoured opponents.

By far the most effective modification was the addition of a single, manually-operated 40mm Bofors on the stern. This excellent weapon was powerful enough to defeat the armour of any potential adversary the PT might encounter close up. Several 80ft boats (*PT 168* and *PT 174* among them) carried an additional 40mm forward, although the 37mm was more common in this position.

By 1945, the standard configuration of a Pacific boat was:

- one 20mm Mk 14 forward, to port
- one 37mm M4 or M9 forward, on the centreline
- two twin Mk 17 .50 calibre mounts
- two eight-barrelled, 5in spin-stabilised rocket launchers forward
- four 22.5in Mk 13 torpedoes in roll-off racks
- one 40mm Mk 3 mount aft.

Few of the Mediterranean boats carried the 37mm, often having only the 20mm fore and

.50 calibre turret, en echelon. The forward turret was mounted on the charthouse to starboard, while the aft turret was fitted to port on the aft corner of the dayroom. This arrangement gave a wider firing arc than the earlier ELCOs and the current Higgins boats. Abaft the dayroom was the engine room hatch, on which were mounted four cowl vents and an access hatch.

The size and placement of the turrets and the access hatch are the primary identifying features between the two series of ELCO PTs. On the first series (*PT 103–196, 314–367*), the forward turret was mounted about 3ft forward of the aft bulkhead of the chartroom, while the access hatch was only slightly raised above the engine room hatch. On the second series (*PT 372–383, 486–563, 565–622*), the turret was moved to the aft bulkhead and the access hatch greatly enlarged to double as a vent.

Power was provided by three supercharged 4M2500 Packard V-12 petrol engines. Initially rated at 1350hp, these engines were eventually rated at 1500hp. To feed these petrol-hungry engines each boat carried 3000 gallons of 100 octane fuel in tanks amidships. Needless to say, fire was a constant threat and a number of boats were lost in this manner.

Armament varied considerably on the 80ft ELCOs, particularly as the war progressed. As designed, the boats carried two twin .50 calibre machine-guns, a single 20mm Mk 4 aft, and four 21in Mk 18 torpedo tubes. Like their earlier sisters, provisions were made for the replacement of the aft tubes with four depth charges. Later, the torpedo tubes were re-

placed by the much lighter roll-off racks for the 22.5in Mk 13 torpedo. This drastic reduction in weight allowed the boats to increase the size and number of automatic weapons carried. This was especially important in the Pacific, where the primary mission of the PTs had moved from sinking capital ships to 'barge busting'.

In order to gain more firepower for this role, experiments in the field included the addition of 37mm anti-tank guns, additional 20mm, .50s and .30s, bazookas, 60mm mortars, rocket launchers, and even 75mm guns. Several boats of RON 9, *PT 157* among them, replaced one pair of their turret-mounted .50s with a single 20mm.

A typical configuration of the 80ft ELCO by the end of the war – PT 596 in August 1945. (Al Ross)

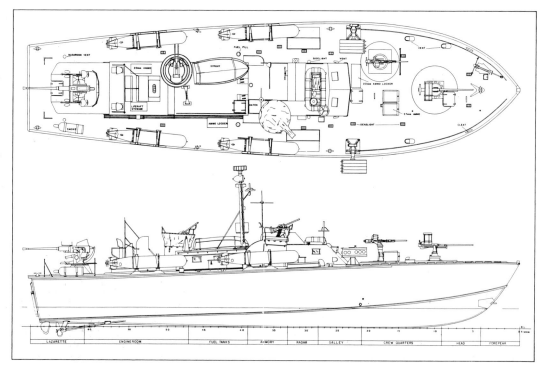

General arrangement of an early 78ft Higgins PT-boat, with augmented armament (PT 209 in August 1944). This boat was one of a number transferred to the Royal Navy. (Al Ross)

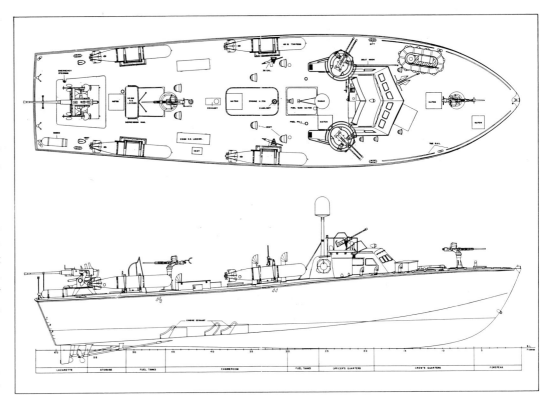

aft. Four RON 29 boats carried the Thunderbolt, the remainder having the 40mm aft.

Radar was important to the success of the PT and the first sets were fitted to the ELCOs in 1943. There were two basic units: SO and SO3. Both units were mounted on a hinged bipod mast fitted on the forward end of the dayroom.

Beginning in 1944, sixty 80ft ELCOs were transferred to the Soviet navy, where they were designated type A 3. ELCO plans for the last batch of these indicate that they were fitted with the Higgins Mk 19 torpedo tubes, rather than the trainable Mk 18 tubes normally fitted.

78ft Higgins PT

Like the ELCO, the 78ft Higgins PT was the result of the design competition sponsored by the US Navy in 1941 and it became the second design standardised upon. Only 2ft shorter than the ELCO, the Higgins was a markedly different craft. Its hard-chine hull, constructed of two layers of mahogany set diagonally to each other, lacked the grace and elegance of the ELCO. Although there was a slight reverse sheer, the hull had nearly 2ft more freeboard forward, less flare to its sides, a short cockpit placed well forward, and no superstructure aft of the cockpit.

The hull was quite conventional in arrangement, with enlisted and officer quarters forward, fuel tanks and engine-room amidships, and lazarette aft. One major difference, however, was that no below-decks access was provided between watertight bulkheads. This may have been due, in part, to the fuel tank compartment arrangement. Access to these compartments was only from hatches on the main deck.

The Higgins PT was powered by three of the same Packard 4M2500 engines that powered the 77ft and 80ft ELCOs. Although several knots slower than the ELCOs, the Higgins had a tighter turning circle, due primarily to the size and placement of its twin rudders.

Armament varied considerably on the 78ft Higgins PT, depending on time period, mission, and theatre of operations. As designed, the boats carried two twin .50 calibre machine-guns, two single 20mm Mk 4 amidships and aft, and four 21in Mk 19 torpedo tubes. These tubes were unique among US PTs, as they were not trainable and launched their torpedo with compressed air rather than by igniting a black powder impulse charge. Later, the torpedo tubes were replaced by the much lighter roll-off racks for the 22.5in Mk 13 torpedo. In many boats, this allowed the introduction of a 20mm on the port side forward, and the addition of a single 40mm Mk 3 aft. Some of the Mediterranean boats carried two 37mm forward in response to encounters with the German Flak lighters, and a number were fitted with 'Mousetrap' style barrage rocket launchers on the bow. Pacific boats tended to be more heavily armed, a typical 1945 configuration being nearly identical to that carried by the 80ft ELCO.

A number of Higgins PTs were transferred to the Royal Navy in 1943 and 1944 for use as MTBs and MGBs. *PT 88*, *90–92*, and *94* became *MTB 419–423* and *CT 16*, while *PT 201*, and *203–217* became *MGB 177–192*. In both cases, they retained the US .50 calibre mounts, while the MTB version replaced the four torpedo tubes with two 21in RN pattern tubes, mounted a twin 20mm over the engine room hatch, and a single 40mm Bofors over the aft fuel tank hatch. The MGBs appear to have retained the two single 20mm.

Fifty-five Higgins PTs were also transferred to the Soviet navy from 1943, where they were designated type *A 2*.

PT 462, a later 78ft Higgins boat. The roll-off racks for the torpedoes are empty, revealing more of the deck details than are usually visible. (Al Ross)

The British steam gunboat SGB 9 *(later* Grey Goose). *The boilers proved very vulnerable to gunfire, but more problematical was the fact that they could only be built by specialist destroyer builders, and destroyers had too high a priority to be replaced by coastal forces. (IWM)*

D 3 MTB

Although a contemporary of the *G 5*, the *D 3* type MTB was a totally different design. Far more conventional in form and construction, the *D 3* had a flush-decked, wooden, hard-chined hull with a relatively narrow beam. Hull planking was oak instead of the more usual mahogany.

Initially powered by the same GAM 34 petrol engines of its stablemate, boats built from early 1943 had three of the powerful Packard 4M2500 engines installed. Armament consisted of two 21in torpedoes in side launching racks and two or three 12.7mm machineguns.

Japanese MTB/MGBs

For an island nation, Japan had surprisingly limited coastal forces. At the beginning of the Pacific War, the Imperial Japanese Navy had only a few captured Chinese MTBs of the CMB and Lürssen types, and a couple of Baglietto-designed hydroplanes. Indigenous

designs did not being to appear until about 1943 and these were a mixed bag of hard-chined MGBs or MTBs of wood or steel construction, ranging from 15m to 18m (49ft–59ft) in length. Powered by a wide range of petrol engines, most were only capable of about 27kts, although there were some notable exceptions. The most significant MTBs were the *T14*, *T35*, *T38*, and *T51* types; for MGBs, the *H35*, *H38*, and *H61* types were produced in the largest numbers.

Typical armament for an MTB included two 45cm (17.7in) torpedoes with side launching gear and one or two 13mm or 25mm guns. MGBs generally were fitted with three 25mm cannon and several depth charges.

Plagued by poor design, shortages of spares,

and unreliable engines, these boats had little effect on the outcome of the Pacific campaign.

Steam gunboats

The seven boats of this group were essentially an experiment that was not overly successful. In 1940, the Admiralty, Yarrow and Denny attempted to design a large, fast but relatively quiet gunboat to counter the *Schnellboote*. The result was a sleek steel hull 145ft in length and powered by two 4000shp steam turbines. Armament was similar to that fitted to the smaller Fairmile 'D' MTB. Unfortunately, the steam power plant proved to be an Achilles heel, being easily put out of action by gunfire.

Al Ross

Coastal Forces: Typical Craft 1906–1945

Boat or Class [Type]	Nationality	Dispt (tons) Normal Full load	Dimensions (loa × breadth × deep draught) Feet–Inches Metres	Armament	Hull	Speed (max design kts)	Launch dates	Numbers built
ML 51 [80ft ELCO ML]	British (US-built)	37	80–0 × 12–3 × 4–0 24.4 × 3.7 × 1.2	1–3pdr	Wood	19	1915–18	530
CMB 40 [40ft CMB]	British	5	45–0 × 8–6 × 3–0 13.7 × 2.6 × 0.9	1–18in TT 2 MGs	Wood	35	1916–20	39
MAS 3 [SVAN type MAS boat]	Italian	16	52–6 × 8–7 × 3–11 16.0 × 2.6 × 1.2	2–17.7in TT or 1–47mm gun, 1/3 MGs, 4/6 DCs	Wood	23	1916–17	20
SC 1 [Submarine chaser]	American	77 85	110–0 × 14–9 × 5–7 33.5 × 4.5 × 1.7	1–6pdr or 3in 2 MGs, 1 Y-gun	Composite	18	1917–19	440
LM 7 [MTB]	German	c7 c15	52–6 × 7–10 × 2–3 16.0 × 2.4 × 0.7	1–17.7in TT 1 MG	Wood	31	1917	4
'G 5' type [MTB]	Russian	14–16	61–8 × 11–2 × 2–4 18.8 × 3.4 × 0.7	2–21in TT 1/2 MGs	Duralumin	45–50	1933–40	295
S 14 [S-Boot]	German	92 114	113–7 × 16–9 × 4–9 34.6 × 5.1 × 1.4	2–21in TT 1–20mm	Composite	37.5	1936–38	4

Boat or Class [Type]	Nationality	Dispt (tons) Normal Full load	Dimensions (loa × breadth × deep draught) Feet–Inches Metres	Armament	Hull	Speed (max design kts)	Launch dates	Numbers built
MTB 1 [BPB 60ft MTB]	British	18	60–4 × 13–10 × 2–10 18.4 × 4.2 × 0.9	2–18in TT 4 MGs, 6 DCs	Wood	38	1936–39	18
MAS 526 [Baglietto type MAS]	Italian	25	61–4 × 15–5 × 4–11 18.7 × 4.7 × 1.5	2–17.7in TT 1 MG, 6 DCs	Composite	44	1938–39	25
'D 3' type [MTB]	Russian	32 35	70–9 × 13–3 × 4–3 21.6 × 4.0 × 1.3	2–21in TT 1/2–20mm or 1/4 MGs	Wood	35–39	1939–45	c130
MGB 50 [BPB 70ft MGB]	British	28 32	70–0 × 19–9 × 4–0 21.3 × 5.1 × 1.2	1–20mm 3/8 MGs, 2DCs	Wood	27–38	1939–41	35
PT 20 [ELCO 77ft type]	American	40 54	77–0 × 19–11 × 5–6 23.5 × 6.1 × 1.7	4–21in TT 5 MGs	Wood	39	1940–41	29
FAIRMILE 'B' type [Motor launch]	British	76 86	112–0 × 18–4 × 4–9 34.8 × 5.6 × 1.5	1–3pdr/2pdr/ 40mm, 1/3–20mm/MGs, 20 DCs	Wood	18	1940–45	c650
ML 1001 [HDML]	British	44 52	72 × 15–10 × 4–7 22.0 × 4.8 × 1.4	1–2pdr/3pdr, 1–20mm, MGs, 8 DCs	Wood	12	1940–45	c450
MTB 73 [Vosper 73ft type]	British	35 44	72–6 × 19–2 × 4–2 22.1 × 5.8 × 1.3	2–21in TT 2/4 MGs, 8 DCs or 4 mines	Wood	37–40	1941–42	51
GREY GOOSE [Steam gunboat]	British	175 255	145–8 × 23–4 × 5–8 44.4 × 7.1 × 1.7	2–21in TT 1–3in, 2/3–2pdr, 2/3–20mm, MGs	Steel	34	1941–42	7
S 62 [S-Boot]	German	92 115	114–8 × 16–9 × 9–6 34.9 × 5.1 × 2.9	2–21in TT 2–20mm	Composite	39	1941–43	38
PT 71 [Higgins 78ft type]	American	45 54	78–6 × 20–1 × 5–3 23.9 × 6.1 × 1.6	4–21in TT 2–20mm, 4 MGs	Wood	39	1941–43	131
VAS Type 1 [Motor ASW boat]	Italian	68	91–10 × 14–1 × 4–5 28.0 × 4.3 × 1.4	2–17.7in TT 1/2–20mm, 2 MGs, 26 DCs	Wood and composite	20	1942	30
PT 103 [80ft ELCO type]	American	51 54	80–3 × 20–8 × 5–6 24.4 × 6.3 × 1.7	4–21in TT 1–20mm, 4 MGs, 8 DCs	Wood	39	1942–43	160
MTB 601 [Fairmile 'D' type]	British	102 118	115–0 × 21–3 × 4–11 35.1 × 6.5 × 1.5	2–21in TT 2–6pdr, 2/3–20mm, MGs, DCs or mines	Wood	29	1942–44	160
110ft SC type [Submarine chaser]	American	121 136	110–11 × 17–0 × 6–0 33.8 × 5.2 × 1.9	1–40mm 3–20mm, DCTs and 2 'Mousetrap'	Wood	21	1942–45	435
R 218 [R-Boot]	German	140 148	129–3 × 18–9 × 5–3 39.4 × 5.7 × 1.6	1–37mm 3–20mm	Composite	21	1943–45	83

Notes:

The data criteria are generally as for earlier tables, but the figures are merely representative as individual craft varied considerably, particularly in respect of armament fit.

9
Amphibious Warfare Vessels

AMPHIBIOUS or combined operations are as old as naval warfare itself, but prior to the twentieth century they did not require specialised ships, although the landing craft themselves may have been modified versions of existing boat types. There are one or two exceptions to this generalisation – medieval horse transports or the purpose-designed craft of the eighteenth century Swedish Archipelago Fleet, for example – but more often than not in the age of sail, landings were performed by the ships' boats of the fleet or squadron. As a result, assaults were not expected to succeed against concerted opposition on the beach-head itself, and were confined to relatively small numbers and limited objectives. Amphibious warfare, therefore, was usually a matter of raiding rather than full-blown invasion, while the introduction of the machine-gun and rapid-fire artillery made the prospects of a successful large-scale landing even less likely using traditional methods.

to a method of getting the troops close to the shore without exposing them unnecessarily. A small steamer, the *River Clyde*, was crudely converted into an assault ship with holes cut in her sides for rapid disembarkation of troops and sand-bagged machine-gun positions on the forecastle for covering fire; ramps and stages were needed to land troops via pontoons on to the beach. At Suvla Bay several months after the initial landings, the British used the hurriedly designed X-Lighter. These craft were of about 160 tons displacement, armoured, and powered with an assortment of engines. They had a ramp, for landing horses and guns, lowered and raised from detachable horns at the bow. Nearly two hundred were built and a few even saw service during the Second World War supplying the British armies in North Africa. Another innovation was the Y-Lighter, a small simple pontoon barge designed to be towed or powered by outboard motors. Both types were rushed into production, and as was to be the cry of all combined operations planners, there were never enough of them.

Another British development was the Great Landing Pontoon of 1917. These monsters were 550ft long, and were pushed by a pair of *Prince Rupert* class monitors lashed together. Trials showed that this unwieldy combination could steam at about 6kts. With a 100ft wooden beaching raft in front, and the length of the 'pusher tug' monitors included, the whole combination was over 1000ft long. Three pontoons were built, and each could carry an assault brigade with artillery and three tanks. They were to have been used for a landing on the Belgian coast, but in late 1917 the operation was cancelled. Plans were also prepared to adapt one of the big-gun monitors to carry 600 troops, fit an assault ramp, and attack the mole at Zeebrugge. This operation was eventually carried out in 1918, but instead of the monitors *Vindicitive*, and old cruiser, was selected and converted into an assault ship, with side ramps, machine-guns, mortars and protection for the landing force.

Britain was not the only country involved with landing craft during the Great War. The

The First World War and after

The stalemate on the Western Front encouraged the Allies, and the British in particular, to consider the use of their superior sea power for amphibious attacks on the flanks of the Central Powers. A grand plan to knock Turkey out of the War was hatched, in which landings on the Gallipoli peninsula would be followed by the capture of Istanbul. Since the landings would have to be made on to an open beach and probably under heavy fire, thought had to be given

The makeshift assault ship River Clyde *at 'V' Beach, Gallipoli. Although a causeway had been built out to the ship by the time this photo was taken, an exploding Turkish shell underlines the vulnerability of the ship and its soldiers during the initial assault across pontoons on to the beach. (IWM)*

Imperial Russian navy carried out several landings on the Turkish Black Sea coast, and converted several shallow-draught *Elpidifor* type merchant vessels into landing ships with infantry gangways forward. They also built 'Russud' type landing craft with a large ramp for guns and horses. The German army used special (unpowered) landing boats in their Baltic campaigns, and the Imperial Japanese forces, whilst occupying the German Pacific colonies, learnt their amphibious lessons very well indeed.

After the War, there were few resources for experimentation in any navy, and as a 'hostilities only' requirement amphibious warfare vessels were inevitably accorded a low priority. However, some far-sighted officers kept the idea of combined operations alive. In the Royal Navy, a recommendation from the first Inter Services Staff Course led to the formation in 1921 of the Landing Craft Committee. From the recommendations of that committee came the Motor Landing Craft Number 1 (*MLC 1*) in 1926 and the improved *MLC 10* in 1929, a 20-ton craft that could carry a 16-ton truck. In 1938 the functions of the Landing Craft Committee were taken over by the newly formed ISTDC (Inter Service Trials and Development Centre). From its headquarters at Hayling Island, it considered future combined operations in the approaching war. Plans were prepared for assault transports (LSIs), landing craft carriers (LSGs and LSSs) and suitable ships were selected for conversion. Industry was consulted, the MLC (now called a Mechanised Landing Craft) was redesigned and an infantry Assault Landing Craft (LCA) produced. Many of the ideas formulated by the ISTDC were to come to fruition later.

In the United States progress was centred on the Marine Corps. Their role was redefined from naval infantry to the amphibious assault arm of the US Navy. The Marine Corps Equipment Board was established in 1933, and this body in conjunction with the Navy De-partment gradually developed the equipment needed. Landing exercises were included in annual fleet manoeuvres and, as in Britain, private industry was involved. This avenue led to the Landing Craft Personnel (Large) or LCP(L), developed from a Higgins Industries logging boat (also reputed to have been used as a rum-runner) and to a very successful MLC design adapted from a Higgins river tug, which was to become the wartime LCM(3). The concept of the fast destroyer transport was evolved and led to the conversion of the 'flush-decker' USS *Manley* as APD 1. Initially carrying whaleboats at its davits, it later carried four Higgins LCP(L)s and a company of marines. Five further flush-deckers were converted to APDs before the outbreak of the Pacific War and twenty-six after it.

In the Pacific, the Japanese built the first purpose-designed landing craft carrier in the world, the 12,000-ton *Shinshu Maru*. In 1937 she was operating in China with her twenty *Daihatsu* type landing craft launched through stern doors (large hatches in the sides amidships allowed loading of the landing craft after launch). Although built for the army, the ship was taken over by the Imperial Navy during construction and gave the Japanese the only prewar specialist amphibious force.

The Second World War

Developments in amphibious technology are usually associated with the Anglo-American preparations for the invasion of Europe and the US island-hopping campaign in the Pacific. However, while the Western Powers were responsible for the definitive types of craft now accepted as essential to amphibious warfare, most of the problems of placing a modern mechanised army on a hostile beach were first faced by the Germans.

The Gallipoli campaign produced an instant call for specialist landing craft and the result was the X-Lighter, a hurriedly built self-propelled barge with a bow ramp. The armoured variant, shown here in a specially constructed dock at Suvla Bay in December 1916, were given numbers prefixed with 'K' and were sometimes referred to as K-Lighters. (IWM)

Operation Sealion

In the Great War the German army had used small numbers of unpowered *Pferdeboote*, or horse transports, with a stern ramp, but there was no real development work between the wars. Therefore, when the Germans reached the French coast in 1940, neither the army nor the navy was in any sense equipped to carry out Hitler's intended invasion of England, codenamed Sealion. However, within a few months a masterly feat of improvisation had produced a fleet of over 4000 vessels – capable of landing nearly 70,000 men and their equipment on the first day of the planned invasion (this was comparable with what was achieved by the Allies on D-Day, but thereafter the German build-up would have been much slower, because of the relative paucity of reserve craft and the extra loading and disembarking time required by these makeshift vessels).

The functions for which they were pressed into service anticipated nearly all of the later Allied types – transports, assault boats, landing craft for infantry, vehicles and tanks, and fire support ships – while their modifications show the Germans to be aware of most of the practical difficulties involved in a large-scale landing. The vast majority of the troops were to be moved in 174 commandeered freighters and small passenger ships which did not require substantial conversion work; some 1600 assorted lesser vessels, ranging from coasters and motor fishing vessels to police and customs launches, were also taken up. Troops from these vessels would have been ferried ashore in small craft.

During the First World War the Germans also developed a ramped landing craft for their Baltic landings. One of these pferdboote ('horse boats') is seen alongside a transport during the occupation of Ösel Island in the Gulf of Riga during October 1917. Presumably the crate contains a horse. The slow pace of landings using this technology made any assault against determined opposition a risky, if not suicidal, venture. (IWM)

However, the centre-piece of the assault was to be a huge force of 2400 barges from the inland waterways of Europe, the bows of which were modified to include a rudimentary ramp, allowing them in theory to land tanks or vehicles directly on to the beach. As with the first British LST designs, much effort was expended on producing a ramp of satisfactory length, since otherwise the draught of the barges meant that vehicles would have to be driven into deep water; eventually the Germans settled for beaching on a falling tide and waiting for the depth of water to reduce. Because many of the barges were unpowered or underpowered, they were to be towed in pairs by tugs, and actually beached by small pusher craft, who would then pull them off with the help of the next tide. To speed up unloading, prefabricated jetties were devised, but they

were too complex to be mass-manufactured.

It is clear from these long-winded arrangements that the Germans did not anticipate continuing resistance on, and off, the beaches themselves, but during the first phase of the landing they planned to use the fast *Pioniersturmboot 39*, an army engineers assault craft powered by a 30hp outboard motor and capable of carrying six troops. Many of the coasters and fishing vessels allocated to the first wave were equipped with slides or ramps for the speedy launching of these craft. They were also carried by specially armoured versions of the barges, destined to carry troops for the initial assault.

Among the most ingenious, though not the most successful, improvisations was a variety of rafts and pontoons, fabricated from an unpromising range of items from seaplane floats

to Bordeaux wine casks. The most practical were based on pairs of pontoons from army bridging equipment with a platform between, and some were powered by old aero-engines with a platform between, and some were powered by old aero-engines driving airscrews. The main variations, known as *schwere Schiffsbrücke*, Herbert- and Siebel-Ferries, were useful for bulky loads and were also intended to carry heavy flak units for the defence of the invasion convoys. Other fire support was provided by converted coasters, five of which were designated heavy gunboats and carried 15cm (5.9in) or 10.5cm (4.1in) guns; there were also twenty-seven light gunboats with a 7.5cm (3in) army gun and some smaller weapons.

From the outset, air supremacy was a recognised *sine qua non* for a successful amphibious assault and when the Luftwaffe failed to achieve it during the Battle of Britain, the invasion was called off.

Early British developments

At the same time as the Germans were expending such vast efforts on their invasion fleet, the British were also giving thought to special ships for amphibious warfare. In April 1940, even before the Dunkirk evacuation, a requirement was promulgated for an LSI (Landing Ship Infantry). At this stage it was not the full-scale invasion of Europe which concerned the planners, but a return to the raiding strategy that Britain had applied against dominant Continental military powers from Louis XIV to Napoleon. Inter-war development had already produced prototype vehicle landing craft (MLC until rechristened LCM, for Landing Craft Mechanised, in 1942), while experiments with assault landing craft (ALC, then LCA) had resulted in a satisfactory design by April 1940. Thus the LSIs were expected to carry

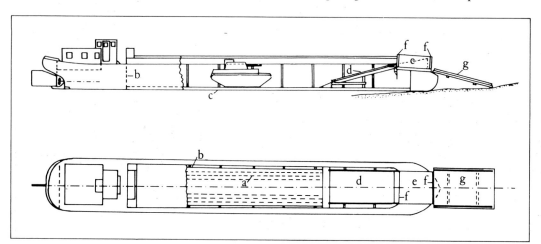

The backbone of the planned 'Sealion' invasion of Britain was a large collection of hastily converted barges from the inland waterways of occupied Europe. The main features of the conversion were: a. longitudinal stiffeners; b. transverse bulkheads; c. layer of concrete; d. internal ramp; e. watertight bow chamber; f. wooden bulkheads; g. external ramp. (From Landing in England by Peter Schenk)

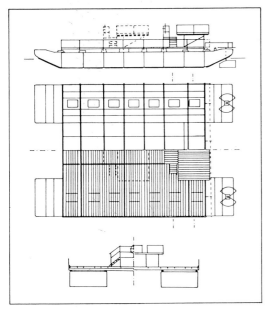

A schwere Schiffsbrücke ferry improvised from army bridging equipment. The dotted outline shows platforms to mount aero engines for airscrew propulsion. (From Landing in England *by Peter Schenk)*

6–12 LCAs under davits and, if possible, a pair of LCMs.

The first ships taken up were three new 9800-ton Glen Line cargo liners, which were given thorough conversions, but more typical were a series of cross-channel and short-sea ships in the 2000/4000-ton range; classified as LSI(M) or (S) for Medium or Small, they carried 200–500 troops as opposed to the 800–1200 of the large LSI(L)s. Eventually, the provision of more powerful davits allowed more – and heavier – LCAs to be carried and the ships in general became more elaborately equipped for their tasks. Even before the Lend–Lease agreement a British supply mission in America discovered the Higgins 'Eureka' hard chine boat, then also under evaluation by the US Navy, and its 18kt speed seemed to make it a superior raiding craft to the 11kt LCA, even though it was unarmoured. The first order was placed in October 1940, and became known as the Landing Craft Personnel (Large); with the later addition of a ramp it became the ubiquitous Landing Craft Vehicle–Personnel, or LCVP, and about 30,000 of these Higgins craft in various versions were produced during the War.

By 1942 the whole coastline of western Europe was German-held, which seemed to offer opportunities to the British for large-scale raiding at considerable distance from their bases. For this they needed something less vulnerable than the LSI/LCA combination and envisaged a so-called 'giant raiding craft' that could carry 2000 infantry at somewhere between 14kts and 20kts, for 500nm, and land them directly on the beach like an LCA. They would necessarily be built of steel, so could not be constructed in Britain without detriment to the destroyer building programme; America was the only alternative supplier so, being too large for deck cargo, the craft would have to be able to cross the Atlantic under their own power. As developed in the United States, the Landing Craft Infantry (Large) had a somewhat ship-like form (the troops landed over gangways rather a bow ramp), a 15kt speed, and the huge endurance of 8000nm or more at 12kts. Although they were never used in their intended role, 1000 were eventually built between October 1942 and October 1944, and proved amenable to a variety of specialist conversions besides their troop-carrying function. A reduced version, called an LCI(S), was built in limited numbers in Britain early in 1943; using the Fairmile wooden prefabrication system, they were lightly armoured and could carry about half the troops of an LCI(L) but had a limited range.

A shortcoming of the early LSIs was the small number of LCMs carried and the time it

A general arrangement of the British 'Glen' class Landing Ship Infantry, Large or LSI(L).

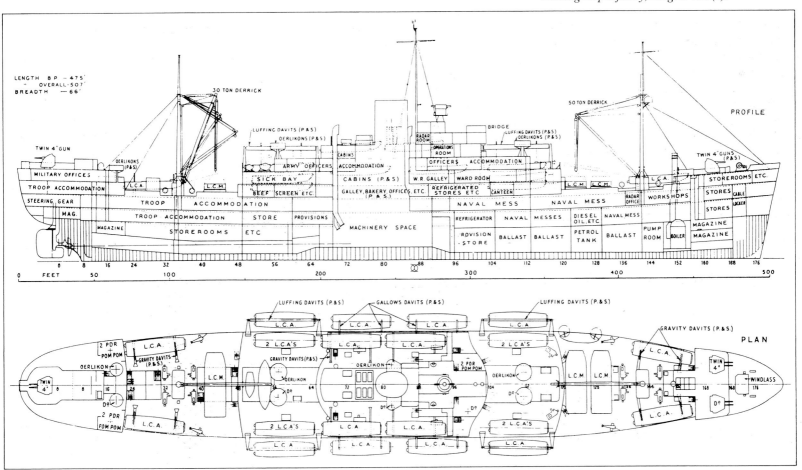

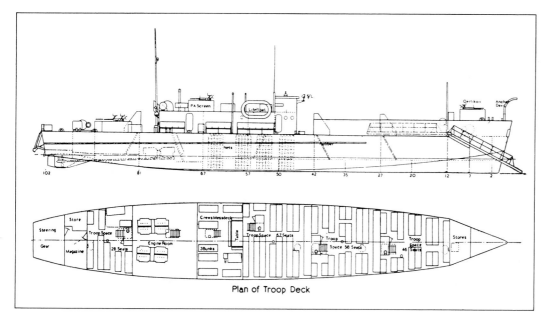

Plan of Troop Deck

took to deploy them (initially with derricks); in a raiding scenario, a number of ferry trips to get equipment ashore – and, more importantly, re-embarked – was not satisfactory. British thinking, therefore, turned towards landing-craft carriers, early ideas producing converted train ferries that could launch loaded LCMs down a stern ramp (Landing Ship Stern Chute or LSS) and modified tankers that stowed the craft on deck and launched them with the aid of large gantries (Landing Ship Gantry). This line of thought culminated in an ingenious Staff Requirement of September 1941 for a fast (17kt) and seaworthy self-propelled floating dock, that could carry the largest tank landing craft fully laden and float them out off a beach-head (although the first tank landing ships were already in prospect, there was some doubt about whether there would ever be sufficient to

hazard them during the assault phase of a landing). In the event the new LSDs (Landing Ship Dock) were built in America and the operational concept was modified during the detail design stage to emphasise the carriage of large numbers of vehicles, with equipment to put them ashore. One of the most successful examples of Anglo-American co-operation in amphibious warfare, the ships proved so versatile in service that the docking concept was adopted by nearly all major amphibious warfare vessels postwar.

The early LCMs were designed to carry a light tank, but after the Dunkirk evacuation Winston Churchill called for proper tank landing craft that could carry armoured vehicles across the English Channel for the eventual invasion of occupied Europe. The design was to carry three heavy tanks at 10kts, to be sea-

worthy enough to reach western France and to be capable of beaching in 2ft 6in of water; known as the Landing Craft Tank, Mk 1 or LCT(1), the prototype was delivered by November, to become the world's first effective heavy landing craft. Enlarged versions followed, there being three further marks developed down to September 1942.

Provoked by the failure of the Dakar expedition in September 1940, Churchill issued an even more demanding requirement for a vessel that could carry tanks anywhere in the world and land them directly on an unprepared beach. The combination of an oceangoing hull with shallow draught was inherently difficult, while detail considerations, like how to ventilate the tank deck (so tanks could run up their engines safely before disembarkation), added novel challenges. Furthermore, the raiding strategy seemed to call for high speed and eventually a 400ft ship, capable of lifting thirteen heavy tanks (plus twenty-seven other vehicles) at 18kts was specified. Three were ordered and were completed as the *Boxer* class in 1943; they were relatively sophisticated, not suitable for mass-production and consequently could not be regarded as expendable, but the biggest drawback was that they could not beach in less than 5ft 6in of water, which meant carrying an elaborate 145ft retractable ramp that took up nearly a third of the tank deck. However, these LST(1)s proved that 'clamshell' type hinged bow doors were a practical proposition, allowing later tank landing ships to adopt a ship-shaped bow, for greater seaworthiness and speed.

Completion was delayed by enemy action and detail design difficulties, but in the meantime a makeshift conversion of three oil tankers was proving most of the operational concepts. These ships were built for the Lake Maracaibo trade where shallow draught was essential, but it was still almost as much as the *Boxers*' and they too needed a complex bow ramp. Nevertheless, beaching trials were successful, and

One of the most original of all Second World War amphibious innovations was the Landing Ship Dock, which could carry fully laden tank landing craft and flood down to float them out of a stern dock. American-built and designed, although initially responding to a British Staff Requirement, this is the first LSD, HMS Eastway at the end of the war. The docking gate is clearly visible at the stern. (IWM)

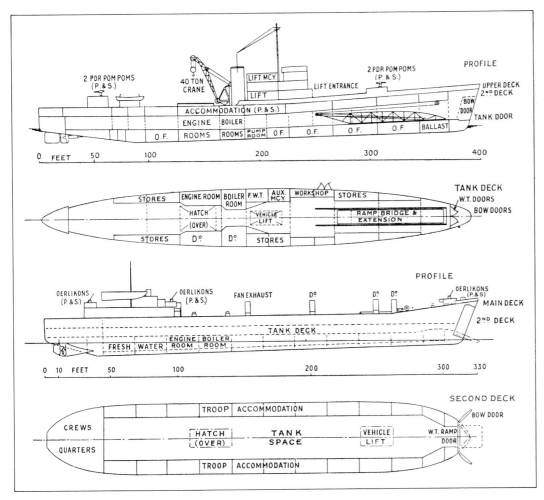

The relatively complex concept of the British Landing Ship Tank, Mk 1 of the Boxer *class compared with the American LST(2) which became the basis of future development. The large area of tank deck taken up by the British ship's bow ramp is evident.*

power. From this requirement for an Atlantic Tank Landing Craft was born the famous Landing Ship Tank, Mk 2 or LST(2), the *Boxers* being regarded as LST(1)s. A 300ft, 10kt vessel with clamshell bow doors, they could carry twenty 25-ton tanks or equivalent on the tank deck, plus a weather deck load, that for delivery purposes might include a complete LCT. The design details were worked out with impressive speed by an Anglo-American team, the first being ordered in February 1942 and completed in November; nearly 900 were completed during the war.

As suggested by the numbers built, they were very successful and surprisingly robust, but their main shortcoming was lack of speed – they rarely reached the design figure, and among their crews the type initials were said to stand for 'Large Slow Target'. The British, therefore, decided to build limited quantities of faster ships, which became LST(3)s; lacking the US lightweight diesels and widespread welding facilities, the ships had to be of riveted construction and powered by frigate-type reciprocating machinery, which gave them a 3kt speed advantage but a poorer payload-to-tonnage ratio. They were also deeper, and usually employed a pontoon causeway to discharge their loads on all but the most steeply shelving beaches.

As well as craft to carry troops and supporting equipment, a need for fire support vessels had been recognised prewar and the initial response was a version of the LCA armed with machine-guns and a smoke mortar to suppress any light opposition on the beaches; the Landing Craft Support (Medium) went through three marks. By December 1940 a craft capable of taking on enemy tanks was requested, but at this time the LSI was still the main delivery vehicle, so weight was restricted by lifting capacity to the 20 tons of an ordinary LCM. The Heavy Support Craft, later to be known as the LCS(L), was given a tank-type 2pdr turret and some light protection, but the first was not completed until April 1943 and trials concluded that it was simply impossible to build a 20-ton boat that could resist a 40-ton tank. Thereafter the British gave up attempts to pro-

they also proved that it was possible to kedge themselves off after beaching (the German expedient of waiting for the tide could not be countenanced given prevailing British strategy).

It soon became clear that victory in the War could only be obtained by re-occupying continental Europe in force, but early calculations of the numbers of tank landing craft needed for the invasion were far beyond British shipbuilding resources. A partial solution was larger landing craft, combined with the provisions of the Lend–Lease Act, which would allow them to be built in America; since there was no spare shipping capacity, this implied that they would have to cross the Atlantic under their own

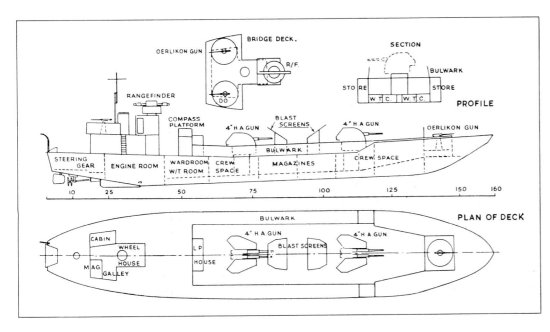

A general arrangement of the remarkably heavily armed British conversions known as Landing Craft Flak, Mk 1s.

The American contribution

Before the outbreak of the European war, American amphibious attention was concentrated on police actions in the Caribbean, and the possibility of having to seize Pacific islands as bases ahead of the fleet advance towards Japan. For both scenarios, the Marine Corps expected to employ shipborne landing craft from transports, similar in concept to British LSIs. There were already the fast destroyer transports (APDs), which would be useful for surprise attacks and raids, but far larger Attack Transports (APAs) and Attack Cargo Ships (AKAs) were developed from prewar troopers (APs) and freighters (AKs); these ships would carry an assault force long distances and put them ashore without chance to regroup, so they had to be 'combat-loaded', with troops, equipment and supplies available in the order of disembarkation. From late 1940 the assault craft were Higgins type LCP(L)s – then also entering service with the Royal Navy – which were handled by davits and loaded from scrambling-nets when afloat. There were also artillery and tank lighters, which needed heavy derricks to both launch and load them. As the British also discovered, this was too time-consuming, and better craft and faster methods of deploying them became essential.

With the provision of Lend–Lease assistance to Great Britain, the USA was to become closely involved with British ideas on amphibious warfare even before Pearl Harbor brought the country into the war. One request from across the Atlantic was for a tank landing craft to carry three 50-ton tanks or equivalent load;

duce shipborne support craft, but early in 1942 the prospect of employing LCIs directly in raids revived the problem of dealing with opposition from enemy tanks and artillery. An LCI(S) conversion was developed, utilising a 6pdr tank-turret, but protection of the wooden hull was inadequate and the LCS(L)2 as it was designated, was also regarded as a failure.

However, the evacuation of Crete in June 1941 brought home the vulnerability of landing craft to air attack, and a pair of special AA vessels were improvised from LCT(2)s under construction. One was given the remarkable armament of two twin 4in and three 20mm Oerlikons, while the second had eight 2pdr pom-poms and four Oerlikons; although perfectly practical, the former pattern was not repeated, whereas a few more of the second type were converted. As the Germans had anticipated with their flak-armed Siebel-Ferries, these Landing Craft Flak (LCF) also proved effective in the surface close-support role.

The 4in armed LCF inspired a Landing Craft Gun or LCG(L) that was to carry two ex-destroyer 4.7in weapons; less valuable than a cruiser or destroyer, they could be risked inshore against fixed coast defences. First conceived during the run-up to the Sicilian invasion in late 1942, they were to become quite sophisticated in terms of armament and protection, but the low trajectory of their weapons confined them to direct fire. The final design, a Landing Craft Gun (Medium), inge-

niously overcame this shortcoming, while meeting an army requirement that the craft be capable of tackling a tank or pillbox and providing fire support to normal (ie beyond line of sight) artillery ranges. The craft were armed with two army 25pdr field gun/howitzers or 17pdr anti-tank guns, depending on mission, and were equipped to flood down and ground at prearranged coordinates so as to be able to fire using map references. A hundred were built but they came too late for the invasion of Europe. In the first major naval venture into rocketry since Congreve, LCTs were also converted for shore bombardments as LCT(R)s, whereby 800–1000 5in rockets were fired electrically in salvoes from static launchers; since the range was fixed at 3500yds, the craft had to be navigated precisely to a pre-arranged firing position.

The attack cargo ship (AKA) USS Rankin *postwar. The large LCMs are visible athwartship both before and abaft the superstructure. (L & L van Ginderen)*

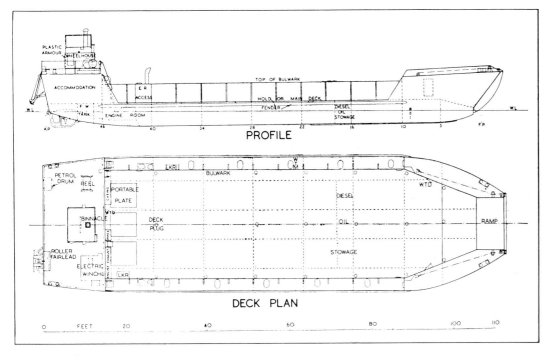

A general arrangement of the Landing Craft Tank, Mk 5. With a loaded displacement of 311 tons they could carry four heavy or seven light tanks. Empty, they could also be transported as deck cargo on LSTs and broadside-launched by heeling the landing ship.

a Thornycroft outline design existed, but in a month following the issuing of the Admiralty Staff Requirement in November 1941, a modified final design was prepared and production followed very rapidly. This LCT(5) was adopted by the US Navy as well, and was the first of a whole series of collaborative ventures whereby British initial concepts were refined by US designers and mass-manufactured by the huge industrial resources of the USA. As already outlined, from this immensely fruitful process came the classic LST(2), LSI(L) and the highly original LSD. It was at this time that the varied British and American designations were standardised into a single integrated series, prefixed by the now-familiar LS or LC plus type and mark number – for example, the American YTL or Yard (*ie* local) Tank Lighter becoming the LCT(5), following the four earlier British tank landing craft designs.

The original sketch for the LCT(5) was a double-ended layout allowing vehicles to be driven on over the stern from an LST and then off on to the beach, but this requirement was dropped during detailed design. However, the succeeding LCT(6) readopted the idea, the superstructure being split down the centreline to permit the kind of operation envisaged for the earlier LCT. Between June 1942 and December 1944, 500 LCT(5)s and 965 LCT(6)s were completed.

The relatively seaworthy Landing Ship Medium began life as a fast LCT. They were a mainstay of the US Pacific amphibious campaigns, nearly 500 being built. LSM 175 in this postwar view, shows clearly the ramp behind the clamshell doors. (L & L van Ginderen)

A larger oceangoing craft was requested early in 1943 which would be fast enough to operate with LCI(L)s and the result was a seaworthy vessel of about 750 tons in beaching mode. Although larger than contemporary British tank landing craft, they were originally designated LCT(7)s, but were soon reclassified as Landing Ships Medium (LSMs), since their seakeeping was significantly better; given a high priority towards the end of the War, nearly five hundred were completed as landing ships and others as fire support vessels.

Apart from conventional land vehicles, the Marines also employed amphibious trucks (DUKWs) and LVT tracked vehicles, which did not require landing craft. In 1943 two 6000-ton minelayers and four similar netlayers were converted to vehicle carriers (LSVs), with

a ramp aft to deploy these vehicles directly into the sea for the rapid reinforcement of a beachhead. Minor landing craft were also modified as war experience accumulated: the LCP(L) was given a ramp so that heavily laden troops did not have to clamber over its 4ft bow, and this LCP(R) was in turn superseded by an LCV with a larger ramp to allow a light vehicle to be carried; over two thousand of each of these types were built before the definitive armoured LCVP version was developed, the wartime production of these last totalling some 22,500.

The versatility of these standard types is witnessed by the number and variety of specialist conversions to which they were successfully adapted. Of the LSTs, eighty-three became battle damage, landing craft or aero-engine repair ships; tenders to PT-boats or salvage craft; stores issuing ships; and even self-propelled accommodation ships. The LCI(L)s were equally adaptable: forty-nine became flotilla flagships for various types of landing craft; forty-two carried mortars for pre-landing barrages; thirty-six were converted for rocket bombardment; eighty-six were fitted for various forms of gunfire support; and five became underwater obstacle locators.

Fire support was probably the largest single mission for which craft were converted. The smallest LCP(L)s existed in a version armed with machine-guns, smoke launchers and rockets for the beach covering role, and over five hundred of these were acquired. As well as the conversions of LCI(L)s mentioned above, 130

Some idea of the sheer numbers of amphibious craft required for the Allied invasion of Europe can be gleaned from this photo of serried ranks of LCTs in a British port in 1944. Note two LCI(L)s converted to leaders in the middle of the foreground 'trot'. All the LCTs have camouflage netting over their tank decks so that aerial reconnaissance could not discover whether they were loaded so as not to help with any analysis of the likely timing of an invasion. (IWM)

Amphibious ships in the Axis navies

Both made their conquests early in the War, and so in direct contrast to the Allies their amphibious preoccupations were largely defensive, and after the abandonment of the German Sealion plan for the invasion of England, outlined above, neither envisaged a major opposed landing for the rest of the War.

The principal German need was craft to support army operations around the fringes of the land war, particularly in the Mediterranean, the Black Sea, the Baltic and Norway, as well as on the larger lakes and rivers. These craft carried out relatively small amphibious operations, kept garrisons supplied, and as the War turned against Germany, were increasingly used to withdraw forces from untenable positions. For most of the War the German army continued to build minor landing craft derived from the 1939 prototype *Pionierlandungsboot 39*, plus a class of small infantry transports, which saw action on inland waters as well around the coasts. The navy's principal contribution to the art was a series of *Marine-*

purpose-designed fire support craft were built using their hull design, but rearranged internally; designated LCS(L)3s, they were in effect all-purpose shallow-draught gunboats armed with a 3in gun, two twin 40mm, plus Oerlikons and rocket launchers. The largest support ships were similarly evolved from the LSM, the first twenty being conversions with a 5in gun aft, four mortars and up to one hundred rockets; forty-eight later units were built from scratch on modified LSM hulls but with the superstructure moved aft and the 5in gun immediately forward of it and the weather deck filled with ten twin automatic rocket launchers instead of the fixed rails of the conversions.

One of the most important lessons learnt about large-scale amphibious operations was the need for elaborate command and control facilities to proceed with the assault forces. The British converted five large headquarters ships – LSH(L)s – from existing merchant auxiliaries and eight specialist fighter direction ships (LSFs) from LSTs and smaller auxiliaries, but superior American resources allowed fifteen command ships (ACGs), combining both functions, to be built on standard mercantile hulls. However, the role was so important that conversions were also undertaken from a

transport, a light seaplane tender and, in 1944, from the six surviving 'Treasury' class Coast Guard cutters.

Although her forces carried out a number of amphibious assaults along its Arctic and Baltic coasts, the Soviet Union made do without specialist landing ships, so the only other wartime developments of note were in the Japanese and German navies.

Although not entirely successful as the prototype tank landing ship, HMS Boxer was converted to fill the equally vital role of fighter direction ship or LSF. The radar and electronics dominate the superstructure and mastheads, necessary to detect enemy and control friendly aircraft over the invasion coast. (IWM)

The unusual Japanese fast transport T 1 *in May 1944. They could carry four landing craft or seven amphibious tanks and later transported midget submarines or human torpedoes.* (IWM)

fährprähme or MFP (naval lighters) of about 250 tons; they had landing craft type hulls and could carry tanks or infantry, but were soon adapted for a range of other duties, including fire support, flak defence, minelaying and *sperrbrecher* mine destruction (about 1200 of all types were completed and they were employed in most theatres of the European war). A noteworthy variation on this general theme was the prefabricated *Marine Artillerie Leichter* (MAL), designed for sectionalised transport by rail; built in three series totalling forty-seven completed units, they were primarily gunfire support ships with a subsidiary transport capability. The Sealion Siebel-Ferry concept was also developed into more seaworthy craft, but they were always vulnerable to attack. No major landing ships were developed or converted by the Germans after 1940.

In contrast to Germany, Japan's conquests were predominantly amphibious, but despite the prewar lead in specialist types, most of her early successes were scored with relatively unsophisciated converted transports and small landing craft. Strategic surprise and the weak state of opposing defences made this possible, but as the offensive ground to a halt in mid-1942 the need for specialist landing ships

became apparent. In August 1943 an important policy decision in effect put Japanese forces on the defensive, and from this stemmed a number of requirements for amphibious craft which could carry out selective counter attacks and reinforce the existing defence perimeter. One particularly important mission stemmed from the Japanese desire to build airfields in areas of Allied air superiority, which was to exert a powerful influence on the designs which followed.

The unsuccessful attempt to support the forces on Guadalcanal cost the Imperial Japanese Navy many front-line warships, and this inspired the concept of a fast transport which could conduct such risky operations. The resulting 1500-ton *T 1* class bore a general resemblance to a destroyer escort with a beaver-tail stern down which *Daihatsu* landing craft or amphibious tanks could be launched; because they were to be employed in areas of high risk, they were given a 22kt speed (to cover as much distance as possible in the hours of darkness) and a powerful armament of a twin 12.7cm (5in) DP gun and three triple 25mm AA, as well as a relatively luxurious electronics suite. They proved versatile ships, which could be used for commando-type raids, escort duties

(they were given depth charges and enhanced AA weaponry) and were eventually employed transporting midget submarines and human torpedoes in the final phase of the Pacific war; twenty-one were completed between early 1944 and July 1945.

A small LST-type vessel was also called for, and it too was to have a relatively high top speed (16kts) and to be highly manoeuvrable. The army was already building the slower (13kt) ES type, but it was not suitable for rapid construction so from late 1944 it was superseded by the navy's new SB type, a 1000-ton vessel with a bow ramp rather than the bow doors of the army type. Generally resembling Allied LCTs, the Japanese craft paid for their higher speed with a much reduced payload-to-tonnage ratio, being narrower and devoting a greater percentage of length to machinery; some had to be fitted with diesels instead of geared turbines so could only reach 13kts. Being designed especially for the calm waters of the South Pacific, they were very lightly constructed and suffered some structural failures when the exigencies of war forced them to operate in rougher conditions, but over fifty were completed for the navy and a further twenty for the army.

At the end of the war, developments were tending towards faster and more seaworthy landing craft in the Allied navies, but the introduction of the helicopter was to make fundamental changes to concepts of amphibious warfare thereafter.

Brian Friend and Robert Gardiner

Amphibious Warfare Vessels: Typical Ships 1906–1945

Ship or Class [Type]	Nationality	Dispt (tons) Normal Full load	Dimensions (loa × breadth × deep draught) Feet–Inches Metres	Armament	Typical maximum load	Speed (max design kts)	Launch dates	Numbers built
X1 [X-Lighter]	British	160	105–6 × 21–0 × 3–6 32.2 × 6.4 × 1.1	Nil	Men, horses or light artillery	?6	1915	200
No1 ['Russud' type]	Russian	225	179–6 × 21–6 × 4–0 54.7 × 6.6 × 1.2	MGs only	520 men (hold); 240 on deck	5.5	1915–16	50
SHINSHU MARU [Landing ship]	Japanese	9000 12,000	492–2 × 72–2 × 26–9 150.0 × 22.0 × 8.2	5–3in AA	20 Daihatsu	19	1935	1
'DAIHATSU' type [Landing craft]	Japanese	20	47–10 × 11–0 × 2–6 14.6 × 3.4 × 0.8	2 MGs or 2/3–25mm	1–7t tank; or 70 men	c8	1935–45	3229 for IJN
TYPE A1 'PENICHE' ['Sealion' barge]	German	360	c126–4 × 16–6 × 7–6 c38.5 × 5.05 × 2.3	Army guns	3–25t tanks	6–8	1940*	1336

Ship or Class [Type]	Nationality	Dispt (tons) Normal Full load	Dimensions (loa × breadth × deep draught) Feet–Inches Metres	Armament	Typical maximum load	Speed (max design kts)	Launch dates	Numbers built
SF01 [Siebel-Ferry]	German	130 c300	79–6 × 44–11 × 3–11 24.3 × 13.7 × 1.2	Various	40/60-ton load	6.6	1940	?
GLENEARN [LSI(L)]	British	9784grt	511–0 × 66–6 × ? 134.2 × 20.3 × ?	6–4in, 2pdr and 20mm	24 LCA, 3 LCM, 1087 men	18	1940*	3
ALC (later LCA) 2 [Assault craft]	British	9 11	38–9 × 10–0 × 4–8 11.8 × 3.0 × 1.4	Nil [MG later]	35 men	11.5	1940–44	2030
LCM 100 [LCM(1) type]	British	36	44–8 × 14–0 × 3–0 13.6 × 4.3 × 0.9	Nil	1–16t tank or 100 men	7.5	1940–44	600
LCT 1 [LCT(1) type]	British	372	152–0 × 29–0 × 4–4 46.3 × 8.8 × 1.3	2–2pdr, 2–20mm	3–40t or 6–20t tanks	10	1940–41	30
BOXER class [LST(1)]	British	3616 beached 5970	390–0 × 49–0 × 5–6 fwd, 13–0 aft 118.9 × 14.9 × 1.7, 4.0 beached	12–20mm, 2 mortars	13–40t tanks and 27–3t trucks	16.25	1942	3
LST 1 [LST(2) type]	American	2366 beached 4080	328 × 50 × 3–11 fwd, 10–0 aft 100.0 × 15.2 × 1.2, 3.0 beached	7–40mm, 12–20mm	20–25t tanks or equivalent load	c10	1942–45	982
ASHLAND [LSD]	American	4032 7930	457–9 × 72–2 × 15–10 seagoing 139.5 × 22.0 × 4.8	1–5in, 12–40mm, 16–20mm	3 LCT(6)s or 2 LCT(3)s	15	1942–46	25
LCI(L) 1 [LCI)L)]	American	238 beached 387	158–6 × 23–8 × 2–8 fwd, 5–0 aft 48.3 × 7.2 × 0.8, 1.5 beached	4–20mm	188 men or 75t cargo	15	1942–44	1000
F811 [MPF type D]	German	168 239	163–6 × 21–7 × 4–5 49.8 × 6.6 × 1.35	1–8.8cm, 1–3.7cm, 2–20mm	3–40t tanks, 200 men or 140t load	10	1942–44	c335
LCG(L) 939 [LCG(L)4]	British	570	187–3 × 38–8 × 4–5 57.1 × 11.8 × 1.4	4–4.7in, 10/14–20mm		10	1943–44	10
LCVP type	American	8	36 × 10–6 × 2–2 fwd, 3–0 aft 11.0 × 3.2 × 0.7, 0.9 beached	2 MGs	36 men or 2.5t vehicle	8	1943–45	22,492
LCT(6)	American	309 beached	119–1 × 32–8 × 3–7 fwd, 4–0 aft 36.3 × 10.0 × 1,1, 1.2 beached	2–20mm	3–50t tanks or 150t cargo	8	1943–44	965
APPALACHIAN [ACG, C2–S–B1 hull]	American	7430 13,910	459–3 × 63–0 × 24–0 max 140.0 × 19.2 × 7.3	2–5in, 8–40mm, 20–20mm	368 HQ staff	17	1943	4
HASKELL [APA, 'Victory' hull]	American	6873 14,800	455–0 × 62–0 × 24–0 max 138.7 × 18.9 × 7.3	1–5in, 12–40mm, 10–20mm	1561 men, 2 LCM, 22LCVP, 2 LCP(L)	16.5	1943–45	116
LSM(R) 401 [LSM(R) type]	American	790 994	206–3 × 34–6 × 6–9 62.9 × 10.5 × 2.1	1–5in, 4–40mm, 10 auto RLs		13	1944–45	48
MAL 13 [MAL type Ia]	German	146	112–6 × 25–11 × 2–9 34.3 × 7.7 × 0.8	2–8.8cm, 1–3.7cm, 4–20mm		8.5	1944	24
T1 [Fast transport]	Japanese	1476 1934	315–0 × 33–5 × 12–6 max 96.0 × 10.2 × 3.8	2–5in, 9–25mm	4 Daihatsu, 260t load	22	1944–45	21
T103 [SB type LST]	Japanese	856 1004 trial	264–0 × 29–10 × 8–10 fwd, 10–6 aft 80.5 × 9.1 × 2.7, 3.2 trial	1–8cm, 6–25mm	9–15t tanks or 250t load	16	1944–45	43 navy 20 army

* Date taken into service as amphibious vessel.

10

Auxiliary Warships

THE world's merchant fleets have always been a strategic reserve for their respective navies, and the wartime conversion of mercantile vessels into fighting ships is as old as naval warfare itself. In the age of sail large merchantmen like East Indiamen made passable if not first class ships of the line, while countries like France had encouraged privateering – essentially free enterprise commerce warfare – into an instrument of national policy. With the growing divergence between warship and merchant ship design following the introduction of steam, the opportunity for such conversions seemed to recede. However, warships simultaneously became more complex, expensive and fewer in numbers, so there was further impetus in times of emergency to supplement regular naval vessels with converted merchant ships. The advent of the armoured ship meant that merchant ships would never again fight in the line of battle, but there were many other roles for which they were suited, from cruisers downwards.

From the American Civil War onwards, attention was paid to the wartime potential of suitable merchant ships and from the 1880s some navies adopted subsidy schemes to encourage shipowners to modify specific ships (principally with strengthened points for gun mountings) in anticipation of their employment in war. However, the two great wars of the twentieth century were both global and virtually unlimited, which increased the demand for ships beyond any reasonable anticipation. Furthermore, new or previously undervalued threats – the mine, the submarine and the air-

craft – also required new types of ships, and more rapidly than the conventional design and construction cycle of a purpose-built warship. All these factors were to promote the employment of auxiliary warships in a variety and quantity never seen in earlier conflicts.

Space precludes all but the briefest survey of the many types, but since all these auxiliaries were essentially substitutes for, or supplements to, regular warships the following sections have been organised accordingly: cruiser substitutes (armed merchant cruisers, boarding vessels and commerce raiders), escort forces (commissioned escorts, armed yachts, AA auxiliaries), aviation ships (seaplane carriers, CAM and MAC ships), and mine warfare vessels (auxiliary minelayers, minesweepers, trawlers, etc). Mercantile conversions for amphibious purposes are too closely linked with the history of combined operations to be separated; they are covered in Chapter 9.

Auxiliary cruiser

The 1856 Declaration of Paris had outlawed the seizure of merchant ships by private vessels operating under a Letter of Marque, thus effectively abolishing the legal basis for privateering.

However, in Europe there was much spec-

ulative building of fast commerce raiders for the Confederate States during the American Civil War. These vessels were of mercantile design in order to deceive the Federal cruisers. The Russians and Germans had taken note of these developments and by 1877, when war between Great Britain and Russia seemed likely the Russians acquired three 13kt vessels building in the USA, for use as auxiliary cruisers. These vessels were of 6000grt, carried 6in guns and had an endurance of 20 days. War, however, was averted and the three vessels acquired were used as part of the newly constituted Russian Volunteer Fleet (RVF), which was used on a regular liner service between Odessa and the Far East in peacetime and in war the vessels supplemented the cruiser squadrons.

Technical developments, including new boiler designs and the adoption of triple expansion engines, gave vessels greater endurance and fuel economy. The construction of the vessels was aided by the adoption of steel instead of iron, which aided carrying capacity. The British Admiralty reached an agreement with the White Star Company to subsidise future vessels strengthened in certain areas to mount guns at times of international tension. The Germans made similar agreements with Norddeutscher Lloyd and Hamburg-Amerika. During 1889–90 the first vessels designed with such strengthening were launched: *Majestic* and *Teutonic* for White Star and Hamburg-

The British armed merchant cruiser (AMC) Avenger; originally the Aotearoa, *she was taken over from the Union Steam Ship Co of New Zealand during building and entered service in 1916 armed with eight 6in guns. Her career was short, being sunk in June 1917 by U 69. Like most AMCs, her modifications were minimal – superstructure cut away in places, boats reduced in number and some protection afforded to the wheelhouse – but from a distance the silhouette remained that of a liner. (CMP)*

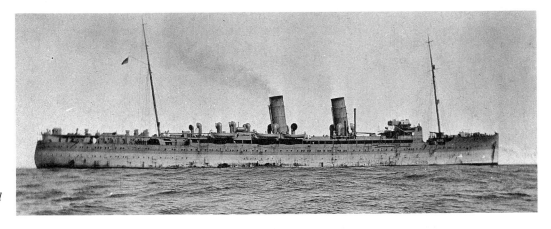

Amerika's *Auguste Victoria, Columbia, Normannia* and *Furst Bismarck*.

The 1890s were to see the Russians develop two standard types for the Volunteer Fleet – a 20kt passenger vessel and a 5000/6000-ton cargo ship. In 1895 the Imperial German Navy chartered the *Normannia* for a 15-day experimental cruise. At this time, the thinking was very much in terms of a conventional cruiser being converted from the large number of passenger vessels then available and not the fast refrigerated cargo vessels that were later used as commerce raiders.

The British Admiralty's philosophy on the use of the armed merchant cruiser (AMC), as these vessels were now termed, was not to alter radically in the next forty years, as Britain's major preoccupation was that of trade protection, where speed, endurance and seakeeping were the qualities required.

Russian policy was also consistent throughout the period with the expansion of the Volunteer Fleet continuing, and by 1902 this fleet consisted of six large and nine small ships. On the outbreak of the Russo-Japanese War in 1904, two of the RVF's largest vessels were stationed in the Red Sea to intercept enemy commerce. However, after the seizure of a British ship, the RVF vessels were withdrawn following diplomatic protests. During this war the Russians commissioned seven auxiliary cruisers, whilst the Japanese replied with twenty 'Commerce Protectors' and a further twenty-two gunboats that had been converted from small steamers. Russia also acquired the *Auguste Victoria, Columbia* and *Furst Bismarck* from Germany, which they operated as the *Kuban, Terek* and the *Don*.

The Hague Convention (1907) restricted the use of converted merchant ships as auxiliary cruisers in the following ways:

1. The converted vessels were required to fly the appropriate naval ensign and her commander's pendant.

2. The vessel's commander had to be appointed by the nation operating the vessel and his name had to appear on the appropriate service list.

3. The vessel's crew had to be subject to service discipline.

4. Vessels' names had to be entered on the country's Navy List.

The Germans made further provision for the use of the auxiliary cruiser, when it was agreed that leading German shipping companies, such as Hamburg-Sud Amerika, joined by the Hamburg-Amerika and Norddeutscher Lloyd lines would commit themselves to the employment of a minimum number of former naval personnel on board their vessels. In 1913, the following specification for new tonnage was also established:

1. A minimum speed of 18kts.

2. A cruising range of 10,000 miles at 10kts.

3. Twin-screw propulsion.

4. Improved sub-division and a double bottom.

5. Adequate pumps and flood control had to be fitted.

6. Two separated and independently operated sets of emergency steam steering machinery, situated below the waterline and protected by coal bunkers, had to be installed.

7. Boilers, engines and high pressure pipes had to be protected by coal bunkers.

8. Decks had to be strengthened for the mounting of two 10.5cm (4in) guns forward and aft and four 15cm (5.9in) guns broadside.

9. An increased number of coal ports were fitted to allow its movement within the ship and expedite stowage from other vessels.

10. Cooling arrangements for ammunition fitted.

11. Provision of additional electrical generators.

12. Provision of tall masts for radio aerials and lookouts.

Thus, it can be seen that at this time the Germans, like the British, were only considering the use of liners.

The outbreak of war in August 1914 initiated rapid changes in the philosophy and operation of AMCs. The following vessels were earmarked for conversion to AMCs at this time:

Great Britain	– 26 ships	(18–25kts)
France	– 9 ships	(17–23kts)
Italy	– 21 ships	(17–23kts)
Japan	– 4 ships	(20–21kts)
Russia	– 4 ships	(19–20kts)
Germany	– 13 ships	(15–23kts)

There were to be distinct differences between the operations of the German and British AMCs. The German vessels were to develop into vessels used to destroy enemy commerce, whilst British AMCs were used solely on trade protection duties.

The armed merchant cruiser in British service 1914–1918

The Royal Navy commissioned or started the conversion of no less than sixty-eight vessels into armed merchant cruisers. The vessels converted ranged from the 2876-ton gross *Calypso*, renamed *Calyx* in service, to the 45,647-ton *Aquitania*. In fact *Aquitania*, with *Lusitania* and *Mauretania* were released after a few weeks because of their heavy fuel consumption and then reverted to commercial use. The typical British AMC evolved into a vessel of some 15,000 tons with a speed of approximately 18kts. The vessels were armed with surplus naval guns, that had been stored at strategic locations for the purpose.

The vessels were employed on escort and patrol duties all over the world, but no fewer than thirty-three of these vessels served with the 10th Cruiser Squadron based at Kirkwall, in the Shetlands, blockading the Denmark Straits, the Iceland-Shetland passages from the threat of German raiders. The AMCs were particularly suited to these arduous duties because of their size, seaworthiness, stability and endurance. The British AMCs were to achieve two successes against German auxiliary cruisers – first when *Carmania* cornered the brand new *Cap Trafalgar* in the vicinity of Trinidad Island in the South Atlantic in the early days of the war. Some eighteen months later in February 1916, the commerce raider *Grief*, after sinking the AMC *Alcantara*, was sunk by the AMC *Andes* and the armed boarding vessel *Dundee* in the North Sea.

Losses were heavy: *Avenger, Bayano, Calgarian, Hilary, India, Marmora, Moldavia, Orama, Otway* and *Patia* and *Viknor* were sunk by submarines; *Clan MacNaughton* and *Laurentic* were mined, and *Oceanic* and *Otranto* were wrecked. *Digby* and *Oropesa* became the French *Artois* and *Champagne* (lost 1917) from the end of 1915 until July 1917. Some thirty AMCs were still operational in November 1918, but were quickly demobilised, with *Arlanza* being the last during June 1920.

Any doubts about the viability of the AMC against the submarine were soon forgotten, but these doubts soon came to fore in the next conflict.

British AMCs: the Second World War

During the winter of 1939–40 fifty-six passenger liners, all twin-screw vessels with a speed of at least 15kts were requisitioned. The Canadians converted three vessels, the Australians *Kanimbla* and *Manoora* and the New Zealanders the *Monowai*. The vessels were generally armed with six or eight 6in guns and a pair of 3in AA guns. Later in the war, this armament was supplemented by 20mm or 40mm weapons when available. Rudimentary fire control equipment was also fitted as was radar, when it became available. Some vessels, especially those serving in the South Atlantic were fitted with catapults and aircraft. To in-

crease the buoyancy of the vessels, if torpedoed, thousands of empty oil drums were stored between decks. (The effectiveness of these measures is shown by the fact that *Forfar*, *Salopian* and *Patroclus* took no less than five, six and seven torpedoes to sink them in 1940–41). *Corfu* was one of the best equipped AMCs and her final armament was nine 6in guns in single mounts, four 4in guns in twin mounts, two 2pdrs, nineteen 20mm as well as an aircraft with catapult. Gunnery control and aerial warning radar was also fitted.

The AMCs were to have a short career in the North Atlantic, as losses were very heavy, with *Rawalpindi*, *Jervis Bay* and *Voltaire* being sunk in surface actions; *Andania*, *Carinthia*, *Dunvegan Castle*, *Forfar* (ex-*Montrose*), *Patroclus*, *Laurentic*, *Rajputana*, *Salopian*, *Scotstoun* (ex-*Caledonia*) and *Transylvania* were sunk by submarine torpedo, whilst *Comorin* was lost by fire. However, AMCs remained in service in the South Atlantic, Indian Ocean and Pacific waters throughout 1942–43. However by January 1943 only seventeen vessels were still in

commission – six in the South Atlantic, eight in the East Indies and three in Australian and New Zealand waters. This had been reduced to eight vessels (four in the East Indies and four in West African waters) a year later. By May 1944 only the damaged *Asturias*, laid up at Freetown, remained.

By this time, these valuable vessels were wanted on other duties and their crews required to man the new frigates and destroyers joining the fleet. Thus passed the AMC from British service. The forty vessels that survived were all to give sterling service in other roles – *Pretoria Castle* was converted to an escort carrier during 1943, *Prince Robert* (RCN), to an auxiliary AA vessel, whilst two others became depot ships, four more repair ships, eight LSIs,

two HQ ships and twenty-two into troopships, *Laconia* and *California* being subsequently lost on trooping duties.

German auxiliary cruisers 1914–1918

At the onset of the war, four auxiliary cruisers sailed for their respective areas of operations and this phase ended with *Kronprinz Wilhelm's* arrival at Newport News, USA in April 1915. These vessels met the traditional ideas of the armed merchant cruiser. The Germans had planned to operate twenty auxiliary cruisers at the beginning of the War; thirteen of these twenty vessels were to be used offensively and the others were to operate as supply vessels. However, of the thirteen, only six were avail-

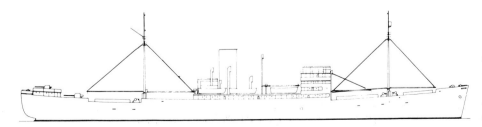

THE CHANGING STYLE OF GERMAN AUXILIARY CRUISERS

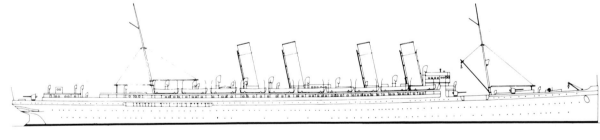

The liner Kaiser Wilhelm der Grosse *in 1914 – large distinctive and vulnerable.*

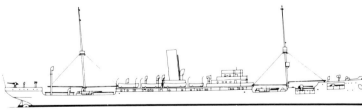

Möwe, the most successful commerce raider of the First World War was an ex-fruit carrier – indistinguishable from many merchant ships and far easier to disguise than unique passenger liners.

The raider Atlantis *in 1940. Continuing the lessons learnt in the First World War, later raiders were ordinary cargo ships. Although the raiders chosen were usually rather Germanic in appearance,* Atlantis *was very similar to Norwegian, Soviet, Japanese and Dutch ships, so was not automatically suspicious.*

able in German ports at mobilisation and of these two were returned to their owners after only a short period of service. Three vessels were not commissioned at all and only *Kaiser Wilhelm der Grosse* was fitted out and sent on her mission from Germany, to be sunk by the cruiser *Highflyer* on 26 August 1914. Three of the remaining seven vessels avoided British patrols and were fitted out in the following ways:

Kronprinz Wilhelm made for New York, but later met the cruiser *Karlsruhe* at a predetermined Atlantic rendezvous, was armed and received additional crew and entered service on 5 August 1914. After capturing and sinking fifteen ships, she arrived at Newport News on 11 April 1915 and was interned.

Cap Trafalgar reached Buenos Aires, but was later equipped by the gunboat *Eber* and commissioned on 31 August 1914. However, a fortnight later, she was sunk by the AMC *Carmania* off Trinidad Island in the South Atlantic.

Prinz Eitel Friedrich, arrived at Shanghai and was later re-armed and re-crewed from the gunboats *Tiger* and *Luchs* at Tsingtao and commissioned on 5 August 1914. After sinking and capturing eleven vessels, she arrived at Newport News on 11 April 1915 and was interned.

Berlin was converted at Wilhelmshaven Dockyard into an auxiliary minelayer and entered service on 29 September 1914. The mines she laid off Tory Island, Ireland led to the sinking of the battleship *Audacious* on 27 October 1914. However, beset by bad weather and a misunderstanding of intelligence led to her commanding officer letting her be interned at Trondheim on 18 November 1914.

It was soon realised that the use of high speed steamers as commerce raiders, led to heavy fuel consumption and consequently the need for fuel supplies completely controlled their commanders' course of action and made these vessels reliant on the capture of enemy colliers. When reports were received on these first operations, the whole policy on commerce raiders was reviewed.

As the last of the old type auxiliary cruisers were being interned at Newport News, the first conversions of what was to become the definitive raiders were under way. This vessel, the *Meteor*, made two cruises during May–August 1915, sinking four merchant ships through the mines she laid as well as the armed boarding vessel *Ramsey* in a surface action, before scuttling herself on the approach of British cruisers on 9 August 1915.

The parameters for the following deep sea vessels had been drawn up by *Oberleutnant zur*

See Theodor Wolf during August 1915 when he proposed that cargo vessels be fitted out as auxiliary cruisers, with the following characteristics: 4600 tons, 150 crew, cruising range of 38,000 nautical miles with an endurance of 140 days. Such vessels would be harder to trace as they were standard cargo vessels, could change their identity more quickly and had long endurance without recourse to refuelling. At this time (November 1915), the German admiralty were still thinking of minelaying as these vessels' principal weapon.

On 4 December 1915 the steamer *Pungo* arrived at Wilhelmshaven for conversion into the raider *Möwe*, and during the next two years these nine raiders had varying degrees of success. The principal naval successes came early with the pre-dreadnought battleship *King Edward VII* sinking off Cape Wrath on 6 January 1916 after hitting one of the mines laid by *Möwe* five days earlier. *Grief* sank the AMC *Alcantara* in action in the northern North Sea. *Möwe* in two cruises from December to March 1915 and November 1916 to March 1917 sank or captured forty ships of some 180,000grt. *Meteor* sank five ships whilst *Wolf* (ii) sank fourteen ships of 38,391 gross registered tons; *Seeadler*, a converted sailing ship, sank sixteen ships of 30,099 tons; *Geier* (ex-*Saint Theodore*) captured and armed by *Möwe* sank two ships of 1442 tons plus nineteen vessels of 96,000 lost by mines laid.

Meteor, *Greif*, *Leopard* and *Iltis* were sunk in action with British vessels, whilst *Wolf* (i) grounded in the Elbe and was written off. *Seeadler* stranded on the island of Mopelia in the Society Islands on 2 August 1917 and was lost; *Geier* was scuttled by *Möwe* as her machinery was worn out on 14 December 1917; *Möwe* and *Wolf* (ii) survived the war.

German auxiliary cruisers in the Second World War

The general principles set by the vessels above were incorporated in the raiders used during the Second World War. Generally the vessels utilised were superior in size, seakeeping characteristics, speed and endurance over those vessels used between 1914 and 1918. The vessels were largely powered by diesel engines to give the extended range required. Generally the main armament consisted of six 150mm, one 75mm and two 37mm, two 20mm, although there were variations in the armament.

The first wave – *Orion*, *Atlantis*, *Widder*, *Thor*, *Pinguin* and *Komet* – sailed in the spring and early summer of 1940. They were to prove successful: *Orion* sank six ships of 39,132 tons

between March 1940 and August 1941, beside sharing the sinking of seven ships of 43,162 tons with *Komet*; *Komet* on her second cruise sank a further three ships of 21,378 tons. *Atlantis* between March 1940 and November 1941 sank twenty-two ships of 145,968 tons; *Widder* sank ten ships of 58,644 tons between May and October 1940; *Thor* on her first cruise sank twelve ships of 96,547 tons between June 1940 and April 1941. Finally, *Pinguin* captured or sank twenty-eight ships of 136,642 tons; on 14 January 1941 she captured the whole of a Norwegian whaling fleet of three factory ships and eleven whalecatchers.

This group of raiders caused the Allies great material loss as well as disruption of their shipping. The Allies were forced to employ large numbers of their scarce cruisers and AMCs on trade protection and search duties.

The second wave, consisting of *Kormoran* (December 1940–November 1941), *Thor* (January–October 1942) and *Michel* (March 1942–March 1943) and again between May–October 1943 and *Stier* (May–September 1942) were as disruptive, but not as successful in terms of sinkings, as Allied intelligence and countermeasures were becoming more effective.

Stier sank four vessels of 30,728 tons including the 'Liberty' ship *Stephen Hopkins* which sank her. *Kormoran* sank eleven vessels of 68,274 tons, before being sunk; she took her assailant, the Australian cruiser *Sydney* to the bottom with her, and this was the only time an auxiliary cruiser sank a regular warship in direct combat. *Michel* sank eighteen ships of over 128,000 tons in her two cruises. In addition to the above litany of loss and disruption, mines laid by *Thor* off the New Zealand coast sank an auxiliary minesweeper, three merchant ships of 27,245 tons and two trawlers. *Pinguin* and *Passat* (an auxiliary armed by *Pinguin*) sank four ships of 18,068 tons off the coast of Australia.

Atlantis, *Pinguin* and *Kormoran* were sunk by British cruisers, *Stier* by the 'Liberty' ship *Stephen Hopkins* in the South Atlantic, *Komet* by MTB 236 in the Channel and *Michel* by the US submarine *Tarpon*. *Thor* was destroyed by an explosion at Yokohama in November 1942. *Coronel* damaged by air attacks off Boulogne on 13 and 26 February 1943, returned to Kiel and was decommissioned. *Hansa* reverted to a fighter direction ship.

The successes of these raiders were concentrated in the early years of the war, when Allied resources were limited and intelligence faulty or sparse. However, as new ships, better intelligence and Admiralty control of shipping movements became tighter, the achievements of these vessels declined. The cost of fitting out eleven such vessels and their maintenance on the sea lanes was not an inconsiderable strain on German resources.

Auxiliary cruisers in service with other nations

The United States was unique in that it did not employ armed merchant cruisers of any kind in either World War. This was a product of the fact that the USA had a relatively small merchant marine and the industrial capacity to build sufficient front-line warships.

The Japanese, however, had requisitioned ten vessels of between 3320 and 6242 gross tons for use during the Russo-Japanese War of 1904–5. Little is known of their armament and all the vessels were paid off at the war's end except *Nikko Maru* (1903, 5823 gross tons), which was wrecked off Pusan in May 1905. The Japanese did not commission any AMCs during the First World War, as she was only lightly engaged in the conflict and her lines of communication were not threatened. However, during the second conflict, the Japanese commissioned thirteen cargo liners and freighters of between 5000 and 11,000 tons, with speeds of between 16kts and 21kts, for use as commerce raiders. The Japanese seemed to have learnt the German lessons of the Great War concerning speed, endurance and size of such vessels. However, these vessels were to be relatively unsuccessful in service. This was because the guns were carried behind fixed shields and could not be concealed and hence these ships could not be disguised when raiding. The success of Allied countermeasures meant that the ten surviving vessels were converted to troop transports during 1942–43. *Akagi Maru* and *Kongo Maru* were sunk by US carrier aircraft, whilst *Hokuku Maru* was sunk in a spirited action by the Indian minesweeper *Bengal* and the Dutch tanker *Ondina* on 11 November 1942 in the Bay of Bengal.

The French navy employed auxiliary cruisers in both World Wars – over twenty in the First, initially as cruisers and later as troopships to the Dardanelles and Macedonian fronts. The vessels used varied greatly in size between the 1380-ton *Golo II* to the 14,900-ton *Gallia*, and in armament – from *Golo II*'s two

65mm and two 47mm to *Provence II*'s three 138.6mm (5.5in) and four 120mm (4.7in). Losses were heavy, with *Burdigala* and *Caledonien* being mined, whilst *Carthage* was torpedoed off Gallipoli and *Golo II* was torpedoed off Corfu, whilst operating as cruisers. *Djemnah, Gallia, Gange, Himalaya, Italia, Polynesien, Provence II, Santa Anna* and *Sontay* were all later lost when trooping.

In the Second World War, France commissioned a further eleven AMCs between September and November 1939 and the *Cap des Palmes* was requisitioned during 1941. The majority of these vessels were paid off following the French defeat in June 1940. However, *Barfleur* was retained as an armed transport and the *Cap des Palmes* was not returned until 1947. *Victor Schoelcher* had originally paid off on 15 October 1940, but was again requisitioned on 27 November 1941 and as *Bougainville* was sunk by Fleet Air Arm aircraft at Diego Suarez on 6 May 1942 during the initial Madagascar landings.

Italy operated numerous AMCs during both World Wars and in the later conflict operated the short-lived raider *Ramb III* as well.

Armed boarding vessels/ocean boarding vessels

These vessels, generally smaller than AMCs, only served with the Royal Navy and performed the necessary but arduous duty as the name implies of boarding neutral vessels at sea to enforce contraband control. These vessels had become necessary after the imposition of the distant blockade as an instrument of policy in 1913. If contraband was found on board, the

neutral vessel was sent to either Lerwick in the Shetlands or the Downs Contraband Control Centre in the Channel for more thorough examination of her cargo, throughout the First World War. However, the station at the Downs only operated during 1939–40, as after the defeat of France it became untenable. Lerwick was still operational, but many of the boarding vessels were transferred to other duties as the German occupation of most of western Europe in 1940, made contraband control obsolete.

During 1914–18, some forty vessels were commissioned as armed boarding vessels, as they were then termed. Most vessels were around 2000 tons, with a fair turn of speed and many cross channel packets were taken up for these duties. The *Duke of Albany* (torpedoed 25 August 1916), *Dundee* (torpedoed 3 September 1917), *Fauvette* (mined 9 March 1916), *Grive* (torpedoed 8 December 1917), *Louvain* (torpedoed 20 January 1918), *Sarnia* (torpedoed 12 September 1918), *Snaefell* (torpedoed 5 June 1918) *Stephen Furness* (torpedoed 13 December 1917), *Tara* (torpedoed 5 November 1915), *The Ramsey* (sunk in action 8 August 1915), *Tithonus* (torpedoed 29 March 1918) were all lost whilst undertaking these unsung, arduous and dangerous duties. The survivors were rapidly demobilised postwar.

A further twenty-eight vessels (sixteen ocean boarding vessels and twelve armed boarding vessels) were commissioned during 1939–40. The need for such vessels ceased in 1940, but the last of the ocean boarding vessels were not returned to their owners or converted to other uses until 1943. The primary distinction between the two types was that the ocean board-

Besides large AMCs, the British also employed boarding vessels to inspect neutral shipping and intercept would-be blockade runners, and commissioned escort vessels. This is Bayano *in First World War camouflage serving as a commissioned escort; the large 6in gun on the forecastle is very obvious.* (CMP)

ing vessels were usually armed with two 6in guns, and were larger – usually around 5000 tons gross, with the *Corinthian* the smallest at 3151 tons and *Lady Somers* of 8194 tons the largest. *Camito, Crispin, Lady Somers, Manistee, Malvernian* and *Patia* had all been lost by the close of 1941.

The armed boarding vessels (ABVs) were to suffer even heavier losses with six of the eleven vessels converted being sunk: *Chakdina, Chakla, Chantala, Fiona* were lost off the North African coast between April and December 1941. *Vandyck* was sunk by air attack off Narvik on 10 June 1940, whilst *King Orry* was lost at Dunkirk on 30 May 1940. Generally the ABVs were considerably smaller vessels, approximately 1600–3000 gross tons, armed with a single 4in or 4.7in gun, but *Vandyck* was a giant at 13,241 tons – the size of an AMC. These vessels were representatives of an earlier era – an age before aircraft had become an efficient weapon and their tasks were overtaken by the strategic changes that followed the defeat of France. The surviving vessels were quickly transferred to other duties – *Fratton* (the smallest) to become a barrage balloon vessel, *Laird's Isle* a headquarters ship, *Goodwin* and *Mona's Isle* to auxiliary AA vessels and *St Tudno* a depot ship.

Auxiliary escort vessels

Most of the major navies requisitioned large numbers of medium and small merchant ships to act as escorts and patrol craft during both World Wars, although the practice was far more widespread in the Second. Britain, for example, took over at least eighty-nine of such craft (varying in size from tugs to coastal passenger ships) between 1939 and 1942 and the vast majority saw service in the Far East. In the run-up to the Pacific War Japan similarly acquired more than eighty merchant ships for use as 'gunboats'; predominantly in the 1000/2000-ton range, thirty-seven of the larger ships were actually employed as minelayers. France, too, developed an auxiliary patrol force, the seven largest vessels of 2500–4000 tons being relatively well armed with five

Most maritime nations took over otherwise unusable pleasure craft during wartime. The largest of these could be almost the size of a sloop – Beryl shown here, for example, measured 1368 tons, and was relatively heavily armed. Built in 1898 the yacht was requisitioned (technically, hired) from January 1915 until March 1919. (CMP)

3.9in guns and a few MGs; eight ex-coasters of around 1000 tons were armed with one 3.9in less, while most of the forty or so trawlers also carried 3.9in guns (three in the largest).

As Germany came to dominate continental Europe, small craft were commandeered in numbers that probably exceeded those of any other nation. It is almost impossible to give anything but the broadest generalisations about all these craft, but since Germany rarely controlled waters beyond the reach of her air power they were essentially coastal vessels. The most capable were rated as *Ujäger* (submarine chasers, numbered with a *Uj* prefix), other larger boats as *Vorpostenboote* (patrol craft; *V, Vp* or *Vs* prefix), and the smallest as *Kustenschutzboote* or *Hafenschutzboote* (coastal or harbour defence craft; prefixed with letters indicating country/area – eg RS = Russia/ Sevastopol). Because the German numbering system included the flotilla number, and ships were renumbered as re-assigned, the actual quantities involved are by no means clear, but the total in all categories runs into many thousands. The *Uj* craft included many captured enemy escort vessels and re-rated KFKs (see below), but most of the mercantile craft were converted deep sea trawlers and whalecatchers, although large motor yachts and coastal ferries also featured, particularly in the Mediterranean. The *V* boats were also largely ex-trawlers and drifters, while the smaller boats could have started life as anything from an inshore fishing boat to a pilot boat, a motor yacht or a tug.

The number of suitable merchant vessels was bound to dry up eventually, and in service flotillas of these heterogeneous types proved a logistic nightmare, so in 1941 a war standard design was drawn up, based on a wooden com-

mercial fishing boat type. Known as the *Kriegsfischkutter* or KFK, nearly 1100 of these 110-ton boats were ordered by the middle of 1944. Like the contemporary British Admiralty MFV (Motor Fishing Vessel), they were purpose-built but followed commercial practice; unlike the British boats, they were employed in a variety of active roles, against submarines and aircraft, as well as in their main task of minesweeping.

Apart from these general purpose patrol forces, there were a few more specialist auxiliary escort roles, and these are outlined in the sections that follow.

Commissioned escort vessels

In both wars a limited number of medium sized merchant vessels with slower speeds than those of AMCs were requisitioned by the Royal Navy to provide more economic escorts for Atlantic convoys than their larger consorts. Thirteen vessels were taken up during 1917–18 and beside their normal armament of obsolete 6in and 4in guns, they were armed with an 11in anti-submarine howitzer. Three of these vessels were lost to torpedo attack: *Bostonian* (ex-*Cambrian*) by *U-53* off Start Point on 10 October 1917, *Mechanician* by *UB-35* off St Catherine's Point on 20 January 1918 and *Quernmore* by *U-82* off Tory Island. *Bayano* was typical, being of 6788 tons and beside her anti-submarine armament she carried four 6in, two 4in at a speed of 14kts and was operational between December 1917 and March 1919.

In the second conflict, only two such vessels were commissioned in late 1940. They were the *Antwerp* and the *Malines* of 2957 and 2980 tons respectively. They operated in the Medi-

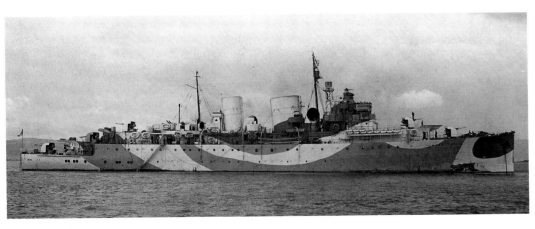

Probably the most battle-worthy of all mercantile conversions in either World War were the British seagoing anti-aircraft ships of 1939–45, designed not for fleet but for convoy duties. Not only were they heavily armed, but they had the fire control equipment of regular warships to make the gunnery effective. One of the most comprehensive was the last, the Canadian former AMC Prince Robert, *converted in 1943. She was so highly regarded that she was selected to serve with the British Pacific Fleet in 1945.* (IWM)

terranean and were moderately armed with one 4in high-angle gun and four 2pdrs. *Malines*, sunk in 1942 was later salvaged and was operational until the war's end. *Antwerp* became a fighter direction ship in 1944.

The armed yacht

The Royal Navy and its daughter services, especially the Royal Canadian Navy, requisitioned a large number of private yachts in the First World War, which were utilised on local escort and patrol duties, relieving other vessels for more hazardous duties.

However in the second conflict yachts were used far more extensively as ASW vessels, on minesweeping and many miscellaneous duties. At the beginning of the war forty-eight yachts were formed into nine ASW groups. These vessels were, however, relegated to subsidiary duties as purpose-built anti-submarine ships came into service. The RCN purchased fourteen yachts in the USA during 1940 to act as ASW vessels; two of them were to become war losses, the *Otter* by fire and *Racoon* by torpedo attack in the St Lawrence on 1 September 1942.

Another fifteen yachts were used as Senior Officer's ships at minesweeping bases or as dan-layers. *Gulzar*, *Sargasso* and *Thalia* did not survive the war. A further seventy-eight vessels were requisitioned during 1939–40 and used on examination duties, as harbour defence craft, on auxiliary patrol duties, as armed boarding vessels, barrage balloon vessels or as targets for the Fleet Air Arm. Several became war losses.

Thirteen of the older yachts, one being built as long ago as 1873 (*Florinda*), were used as accommodation ships for patrol vessels and were generally not commissioned and were all paid off at the end of the war.

The Dominion navies acquired over eighty vessels for coastal escort duties and were generally armed with a 12pdr on 4in gun, supplemented later by light AA guns, depth charges and Asdic. The majority of such vessels acquired for the Royal Navy were operated in the Far East. These ranged from tugs to coastal passenger vessels and a few of the larger and faster vessels were as capable as similar naval vessels. As naval construction rose, these requisitioned vessels were gradually returned to their owners; the forty-eight such vessels in service in December 1943 had been reduced to thirty-five by September 1945.

During the Second World War the US Navy requisitioned literally hundreds of yachts, which varied greatly in size and consequently in designation. The largest were rated as gunboats (PG), followed by the 'patrol yacht' (PY) category, with the smallest regarded as coastal patrol yachts (PYc); even smaller cabin cruisers became local patrol craft (YP). Their duties were humdrum and few were lost, but a number of the larger vessels served in specialist roles – three became PT-boat tenders, one a survey ship, and *Vixen*, the largest of all, was the flagship of the Atlantic submarine force.

German fast escort vessels

With its shipping rapidly driven from the high seas in both World Wars, Germany had little need for seagoing auxiliary escorts. However, from 1943 a small group of five well armed auxiliaries was operated in the Mediterranean for coastal convoys. Officially rated as *Schnelle Geleitfahzeuge* (fast escorts), they were converted French reefers (refrigerated fruit carriers) or small liners of 2500–3700 tons, armed with two or three 10.5cm (4.1in) guns, four 3.7cm and sixteen to eighteen 20mm AA, plus depth charges; mines were added later to the survivors. Most were sunk fairly quickly, one surviving to be scuttled at Marseilles in August 1944.

Anti-aircraft auxiliaries

The primitive characteristics of early aircraft gave warships relative immunity from attack during the first conflict. The British Grand Fleet completed a programme of fitting anti-aircraft guns and platforms for fighters, when the development of the Zeppelin airship increased the threat of air attack above nuisance value; 'Insect' class gunboats were used as AA guardships on the east coast, but little else was required. During the inter-war years, aircraft developed quickly and by the late 1930s the fast twin-engined monoplane bomber, such as the British Blenheim and the German Ju 88, were far faster than most current fighter aircraft. The Royal Navy was to be poorly equipped to face these developments, because of delays with the rearmament programme. However, it had developed the excellent Mk XVI twin 4in HA/LA gun on the XIX mounting, but attempts to develop the multiple 2pdr pom-pom produced an over-complex and ineffective weapon. This weapon was to be replaced by the imported 20mm Oerlikon and later the 40mm Bofors gun during the Second World War.

The Royal Navy had realised that its new construction programme would not be sufficient for its needs and had made plans prewar for the conversion of a number of vessels to act as AA vessels. These vessels were not intended as fleet escorts but for convoy protection duties only. The vessels were to have the following characteristics:

1. To be armed with the Mk XVI 4in gun on Mk IX mounting, with a director.

2. Point defence was to consist of quadruple 2pdrs, 0.5in machine guns and later 20mm Oerlikons under local control.

3. The vessels were to be diesel-engined to provide the necessary range.

4. The conversion was to give the vessels all the attributes of a warship, except sub-division, protection and speed.

These were among the most radical conversions of a merchant ship undertaken: usually all the superstructure was removed, a warship-type bridge constructed, and holds converted to magazines. Amongst the vessels converted were:

Foylebank converted between September 1939 and June 1940; she was sunk by twenty Ju 87s at Portland whilst on trials on 4 July 1940.

Alynbank converted between October 1939 and August 1940; she then served in the Irish Sea, on Arctic convoy duty and then in the Mediterranean until paid off during October 1943.

Springbank's conversion was started in October 1939, but she never served as an AA vessel and commissioned on 23 April 1941 as a fighter catapult ship. She was sunk on 28 September 1941 in the Bay of Biscay after being torpedoed by *U 201*.

Pozarica: Converted between June 1940 and March 1941, her armament consisted of six 4in HA/LA guns, eight 2pdrs, two single 20mm, eight 0.5in machine guns. She also carried radar, Asdic, echo-sounder and depth charges. She operated in the Western Approaches and in the Arctic before being torpedoed by aircraft off Bougie on 29 January 1943 during the 'Torch' operations. Although beached she capsized during salvage operations 15 days later and became a total loss.

Palomares, a sister of *Pozarica*, served on Arctic convoy duties for a year after commissioning during September 1941 following conversion work that had lasted 13 months. She returned to the UK following aircraft torpedo damage during the Operation Torch landings on 9 November 1942 and was immediately converted into a fighter direction ship.

Ulster Queen was converted between August 1940 and November 1941 and was the most thorough of all the conversions undertaken. Modifications included the fitting of a cruiser bridge, three gun platforms and two tripod masts. She served with the Irish Sea Escort Force, apart from detached service with convoys PQ15, QP12, PQ18 and QP15. She was then converted to a fighter direction ship.

Tynwald converted between July 1940 and September 1941, but was to see scarcely a year's service before being mined and sunk off Bougie on 12 November 1942.

The only other vessel utilised was the former Canadian AMC *Prince Robert*, which was converted at Burrard Dry Dock between January and July 1943. The conversion was extensive, with a new bridge and operations room, Type 285 radar, five twin 4in guns, two quadruple 2pdr and six 20mm Oerlikons being fitted. She escorted Gibraltar convoys up to September 1944 and then refitted for service in the Pacific, where she operated after July 1945.

These were the most capable Second World War AA conversions but the British also converted thirty-two small excursion ships and ferries to far more makeshift coastal anti-aircraft ships. All but six were paddle steamers, the vast majority of less than 1000 tons, and many had already done duty as auxiliary minesweepers. They had no HA control arrangements so the *ad hoc* collection of 2pdrs, 20mm Oerlikons, machine-guns and rocket projectors were none too effective. However, since coastal convoys were often confined to narrow channels, breaking up an attack or even putting a pilot off his aim was a worthwhile achievement. For such a hazardous duty, it is surprising that only four were lost.

There were no precise equivalents of these specially converted AA escorts in other navies, but Germany modified some of her *Ujäger* and *Vorpostenboote* to carry heavier AA weapons and rerated them *Flakjäger* or *Flak korvetten* later in the war. She did have a series of very heavily armed AA floating batteries, but these were all converted from old warships rather than merchant ships; more interesting were a number of fighter direction ships based on merchant ship hulls. Operational conditions in the Mediterranean rendered the first conversions useless, but in Germany itself the ex-raider *Coronel* underwent a substantial refitting to carry *Freya* and *Wurzburg-Gigant* long range air surveillance radars, and an impressive battery of light AA guns for self-defence. Reverting to her original name of *Togo*, the ship commissioned in October 1943 and was used to fill the Skagerrak gap in the line of early warning radar stations protecting Germany from Allied bomber raids.

The United States Coast Guard

The service, formed in 1915 by the amalgamation of the Revenue Cutter Service originally founded in 1790 and the Life Saving Service, was a unique force until recent years. It provides the United States with a second naval force in time of war, when it is incorporated into the navy. However, in peacetime, the service is part of the civil government.

During the First World War most of the larger vessels had been armed with one or more 3in, two 6pdrs and two machine-guns. Six vessels were fitted for anti-submarine duties. During the conflict three cutters were lost: *McCullough* and *Mohawk* by separate collisions during October 1917 and the *Tampa* torpedoed by a U-boat whilst on escort duties in the English Channel on 26 September 1918. By 1919, the Coast Guard consisted of twenty-two cruising cutters, fifteen harbour cutters and eleven launches.

The inter-war years were to see the Coast Guard expanded rapidly to fight 'rum running' during the Prohibition era. Twenty old destroyers were transferred from the US Navy in 1924, with five more transferred two years later. In 1930 six flush-decked destroyers replaced some of the earlier vessels. In addition over two hundred 74ft 11in patrol boats were also built to fight the smugglers. On the ending of Prohibition many of these patrol vessels were transferred to Reserve training duties.

The Second World War

The Coast Guard came under naval jurisdiction on 1 November 1941 and at this time consisted of the following vessels:

Largest of the inter-war US Coast Guard cutters was the 2350-ton 'Treasury' class (George W Campbell is seen here in peacetime guise in 1937). During the war they served as effective North Atlantic convoy flagships until 1944 when they were converted to amphibious force flagships for the Pacific campaign. They were returned to the Coast Guard after the war and some served into the 1980s. (L & L van Ginderen)

Northland of 1927 – 1785 tons and two 6pdrs and one 1pdr.

Seven 'Treasury' class (launched 1936–37) of 2350 tons with two 5in guns and two 6pdrs.

Six *Algonquin* class (launched 1932–34) of 1005 tons with two 3in guns.

Seventeen *Thetis* class (launched 1931–34) of 334 tons with two 3in guns, twenty 20mm, 2 DC tracks.

Thirty-three *Active* class (launched 1926–27) of 232 tons with two 20mm guns.

The ten 'Lake' class launched between 1927 and 1931, of 1662 tons, armed with one 5in, one 3in gun and two 6pdrs had all been transferred to the Royal Navy under Lend–Lease during 1941. Three of these vessels were to become war losses.

During the war, the Coast Guard fleet was supplemented by the completion of thirteen *Owasco* class large cutters, three 'Wind' class icebreakers and over 230 83ft patrol boats. The Coast Guard was also an invaluable source of manpower to the US Navy providing crews for thirty destroyer-escorts, seventy-five frigates, fifty-one transports, eighteen petrol tankers, seventy-six LSIs, twenty-eight LCIs as well as some three hundred small navy and army vessels. Later, several of the 'Treasury' class cutters served as command ships for amphibious operations in the Pacific. The Coast Guard was relatively unscathed by the war with war losses being confined to *Alexander Hamilton* (torpedoed by *U 132* off Iceland and sinking in tow on 29 January 1942) and *Acacia* (sunk by gunfire of *U 161* south of Haiti on 15 March 1942). *Beoloe*, *Bodeca*, *Dow*, *Escanaba*, *Jackson*, *Magnolia*, *Natsek* and *Wilcox* were all lost through marine causes.

Auxiliary aviation ships

All early aviation ships were converted merchantmen, but the first seaplane carriers are so important to the history of aircraft carrier development that they are more properly covered in that section; suffice to say, that although the British made all the running initially with their converted short sea ships, other nations made similar conversions. France had a converted cargo liner, the *Campinas*, by late 1915, joined by a pair of ex-cross channel paddle steamers by 1916; Germany modified three cargo-passenger liners to seaplane carriers, but they were too slow for offensive operations and in practice acted more as aviation depot ships than fighting vessels; Japan had a single seaplane carrier, the *Wakamiya* a converted freighter, but she too was more of a depot ship, although her aircraft were to see action over Tsingtao in 1914. Perhaps the most advanced naval aviation force outside the Royal Navy in the First World War was the Russian, which had a force of six seaplane carriers in the Black Sea (four on loan from Romania) and one in the Baltic, all fairly basic conversions from small passenger-cargo vessels.

Besides heavier-than-air craft, the Allied navies also employed balloons, principally for artillery spotting. These could be carried with very little alteration to a ship, but the British alone developed a force of five ex-cargo ships specially converted to carry, maintain and operate kite balloons. This involved equipment to generate hydrogen and inflate the balloon, gear to control its ascent and descent, and some form of shelter. The ships were first employed off Gallipoli.

Seaplane tenders

Between the wars the popularity of the seaplane carrier declined as performance of wheeled aircraft began to noticeably exceed that of floatplanes and flying boats, making the flight deck aircraft carrier the only viable projector of front line naval air power. However, both the Japanese and the Americans believed that in the vast areas of the Pacific there was still a specialist role for the seaplane. Fleet carriers would always be in short supply, and any advance across the Pacific island chains might be delayed if it was necessary to wait for airstrips for land planes to be built; if self-contained, seaplane tenders could carry, maintain and operate their aircraft from any suitably sheltered lagoon.

Most American tenders were purpose-built or converted warships, but even US resources did not run to the numbers required, so Maritime Commission C3 hulls were employed. Ten were ordered, of which two were converted from completed ships and the rest built on bare hulls; two were cancelled towards the end of the war, when it was clear that air bases could be constructed very rapidly and the strategy was outmoded.

Although the prototypes, *Notoro* and *Kamoi*, were converted oilers, most of Japan's interwar seaplane carriers were purpose-built. However, nine merchant ships were also taken over between 1937 and 1942; they were 6000–9000grt and carried up to eight seaplanes, which could be launched from two catapults in a well deck aft.

CAM ships and MAC ships

By the outbreak of the Second World War the performance of aircraft had advanced to the point where deployment from merchant ships was no longer a matter of relatively simple conversion – unless considerable sacrifice was contemplated. Probably the most drastic measure was the British Catapult Armed Merchant ship (CAM ship), which entailed fitting a fixed forward-facing catapult over the forecastle to launch a fighter (usually a Hurricane) on a one-way mission. The aircraft had no floats and the pilot was expected to ditch or parachute into the sea after his sortie. It was intended to fill the gap where air cover could not be provided, but where German air reconnaissance might threaten to bring down more powerful forces on the convoy; it might therefore be effective against individual aircraft, but was clearly a desperate measure.

The ultimate solution was the escort carrier, the first of which, the *Audacity*, was converted from a captured German merchant ship in 1941; she had no lift or hangar but could carry six aircraft on deck. More sophisticated conversions followed and soon the USA was geared up for the large scale production for both navies of such ships, which were based on mercantile hulls but were closer to warships in sophistication of armament and fittings.

However, there were teething troubles with the early units and escort carriers were still in short supply at the height of the Battle of the Atlantic. Reverting to a simpler approach, the British devised the Merchant Aircraft Carrier (MAC ship), which entailed building a flight deck over a bulk carrier – oil tanker or grain ship – that continued to operate as a merchant ship, flying the Red Ensign and carrying a full cargo. Nine tankers were converted in 1942–43 (two of which flew the Dutch flag), and four more under construction were completed as MAC ships; they carried four aircraft on deck. This was followed by a more sophisticated conversion of six grain carriers, which incorporated a hangar and lift for the four aircraft, still without detriment to the ships' carrying capacity. Invaluable at the time, they could not be as effective as purpose-built escort carriers, and when the supply of the latter increased in 1943, MAC ship conversions ceased.

The Japanese converted a few tankers to a basically similar aircraft transport configuration, some of which had a hangar, but they did not operate as merchant ships.

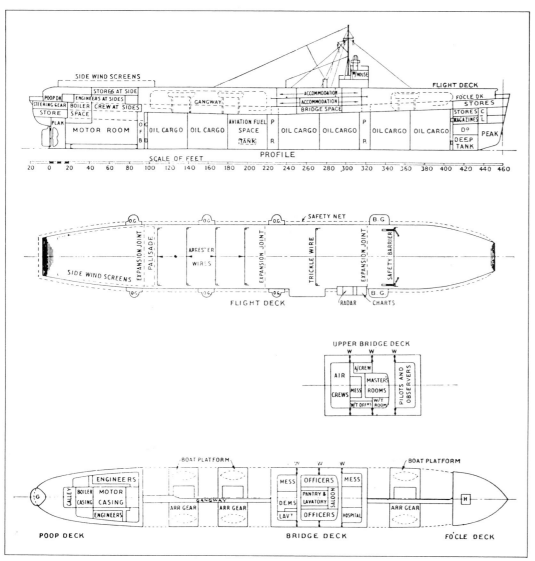

The British MAC ship (merchant aircraft carrier) was an ingenious method of providing convoys with minimum air cover. The absence of the need for general handling facilities – large hatches, derricks, etc – made it possible to build a flight deck over tankers and bulk carriers. This is the general arrangement of the converted tanker Rapana, *which had no hangar.*

into minelayers, from the cross channel ship *Biarritz* of 2495 tons, armed with two 12pdrs and fitted to carry 180 mines, which served between March 1915 and November 1919, to the liner *Orvieto* of 12,130 tons, armed with four 4.7in one 3pdr and 600 mines that operated between January 1915 and May 1916. The obsolete battleship *London* and cruiser *Euryalus* were also converted.

These vessels were employed in laying defensive barrages in the North Sea barrier, as their speed was insufficient to be used on offensive minelaying sorties. The Royal Navy was supported in the huge task of laying the North Sea Barrage by nine US minelayers: the converted liners *Shawmut* and *Aroostook*, the cruisers *San Francisco* and *Baltimore* and the former liners *Canandaigua*, *Canonicus*, *Housatonic*, *Quinnebaug* and *Roanoke*.

The German navy used its cruisers, destroyers, torpedo boats and submarines as the principal means of laying offensive minefields. They were aided by the auxiliary minelayer *Meteor* and the auxiliary cruiser *Wolf*, but there were also about a dozen converted short sea ships, of which the best known is the *Königen Luise*, which was sunk in action with the British cruiser *Amphion* in August 1914.

During the 1920s and '30s, the Royal Navy remembered the lessons of the war and although constrained by finance, constructed the minelaying cruiser *Adventure* and made provision for destroyer minelaying. The navy was building four *Manxman* class fast minelayers and two sisters were ordered under the War Emergency Programme, but on the outbreak

Mine warfare auxiliaries

Minelayers

Mines of various descriptions had been used since the Crimean War and the Russians had been experimenting with the purpose-built minelayers *Bug* and *Dunai* since the early 1890s. The Royal Navy having a considerable number of obsolete cruisers with considerable hull life left, converted seven vessels of the *Apollo* class between 1906 and 1910. These vessels were rearmed with four 4.7in guns and two

minelaying tracks with a capacity of 140 mines. These vessels were extensively used during 1914–15, when they laid some 8000 mines in twenty-two operations. Offensive minelaying was undertaken by the fast light cruisers and destroyers of the Grand Fleet and Harwich Flotilla.

The Admiralty converted or considered converting a further thirteen mercantile vessels

Being relatively fast, capacious and unemployed in wartime, short sea passenger ships and ferries made reasonable minelayer conversions in many navies. This is the British Princess Margaret, *which served right through the First World War, and was so successful that she was purchased outright in 1919. A 6000-ton ship capable of more than 20kts with a 500-mine load, her capabilities were not exceeded until the purpose-built minelaying cruiser* Adventure *entered service in 1927.* (CMP)

One of the great undertakings of the First World War at sea was the North Sea anti-submarine mine barrage, a significant part of which was laid by US ships. This is the converted coastal liner USS Shawmut *in September 1918, actively engaged in this task. She and her sister* Aroostook *later became flying boat tenders. (IWM)*

of war, the Royal Navy immediately requisitioned nine vessels for service as auxiliary minelayers to be used in laying protective mine fields in home waters. Two types of vessel were used: ex-cross channel ferries such as the *Hampton Ferry* and *Shepperton Ferry* of 2839 tons completed in 1934–35 and each converted to carry 270 mines, and the newly completed *Princess Victoria* of 2197 tons; the other vessels taken from trade were cargo vessels and consisted of the Holt sisters *Agamemnon* and *Menestheus* of 7593 tons and 7493 gross tons respectively and converted to carry 530 and 410 mines respectively, while the Port Line vessels *Port Napier* and *Port Quebec* were converted to carry 550 mines each. The largest vessel to be converted was the whale factory ship *Southern Pride*, built in 1929 of 10,917 gross tons, which carried 562 mines. Finally *Teviotbank* of 5087 tons completed in 1938 was converted to carry 272 mines.

During 1940–41, these vessels, under heavy escort, laid a series of defensive barrages at night. From early 1941 until October 1943, when the minelaying squadron was disbanded, these vessels laid and then maintained the Northern barrage and fields around the Orkneys, Shetlands, Faeroes and Iceland from a base at Ullapool. On demobilisation, these vessels were retained by the Admiralty for subsidiary purposes, except the war losses *Princess Victoria*, *Port Napier* and *Shepperton Ferry*. Another war loss was the locally requisitioned and converted *Kung Wo* near Singapore during February 1942.

Although the Germans maintained their earlier policy of fitting most regular warships for minelaying, around forty merchant ships of assorted types were also taken up for this duty. Destroyers and S-boats laid fields in the most hazardous areas (and U-boats and raiders in distant parts of the world) but that still left many areas where auxiliaries might operate with success. The ships themselves had little in common, except that most were taken from the merchant fleets of occupied countries or were war prizes; many were short sea ships or ferries, but a few were small freighters in the 3000-ton range. Armament and mine capacity varied enormously: *Cobra*, a converted excursion steamer of 2131grt, could carry 150 EMC mines and was armed with two 8.8cm AA, one 3.7cm and two 20mm guns; *Ulm*, a small cargo liner of 3071grt, could carry 355 UMB or 482 EMC type mines and was armed with one 10.5cm (4.1in), one 3.7cm AA and four 20mm.

The other navy in which auxiliary minelayers played a significant part was the Imperial Japanese. During the First World War a large number of steam trawlers was taken up for this duty, of which thirty-three continued to serve postwar. During the Second World War, two standard Type 2D freighters were converted to carry 380 mines, and a series of small dual purpose tug-harbour minelayers were built (about thirty of the 100 and 150-ton type and sixteen of the 175-ton class); seven large cargo ships of around 7000 tons were also taken up for the minelaying role before the actual outbreak of war.

Mine countermeasures auxiliaries

British and German expertise in this form of warfare is notable, although the Russians had been experimenting with mines since the Crimean War and had great experience both in minelaying and sweeping. Russia had designed the first purpose-built minesweepers, the *Fugas* being launched as early as 1910. Despite losing the battleships *Yashima* and *Shikishima* to mines during the Russo-Japanese War, Japan never showed much interest in defensive warfare and this is shown by their lack of escort and minesweeping vessels at the start of the Pacific War.

The whole of the Royal Navy's minesweeping capacity on the outbreak of war in August 1914 was a force of ten converted gunboats, but the early losses of the superdreadnought *Audacious* and cruiser *Amphion* by mines led to the rapid expansion in Britain's minesweeping fleet. The first conversions were four *Halcyon* class gunboats in 1914–15 followed by the requisitioning of twelve screw steamers and seventy shallow draft paddle steamers as sweepers. The Admiralty then ordered a large number of trawlers, built to commercial lines, to provide cheap and expendable minesweeping, anti-submarine and patrol vessels. These vessels were characterised by their robust construction, seaworthiness, with machinery that could be used readily by Reservists. However, the largest source of minesweepers were the vessels of Britain's huge fishing fleet. In all, over 1400 trawlers and a 1000 drifters, plus 42 ex-German and Russian vessels were requisitioned.

However, the realisation that the requisi-

Shallow draught paddle excursion steamers found wartime employment in the role of minesweeper during both World Wars. In the First, the main target was the moored mine which was cut free by gear streamed from gallows at the stern of the vessel; it then floated to the surface where it could be disposed of (mines were usually set off by well directed rifle fire from a safe distance). The crew of this paddle minesweeper are investigating a floating mine. (CMP)

tioning of further trawlers for naval use, plus heavy losses, would drastically reduce the amount of fish landed at a time of potential food shortage, led to large orders for commercial-type trawlers being made by the Admiralty. These vessels were ordered in three batches: 250 in November 1916, a 150 further vessels during 1917, and the final batch of 140 the next year. The vessels ordered were in three distinct groups in order to facilitate construction at all the trawler-building yards.

156 'Mersey' class of 438 tons, with one 12pdr and a speed of 11kts (69 completed by November 1918).

217 'Castle' class of 360 tons, with one 12pdr and a speed of 10.5kts (127 completed by November 1918).

167 'Strath' class of 311 tons, with one 12pdr and a speed of 10kts (89 completed by November 1918).

There were also two types of naval drifter: a wooden-hulled version of which 91 were built in Britain at the end of the war and 100 in Canada; and steel-hulled type, of which 123 were completed from some 170 ordered. Although there were some cancellations at the wars' end, the majority of incomplete hulls were sold off to the fishing industry to make up

The principal source of most navies' auxiliary minesweepers was the national fishing fleet, but in both wars the British also built mercantile-type trawlers specifically for naval use. This is HMS Cherwell, which belonged to the largest standard type of the First World War, the Mersey class.

for war losses as were most of the commissioned vessels.

Apart from the distant blockade of the Grand Fleet, Germany quickly found her coastal waters and estuaries under threat from British offensive minelaying. She responded with the somewhat desperate-sounding *Sperrbrecher* concept (literally 'barrage breaker'), whereby old and expendable merchant ships preceded more valuable targets to sea in order to set off any mines in the channel. At first these ships had no protection whatever, but slowly their survivability was improved by using sand to dampen blast, by filling the holds with empty drums and timber to increase buoyancy, and eventually fitting various bow

protection devices and actual sweeping gear. There were twelve numbered *Sperrbrecher* units, each allocated a single vessel and organised into three active and one reserve groups; nearly forty ships were so employed, some in more than one unit during their careers. Only five were actually sunk by mines, but others fell victim to British submarines.

France had similar problems to Britain and met the challenge by building or projecting sixty-four minesweepers of the *Camella*, *Ajong*, *Fanfaron*, *Amandier*, *Campanule* and *Briseard* classes. Again, many of these vessels were not completed until postwar. Additionally, the French purchased over 50 trawlers and requisitioned a further 450 trawlers for minesweeping and other duties.

Russia had followed the *Fugas* class with a series of thirteen vessels under the massive 1912 building programme. The war saw these vessels being supplemented by the thirteen British-built *T 13* class trawlers, as well as the requisitioning of over 160 auxiliary minesweepers. The USA did not have a requirement for auxiliary sweepers, since there were enough 'Bird' class minesweepers in service by the end of the war to fill its needs.

Postwar, all navies rapidly demobilised requisitioned vessels and sold large numbers of their minesweeping trawlers for further mer-

Trawlers could perform seagoing naval duties but there was also a need for a less capable drifter, which was eventually built in wooden and steel-hulled versions. This is the steel drifter HMS Dew *about 1918. (CMP)*

cantile service. The need for a viable minesweeping force was hardly met by retention in the Royal Navy by 1938 of twenty-two vessels of the 'Axe' (ex-Russian), 'Strath', 'Castle' and 'Mersey' classes, supplemented by twenty commercial trawlers purchased during the Abyssinian Crisis in 1935–36 and the twenty-one fleet minesweepers of the *Halcyon* class completed between 1933 and 1939. Later large numbers of fleet minesweepers of the *Bangor* (113 built), *Bathurst* (60) and *Algerine* (110) classes were completed for the Royal and Dominion Navies. To this substantial programme of fleet sweepers, hundreds of wooden American YMS type and British MMS motor minesweepers were also completed for inshore duties to sweep the influence and magnetic mines then used by the Germans. The Royal Navy was supplemented by the purchase of a further twenty-one commercial trawlers in 1938–39 and the construction of over 240 trawlers of the 'Tree', 'Dance', 'Shakespearian', 'Isles', 'Professor', 'Hills', 'Round Table', 'Fish' and 'Military' classes between 1939–1945. Again, the commercial fisheries were utilised as a source of auxiliary vessels with over 1300 trawlers being used on minesweeping, escort and patrol duties. In September 1939 only thirty-one trawlers with a further ninety-eight under conversion, were employed as sweepers in Royal Navy service, but by May 1944 over 650 trawlers were being utilised on sweeping duties alone.

In the winter of 1939–40, several coastal vessels were converted and used as mine destructor vessels, against the magnetic mines then

Second World War British naval trawlers were less mercantile in appearance, perhaps influenced by the corvette (itself derived from a whalecatcher design). This postwar view of the 'Isles' class Wiay *shows the naval style bridge positioned further forward than is usual trawler practice, and the extended deckhouse. (L & L van Ginderen)*

being laid in British coastal waters. These vessels were degaussed and were fitted with 300-ton electro magnets in the bows, but this could not generate a field that would explode a magnetic mine far enough from the ship to prevent damage. As a result their losses were heavy and this approach was soon replaced by the more effective LL sweep. Later during 1943–44 two special vessels, the *Cyrus* and *Cybele* were constructed in great secrecy to sweep the almost unsweepable pressure mine.

Nevertheless, commercial requisition was still necessary and eighty-six highly varied small ships were taken up by the Royal and Dominion Navies for auxiliary minesweeping duties; a further thirty-nine paddle steamers (excursion ships and ferries) served in this role in coastal waters, but twenty of these were further converted to AA ships (as mentioned in an earlier section).

In the Second World War Germany revived the *Sperrbrecher* concept, but on a far larger scale. The initial nine freighters requisitioned were unarmed but thereafter the service became less sacrificial in character, with the Great War measures being readopted. They were equipped with more modern paravane-type gear and eventually magnetic and acoustic countermeasures; the ships were also armed and as the war progressed the AA guns in particular became more numerous. They were divided into four classes by size: there were about forty-eight large (above 2500grt) vessels, armed in 1943 with two 10.5cm (4.1in), six 3.7cm AA, fourteen 20mm AA and four MGs; fifteen of medium (1500–2500grt) size, with a standard armament in 1943 of two 10.5cm, two

3.7cm AA, seven 20mm and three MGs; over fifty small vessels of less than 1500grt, armed with a 10.5cm (or one/two 8.8cm) guns, one/ two 3.7cm AA and eight/ten 20mm and two MGs; and finally about fifteen even smaller craft were employed in river estuaries. A war emergency *Kriegs-Sperrbrecher* of about 1750 tons displacement was designed in 1943, but of twenty-seven planned none was ever completed.

Germany also impressed large numbers of commercial craft as more conventional minesweepers; these were predominantly fishing craft, and losses of over 200 are recorded although the exact quantity that served is not certain. Other countries with a fishing fleet responded to the mine war in the same way, although to differing degrees. Japan, for example, prepared for hostilities by taking over 110 vessels (mostly trawlers and whalecatchers in the 200/300-ton range) well before Pearl Harbor; France acquired even more (they number up to over 400, but again exact figures are lacking). Despite its huge industrial base, even the United States was forced to requisition civilian craft for minesweeping. This was a short term stop-gap measure until the vast war programmes could start to supply regular warships, but in the early months of American involvement a large number of such craft were taken up. Twenty steel trawlers were acquired as fleet sweepers (classified AM), while over forty wooden fishing craft became coastal sweepers (AMc). The US Navy also built seventy 97ft boats designed along the lines of tuna fishing boats and armed with two MGs.

John English

Auxiliary Warships: Typical Vessels 1906–1945

Ship or Class [Type]	Nationality	Dispt (tons) Normal Full load	Dimensions (loa × breadth) Feet–Inches Metres	Armament	Speed (max kts)	Launch dates	Original employment [Date taken up]	Numbers converted or built*
ORAMA [AMC]	British	12,927grt	569–0 × 64–4 173.4 × 19.6	8–6in	18	1911	Liner [1914]	68
BERLIN [Commerce raider]	German	23,700 17,324grt	610–3 × 69–10 186.0 × 21.3	2–10.5cm 6–3.7cm	16.5	1908	Liner [1914]	17
IMPERATOR NIKOLAI I [Seaplane carrier]	Russian	9230	381–0 × 52–0 116.0 × 15.8	6–4.7in 4–3in 6/8 aircraft	13.5	1913	Cargo liner [1915]	3
SHAWMUT [Minelayer]	American	3800	395–0 × 52–3 120.4 × 15.9	1–5in 2–3in	20	1907	Coastal liner [1917]	2
MERSEY class [Naval trawler]	British	438 665	136–6 × 23–9 42.2 × 7.2	1–12pdr or 4in	11	1917–18	—	77*
GLEN AVON [Paddle minesweeper]	British	509grt	220–0 × 27–0 67.1 × 8.2	1–12pdr 1–6pdr	17	1912	Excursion steamer [1914]	70
NOTORO [Seaplane tender]	Japanese	14,050	455–8 × 58–0 138–9 × 17.7	2–12cm 2–8cm 10 seaplanes	12	1920–21	Fleet oiler [1924]	2
JERVIS BAY [AMC]	British	14,164grt	548–6 × 68–3 167.2 × 20.8	8–6in 2–3in	15	1922	Liner [1939]	56
ATLANTIS [Commerce raider]	German	7862grt 17,600	508–6 × 61–4 155.0 × 18.7	6–15cm 1–75mm 6 AA, 4TT	16	1937	Freighter [1939]	10
PHILANTE [Armed yacht]	British	1629tm		1–4in 2–20mm, 4 MGs		1937	Motor yacht [1939]	c123
SPERRBRECHER 3 [Mine destructor, large]	German	4418grt 9100	424–10 × 55–6 129.5 × 16.9	2–10.5cm 4–3.7cm 3/5–2cm	14.5	1937	Freighter [1940]	37
ALYNBANK [Seagoing AA escort]	British	5151grt	434–0 × 54–0 132.3 × 16.5	8–4in 8–2pdr 2–20mm	12	1925	Freighter [1940]	8
JEANIE DEANS [Coastal AA escort]	British	635grt	257–6 × 30–0 78.5 × 9.1	2–2pdr 4–20mm 16 MGs	18	1931	Excursion steamer [1941]	26
'TREASURY' class [Convoy flagships]	American	2350 trial	327–0 × 41–0 99.7 × 12.5	2–5in 2–6pdr 1–1pdr	19	1936–37	Coast Guard cutter [1941]	7
KFK 1 [Kriegsfischkutter]	German	110	78–9 × 21–0 24.0 × 6.4	1–3.7cm 2–2cm	9	1942–45	—	c950*
'ISLES' class [Naval trawler]	British	545 770	164–0 × 27–8 50.0 × 8.4	1–12pdr 3–20mm 30 DCs	12	1940–44	—	145*
RAPANA [MAC ship]	British	8000grt 16,600	481–0 × 59–0 146.6 × 18.0	1–4in 8–20mm 4 aircraft	13	1935	Oil tanker [1942]	13

Notes:

Because of the mercantile origins of most of these vessels, the measurement criteria of the above figures are less consistent than in previous tables: grt = gross registered tons; tm = Thames measurement.

11

The Fleet Train

WITH the advent of steam power, navies lost the global mobility they had enjoyed under sail. British ships were regularly stored for '6 months Foreign Service' and longer voyages, even all the way around the world, were achieved. Ships were nearly self-sufficient, carrying cordage and canvas, and picking up wood in forests ashore. There were overseas naval bases, but they were more protected harbours in forward areas, and apart from a few Spanish yards, lacked the facilities and stores of the home posts. The creation of the fleet train, particularly by the US Navy, was intended to restore the mobility of the earlier age. It was justified in 1944–45, when the US fleet operated continuously against Japan, at distances from its forward base comparable to the distance all the way across the Atlantic. Modern fleet trains derive largely from this experience.

Both steam propulsion and modern naval guns rapidly consumed what a ship could carry. Moreover, modern warships could not be totally self-repairing; they required special industrial facilities. As she entered the industrial age, Britain developed a simple solution to the problem of maintaining the mobility of her fleet: a network of coaling stations and navy yards on her expanding colonial territory. Ships could steam from one such station to another. Indeed, the distance from one British possession to another set the endurance required of British warships. For other navies, the availability of comparable facilities largely determined the extent to which they could threaten British seaborne trade, particularly in an era of inefficient steam engines.

Although neutrals might, in theory, coal belligerent warships in wartime, that could never be taken for granted. These considerations had very practical consequences. In 1904 the Russian Baltic Fleet began an ultimately futile cruise half way around the world to relieve the besieged Russian fleet at Port Arthur. Denied British coaling facilities (Britain was allied to Japan, though not a belligerent), the Russian fleet had to carry unusually heavy deck loads of coal from those few French colonial ports (Russia was allied to France, though France was not a belligerent) at which it called. One consequence was that the fleet was unable to conduct battle practice en route to its destruction at Tsushima.

The origins of the US Fleet Train

The US Navy found Tsushima particularly sobering, because it, too, had to contemplate a long voyage from base to battle, with few if any coaling stations en route. That was particularly the case in the Pacific. The latent Japanese threat to the US-owned Philippines was probably the central US naval problem from the seizure of the islands in 1898. It could not be met by stationing a powerful battlefleet there,

Before 1945, US concepts of fleet operations required that the fleet itself set up an advanced base in some unimproved spot. Tenders were the mobile equivalents of work shops and other facilities which might be found at, say, a major overseas British base in a colony. Here the submarine tender Camden *lies alongside a pier in May 1927, servicing two fleet submarines ('V' class) and two smaller submarines ('S' class). The base is probably San Diego. (USN)*

The fleet could secure really long range only if it could be fuelled en route. Coaling at sea was difficult but not impossible, as this 1914 photograph (of an experimental rig) shows. The collier Cyclops *shows the characteristic US arrangement of special gantries and cranes; the lines rigged could carry over two 800lb bags at a time. The method was too slow to be practical, but the line transfer used was later the basis for current US underway replenishment techniques for ammunition and other large objects.* (USN)

so many thousands of miles from the US industrial base needed for long-term support. Moreover, the Japanese threat was hardly the only one taken into account by US naval planners. Early in this century war games showed that unless the battlefleet were concentrated, it could easily be defeated in detail. From about 1905 on, then, US strategy for a Pacific war always entailed a long battlefleet cruise out to the western Pacific, to destroy the Japanese fleet and relieve or recapture the Philippines. The cruise might be direct (such plans were sometimes called the 'through ticket to Manila') or, more likely, conducted in stages. Either way, Tsushima was a reminder of what happened to a fleet fighting too far from bases and supplies.

In 1907–9 the US fleet did steam around the world to demonstrate that it could arrive in the western Pacific in better fighting trim than had the Russians, but even so it clearly lacked the inherent endurance to fight for very long in those waters. That required an advanced base, from which the fleet could sortie and to which it could retire after battle. Such a base would have to be extemporised (it could be assumed that the Japanese would destroy the limited facilities in the Philippines when they struck). For a time it seemed that the United States might build up a fortified advanced base on Guam, comparable in concept to Singapore, but Congress was unenthusiastic. The opportunity vanished when the Washington Treaty (1922) forbade fortification of islands in the

western Pacific. Even after the treaty lapsed in 1936, Congress refused to sanction development, partly because money was so scarce (and partly to avoid irritating Japan, the obvious target of any fortification).

The fleet would have to bring with it whatever was needed to create the base from which it would fight its decisive battle or battles.

US naval thinking on operations in distant waters were first formed by the experience of the Spanish-American War in the Philippines. The small US Asiatic Squadron, which won at Manila, had to steam out of its only friendly port, Hong Kong, at the outbreak of war (Britain was neutral). Once Manila had been seized, the squadron had to rely on the inadequate facilities at Cavite, pending its long-term

development as a US base. The senior US naval advisory group, the General Board, recommended the urgent construction of support ships to turn the harbour at Manila into an effective fleet operating base: an ammunition ship and a repair ship (contemporary warship machinery could not run at high speed for very long without extensive repairs). They had to be in place even in peacetime because Cavite was so far from the United States and because an unstable Far East could explode so suddenly. The then Bureau of Steam Engineering preferred to build up the repair plant at Cavite, but it wanted repair ships with the deployed squadrons to reduce overall repair bills (commercial yards were quite expensive).

With the fleet concentrated in home waters after 1905, the General Board, which was also the war planning agency, expected the fleet to proceed overseas in stages, each comparable to the steaming radius of a battleship (*ie* about 3300nm). It would have to establish an advanced base (preferably in an uninhabited but

The battleship New York *coals more conventionally from a large fleet collier; note the gantries visible beyond her. This is almost certainly an early postwar photograph (as witness the bridges and tops of the battleship). No matter how it was conducted, coaling was inherently very slow, and virtually impossible to interrupt. Oil fuel was infinitely more convenient.* (USN)

The large purpose-built submarine tender USS
Bushnell, *one of a class of seven ships, was built to a
prewar design although not launched until 1942. They
were better equipped than equivalent mercantile
conversions.* (L & L van Ginderen)

naturally protected anchorage) before engaging an enemy fleet. For example, ships
damaged in battle would be repaired at the advanced base. This concept required the fleet to
steam out convoying not only its fuel (it would
have to refuel *en route*) but also its spare ammunition and its repair and maintenance facilities in shipborne form (its train). The
convoyed ships would be dropped off at the
advanced base, which would have to be protected against enemy land and sea attack.

The General Board concluded, then, that
the fleet would require a considerable train, the
ships of which would have to match its own
cruising speed (14kts): colliers (the fleet burned
coal), stores ships (for frozen and dry food),
distilling ships (for water), ammunition ships,
repair ships, destroyer and submarine tenders,
hospital ships. Transports were intended to
carry the regiments of marines who would
guard the advanced base, together with naval
guns for emplacement ashore and mines to
protect against enemy warships. Of these types,
only the requirement for distilling ships was
eventually dropped; the newer battleships
could distill enough water for themselves, and
the destroyer and submarine tenders could
provide for their charges.

Although some of the ships might have
seemed similar to contemporary merchant
ships, in fact they were quite different. For example, a merchant ship might carry refrigerated cargo from point of origin to point of
sale, but her holds would be sealed en route
(saving considerable cooling energy). A stores
ship would open her holds almost constantly,
to replenish warships. Transports superficially
resembled liners, but (at least in theory) they
had to be able to discharge their marines in
something resembling combat order. The train
speed, 14kts, was high by contemporary merchant ship standards.

The destroyer and submarine tenders were
necessary because these classes were not intended to be self-sustaining or self-repairing
on any large scale; by about 1910 the General
Board was advocating heavy gun armament for
destroyer tenders on the ground that experience showed that the destruction of a tender
would also destroy the efficiency of her flotilla.

Tenders, particularly for submarines, were
attractive even to a fleet defending the US
coast, because they could operate away from

fixed naval bases to respond to unexpected circumstances. For example, in the period before
1914, the US Navy decided to adopt submarine tenders instead of building submarine
bases, on the theory that the combination of
submarines and tender was much more mobile
and flexible. Tenders typically incorporated
specialised workshops, and they carried reload
weapons, particularly torpedoes, which their
charges could not carry. In many cases crews
(or replacement crews) lived on board when
their torpedo craft were in harbour.

This fleet burned coal; it could not fuel underway. Instead, it would stop periodically in
isolated bays to fuel from the colliers accom-
panying it (one day per battleship per collier).
Fuel requirements could be enormous; in 1910
it was estimated that a twenty-battleship fleet
steaming from the US East Coast to the western Pacific would require a total of 149,645
tons of coal (the largest special naval colliers
carried about 10,000 tons of coal). At that time
the capacity of the US collier fleet was about
95,000 tons, and two of the ships were considered unsuited to their task (they were converted to repair ships). The experience of the
round-the-world cruise (1907–09), which was
essentially a test of US ability to operate in the
western Pacific in wartime, shaped the large
colliers bought from 1908 to 1912, with their
distinctive engines-aft design. They were built
with continuous coal holds and with tall king-
posts from which coal could be drawn directly
from the deep holds, and then swung over a
battleship's deck. Special efforts were made to
coal more quickly, but the need to coal limited
fleet flexibility: moreover, neutrals might make
those fuel stops difficult.

Beginning with the *Nevada* class battleships,

the US Navy switched to oil fuel (older battleships were not converted until after the First
World War; destroyers already burned oil).
Fleet tanker construction began with the 1913
programme. It was not yet realised that ships
could fuel underway; like the colliers, the tankers were designed to fuel divisions of four battleships each (they had fuelling connections at
bow, stern, and on each side). On the other
hand, a ton of oil fuel provided far more energy
than a ton of coal, so battleship endurance increased considerably (to about 8000nm) once
oil was introduced. That considerably reduced
the expected load on fuelling ships. By the
middle of the First World War, at least the
smaller ships were expected to fuel underway
on a regular basis: that was how the destroyers
made it to Ireland in 1917.

The advanced base concept worked. Two
destroyer tenders very successfully supported
the US destroyers deployed to Queenstown,
Ireland (which had virtually no other support
facilities), in 1917–18. In Brest, the navy's repair ship, USS *Bridgeport*, managed to conduct
hull repairs on at least one severely damaged
merchant ship and also on two destroyers
(earlier repair ships had been confined largely
to machinery repairs). Inspired by these examples, the US Navy established a Base Force
after the war. It controlled the tankers, fresh
and frozen food ships, repair ships, target repair ships, and tugs; ammunition ships were
controlled separately, as were the tenders.
Congress was convinced to authorise destroyer
and submarine tenders and a repair ship, all of
which shared a common hull design. Existing
tug-type minesweepers were converted to seaplane tenders. This programme ended with the
Great Depression.

The ultimate US seaplane tenders were the four ships of the Currituck *class, launched in 1943–4. Relatively fast, (19kts) and well protected, they were intended for independent operations from remote anchorages. This is a postwar view of* Pine Island. *(L & L van Ginderen)*

US prewar planning

Work on auxiliary ship designs resumed in 1933–34. The planned fleet speed was now 15kts, and standard tender sea speed was increased to 16.5kts. A new common hull design was prepared, and prototype destroyer and submarine tenders and repair ships were all completed before the United States entered the Second World War. By 1940 it was clear that they could not be built quickly enough to provide the numbers needed. Fortunately, the US Maritime Commission had been formed in 1936 to revitalise the US merchant fleet; it was also intended to build sufficient ships for wartime conversion, to fill out mobilisation requirements. Numerous wartime tenders and repair ships were built on these standard hulls.

By the mid-1930s the planned fleet moving across the Pacific had a new element: long range seaplane patrol bombers. The US Bureau of Aeronautics argued that such aircraft, flying from unimproved atolls, would be a most valuable complement to the aircraft on board units of the battlefleet (carriers, cruisers, and battleships). They would be supported by their own tenders. However, these tenders probably would not be part of the advanced base. Instead, they would moor in small isolated anchorages. The new large seaplane tenders of the late prewar period (and of wartime construction) were therefore provided with higher speed (to get to their bases) and with a considerable degree of protection, not very much less than what a carrier required.

Floating dry-docks suitable for long-distance towing in the open sea became an essential element of the planned fleet train, particularly after the Washington Treaty made it unwise for the United States to build fixed docks in her western Pacific possessions (they could not be fortified to protect the docks). Unfortunately there was no hope of towing a battleship-sized dock at fleet speed. US post-First World War planners had to accept that the fleet and its train would steam west in sev-

eral groups, one comprising the fleet itself and the fast tenders, then several slow convoys (including floating dry-docks as well as slow merchant ships carrying replenishment supplies). Characteristics for floating dry-docks with capacities of 3000 tons to 50,000 tons were debated as early as 1923, but the first small prototype dock, *ARD-1*, was completed only in 1936. The docks were essential: without them, no forward base could sustain the fleet for any length of time,ʼor deal with major battle damage. Only three special forward-area docks were authorised before the outbreak of war, but thirty, including three battleship docks, were in service in the western Pacific in 1945.

The wartime fleet train also included an extensive repair and salvage organisation, most of whose ships were newly built or converted. Prewar repair ships were intended primarily to work on ships' steam machinery. Prompted in part by the experience at Brest, one of the new ones was completed as a heavy hull repair ship,

the main change being increased provision for welding.

The fleet contemplated before the late 1930s was exclusively steam-powered. The fleet which fought in the Second World War, however, included many ships powered by diesels and even craft with gasoline power. These internal combustion engines required their own specialist repair ships, most of them improvised on 'Liberty' ship and LST hulls. Some of the small craft, such as tugs, used at forward bases lacked distilling facilities, and in 1944 three ships were converted to provide fresh water. There were also specialised repair ships for battle damage, for landing craft, for aircraft engines, and for electronics. None of these types had been contemplated prewar. All were essential for sustained operations.

The main difference between prewar US thinking and wartime practice was that the advance during the Second World War was sequential; there were several advanced bases.

Along with submarine and destroyer tenders, the US Navy designed a somewhat similar specialist repair ship, the Vulcan *class of which this is* Ajax. *Equipped with elaborate machine shops, they could cope with most emergencies except heavy battle damage. (L & L van Ginderen)*

Underway replenishment made it possible for the US fast carrier task forces to remain at sea more or less continuously in the western Pacific in 1944–5. Here a tanker fuels the battleship Missouri *(note the fuelling hoses suspended from the boom at the left). Note, too, that the tanker is also carrying other stores, which must be transferred by crane, on the false deck visible at right. Ships like* Missouri *had not been designed specifically for underway replenishment. They lacked the appropriate cranes and also the open deck spaces needed to land stores aboard before they could be struck below. The requirements of underway replenishment explain much of the empty look of modern US warships.* (USN)

Each had to be maintained as a stepping-stone to the next, but there were never enough ships to equip all. The solution was to use the base ships initially, then build up most base facilities ashore (the most important exception was dry-docks, which would have taken too long to build in place: towable floating dry-docks were used instead). The bases themselves were, in effect, pre-packaged (they were called Lions). They were sustained by point-to-point shipping from the United States.

Underway replenishment

The prewar concept of relatively short-term operations from bases survived until late 1944. In the Central and South Pacific, the fleet seized a base, then sortied to seize the next to support the next sortie. However, after mid-1944 the fast carrier task force remained at sea for extended periods, thousands of miles from its advanced bases at Ulithi and Manaus. It required a different sort of logistic support. Continuous air operations in particular quickly exhausted not merely ship and aircraft fuel storage but also magazine and even food space aboard carriers. For example, carriers normally carried no more than a few days' worth of aviation gasoline. Aircraft themselves were used up.

The solution was to adapt point-to-point ammunition and stores ships so that they could transfer their loads underway. The same tankers which fuelled the carriers also provided aviation gasoline. The replenishment rigs were not suited to operation at high ship speeds. Typically a carrier task group would conduct several days of strikes, then retire to a safer area further from the target to replenish. The replenishment groups shuttled between the forward bases and the task groups.

Fuelling at sea of course was not new; throughout the inter-war period it was a standard exercise in the US Navy. Wartime operations required high speed runs (and other inefficient operating practices, such as running

with split plants) which greatly reduced the distance ships could steam without refuelling. Ships had to refuel at sea, and special underway replenishment groups were formed to service them. However, this type of replenishment supported the type of limited-endurance sortie contemplated before the war, not the sustained steaming actually accomplished in 1944–45.

Similarly, from about 1942 on, many commercial tankers were adapted to fuel Allied convoy escorts at sea. That made it possible for escort groups to remain with a convoy all the way across the Atlantic, instead of shifting over to other groups based in Iceland and in Great Britain. Later escort carriers often fuelled

escorts. Although such ships were never considered part of the fleet train, they were quite analogous to the underway replenishment tankers used by the main fleet.

The great defect of the system was the need for several different kinds of replenishment ships: fast tankers for fuel, ammunition ships, stores (mainly food) ships, and aviation stores ships (aircraft spare parts); there were even small carriers detailed to deliver replacement aircraft. Full replenishment required a ship to go alongside each in turn. Although it might be conducted in relatively safe waters, replenishment always carried some vulnerability, for example to submarine attack (because it had to be

Depot ships allowed submarines to operate from secluded waters in wartime. This is HMS Forth *with boats of the Third Flotilla based in Holy Loch, the Scottish inlet that was later to become home for US Polaris submarines during the 'Cold War'. (CMP)*

done at low speed). Moreover, the longer it took, the more it detracted from the overall mobility of the fast carrier task force. Postwar, then, the US Navy looked towards the development of faster 'one stop' replenishment ships which could supply several consumables at once. They eventually materialised as the current fleet of AOEs and AORs.

Ironically, the US Navy emerged from the Second World War with what amounted to a British-style world-wide chain of bases. Improvised forward bases no longer seemed terribly important, although the war-built ships and floating docks designed for the prewar policy survived. Within a decade of the end of the war, the US approach to naval logistics emphasised, not the seizure of the bases, but the underway replenishment techniques of 1944–45.

Other navies

Other navies bought tenders and repair ships, but not in the numbers or with the sophistication which the US Navy sought and eventually got during the Second World War. For example, before the First World War the General Board noted that *Cyclops*, the British repair ship, was built in the sort of secrecy normally accorded a battleship. During that war the British in particular were embarrassed because Scapa Flow and the other important wartime ports (such as Harwich) had never been built up as bases (base development had been directed against France, hence in the south, until 1905); they needed both tenders and repair ships there. Numerous obsolete light cruisers were adapted as destroyer flotilla depot ships.

The Japanese seaplane tender Chitose *in 1938. She was modified in 1941 to launch midget submarines, and was eventually converted into a light fleet carrier to offset Japanese losses in the battles of 1942. (CMP)*

Moreover, by using tenders (depot ships) and repair ships to provide many fleet services at minor British-controlled ports, the British could avoid major fixed investments. In this sense British policy was not altogether different from that of the US Navy, except that the Royal Navy expected at least some facilities, including those for base defence, to be available when the fleet arrived. They had little interest in very long-range operations requiring underway support. The British did con-

sider the construction of a base ship, which could be deployed to a port while naval base facilities were built up. This project seems to have originated in the experience of operating out of the Greek port of Suda Bay during the First World War; for a time the battleship *Agincourt* was scheduled for conversion. The idea was revived in 1935 after the Abyssinian War scare showing that it was still badly needed.

The lack of a US-style fleet train showed when the British had to improvise one to support their Pacific Fleet in 1944–45 (US naval logistics was too badly stretched to take on this extra load).

The prewar Imperial Japanese Navy enjoyed

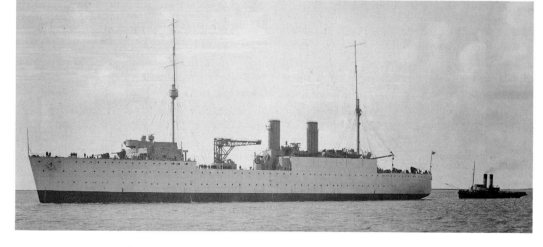

Despite the network of overseas bases, the Royal Navy foresaw the need for mobile repair facilities and in 1928 launched the Resource, *its first purpose-built repair ship. This ship and the contemporary submarine depot ship* Medway *were later to influence the design of the Japanese* Akashi. *(CMP)*

the sort of island base structure which the US Navy lacked; it did not need an elaborate fleet train. Some ships nominally rated as fast tenders had combatant roles. For example, three fast seaplane tenders had wartime roles as carriers of midget submarines (they were intended to launch the midgets into the path of an enemy fleet). Other submarine tenders were intended more as flagships for ocean-going submarine flotillas.

The German situation was somewhat different. In both World Wars she planned extensive raiding operations against British trade. During the First World War special covert stores ships operated from many neutral ports abroad. This covert sort of fleet train was revived during the Second World War, when Germany again had to rely on solitary surface raiders. This time the replenishment ships were essentially tankers (for fuelling) with the capacity to supply whatever else was needed. The *Altmark*, surprised in Norway by *Cossack*, was typical. Postwar, both the US Navy and the Royal Navy tested captured German replenishment ships as prototypes of fast 'single stop' replenishment ships. The Germans also developed special logistic support submarines for analogous support of deployed U-boats.

Norman Friedman

The Fleet Train: Typical Vessels 1906–1945

Ship or Class	Nationality	Type	Dispt (tons) Light Full load	Dimensions (loa × breadth × draught) Feet Metres	Speed (max kts)	Launch dates	Numbers built
JUPITER	American	Collier	6860 19,360	542 × 67 × 27 165 × 20 × 8	14	1912	1
MAUMEE	American	Tanker	5425 14,500	476 × 56 × 26 145 × 17 × 8	14	1914–16	3
CIMARRON	American	Tanker	7136 23,000	553 × 75 × 30 169 × 23 × 9	18.9	1939–40	12
PATAPSCO	American	Gasoline tanker	2020 4142	311 × 49 × 15 95 × 15 × 5	14	1942–45	23
MELVILLE	American	Destroyer tender	5250 7150	417 × 54 × 20 127 × 16 × 6	15	1915	1
DOBBIN	American	Destroyer tender	8325 12,450	484 × 61 × 24 148 × 19 × 7	16	1921–23	2
DIXIE	American	Destroyer tender	9450 17,176	531 × 73 × 20 162 × 22 × 6	18	1939–43	5
KLONDIKE	American	Destroyer tender	8180 16,635	492 × 70 × 18 150 × 21 × 5	16.5	1944–45	10
CURTISS	American	Seaplane tender	8625 13,475	527 × 69 × 20 161 × 21 × 6	18	1940	2
WHITING	American	Seaplane tender	8000 14,000	492 × 70 × 23 150 × 21 × 6	16.5	1943–44	4
APPLELEAF	British	Tanker	12,300	405 × 55 × 26 123 × 17 × 8	10	1916	17
WAR AFRIDI	British	Tanker	11,600	415 × 53 × 24 127 × 16 × 7	10	1918–20	22
WOOLWICH	British	Destroyer tender	8750	610 × 64 × 15 186 × 20 × 5	15	1934	1
FORTH	British	Submarine tender	8900	531 × 73 × 17 162 × 22 × 5	17	1937–38	2
ALTMARK	German	'One-stop' support ship	12,670 22,850	584 × 72 × 16 178 × 22 × 10	21	1937–39	2

Notes:
The four destroyer tenders represent four generations of designs, and thus are not too different from contemporary submarine tenders and repair ships: pre-1914; First World War wartime design; immediately before the Second World War; and wartime converted standard Maritime Commission designs. *Whiting* was also a modified Maritime Commission design.

12

Naval Weapons

IN 1906 the standard heavy gun calibre in all major navies except the German was 12in (304.8mm or in France 305mm) while Germany favoured 11in, actually 283mm (11.14in). In the period to 1918 Britain went to 13.5in (342.9mm) and then to 15in (381mm) with three 18in (457.2mm) in special ships. It should be noted that 14in (355.6mm) was not at this time a regular British calibre, all these guns having been built for foreign countries and taken over. Germany went from 11.14in to 12in (305mm) and then to 14.96in (380mm), 13.78in (350mm) being a later calibre for a class of uncompleted battlecruisers while 16.54in (420mm) was chosen for projected ships of 1918. The United States went to 14in (355.6mm) and then to 16in (406.4mm) for some of the ships under construction in 1918, though a prototype had been in existence since 1914. Japan likewise went to 14in and to 16.14in (410mm) for ships building in 1918.

In the second rank of major navies France went to 13.39in (340mm) and Italy straight to 15in (381mm) though this was limited to powered floating batteries among completed ships. Neither Russia nor Austria-Hungary, which cannot be called a major navy in 1906, completed any ships with larger guns than 12in (305mm Austria) but Russia had some 14in (355.6mm) and Vickers built a prototype 16in (406.4mm) which was never delivered, while Austria would have gone to 13.78in (350mm).

The nominal length in calibres indicated bore in most navies, but overall in the German, Russian and Austrian. Most guns were about 45 calibres, but some were around 50 and a few down to 40 calibres. In longer guns the propellant gases could act over a greater distance but rigidity suffered.

British guns, as well as Japanese and Italian guns designed according to British ideas or made in Britain, were wire-wound while others were built up in various ways without wire. The main, 'A', tube of heavy guns, which often contained an inner 'A' tube or liner, driven and/or shrunk into position, had to be compressed on the outside to withstand the internal gas pressures with the desired factor of safety, and the simplest way of achieving this was to wind layers of wire over the length, or sometimes the breech-end half, of the 'A' tube. The wire did not contribute appreciably to longitudinal strength or to rigidity which was supplied by the 'A' tube and the 'B' tube and jacket over the wire. In built-up guns the 'A' tube was supported by shrunk-on tubes or hoops in more than one layer. The usual criticism of lack of longitudinal rigidity and excessive muzzle droop in wire-wound guns does not seem to be justified, and many built-up guns suffered from too many relatively short reinforcing tubes. More valid criticisms of British guns were the unnecessarily large factor of safety, too large chambers and too narrow rifling lands. Their weight was also high, the British 15in weighing with breech mechanism 100 tons (101,605kg) compared to the German 14.96in (380mm) 76.57 tons (77,800kg), but this reduced recoil energy and some of the weight was added to move the centre of gravity of the gun towards the breech end and thus reduce turret size.

The German and Austrian navies used brass cartridge cases for at least part of the propellant charge even in the largest guns, and favoured a horizontally moving wedge breech block, while in others a Welin type stepped interrupted screw block was used with the charge in bags, usually silk.

Naval guns 1919–1945

In 1919 only Britain, the United States and Japan were still concerned with heavy naval guns, though two 17.72in (450mm)/45-calibre guns were authorised in France in 1920 for experimental purposes. The United States already had the 16in Mk 2/50-calibre gun first proved in April 1918, which was to arm the new battleships and battlecruisers and in early 1919 design work began on an 18in (457.2mm)/48-calibre. Japan was to use the 16.14in (410mm)/45 in new ships, but an experimental 18.9in (480mm)/45 was built though this was thought too large, and an 18.1in (460mm)/45 envisaged for projected ships. In Britain three experimental 18in/45 were ordered, one fully wire-wound, one partly and one without wire so that the most suitable

The construction of a typical heavy gun of the First World War period (a British 15in Mk I) It shows full length wire-wound construction, though in later designs the wire was wound in a single length with one start and finish, known as taper winding. As was normal in British heavy guns, an inner 'A' tube is fitted.

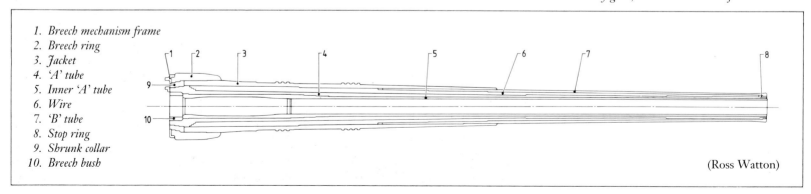

1. Breech mechanism frame
2. Breech ring
3. Jacket
4. 'A' tube
5. Inner 'A' tube
6. Wire
7. 'B' tube
8. Stop ring
9. Shrunk collar
10. Breech bush

(Ross Watton)

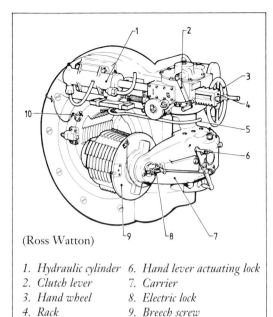

(Ross Watton)

1. *Hydraulic cylinder* 6. *Hand lever actuating lock*
2. *Clutch lever* 7. *Carrier*
3. *Hand wheel* 8. *Electric lock*
4. *Rack* 9. *Breech screw*
5. *Air-blast pipe* 10. *Breech safety contact*

Typical breech mechanism for a heavy gun (British 15in Mk I).

construction could be determined. However the first new capital ships were to be battle-cruisers and the size of an 18in ship would be too great so that priority was given to a wire-wound 16in/45.

Under the 1922 Washington Treaty the maximum bore of naval guns was limited to 16in and the above 45-calibre gun was used to arm the *Nelson* and *Rodney*. During the 1920s there were two interesting experimental guns: the American 18in was converted to a 16in/56 to explore high velocities in heavy naval guns, and a British 12in (304.8mm)/50 known as the Mk XIV, was built to test wire-free con-struction. There was a remote possibility that the Washington limit might be reduced to 12in but after various negotiations which cannot be described here, it was reduced to 14in (355.6mm) subject to various conditions. In the event only Britain complied with this.

Meanwhile the Germans, limited to 11in by the Versailles Treaty, introduced an 11.14in (283mm)/52 in their new 'armoured ships', fol-lowed by a 54 calibre. The French replied with a 13in (330mm)/50 and in the first full size ships since the *Nelson* class, the Italians intro-duced a 15in (381mm)/50.

To summarise heavy naval guns from 1935

The design and manufacture of a heavy gun often took longer than the capital ship to carry it. In this view of the Italian Ansaldo gunshop a pair of 15in (381mm) guns, destined for the monitor Faa' di Bruno *is nearing completion in 1916. (By courtesy of John Campbell)*

to 1945, Britain had the 14in/45 Mk VII, to be succeeded by new 16in/45, never afloat; the United States had new designs of 16in/45 and /50 as well as a 12in/50 for large cruisers in service, and the 16in/56 was reconverted to an 18in/47 in 1941/2 for experiments. Japan, the only country actually to build very large battle-ships, had an 18.1in (460mm)/45 with a 20.1in (510mm)/45 designed, as well as a 12.2in (310mm)/50 for projected large cruisers. Ger-many had a 14.96in (380mm)/51 afloat, and made a few 16in/51 as well as one 21in (533.4mm)/52. Finally France had a 14.96in/45 in service and Russia made a few 16in/50 and 12in/54.

Except for those of the Japanese all these guns were of built up construction with fewer and longer tubes than in older guns though the French still had short ring-hoops over the 'A' tube. Loose liners were in some of the Italian 15in, the French 14.96in and both types of German 11.14in as well as those 14.96in in ships. The German 16in had a loose barrel and a loose liner as did later 14.96in, and the last of the British 16in, the Mk IV, a loose barrel. The normal liner or inner 'A' tube was firmly secured in the 'A' tube and the gun had to be dismounted and sent to a heavy gun factory for relining. There was a clearance between the loose liner and 'A' tube which was taken up by elastic expansion of the liner under the press-ure of the propellant gases, and relining only required the removal of locating bushes or col-lars. Similarly, a loose barrel ('A' tube) had a clearance between it and the jacket or other outer tube and could be replaced like a loose liner. The Japanese 18.1in and 20.1in were wire-wound for at least part of their length and had the inner 'A' tube expanded into place un-der hydraulic pressure, which meant that it had to be bored out if renewal was required. Ger-man guns retained metal cartridge cases and a horizontal wedge breech block but otherwise the Welin screw block was used with bag charges.

Projectile weights

As the weight of shells of identical proportions increased as the cube of the bore, there were advantages in using as large a calibre as poss-ible, though muzzle velocity was usually lowered in the interest of reduced wear and longer barrel life in the largest guns. There were considerable differences in the projectile weight adopted for the same calibre in dif-ferent navies, and the precise reasons are not always clear, though lighter shells saved am-munition weights and space, and the higher velocity in a given gun improved performance against armour at shorter ranges. Thus in the 1906–1918 period the nominal weight of 12in (304.8/305mm) armour piercing (AP) shell varied from 850lb (386kg) in Britain to 1038lb (471kg) in Russia, the average for the eight ma-jor navies being 934lb (424kg), and the four highest being those last to introduce dread-noughts. For larger guns, the British 13.5in (342.9mm) fired a 1250lb (567kg) shell, in-creased in later ships to 1400lb (635kg), which was in line with the 15in (381mm) at 1920lb (871kg) and 18in (457.2mm) at 3320lb (1506kg). German shells were lighter, the 14.96in (380mm) being only 1653lb (750kg)

and relatively heaviest the 12in (305mm) at 893lb (405kg). The United States favoured fairly light shells at this time, the 14in (355.6mm) being 1400lb (635kg) and the 16in (406.4mm) 2100lb (953kg), as did Japan and also France after their 12in. The Italian 15in was heavy as were the Russian proposed 16in and 14in with the Austrian 13.78in (350mm) apparently intermediate.

Curiously the British 16in/45 Mk I had a shell of only 2048lb (929kg) and the 18in/45 was to have one of 2916lb (1323kg). The reason seems to have been that some erroneous tests showed that short AP shells behaved best at oblique impact, but one suspects that the light German 14.9in shell had some influence. British guns of 1935–1945 had heavier shells, 1590lb (721kg) in 14in and 2375lb (1077kg) in 16in Mks II and III. The French 14.96in and the Italian 15in had shells of 1950lb (884kg), but the Japanese were lighter with 3219lb (1460kg) in the 18.1in (460mm) and 2249lb (1020kg) in 16.14in (410mm). The German weights were similar: 1764lb (800kg) in 14.96in and 2271lb (1030kg) in 16in. The United States introduced very heavy AP shells for their new guns; 2700lb (1225kg) for 16in, 1140lb (517kg) for 12in, and 3848lb (1745kg) for the experimental 18in, though these were too large for 16in in older mountings for which the shell was increased to 2240lb (1016kg) in line with 1500lb (680kg) for 14in.

Muzzle velocities depended on the weight of projectile, and to a first approximation for the same gun and propellant charge, the square of the muzzle velocity is inversely proportional to the weight of the projectile plus one-third of the propellant charge. With a few exceptions new-gun muzzle velocities varied from 2472 to 2920fps (753 to 890mps).

In the First World War period, most American and German guns (the 14.96in being a notable exception) had increasing twist rifling and other navies uniform, but later US guns had uniform twist though German still had increasing. The amount of twist was typically 1 in 30, sometimes 1 in 25, while the German 16in had 1 in 40 to 1 in 32. Grooves were of rectangular cross section neglecting chamfers and radii, though in 1906 some American 12in had hook section grooves. Reducing the width of the groove and increasing that of the land from the start of the rifling to the muzzle, was used in some US 14in and 12in and in the German 14.96in/45.

Depth of the grooves was often about 1/100 of the bore in later guns reaching 0.189in (4.8mm) in the German 16in but not over 0.135in (3.43mm) in any British 16in. Chro-mium plating of the rifled bore from shot seating to muzzle was very successful in later US guns in increasing gun life but other navies seem to have found little advantage in this.

Propellant

The size and form of the propellant ('powder') chamber depended on the calibre and performance of the gun which in turn depended on the weight of the propellant charge, and its thermochemical properties and grain size and shape. Differences in chamber volume were greatest in the earlier guns of the period. For example the British and German 12in/50 were of similar performance but the respective chamber volumes were 23,031cu in (377.4dm³) and 12,205cu in (200dm³). Another pair of guns of similar performance, the British 15in/42 and German 14.96in/45, had chambers of 30,650cu in (502.3dm³) and 16,476cu in (270dm³).

It was initially believed in Britain that propellant with cord grain form would lead to the smallest charge weight for a given performance and though this was not necessarily so, Britain and Japan retained cord grain form, while the United States favoured multi-tube with seven holes in a short grain, Germany, Italy, Russia and Austria single tube and France strip (changed to single tube in the 1930s). On the whole single tube was the best form for heavy guns. Pure nitrocellulose (NC) with a small amount of diphenylamine as stabiliser was favoured by the United States, France for strip and Russia, but other navies used nitroglycerin (NG)/NC compositions which could produce more energy per unit weight but also hot and erosive gases which reduced gun life. In all earlier propellants solvents for NC had to be added to produce a gel and then slowly removed with c25 per cent shrinkage. German propellants were usually the most advanced, and RPC/12, the standard German propellant of the First World War, was 'solventless', the NC being dissolved by a NG/Centralite (symmetrical diphenyl diethyl urea) mixture which did not require removal. Later German propellants produced cooler gases and in RPC/38 NG was replaced by DGN (diethylene glycol dinitrate).

Flashless propellants for heavy guns belong to the post-1945 period, though fairly satisfactory charges for 6in (152.4mm) and smaller were developed, particularly reduced charges for star shell.

In the Austrian 12in the whole charge was in a brass cartridge case, but German practice was to have the rear part of the charge in a brass case and the rest in a double silk bag with some brass stiffening. During the Second World War steel cartridge cases were introduced, and in some of the largest charges the brass stiffening was replaced by a cylinder of propellant between the silk bags and the rest of the

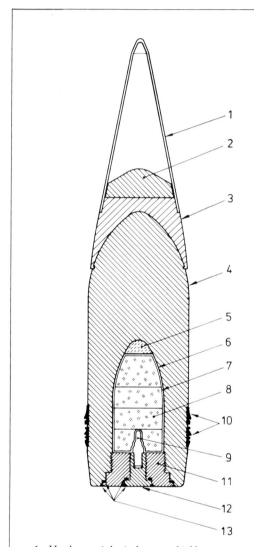

A cross section of a Japanese Type 91 46cm (18.1in) AP shell, the largest calibre actually taken to sea by a capital ship (Yamato and Musashi).

1. *Hood – special wind-water shield*
2. *Cap head*
3. *Cap*
4. *Body*
5. *Aluminium 'anti-inertia' block*
6. *Cork lining*
7. *Wool wrap around filler*
8. *Trinitroanisol filler*
9. *Fuse – Type 13 Mk 5 short delay base fuse*
10. *Copper rotating bands*
11. *Base*
12. *Fuse adaptor*
13. *Copper gas-check rings – copper caulking*

(Janusz Skulski)

charge. With RPC/12 only a single black powder igniter was needed at the base of the rear charge but with cooler propellants further igniters were required. In other navies the charge was in fabric bags, usually silk, with a black powder igniter on each bag. The number of bags per charge was generally four but six in the largest guns afloat.

Shell characteristics

The projectile weights quoted above apply to APC (armour piercing capped) shell which in most navies was heavier than other types, though usually of similar weight in Britain and Germany. APC was typically made from a fairly high carbon nickel chromium steel heat treated to give a hard nose and softer tough body. Until 1918 caps were of soft mild steel but Britain then introduced hard alloy steel caps and this was followed by all. The precise action of the cap when a shell struck armour is not easy to determine but it served to protect the nose of the shell proper from destruction by hard faced plates. Blunt cap and shell noses were best, but their aerodynamic form was poor and ballistic caps (windshields) first introduced by the United States were universal in the latter part of the period. Explosive charges were reduced in most navies, typically from around 3 to 2–2½ per cent, though to 1½ per cent in the United States and Japan. First World War British APC used Lyddite (picric acid) as the burster, a most unsatisfactory choice, replaced by Shellite (latterly 70 picric acid, 30 dinitrophenol). TNT was the most widely used burster often desensitised by beeswax, but the United States favoured ammonium picrate and Japan TNA (trinitroanisole).

Base fuses with a typical delay of 35 milliseconds were used and detonation of the shell filling was preferable to explosion though often not attained. Coloured dyes to distinguish the shell splashes of individual ships (K shells), were introduced by France and by 1942–43 were in general use. Later Japanese shell differed in being designed for a stable underwater trajectory, the ballistic cap and cap head being removed on impact on the water and the flat nose of the remaining part of the cap giving a better underwater course. To allow for underwater penetration by near-misses fuse delays were 400 milliseconds. France had done some work on underwater trajectories about 1914, but it was not realised in Britain until 30 years later that special shells would be needed.

Shells intended to pierce lighter armour included the British CPC (capped pointed common) widely used in the First World War.

This had a 6.8 to 9.4 per cent black powder filling which gave some delay apart from the fuse, and was on occasion surprisingly successful, the large fragments being very destructive. Germany used a base fused shell with 6.5 to 9 per cent TNT filling for 12in and 14.96in guns in the First World War and a later version with 4.4 per cent filling and in 14.96in and 16in a cap, for all heavy guns in the second. Larger capacity shell known variously as HE, HC or bombardment shell, with nose or sometimes nose and base fuses, was supplied in the Second World War for ships on bombardment duties, and was also carried for all German heavy guns at that time. The burster, usually TNT, was generally 6–10 per cent. Up to the latter part of the First World War British 12in and 13.5in guns had nose fused HE with 12.5–14.7 per cent Lyddite or TNT filling as part of their standard outfit but its effect against 4in armour was small. Japan and Russia also had shells with 10–12.5 per cent bursters at this time but favoured base fuses.

In the Second World War Japan used an incendiary shrapnel in all heavy guns with 996 incendiary tubes in the 18.1in. The burst was spectacular but usually too low for optimum AA effect, though the 14in version was destructive in airfield bombardment at Guadalcanal.

Gun mountings

Turret mountings for heavy guns incorporated a fixed armoured barbette, and a revolving armoured turret. This contained two, three or four guns, or exceptionally, for the British 18in in *Furious* in 1917, only one. (The 18in mountings in monitors were of modified land pattern). The more guns to a turret, the less was the weight and space per gun, but the concentration of weight could be difficult with very large guns. Ammunition supply was easiest in twins and if a turret was disabled or jammed only two guns were lost compared with three or four. Apart from the above exception, British ships had twin turrets until 1919–20 when new designs were to have triples as did the *Nelson* class laid down in 1922. Quadruples combined with a twin for reasons of weight, were introduced in the *King George V* class, but later designs would have had triples, except the *Vanguard* with a return to twins to use existing turrets. German ships had twins until their 'armoured ships' and the *Scharnhorst* class of the 1930s which had triples, but later ships and designs had twins. The United States used twins until the *Nevada* class laid down in 1912 which had two triples and two twins. Later ships had triples with an interesting return to

twins in the *Maryland* class laid down in 1917–20 and the cancelled *Lexington* class battlecruisers as four turrets were then preferred to three.

Japan favoured twins until the *Yamato* class which had triples, but France went from twins to quadruples in the ships cancelled because of the First World War, and used them in their ships of 1930s design even though this meant only two turrets. In contrast Italy, Russia and Austria-Hungary all favoured triples though the projected Austrian ships of 1914 and five of the six Italian dreadnoughts of 1914–18 had triples and twins because of topweight problems. The cancelled Italian ships of 1914–15 would have had four twins rather than three triples, but twenty years later the *Vittorio Veneto* class had three triples. The United States used the terms two-, three- or four-gun if the guns were in separate cradles, but triple for those with a single cradle, an unsatisfactory arrangement limited to the *Nevada* and *Pennsylvania* classes. If guns in a turret were to be fired together it was important to limit interference by time delays or better to space the guns as far apart as possible though this caused space and weight problems. In the US 14in three-gun turrets of 1915–18 the spacing between gun axes was only 71in (1.80m) but 117in (2.97m) in the 16in of 1940. In the contemporary German 14.96in two-gun turret the spacing was 147.6in (3.75m), slightly more than in the 1914–16 turret.

In Britain it was usual to power turrets from a hydraulic main with steam driven pumps, but the *Nelson* class had individual steam driven pumps for each turret. Electric mountings were tried in *Invincible* but converted to hydraulic in 1914. Japanese and earlier Italian turrets followed the usual British practice but other navies favoured electric. In Germany training was always electric but increasing use was made of individual hydraulic units for other purposes. German, Austrian, most Russian and the French 13in quadruple turrets were supported on ball races but otherwise rollers were used.

In the First World War period the usual maximum elevation was 13½ to 20 degrees though Japan and Russia went to 25 degrees and some British 'specials' to 30 degrees. Later turrets allowed from 30 to 45 degrees. Loading in earlier British, Japanese and Italian turrets and in all French, was at any angle of elevation though probably not beyond 20 degrees in practice. Run-out was liable to be very slow in British turrets which did not have pneumatic accumulators until 1918 or 1919 and it was found better to use an angle of about 5 degrees.

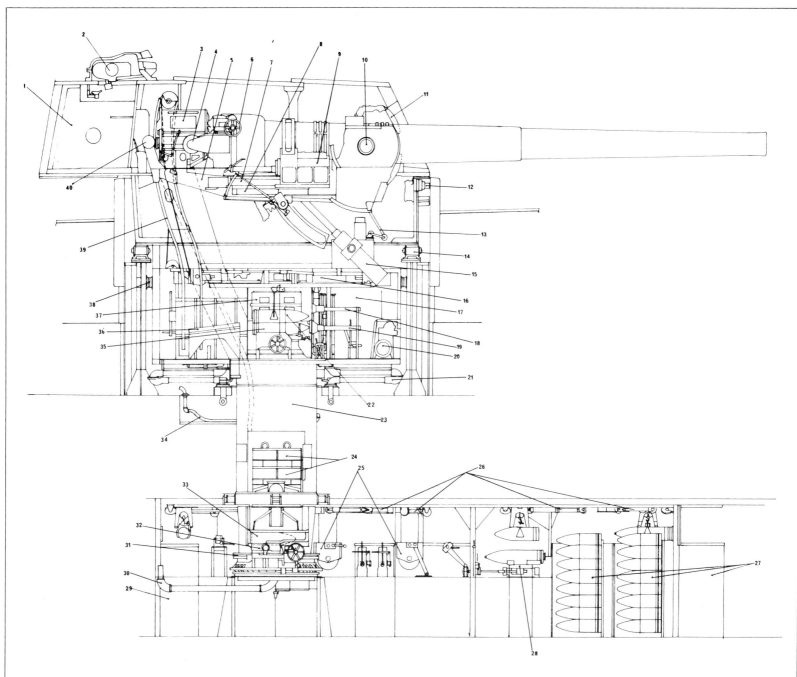

1. Officers' cabinet
2. Rangefinder
3. Gun loading cage
4. Breech (open)
5. Loading arm (attached to gun slide)
6. Breech operating hand wheel
7. Run-out cylinder
8. Chain rammer casing
9. Gun cradle and recoil cylinder
10. Trunnion
11. Splinter shield to gunport
12. Turret training locking bolt
13. Walking pipes (hydraulic power to elevating structure)
14. Roller path
15. Elevating cylinder
16. Ammunition hoist lifting gear
17. Working chamber
18. Cordite rammers (hoist to cage)
19. Shell rammer (hoist to cage)
20. Electric pump
21. Walking pipes (hydraulic power from fixed to revolving structure)
22. Shell suspended from radial transport rail (ready use)
23. Trunk (containing shell and cordite hoists)
24. Cordite hoppers
25. Shell traversing winches
26. Hydraulic shell lifting and traversing gear
27. Shell bins
28. Shell traversing bogie
29. Shell bin
30. Electric cables
31. Shell bogie ring
32. Revolving shell bogie
33. Shell on bogie
34. Flexible voice pipe (fixed to revolving structure)
35. Shell waiting position
36. Shell waiting tray (ready use)
37. Cordite waiting position
38. Training rack
39. Gun loading cage rails
40. Rammer motor

(John Roberts)

Typical heavy gun mounting of the First World War period (British Mk II mounting for Mk I 15in gun as in HMS *Hood, 'Y' mounting).*

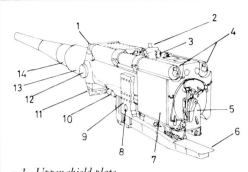

1. Upper shield plate
2. Depression buffer
3. Yoke locking link
4. Counter-recoil (run-out) cylinders
5. Downward opening breech
6. Loader's platform
7. Yoke
8. Slide locking pin
9. Rear end bracket
10. Recoil system expansion tank
11. Lower shield plate
12. Slide trunnion
13. Neoprene gun cover
14. Gun slide cylinder

(Peter Hodges)

A perspective view of the US 16in/50 Mk 7 gun with its slide or cradle.

In all later turrets, except French, loading was at a fixed angle of +1 to +5 degrees though the last Italian turrets loaded at +15 degrees.

Although the US 16in/50 three-gun turret was one of the most compact, revolving weight was 1701–1708 tons (1728–1735t) and barbette internal diameter 37ft 3in (11.35m). The largest ever in a ship, the Japanese 18.1in, had a revolving weight of 2470 tons (2510t) and barbette internal diameter of 45ft 8in (13.93m).

Improvements

The main development in the period, particularly in the years after 1916, was improved safety for propellant charges at all stages from magazine to gun. Inadequate provision for this caused the loss of three British battlecruisers at Jutland and very serious fires in German ships and also at Dogger Bank. Turret and barbette armour was often thicker in recent turrets particularly that on turret crowns. Remote power control (RPC) from the central fire control position, was installed in the later US turrets and in those of the three most completely reconstructed ships. It was also in German Second World War turrets for elevation only, and in French for training also, though it is doubtful if their system was fully satisfactory. In Britain RPC was only introduced for heavy guns in *Vanguard* completed after the war.

Range

Maximum range depended on the allowable elevation of the gun, its muzzle velocity and the air-resistance of the projectile. This last depended on the weight, the cross-sectional area and the form, long nose ones having the least resistance. Actual maximum range with new guns in later turrets varied from 36,900yds (33,740m) at 45 degrees elevation in the US 16in/45 to 46,800yds (42,800m) at 36 degrees in the Italian 15in/50.

Of earlier turrets in battleships and battlecruisers, maximum range varied from 14,765yds

The three-gun turret for the US 16in/50 Mk 7 as used in the battleships of the Iowa *class.*

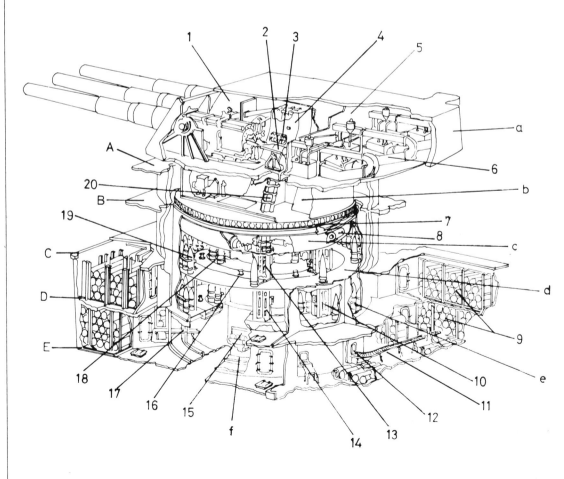

1. Longitudinal flashtight bulkhead
2. Shell cradle
3. Powder charge door
4. Powder trunk
5. Lateral flashtight bulkhead
6. Rammer casing
7. Turret rollers
8. Training buffer
9. Upper and lower powder stowages
10. Centre gun lower shell hoist shutter casing
11. Roller conveyor
12. Powder scuttle
13. Left gun upper shell hoist shutter casing
14. Left gun lower shell hoist shutter casing
15. Powder hopper
16. Shell transfer capstan
17. Powder transfer tray
18. Upper revolving shell-ring
19. Upper fixed shell stowages
20. Shell hoist trunking
A. Main deck
B. Second deck
C. Third deck
D. First platform
E. Second platform
a. Gunhouse
b. Pan floor
c. Machinery floor
d. Upper projectile handling floor
e. Lower projectile handling floor
f. Powder handling floor

(Peter Hodges)

German twin 15cm (5.9in) Drh LC/34 turret as mounted as secondary armament in the Bismarck *and* Scharnhorst *classes.*

(13,500m) at 12 degrees in the 12in/45 of the French *Courbet* class to 28,400yds (25,970m) at 25 degrees in the 12in/50 of the *Kawachi* class. The French shell had a form of high air-resistance. Some monitors had greater ranges, and the 18in/40 with a shell of similar form to those in later guns, ranged to 40,280yds (36,830m) at 45 degrees.

Medium calibre guns, 8in to 6in

Due to the introduction of dreadnoughts and battlecruisers there was little need for guns from over 6in (152.4mm) to 10in (254mm) in the earlier part of the period. The British re-introduced a 7.5in (190.5mm)/45, ballistically the same as a gun of the early years of the century, in the cruisers of the *Hawkins* class, built slowly from 1916, but it was not until the Washington Treaty's limit of 8in (203.2mm) guns for cruisers and aircraft carriers that new guns appeared. Initially Japanese guns were 7.874in (200mm) but others were a full 8in. Russia used a 7.09in (180mm) of Italian influence. Lengths were about 50 to 60 calibres, the German being the longest.

Most guns were of fairly simple built-up type, but the majority of British guns were wire-wound as were the Japanese 7.87in and some of the 8in for at least part of their length. German guns had loose barrels, Italian 53-calibre and Russian 7.09in loose liners, and later US guns had chromium plated bores. German guns had a horizontal sliding breech block with metal cartridge case, but others the Welin screw block with the charge in bags. The US Mk 16 with metal case and vertical sliding block was not in service until 1948.

The 8in shells were typically about 270lb (122kg) with muzzle velocities 2756 to 3035fps (840 to 925mps), but later US cruisers fired a 335lb (152kg) shell at 2500fps (762mps).

Unlike the position with heavy guns the smallest chamber in an 8in was the British of 3646cu in (59.75dm³) and the largest the French of 5595cu in (91.7dm³). The outfit in most navies was APC and HE(HC) but German 8in also had base fused HE as for heavy guns, and the Japanese carried some incendiary shrapnel while their 8in AP lacked a true cap. British 8in had capped semi armour piercing (SAPC) with about 4.5 per cent burster instead of APC, and also carried HE(HC).

Turrets in cruisers were twins in most navies

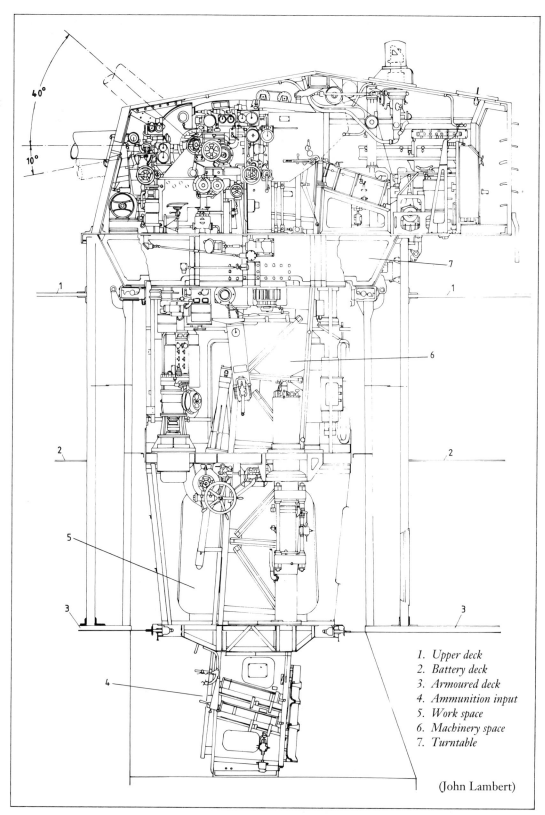

1. Upper deck
2. Battery deck
3. Armoured deck
4. Ammunition input
5. Work space
6. Machinery space
7. Turntable

(John Lambert)

but triple or three-gun in the United States, except for the *Pensacola* class which had twins and triples, while the Japanese *Kako* class originally had single 7.87in turrets, later altered to 8in twins.

In British and German turrets the gun axes were 84–85in (2.13–2.16m) apart but less in others with only 39.4in (1.0m) in Italian tur-

rets, and the Russian 7.09in were even closer at 32.3in (82cm). British and Japanese turrets were hydraulic with individual pumps, German electric and hydraulic as for heavy guns, and the rest electric. Maximum elevation was +70 degrees in nearly all British and some Japanese turrets, and in others +37 to +55 degrees. Loading was at any angle of elevation in later

Italian turrets but otherwise at a fixed angle of +3 to +10 degrees. RPC was in all but one of US 8in cruisers in 1945, in German for eleva-tion and had been in some French for training. Maximum ranges varied from 30,050yds (27,480m) to 36,680yds (33,540m).

Medium calibre guns, 6in and below

With hand loaded guns the shell was limited to about 100lb (45kg) unless it was carried by two or more men, and for many years this was the usual weight for a 6in (152.4mm) gun, though latterly with power loading, heavier shells were favoured. Many different guns of 6in (152.4mm), rarely 6.1in (155mm), or less were used in the 1906–1945 period. AA guns are considered below, and guns forming the sec-ondary armament of capital ships and the main armament of light cruisers and destroyers are briefly noted here. It is convenient to divide

Probably the most effective of all pre-1945 medium calibre DP weapons was the US 5in/38 represented here by the twin Mk 32 mounting, which was widely employed on US Navy ships from battleships and carriers to destroyers.

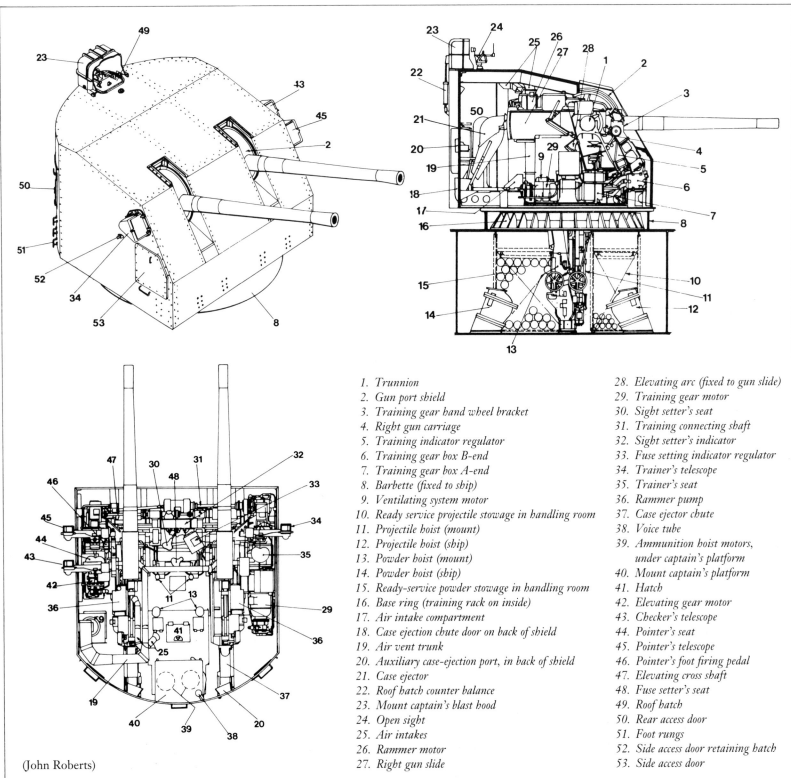

1. Trunnion
2. Gun port shield
3. Training gear hand wheel bracket
4. Right gun carriage
5. Training indicator regulator
6. Training gear box B-end
7. Training gear box A-end
8. Barbette (fixed to ship)
9. Ventilating system motor
10. Ready service projectile stowage in handling room
11. Projectile hoist (mount)
12. Projectile hoist (ship)
13. Powder hoist (mount)
14. Powder hoist (ship)
15. Ready-service powder stowage in handling room
16. Base ring (training rack on inside)
17. Air intake compartment
18. Case ejection chute door on back of shield
19. Air vent trunk
20. Auxiliary case-ejection port, in back of shield
21. Case ejector
22. Roof hatch counter balance
23. Mount captain's blast hood
24. Open sight
25. Air intakes
26. Rammer motor
27. Right gun slide
28. Elevating arc (fixed to gun slide)
29. Training gear motor
30. Sight setter's seat
31. Training connecting shaft
32. Sight setter's indicator
33. Fuse setting indicator regulator
34. Trainer's telescope
35. Trainer's seat
36. Rammer pump
37. Case ejector chute
38. Voice tube
39. Ammunition hoist motors, under captain's platform
40. Mount captain's platform
41. Hatch
42. Elevating gear motor
43. Checker's telescope
44. Pointer's seat
45. Pointer's telescope
46. Pointer's foot firing pedal
47. Elevating cross shaft
48. Fuse setter's seat
49. Roof hatch
50. Rear access door
51. Foot rungs
52. Side access door retaining hatch
53. Side access door

(John Roberts)

the period into 1906 to 1922 and 1923 to 1945. From 1906 the secondary guns of British capital ships went from 3in (76.2mm) to 4in (101.6mm) and then to 6in, all in single mountings. There was a return to 4in in triple shields in four battlecruisers or large cruisers, followed by 5.5in (139.7mm) in two more in single mountings, but the Washington Treaty cancellations and the *Nelson* class had 6in in twin turrets. All German ships had 5.87in (149.1mm), with in the earlier ones also 3.465in (88mm). As in the following navies except where mentioned, all mountings were single. The United States went from 3in to 5in (127mm) with 6in only in the Washington Treaty cancellations. Japan reduced from 6in to 5.51in (140mm), France remained with 5.457in (138.6mm), Italy increased from 4.724in (120mm) to 6in with a mixture of single mountings and twin turrets in one ship with the former gun. Russia had 4.724in and then 5.118in (130mm) and Austria 5.87in. The reason for these increases was the longer range of torpedoes and the greater size of torpedo craft, but some opinion considered 6in too large and 5.5in or 5in to be preferred.

Single mountings were the rule in light cruisers and calibres often as above. Thus Britain went from 3in to 4in to 6in, some having mixed 4in and 6in, with 5.5in in two requisitioned foreign ships. The United States, which built few light cruisers, had mixed 5in and 3in, altered to 5in only, with 6in, some in twin mountings, in the *Omaha* class. Japan went from 6in to 5.51in, Italy had 4.724in and Russia, which completed none in the period, 5.118in. Of the others Germany used 4.134in (105mm) and then 5.87in, Austria 3.937in (100mm) and France which laid down no light cruisers until 1922–23, 6.1in in twin mountings.

Most guns were BL (bag loading) but German and Austrian had brass cartridge cases (QF) as did 3in, some British 4in, for a time some US 5in, and French 5.457in. Typical guns were the British 6in Mk XII and the German 5.87in SKL/45, noted in the Table below. The former was a wire-wound construction, and the latter built-up. Ranges in later light cruisers of the period, where more elevation was allowed than in battleships, were about 18,800yds (17,190m) at 27–30 degrees elevation.

The most widely used British heavy AA gun was the 4in Mk XVI in twin Mk XIX mountings. This photograph shows the difficulties of designing a genuine dual-purpose weapon where it would be possible to load the shells by hand at any angle of elevation. (CMP)

By 1922 more powerful guns were favoured, the 6in/50 Mk XXII in *Nelson* firing a 100lb (45.36kg) shell of better form at 2960fps (902mps) with a maximum range 25,800yds (23,590m) at 45 degrees, and the US 53-calibre Mk 12 105lb (47.6kg) shell at 3000 fps (914mps) to 25,300yds (23,130m) at 30 degrees.

British destroyer guns increased from 3in to 4in and then to 4.724in with one 6in only in *Swift* as rearmed. Germany went from 3.465in to 4.134in with light 5.87in in the largest, the United States from 3in to 4in with 5in in a few, while Japan used 4.724in as their principal gun, France and Austria 3.937in, Russia 4in and Italy 4in or 4.724in with 6in in a few of the largest. Most guns were QF but early British 4in were BL as were 4.724in and 6in. The US 5in was BL as was one of the Italian 6in. Twin mountings were limited to some Italian and two US destroyers. The performance of 4–4.134in guns varied widely with shell weights of 31 to 39lb (14.1 to 17.7kg) and muzzle velocities of 2133 to 2900fps (650 to 884mps), the Russian gun being the most powerful. The British 4.724in fired a 50lb (22.68kg) shell at 2683fps (818mps).

From 1923 to 1945 6in (152.4mm) or 6.1in (155mm) in Japan and 5.87in (149.1mm) in Germany, were used for the armament of cruisers and also the secondary guns of battle-ships, except in Britain, the United States and the French *Dunkerque* class where the primary consideration was AA defence. It was intended that the 6in in the *Richelieu* would serve as an AA gun but it was not a success in this role. The smaller British and US cruisers also had AA guns as their main armament while the Japanese *Agano* class had an elderly 6in not further considered, and the Italian *Regolo* class 5.315in (135mm), not AA.

Bore length of the 5.87–6.1in varied from 47 to 60 calibres. Some Italian guns had loose liners, German and French loose barrels and the US a monobloc barrel, chromium plated in the bore. British and Japanese guns were BL and the rest QF. Piercing and HC shells of various types were carried, the latter being often lighter. Piercing shells were from 100 to 130lb (45.5–59kg) and muzzle velocities from 2500 to 3150fps (762–960mps).

Turret mountings were triple in the United States, Japan and France while other navies had twin and triple. Maximum elevation varied from 40 degrees to 60 degrees with 90 degrees in the *Richelieu*, reduced to 75 degrees. Maximum ranges were from 24,700 to 29,960yds (22,600–27,400m) at 45 degrees elevation.

In destroyers, all navies had twin and single mountings, the former being usually most favoured. All guns were QF except the Japanese 5in (127mm). In Britain a 4.724in

The most common close range AA weapons of the Second World War were produced by neutral nations: the larger was the Swedish Bofors 40mm cannon (seen here in a US quad Mk 2 mounting aboard the battleship Arkansas) which was used by most Allied navies; the smaller Swiss 20mm Oerlikon was widely employed by the forces of both sides in licensed versions. (CMP)

(120mm)/45 of slightly lower performance than the previous BL, was succeeded in twelve destroyers by a 50-calibre gun with 62lb (28.1kg) shell, and then by a 4.45in (113mm)/45 noted below under AA, though in most destroyers it had limited AA capacity. The United States used a 5in (127mm)/38 with full AA capacity in all but a few. Japan had a 5in/49.3 in mountings which allowed 40 to 75 degrees maximum elevation but trained too slowly for AA, and in one class 3.937in (100mm)/65 AA guns formed the main battery. Germany favoured 5.04in (128mm)/45 and then 5.87in (149.1mm)/48, France 5.118in (130mm) and 5.457in (138.6mm) in their largest destroyers of 40 to 45.4 and 40 to 50 calibres respectively, Italy 4.724in/50 and Russia 5.118in/50. None of these had AA capacity though the German 5.87in twin elevated to 65 degrees.

Anti-aircraft guns

Naval AA guns were developed from 1914 and attained their greatest importance in the 1939–1945 war in line with that of aircraft. Britain went from 3in (76.2mm)/45 to 4in (101.6mm)/45, then also to 4.724in (120mm)/40, and later to a new 4in/45, 4.45in (113mm)/45, used also for the main armament of destroyers, and 5.25in (133.35mm)/50 for the secondary armament of battleships and main armament of smaller light cruisers. The United States began with 3in/50 followed by the short 5in (127mm)/25 and then the 5in/38, also used as the British 4.45in and 5.25in. Japan began with 3in/40 after the 1914–1918 war and then 4.724in/45, 5in/40 and 3.937in (100mm)/65, also as the main battery of some destroyers. Germany went from 3.465in (88mm)/45 to /76 of two different types and then to 4.134in (105mm)/65 and /45 for smaller ships. In other navies the most interesting guns were the French 5.118in (130mm)/45.4 in the *Dunkerque* class, the Italian 3.543in (90mm)/50 and the Russian 3.937in/56.

The most powerful was the British 5.25in with an 80lb (36.3kg) shell, a ceiling of 46,500ft (14,170m) at 70 degrees and maximum range of 24,070yds (22,010m) at 45 degrees elevation. In comparison the US 5in/38 had a 55lb

(24.85kg) shell a ceiling of 37,200ft (11,340m) at 85 degrees and maximum range of 18,200yds (16,640m) at 45 degrees. These performance figures were considerably higher than those of the Japanese 5in/40, but lower than those of the British 4.45in which had the same weight of shell as the US gun. Some of the smaller calibre guns had much higher velocities. Thus the Japanese 3.937in/65 fired a 28.7lb (13kg) shell at 3314fps (1010mps), with a ceiling of 42,650ft (13,000m) at 90 degrees and maximum range of 21,300yds (19,500m) at 45 degrees.

The usual shells were HC (HE) originally with powder composition time fuses, then mechanical time fuses and from January 1943 in the US Navy proximity fuses (VT, variable time) based on a very small and rugged radar in the shell nose. These were later supplied to Britain, and were a very great improvement. Most guns fired fixed ammunition, with shell and cartridge case as a unit, but the British 5.25in, 4.45in in destroyers and US 5in/38 had separate cartridge cases.

Most mountings were twin but singles were not unusual and some quadruples were in the

Dunkerque class. Theoretically triaxial mountings with a cross-levelling axis were best, but the extra complications meant that they were only used by Germany for the larger AA guns, though Italy had a quadraxial mounting with separate roll and pitch correction axes for their 3.543in (90mm).

A rough indication of the effectiveness of powered mountings was given by the maximum training speed. This was 25 to 34 degrees per second in the US 5in/38in, up to 16 in later Japanese mountings and not much over half this in German. In the British 5.25in and 4.45in the figure was 20 degrees per second in later mountings but otherwise 10–15 degrees.

Close range automatic AA guns

These date from the First World War, though the first recoil operated water-cooled 37mm (1.457in) guns were introduced in some navies in the previous century. The Vickers 40mm (1.575in), known as the 2pdr pom-pom, was of the above type and fired a 2lb (907 gram) shell at 2040 fps (622 mps) with a fabric belt holding 25 rounds. It was used by Britain and in limited

A US Mk 33 dual-purpose director in the carrier USS Ranger. (USNFI)

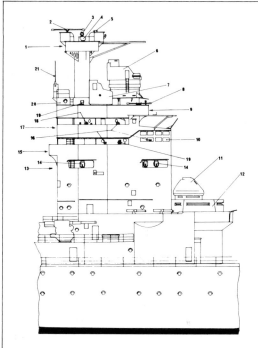

numbers by Italy and Russia while the United States mounted some 37mm of similar type. All were in single mountings.

In the Second World War the Vickers 40mm was widely used by Britain in eight- and four-barrel mountings as well as in singles. Fabric belts were replaced by 14-round metal ones of which ten could be linked together in some mountings, and ammunition was altered to a 1.684lb (764-gram) shell at 2400fps (732mps). In the latter part of the war it was supplemented and in part superseded by the much superior 40mm Bofors noted below.

The United States had a four-barrel 27.94mm (1.10in) but this was replaced by the Bofors. The Japanese favoured a 25mm (0.984in) of Hotchkiss type in one-, two- or three-barrel mountings, and other navies 37mm. All navies had many automatic 20mm (0.787in) guns such as the Oerlikon, and machine-guns of 13mm (0.5in), but their destructive power was limited and as in 1914–1918 rifle calibre machine-guns were virtually useless as naval AA.

The 40mm Bofors had a bore of 56.25 calibres and was recoil operated. The ammunition was in 4-round clips of which two could be accommodated in the gun, but with a skilled loader 24 rounds could be fired continuously at about 120rpm. The shell weighed 1.985lb (900 grams) and muzzle velocity was 2890fps

(881mps). Guns in single mountings were air-cooled, but water-cooled in twins and quadruples. These were introduced in US ships in mid-1942 and supplied to Britain in 1943. The twin triaxial Hazemeyer mounting, developed from that in a Dutch ship in 1940, was introduced to the Royal Navy in late 1942, and a simpler twin biaxial mounting in early 1945.

The shell was too small for existing proximity fuses, and also to disintegrate a Kamikaze so that its ballistic trajectory would fall short of its target. For these reasons the United States intended to introduce a 3in (76.2mm)/50 with loading gear to give 45/50rpm, but this was too late for the War.

The control positions of HMS Rodney, *1928.*

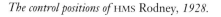

1. AA control platform
2. 12ft high angle rangefinder
3. Bearing sight
4. High angle director
5. Dumaresq
6. Main director control tower with 15ft rangefinder
7. Secondary armament director control tower with 12ft rangefinder
8. 9ft rangefinder
9. Director platform
10. Compass platform
11. Revolving armoured director hood
12. Conning tower
13. Searchlight platform
14. 18in searchlights
15. Captain's bridge
16. Bearing sights
17. Admiral's bridge
18. Torpedo sights
19. Searchlight control
20. High angle calculating position
21. Short range radio aerial

Fire control

The basic requirement of fire control against surface targets was to determine the range and bearing at the time that the shells from the firing ship arrived. Range before firing could be determined by optical rangefinders on coincidence or stereoscopic principles, the latter used by Germany in 1914–1918 and in 1939–1945 by most navies, sometimes in combination with coincidence, except the British. The base size increased from 9ft or 10ft (2.7–3m) to 35–49ft (10.5–15m), but by the end of the Second World War optical instruments took second place to radar, at least in Britain and the United States, as the former were much affected by poor visibility, and the electrical unreliability of early radars was improved, along with accuracy and target resolution. The rate of change of range would determine the difference between measured range before firing and that at the fall of shot. This was originally found by estimation with the aid of simple course and speed resolvers, a process little better than intelligent guessing. Range plots were favoured in Britain in the First World War, but depended on good range readings and many navies did not use them. Later computers of increasing complexity as further variables were taken into account, supplemented by spotting corrections were favoured. The later gunnery radars gave continuous range measurement, could determine the target bearing and spot heavy gun salvoes for range out to 34,000yds (31,000m).

British practice was to fire the guns from a director or director control tower (DT or DCT), the first introduced in capital ships from 1911 to 1916, and the latter which combined the main fire control position, in the *Nelson* class completed in 1927. Stabilised gyro-sights which fired the guns at the correct moment in the roll, were first introduced in 1915–17. Information was fed from the fire control plot or computer in the transmitting station below the armour deck. In 1914–1918 the German navy used a director for training only and the guns were fired independently. The US Navy tended to give more emphasis to the 'control' (transmitting station) and less to the directors and guns were also fired independently.

AA fire control was a much more difficult problem with target motion at high speed in three dimensions, and serious elevation and training errors from a rolling and pitching ship as elevation approached 90 degrees. All the better systems were tachymetric – that is the target speed was measured by instruments depending on constrained gyros – but owing to a most unfortunate error Britain did not adopt this system and none of the tachymetric additions were really satisfactory. The first effective heavy AA director was the US Mk 19 for the 5in/25 gun at sea from 1928, and the best of the Second World War the US Mk 37, first tested in 1939. This had the computer and stable vertical below deck and had triaxially stabilised sight prisms. It incorporated a 15ft (4.6m) stereoscopic rangefinder and later radar, and required a crew of seven. It should be noted that triaxial stabilisation was reduced to the minimum in contrast to German practice where the whole director was so stabilised resulting in a weight less amplifiers and generators, of up to 40.4 tons (41,000kg).

Torpedoes

The development of these between 1906 and 1945 was very great and much work was in progress, particularly in Germany, during the latter part of the Second World War. Only weapons actually in service are considered here. In 1906 the normal size was 17.7in (45cm) diameter, usually called 18in, and this was succeeded by 21in (53.3cm) with 19.7in (50cm) in the German First World War navy and 21.7in (55cm) in the French after that war. Larger torpedoes included the German 23.6in (60cm) of 1916–18, and the British 24.5in (62.2cm) of the 1920s but only Japan standardised on 24in (61cm) from about 1921. These large torpedoes were too bulky for submarines, and for aircraft 17.7in remained the usual size, the most notable exception being the US short 22.4in (57cm).

Surface ship torpedoes

The 17.7in (45cm) torpedoes of 1906 such as the British RGF Mk VI* or Fiume Mk III**, had a 200lb, later 255lb (91,116kg) explosive charge and ranges of 1000yds (914m) at 35kts, 2000yds (1830m) at 28¾kts, and 4000yds (3660m) at 21kts, while the Japanese 24in (61cm) Type 93 of 1941–45 had a 1058lb (480kg) charge and ranges of 21,900yds (20,000m) at 49kts and 43,700yds (40,000m) at 37kts. Clearly this was not due just to increase in size, or to a 50 per cent increase in air (oxygen) pressure, but mainly to the propulsion system.

In 1906 compressed air was fed to the engine via an adjustable reducing valve, and to cure

freezing on the expansion phase of the engine, heating of the air was first introduced. Fuel (usually alcohol) was mixed with air on the exit side of the reducer, and this was known as a dry heater. With higher energy fuel such as kerosene or in Britain 'Broxburn Lighthouse Shale Oil', it was desirable to cool the combustion chamber by water swirled round the walls. This was the wet, sometimes called steam, heater. The United States who alone used turbines, retained alcohol as the wet heater fuel. The Fiume Mk III** converted to dry heater, had a range of 3000yds (2740m) at 29kts and the RGF Mk VI* converted to wet heater, up to 6000yds (5490m) at 29–30kts. With increased air pressure and larger air vessel, this could be improved as in the French 17.7in M1912D with 324lb (147kg) charge and range 9300yds (8500m) at 28kts, but a better solution was to increase diameter.

The British 21in (53.2cm) Mk IV of 1917–18 had a 500lb (227kg) charge and ranges of 11,000yds (10,060m) at 29kts, 15,000yds (13,700m) at 25kts and 18,000yds (16,460m) at 21kts. The German 19.7in (50cm) G7*** had a similar performance but 434lb (197kg) charge, and the 23.6in (60cm) H8 ranges of 14,220yds (13,000m) at 28.5kts and 18,040yds (16,500m) at 25.5kts with 540lb (245kg) charge.

In the 1920s Britain introduced air enriched to about 58 per cent oxygen by volume with 50 per cent alcohol-water fuel to avoid ignition difficulties. The 24.5in (62.2cm) had ranges of 15,000yds (13,700m) at 35kts and 20,000yds (18,300m) at 30kts and the 21in Mk VII 16,000yds (14,600m) at 33kts. Charges were 743–740lb (337–336kg) in both. Oxygen enrichment was not liked, and the introduction of the burner-cycle engine – in effect a semi-diesel, with natural air – replaced it. The 21in Mk IX of the Second World War had ranges of 11,000yds (10,050m) at 41kts and 15,000yds (13,700m) at 35kts with 810lb (367kg) charge. This performance was a little inferior to that of the Japanese 24in (61cm) Type 90 of 1933 which used natural air, but no torpedo in service in 1945 approached the 24in Type 93 noted above. This used pure oxygen with kerosene as fuel and sea water in the combustion system, and ignition was with air before any oxygen was delivered. The dangers of this system are obvious, but results made it well worthwhile to the Japanese.

The Japanese light cruiser Jintsu *launching 61cm (24in) 8th Year (1919) type wet-heater torpedoes. The later oxygen-propelled Type 93 was a massive improvement and probably the best surface ship torpedo of the Second World War. (CMP)*

The standard German U-boat torpedo of the Second World War was the G7a, an example of which is here being loaded aboard U 14, *an early Type II boat. In 1939 performance was reckoned to range between 12,500m (13,750yds) at 30kts and 5000m (5500 yds) at 44kts.* (CMP)

Submarine torpedoes

The foregoing torpedoes were for destroyers and larger vessels, though some were also employed in submarines as well as shorter versions with reduced maximum range and high speed close settings. The British burner-cycle 21in Mk VIII** of the Second World War ranged 5000yds (4570m) at 45.5kts or 7000yds (6400m) at 41kts with an 805lb (365kg) charge, while the Japanese contemporary oxygen 21in Type 95/1 ranged 9850yds (9000m) at 50kts or 13,100yds (12,000m) at 46kts with an 893lb (405kg) charge. All torpedoes so far noted left a track, much reduced in those using oxygen, but electric torpedoes were trackless and though performance was low, they became the principal submarine weapon in Germany and the United States; Japan used some, though the British 21in Mk XI was never in service during the war. The German 21in G7e T2 was developed in the 1920s from an electric torpedo issued in 1918 but never used. The British knew nothing of this until parts were recovered from the wreck of the *Royal Oak* in 1939. The T2 had lead/acid accumulators and range 5470yds (5000m) at 30kts with a 661lb (300kg) charge, while the T3a with a redesigned battery attained 8200yds (7500m) at 29–30kts.

T5, known as 'Zaunkönig 1', introduced in September 1943 was a passive acoustic homer with speed reduced to 24–25kts to reduce self-noise and a range of 6230yds (5700m) or 8750yds (8000m) at 22kts in T5a and b respectively. It was intended to attack convoy escorts

proceeding at 10–18kts but could be countered by towed noise-makers ('Foxer') and by tactical avoidance ('step aside'). Many other German homing torpedoes were under development.

The US 19in (48.3cm) Mk 27 was a development of the airborne Mk 24 described below, with guide rails to suit 21in torpedo tubes. It was a passive homer used against Japanese escorts by submarines in 1944–45 with considerable success.

Airborne torpedoes

The airborne torpedoes used by Britain in 1915 were old cold air 14in (35.6cm) weighing about 810lb (367kg) with a 94lb (43kg) charge and capable of 1000yds (914m) at 24kts. Suitable British aircraft in 1918 were not able to lift heavy loads, and the wet-heater 17.7in (45cm) Mk IX weighed only 1080lb (490kg) with a 250lb (113kg) charge and a range of 2000yds (1830m) at 29kts. The larger German seaplanes in 1917 could take the Fiume wet-heater 17.7in G/125 of 1681lb (762kg) with a 348lb (158kg) charge and a range of 2190yds (2000m) at 36kts and these figures were not surpassed by a British airborne torpedo until the burner-cycle 17.7in Mk XII of 1937 – 1548lb (702kg) weight, 388lb (176kg) charge, range 1500–2000yds (1370–1830m) at 40kts. The Mk XV of 1942 weighed 1801lb (817kg) with a charge of 545lb (247kg) and a range of 2500yds (2290m) at 40kts if carried by land aircraft, but carrier planes were limited to 433lb (196kg)

charges for reasons of weight. The same applied to the Mk XVII in production in 1945, where land aircraft had a 600lb (272kg) charge.

The Japanese had tried pure oxygen in airborne torpedoes but found it not worth the complications, and retained the wet heater air type. Ranges were 2200yds (2000m) at 42kts until 1944 when they were reduced to 1640yds (1500m). The problems of air trajectory and conditions at impact on the water, had received more attention than in other navies and by 1941 the preferred dropping speed and height was 180kts at 330ft (100m), and the torpedoes could stand 250–260kts at 1000ft (300m). No other navy at this time approached these figures. By 1944–45 Japanese torpedoes could stand 300–400kts compared with 270kts for the British Mk XV, 350kts for Mk XVII and 180–200kts for the German F56.

Dates, weights and charges for the various Japanese torpedoes were as follows:

Type 91 Mod 1 – 1931, 1728lb (784kg), 331lb (150kg); this was used by the older planes in sinking *Prince of Wales* and *Repulse*.
Mod 2 – April 1941, 1841lb (835kg), 452lb (205kg); used by later planes in above sinking and at Pearl Harbor.
Mod 3 – latter part 1942, 1872lb (849kg), 529lb (240kg); there were strengthened versions in 1943–44.
Mod 4 Strong – 1944, 2030lb (921kg), 679lb (308kg).
Mod 7 Strong – 1944, 2319lb (1052kg), 926lb (420kg).
Type 4 Mks 2 and 4 of 1944–45 had similar charges to the last two but were about 125lb (57kg) heavier.

The US 22.4in (56.9cm) was developed into a highly effective torpedo. It was turbine driven, only 13ft 5in (408.9cm) long and later versions weighed 2216lb (1005kg) with 600lb (262kg) charges and a range of 6300yds (5760m) at 33.5kts. In 1942 dropping conditions were 110kts at 50ft (15m), but by February 1944 it could be dropped at 1000ft (300m) and at the end of the war at 410kts and 2400ft (730m).

An entirely different airborne torpedo was the electric 19in (48.3cm) Mk 24. This was a passive acoustic homer used with great success by the United States and Britain against

U-boats in the Atlantic from summer 1943. It was 7ft (213.4cm) long, 680lb (308kg) in weight, with a 92lb (42kg) charge and a range of 4000yds (3660m) at 12kts. Dropping was at 125kts and 250ft (76m).

Torpedo charges and detonators

Explosive charges in torpedoes were initially wet gun-cotton replaced by TNT or amatol because of shortage of TNT, and in Germany by a mix of 65 per cent hexanitro-diphenylamine to 35 per cent TNT. After the First World War more powerful explosives were developed by the addition of aluminium powder and in Britain and the United States from 1943 by the use of 'Torpex' (37/41 per cent TNT, 41/45 per cent cyclomethylene trinitramine (cyclonite), 18 per cent aluminium) if supplies were available.

The usual impact or inertia pistols were replaced to a large extent by magnetic pistols intended to explode below the hull, but Britain, the United States and Germany experienced much trouble with these which were taken out of service for much of the Second World War.

Mines

Although mines had been highly successful in the Russo-Japanese War of 1904–5, in 1914 they were still neglected by most navies, except the Russian and perhaps the German. Thus Britain had a stock of only about 4000, and the United States, France and Italy fewer. By the end of the First World War Britain had laid 130,066 excluding net mines, more than 2¼ times the total by any other navy. In terms of numbers sunk, mines were the most effective anti-submarine weapon of this war.

First World War mines

The most widely used type of mine was the moored contact, and there was a great difference between mining conditions in the strong tidal waters of the North Sea and other waters round the British Isles, and those in the Baltic, Black Sea and Mediterranean. Much improvement was needed in sinkers and also mooring wires for tidal conditions. Mechanical firing by lever or similar system was generally much inferior to Herz horns, used for a long time by Germany and Russia but not introduced in Britain until 1917. Herz horns were made of metal, covering a glass tube containing battery electrolyte which activated the firing gear when broken. Pendulum inertia pistols could be made more sensitive and were used by Russia and Germany in the Baltic, but were not suited to the North Sea.

The British HII was a moored Herz horn mine of spherical shape 38in (96.5cm) diameter with a 320lb (145kg) amatol charge. The mine weighed 650lb (295kg) with 400lb (181kg) buoyancy, and the standard sinker weighed 950lb (431kg) in air. The normal mooring wire was 60 fathoms (110m) but deep water modifications had up to 200 fathoms (366m). HII* was an anti-submarine version with a 170lb (77kg) charge and practical depth limit for the mine of 240ft (73m).

SIV was designed for laying by 'E' class submarines and was of cylindrical form 20.85in (52.96cm) in diameter to fit the chutes. The charge was 210/220lb (95/100kg).

The method of laying a British moored mine on a Mk VIII sinker, 1914–18 period.

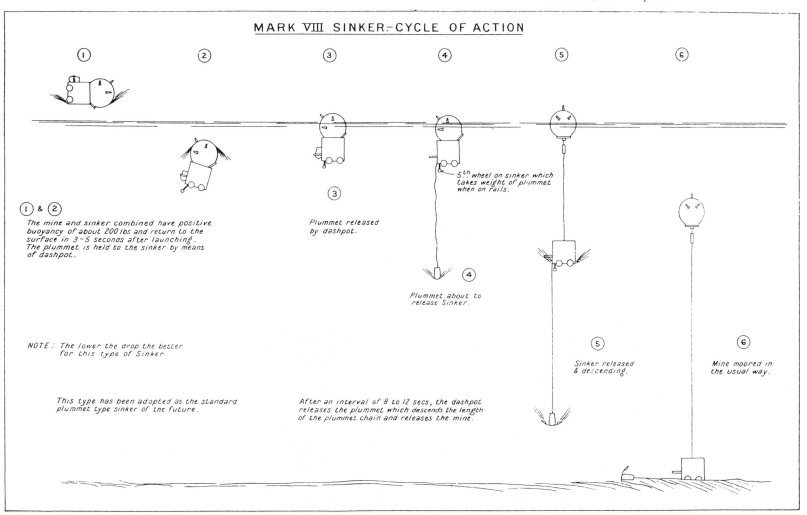

MARK VIII SINKER – CYCLE OF ACTION

(1) & (2)
The mine and sinker combined have positive buoyancy of about 200 lbs and return to the surface in 3–5 seconds after launching. The plummet is held to the sinker by means of dashpot.

(3)
Plummet released by dashpot.

(4)
Plummet about to release Sinker.

5th wheel on sinker which takes weight of plummet when on fails.

NOTE: The lower the drop the better for this type of Sinker.

This type has been adopted as the standard plummet type sinker of the future.

After an interval of 8 to 12 secs, the dashpot releases the plummet which descends the length of the plummet chain and releases the mine.

(5)
Sinker released & descending.

(6)
Mine moored in the usual way.

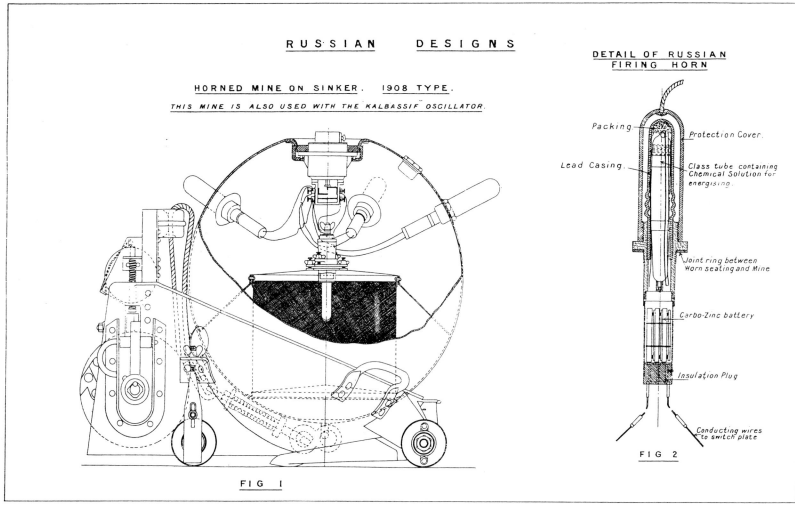

RUSSIAN DESIGNS

HORNED MINE ON SINKER. 1908 TYPE.

THIS MINE IS ALSO USED WITH THE KALBASSIF OSCILLATOR.

FIG I

DETAIL OF RUSSIAN
FIRING HORN

Packing.

Lead Casing.

Protection Cover.

Class tube containing
Chemical Solution for
energising.

Joint ring between
Horn seating and Mine

Carbo-Zinc battery

Insulation Plug

Conducting wires
to switch plate

FIG 2

A Russian 1908 design for a moored mine with details of its firing horn.

Moored acoustic mines were ready in November 1918 but never used and moored magnetic mines were under development. Sinker Mk I (M) was a ground magnetic mine in the form of a truncated cone, principally made of concrete. The charge was 1000lb (454kg) crude TNT. Premature explosions and counter-mining were frequent and only 472 were laid in August–September 1918. A submarine, destroyer, torpedo boat and trawler were sunk.

The US Mk 6 was a moored antenna mine with a copper antenna latterly c35ft (11m) long, and float to keep it above the mine. The potential in sea water between copper and the steel hull of a submarine operated a relay which fired the mine. During the war 102,490 were made of which 56,611 were laid in the anti-submarine barrage between the Orkneys and the Utsire Light, the mines being at various depths down to 260ft (79m). The mine weighed 584lb (265kg), was of 34in (86.4cm) diameter and contained 300lb (136kg) TNT or TNT/TNX. Only 38 per cent remained in place when the field was swept in 1919 and it is likely that six submarines were sunk.

The standard German moored horned mine was E150 introduced in 1912. It was of cylindrical form with rounded ends, and heavier and of less buoyancy than the British HII, and contained 331lb (150kg) TNT or wet gun-cotton in early mines; sinkers were up to 1234lb (560kg). UC200 for laying by submarines in the latter part of the war, was generally similar but heavier at 835lb (379kg) with a 362lb (164kg) TNT charge.

T1 and T2 mines were for laying from a submarine's torpedo tubes. The charge was 187lb (85kg) TNT and they could also be carried by the large torpedo seaplanes, which laid 70 in the Baltic in 1917, sinking the Russian destroyer *Ochotnik*, the first warship so lost.

Other types of mine were used by navies in this war including oscillating and shore controlled (observation) mines.

Second World War mines

There was a great advance in the use of influence mines, magnetic, acoustic or combined in 1939–45. Pressure-sensitive mines for which there was no known method of sweeping, were

developed but for various reasons little used. Many of the above were ground mines and often laid by aircraft. In moored contact mines the trend, except in Germany, was to replace Herz by switch horns.

The first airborne British magnetic mines were laid in April 1940, acoustic in September 1942 and combined in April 1943. A few magnetic/pressure mines were ready in spring 1945 but never used. The Germans laid their first magnetic mines in 1939 and acoustic in August 1940, in both cases before stocks were adequate. Pressure mines could have been laid in quantity in autumn 1943, but fears that they might be recovered, copied and dropped in the U-boat training areas in the Baltic, prevented their use until June 1944.

Of moored contact mines the British Mk XVII had eleven switch horns, a charge of 320 or 500lb (145 or 227kg) and could be laid in 500 fathoms (915m). There were moored magnetic, acoustic and antenna mines (Mks XX, XXII) with similar charges. German contact mines of the EM series generally had charges

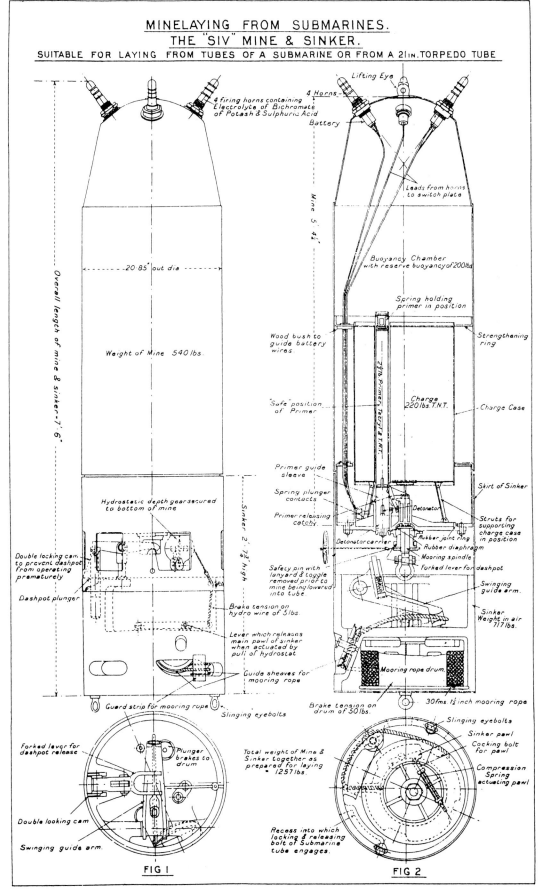

MINELAYING FROM SUBMARINES.
THE "SIV" MINE & SINKER.
SUITABLE FOR LAYING FROM TUBES OF A SUBMARINE OR FROM A 21in. TORPEDO TUBE

The British S IV mine designed for laying from the tubes of 'E' class submarines. From a First World War manual.

of up to 661lb (300kg). Ship laid influence mines included the British M Mk III with a charge of up to 1750lb (794kg) minol, and from February 1943 additional acoustic firing. The US Mk 12/3 for laying from submarine torpedo tubes had a charge of 1200lb (544kg) Torpex, while the similarly used German TMC had a charge of up to 2050lb (930kg). Airborne influence mines were at first laid from low altitude but latterly parachutes were used and they could be dropped from 15,000ft (4500m), albeit with some loss of accuracy. British mines of the 'A' series had minol charges of up to 1100lb (499kg), US Mks 12/4 and 25 1200–1274lb (544–578kg) Torpex and German LMB a charge of 1554lb (705kg) though others of the LM series had 639–661lb (290–300kg). BM 1000 intended for use without parachute, had a 1499lb (680kg) charge and could apparently be dropped from 19,700ft (6000m) in 19 fathoms (35m) and from 1640ft (500m) in 20ft (6m) water. German mine explosives were generally similar to those in torpedoes.

Anti-submarine weapons

The development of these is mostly associated with the British and secondly the US navies in the two world wars. The most important in the first was the depth charge (DC), second only to the mine as a destroyer of submarines in this war.

First World War weapons

Type D issued in early 1916 was the only effective DC, but it was not available in adequate quantities until 1918. This had a charge of 300lb (136kg) TNT or amatol with total weight 430lb (195kg) and 200lb (91kg) negative buoyancy. The hydrostatic pistol was usually set for 150ft (46m) by day and 100ft (30m) at night, with a maximum of 200ft (61m) or 300ft (91m) after the war. The DC's were dropped over the stern or fired on the beam to 40yds (37m) by a Thornycroft DC Thrower, a 9.45in (240mm) mortar with the DC on an expendable tray and arbor. The number of DCs in anti-submarine vessels increased from 2 to 30–50 during the war, and more than the last number might be needed to disable a submarine.

The US Mks 2 and 3 were similar to the

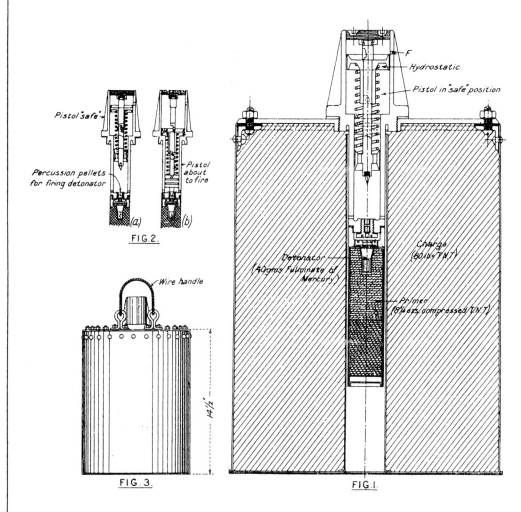

DEPTH CHARGE—ITALIAN DESIGN.

TO FIRE AT DEPTHS FROM 35 TO 45 FEET.

An early shallow draught (35ft–45ft) Italian depth charge, similar in conception to many of the period.

above, but the Thrower (known as a Y-gun or ASW Projector Mk I) had two barrels set at 90 degrees to each other and at 45 degrees to the vertical, so that a single DC was projected to port and starboard at ranges adjusted by the propellant charge to 50, 66 or 80yds (46, 60 or 73m). The US Mk 4 was a larger DC with twice the charge, but only 1000 were made in late 1918.

Explosive sweeps with single or multiple towed charges were favoured by some but were of relatively little use. Anti-submarine howitzers of up to 11in (279.4mm) calibre and bomb-throwers were developed by Britain in particular, as were stick bombs for firing from conventional guns and some of the above special weapons. Further development was needed in all.

Second World War weapons

The standard British DC of 1939, the Mk VII, was similar to Type D, and was replaced from the end of 1940 by the Mk VII Heavy with a 150lb (68kg) cast-iron weight attached increasing the terminal velocity from 9.9 to 16.8fps (3.0–5.1mps). Maximum settings of the hydrostatic pistol were increased to 600ft (183m) and later to 900 or 1000ft (274 or 305m), and from December 1942 the usual amatol charge was improved by adding about 20 per cent aluminium (minol).

The Mk X was a very large DC with 2000lb (907kg) charge. It was introduced in March 1942 but was not much used.

Anti-submarine bombs were far less effective than airborne DCs. The latter included a version of the Mk VII and the smaller Mks VIII and XI with 170lb (77kg) charge, made more effective by the use of Torpex.

US DCs included Mks 6 and 7 (redesigned 3 and 4), Mk 8 with a magnetic pistol and not very successful, and Mk 9 of 'teardrop' shape with angled tail fins. This was standard from spring 1943 and had a 200lb (91kg) Torpex charge. The hydrostatic pistol was set to 600ft (183m) maximum or later in some to 1000ft (305m); sinking speeds were up to 22.7fps (6.9mps) in some.

The Y-gun was found to occupy too much centreline space, and was replaced by the single-DC K-gun with a range of up to 150yds (137m). US anti-submarine bombs and airborne DCs were allocated Mark numbers in the bomb series. Mk 54 with 250lb (113kg) Torpex charge and tail hydrostatic fuse was in service for over 30 years after the war.

The principal British ahead-throwing weapons were 'Hedgehog' and 'Squid'. The former

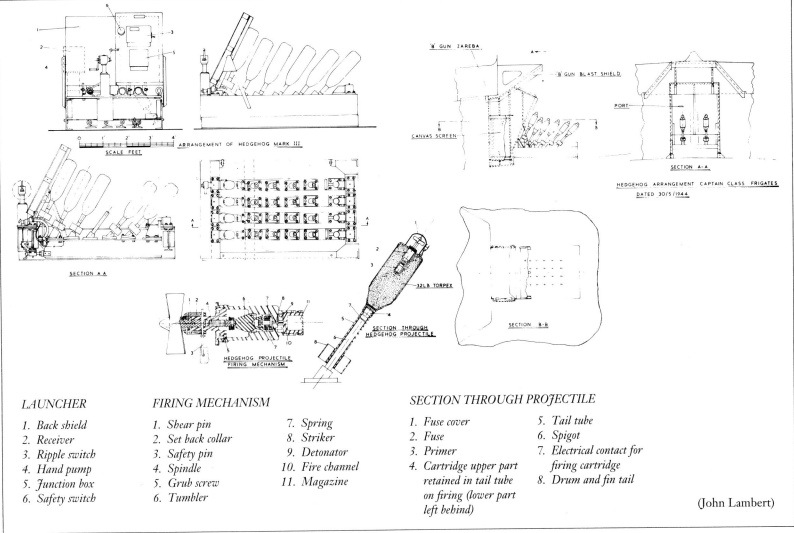

SCALE FEET

ARRANGEMENT OF HEDGEHOG MARK III

SECTION A A

'B' GUN ZAREBA

'B' GUN BLAST SHIELD

PORT

CANVAS SCREEN

SECTION A-A

HEDGEHOG ARRANGEMENT CAPTAIN CLASS FRIGATES
DATED 30/5/1944

32LB TORPEX

SECTION THROUGH
HEDGEHOG PROJECTILE

SECTION B-B

HEDGEHOG PROJECTILE
FIRING MECHANISM

LAUNCHER

1. Back shield
2. Receiver
3. Ripple switch
4. Hand pump
5. Junction box
6. Safety switch

FIRING MECHANISM

1. Shear pin
2. Set back collar
3. Safety pin
4. Spindle
5. Grub screw
6. Tumbler

7. Spring
8. Striker
9. Detonator
10. Fire channel
11. Magazine

SECTION THROUGH PROJECTILE

1. Fuse cover
2. Fuse
3. Primer
4. Cartridge upper part retained in tail tube on firing (lower part left behind)

5. Tail tube
6. Spigot
7. Electrical contact for firing cartridge
8. Drum and fin tail

(John Lambert)

Escorts lost sonar contact with their targets when they passed over them so various forms of 'ahead throwing weapons' were developed to fire over the bow of the attacking ship. The most successful of the first generation was the British Hedgehog, a spigot mortar that fired a pattern of projectiles that only exploded on contact; it was widely used by the Royal and US Navies.

was a 24-spigot mortar firing 7in (177.8mm) contact-fused projectiles of 65lb (29.5kg) with 35lb Torpex charge. The spigots were angled to give a 40yd (37m) diameter circle about 200yds (183m) ahead of a stationary ship. Over one hundred ships had been fitted by the end of 1942 but it was not really successful until 1944.

'Squid' was a 3-barrelled 12in (304.8mm) mortar firing 390lb (177kg) projectiles with 207lb (94kg) minol charges, and clock time fuse set automatically from the depth recorder to 900ft (274m) maximum. It was automatically fired from the sonar range recorder and was first afloat in 1943. The first 'kill' was on 31 July 1944, and each ship usually had two 'Squids'. Though only sixty to seventy ships

had been fitted by the end of the war, it was considered the best surface ship ASW weapon in Britain.

The US version of 'Hedgehog' was in production from late 1942 and was more popular and generally more successful than in the Royal Navy, whereas 'Squid' was tried in 1944 but not adopted.

Manned torpedoes

An Italian device known as *Mignatta* (Leech) based on a 14in (35.56cm) torpedo, steered by two swimmers and with two 385lb (175kg) charges, attacked Pola harbour in November

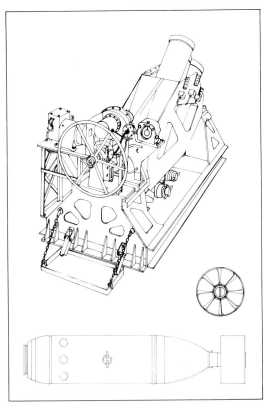

Hedgehog was followed by a larger three-barrelled mortar called 'Squid' which fired time-fused bombs set automatically from a depth recorder. They were very successful in the Royal Navy towards the end of the war, but not adopted by the US Navy. (John Lambert)

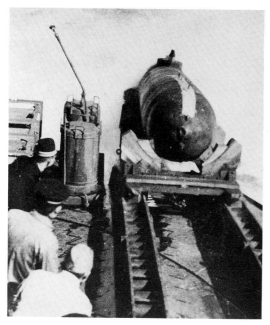

A Japanese Kaiten *human torpedo being launched from the converted light cruiser* Kitakami. *(CMP)*

1918. One charge sank the Austro-Hungarian battleship *Viribus Unitis* and the other an accommodation ship. Italian Second World War weapons of this type known as *Maiale* ('Pig'), or 'Chariot' for the British copy, had charges of 485 to 661lb (220–300kg) and were ridden by the crew of two. Their greatest success was to disable the battleships *Queen Elizabeth* and *Valiant* in Alexandria harbour in December 1941.

The Japanese *Kaiten* was a different concept based on a 24in (61cm) torpedo with a suicide pilot; the charge was 3420lb (1550kg). Later developments did not enter service, but there seems to have been only two successes, a fleet oil tanker and a destroyer escort, from the 330 that did.

Rockets and guided weapons

Rockets

None of the various naval anti-aircraft rockets whether with HE heads or parachute and cable devices, were of much effect in 1939–1945 though some Japanese ships later in the war had 4.724in (12cm) rockets in launchers taking 28. The incendiary shrapnel head had a fuse set to 1100yds (1000m) or 1640yds (1500m). Considerable use was made by Britain and the United States of 4.5in (114.3mm) or 5in (127mm) rockets for shore bombardment in landing operations. Airborne anti-submarine

Naval Guns: Typical Weapons 1906–1945

Gun	Bore Inches (Millimetres)	Length bore Calibres	Weight of gun incl. breech mechanism Tons (Tonnes)	Shell-weight Pounds (Kilos)	Muzzle velocity Feet (Metres) per second	First in service
Great Britain						
18in Mk I	18 (457.2)	40	149 (151.39)	3320 (1506)	2420 (738)	*Furious* 1917
16in Mk I	16 (406.4)	45	108 (109.73)	2048 (929)	2586 (788)	*Nelson* 1927
15in Mk I	15 (381)	42	100 (101.6)	1920 (871)	2472 (753)	*Queen Elizabeth* 1915
14in Mk VII	14 (355.6)	45	78.99 (80.26)	1590 (721)	2483 (757)	*King George V* 1940
13.5in Mk V	13.5 (342.9)	45	76.13 (77.35)	1250/1400 (567/635)	2582/2498 (747/761)	*Orion* 1912
12in Mk X	12 (304.8)	45	57.66 (58.59)	850 (385.6)	2725 (831)	*Dreadnought* 1906
8in Mk VIII	8 (203.2)	50	17.20 (17.48)	256 (116.1)	2805 (855)	*Cumberland* 1928
6in Mk XII	6 (152.4)	45	6.89 (7.0)	100 (45.4)	2825 (861)	*Birmingham* 1914
6in Mk XXIII	6 (152.4)	50	6.91 (7.02)	112 (50.8)	2758 (841)	*Leander* 1933
5.25in QF Mk I	5.25 (133.4)	50	4.293 (4.362)	80 (36.3)	2672 (814)	*Bonaventure* 1940
4in BL Mk VII	4 (101.6)	50.31	2.092 (2.126)	31 (14.06)	2864 (873)	*Bellerophon* 1909
4in QF Mk XVI	4 (101.6)	45	2.007 (2.039)	35 (15.88)	2660 (811)	*Penelope* 1936
USA						
16in Mk I	16 (406.4)	44.7	105.27 (106.96)	2100 (953)	2600 (792)	*Maryland* 1921
16in Mk 7	16 (406.4)	49.7	106.8 (108.5)	2700 (1225)	2500 (762)	*Iowa* 1943
14in Mk 4	14 (355.6)	49.7	80.53 (81.82)	1400 (635)	2800 (853)	*Mississippi* 1917
8in Mk 12 (Heavy shell)	8 (203.2)	54.7	17.14 (17.42)	335 (152)	2500 (762)	*Baltimore* 1943
6in Mk 16	6 (152.4)	47.04	6.49 (6.59)	130 (59)	2500 (762)	*Brooklyn* 1938
5in Mk 7 (BL Mods)	5 (127)	50.06	5.027 (5.107)	50 (22.7)	3150 (960)	*Texas* 1914
5in Mk 12	5 (127)	38	3.200 (3.251)	55 (24.95)	2600 (792)	*Farragut* 1934
Germany						
38cm SKL/45	14.96 (380)	42.4	76.57 (77.8)	1653 (750)	2625 (800)	*Bayern* 1916
38cm SKC/34	14.96 (380)	48.4	109.2 (111)	1764 (800)	2690 (820)	*Bismarck* 1940
30.5cm SKL/50	12.01 (305)	47.4	51.03 (51.85)	893 (405)	2805 (855)	*Ostfriesland* 1911
28cm SKL/45	11.14 (283)	42.4	39.17 (39.8)	666 (302)	2805 (855)	*Nassau* 1909
20.3cm SKC/34	7.99 (203)	56.7	20.4 (20.7)	269 (122)	3035 (925)	*Admiral Hipper* 1939
15cm SKL/45	5.87 (149.1)	42.4	5.73 (5.82)	99.9 (45.3)	2740 (835)	*Nassau; Blücher* 1909

Gun	Bore Inches (Millimetres)	Length bore Calibres	Weight of gun incl. breech mechanism Tons (Tonnes)	Shell-weight Pounds (Kilos)	Muzzle velocity Feet (Metres) per second	First in service
15cm SKC/25	5.87 (149.1)	57.5	11.78 (11.97)	100.3 (45.5)	3150 (960)	Königsberg 1929
10.5cm SKC/33	4.134 (105)	60.5	4.49 (4.56)	33.3 (15.1)	2953 (900)	Admiral Graf Spee 1936
Japan						
46cm Type 94	18.11 (460)	44.5	162.4 (165)	3219 (1460)	2575 (785)	Yamato 1941
40cm 3rd Yr Type	16.14 (410)	44.6	100.4 (102)	2205 (1000)	2592 (790)	Nagato 1920
14cm 3rd Yr Type	5.51 (140)	50	5.61 (5.7)	83.8 (38)	2789 (850)	Ise 1917
12.7cm 3rd Yr Type	5 (127)	49.3	4.18 (4.245)	50.7 (23)	3002 (915)	Isonami 1928
10cm Type 98	3.937 (100)	65	3.005 (3.053)	28.7 (13)	3314 (1010)	Akizuki 1942
France						
380mm M1935	14.96 (380)	45.4	92.64 (94.13)	1949 (884)	2723 (830)	Richelieu 1940
340mm M1912	13.39 (340)	45.5	65.23 (66.28)	1186 (538)	2625 (800)	Provence 1915
152.4mm M1930	6 (152.4)	55.05	7.657 (7.78)	119.4 (54.17)	2854 (870)	Emile Bertin 1934
138.6mm M1929	5.457 (138.6)	50	4.207 (4.275)	89.5 (40.6)	2625 (800)	Le Terrible 1935
Italy						
381mm M1934	15 (381)	50	100.8 (102.4)	1951 (885)	2854 (870)	Vittorio Veneto 1940
12in Patt T	12 (304.8)	46	62.52 (63.52)	997 (452)	2756 (840)	Dante Alighieri 1913
203.2mm M1927	8 (203.2)	53	19.2 (19.5)	276.2 (125.3)	2953 (900)	Zara 1931
Russia						
180mm B–27*	7.09 (180)	55.5	14 (14.2)	215 (97.5)	3018 (920)	Kirov 1938
102mm Obuch M1912	4 (101.6)	58	2.17 (2.20)	39 (17.7)	2700 (823)	Novik 1913
Austria–Hungary						
30.5cm K 1910	12.01 (305)	42	53.44 (54.29)	992 (450)	2625 (800)	Erzherzog Franz Ferdinand 1910

Notes:

* The gun in *Krasnyi Kavkaz* (1932) was 3 calibres longer and suffered from excessive muzzle velocity and wear. In no other ship.

rockets which could easily hole the pressure hull, were first used successfully by Britain in May 1943. These had 3.5in (88.9mm) 25lb (11.3kg) solid heads and of velocity around 1175fps (358mps). The United States first used similar rockets in January 1944 and both navies also used airborne 5in rockets on more general targets. The United States also made limited use of an 11.75in (298.5mm) airborne rocket known as 'Tiny Tim'.

Guided weapons

The Japanese *Kamikaze* was a form of guided weapon, but only possible for a nation holding their philosophy of war. It was used from late 1944 and the approximately 2550 expended sank 3 escort aircraft carriers and 13 destroyers and inflicted much damage to fleet aircraft carriers. The Oka 11 was a rocket propelled piloted glider bomb capable of up to 540kts in a dive and with a 1135lb (515kg) burster. Manoeuvrability was poor and the Japanese had no suitable parent aircraft. The only notable success was to sink a previously damaged destroyer in April 1945.

The other important guided weapons were German. The FL motor boat of 1916–17 had a 1543lb (700kg) charge and speed of 30kts. It was controlled by 16 (later 27) sea miles of cable from a shore station with corrections wirelessed back by aircraft. One hit the monitor *Erebus* amidships in October 1917 but her bulge limited damage.

The FX-1400 guided bomb had course correction by radio from the parent aircraft and a tail flare to aid visual steering. It was dropped at 12,000–19,000ft (3700–5800m) and the parent had to hold a straight and level course at reduced speed after release. This is perhaps why only 400–500 were made. The bomb had a hardened head and weighed 3090lb (1400kg) with a 660lb (300kg) burster. It sank the new Italian battleship *Roma* while steaming at 30kts in the middle of a 90 degree turn, and very seriously damaged the battleship *Warspite* and the cruisers *Savannah* and *Uganda* off Salerno.

Hs 293 was a small monoplane with a simple hydrogen peroxide rocket motor, and was controlled by radio and tail flare from the parent aircraft. Operational range was up to 22,000yds (20,000m) and speed 300–400kts. The burster was 683lb (310kg), and the missile was effective against shipping, though the largest warship sunk was the British light cruiser *Spartan*. Once jamming equipment with skilled operators was available, its effectiveness was much reduced.

John Campbell

13

Electronics and Navies

ELECTRONICS had two main aspects during the period covered by this book. First, in 1887 Heinrich Hertz demonstrated that very rapid electrical oscillations in a wire could cause energy to be radiated into space at the speed of light. That energy could be detected at a distance. The application to communication was obvious and primitive radios were in service in several navies soon after 1900; for example, the first US tests were conducted late in 1899. As early as 1904 a German, Christian Hulsmeyer, observed that radio waves would be reflected by solid obstacles, and patented a form of radar. It bore no fruit at the time, but the radar concept was rediscovered during the inter-war period.

The other aspect of electronics was a consequence of the discovery of the electron itself, a lightweight particle carrying a negative electric charge. Only at the very end of the last century was it discovered that electrons could be isolated by boiling them off a cathode (whence the cathode ray tube, the CRT, the standard radar and then television and computer display device). What mattered was that electrons were so light that they could easily be manipulated by relatively small electric and magnetic fields. This manipulation in turn could be used as a valve to control quite powerful electric currents. The three-element tube ('valve' in British parlance) operating this way, and thus suitable for amplification, was invented by Lee

DeForest in 1906, but the corresponding amplifier appeared only in 1912, and the corresponding oscillator in 1913.

The two phases of electronic development correspond to two quite different kinds of physics, classical and early modern; modern solid-state devices are perhaps the most important application of yet another type of physics, quantum mechanics (ironically, it turns out that the pre-tube radio signal detectors were solid-state devices not entirely

Radio was the first naval employment of electronics, externally manifested in tall topmasts and long wire antennas – visible in this view of the Australian cruiser Sydney *at the end of the First World War. (RAN, by courtesy of Vic Jeffrey)*

divorced from modern transistors; the difference is that no one knew just why they worked).

Tube (or valve) electronics made two things possible: the generation of strong signals at very much higher frequencies (the tube could oscillate very much faster than a circuit made out of more conventional elements) and the detection and use of very much weaker signals.

Higher frequencies initially meant much greater radio range. High frequency (HF) radio signals could bounce off the ionosphere to reach surface receivers many thousands of miles away. These are the 'short wave' radio signals by means of which overseas stations often communicate. The waves are shorter than those of the low and medium frequency radios used before and during the First World War, but their wavelengths are still between 10 and 100 metres (corresponding frequencies are 3 to 30MHz). Even higher frequencies were adopted during the Second World War because their signals generally would *not* propagate much beyond the horizon and thus could be considered relatively safe from eavesdroppers. Wartime short range tactical radios typically operated at VHF (very high frequency, 30 to 300MHz); postwar navies shifted to UHF (300 to 3000MHz, *ie* 10cm to 1m).

Radio

The advent of radio had revolutionary implications for navies. Before, a ship beyond the horizon was, in effect, completely isolated. Her commander had to rely on written orders issued before he sailed (and often themselves based on intelligence weeks or even months old), and on whatever he could learn from ships he chanced upon. The independence, and the risks, attendant upon limited communications shaped British and American naval traditions of command and control.

Then the overseas telegraph appeared. It provided more or less instantaneous communication, but only when the ship was in some foreign port, *ie* only intermittently. Even that very limited link with home authority seemed new and very unwelcome when it was first introduced in the mid-nineteenth century – the senior French Admiral in the Crimea balked at operating 'at the end of a telegraph line' (the end of the telegraph was connected to deployed ships in the Black Sea by despatch boats). Once radio appeared, this sort of control was no longer intermittent, except when

ships passed out of radio range altogether. Long-haul radio became so important so quickly that destruction of the German naval radio stations in the Pacific was an important British goal when war broke out in 1914.

There were also short-haul (tactical) radios. Without them, ships in a scouting line had to remain within visual range of each other, since they were also the line down which notice of contact had to come. Any fleet trying to intercept an enemy needed numerous pickets to cover even a narrow frontage. A chain of others (or a very fast despatch boat) had to be available to transmit that sighting report back to the main body of the fleet. Scouts equipped with radio could operate much further apart. For example, a few Japanese cruisers sufficed to cover all the routes the Russian fleet could have taken before the Battle of Tsushima in 1905. The Japanese could not have deployed enough cruisers to do anything like the same job without radio. Eleven years later, radio made it possible for Jellicoe to receive reports from scouting forces operating well beyond the horizon as they drew out the German fleet at Jutland.

Radio signals could be intercepted by anyone with the appropriate receiver. Since they spread well beyond the horizon, they became an important source of long range intelligence. At the least, a direction finder (DF) cut could indicate the direction of the signal, and analysts could draw conclusions from the rise and fall of activity on a given net. By 1914 naval signals were generally coded, but during the First World War the British managed to obtain keys to all the German codes. Code-breaking and other signals intelligence first revealed that the German fleet was at sea before Jutland. Given its immense success in using signals intelligence during the First World War, the Royal Navy adopted a policy of virtually complete radio (and radar) silence at the outset of the Second World War (there is some evidence that radar silence cost *Hood* the chance of accurately ranging on the German battleship *Bismarck* in May 1941).

Medium and low frequency radio signals have very long wavelengths, so there is little hope of building highly directional shipboard DF antennas at these frequencies. However, at relatively short ranges even an inefficient antenna will work, because enough signal strength will be present. Most warships of the inter-war period were fitted with 'loop' direction finders whose antennas consisted of a pair of crossed loops. Although generally described as navigational (to pick up coastal radio beacons), they must have been conceived

largely as a means of detecting enemy transmitters just beyond the horizon.

The extension to useful high frequency direction finding (HF/DF) proved difficult but extremely important. The Royal Navy began fitting HF direction finders to its cruisers in 1935; it placed such devices aboard its escorts during the Second World War. The US Navy followed suit, though it used a slightly different technology. HF/DF ('huff-duff') was important because the German U-boats transmitted their tactical messages home using this frequency. Ships equipped with HF/DF could detect them, beyond the horizon, at ranges as great as about 30 miles. No other beyond-the-horizon detector existed.

Interception and DF exemplify another form of electronic weaponry: countermeasures. They are passive techniques; in the radar world they would be called electronic support measures (ESM). Clearly it is also possible to jam radio or radar or sonar signals, a possibility realised about as soon as naval radios appeared. Jamming and active electronic deception are generally classed as electronic countermeasures (ECM), although ECM sometimes embraces ESM (passive ECM) as well.

The German use of HF exemplified a radical change in the style of naval warfare, in which ashore commanders gained far more operational control over ongoing battles. Perhaps the most famous example of such control was the scattering of Convoy PQ17 in 1942 at the behest of the First Sea Lord, Admiral Sir Dudley Pound, sitting in the Admiralty over a thousand miles from the convoy. His decision, moreover, exemplified the use of passive radio intelligence. By 1942 the British were regularly decoding German naval radio signals. The Admiralty's Operational Intelligence Centre (OIC) was tracking the German fleet and, with the aid of decrypted signals (and other forms of intelligence) had gained considerable insight into German operational thinking and intentions. Admiral Pound might well therefore have considered himself better placed than his deployed commanders to appreciate the situation as a whole. At least one experienced commentator, the late Cdr Patrick Beesly, RN (Ret), thought that Admiral Pound's disastrous decision resulted from insufficient appreciation of the nature of the intelligence the OIC had produced. The point, however, is that the Germans' use of radio made it possible for an Admiral in London realistically to make hour-to-hour tactical decisions; and that British radio permitted him to transmit those decisions to commanders at sea in time for them to have real effect.

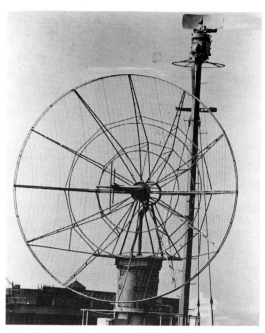

The first important radar function was search, both for surface targets and for aircraft. Two standard US Second World War sets were SG (surface) and SK-2 (air search), shown here aboard the new amphibious command ship (AGC) Mount McKinley, May 1944. They are very different sizes because the wavelength of SG was about 1/15th that of SK-2; it took a much larger antenna to make a narrow beam at the longer wavelength. (USN)

Radar

Because their wavelengths are short, high frequency signals can be used to form precise directional signals. For a given antenna, the width of the beam depends upon the size of the antenna in wavelengths: a large antenna generates a narrow beam. That was not too important for radio, but it was extremely important for radar. A radar set measures distance by timing a pulse out to a target and back. It determines the *direction* of the target by pointing the beam at it. The narrower the beam, the more precisely the target is located (and the less the likelihood that other targets will find themselves in the same beam to confuse the system). HF radar could be built, but only ashore, because no ship could carry a large enough antenna to generate a beam of useful width. One key to radar, then, was the ability to generate signals well above HF. For example, many US naval radars of the Second World War operated at about 200MHz, *ie* at a wavelength of about 1.5 metres. The Royal Navy, which began using radar somewhat earlier, had to use somewhat lower frequencies and thus rather less directional search radars.

Radars produce particularly weak signals,

because their pulses must travel out to the target and then back (radio is a one-way proposition). Tube amplifiers made it possible to detect and use these weak signals; CRTs made it possible to display them.

Between the two World Wars, radars were developed independently in Britain, France, Germany, Italy, Japan, the Netherlands, the Soviet Union, and the United States. In each case, they seemed the obvious solution to the very serious problem of detecting oncoming aircraft in time to intercept them. They were, in fact, so important that each country kept the idea very secret.

Information handling systems

It turned out that radar itself was not enough. The data it produced had to be collated. That is, radar was only part of a means of presenting

some decision-maker (such as a fighter-intercept officer) with a usable tactical picture. A search radar presented the current situation in terms of current (or nearly current) locations of nearby aircraft. That was not what the decision-maker needed. He was much more concerned with vectors: with the course and speed of each of the aircraft displayed. For example, he would react very differently to an aircraft heading for a target than to one passing by it, or heading away from it. The vectors could only be estimated by examining the behaviour of each target over time; by maintaining a current plot of target positions. The

The British equivalents to SG and SK-2 were Type 271 (in the lantern) and Type 281 (the four dipoles on the mast). The lantern was chosen to conceal the existence of a British microwave surface search radar. Both are shown aboard the US-built escort carrier, HMS Attacker, 26 November 1942 at Mare Island. (USN)

The Combat Information Center (CIC) was the key to effective use of radar information: this one is in the US aircraft carrier Yorktown *(CV 10). The three blackboards were status boards, to summarise the condition of combat air patrols and offensive strike aircraft (including how much fuel they had left). The large vertical screen was used to plot a summary of the air and surface situation, the plotters standing behind it. Radar monitors, such as the one in the foreground, fed data into the CIC. (USN)*

British were not the first to invent radar, but they were the first to conceive the filter centre, the room in which successive radar detections (and other available information) could be plotted and collated.

The combination of radar and filter rooms proved decisive in the Battle of Britain in 1940. Naval radar in Britain and in the United States came of age when similar organisations went to sea in the form of the Action Information Organization (AIO: British) and the Combat Information Center (CIC: US). These seaborne filter centres would collate information from several radars on board a ship, and combine it with information from other ships (*ie* from their CICs or AIOs) and with information from other sources (such as intelligence and radio and radar intercepts). The output would be a 'compiled' tactical picture making sense out of a confused tactical situation, and thus

suitable for decision-making. Remarkably, none of the Axis navies, all of which had radar in some form, seems to have created anything like a CIC/AIO.

In effect the CIC or AIO made it possible for a ship to locate distant air contacts *and* to guide aircraft to deal with them. It integrated a ship with fleet aircraft and extended her effective horizon a hundred miles or more. This capability was most dramatically demonstrated at the Battle of the Philippine Sea in June 1944, when the US carrier fighters destroyed the bulk of a Japanese air attack force in the air (the 'Marianas Turkey Shoot'). CICs also proved extremely effective both in dealing with enemy air attacks and in handling the confused tracks of ships in night engagements, as in the Solomons in 1942–44. The advent of CICs in US destroyers made it possible for the US forces finally to deal with fast-moving Japanese cruisers and destroyers without fear of attacking each other.

The wartime CIC did have its limits. Each radar operator at his scope would call out a plot (a position), and there would be a time lag while a plotter marked it in grease pencil on the overall ('compiled' in British parlance) plot. Target courses and speeds were measured by connecting up the plotted points. A typical wartime air search radar, such as the US SK,

rotated 4 times per minute, so that it could check an aircraft's position every 15 seconds. During that time an aeroplane flying at 200kts would move less than a mile. If every detection

Besides search, the other main wartime radar application was fire control. This Mk 8 radar is mounted atop a Mk 34 director on board the light cruiser USS Mobile, *shown on 18 July 1943. By the end of the war radar was considered so reliable that the next cruiser director, Mk 54, did away with the optical rangefinder so prominent here. (USN)*

were plotted, then, the aircraft's course could be quite accurately depicted, certainly well enough for interception. However, as more aircraft came into the area around the ship, the number of plots (detections) would increase. The plotters with their grease pencils would not be able to keep up. They would fall behind imperceptibly.

At the Philippine Sea, the plotters triumphed because, although the Japanese flew in great numbers, they flew in tight formations. The had to: they knew that it would take numerous aircraft attacking nearly simultaneously to break through the inner anti-aircraft defences (the guns) on board the carriers which were their main targets. A few months later, however, the Japanese adopted kamikaze tactics. Aircraft approached almost randomly, on the theory that a single kamikaze pilot, undeterred by shipboard fire, might well be able to break through. Now the fleet's CICs were faced by very large numbers of separate targets. They were saturated. Desperate expedients were tried, among them dividing up air control sectors so that individual CICs could no longer be saturated (but also so that no single CIC could concentrate fleet defensive resources).

Postwar experiments confirmed this wartime experience: manual CICs were quite limited. Much of the postwar push towards combat data automation was an attempt to solve the saturation problem by using a computer to compile the tactical picture (the radar operators inserted their detections directly, without passing their data through separate plotters). It took about fifteen years for such systems, like the US NTDS and the British ADA, to enter service.

Wartime developments

By 1939–40 both the Royal and US navies had operational air search ('air warning' in British parlance) radars, operating at metric wavelengths. This wavelength was important because it precluded making narrow enough beams to avoid much sea clutter, and thus to search for surface targets. In 1940, however, British scientists developed the magnetron, which could generate useful amounts of energy at frequencies high enough (3000MHz and above, for centimetric wavelengths) for effective surface search.

During the Second World War, both the metric and the centimetric sets proliferated in the Royal and US navies. Search radars were joined by fire control sets, so that ultimately a ship could locate and destroy targets in conditions of zero visibility. It therefore became im-portant to be able to identify the targets, or at least to distinguish friend from enemy. Hence the development of IFF (identification, friend or foe) systems, in which a search radar automatically sends out an interrogating pulse. At least in theory, a friendly target automatically replies, and the reply is visible on the radar display.

The German, Italian and Japanese navies all deployed radars of their own, but they were generally substantially less advanced and much less effective than those of the Allies. For example, neither the Germans nor the Italians deployed centimetric radars in any numbers (the Germans did capture a magnetron, but only in 1943). In the case of the Germans, a substantial radar industry had to be devoted largely to fending off the Allied bomber offensive.

Sonar

Sonar is similar in concept to radar. It was invented earlier, in 1918 (in fact the first German radars were built by the German sonar factory). Radio waves, at least those at useful frequencies, will not penetrate very far in water. Sound will. During most of the First World War, the only useful submarine locators were low frequency sound receivers (hydrophones; low frequency sound travels furthest). They depended on just how noisy the target submarine was (the Germans learned to rig for silent running), and they could not actually locate a submarine, since they could only measure target bearing. The Allies sought something better: sonar. Certain materials change shape when electric currents pass through them, and this change can produce a sharp pulse of sound (a 'ping'). Similarly, when a sound wave hits such materials, it deforms them and creates a weak electric current. The special materials are called transducers: they switch between two forms of energy, mechanical and electrical. Sonar could operate whether or not the target chose to make noise. If it worked at high enough frequency (typically about 30kHz in early sonars), a transducer of manageable size could produce a beam of useful width (typically about 15 degrees wide). As in radar, the time for the ping to make a round trip between projector and target was a measure of target range.

Second World War sonars (the British called theirs Asdics; the name sonar was invented to reflect the similarity to radar) produced a single narrow searchlight-like beam. The operator pointed his transducer in one direction, sent out a sharp 'ping', and waited for an echo before searching in another direction. Maximum effective range was about 2000yds, although it could vary with water conditions. Tactically, such a sonar was very useful for attack but not for search (since it could not look very rapidly in many directions). Typically, then, a submarine would first be detected when she fired a torpedo. Sonar would search the small area in which the submarine had to be, and then would allow a ship to keep or regain contact after attacking with depth charges. Only at the end of the Second World War did true search sonars, with all-round capability, appear.

During the war, the Allies and the Japanese all used active sonar. The Germans had active sets, but they preferred low frequency passive sets, which had longer inherent range (and which U-boats could use to detect and locate surface targets). These passive sets became the basis for important British, Soviet, and US submarine sonars. It appears that the Italians also relied entirely on hydrophones.

Although a sonar could, in theory, have operated purely mechanically, realistically it required electronic amplification to detect the tiny echo current in the transducer.

Electronics and Naval Warfare

Radar is searchlight sonar using radio waves, which move more than 100,000 times faster. Just like a searchlight sonar, a radar set sends out a pulse and waits for the echo before looking elsewhere. However, because radio waves move so fast, the wait is nearly imperceptible, so a searchlight radar can search quite effectively. Indeed, radar was initially used both in Britain and in the United States to detect aircraft and thus to provide ships with sufficient early warning of fast attackers (visual warning ceased to be practical when aircraft speeds went much above 150mph and when aircraft began to make their approaches above cloud layers).

Radio, radar, and sonar, the three fruits of the electronic revolution of this century, all had profound effects on naval warfare. Collectively, they made it possible for ships and fleets to operate over much larger areas (in modern terms, they greatly expanded the usable battle space). That was essential, because they appeared just as aircraft and submarines expanded the space ships and fleets had to dominate. For example, in the late nineteenth

century, ships engaged at ranges of a few thousand yards or less. They could be seen on the horizon, then, long before they could begin to shoot. A senior officer could make his tactical decisions during the approach. That became more difficult as better optics and simple mechanical computers increased battle range nearly to the horizon during the First World War. As the outcome of the Battle of Jutland showed, existing means of detecting and tracking ships did not match the capabilities of the weapons. Fast aircraft completely overthrew the existing order. They could not be seen nearly soon enough to be intercepted. Hence, for example, the British decision in the late 1930s to abandon any attempt at interception by fleet fighters in favour of armoured carriers (which could, in theory, ride out attacks).

Radio made scouting and fleet tracking possible. Jutland was an unwieldy battle, but it was possible to fight only because units beyond each commander's horizon could still communicate with him (it can be argued that Admiral Sir John Jellicoe was cheated of decisive victory only because most of his scouts did not report effectively). Radar solved the problem of the fast aeroplane. Sonar is an intermediate case: it made anti-submarine warfare practicable, where there was really no pre-sonar alternative.

Radio and radar had very visible impacts on the shape of warships. Particularly before 1914, many ships were given very high masts because raising antennas made for greater radio range. It also made ships visible at greater distances, and long wire antennas were particularly vul-

nerable to gunfire. Later, they tended to foul anti-aircraft arcs of fire. During the Second World War, the US Navy adopted much less efficient 'whip' radio antennas because they created so many fewer problems in topside arrangement.

By this time there was a new problem. Radio communication was so important that each ship had numerous separate sets, operating, in many cases, at very different frequencies. Space had to be found for all their antennas, and the antennas had to be arranged so as to avoid either mutual interference or interference with the ship's radars. The problem only began to disappear in the 1950s, with the advent of new types of broadband radio antennas, each of which could serve several sets simultaneously.

By that time radars had come to dominate the topside appearance of many ships. There were many of them, and they all competed for the few places giving wide arcs: air and surface search sets, pencil-beam sets capable of determining the altitude of a target, and numerous fire control sets atop main and lesser calibre directors. Many ships also had special aircraft homing beacons, which were essential for fighter control (the pilots needed a point of reference). Ideally, the number of radars could have been reduced by combining roles, but that was not really practicable, at least with existing technology: different roles really seemed to need sets operating at quite different frequencies, and even at different scan rates.

Few warships completed before the end of the Second World War had been designed with radar or CIC/AIO operation in mind. For all the others, radars had to be mounted where space was available. Sometimes that meant adding a mast. On board US carriers, it meant accepting severe funnel gas and heat damage to antennas (not to mention very limited clear arcs in many cases). CIC location was a particular problem because long leads from the antennas often had to be avoided (weak signals would further decay in this wiring). For example, most US *Essex* class carriers had their CICs fitted on the gallery decks immediately

Radar beacons also became important. Aircraft launched to great distances used them to locate carriers which could not always maintain predetermined courses. The mast on the funnel of USS Enterprise *carries such a beacon. The 'Stovepipe' forward of it is an IFF (identification) transponder. This photograph was taken in 1943.* (USN)

under their unprotected flight decks, where they (and the nearby ready rooms for pilots) were particularly vulnerable to kamikaze hits. The alternative, the island, just did not have enough space to accommodate an efficient CIC.

This vulnerability had to be accepted to avoid the surer worse fate associated with not having a CIC at all. That was the beginning of the present era of warship design, in which electronic vision is extraordinarily effective, but also in which a single hit in the nerve centre renders even a large and nominally well-protected ship nearly helpless. It will remain for the next era, then to combine electronic vision with the degree of armour protection ships used to enjoy.

Norman Friedman

Naval Radars: Typical Sets 1939–1945

Radar	Nationality	Date	Wavelength	Employment	Beam width (degrees) Horizontal × Vertical	Peak power (kW)	Pulse length (microsec)	Effective range (nm) on (target)
Air Search Sets								
Type 79	British	1939	7m	Large ships	75 × —	90	8–30	50 (bomber)
Type 281	British	1941	3.5m	Large ships	35 × —	350	12	88–115 (bomber)
Type 291	British	1942	1.5m	Destroyers	40 × —	100	1.1	15 (bomber)
CXAM	American	1940	1.5m	Large ships	14 × 70	15	3.0	70 (bomber)
SK	American	1942	1.5m	Large ships	20 × 17	200	5.0	100 (bomber)
SC–2	American	1942	1.5m	Destroyers	20 × 50	20	4.0	80 (bomber)
Type 3	Japanese	1944	2m	Battleships	68 × 35	10	5	27–54
Surface/Low Air Search								
Type 271	British	1941	10cm		1 × 20	70	1.5	13 (battleship)
Type 277	British	1944	10cm		4.5 × 4.5	500	1.5/1.9	23 (battleship)
SG	American	1942	10cm		5.6 × 15	50	2.0	22 (battleship)
SM	American	1943	10cm	Height-finder	2.7 × 2.7	600–700	1.0	50 (bomber)
Gunnery Sets								
Type 285	British	1942	50cm	Medium calibre	18 × 43	25	1.7	7 (large cruiser)
Type 275	British	1945	10cm	Dual-purpose	6 × 8.2	400	0.5	18
Mk 8	American	1943	10cm	Heavy calibre	2 × 3	15–20	0.4	20 (battleship)
Mk 12	American	1943	33cm	Dual-purpose	10 × 10	100–110	0.5	22.5 (air target)
Mk 34	American	1945	3cm	Light AA	3 × 3	25–35	0.3	12.5
Seetakt	German	1936	80cm	Pocket battleships		7		10 (battleship)
FuMO 22	German	1940	80cm	Battleships	5 × ?	8	5	13 (battleship)

Note:
Wavelength indicates precision; 3cm and 10cm are microwave radars.

14

Camouflage and Deception

MARINE camouflage was introduced as a means of protecting ships from, initially, torpedo or surface attack, and later from attack from the air. The advances in naval gunnery and the development of the self-propelled torpedo, from the mid-Victorian era onwards, meant that for the first time ships could be engaged when they were as far away as the horizon. At such extreme ranges target visibility became a major issue so that attention was focused on reducing vessels' conspicuousness to afford them a measure of protection. Thus, from around the turn of the twentieth century, neutral colours and camouflage paint schemes were increasingly adopted for warships and naval auxiliaries. This involved the application of paint in such a way that it would either conceal a ship, as far as that was possible, or make it difficult to accurately determine its range and bearing for the purposes of taking aim. Later, when ships became exposed to aerial attack, additional camouflage measures were evolved to respond to this threat.

Deception is a strategem for fooling an enemy in order to gain tactical advantage during a situation of attack or by causing him to adjust his offensive or defensive intentions as a result of the misinformation that he is being fed. In parallel with the adoption of painted camouflage, deception was also practised more widely in naval combat.

In spite of their apparently close association as subjects, the purposes for which camouflage and deception were respectively adopted and the reasons behind their development were quite different.

In simple, general terms camouflage can be described as the art of hiding the act of hiding.

Where ships at sea are concerned it might be more accurately described as trying to conceal the unconcealable. Consequently, the science of naval camouflage has been characterised throughout by much research and experimentation in the search for protective measures that would be effective in the ever changing conditions of light, weather and sea state that are typical of the marine environment. For half a century this was an objective that taxed the minds of scientists and artists alike.

By contrast, deception is concerned only with feeding an enemy with misleading information for any of a number of reasons. Quite correctly, therefore, it comes under the heading of 'ruses de guerre'. Unlike camouflage, deception can and has been effectively applied in sea warfare without any requirement for extensive research or specialised methods of application.

In considering camouflage and deception more closely, it can be seen that both, in fact, have a number of subsidiary aspects, each concerned with achieving different objectives. Camouflage can be further subdivided into concealment and confusion, or disruption, while deception also covers disguise, distraction and the utilisation of decoys and lures.

Concealment in a dynamic sense can be most readily recognised in the form of smoke screens. Equally, in complete contrast, it covers the use of smokeless fuels. It also refers to the application of all those, so-called static or painted camouflage schemes that are concerned with minimising conspicuity. These cover everything from counter-shading to neutral shades, all intended to reduce visibility.

Confusion acts in the completely opposite way. It is based on the assumption that it is an impossible objective to hide a vessel or, in some way, render it as less distinct when viewed against the ever-changing backdrop of the seascape. Instead, confusion aims to make it difficult to launch a successful attack against a ship, once sighted. The technique of dazzle or disruptive painting is the best known of these confusion measures, but also covered under this heading are any of a number of physical subterfuges designed to interfere with the normal perspective of a ship so as to prevent or delay the accurate determination of its position, speed or bearing, in relation to the horizon.

Disguise, as one of the aspects of deception, is very much a defensive trick concerned mainly with altering the appearance of a ship to make it look like another, usually an innocent or neutral vessel. It can also be considered as covering such actions as the painting of false ships and fake bow waves on the sides of ships in order to deceive an adversary.

Distraction, as the term plainly implies, is concerned with drawing attention away from vessels having a vital or sensitive importance in much the same way that a diversionary tactic would be launched during an offensive, to dilute the defences protecting a primary target or to permit a hostile intention to be disregarded for as long as possible to allow it to be carried out more effectively.

The most dramatic of First World War camouflage measures was the so-called 'dazzle pattern' type, seen here on the primitive aircraft carrier HMS Furious *in 1918. Designed to make it more difficult to estimate a ship's speed and bearing, the pattern was directed particularly against U-boats, which could only afford a brief periscope view of an intended target.* (CMP)

When decoys are used in naval war to deceive an enemy, the intention is rather different. Their use is directed as misguiding enemy intelligence on naval strength or dispositions. Alternatively, as in the case of the Q-ships, the intention was to attract target vessels to within a fatal distance of these seemingly innocent but, in reality, quite lethal warships by offering the vessels themselves as the bait or lure.

Early attempts at camouflage

The functional use of camouflage in the natural world can be traced back to the very dawn of animal life. Some of the most primitive of creatures, such as the cuttlefish and the chameleon, depend for their survival on the ability to conceal themselves within their surroundings. By comparison, the adoption of camouflage for military purposes and specifically for the protection of warships and naval auxiliary vessels is of much more recent origin. Up to the late 1800s, the selection of the colours in which warships were painted was made without any consideration for the needs of concealment or protection. British warships of the time had black hulls, white superstructure and buff funnels. Many contemporary German naval vessels were painted white overall. The ships of other nations displayed similarly ostentatious colour schemes.

The date from which the thinking on warship colouring appears to have changed is 1895. At the time of the official opening of the Kiel Canal, during that year, some of the attendant warships assembled to commemorate the occasion were seen to have adopted obliterative colouring. Ships of the German High Seas Fleet had been painted in a uniform shade of warm grey while their French counterparts had been treated similarly, although in their case the colour was dark grey. During the Spanish-American War of 1898, the United States Navy turned to a neutral grey colour scheme for its ships and the Royal Navy followed suit in 1903. Subsequently all the other major naval powers made similar changes so that, well before the outbreak of the First World War, grey was already recognised as the correct and appropriate colouring for warships of all types.

This simple form of concealment, while not rendering ships invisible, certainly reduced their visibility in a wide variety of sea and weather conditions, in comparison with earlier colour schemes. For this reason, this basic scheme was frequently reverted to and, to this day, remains the preferred colouring of all warships, virtually without exception. From an economic point of view, overall grey is a simple and cheap colour to apply and maintain; from a camouflage point of view, it provides the best all round protection in average conditions.

Even as uniform grey was being adopted, attempts were made to elevate maritime camouflage thinking to an even higher level by linking it more directly to the principles of camouflage in nature. Among those leading the study of natural protective colouring, with a view to applying it to ships at sea, was the American painter Abbott Henderson Thayer. Thayer had made a detailed investigation of the subject, resulting from which a number of proposals on alternative colour schemes for ships were presented to the United States Navy.

In particular, he concentrated his efforts on developing effective counter-shading measures. Widely utilised in nature, counter-shading reduces the visibility of animals by neutralising the contouring shadows that emphasise their three-dimensional shape. The theory is that, by flattening their body contours, counter-shading assists in concealing them within their background. Thayer suggested that it was possible to achieve much the same effect with ships by darkening their light, exposed surfaces and painting all shaded areas white or very light grey.

Among his other contributions, Thayer also proposed, as a hull colouring scheme, a mixture of white and pale blue (a shade called Thayer Blue was recommended) applied in stripes. This was the first recognition that ships were in fact better protected with colour schemes that were generally light rather than dark. It also exploited the optical principle known as the Purkinje Effect in which the eye perceives blue shades somewhat less favourably than other colours in fading light, as at sunset.

The First World War

On the outbreak of the World War in 1914, the United States was not immediately involved, but for Great Britain, Germany, France and the other countries concerned, who were confronting the prospect of total naval warfare, the opportunity to examine the effectiveness of colouring systems in combat conditions presented itself.

Perhaps the best known British personality from the First World War period, who completely revolutionised marine camouflage, was Norman Wilkinson, a well-known marine artist and, at the time, a Lieutenant-Commander in the Royal Navy Volunteer Reserve. He is credited with having conceived the radical technique of dazzle painting.

Having concluded that it was impossible to render a ship anything like totally invisible when seen from periscope level against a sky background, Wilkinson directed his efforts at making it difficult to attack ships successfully by confusing the attacker's aim. Ships, as objects seen from afar, already have a recognisable texture formed from the lines and shadows of their structural details and deck fittings; this is known as the structure pattern. By adding to this a violently different, painted pattern constructed of bold geometric lines and shapes in

There were numerous forms of dazzle patterns, those based on stripes being a popular variation, as demonstrated here by the British transport Euripides. (David L Williams)

vivid, contrasting colours, the ship's recognisable structure is broken up. It was claimed that, when these painted patterns were applied according to carefully calculated principles, confusion over target bearing and speed was also caused.

Patrolling U-boats carried a limited number of torpedoes and, for maximum effectiveness, each one had to be made to count. Already, the decision of when to fire and in which direction had to be made after restricted opportunity for observation. The submarine had to be constantly alert to the risk of counter attack and the target itself was frequently obscured by the motion of the waves. In these circumstances, the artifice of dazzle painting was intended to make a hard task significantly harder.

With the full support of the Admiralty, Wilkinson was provided with his own department and staff, based at the Royal Academy, plus a group of artists located at docks and ports all around the coast. The latter were engaged to supervise ships' companies in the application of the camouflage schemes that were devised and evaluated by the team centred in London.

As the war progressed, debate over the value of competing camouflage schemes developed and intensified. Efforts were made to measure the effectiveness of different systems, to draw conclusions in support of future policy. Most of these studies were inconclusive because the criteria of measurement were inconsistent or because the sample cases examined were not sufficiently large to permit balanced conclusions to be drawn. To some extent, it might be said, the results were even contrived to support the views of their respective sponsors.

Germany did not attach the same degree of importance to camouflage as did her opponents, no doubt because, following the Battle of Jutland, she conducted an almost exclusively submarine war. The French and Italian navies followed the lead of the British and at first, after entering the conflict in 1917, so did the United States Navy.

Prompted by the Submarine Defense Association, the US Navy Department had committed itself to a thorough study of camouflage. For this a camouflage research centre was established, attached to the Eastman Kodak film laboratories at Rochester, New York. A leading physicist, Loyd Ancile Jones, was appointed to run the research centre. The team of scientists assembled under his leadership pioneered the investigation of the principles and mechanism of visibility as the basis of devising effective camouflage measures. They also formulated the very first methods of reliably assessing the performance of different camouflage schemes in quantitative and comparative terms. Even as this work was progressing, a number of camouflage measures, proposed by contemporary artists and naval personnel, were approved for adoption by US warships and merchant vessels. These schemes were the only painted protection measures from the First World War to be specifically identified and listed:

Title (Type)	Function	Colours/Pattern	Application
Brush (counter-shading/ low visibility)	anti-submarine	blacks/whites/ greys	various types, naval and mercantile

| Fleet System (confusion) | anti-range finding | dazzle or confusion patterns with horizontal sawtooth design along the weather decks | battleships |
| Herzog (low visibility/ confusion) | anti-submarine | blue and green arcs and curves over violet/grey base | various types, naval and mercantile |

| Mackay (low visibility) | anti-submarine | red, green and violet in speckles | patrol vessels and transports |

| Mackay (low visibility/ confusion) | anti-submarine | green, orange, white and blue in bold, undulating shapes | patrol vessels, transports and battleships |

| Thayer (low visibility) | anti-submarine | white and blue in broad bands or chevrons | patrol vessels and escorts |
| Toch (low visibility/ disruptive) | anti-submarine | light blue-grey, dark blue-grey, dark green and light pink-purple in abstract designs | patrol vessels and NOTS ships |

| Warner (dazzle confusion) | anti-submarine | red, blue, grey, green and white in contrasting large irregular patterns | NOTS ships and transports |

| Watson/Norfolk (dazzle confusion) | anti-submarine | dark and light colours in bold geometric patterns | cruisers and battleships |

Note: NOTS = Naval Overseas Transportation Service

By the end of the war, some 495 different camouflage designs had been prepared by the United States Navy's Camouflage Research Center for a variety of objectives. Of these, 193 were applied to naval vessels and 302 to merchant types or naval auxiliaries.

Following the end of the Great War, the Camouflage Research Center was closed down but it provided the embryo for the US Navy's Camouflage Training School, created soon after. This remained the only active establishment concerned with the protective colouring of ships that continued in being throughout the inter-war period.

The use of deception

The use of deception in the war at sea during the First World War can be best highlighted with three examples. These are the German commerce raiders, whose exploits were legion, the notorious Q-ships and the group of dummy battleships and battlecruisers that were commissioned by the Royal Navy.

Germany's naval policy called for the use of submarines and surface raiders to attack the United Kingdom's supply lines. In preparation for this, 42 suitable surface ships had been stationed around the world while a number of others were earmarked for conversion for this work. A network of safe ports had been identified and supply vessels, loaded with stores and ammunition and fitted with workshops, had been sent to sea in readiness.

The main obstacle to conducting this form of naval warfare was the British blockade that was introduced to prevent raiders getting to sea in the first place or from breaking through to neutral or friendly ports to seek replenishment or rest. As a means of avoiding interception, surface raiders resorted to disguises of one sort or another. Painted disguise was the most common, usually in the colours of neutral or British ships. In 1915, the auxiliary cruiser *Kronprinzessin Cecilie* was thinly disguised as the White Star liner *Olympic* but still, ~~in~~ this sham livery, managed to evade capture and reach the safety of the neutral waters of the United States.

More sophisticated was the disguise of the *Cap Trafalgar*. Her funnels were reduced in

The Q-ship was a widely used anti-U-boat measure during the First World War. These two views show Underwing *in two guises. In the zebra-striped view, the normally concealed armament is visible aft and under the bridge, and quite properly the ship is flying the naval ensign; in the other view the ship might be any harmless merchantman. (IWM/CMP)*

number and other structural alterations made to render her quite unidentifiable. It should be said that British ships, likewise, turned to these sorts of tricks in order to confuse the pursued as to the identity of the pursuer.

Though much vaunted in epic and dramatic accounts published after the war, the Q-ships were not in fact a success. First introduced in November 1914, a total of 180 of these vessels, mainly converted coasters, tramps and colliers, were equipped as decoys. Between them they managed to sink eleven U-boats but this was achieved at the price of thirty-one losses from their own number.

The outward impression deliberately presented by the Q-ships was that of lone, defenceless cargo ships – sitting ducks which U-boats could safely attack on the surface with their guns, allowing them to save their torpedoes. All evidence of the Q-ships' special role was carefully concealed. Their guns, their only means of salvation, were hidden behind bulwarks and in cargo holds but in such a way that they could be rapidly deployed.

The idea was to entice a U-boat to within a range where, in effect, the roles could be reversed and the submarine became the more vulnerable target. At these distances, it would be overwhelmed by fire in a swift surface exchange. The hoax extended beyond the Q-ships themselves too, for the crews would go through a well-rehearsed and suitably convincing performance in order to dupe U-boats.

Following the initial attack by the submarine, invariably shellfire aimed from a safe distance inflicting a certain amount of damage, which by necessity had to be sustained, the Q-ship would stop dead in the water and commence to blow off steam to give the impression that she had been fatally impaired. Simultaneously, boats would be lowered, taking off a large portion of the crew, suggesting that the ship was being abandoned. As the U-boat circled her prey, growing less cautious by the minute and coming closer into range, the crew remaining hidden aboard the Q-ship prepared for the instant of surprise. On the order of the Captain, the White Ensign would be run up, guns uncovered and the U-boat's fate settled in a flash.

This, of course, was the planned course of events but the statistics demonstrate that all too often the U-boat saw through the disguise and either fled or dealt with the Q-ship before it could carry out its intentions.

From late 1914, the Royal Navy created a group of dummy capital ships to deceive the Germans on naval strength and dispositions. All of the fourteen ships concerned were converted from passenger vessels, each carefully remodelled to individually mimic one of the battleships or battlecruisers of the Grand Fleet. With the use of wood, canvas and other simple construction materials, but with a close attention to detail, a quite convincing resemblance was achieved in most cases. Additional funnels were erected, wooden turrets assembled on

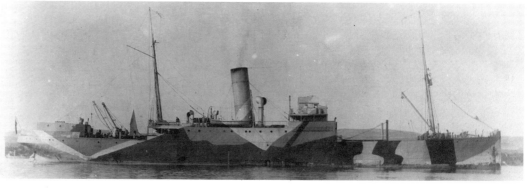

The US Measure 32 was somewhat similar to earlier dazzle designs and was employed in the Pacific towards the end of the war. This is the destroyer Davis *in 1944. (USN)*

deck, bow and stern shapes remodelled and ballasting modified, all to realise the desired effect. Whatever the impact these dummy warships may have had, after only a year in service they were all disposed of or re-converted for other duties, with the exception of the *Merion* ('HMS *Tiger*'), which was torpedoed and sunk in the Mediterranean.

In the Second World War the dummy warships tactic was re-introduced, though on a much smaller scale, to deceive the Luftwaffe when bombing attacks were made on naval bases. Among the vessels adapted for this purpose were three Shaw Savill ships, the *Pakeha* and *Waimana* as the dummy battleships HMS *Revenge* and HMS *Resolution*, respectively, and the *Mamari* as the dummy aircraft carrier HMS *Hermes*. Also, the First World War battleship

Centurion, which had been represented in dummy form in that conflict by the ex-*Tyrolia*, was herself remodelled as a dummy of a *King George V* class battleship.

The Second World War

American development of camouflage schemes

Apart from the continuing instruction on camouflage technique that was imparted to United States naval personnel by the Camouflage Training School and a programme of low vis-

ibility camouflage tests undertaken by the Naval Research Laboratory at San Diego, California, commencing in 1935, all other camouflage research and practice was abandoned between the wars. However, resulting from the continued interest in the development of effective ship colour schemes that persisted in the United States, a list of formalised specifications and application instructions was issued to ships' commanders prior to American entry into the Second World War. Like the numbering codes introduced in 1936 for standard ships built for the United States Maritime Commission, the method of identification that was created for painted concealment and deception measures was detailed and comprehensive. Each scheme was identified as a Measure with its own individual number. The paint colours called up under each measure were also standardised, each allocated its own title and specification number. Also, for each measure, a range of designs for different ship types was also conceived and these too were referenced by a special alpha-numeric coding system that permitted each one to be precisely identified.

These United States Navy Official Measures, which were added to right up to the end of the Second World War, are listed in their entirety:

Title (Type)	Function	Colours/Pattern	Application	Title (Type)	Function	Colours/Pattern	Application
Measure 1 Dark Grey System		dark grey overall except white masts and funnel tops	cruisers and transports	Measure 6 6in cruiser simulating 8in cruiser	deception	dark grey, light grey	cruisers
Measure 2 Graded System (concealment)	anti-submarine	dark grey, ocean grey, light grey	cruisers and destroyers	Measure 7 4-funnel cruiser simulating 4-funnel destroyer	deception	dark grey, light grey	cruisers
Measure 3 Light Grey System (concealment)	anti-submarine	light grey overall	various types, both naval and mercantile	Measure 8 6in cruiser simulating 2-funnel destroyer	deception	dark grey, light grey	cruisers
Measure 4 Black System - Destroyers		black overall	destroyers	Measure 9 Black System - Submarines		black overall	submarines
Measure 5 Painted Bow Wave	deception	dark blue with white or light grey	cruisers and destroyers	Measure 10 Grey System - Submarines		ocean grey overall	submarines

Title (Type)	Function	Colours/Pattern	Application
Measure 11 Sea Blue System (concealment)	anti-aircraft – Pacific and Mediterranean	sea blue overall	battleships, cruisers and destroyers
Measure 12 Graded System with Splotches (concealment)	anti-submarine anti-range finding – Atlantic and Pacific	sea blue, navy blue, haze grey, ocean grey – dark and light colours separated by an irregular line along the weather decks	aircraft carriers, battleships, cruisers and destroyers
Measure 13 Haze Grey System (concealment)	anti-submarine anti-aircraft	haze grey overall	various types, both naval and mercantile
Measure 14 Ocean Grey System (concealment)		Ocean grey overall	various types including aircraft carriers, USMC vessels, eg 'Liberty' ships and 'Victory' ships
Measure 16 Thayer System (concealment)	anti-submarine – North Atlantic and North Pacific	Thayer blue and white in broad bands or chevrons	cruisers and destroyers
Measure 21 Navy Blue System (concealment)	anti-aircraft – Pacific	navy blue overall	aircraft carriers, battleships and destroyers

Title (Type)	Function	Colours/Pattern	Application
Measure 22 Graded System (concealment)	anti-range finding, anti-aircraft – Atlantic and Pacific	navy blue, haze grey – dark and light colours separated by a straight line along the main or first continuous deck	battleships, cruisers, destroyers and transports
Measure 23 Light Grey System (concealment)	anti-submarine	light grey overall	
Measure 31 Dark Pattern System (disruption)	anti-aircraft – inshore, as with invasion forces	navy green, ocean green, haze green, navy blue, black and browns in irregular patterns	landing craft and other amphibious vessels, PT-boats, escort vessels and small transports
Measure 32 Medium Pattern System (disruption/ dazzle)	anti-submarine and delayed recognition post-radar detection	pale grey, haze grey, ocean grey, navy blue, black or greens in bold angular or splinter patterns	aircraft carriers, battleships, cruisers, destroyers and transports
Measure 33 Light Pattern System (concealment/ disruption)	anti-submarine and anti-range finding – North Pacific and North Atlantic	pale grey, haze grey, ocean grey or ocean green and haze green in irregular patterns	cruisers and transports

Camouflage and the response to wartime conditions

No other country had so conscientiously prepared itself for war, as far as protective colouring schemes were concerned, as had the United States. Those nations that stood against one another in the autumn of 1939 for the most part left their warships in the colours they already carried, adopted *ad hoc* schemes, as seemed appropriate, or referred back to the experience of the First World War, in so far as this was possible.

As the war progressed and the issue of camouflage protection for ships of all kinds became a matter of real concern, more effort was concentrated on devising effective, multi-condition schemes. Three developments had taken place between 1919 and 1939 that had a significant bearing on how camouflage practice should be conducted in this new war. In a general sense, the physical and analytical sciences had advanced considerably in those twenty years and tools were now available to researchers that permitted far more accurate evaluation of projected designs and colour

combinations. The other key developments involved aircraft and radar. From being only a minor irritation, in military terms, usually engaged in patrol duties as the 'eyes of the fleet', naval aircraft had become major offensive weapons. Inter-war trials were believed to have demonstrated beyond question just how vulnerable ships were to concerted air attack and the threat posed to shipping by the offensive use of aircraft was now rated as high as the submarine menace. At the outbreak of war, radar was still in its infancy but the potential of this device in locating ships that were not vis-

ible to the naked eye, as well as in pinpointing their bearing and range was immediately appreciated.

Thus, the thinking on camouflage was as much directed at developing protective measures that were appropriate to these new conditions as to any of the already recognised threats to ships, as the US Navy's measures, already described, indicate.

British camouflage schemes

Once the British administration of the war effort had been organised on a proper footing, the direction of camouflage research became clearer and more purposeful. The leading British personalities involved in maritime camouflage research in the Second World War were Alphonse Emil Schuil, a promising young physicist, and Lieutenant Oliver Grahame Hall, RNVR, who cemented a close and valuable partnership after the former was attached to the Admiralty's Training and Staff Duties Division in 1942.

Schuil had already designed the optical systems for the Naval Camouflage Viewing Range that had been constructed at Leamington Spa for the Directorate of Camouflage. This laboratory pioneered new standards in camouflage assessment at a level that was markedly superior to that which had been possible by the Royal Academy team in the Great War. (Sadly, Alphonse Schuil was killed in October 1943 when the submarine *P 615*, from aboard which he was conducting full-scale camouflage trials, was torpedoed and sunk.)

While the scale of British camouflage work was relatively minor when compared with the extensive American activities, the Admiralty also published both standard camouflage colours, which could be identified by an alphanumeric designation and a pattern number, as well as a list of specific disruptive patterns and standard colour schemes:

Title (Type)	Function	Colours/Pattern	Application
Western Approaches anti-submarine Scheme – official; known as the Peter Scott scheme (concealment)		white, light sea blue, light sea green and darker blues, the darker colours on the hull and the rest of the ship painted white	destroyers and escort vessels
Western Approaches anti-submarine Scheme – unofficial; known as the Louis Mountbatten scheme (concealment)		'Mountbatten Pink' (grey/pink) overall	destroyers and escort vessels
Admiralty Light Disruptive Pattern (concealment/ disruption)		blues, greys and greens in bold, irregular patterns	various types, both naval and merchant auxiliaries
Admiralty Intermediate Disruptive Pattern (concealment/ disruption)		as above	as above
Admiralty Dark Disruptive Pattern (concealment/ disruption)		as above	as above
Home Fleet Destroyer Scheme	anti-submarine	dark blues and greys aft, light blues and greys in irregular patterns forward	destroyers
Admiralty Standard Scheme	anti-submarine and anti-range-finding	sea blue in a panel over an otherwise all light grey hull with light grey superstructure	various types, both naval and merchant auxiliaries
Admiralty Alternative Scheme	anti-range-finding and anti-aircraft	light grey upperworks, dark grey hull and decks	various types, both naval and merchant auxiliaries

Other naval camouflage schemes

Apart from the vessels of the Royal Navy and United States Navy, the ships of other combatants also adopted painted camouflage measures of varying degrees of complexity during the Second World War.

Although many German warships retained their prewar colouring of light grey superstructure and dark grey hull, others adopted splinter or dazzle patterns based on the use of pale grey, dark grey and sea blue or mottled designs of pink, blue and green with light grey. This was true of certain smaller units, including S-boats, as well as heavier types, also troop

The French cruiser Gloire *in her unique wartime zebra camouflage, an extreme form of the dazzle pattern.* (CMP)

transports and the numerous vessels gathered along the Channel coast for the threatened invasion of Great Britain, Operation Sealion. In some schemes, attempts were made to paint out the bows and sterns to foreshorten the vessel. In other cases, an overall scheme of extremely light, pale grey was introduced as an overall colouring, which was particularly effective as a concealment from submarines.

During the War, considerable effort was made in Germany to investigate the phenomenon of camouflage to determine more effective colouring practices. Much of this research material was captured at the end of the war, revealing that significant interest had been placed in two concepts in particular. One was disruption colour schemes, of various types, which were collectively described as *flimmestarmung*. The other was the idea of painting false ships on the sides of vessels. In some cases these were suggested in dark colours against a light hull background and in other cases with the tones reversed.

The Italian navy also adopted numerous true camouflage paint schemes during the war, dazzle or disruption variants being prominent among them. These utilised dark grey, light grey, light sea blue and light sea green shades and were largely confined to the bigger naval units such as the battleships and cruisers, for each of which completely unique designs were conceived. Many smaller Italian vessels also remained in their peacetime colours of overall light grey throughout the period 1940–43.

The camouflage practices of two other combatants deserve to be mentioned here, though they were not, in practice, as widely employed as those of the four nations already described.

The French navy had little opportunity to experiment with protective camouflage before the country was compelled to agree terms with the rapidly advancing German army. However, a great many French vessels, which were not in home ports at the time, joined the Free French forces and operated with their Royal Navy and US Navy counterparts.

Depending on which of these affiliations applied in practice, French vessels were invariably recoloured accordingly. The smaller ships, which assisted in patrolling the Western Approaches or which were attached to amphibious operations, were mainly repainted in Admiralty colour schemes. Those that operated in conjunction with American warships or which were refitted in the United States generally

took the United States Navy's official Measure 22 unless it was inappropriate to the sea area in which they were based.

There were some notable exceptions to this. Some French ships were painted in much more striking colour schemes such as the aircraft carrier *Béarn*, which received a bold Measure 33 livery, and the cruiser *Gloire*, which was given a unique and very vivid 'zebra stripe' camouflage pattern.

For the most part, the smaller ships of the Imperial Japanese Navy remained in their prewar colouring, of dark blue grey painted overall, for the duration of the conflict. Many of the larger Japanese ships, such as the aircraft carriers, battleships and cruisers, were painted in a dark sea green colour. Other cruisers received a vague form of disruptive pattern but the utilisation of true confusion colour schemes, mostly developed in isolation by the shipyards, was largely confined to mercantile auxiliaries. An attempt was made on a number of Japanese aircraft carriers to deceive American navy pilots by painting the structure of a battleship or cruiser on the flight deck. The superstructure was projected as it would have been seen from above, including turrets and gun barrels complete with contouring shadows and other features designed to give the impression that a ship other than a carrier was being attacked.

Deception

In contrast with the First World War, the practice of deception in the war at sea in the Second was not characterised by such distinct and widespread examples. Nevertheless, there were interesting cases of the use of this stratagem which serve to demonstrate that it continued to have a value in the conduct of naval operations.

The Japanese worked a ruse in which converted merchant auxiliaries were registered as hospital ships and then used to ferry troops, ammunition and other war materials under the

blessing of safe conduct that was afforded to vessels painted in Red Cross colours.

Q-ships were reintroduced but on a much smaller scale and for only a comparatively brief period. Six small merchant ships were equipped in this fashion and sent out into the Western Approaches to counteract the German submarines operating in the area. After two were sunk, however, with no corresponding successes, the remainder were withdrawn in March 1941.

A number of other special service vessels were operated during the war for which deception techniques were regularly employed as a means of making their activities covert. In March 1942, the former American Lease-Lend destroyer HMS *Campbeltown* was laden with explosives and used as a blockship to destroy the dry-dock entrance at Saint Nazaire. Deception measures were again resorted to as a means of distracting German shore defences from her intentions, her silhouette being altered to approximate that of a *Möwe* class torpedo boat.

With the end of the Second World War, the practice of camouflage once more fell into disuse. As before, the prospect of a future conflict in which such a requirement might arise was not a matter of immediate consideration even though the Cold War confrontation of East and West had already commenced in earnest. As radar and other electronic devices were rapidly developed and refined, the visual location and recognition of ships, or any other fighting vehicles for that matter, was no longer an issue of concern. The problem of the day became the prevention of identification by radar or infra-red sensors or other electronic surveillance devices. Though the principle was the same, this resulted in the practice of camouflage and deception in a way that was somewhat different, certainly more sophisticated, than the comparatively crude techniques that had been appropriate up to 1945.

David L Williams

Bibliography

Compiled by Robert Gardiner, with the assistance of the contributors. After the first section containing books of general relevance to the contents of the volume as a whole, the list division reflects the order of chapters.

GENERAL

These works are the best available sources of basic data, either on warships generally, or on the ships of a specific navy, for the 1906–1945 period.

SIEGFRIED BREYER, *Enzyklopädie des sowjetischen Kriegsschiffbaus*, 3 vols continuing (Herford 1987–).

A technical survey of Russian warship design and construction since 1917, based largely on material recently published in Soviet journals. First three volumes take the story up to about 1937, with three further volumes in prospect. An English translation is underway.

EDWARD C FISHER *et al* (eds), *Warship International* (Toledo, Ohio, quarterly since 1964).

From humble beginnings as a club magazine, '*WI* (not to be confused with *Warship* – see below) has become an important periodical for warship studies, publishing many major features. The most relevant are listed in individual sections below.

ROBERT GARDINER and RANDAL GRAY (eds), *Conway's All the World's Fighting Ships 1906–1921* (London 1985).

ROBERT GARDINER and ROGER CHESNEAU (eds), *Conway's All the World's Fighting Ships 1922–1946* (London 1980).

These two volumes form probably the best available single source of basic data on the world's warships, although some minor craft and auxiliaries are excluded. The introductory essays to each navy are useful resumés of economic, political and technical developments.

ERICH GRÖNER (updated by DIETER JUNG and MARTIN MAASS), *Die Deutschen Kriegsschiffe 1815–1945*, 8 vols (Munich and Koblenz 1982–).

The most comprehensive work on German warships, covering every craft of remotely military significance. Data rather than evaluation, but useful sections on handling and seaworthiness. Very difficult to use but being translated in a less abstruse form as *German Warships 1815–1945* (2 vols published to date, London 1990 and 1991).

FRED T JANE *et al* (eds), *Jane's Fighting Ships* (London, annually since 1898).

The best known naval reference work, but largely superseded by later studies based on accurate sources; of interest in as far as *Jane's* published the official figures of the time, when many countries released deliberately misleading data.

H JENTSCHURA, D JUNG and P MICKEC, *Warships of the Imperial Japanese Navy 1869–1945* (London 1977).

A well illustrated reference book on the characteristics of Japanese warships, including very small craft and auxiliaries.

L L VON MÜNCHING, *Schepen van de Koninklijke Marine in de Tweede Wereldoorlog* (Alkmaar 1978).

A detailed reference for all Dutch ships that fought in the Second World War, including auxiliaries and transfers from other navies. Dutch text but many data tables and photographs.

ANTONY PRESTON *et al* (eds), *Warship* (London, quarterly 1977–88, annually since then).

One of the two important periodicals in the field, this journal pioneered a more sophisticated approach to the study of warship history. Has published many significant articles, relevant titles being listed in specific sections below.

JOHN WINGATE and ANTONY PRESTON (series eds), *Warship Profiles* (London c1970–1974).

An influential publishing concept, this series of short technical monographs on famous warships spawned many similar publications; the series reached forty titles (mostly covering larger vessels) before it ceased publication and with a variety of authors, the quality of the coverage was naturally varied. These were followed by the more detailed 'Ensign' series (1972–1978), which tackled its subjects by class and concentrated on British Second World War designs; the series in effect carried on for a few years in the United States under the 'Man o' War' heading. A similar approach was the American 'Ships' Data' series (1973–c1980) that dealt with major US warships, while the Italians have persevered with the rather more substantial 'Orizzonte Mare' series, which to date have covered most Italian major warship classes of the Second World War period. Of all these series, only individual titles which fill real gaps are listed below even though many more were valuable, if small-scale, contributions to their fields.

INTRODUCTION

Since the opening section necessarily touches on many topics covered in more detail in the following chapters, the titles listed here are only those of specific relevance to the points made in the Introduction.

DAVID K BROWN, 'Attack and Defence', *Warship* 24 (1982).

First of a series of articles concerned with British weapons trials against ships.

——, 'Sustained Speed at Sea in the RN', *NEC 100* (Newcastle 1984).

——, 'Attack and Defence prior to World War I', *Warship* 33 and 34 (1985).

——, 'R E Froude and the Shape of Ships', *Warship Technology* 1 (1987).

——, 'The Torpedo Boat Destroyer Committee 1903', *Warship Technology* 2 and 3 (1987 and 1988).

——, 'The British Ship Catapult', *Warship* 49 (1989).

——, 'The Technology of Submarine Design', *Interdisciplinary Science Review* (1990).

——, 'The Surface Fleet of World War I', *Les Marines de Guerre du Dreadnought au Nucleare* (Paris 1991).

——, 'Naval Rearmament 1930–1941: The Royal Navy', *Revue Internationale d'histoire militaire*, 1991.

STANLEY V GOODALL, 'Uncontrolled Weapons and Warships of Limited Displacement', *Transactions of the Institution of Naval Architects* 79 (1937).

An essay on the effects of treaty limitations on warship design, by a prominent British warship designer.

WILLEM HACKMANN, *Seek and Strike: Sonar, Antisubmarine Warfare and the Royal Navy, 1914–1954* (London 1984).

The title is an understatement since it also describes sonar development in other navies. For the Royal Navy, it shows the relationship between sonar characteristics and tactics.

INGVAR JUNG, *The Marine Turbine*, National Maritime Museum Monograph (London 1982).

LOUIS LE BAILLY, *The Man Around the Engine* (Emsworth 1990).

Ostensibly the autobiography of an eminent engineering officer, but in passing a useful review (and critique) of British naval engineering practice in the Second World War and earlier.

A NICHOLLS, 'The All Welded Hull Construction of HMS Seagull', *Transactions of the Institution of Naval Architects* 81 (1939).

NATHAN F OKUN, 'Face Hardened Armour', *Warship International* XXVI/3 (1989).

A brief, but rather technical, history of armour.

P M RIPPON, *The Evolution of Engineering in the Royal Navy* (Tunbridge Wells 1988).

Inadequate in many ways, but the only survey of British naval engineering; a promised follow-up on later developments has not been published to date.

ALFRED J SIMS, 'The Habitability of Naval Ships under Wartime Conditions', *Transactions of the Institution of Naval Architects* 87 (1945).

EDGAR C SMITH, *A Short History of Naval and Marine Engineering* (Cambridge 1937).

HARRY D WARE, 'Habitability in Surface Warships', *Transactions of the Institution of Naval Architects* 128 (1986).

GENE T ZIMMERMAN, 'SMS Ostfriesland', *Warship International* XII/2 (1975).

Particularly useful on the bombing trials of July 1921 from which so many dubious conclusions were drawn.

THE BATTLESHIP AND BATTLECRUISER

The number of books, articles and papers on the capital ship can be gauged from the fact that a recent bibliography solely devoted to the subject (by Myron J Smith, Jr – see below) has around 5500 entries. Therefore, this selection is confined to the most important technical histories, generally avoiding purely operational accounts, but attempting to give the reader a starting point for further reading about the battleships of all the major navies.

SIEGFRIED BREYER, *Battleships and Battle Cruisers 1905–1970* (London 1973).

Probably the best one-volume technical history of capital ships in its day, but surpassed by later works on many navies.

D K BROWN, 'The Design and Construction of the Battleship Dreadnought', *Warship* 13 (1980).

R A BURT, 'The Royal Sovereign Class Battleships', *Warship* 34–36 (1985).

——, *British Battleships of World War One* (London 1986).

A class-by-class design history from *Dreadnought* onwards; much detail but lacks analysis.

N J M CAMPBELL, 'Washington's Cherrytrees', *Warship* 1–4 (1977).

A in-depth study of the cancelled British capital ship designs of 1921–22.

——, *Battlecruisers* (London (1978).

A monograph on British and German battlecruisers of the First World War; very detailed description of armour schemes and armament.

ANTHONIE VAN DIJK, 'The Drawingboard Battleships for the Royal Netherlands Navy', *Warship International* XXV/4 (1988), XXVI/1 and /4 (1989).

Study of the many unbuilt Dutch battleship designs.

R DULIN, W GARZKE and R SUMRALL, *Battleships: United States Battleships in World War II* (Annapolis 1976).

A detailed overview of post-Washington Treaty American capital ships, emphasising technical description rather than evaluation.

R DULIN, W GARZKE and T WEBB, *Battleships: Allied Battleships in World War II* (Annapolis 1980).

A similar volume to the above, featuring British, French, Soviet and Dutch designs.

——, *Battleships: Axis and Neutral Battleships in World War II* (Annapolis 1976).

The final volume in the trilogy, covering the ships of the remaining navies.

ROBERT DUMAS, 'The King George V Class', *Warship* 9–12 (1979).

——, 'The French Dreadnoughts: The Courbet Class', *Warship* 35 and 36 (1985).

——, 'The French Dreadnoughts: The Bretagne Class', *Warship* 38 and 39 (1986).

ROLF ERIKSON, 'Soviet Battleships', *Warship International* IX/4 (1972) and XI/2 (1974).

NORMAN FRIEDMAN, 'USS Nevada: The "All or Nothing" Scheme of Protection', *Warship* (1977).

——, *Battleships: An Illustrated Design History* (Annapolis 1985).

Probably the best overall account of US battleship design and construction, with a coherent view of the design background.

——, *Battleship Design and Development 1905–1945* (London 1978).

A general analysis of the varied and competing factors that influenced capital ship design. The first of a new style of warship history that looked beyond data to the policy, strategy and tactics that constrained designers.

SHIZUO FUKUI, *Japanese Naval Vessels Illustrated, 1869–1945. Vol 1: Battleships and battlecruisers* (Tokyo 1974).

A magnificently complete collection of photographs; text and captions in Japanese but some data in English.

GIORGIO GIORGERINI, 'The Cavour and Duilio Class Battleships', *Warship* 16 (1980).

RICHARD HOUGH, *Dreadnought: A History of the Modern Battleship* (London and New York 1964).

A superficial but readable popular history of the 'Dreadnought era'.

HANS LENGERER, 'The Japanese Super Battleship Strategy', *Warship* 25–27 (1983).

HENRI LE MASSON, 'The Normandie Class Battleship with Quadruple Turrets', *Warship International* XXI/4 (1984).

——, 'The Lyon Class Battleships', *Warship International* XXII/1 (1985).

A NANI and GIORGIO GIORGERINI, *Le Navi di Linea Italiane 1861–1961* (Rome 1962).

The official history of Italian battleships; well detailed but not very analytical.

OSCAR PARKES, *British Battleships 1860–1950* (London 1957, reprinted 1990).

The first serious historical study of British capital ships, in great detail and showing real insight. For later ships now superseded by Raven and Roberts (see below), but a monumental achievement in its day and still very useful.

FRIEDRICH PRASKY, 'The Viribus Unitis Class', *Warship* 6 (1978).

ALAN RAVEN and JOHN ROBERTS, *British Battleships of World War Two* (London 1976).

A detailed technical history of all British capital ships designed or operational during the 1939–45 conflict (including the First World War ships), with much information on modifications and war lessons.

JOHN ROBERTS, 'The Design and Construction of the Battlecruiser Tiger', *Warship* 5 and 6 (1978).

——, 'Penultimate Battleships: The Lion Class of 1937–1946', *Warship* 19 and 20 (1981).

MYRON J SMITH, JR, *Battleships and Battle Cruisers, 1884–1984: A Bibliography and Chronology* (New York and London 1985).

A monumental listing of some 5500 published items relating to capital ships.

ROBERT F SUMRALL, *Iowa Class Battleships: Their Design, Weapons and Equipment* (London 1988).

A comprehensive technical description of the last surviving battleship class, with many outstanding illustrations.

DAVID TOPLISS, 'The Brazilian Dreadnoughts 1904–1914', *Warship International* XXV/3 (1988).

THE AIRCRAFT CARRIER AND NAVAL AVIATION

Generally, though not universally, accepted as the capital ship of the present day, the carrier and its aircraft are still important and controversial issues, and consequently have inspired a number of fine studies of their history and rationale. The most significant gap is a major work on Japanese naval aviation, one of the 'big three' carrier navies of the inter-war years.

J D BROWN, *Carrier Operations in World War II*, 2 vols (London 1968 and 1974).

Includes lengthy accounts of relatively unknown British and US operations.

——, *Carrier Fighters* (London 1975).

Useful for a detailed account of carrier fighter tactics, including night-fighter operations.

ROGER CHESNEAU, *Aircraft Carriers of the World* (London 1984).

A unique compendium of all the carriers built up to the date of publication. It is particularly important because as yet there is no good account of the Japanese carriers; Chesneau places them in context, and facilitates comparison with their British and American contemporaries.

F DOUSSET, *Les Portes-Avions Français* (Brest 1978).

This is the only account of the French carrier force and its aircraft; drawn from official documents, it describes many abortive projects, including carriers designed while France was occupied.

RENÉ FRANCILLON, *Japanese Aircraft of the Pacific War* (London 1987).

Includes descriptions of the long range land-based aircraft intended to make up for the shortage of carriers.

NORMAN FRIEDMAN, *Carrier Air Power* (London 1981).

Carrier design considerations, including the interaction of carrier and naval aircraft design. The best general introduction to the subject.

——, *US Aircraft Carriers: An Illustrated Design History* (Annapolis 1983).

An authoritative study drawn from official US Navy documents; includes abortive design projects.

——, *British Carrier Aviation* (London 1988).

Drawn from official British naval documents, this book describes the evolution of both the carriers and their aircraft; it also takes British naval tactical concepts into account. Many abortive ship and aircraft projects are included.

W HADELER, *Der Flugzeugtrager* (Munich 1968).

Hadeler designed the never-completed German carrier *Graf Zeppelin*; this book describes his design rationale.

VICE-ADMIRAL SIR A HEZLET, *Aircraft and Sea Power* (London 1970).

One of three excellent books on what Hezlet sees as the three revolutionary naval technical developments of this century: aircraft, the submarine, and electronics. Hezlet is particularly concerned with how these developments were integrated into contemporary navies for maximum effect.

W P HUGHES, *Fleet Tactics* (Annapolis 1986).

A valuable corrective to the view that carriers ought to have displaced battleships far earlier. Hughes shows how they fit the tactical and technical realities of 1939–41.

R D LAYMAN, *To Ascend From a Floating Base* (Cranbury 1979).

The pre-history of carriers, mainly before 1914.

——, *The Cuxhaven Raid* (London 1985).

Cuxhaven was the first carrier air raid.

——, *Before the Aircraft Carrier* (London 1989).

An account of the aircraft-supporting ships which preceded true carriers; in some ways a valuable complement to the two books listed above.

——, *The Hybrid Warship* (London 1990).

Hybrid gun-and-aircraft ships were very popular between the two World Wars.

C M MELHORN, *Two-Block Fox: The Rise of the Aircraft Carrier, 1911–1929* (Annapolis 1974).

The carriers in question were operated by the US Navy. Melhorn sees the Washington Conference as a major factor in the rise of the carrier.

STEPHEN ROSKILL, *Naval Policy Between the Wars* (London 1968 and 1976).

Naval policy here is largely British; Roskill is often concerned with the British attempt to avoid escalating naval costs by pursuing treaty limitation, which in turn deeply affected carrier evolution. He is also much concerned with the Royal Navy's struggle to regain control over naval aircraft.

GEOFFREY TILL, *Air Power and the Royal Navy* (London 1979).

This is largely an account of the struggle for control of the Fleet Air Arm, which in turn deeply affected the Royal Navy's interest in building and operating carriers. There is also an account of the Royal Navy's interwar air tactical concepts, both offensive and defensive.

THE CRUISER

The literature on cruisers is nowhere near as fulsome as that for battleships or carriers; in fact, considering their relative importance they have been surprisingly little studied. There is no general history of their developmnt and only American and Second World War British ships have received adequate treatment (Friedman and Raven/Roberts – see below). However, numerous articles and monographs fill some of the more obvious gaps: there are, for example, 'Profiles' devoted to the Italian *Zara*, the German *Emden* and *Prinz Eugen*, and Dutch *De Ruyter*. Italian cruisers are well covered by the 'Orizzonte Mare' series of well detailed design and operational histories.

ELIO ANDO, 'Capitani Romani', *Warship* 7 and 8 (1978). Italian light cruisers.

RENÉ BAIL and JAN MOULIN, *Les Croiseurs 'De Grasse' et 'Colbert'* (Paris 1984).

A monograph on the last French cruisers, a wartime design although neither ship was completed until the 1950s.

NORMAN FRIEDMAN, *US Cruisers* (Annapolis, 1984).

Very detailed survey of the design of all US cruisers also covering modifications and an outline of operational history. Preferred source for US data.

SHIZUO FUKUI, *Japanese Naval Vessels Illustrated, 1869–1945. Vol 2: Cruisers, Corvettes and Sloops* (Tokyo 1980).

A superb pictorial portfolio of Japanese cruising ships. Captions in Japanese but English data tables.

GIORGIO GIORGERINI and AUGUSTO NANI, *Gli Incrociatore Italiani 1861–1975* (Rome 1976).

Well illustrated Italian official history of cruisers. Not very enlightening about design philosophy and, being official, rather uncritical.

E LACROIS, 'The Development of the "A Class" Cruisers in the Imperial Japanese Navy.' *Warship International* XIV/4 (1977), XVI/1 and 4 (1979), XVIII/1 and 4 (1981), XX/3 (1983) and XXI/3 (1984).

Indispensable reference for both design and operational careers of Japanese cruisers. Very considerable detail on weapons, machinery etc as well as ship. Preferred source for Japanese data.

HANS LENGERER, 'Tone: A Different Approach to the Heavy Cruiser', *Warship* 41–44 (1987).

HENRI LE MASSON, 'The Complex Development of the French Light Cruiser 1910–1916', *Warship International* XXII/4 (1985) and XXIII/2 (1986).

DAVID LYON, 'The First Town Class 1908–1931', *Warship* 1–3 (1977).

ALAN PAYNE, 'The Improved Leander Class', *Warship* 17 (1981).

ALAN PEARSALL, 'Arethusa Class Cruisers', *Warship* 31 and 32 (1984).

ALAN RAVEN and JOHN ROBERTS, *British Cruisers of World War Two* (London 1980).

An excellent account of the design history and subsequent modifications to British cruisers from 1912. Preferred source for British data.

M J WHITLEY, *German Cruisers of World War Two* (London 1985).

An illustrated design and operational history of the relatively few ships built by Nazi Germany.

CHRISTOPHER C WRIGHT, 'Soviet Cruisers', *Warship International* XV/1 (1978).

COAST OFFENCE AND DEFENCE VESSELS

The literature on these ships is sparse. British monitors are well covered by Ian Buxton's book listed below, but there is no equivalent work for coast defence ships. Information on the development of Scandinavian navies is available in a series of articles in the early issues of *Warship International*: Swedish coast defence ships (Spring 1966); Danish (Summer 1966); Norwegian (Spring 1967); Finnish (Summer 1967).

IAN BUXTON, *Big Gun Monitors* (London 1978).

A comprehensive history of the design, construction and operation of British monitors.

STEPHEN S ROBERTS, 'The Thai Navy', *Warship International* XXIII/3 (1986).

Includes details of Thai coast defence ships.

THE DESTROYER AND TORPEDO BOAT

The destroyer chapter in this book was largely based on the technical records of the British Admiralty (plans and, especially, the 'Ships Covers' – the bound files of the Director of Naval Construction's Department – which include much information on foreign as well as British designs) and the records (both plans and documents) of the specialist destroyer-building firm, John I Thornycroft, held at the National Maritime Museum, Greenwich. There is no good single volume history of the type, although destroyers have received a lot of attention in print. The volumes on individual classes of destroyers in the 'Profile', 'Ensign' and 'Man o' War' series are mostly good. Relevant articles can also be found in back numbers of *Warship* and *Warship International* magazines.

PETER DICKENS, *Narvik: Battles in the Fjords* (London 1974).

An all too short but well written account not only of what happened in these destroyer battles of 1940 but also of why it happened that way. The literature on destroyers in action is large and steadily increasing, but this and the 'Taffrail' volumes can be singled out for their valuable insights into what destroyer fighting actually involved.

G FIORAVANZO et al, *I Cacciatorpediniere Italiani* (2nd ed, Rome 1969).

The Italian Naval Historical Branch's excellently illustrated and thorough history of Italian destroyers.

HARALD FOCK, *Schwarze Gesellen* (Herford 1979).

Good for earlier German destroyers and torpedo boats.

NORMAN FRIEDMAN, *US Destroyers* (Annapolis 1982).

Very useful design history of American flotilla craft.

PETER HODGES and NORMAN FRIEDMAN, *Destroyer Weapons of World War 2* (London 1979).

British and American weaponry contrasted; good level of technical detail.

P INSULANDER et al, *Jagare* (Karlskrona 1963).

Well illustrated account of Swedish destroyers.

HENRI LE MASSON, *Histoire du Torpilleur en France* (Paris 1963).

A history of French torpedo boats and destroyers and a valuable insight on what the French themselves thought of their ships as well as a good general history.

EDGAR J MARCH, *British Destroyers* (London 1966).

Unreliable and a prime example of how not to use original material. A good history of British destroyers remains to be written.

ANTONY PRESTON, *V and W Class Destroyers 1917–1945* (London).

Perhaps *the* classic destroyers built before the threats from the air and beneath the sea seriously affected design; this is possibly the best of the numerous books devoted to individual destroyer classes.

—— (ed), *Super Destroyers* (London 1978).

A series of essays on the large destroyers built between the wars for most of the major navies.

'TAFFRAIL' [TAPRELL DORLING], *Endless Story* (London 1931).

The operational story of British destroyers in the First World War by someone who had served in them.

M J WHITLEY, *Destroyer! German destroyers in World War II* (London 1983, revised 1991).

A technical and operational history of later German torpedo craft.

SUBMARINES

There is no shortage of good works on submarines, most services having at least one book devoted to its craft, so the following list is confined to the more general titles. There are many more monographs on individual classes or boats available.

JOHN ALDEN, *The Fleet Submarine in the US Navy* (Annapolis and London 1979).

A history of the fleet submarine in the US Navy from before the First World War to 1975 showing the link between operational necessity and advancing technology. The text is amplified with data tables, appendices and sketch plans.

ERMINIO BAGNASCO, *Submarines of World War Two* (London 1977).

Details of all submarines involved in the Second World War together with their fate. Additional information traces the development of national submarine forces.

RICHARD COMPTON-HALL, *Submarine Warfare: Monsters & Midgets* (Poole 1985).

As the title indicates the first half of the book is an interesting and well documented story of the several large submarine types developed by the many nations, dispelling several myths. Well illustrated.

NORMAN FRIEDMAN, *Submarine Design and Development* (London 1984).

A detailed survey of the development of submarine warfare showing the relationship between technology and tactics.

A N HARRISON, *The Development of HM Submarines 1901–30* (London 1979).

A comprehensive study of all the submarines built for the Royal Navy from the *Hollands* to the 1930s. Many appendices give detailed additional technical information on each specific class in addition to the abundant line diagrams. Official publication (*BR3043*).

HENRI LE MASSON, *Les Sous-Marins Français* (Brest 1980).

An authoritative review of French submarine development from 1863 to the nuclear age, reworking an earlier book by the author; extensive appendices of submarine details.

NORMAN POLMAR and DORR CARPENTER, *Submarines of the Imperial Japanese Navy, 1904–45* (Annapolis and London 1986).

The technical details and operational story of the Japanese submarine fleet to 1945 with full details of each class and type.

NORMAN POLMAR and JURRIEN NOOT, *Submarines of the Russian and Soviet Navies 1718–1990* (Annapolis 1990).

A comprehensive technical history covering both design and operations.

EBERHARD RÖSSLER, *The U-Boat* (London 1981).

A detailed study of all U-boats built, or planned. Copiously illustrated and with numerous line drawings and tables.

M WILSON, 'Submarine Minelayers of the Royal Navy', *Warship* 49 (1989).

A brief description of the building and operations of British submarine minelayers in both World Wars.

MINE WARFARE AND ESCORT VESSELS

Neither anti-submarine ships nor mine warfare vessels have ever inspired a good general study, the nearest being Elliot's book on Second World War escorts (see below), which gives no real sense of overall development. No major navy's individual efforts have been analysed either, so the reader seeking further information has to look to monographs and articles on specific classes.

ELIO ANDO, 'The Gabbiano Class Corvettes', *Warship* 34 and 35 (1985).

PRZEMYSLAW BUDZBON and BORIS LEMACHKO, 'The Bad Weather Flotilla', *Warship* 22–24 (1982).

A design history of the first major Soviet warship programme, the *Uragan* class escorts.

TOM BURTON, *Abdiel-Class Fast Minelayers*, 'Warship Profile 38' (London 1973).

PETER ELLIOTT, *Allied Escort Ships of World War II* (London 1977).

A survey of all British and American war-built escort classes, with a strong emphasis on statistical aspects of the construction programme; also details of armament and electronic equipment.

HANS LENGERER, 'Japanese "Kaibokan" Escorts', *Warship* 30–32 (1984).

The belated war-standard escort programme analysed.

KEITH MCBRIDE, 'The First Flowers', *Warship* 1989 (London 1989).

A design history of the British Great War fleet minesweeping sloops.

PAUL H PAIST, 'Henry Ford's Navy', *Warship* 41 (1987).

The story of the US 'Eagle' Boats of the First World War.

ALAN RAVEN and ANTONY PRESTON, *Flower Class Corvettes*, 'Ensign 3' (London 1973).

A W WATSON, RCNC, 'Corvettes and Frigates', *Transactions of the Royal Institution of Naval Architects* 89 (1947).

An important postwar paper summarising British work on escort vessels during 1939–1945; reprinted in *Selected Papers on British Warship Design in World War II* (London 1983).

ANTHONY WATTS, *The U-Boat Hunters* (London 1976).

An operational history of the Battle of the Atlantic, but with a bias towards the ships and equipment.

M J WHITLEY, 'The Type 43 Minesweepers', *Warship* 27 and 28 (1983).

A history of the multi-purpose wartime German minesweeper/escort.

——, 'The Kriegsfischkutter', *Warship* 39 (1986).

The German utility escort based on a fishing boat hull.

——, 'F Boote of the Kriegsmarine', *Warship* 45 (1988).

The unsuccessful German fast escort.

COASTAL FORCES

The speed and dash of the smallest genuine warships has produced a substantial literature; much of it relates to the more exciting aspects of operations, but there are a number of good technical histories.

ANON, *A Short History of the Revival of the Small Torpedo Boat during the Great War* (London 1918).

A company history of 40ft and 55ft CMBs produced by Thornycroft.

ERMINIO BAGNASCO, *Le Motosiluranti della Seconda Guerra Mondiale* (Parma 1977).

A good Italian language general history of Second World War MTBs in all the major navies.

——, *I MAS e le Motosiluranti Italiane* (Rome 1969).

The Italian official history of their coastal forces; heavily illustrated.

FRANZ BILZER, 'Versuchgleitboot: the World's First Hovercraft', *Warship* 17 (1981).

The experimental Austrian air-cushion MTB of the First World War.

ROBERT J BUCKLEY, *At Close Quarters* (Washington 1962).

An official history of US PT-boat development and operations during the Second World War.

PRZEMYSLAW BUDZBON, 'The Beginnings of Soviet Naval Power', *Warship* 8 (1978).

A well illustrated piece on Soviet 'G-5' class MTBs; see also additional information on inter-war Soviet craft in articles by René Greger in *Warship* 33 and 46.

PETER DU CANE, *High-Speed Small Craft* (London 1951).

A textbook on design by a man who did much brilliant work for Vospers; naturally includes material on MTBs.

DAVID COBB, *HM MTB/Vosper 70ft*, 'Warship Profile 7' (London 1971).

A monograph of the 'standard' British MTB by a well known marine artist who served in boats of this type during the war.

BOB FERRELL and AL ROSS, *Early ELCO PT-Boats* (Memphis 1980).

A heavily illustrated description of 70ft and 77ft ELCO craft produced for the PT-Boat Museum.

HARALD FOCK, *Fast Fighting Boats 1870–1945* (Lymington and Annapolis 1978).

A comprehensive history of development in all major countries, with many plans and photos; originally published in German.

NORMAN FRIEDMAN, *US Small Combatants* (Annapolis 1988).

The best explanation of the rationale of 'mosquito fleets' in any navy so far published, and essential reading for anyone interested specifically in US developments.

W J HOLT, RCNC, 'Coastal Forces Design', *Transactions of the Royal Institution of Naval Architects* 89 (1947).

One of a series of important postwar papers by men most closely involved summarising British work on various warship types during 1939–1945; reprinted in *Selected Papers on British Warship Design in World War II* (London 1983).

JOHN LAMBERT and AL ROSS, *Allied Coastal Forces of World War II*, Vol 1 (London 1990).

The first of a three-volume series which will cover American and British small craft, type by type in great depth; mostly based on numerous detailed drawings but including short histories. This volume is devoted to Fairmile designs, HDMLs and US *SC 497* class submarine chasers.

ADRIAN RANCE, *Fast Boats and Flying Boats* (Southampton 1989).

An illustrated history of Hubert Scott-Paine's British Power Boat Company.

AMPHIBIOUS WARFARE VESSELS

There is no technical history of these vessels, although Ladd (see below) is a good popular survey. Most of the general histories of amphibious warfare make more than passing reference to the craft so the more important of these are listed here.

ANON, 'WWII Japanese Landing Craft', *Warship International* XI/3 (1974).

R BAKER, RCNC, 'Ships of the Invasion Fleet', *Transactions of the Royal Institution of Naval Architects* 89 (1947).

An important postwar paper by the man most closely involved summarising British work on amphibious vessels during 1939–1945; reprinted in *Selected Papers on British Warship Design in World War II* (London 1983).

——, 'Notes on the Development of Landing Craft', *Transactions of the Royal Institution of Naval Architects* 89 (1947).

A companion piece to the above dealing with wartime work on small landing craft during 1939–1945; reprinted in *Selected Papers on British Warship Design in World War II* (London 1983).

MERRILL L BARTLETT, *Assault from the Sea* (Annapolis 1983).

A series of essays on various aspects of the history of combined operations.

K J CLIFFORD, *Amphibious Warfare Development in Britain and America from 1920–1940* (New York 1983).

An academic study of the inter-war background.

DIVISION OF NAVAL INTELLIGENCE, *Allied Landing Craft of World War Two* (London 1985).

A reprint of an official US Navy Second World War manual, ONI 226; data, drawings and photos of all types of amphibious warfare ships, craft and vehicles.

NORMAN FRIEDMAN, 'Amphibious Fire Support', *Warship* 15 (1980).

Very enlightening on other aspects of US Navy amphibious doctrine besides fire support.

BRIAN FRIEND, 'Landing Craft through the Ages', *Warship* 45 and 46 (1988).

A good introductory survey.

——, 'Maracaibo Class Landing Ships of the Royal Navy', *Warship* 47 and 48 (1988).

The first experiments in LST design.

RANDOLF KUGLER, *Das Landungswesen in Deutschland seit 1900* (Berlin 1989).

A narrative history of amphibious warfare in Germany since 1900.

J D LADD, *Assault from the Sea 1939–1945* (Newton Abbot 1976).

A general history of amphibious warfare craft, but largely devoted to Allied efforts.

HANS LENGERER *et al*, 'The Special Fast Landing Ships of the Imperial Japanese Navy', *Warship* 38–40 (1986).

NORMAN POLMAR and JOHN J PATRICK, 'Amphibious Command Ships', *Warship* 23 and 24 (1982).

NORMAN POLMAR and PETER MERSKY, *Amphibious Warfare: An Illustrated History* (Poole 1988).

Useful for photographs of the various types of craft in action.

PETER SCHENK, *Invasion of England 1940: The Planning of Operation Sealion* (London 1990).

Although it is a general history, the book contains much detail on the ships and craft fabricated for the attempt to invade Britain, as well as their intended mode of operation.

M J WHITLEY, 'Marine Artillery Leichter', *Warship* 29 (1984).

The German modular landing craft design.

AUXILIARY WARSHIPS

Given that this is a huge and fragmented topic, it is not surprising that there has never been an attempt to study more than a specific type or class – and most of these are no larger in scale than an article. Except for German ships (courtesy of Gröner), even full listings of the ships are problematical: of the series of pocket books on First and Second World War warships published by Ian Allan in the 1960s and 1970s, Paul Silverstone's *US Warships* does not include all ships taken up from trade; J L Couhat's *French Warships* and A J Watts' *Japanese Warships* do not cover all auxiliaries; while Aldo Fraccaroli's *Italian Warships* contains no real auxiliaries at all; the equivalent *British and Commonwealth Warships* volume by H T Lenton and J J Colledge is better, but it is necessary to turn to the last author's dictionary-like *Ships of the Royal Navy* Vol 2 (Newton Abbot 1970) for data on all the vessels.

PETER ARNDT, *Deutscher Sperrbrecher 1914–1945* (Stuttgart 1979).

A very thorough history of the Sperrbrecher concept, with details of the specifications and careers of all ships.

JOHN ENGLISH, 'Royal Navy Anti-Aircraft Ships', *Warship 1989* (London 1989).

Includes the seagoing mercantile conversions.

J LENAGHAN, 'Merchant Aircraft Carrier Ships', *Transactions of the Royal Institution of Naval Architects* 89 (1947).

An important postwar paper by someone closely involved with the wartime programme; reprinted in *Selected Papers on British Warship Design in World War II* (London 1983).

FRASER M McKEE, 'Princes Three', *Warship International* VII/1 (1970).

The careers of the RCN's *Prince Robert* class as AMCs, LSIs and auxiliary AA ships.

KENNETH POOLMAN, *Armed Merchant Cruisers: Their Epic Story* (London 1985).

Concentrates on the more spectacular operations, but there is nothing else.

ROBERT L SCHEINA, *US Coast Guard Cutters & Craft of World War II* (Annapolis 1983).

Complete data on all cutters (some 400) with outlines of operations; also lists about 4000 small craft under USCG control during the war.

THE FLEET TRAIN

There is no history of the US fleet train. Most of this book's chapter is based on the files of the General Board (series 420–5), supplemented by standard sources on ships actually built for the US Navy.

REAR-ADMIRAL W R CARTER, *Beans, Bullets, and Black Oil* (Washington 1952).

Pacific Fleet logistics in the Second World War.

——, *Ships, Salvage and Sinews of War* (Washington 1954).

Fleet logistics in the Atlantic and Mediterranean during the Second World War.

D JUNG, M MAASS and B WENZEL, *Tanker und Versorger der Deutschen Flotte 1900–1980* (Stuttgart 1981).

German naval tankers and supply ships.

E E SIGWART, *Royal Fleet Auxiliary: Its Ancestors and Affiliations* (London 1969).

A general history of the organisation that provides the British fleet train.

NAVAL WEAPONS

At the level of the general reader there is not very much published material; guns are better covered than other weapons, but there is no layman's introduction to the development of naval weaponry in general and fire control in particular. The essential data can be found in N J M Campbell's encyclopaedic works listed below, and for the USA Norman Friedman provides a coherent overview, but otherwise there is little available.

ERMINIO BAGNASCO, *Le Armi della Navio Italiane nella Seconda Guerra Mondiale* (Parma 1978).

A well illustrated history of Italian naval weapons employed in the Second World War, including many of the older types.

N J M CAMPBELL, 'British Naval Guns 1880–1945', *Warship* 9–38 (1979–1986).

A series describing every Mark of every British naval gun down to 4in calibre.

——, *Naval Weapons of World War Two* (London 1985).

A comprehensive and detailed listing of the world's naval guns, torpedoes, mines, anti-submarine and air-launched weapons.

——, *Naval Weapons of World War One* (in preparation).

A companion volume to the above.

NORMAN FRIEDMAN, *US Naval Weapons* (London 1983).

More than just a catalogue of weapon systems since 1883, the book also gives an idea of technical and tactical concepts influencing developments.

PETER HODGES, *The Big Gun: Battleship Main Armament 1860–1945* (London 1981).

Concentrates on gun mountings more than guns, and stronger on British developments than those of other navies.

PETER HODGES and NORMAN FRIEDMAN, *Destroyer Weapons of World War 2* (London 1979).

An analysis of the weaponry of British and American destroyers (inter-war and war-built classes), including fire control equipment. The British section has more detailed material on individual pieces of equipment, whereas the American section is stronger on the rationale of weapons development.

HANS LENGERER *et al*, 'Anti-Aircraft Gunnery in the Imperial Japanese Navy', *Warship 1991* (London 1991).

An account of Japanese AA guns and fire control.

——, 'Japanese Oxygen Torpedoes and Fire Control Systems', *Warship 1991* (London 1991).

A description of all Japanese oxygen powered torpedoes, including the famous 'Long Lance'.

M P PEIRA, *Historique de la Conduite du Tir dans la Marine 1900–1940* (Paris 1955).

A history of French naval fire control.

EBERHARD RÖSSLER, *Die Torpedos der Deutschen U-Boote* (Herford 1984).

Very narrow in scope, but useful for 1939–1945 torpedo developments in general.

PAUL SCHMALENBACH, *Die Geschichte der Deutschen Schiffsartillerie* (Herford 1968).

A history of German naval gunnery by a retired *Kriegsmarine* gunnery officer.

RADIO, RADAR AND ELECTRONICS

Only works of value to the general reader are listed below, the more technical textbooks being avoided in favour of those with an historical approach.

PATRICK BEESLY, *Very Special Intelligence* (London 1977).

The application of signals intelligence, largely to the U-boat war, during the Second World War, told by the master of this subject. Beesly was a major participant in the events he describes.

——, *Room 40* (London 1982).

Naval signals intelligence during the First World War, including the failure to protect the *Lusitania*.

R BURNS (ed), *Radar Development to 1945* (London 1988).

Technical papers on different aspects of the subject.

NORMAN FRIEDMAN, *Naval Radar* (London 1981).

A compendium on naval radar, past and contemporary, with an appended catalogue of radars.

——, *US Naval Weapons* (London 1983).

Includes applications of naval radars and of sonars, and also a catalogue of US sonars and naval airborne radars.

L A GEBHARD, *Evolution of Naval Radio-Electronics and Contributions of the Naval Research Laboratory*, NRL Report 8300 (Washington 1979).

NRL invented the first US naval radar, CXAM, and developed many of its successors. This account was assembled from official reports. Its only defect is that it provides little context; the reader gets the impression that NRL was the only US wartime technical development organisation, which was hardly the case.

H GUERLAC, *Radar in World War II*, 2 vols (New York 1987; reprint of 1947 report).

This report, based on wartime work, is still probably the only connected account of wartime and prewar radar development both in the United States and abroad. It includes some accounts of radar applications.

WILLEM HACKMANN, *Seek and Strike: Sonar, anti-submarine warfare and the Royal Navy, 1914–1954* (London 1984).

See under Introduction for description.

VICE-ADMIRAL SIR A HEZLET, *The Electron and Sea Power* (London 1975).

An excellent account of the impact of all forms of electricity and electronics on naval warfare up to about 1960. Hezlet is as interested in the tactics of searchlights in the First World War as he is in signals intelligence and in the later radars and sonars. This is a companion to similar books on the impact of aircraft and of submarines.

ALASTAIR MITCHELL, 'The Development of Radar in the Royal Navy 1939–45', *Warship* 13–14 (1980).

A potted history of British naval radar development in the Second World War.

J ROHWER, *The Critical Convoy Battles of March 1943* (London 1977).

A convoy battle is described from the signals intelligence point of view, the commanders on both sides making their moves and countermoves based largely on radio direction finder and code-breaking information. This book is also a marvellous account of the application of Murphy's Law to combat.

ERWIN SIECHE, 'German Naval Radar to 1945', *Warship* 21–22 (1982).

An outline of German surface ship active radars.

——, 'German Naval Radar Detectors', *Warship* 27 (1983).

A short piece on the passive detectors so important to the U-boat campaign in particular.

CAMOUFLAGE AND DECEPTION

A comprehensive history of naval camouflage has yet to be written, but the subject has provoked a lot of interest, particularly among the modelmaking fraternity. As a result many monographs on particular ships or classes often contain information on protective colour schemes, and readers are directed to these as well as the titles listed below. Deception is an altogether wider topic and it also awaits a coherent history.

ADMIRALTY, *History of Sea-Going Camouflage* (London 1946). Postwar British official assessment of naval camouflage.

BUREAU OF SHIPS, CAMOUFLAGE SECTION, *Handbook of Ship Camouflage* (Washington 1937 and later supplements). Official US Navy guide.

——, *A Pictorial Report on Japanese Ship Camouflage* (Washington 1945).

A US naval intelligence handbook on Japanese measures.

GUY HARTCUP, *Camouflage – A History of Concealment and Deception* (London 1979).

A general account of the military applications of camouflage.

LOYD A JONES, *Protective Coloration as a Means of Defense Against Submarines* (New York, c1920).

A seminal work by an important pioneer.

DIETER JUNG *et al*, *Anstriche und Tarnanstriche der Deutschen Kriegsmarine* (Munich 1977).

A small guide to German navy camouflage and paint schemes, principally during the Second World War.

ALBERT ROSKAM, *Dazzle Painting – Kunst als Camouflage* (Rotterdam 1987).

A book associated with an exhibition looking at the aesthetic aspects of camouflage.

LAWRENCE SOWINSKI and TOM WALKOWIAK, *United States Navy Camouflage of the WW2 Era* (Philadelphia 1976).

A useful well illustrated booklet outlining US camouflage schemes.

——, *United States Navy Camouflage of the WW2 Era 2: Fleet Carriers* (Philadelphia 1976).

In the same format as the previous title but concentrating in greater detail on fleet and light fleet carriers.

ROBERT F SUMRALL, 'Ship Camouflage (WWI): Deceptive Art', *United States Institute Proceedings* (July 1971).

——, 'Ship Camouflage (WWII): Deceptive Art', *United States Institute Proceedings* (February 1973).

LINTON WELLS, 'Painting Systems of the Imperial Japanese Navy 1904–1945', *Warship International* XIX/1 (1982).

NORMAN WILKINSON, 'The Puzzle Painting of Ships', *Transactions of the North East Coast Institution of Engineers and Shipbuilders* (1919).

A first-hand account by one of the pioneers of dazzle camouflage.

DAVID L WILLIAMS, *Liners in Battledress* (London 1989).

Although primarily concerned with merchant ships, this book is valuable for its account of the principles of camouflage and the general background to its naval use.

Glossary of Terms and Abbreviations

This glossary, compiled by David K. Brown, refers only to terms and abbreviations used in this volume.

A tube. The inner tube of a built-up gun.

AA. Anti-aircraft (as of gun or control). If the trunnion of an AA gun was positioned so that, at high elevation, the breech was in an easy position for hand loading, it could be too high to load at low angles. Attempts were made to provide portable platforms for low angle loading but the true dual purpose (DP) gun had to await power loading. AA fire control was tachymetric except in the Royal Navy (*see* Chapter 12).

ABV. Armed Boarding Vessel. Medium sized merchant ships, usually with two guns, used by the British to implement blockade by stopping and searching.

acoustic mine. Mine actuated by the sound radiated by a ship, usually from the propeller.

Action Information Organization (AIO). In US Navy terminology, the CIC or Combat Information Center. Based on the operations room, the AIO received data on the position of enemy forces and own forces from radar, sonar, HF/DF etc and plotted their position and course eventually leading to a firing solution for own weapons.

ADA. Action Data Automation. Royal Navy computer based, automatic AIO.

AIO. *See* Action Information Organization.

AMC. Armed Merchant Cruiser. Auxiliary cruiser, used in both world wars, converted from a liner with about eight 6in guns (or smaller). In the Second World War some carried heavy AA armament and aircraft. The guns were from store and usually ancient. (Said by cynics to stand for 'Admiralty Made Coffin'!)

antenna mines. A moored mine held some distance below the surface used against submarines. A small float carried a copper wire above the mine and if a steel hull contacted this wire it would form a battery generating a charge which would explode the mine. Used in large numbers by the US Navy in the Northern Barrage during the First World War but to little or no effect.

AOE. US fast combat support ship. Can replenish oil and ammunition.

AOR. Replenishment ship for oil, solids and ammunition (modern American term also used by Royal Navy).

AP. Armour Piercing (shell). A hard nose protected by a cap with a softer body. The explosive charge was small. *See* Chapter 12.

APC. Armour Piercing (Capped). All AP shells were capped.

armour. Thick armour, over 3in, was cemented, with a hard face supported by a tougher back. Virtually all First World War armour used Krupp patents and hits in action showed there was little difference in quality. From about 1930 Britain and Germany alone developed a much improved material with a deeper face, slightly less hard, giving a 25 per cent improvement in resistance. Thick armour was applied over the side, usually between the end turrets, and extending well below the waterline.

Thinner armour was of much the same composition but without the hard face. It was used on decks and sometimes toward the end of battleships and also as belt armour on cruisers.

Asdic. A British term for what is now called active sonar. The interpretation is the subject of much argument (*see* W Hackmann, *Seek and Strike*). 'Asd' probably stands for anti-submarine detection: it is almost certain that the 'ic' does *not*, as is usually stated, refer to 'investigation committee'.

ASW. Anti-Submarine Warfare.

Atlantic bow. German cruisers and battlecruisers in the 1930s had low freeboard and a straight stem, proving very wet in head seas. To improve them, they were fitted with the so-called Atlantic bow with more sheer, giving greater freeboard forward and a raked stem with increased flare. This was a palliative, giving some improvement, but they were still wet.

Avgas. *Av*iation *gas*oline (aircraft petrol).

Baglietto. Designer and builder of Italian small craft.

barbette. During this era, the barbette was the fixed cylinder, usually armoured, on which the turret rotated. It contained the ammunition supply hoists which, to varying extents, were protected against flash. Barbette armour was much reduced behind side armour.

battlecruiser. An armoured scout, carrying battleship sized guns, which sacrificed armour or number of guns to obtain higher speed. Designs, not built, after the First World War retained armour and gun power, obtaining speed by increasing size and hence cost.

battlefleet. The main fleet, centred on the battleship force, accompanied by battlecruisers, cruisers, destroyers and, latterly, aircraft carriers.

beaver-tail stern. Descriptive term for a stern in which the deck sloped rapidly down at the aft end to the waterline.

biaxial mounting. One in which the gun could be turned in train and elevation only (*see also* triaxial).

BL. Breech-Loading. The shell and propellant were loaded separately, the latter being contained in a bag (usually silk) rather than a brass case.

blisters. *See* bulge.

Bofors. Swedish gun manufacturer, famous for its 40mm anti-aircraft weapon used through the Second World War and up to the present.

bombardment shell. Light case shell with big high explosive filling.

bore. The inside diameter of a gun.

British Power Boat Company (BPB). Designers and builders of light coastal craft.

bulges. Invented by Sir Eustace Tennyson d'Eyncourt, this was a protrusion beyond the shell of a ship designed to explode torpedoes away from the hull. Usually the bulge was divided longitudinally, the outer space being water-filled to absorb splinters from the explosion, the inner being air-filled to diffuse blast. They proved very successful; bulged ships hit by torpedoes all survived. Fitted to a battleship, bulges would reduce speed by 1–2kts. Sometimes, incorrectly, called blisters.

bulkhead. Partition to prevent flooding spreading from one compartment to another and to provide strength; usually transverse.

calibre. Strictly the bore of a gun. Length was often quoted in calibres – *eg* 50-calibre, or length 50 times the bore. See Chapter 12 for slight national differences in interpretation.

CAM ship. Catapult Armed Merchant ship. An ordinary cargo vessel fitted with a fixed catapult on the forecastle which could launch a fighter against an enemy aircraft. A short-lived British expedient.

cannonieri. Italian gunboats.

carrier task group. A group formed round a small number of fleet aircraft carriers (typically four) forming an element of a larger force.

catapults. A device for rapidly accelerating an aircraft to flying speed. The plane would be connected to a ram driven in this period by cordite or compressed air.

cathode ray tube. Electronic screen as in a television screen.

CCA. Carrier Controlled Approach. Radar guided system to bring a plane down to a flight deck in bad visibility.

Celli. Designer and builder of Italian fast motor boats.

CIC. Combat Information Center. US Navy term corresponding to British Action Information Organisation or operation room (*see also* AIO).

CIWS. Close In Weapon System, a postwar term.

CMB. Coastal Motor Boat. British motor torpedo boat (or minelayer) of the First World War designed by Thornycroft in three sizes. All were stepped-hull hydroplanes. A few similar craft were built in the Second World War and some surviving Great War craft were used but were classified as motor torpedo boats.

CNA. Costruzioni Navali e Aeronautiche, Rome. Designer and builder of Italian fast motor boats.

Combat Information Center. *See* CIC.

condenseritis. Impingement attack on the brass tubes of condensers allowing salt water to enter the feed water, damaging boilers.

Condottieri. Generic names for four classes of Italian light cruisers named after Renaissance war leaders.

contact mines. Mine exploded by contact; usually a horn would be broken, releasing acid into a battery which would fire the mine.

contre-torpilleur. French term for a very big destroyer.

cord grain. Cordite or similar propellant extruded in the shape of fine cords.

corvette. British name, suggested by Winston Churchill, for small anti-submarine vessels based on a whalecatcher design.

CPC. Capped, Pointed, Common (shell). Moderate sized black powder filling producing large, very damaging splinters.

CRDA. Cantieri Riuniti dell'Adriatico. Italian shipbuilder at Trieste and Monfalcone.

cruiser. Medium sized ship (3000–10,000 tons) for fleet scouting, trade protection and for use as a 'capital ship' in areas distant from main operations.

CST. Contractor's Sea Trials, prior to acceptance to ensure that everything worked.

dazzle. Confused paint scheme of highly contrasting colours intended to break up the outline of a ship and, in particular, to make it difficult to recognise its course for torpedo fire control purposes.

DCT. Depth Charge Thrower. A mortar which could throw a depth charge some distance to the side of a ship.

DE. Destroyer Escort (US Navy). Roughly equivalent to a British frigate.

degaussed. Fitted with wire coils through which a current ran, neutralising the magnetic field of the ship in both vertical and horizontal planes.

depth charge. A cylinder containing about 300lbs of high explosive which would explode at a pre-set depth.

destroyer. Originally a torpedo boat destroyer, it usurped that role and became a general purpose, small, fast warship carrying out torpedo attacks against enemy ships while protecting its own forces. Later gained ASW and AA capability.

destroyer escort. *See* DE.

DF. Direction Finding – of radio transmissions.

DGN. Official French naval ship design organisation.

diesel-electric. Propulsion plant in which diesels drive electric generators which, in turn, drive electric motors connected to the propeller shaft.

direction finder. Device for identifying the direction from which a radio transmission is coming.

director control. Guns controlled and fired from a master sight, the 'director' high in the ship.

displacement. The weight of a ship, which is equal to the weight of water which is displaced by the underwater hull.

– deep or full load. Weight fully equipped.

– light. Displacement with all fuel, stores, ammunition etc removed.

– normal. In the First World War, most navies quoted a normal displacement with half to two-thirds fuel on board.

– 'standard'. Defined by the Washington Treaty as fully loaded, less all liquids, fuel, ballast, fresh water and water torpedo protection systems.

disruption. Painting scheme to make the features of a ship less conspicuous. (*See also* dazzle).

DNC. Director of Naval Construction. In Britain responsible for the design and building of all warships and auxiliaries. He was also the Principal Professional Adviser to the Board of Admiralty.

double-hull boats. Submarines with a complete ring of ballast tanks round the pressure hull, the outer plating of the ballast tanks forming a 'second hull'.

DP (gun). Dual Purpose (gun). Capable of both low angle and high angle fire which usually required power loading.

E-boat. British term ('Enemy' boat), for German fast, or motor torpedo boat (S-boat or *Schnellboote* to the Germans).

Eagle boat. US Navy anti-submarine vessel of First World War built by Ford Motor Company. Only one completed before the armistice.

ECM. Electronic Countermeasures, including jamming, emission reduction and location measures. Sometimes called Electronic Support Measures (ESM) in recent years.

ELCO. Electric Launch Company. US builder of motor torpedo boats.

electronic countermeasures. *See* ECM.

electronic support measures. *See* ECM.

escort carrier (CVE). Small aircraft carrier to escort convoys based on merchant ship style hull. Later, purpose-built US Navy escort carriers used merchant ship practice and construction techniques.

esploratori. Generic name for classes of large Italian destroyers (literally 'scouts').

Fairmile. British design organisation for light coastal craut. Independent but effectively Admiralty controlled.

fire control. A system to accept ranges and estimates of enemy course and speed, together with own ship movements and so estimate the gun angles required to hit the target. Expression is also applied to torpedoes.

fiume wet-heater. Torpedo motor using heated gas together with water injection.

FL motor boat. German radio controlled explosive boat ('*Fernlenkboot*') of the First World War.

flak lighter. German lighter, often designed as landing craft, carrying a heavy battery of light anti-aircraft (flak) guns.

flare. Outward curvature of hull section, particularly forward. Intended to throw spray and heavy seas clear of the deck.

Fleet Air Arm. The air arm of the Royal Navy. Formed in 1918 as part of the Royal Air Force replacing the seaborne component of the Royal Naval Air Service. Taken into the RN in 1938.

fleet auxiliary. Support vessel such as tanker, ammunition ship etc. Specifically in British service manned as a merchant ship in the Royal Fleet Auxiliary.

fleet train. The auxiliary and support vessels, repair ships, depot ships as well as tankers etc needed to operate a fleet away from the main base.

flimmestarmung. German disruptive camouflage scheme.

floatplane. American term. Aircraft capable of operating from water with one or two floats instead of wheels. Seaplane in British usage.

flotilla. An operational formation of small vessels, destroyers and smaller. In British practice, typically about sixteen ships in the First World War, eight in the Second and ever fewer in recent years, though numbers always varied.

flotilla vessel. Small warship, destroyer etc administered in a flotilla (*qv*).

flush-decked. No break in the uppermost deck, *ie* no forecastle or poop.

flush-deckers. Popular term for a big group of US Navy destroyers built at the end of the First World War which had no forecastle but a flush upper deck.

four-stackers. Another nickname for the US Navy flush-deckers, derived from their four thin funnels.

foxer. A noise-maker towed astern to attract acoustic homing torpedoes away from the ship. Use was limited as it interfered with the functioning of the sonar.

FPB. Fast Patrol Boat. British term used after the Second World War to replace both MTBs and MGBs (*qv*).

freeboard. Height from upper deck to waterline. If freeboard is too low, the ship will be wet and may lack stability at large angles of heel. The use of the term often implies freeboard at the bow, where it was greatest.

grt. Gross registered tonnage; a measure of internal volume, principally used for merchant ships. 1 ton = 100 cubic feet.

gunnery control. The control of guns from a central position which accepts ranges measured from one or more rangefinders, data on own course and space and estimates of those of the enemy, making an estimate of the angles of train and elevation at which the guns are to be fired to hit the target.

Hazemeyer mounting. A Dutch mounting carrying two 40mm Bofors and a predictor. British copies had an integral radar set. It was the first triaxial mounting (*qv*) in service.

HC. High Capacity (of shell). Thin wall with big high explosive filling.

HDML. Harbour Defence Motor Launch (Royal Navy usage).

HE. High Explosive, usually of shell filling.

HE shell. Thin wall shell with big high explosive filling.

hedgehog. Spigot mortar used to fire patterns of small (65lb) contact-fused anti-submarine projectiles ahead of the ship (used by Royal and US Navies).

hein mat. A stiffened mat, towed behind the ship, to smooth out the surface for seaplane launching.

Herbert ferry. German double pontoon landing craft, originally based on army bridging equipment.

herz horns. A lead horn protruding from a moored mine. If the horn was bent by contact with a ship, an inner glass tube would break, releasing acid into a battery which would fire the mine electronically.

HF/DF. High Frequency Direction Finding. One of the greatest British electronic achievements of the Second World War, it could determine the bearing of an HF transmitter with great accuracy, a feat so difficult that the Germans remained convinced it was impossible.

Higgins. US builder and designer of light coastal craft.

Holland design. Early submarine designed by the American J P Holland.

horsepower. The rate of doing work. One horsepower = 550 foot pounds per second. Early steam engine builders equated ihe power of their engines to that of a horse, showing how many they could replace. They chose weak horses to enhance the value of their engines and initially, the numerical value differed. Eventually the formula given above, due to James Watt, became universal. The horsepower in a propulsion plant will depend on where, and to some extent how, it is measured.

– brake horsepower (bhp). The power at the output of the engine measured by a mechanical dynamometer, known as a brake. Usually only given for internal combustion engines.

– indicated horsepower (ihp). This measures the pressure and volume of the gas within a cylinder and gives the power available within the engine. This power is then reduced by internal losses (such as friction) and by the power needed to work auxiliaries such as the fuel pump, air extraction pump, etc; ihp may be some 25 per cent more than the power output. It is normally only quoted for steam reciprocating engines though it can be measured for internal combustion engines.

– shaft horsepower (shp). The power at the forward end of the propeller shaft. Will only differ significantly from bhp if there is a gear box (with power losses) between the two points of measurement.

To complete the complicated story there are often 'horsepowers' used by the designer.

– delivered horsepower (dhp), measured at the propeller and at the shaft, differing from the shp by power losses in the bearings and their gland.

– effective horsepower (ehp). The power required to tow a hull, without appendages, using a 'tug' which does not disturb the flow round the hull.

Note: until well after the Second World War it was customary to use capital letters in abbreviating horsepower. Lower case letters are now formally standardised.

– thrust horsepower (thp). The power generated by the propeller differing from dhp by propeller efficiency and some complicated effects due to the interaction of the flow round the propeller and that round the hull.

Hotchkiss. A make of gun, often a machine-gun or cannon.

HSL. High Speed Launch, usually referred to RAF air sea rescue craft.

HTP. High Test Peroxide, near pure hydrogen peroxide, (H_2O_2) which, passing over a catalyst, would break down into steam and oxygen. Fuel would be injected to burn in the oxygen and the hot gases and steam would pass into a turbine to drive a submarine or missile. HTP is very difficult to store as most substances explode or burn with great vigour if in contact.

Huckins. US builder of small craft.

Huff Duff. Phonetic name for HF/DF (*qv*).

hydrophone. Listening device for submarines. First World War term – eventually developed into passive sonar.

immune zone. At long range, an armoured deck can be penetrated by shells falling at a very steep angle while at close range the side armour can be pierced by shells travelling close to the horizontal. The immune zone is the space between, where neither deck nor side armour can be penetrated by a like adversary. Of course, in a weakly protected ship there may be no immune zone.

The concept can be extended to a diagram showing either adversary on any course. The concept was central to the US 'all or nothing' armouring scheme.

inertia pistol. A pistol, used to fire a main charge, operated by the shock of impact – usually some form of pendulum.

IvS. Ingenieurskantor vor Scheepsbouw. A covert German design bureau established in the Netherlands to circumvent Versailles Treaty restrictions. It enabled German naval architects and engineers to gain experience in submarine design in particular.

J S White. A British designer and builder of light coastal craft (and builder of large ships).

K-amt. The German navy ship design department.

K-gun. Type of US Navy depth charge thrower.

Kamikaze. Suicide bomber, named after the 'divine wind' which had dispersed a medieval Korean fleet intent on the invasion of Japan and intended to repeat this feat.

kango hammer. A pneumatic hammer, derived from a road drill, which hit a diaphragm repeatedly, setting off primitive acoustic mines at a safe distance.

KFK. Kriegsfischkutter. A German purpose-built patrol craft based on an inshore fishing craft. Also applied to converted armed trawlers.

kites. Used to pull a mine sweep out to the side of the ship.

Korting paraffin engines. Make of internal combustion engine used in early German submarines.

kriegsfischkutter. *See* KFKs.

lance bomb. Bomb with long handle, thrown by hand at submarines during the First World War.

Laubeuf design. Type of French submarine.

Laurenti design. Type of Italian submarine.

LCA. Landing Craft Assault (British). Designed by Thornycroft it carried about thirty men with light protection.

LCI. Landing Craft Infantry.

– (L). Large, US built.

– (S). Small, British built.

LCM. Landing Craft Mechanised. Many marks built in both Britain and USA to carry a small tank.

LCP. Landing Craft Personnel.

– (L). Large, the most common type. Built in US to carry a platoon; fast but unprotected.

– (M). Medium.

– (S). Small.

Both smaller, British types built in small numbers.

LCT. Landing Craft Tank. Mks I–IV, VII British built, Mks V–VI US built; designated by arabic numbers in parentheses after the type code, *eg* LCT (8) was a Mk VIII.

LCVP. Landing Craft Vehicle and Personnel (US Navy). Adaptation of LCP (L) to carry a small vehicle such as a jeep.

lend-lease. US legislation to get round the neutrality act so that supplies could be sent to Britain and her allies, in return for lease on bases in the Americas. Effectively gave generous supplies free of charge.

Letter of Marque. In earlier wars, privately owned ships could be given a licence – a Letter of Marque – to take prizes from the country's enemies. Outlawed in the late nineteenth century.

LM. *See* luftschiffmotorboot.

London Naval Treaty. The most important London Treaty was signed in April 1930, extending and modifying the Washington Treaty. Battleship building was prohibited until 1936, aircraft carriers were redefined and total limits imposed on cruiser tonnage, the proportion of 8in to 6in ships varying from one country to another. Another London conference was planned in 1936 but in 1934 Japan gave formal notice that she was withdrawing from all treaty obligations. A treaty, which did little more than clarify definitions, was signed by France, Britain and the USA in 1936.

Long Lance. Code name for Japanese long range, oxygen torpedoes.

loose liner. The inner tube of a gun barrel, manufactured with tiny clearance to allow easy changing when worn; normally locked in position, on firing the liner expanded to take up the clearance.

LSG. Landing Ship Gantry (British). Converted Royal Fleet Auxiliary tankers with a gantry crane to lower their cargo of small landing craft (LCM) into the sea.

LSI. Landing Ship Infantry. Ranged in size from small cross channel ships to ocean liners, differentiated by (L), (M) or (S) suffixes as large, medium or small. Carried small landing craft (LCA, LCP) in davits and sometimes LCM as well.

LSS. Landing Ship Stern chute (British). Converted train ferries with a stern ramp down which landing craft (usually LCM) could be launched.

LST. Landing Ship Tank. The earliest prototypes were converted from shallow draft oil tankers by the Royal Navy. There were also:
– **LST(1).** *Boxer* class, three ships, Royal Navy.
– **LST(2).** Built in US to Anglo-American design in very large numbers and served in both navies.
– **LST(3).** British design with frigate steam machinery built to supplement limited numbers of LST(2).

luftschiffmotorboot. Small German motor torpedo and gunboats of the First World War, named because they were propelled by spare airship (*Luftschiffe*) engines.

Lürssen. German builder of fast motor torpedo boats (*Schnellboote*).

M-Sinker. Code name for the Royal Navy's magnetic mine of the First World War, the first such mine.

MAC ship. Merchant Aircraft Carrier. British bulk cargo ships (oil or grain) fitted with a flight deck to carry a few Swordfish aircraft. Their cargo capacity was unaffected and they remained under the mercantile Red Ensign.

magnetic mine. Any mass of metal moving in the earth's magnetic field will generate its own field and, in addition, a ship will usually become a weak permanent magnet during construction. These fields can be detected and used to activate a mine. Early British mines in the First World War and German in the Second used the vertical component of the field. Later types used the horizontal component (or its rate of change) which were difficult to neutralise.

MAN. A German manufacturer of excellent diesel engines.

marinefährprähme. German naval lighter or ferry; essentially a purpose-built landing craft that was convertable to a number of roles.

MAS. Italian fast motor craft. The initials changed their meaning over the years: originally it was *Motobarca Armata SVAN* (after the Venetian yard that built them); later *Motobarca Anti-Sommergibile* (motor anti-submarine boat); but most commonly *Motobarca Armata Silurante* (motor torpedo boat).

MASB. Motor Anti-Submarine Boat (British). Late 1930s craft, not successful in design role and converted to gunboats.

Measure. Numbered US camouflage scheme.

merchant aircraft carrier. *See* MAC ship.

Metox. German radar detector carried in submarines. Could not detect centimetric radars.

MFP. *See* marinefährprähme.

MFV. Motor Fishing Vessel (British). Trawler-derived naval auxiliary.

MG. Machine-Guns.

MGB. Motor Gun Boat. Fast Royal Navy craft with gun armament and automatic weapons.

mignatta. Italian 'human torpedo' of First World War vintage.

mine sinkers. A moored mine is buoyant and is kept in place by a heavy weight, the mine sinker, resting on the sea bed to which it is connected by a cable.

minensuchboot. German designation for minesweeper (*qv*).

minesweeper. Vessel used to sweep mines either moored with a wire sweep, magnetic with an influence sweep or acoustic with a noise-maker (or any combination of these).

Mk. Mark.

ML. Motor Launch.

monitor. British term for a shallow draft vessel carrying a few (usually two) heavy guns for shore bombardment.

monobloc barrel. A gun built from a single tube apart from the breech ring and mechanism.

motor anti-submarine boat. *See* MASB.

motor fishing vessel. *See* MFV.

mousetrap. A US anti-submarine weapon firing a number of small, rocket propelled charges over the bow.

MS boat. Italian motor torpedo boats (*motosiluranti*); larger and slower but more seaworthy than MAS boats (*qv*).

MTB. Motor Torpedo Boats (Royal Navy). Fast motor boat armed with torpedoes. About 1944 most remaining motor gunboats were given torpedo tubes and re-classified as motor torpedo boats.

MTK. Austro-Hungarian fast craft.

navigatori. Class of Italian destroyers names after famous navigators (explorers).

NC. (i) Non-cemented armour (British). Tough nickel steel without a carburised face. Used for decks, turret roofs and any protection less than 3in thick.
(ii) Nitrocellulose. Explosive used in propellants.

NG. Nitroglycerine. Explosive used in propellants.

nm. Nautical mile; standard distance is usually quoted as 6080ft (1852m) but actually varies slightly according to latitude, being shortest at the Equator.

NTDS. Naval Tactical Data System. An early US Navy automated operation room system.

Oerlikon. Swiss gun-maker. The most commonly used of their products was the 20mm gun.

optical rangefinders. Measures range by measuring the angle to the target at each end of the rangefinder.

Oropesa sweep. Early British wire sweep to cut cables of moored mines. Introduced early in the First World War and named after the ship, *Oropesa*, used in trials.

P-boat. Patrol boat. A British First World War design, with very low freeboard and a narrow, high superstructure. In bad weather water would wash over the deck damping out pitch, heave and roll motions. They were moderately successful.

pair sweep. A wire sweep, towed between a pair of vessels (often trawlers) to cut the cables of moored mines.

panzerschiff. Literally 'armoured ship'. The correct German name for what were popularly known as 'pocket battleships'.

paravane. A mechanical 'fish', which supported and controlled the outboard end of each of a pair of wires streamed from the bow of a ship to protect it from moored mines.

PC-boat. A modification of the P-boat design (*qv*), designed to look like a small merchant ship – though the shallow draft, P-boat hull presented considerable difficulties round the counter. The PC-boats' higher freeboard made them much dryer and better seaboats than the original P-boat.

PCE. Small US Navy anti-submarine vessel of the Second World War (a version of the 180ft minesweeper design). Some served in the Royal Navy as the 'Kil' class.

PCS. Small US Navy anti-submarine vessel based on YMS (*qv*).

periscope. An optical tube enabling submarines to see above the surface of the sea. There were usually two, one a search periscope giving optimum vision (usually with two magnifications) which could also be elevated to look for aircraft. The attack periscope had a much narrower tube; it made less spray and was less likely to be seen but had poorer view capability. The maximum speed at which periscopes could be used was limited by vibration, caused by eddies resulting from the movement of the tube through the water.

pferdeboot. German horse lighter with stern ramp of First World War vintage.

PG. US Navy Patrol Gunboat.

PGM. A small US Navy motor gunboat.

Picchiotti. Italian light coastal craft builder.

pionierlandungsboot. German Army engineers' landing craft. A 1939 prototype.

plough bow. Description of a stem shape, concave from deck to just above water, convex to keel.

pocket battleship. *See* panzerschiffe.

pom-pom. Vickers designed an automatic 2pdr gun early in the century which was used extensively as an AA gun in the First World War. During the 1920s a multiple mounting with eight barrels (later an alternative with four barrels) was developed. At this time it was by far the most advanced light AA weapon in the world but shortage of funds made it slow entering service. By the Second World War it was becoming obsolescent, particularly due to a low muzzle velocity, and though used extensively in improved versions it was never as good as the much more modern Bofors.

PQ. Used incorrectly for PC-boats (*qv*), disguised as merchant ships.

psi. A measure of pressure – pounds per square inch.

PT-boat. US Navy term for motor torpedo boat, standing for Patrol, Torpedo.

PTC. Anti-submarine version of US Navy PT-boat, equivalent to British MASB (*qv*) and likewise unsuccessful.

PV 70. A British Power Boat Company Private Venture boat of '70ft' length. Served in the US Navy as *PT 9*. Modified versions, much strengthened, served in the Royal and US navies.

PY. US Navy Patrol Yacht. Requisitioned yacht armed as patrol boat.

PYc. Small PY, 'c' standing for coastal.

Q-ship. In First World War the British used a considerable number of merchant ships, including trawlers and sailing vessels, as traps for German submarines attacking on the surface. If the submarine got into a suitable position, the flag would be replaced by the White Ensign and concealed guns opened fire. Initially, they scored some successes but as soon as German commanders were aware of their use, their value virtually disappeared.

QF. Quick-Firer (of gun). In US terminology 'rapid-fire'.

quadaxial mounting. A gun with four axes of rotation enabling the combination of training and elevation to be carried out more quickly and accurately. A few Italian mounts used the system. *See* biaxial and triaxial.

R-boats. *See* räumboote.

radar. Acronym for *ra*dio *d*etection *a*nd *r*anging. Electro magnetic device which sent out pulses of radiation and timed the return of the echo giving range. Prototype sets were in use before the Second World War but were not common until 1941.

rake tactic. *See* rudeltaktik or wolf pack.

raked stem. A stem sloping forward from waterline to the deck. Helps to reduce deck wetness.

ram bow. During the nineteenth century most major warships had a reinforced ram projecting from the stem below water. In the early twentieth century ramming was abandoned as a tactical manoeuvre but it was found that the ram shape was beneficial to top speed and many ships (for example the battleship HMS *Queen Elizabeth*) were built with a ram shape, but not reinforced. It was an early bulbous bow.

räumboot. German motor minesweeper. Often heavily armed and used as escort vessel.

reciprocating engines. Steam piston engines. In the twentieth century, almost invariably triple expansion (*qv*) with three or four cylinders, some have a split low pressure cylinder. Diesel and petrol engines were also 'reciprocating' but the word is not usually applied to them as, in this era, all internal combustion engines were reciprocating.

RPC. Remote Power Control (of guns) Power trained and elevated from the director.

RPC/12. German First World War propellant.

RPC/38 NG. German Second World War propellant.

rpm. Rate at which shaft turns, Revolutions Per Minute. In gunnery, Rounds Per Minute.

rudeltaktik. German description of 'wolf pack' tactics (*qv*), translated literally as 'rake tactics'.

RVF. Pre First World War Russian Volunteer Fleet; warships taken up from trade in wartime.

S-boat. *See* schnellboot

saddle tank construction. Submarine with light ballast tanks, external to the pressure hull, along the sides only; *ie* not all the way round as in double hull.

SAP. Semi Armour Piercing shell with thinner walls and larger charge (4.5 per cent by weight) than a true AP shell.

SAPC. Semi Armour Piercing, Capped shell.

SC. Submarine Chaser. Navy designation of both world wars.

schnellboot. Literally 'fast boat', German motor torpedo boat of Second World War.

schnorkel. Breathing tube to enable a submarine to run its diesels whilst submerged. Initially fitted in new Dutch submaries about 1940, adapted and fitted widely to German submarines in 1944. Had a ball valve (as in lavatory cistern) at the top to prevent water flooding down.

schwere schiffsbrücke. Type of German Second World War twin pontoon landing craft, based on army bridging equipment.

seaplane. An aircraft designed to land and take off from water using floats separate from the main fuselage. Often interchangeable with a wheeled undercarriage. Floats did not greatly reduce speed but they markedly reduced range and load carrying.

SGB. Steam Gun Boat (British). Designed to hunt and destroy E-boats; their lightweight, steam machinery was complex and easily disabled by small arms. By the time the machinery had been protected, weight had increased so much that they were too slow.

short grain. Cordite in which the 'cords', individual strands, were short.

Siebel-ferry. German catamaran, shallow draught transport/landing craft. Many were heavily armed and used to escort coastal convoys.

single-hull construction. Submarine in which ballast tanks were internal to the pressure hull.

SK. Russian initials for US-built submarine chaser.

sonar. Second World War, US Navy term for the ultrasonic detection of submarines, known as Asdic (*qv*) to the British.

sperrbrecher. German mine clearance vessel, usually a converted merchant ship. Intended to explode mines by its own influence, acoustic and magnetic, and strong enough to resist the explosion.

spindle form. Descriptive of early submarines, a body of revolution, pointed at either end with little external structure.

Squid. British three-barrelled anti-submarine mortar firing ahead under Asdic control.

staff requirement. A list of the features seen by the naval staff as desirable in a new ship including armament, speed, endurance etc. Sometimes a cost target would be included.

standard displacement. Defined in the Washington Treaty – the weight of the ship fully equipped, but with all liquids (fuel, fresh water, ballast, reserve freshwater removed). Given in Imperial units of 2240 pounds.

steam turbine. Steam engine in which steam is passed over sets of blading, alternately fixed and rotating, which by changes in pressure over the blading causes the shaft to rotate.

superfiring. Arrangement of guns in which one mount is at a higher level, firing over the other. The lower mounting is exposed to considerable blast from the upper guns and special measures, such as blast screens, are needed to alleviate the effects.

SVAN. Società Veneziano Automobili Nautiche. Designer and builder of Italian fast light craft.

sweeping. Originally sweeping for mines with a wire which cuts the mooring or guides the mooring into a cutter. Extended to cover the use of magnetic and acoustic 'sweeps' which simulate the signature of a ship. The majority of modern mines (1992) are effectively unsweepable though many older mines remain in service which can be swept.

TB. Torpedo Boat

TBD. Torpedo Boat Destroyer, eventually shortened to destroyer.

TGB. Torpedo Gun Boat. A small, fairly fast vessel intended to destroy torpedo boats. They were thought to be too slow and the task was taken over by the torpedo boat destroyer, themselves based on enlarged torpedo boats. The speed of destroyers was illusionary and trials showed that, in a seaway, they were slower than torpedo gunboats.

TNA. Trinitroanisole – a high explosive used for filling shells.

TNT. Trinitrotoluene – a high explosive used as filling in shells and torpedoes.

Tomahawk cruise missile. A US weapon which can be launched from surface ships or submarines, using terrain following to find its target. May have nuclear or high explosive head.

torpedo. Originally any underwater explosive device (*ie* including mines). Now used for self-propelled 'fish', carrying a high explosive (or nuclear) charge which will explode in contact with, or beneath the keel of, an enemy. May be free running, homing or guided.

torpedo boat. Small, fast steam boat carrying torpedoes.

torpedo gunboat. *See* TGB.

Torpex. A high explosive filling used in torpedoes and some other underwater weapons. (Composition 37–41 per cent TNT, 41–45 per cent cyclonite, 18 per cent aluminium).

transom stern. Stern ending in a vertical, virtually flat, surface like a bulkhead. The flow past such a stern is equivalent to that past a longer ship giving a slight increase in speed. The broad stern associated with a transom makes easier the arrangement of such features as twin rudders, helicopter deck, mooring arrangements etc, and improves stability, particularly after damage in the after half of the ship.

trawler bow. A vague, descriptive term used in the First World War to describe increased upper deck sheer forward.

triaxial mounting. Gun or director which can turn about three axes, each at right angles to the other two. Gives quick and accurate pointing against aircraft targets.

triple expansion engine. Steam is expanded, doing work, in three stages. Initially, each stage of expansion was carried out in a single cylinder but, in many later engines, the large, low pressure cylinder was replaced by two cylinders of more moderate size.

turbine. *See* steam turbine.

turbo-electric. A propulsion system in which a steam turbine drove an electrical generator which, in turn, supplied power to an electric motor connected to the propeller shaft. It was used extensively in big US Navy ships of the First World War, mainly because of a shortage of gear cutting machinery but it was heavy and inefficient.

turtleback bow. A forward deck in which the centreline rose sharply moving aft from the stem, associated with a sharply rounded transverse section. It was intended to drain off rapidly water coming over the bow but, since it reduced freeboard at the stem and deck edge it made such wetness more likely.

Though not totally proven, it is generally accepted as unsuccessful and expensive.

Unterseeboot. 'Under see boat'. German word for submarine, hence 'U-boat'.

'V & Ws'. Big class of British destroyers built at the end of the First World War carrying names beginning with the letters 'V' and 'W'. Arguably the most successful destroyer design of all time, their main features were copied in many countries until the late 1930s.

VAS. Vedette antisommergibili – large Italian ASW motor launches.

Versailles Treaty. The peace treaty at the end of the First World War between Germany and the Allies. Its clauses limited the number and size of German warships. The biggest permitted was 10,000 tons which led to the 'pocket battleship' design which were actually of about 11,500 tons.

versuchsgleitboot. Austro-Hungarian torpedo-carrying craft of First World War, operating on the hovercraft principle.

vorpostenboot. German auxiliary patrol craft or minesweeper; some, in the Second World War, were uprated to flak korvette (anti-aircraft escort).

Vosper. British designer and builder of motor torpedo boats.

VT. Variable Time – a code name to conceal the function of radar proximity fuses in AA shells.

Walter turbine. Herr Walter designed a propulsion system for submarines in which HTP (*qv*) was decomposed into steam and oxygen. Fuel was then burnt in the oxygen and the mixture of hot gases passed through a turbine to drive the propeller. The Germans completed some experimental craft (one of which, *U 1407*, became HMS *Meteorite* after the Second World War) but were some way from perfecting operational submarines using the system.

War Emergency Programme. British naval building programme authorised soon after the outbreak of war in September 1939. Sometimes, loosely, used to apply to 1940 and later wartime building programmes.

Washington Treaty. Naval limitation treaty signed in 1922 by Britain, USA, Japan, France and Italy. May be summarised as: No battleship building for 10 years (except Britain, allowed to build 2); new battleships not to exceed 35,000 tons standard displacement (*qv*) or carry guns bigger than 16in; new cruisers not to exceed 10,000 tons with 8in guns. The total battleship (and battlecruiser) tonnage was fixed with a ratio of 5:5:3 for Britain, USA and Japan with a smaller equal limit for France and Italy.

Welin. Type of breech block used in British guns.

well deck. Lowered portion of deck between superstructures such as forecastle, bridge and poop.

wire-wound. Gun in which the inner barrel was reinforced against hoop stresses by a wire coiled round it under considerable tension.

wolf pack. An operation unit of German submarines which, initially, would be deployed in an extended line to search for a convoy. When found and reported to U-boat command, the pack would be ordered to concentrate for a massed night attack on the surface. The success of wolf packs depended on the ability to use HF radio links between U-boats and headquarters which the Germans believed could not be located by direction finders (HF/DF), but British ships were fitted with effective HF/DF by 1941.

Y-gun. AWS mortar with two barrels pointing one to port and one to starboard firing depth charges.

YMS. US motor minesweeper, standing for Yard (*ie* harbour) Mine Sweeper. A very successful Second World War design.

YP. US Navy motor launches, mainly for training but with some patrol capability.

Index